RAMSEY ZARIFEH was born in Kent but has spent most of his working life outside the UK. In 1993 he took a year off to teach English in Germany and for a holiday job at Disneyland Paris before going up to Magdalene College, Cambridge, where he graduated in English. He then spent two years in Japan, teaching on the JET programme.

After a short spell at Reuters in London he returned to Japan to research this guide. Whilst there he was also a contributor to *Up All Night* on BBC Radio 5 Live and a correspondent for Radio 2's *Steve Wright In the Afternoon*.

He currently lives in Switzerland where he is a journalist at swissinfo – Swiss Radio International.

Japan by Rail
First edition: 2002; reprinted with amendments July 2004

Publisher (all countries except Japan)
Trailblazer Publications
The Old Manse, Tower Rd, Hindhead, Surrey, GU26 6SU, UK
Fax (+44) 01428-607571
info@trailblazer-guides.com   www.trailblazer-guides.com

Publisher (Japan)
ICG Muse, Inc.
5-10-33 Roppongi, Minato-ku, Tokyo 106-0032
Tel 03-5414-5530 Fax 03-5414-5247
orders@tuttlebook.co.jp www.tuttlebook.co.jp

British Library Cataloguing in Publication Data
A catalogue record for this book is available from the British Library

ISBN 1-873756-23-2

Text © Ramsey Zarifeh 2002

Maps © Trailblazer 2002
Colour photographs © as credited
B&W photographs © Kazuo Udagawa

The haiku at the start of each chapter in this book is reproduced with permission of:
Tohta Kaneko: p9; Minako Kaneko: p362; Kazuko Konagai: p66; Professor Makoto Ueda
and University of Toronto Press (*Modern Japanese Haiku – An Anthology)*: p32 & p321

Editor: Anna Jacomb-Hood
Series editor: Patricia Major
Layout: Anna Jacomb-Hood
Japanese typesetter and proof-reader: Sachiko Shinohara
Cartography: Nick Hill
Index: Jane Thomas

Printed on chlorine-free paper by
D²Print (☎ +65-6295 5598), Singapore

JAPAN
BY RAIL

RAMSEY ZARIFEH

TRAILBLAZER PUBLICATIONS
ICG MUSE INC

Acknowledgements

Special thanks are due to the Central Japan Railway Company (JR-Tokai), without whose generous support this book would never have been written. JR-Tokai staff in London (Kunihiro Kondoh, Shuzo Kitade and Goro Yayama) were all very helpful, as were David Hodgson and Jackie Hammond at the Japan National Tourist Organization (JNTO) and Kikuko Ota of All Nippon Airways (ANA).

In Japan, thanks to: Mari Watanabe in Sapporo, Tamami Yamaguchi in Otaru, Matsuyama-san in Asahikawa, Rumi Saito in Onuma-Koen, Satoshi Ichitani and Yoshiko Matsubara in Nara, Yasushi Shioda in Takaoka and Keiko Kuromizu in Miyazaki. Many of the JET programme CIRs were a great help, including: Fiona Keyes in Matsue, Eleanor Robinson in Aomori, Chris in Niigata, Hillary Pedersen in Taki, David Matsuda in Hakui, Eleanor Oguma in Takada, Rachael Leighton in Naoetsu, Owen Rosa in Hanamaki, Jason Grave in Minamata, Adam Newman in Shizuoka, Ryan Armstrong in Takamatsu and Lisa Farley in Okayama.

Thanks also go to: Anthony Robins in Nagoya for patiently answering all my rail-related questions, Akira Shirai of the Oigawa Railway, Yoko Konishi of Shingu Tourist Association, Takahashi-san of the Japan Economy Hotel Group and Takenobu Higashimoto (former manager of the Welcome Inn Reservation Center), Graham Fry, Sir Hugh Cortazzi, Julie Hensley and Allister McRae, Mikiko Kawano, Clive Allnutt, Hironobu Tomitaka, Noboru Kawano, Miyuki Nasu, staff and students of Nobeoka High School, Yuji Nakayama, Ian Mutsu, Jin Koyanagi and Jun Koshio of Odakyu Railway, and Kazuho Wapo Hirai.

I am also grateful to Richard Brasher for taking many of the photos, and to everyone else I met along the way for giving me advice and telling me about their own experiences of travelling in Japan.

Special thanks to Anna Jacomb-Hood for her meticulous editing and for taking on the task of sorting out the timetables and appendix; thanks also to Kazuo Udagawa for his help and advice, and to the rest of their family (Kenichi and Rikki) for volunteering to help as well.

For the poetry at the start of each chapter I am grateful to the President of the Modern Haiku Association (Japan), Tohta Kaneko; to the President of the British Haiku Society, David Cobb, whose introductions, haiku suggestions and general advice were invaluable; to Kazuko Konagai for supplying and translating a wide range of appropriate haiku; and to series editor Patricia Major for liaising with everyone above and for making the final selection.

My thanks are also due to Ichie Uchiyama for providing the calligraphy for the book title, to Nick Hill for drawing the maps, Jane Thomas for the index, and also to the publisher, Bryn Thomas. Finally, thanks to my brothers Alex and Andrew, and to my parents, who kept me financially afloat and to whom I will literally always be indebted.

A request

The author and publisher have tried to ensure that this guide is as accurate and up to date as possible. Nevertheless things change. If you notice any changes or omissions that should be included in the next edition of this book, please write to Ramsey Zarifeh at Trailblazer (address on p2) or email him on ramsey.zarifeh@trailblazer-guides.com. A free copy of the next edition will be sent to persons making a significant contribution.

www.japanbyrail.com

To listen to radio interviews with the author, and for more photos and web links see Ramsey Zarifeh's website: www.japanbyrail.com.

Cover photo: Bullet train (Nozomi shinkansen 700 series) passing Mt Fuji
© Central Japan Railway Company (JR-Tokai)

CONTENTS

MAP KEY

Symbol	Description	Symbol	Description
⇧	Where to stay	▭	Park
O	Where to eat	⛴	Ferry/river cruise
⊠	Post office	Ⓑ	Bus station
ⓘ	Tourist Information	✕	Airport
📖	Bookstore/Internet	—Ⓢ—	Subway
🏛	Museum	—Ⓣ—	Tram
⛩	Shrine	·—•—·—•—·	Private/Local Rail Line
🛕	Temple	+—•—+—•—+	JR Rail Line
✚	Church/Cathedral	●●●●●●●●●●●	Shinkansen Line
●	Other	→)—•—+—•—(←	Underground Rail Line

INTRODUCTION

Think of Japan and one of the first images you're likely to conjure up is that of the bullet train speeding past snow-capped Mt Fuji. For many, what lies beyond the frame of this image is a mystery. But step inside the picture, hop on board that train and you'll quickly discover the true scope and variety of what the country has to offer.

The fascination of Japan lies in its diversity: remote mountain villages contrast with huge neon-lit cities that never sleep; the vast natural landscape of unspoilt forests, volcanoes and hot springs more than compensate for the occasional man-made eyesore; the silent oasis of a Shinto shrine or a Buddhist temple is not far from the deafening noise of a virtual-reality games arcade. Nowhere else in the world do past and present co-exist in such close proximity as in this relatively small country.

The ideal way of seeing it all is by rail, whether it's on one of the world-famous bullet trains (*shinkansen*) or on the wide network of local or express trains, or even on one of the many steam trains. A turn of the century guide advises visitors to 'make travel plans as simple as possible. The conditions of travel in this country do not lend themselves to intricate arrangements'. Today, however, nothing could be further from the truth. Trains run not just to the minute but to the second, so itineraries can be as complicated or minutely timetabled as you wish. Or you can simply turn up at the station and plan your journey as you go. Most Japanese travel by train, so it's the ideal way to meet the people and find out what life is really like for at least some of the 127 million who live here.

The real secret to touring the country is the Japan Rail Pass, deservedly recognized as the 'bargain of the century'. Rail-pass holders can travel easily almost anywhere on the four main islands over a network that stretches for 20,000km. Take advantage of the freedom it confers to explore on and off the beaten track beyond the Tokyo metropolis and the tourist capital of Kyoto.

Japan can be expensive but, apart from your rail pass, you can cut costs even more by staying in youth hostels or in B&Bs (*minshuku*). *Ryokan* (upmarket B&Bs) are also good value and welcoming but if you prefer and can afford it there are world-class five-star hotels throughout the country.

Unexpected pleasures also await the traveller: where else can you enjoy a massage while hurtling along at 300kph on a shinkansen, buy cans of hot coffee from a vending machine at the top of a mountain and take a crash course in Zen meditation inside a temple, all in the space of a week? It's said that no *gaijin* (outsider) can ever fully know Japan but only by visiting and seeing for yourself can you discover what the country is really like: somewhere between the images of traditional past and high-tech future which flicker worldwide on the small screen.

Routes and costs

ROUTE OPTIONS

So you know you're going to Japan: the next step is to work out what you want to see and how much ground you want to cover once you've arrived. This guide shows you how travelling around Japan by rail is the best way of seeing as much as possible in a short space of time. Travelling by air may be quicker but only by rail can you see the country close up and in full colour. And there are few places in the world where the trains virtually always run on time, travelling at speeds of up to 190mph (300kph); where smartly-dressed conductors doff their caps and bow to the whole carriage before checking tickets, and where it really can be as much fun to travel as it is to arrive. Welcome to Japan by rail.

Japan Rail (JR) boasts that its network covers every corner of the four major Japanese islands. If you looked at the maps in JR's timetable you'd see what appears to be a close approximation to a bowl of spaghetti. The choice of routes is, if not infinite, at the very least overwhelming.

To simplify travel planning and to reassure the first-time visitor that a qualification in orienteering is not needed to negotiate your way round the country, this guide splits Japan into seven regions: Central Honshu (see p109), Western Honshu (p202), Northern Honshu/Tohoku (p242), the Kansai region (p165) which includes the cities of Kyoto, Nara and Osaka, Kyushu (p321), Shikoku (p362) and Hokkaido (p281). To help plan a trip, sample itineraries are provided (see p16) as well as information on using the route guides (see p84).

COSTS

Contrary to popular belief, a visit to Japan doesn't have to be expensive but it is important to plan your budget as it is an easy country to spend money in.

Package tours which include travel by rail (see p24) rarely offer better value than organizing an independent trip. From the UK, you'd be unlikely to pay anything less than £2000 for a 14-day tour including return flights, rail travel, accommodation in basic Japanese inns, some meals and the services of a tour guide. This may be an option if you prefer to let someone else do

きよお！と喚いてこの汽車はゆく新緑の夜中

*Kyoh! screaming aloud
this train runs into
the fresh green midnight*
(Tohta Kaneko)

all the planning and route selecting but given the price of a 14-day rail pass (£260/US$379) it would certainly be more cost effective (as well as more fun!) to organize your own trip.

Though the initial cost of a Japan Rail pass (see box p12) may seem a lot, bear in mind also that a return ticket on the shinkansen between Tokyo and Kyoto costs ¥26,440; since a one-week rail pass costs ¥28,300 the pass almost pays for itself from this one trip. Take just one additional journey and the pass really begins to save you money. The return fare from Tokyo to Hiroshima by shinkansen is ¥36,100, well over the cost of a one-week pass. A return journey to Sapporo in Hokkaido from Tokyo by a combination of shinkansen and limited express works out at ¥44,860, a fraction under the cost of a two-week pass.

So, a rail pass turns travelling around the country into a real bargain, but what about all the other costs? One couple boast on the web that they live in Japan on ¥500 (£3/$4.20) a day, though their tips for survival include 'pot noodle', 'hide in the toilets on long-distance trains' to avoid buying a ticket, and for accommodation 'cardboard boxes and newspaper make really good insulation'. This is definitely not recommended. For a better idea of what you're likely to be spending per day, see the box below. Alternatively, check ⌨ www.price

---

❏ SAMPLE DAILY BUDGETS

Low

Accommodation	¥2600 (£15/US$22) hostel without meals
Breakfast	¥500 (£3/US$4.20) coffee and toast
Lunch	¥500 (£3/US$4.20) sandwich or convenience store snack
Dinner	¥1100 (£6.35/US$9.24) noodles/pasta or a hostel meal
Sightseeing	¥1700 (£10.30/US$14.30) less if you only visit free attractions
Total	**¥6400 (£37.65/US$52.10)**

Mid-range

Accommodation	¥5300 (£30/US$42.70) basic business hotel (no meals) or Japanese inn with two meals
Breakfast	¥890 (£5.15/US$7.48) egg, ham, toast and coffee
Lunch	¥1100 (£6.35/US$9.24)) lunch deal in a café/restaurant
Dinner	¥1600 (£9.25/US$13.45) set evening meal at a restaurant or in hotel
Sightseeing	¥1700 (£10.30/US$14.30) more if you visit lots of galleries and museums
Total	**¥10,590 (£61.20/US$88.99)**

High

Accommodation	¥16,000 (£92.50/US$134.50) upmarket hotel
Breakfast	¥2140 (£12.37/US$17.98) buffet breakfast
Lunch	¥3570 (£20.64/US$30) three courses
Dinner	¥6250+ (£36+/US$52+) à la carte
Sightseeing	¥9000+ (£52+/US$75+) guided city tours of Kyoto/Tokyo and entry fees
Total	**¥36,960+ (£213+/US$310+)**

checktokyo.com, where you'll find lists of up-to-date prices for everything from beer to butter, toothpaste to toilet paper in Tokyo, though the prices seem applicable for the country as a whole.

When to go

In general, Japan has a mild climate, though it's difficult to talk at all generally about a country which stretches for some 3000km north to south. It can be below freezing and snowing in Hokkaido, while southern Kyushu is enjoying sunshine and mild temperatures. Spring is considered the best time to visit, when the worst of the Hokkaido winter is over and the rest of Japan is not yet sweltering in humidity. Cherry blossom viewing takes place in April/May.

The rainy season in June marks the change from spring to summer but the squalls and showers soon dry up to be replaced by heat and humidity. Hokkaido is by far the coolest place in summer but this also makes it one of the busiest. The high temperatures and – particularly in the south – sweltering heat can last well into September but things usually cool down by the beginning of October.

Autumn is another pleasant season, though October/November are the 'leaves viewing' months, when people flock to see temple grounds covered in fallen leaves. The main areas for skiing are central Japan and Hokkaido. If you don't mind the cold, late autumn/early winter can be a peaceful time to visit.

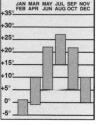

Sapporo

Try to avoid Japan's national holidays, in particular **Golden Week** (April 29th-May 5th), when it seems as if the entire country is on the move, hotels and trains are booked out and prices rise to meet demand. The school holiday season in August is another busy time, particularly around mid August during the **obon** festival when people head back to their home towns.

Temperature charts – max/min °C centigrade

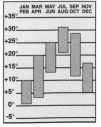

Tokyo

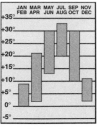

Fukuoka

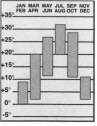

Takamatsu

Rail passes

The original and still the best-value rail pass available to visitors is the national Japan Rail Pass. In the last few years, some of the regional JR companies have introduced their own passes which compliment the existing national pass. The regional passes (see pp13-15) are a cheaper alternative and may be of interest to anyone intending to focus their travel on a specific area. With one exception, the JR passes must be purchased before arrival in Japan (for full details, see p15).

Travel by rail becomes much more expensive without the rail pass, but there are still some discounts and bargain tickets to be had (see p77).

THE JAPAN RAIL PASS

The Japan Rail Pass is truly the bargain of the century. It entitles the pass holder to travel freely on almost all JR services, including most shinkansen (the bullet train). The only exceptions are the *Nozomi* (super-express) shinkansen and some overnight services. Having a rail pass means you can travel almost everywhere without having to buy a ticket.

Who can use the pass?
The rail pass can be used by any non-Japanese tourists visiting Japan under 'temporary visitor' status. Some Japanese nationals not residing in Japan can use a rail pass but all other Japanese cannot. The pass cannot be used by anybody arriving in Japan for employment.

Buying the pass
The most important rule concerning use of the rail pass is that it **cannot** be purchased in Japan. It is sold, in the form of an exchange order, at authorized agents (see p22) outside Japan. Before contacting an agent, work out what kind of pass

---

❏ **Japan Rail Pass – costs**

Days	Ordinary Class	Green Class
7 days	¥28,300 (£163/US$238)	¥37,800 (£219/US$318)
14 days	¥45,100 (£260/US$379)	¥61,200 (£354/US$514)
21 days	¥57,700 (£333/US$484)	¥79,600 (£460/US$669)

Children aged under 6 travel free providing they do not occupy a seat; those aged 6-11 pay half. Prices are fixed in yen, but the charge is payable in local currency. The prices in brackets are for rough guidance only. The exact cost depends on the exchange rate in your home country at the time of purchase. It's worth shopping around as travel agencies apply different exchange rates.

you will need. First decide whether you would like a **7-day**, **14-day** or **21-day** pass. The pass runs on consecutive days from the date you first use it but there is no limit to the number of passes you can buy.

Once you've decided the length of pass you want, the next step is to decide what class you'd like to travel in. There are two types of rail pass: The **Ordinary Pass** is valid for standard-class rail travel, which is likely to be more than adequate for most people. Seats in ordinary class are very comfortable and on some trains are as good as first-class rail travel elsewhere in the world. For those used to luxury and wishing to travel in a bit more style, the **Green Pass** is the one to get. Green-class carriages (known as 'Green Cars') offer much wider seats, more legroom, and often include extras like slippers, personal TVs and free coffee. Note that local trains in Japan have standard class only but all limited expresses and shinkansen convey Green cars.

REGIONAL JAPAN RAIL PASSES

In addition to the pass for nationwide travel, some companies in the JR Group have introduced regional passes; these are a cheaper alternative if you're planning to restrict your travel to specific areas. Note that none of the regional passes includes travel on the bullet train between Tokyo and Kyoto, so you need to buy the national pass if planning to take this route or be prepared to pay the cost of the ticket. With one exception (see p14), regional rail passes must also be purchased before arrival in Japan.

⛩ **Overcoming the language barrier**
One of the biggest worries for first-time visitors to Japan is the language barrier. How easy is it to make yourself understood and navigate your way around the country? The answer is that it's surprisingly easy; most Japanese can understand some English, even if not everybody speaks it.

You don't need to be able to read Japanese characters to find your way around; station (place) names are written in English on every platform, and on-board announcements are made in English on all shinkansen and some limited express trains; the vast majority of hotels and ryokan have their names written in English outside, and in most towns and cities, road signs and street names are in both Japanese and English.

However, it's always useful to have the name of the place you're heading for written on a piece of paper, so you can show it to taxi drivers or passers-by when asking for directions. Ask hotel reception or tourist information staff to write down in Japanese all the places you're planning to visit during the day.

For more details about English on the railways, see p81.

❏ **JR East Rail Pass**

Days/class		Adult	Youth (12-25)
5-day	Ordinary	¥20,000 (£116/US$168)	¥16,000 (£92/US$134)
	Green	¥28,000 (£162/US$235)	n/a
10-day	Ordinary	¥32,000 (£185/US$269)	¥25,000 (£144/$210)
	Green	¥44,800 (£259/US$376)	n/a
Flexible 4-day	Ordinary	¥20,000 (£116/US$168)	¥16,000 (£92/US$134)
	Green	¥28,000 (£162/US$235)	n/a

Children aged under 6 travel free providing they do not occupy a seat; those aged 6-11 pay half the ordinary/green adult rate.

JR East Rail Pass

Valid for travel on the JR East network, which extends east of Tokyo and includes the route around Tohoku (see pp242-265) as far as the northern tip of Honshu, but does not include Hokkaido. The pass is also valid for travel from Tokyo into the Japanese Alps, as far as Nagano (see p145) and Matsumoto (see p150). It also includes travel on the Tohoku, Nagano and Joetsu shinkansen, the Narita Express train from Narita Airport to downtown Tokyo, and JR services in the Tokyo metropolitan area. Passes are available in **5-** and **10-day** varieties, or the **flexible 4-day** ticket is valid for any four days within one month from the first date of use. The pass is an especially good deal if you're aged between 12 and 25 because there is a youth rate.

JR West Rail Pass

There are two types of JR West Rail Pass: the Sanyo Area Pass and Kansai Area Pass. Both are available in ordinary class only. These passes are the exception to the rule and can be purchased in Japan as well as overseas but you still need to show your passport with 'temporary visitor' stamp.

The **Sanyo Area Pass** is valid only for stops on the Sanyo line between Shin-Osaka and Hakata (Kyushu). The pass permits travel on: all shinkansen services on this route (including the Nozomi) as well as local trains, the JR ferry service to Miyajima (see p235), and the journey from Kansai Airport to Osaka. It is **not** valid for journeys to Kyoto. To buy this pass (4-day or 8-day) visit a JR travel service centre at any main station between Shin-Osaka and Hakata.

The **Kansai Area Pass** is useful if you're spending only a few days in and around Kyoto and plan to make a couple of short excursions. It covers travel on local trains only between Kyoto, Osaka, Kobe, Nara, Himeji and Kansai Airport and is valid for **one day** or **four days**. To buy this pass, visit a JR travel centre at either Kansai Airport, Kyoto or Shin-Osaka station.

JR Kyushu Rail Pass

Valid for travel on all JR Kyushu lines so the pass is useful for the Kyushu route guide (see pp321-336), but cannot be used on the shinkansen. Rail travel to

❏ Sanyo Area Pass		Kansai Area Pass	
Days	**Adult**	**Days**	**Adult**
4-day	¥20,000 (£116/US$168)	1-day	¥2000 (£12/US$17)
8-day	¥30,000 (£173/US$252)	4-day	¥6000 (£35/US$50)

Children aged under 6 travel free providing they do not occupy a seat; those aged 6-11 pay half the adult rate.

Kyushu from elsewhere in Japan is not included. This pass is available in two varieties: a **5-day pass** costs ¥15,000 (£86.70/US$126) and a **7-day pass** ¥20,000 (£116/US$168). Children aged under 6 travel free providing they do not occupy a seat.

EXCHANGE ORDERS

For both the national and regional rail passes, what you actually buy before departure is not the pass itself, but an Exchange Order; you can turn this in for the real thing once in Japan. Exchange orders are valid for three months from the date of issue, so only purchase one less than three months before you plan to start travelling by rail. When purchasing the exchange order, you should also receive a guide to using the pass and a timetable of main rail services in Japan. If not, JNTO (see p23) offices have supplies of both.

How and where to turn in the exchange order

Once in Japan, take your exchange order to any **JR Travel Service Center** authorized to handle the Japan Rail Pass. The most obvious ones are at the JR stations in Narita (Tokyo) and Kansai (Osaka) airports. Major JR stations such as Tokyo, Nagoya, Kyoto, Osaka, Shin-Osaka, Sapporo and Hakata have travel service centres, but it's often easiest to sort your pass out at the airport offices, even if you're not going to start travelling immediately.

At the time of exchange JR staff will ask to see your passport to check that you have been admitted on 'temporary visitor' status. You'll also be asked to specify the day you want to start using the pass; this can be any day within one month of the day you turn in the exchange order. Once a date has been stamped on the rail pass it cannot be changed. JR will not replace lost passes.

HOW TO USE THE RAIL PASS

Once you've received the pass, all you do is show it whenever you pass a ticket barrier and JR staff will wave you through. Since the pass is not computerized it cannot be fed through automatic wickets but this is not a problem as there is always a staff member around.

Seat reservations are not necessary as you can just turn up for any train and sit in the unreserved carriages. However, on some trains, and at certain times of the year (see p11), it's a good idea to make a reservation in order to guarantee a seat if the unreserved carriages are full. Since rail-pass holders can make any number of seat reservations for free (see p79 for details) it's worth doing so in any case.

A few JR trains run on sections of track owned by private companies. Rail-pass holders are supposed to pay a supplement for the section of journey over non-JR track. In practice, you will only have to pay if a conductor is checking tickets at the time the train is running along the non-JR track. Any instances where this occurs are referenced in the route guides.

For details of other rail passes/special tickets see p77.

Suggested itineraries

With such a vast network of rail services, one of the hardest tasks in planning a trip to Japan is working out how much you can fit in. **One week** is really too short to attempt anything more than a quick shuttle between Kyoto and Tokyo, with perhaps a day trip to Nara (see p195) or Hiroshima (see p230). To get anything like a sense of what the country is really about, and to give yourself time to get over jet lag and/or culture shock, plan for at least **two** or **three** weeks.

The following itineraries are neither prescriptive nor are they intended to be the last word on rail travel in Japan. Their purpose is to give a flavour of what can be accomplished. Unless otherwise stated, the routes below assume arrival in and departure from Tokyo and do not include days before/after the rail pass is used.

GENERAL ITINERARIES

A one-week itinerary
Day 1 Take the shinkansen from Tokyo to Kyoto (p180); afternoon and overnight in Kyoto.
Day 2 Spend day in Kyoto and consider a half-day trip to Nara (p195), then back to Kyoto for second overnight stay.
Day 3 Pick up the shinkansen to Hiroshima (p230), perhaps stopping along the way for half a day in Okayama (p225). Overnight in Hiroshima.
Day 4 Spend day in Hiroshima and second overnight.
Day 5 Board a Sanyo line train from Hiroshima for Miyajima-guchi and transfer to the JR ferry to Miyajima Island (p235). Spend the rest of the day touring the island and overnight here.
Day 6 Take ferry back to Miyajima-guchi, return to Hiroshima and transfer on to shinkansen back towards Tokyo. Stop off along the way at Shizuoka (p134), from where you can make a side trip to Kunozan Toshogu Shrine.
Day 7 Morning in Shizuoka, then board a shinkansen for the last part of the journey back to Tokyo (p85).

☖ **An itinerary for the enthusiast**

Rail enthusiasts and anyone else wanting to get maximum use out of the rail pass might consider the following one-week itinerary, a non-stop tour of the country from Sapporo in Hokkaido to Kagoshima on the southern tip of Kyushu. Take a deep breath and watch the kilometres clock up from the comfort of your train seat!

Day 1 (479km) Starting in Sapporo (see p309), take a Super Hokuto LEX to Hakodate and then the Hatsukari LEX from Hakodate to Aomori. Spend the night in Aomori.

Day 2 (1040km) An early start from Aomori, as you take the Inaho LEX leaving at 6:11am, arriving in Niigata (see p275) at 12.17pm. Spend just over three hours in Niigata before boarding the Raicho LEX at 3:41pm; this runs direct to Osaka via Kanazawa and Fukui, arriving at 10.11pm.

Day 3 (447km) Enjoy a (brief) lie-in after the marathon journey of day two, before boarding a westbound shinkansen from Shin-Osaka to Okayama, where you could stretch your legs in the gardens of Korakuen (see p228). Head next for Shikoku by taking a train across the Inland Sea from Okayama to Takamatsu (see p375). Visit your second garden of the day at Ritsurin-kocn (see p376) or take a side trip to nearby Yashima (see p380). As evening falls, take a westbound limited express to Matsuyama (see p385).

Day 4 (408km) Get up early, take a short tram ride from Matsuyama to nearby Dogo Onsen (see p386) for an early morning bath, before boarding the limited express back to Okayama. From here transfer to the shinkansen and continue west to Hiroshima. Before dusk, take a local train west to Miyajima-guchi and cross via the JR ferry to Miyajima Island (see p235). You should just have time to see the island before crashing out for the night.

Day 5 (458km) Backtrack to Hiroshima, transfer to the shinkansen and travel all the way to the Hakata terminus, on the tip of Kyushu. Fukuoka/Hakata has enough shops and museums to keep most people happy for an afternoon. As evening falls, board a limited express for Nagasaki.

Day 6 (414km) Spend the morning in Nagasaki (see pp343-350) before taking a limited express back towards Hakata, transferring in Tosu for the final part of the journey south to Kagoshima (see p355). If feeling particularly ambitious, you could stop off in Kumamoto for a couple of hours to take in the city's castle (see p350).

Day 7 Walk to the ferry terminal (see p361) and catch a ride to Sakurajima. Rent a cycle or car and head for the hot springs at Furusato Kanko Hotel which overlook the sea. Take a long hot soak in the outdoor tub, stare out over the water, contemplate the 3246km journey you've just completed and consider that this is how the Japanese like to travel.

Two-week itinerary: into the mountains and along the coast

Day 1 Take the Asama shinkansen from Tokyo (p85) to Nagano (p145); spend the day and overnight in the Olympic city.

Day 2 After a dawn visit to Zenko-ji temple (p145), take the Shinano LEX to Matsumoto (p150), a city which is home to one of Japan's best preserved castles. Overnight here.

Day 3 Picking up the Shinano once more, continue further south to Shiojiri and change to a local train to reach the old post town of Narai (p119). By late afternoon, pick up the train and continue as far as Nagiso (p121), from where it's a short bus ride to Tsumago, another post town where a number of traditional inns offer the weary (rail) traveller a chance to rest.

Day 4 After an early morning wander around Tsumago (before the tour buses arrive!), return to Nagiso and continue south to the terminus of the Shinano in Nagoya (p139). Afternoon and overnight here.

Day 5 Head west along the Tokaido shinkansen line to Kyoto (p180), Japan's ancient capital. Take in a couple of the city's famous sights or follow one of the half-day side trips by rail described on p191.

Day 6 Spend a second day in Kyoto or take the train to nearby Nara (p195). Overnight in Kyoto or Nara.

Day 7 From Kyoto, it's a brief hop on the shinkansen to Osaka (p101). Though a city of commerce rather than tourism, Osaka is worth a half-day stop; theme park enthusiasts will want to head to the new Universal Studios Japan (p105). Overnight here or in Kobe (p219), one stop along the shinkansen line.

Day 8 Spend a couple of hours in Kobe or press on to nearby Himeji (p204), fêted for its picture-postcard castle, one of the country's most visited tourist attractions. Pick up the shinkansen again and continue on to Okayama (p225) in time for an overnight stay.

Day 9 Early morning is the best time to visit Okayama's stroll garden and castle. In the afternoon pick up a westbound shinkansen and alight in Hiroshima (p230). Overnight here.

Day 10 Spend day in Hiroshima and second overnight.

Day 11 Take a Sanyo line train to Miyajima-guchi, then transfer to the JR ferry to reach Miyajima Island (p235).

Day 12 Opportunity for an early morning hike up Mt Misen (p236) before taking the ferry back to the mainland, retracing your steps to Hiroshima and picking up a westbound shinkansen to Hakata/Fukuoka (p336) in Kyushu.

Day 13 Spend day in Hakata/Fukuoka or (if feeling ambitious) take an early train and pack in a day trip to Nagasaki (p343).

Day 14 Finally retrace your steps by riding the shinkansen all the way back to Tokyo, covering a distance of 1175km in just over six hours.

If you prefer to have more time in Tokyo it might be best to cut out the trip to Hakata/Fukuoka in Kyushu.

Three-week itinerary

Make the most of a three-week rail pass by combining the two-week itinerary outlined above with a week focusing on one of the regions described below.

The two-week itinerary ends in Hakata, capital of Kyushu (p336), so you're perfectly placed to continue with a third week of travel around the island. If you prefer to spend the extra week exploring Shikoku (p362), the starting point is Okayama (reached on day 9 of the two-week itinerary). Another option would be to explore the less developed side of Western Honshu (p202) away from the Sanyo coastline. In this case, follow the two-week itinerary as far as day 12, then the Western Honshu regional itinerary.

REGIONAL ITINERARIES

Regional itineraries assume use of a one-week rail pass. If you have the luxury of more time to focus on a particular region, one week can easily become two or three by slowing down the pace and including a number of side trips along the way. For more details about each region, see the introduction to the individual route guides.

Central Honshu (see pp109-165)

Day 1 Board a Tokaido shinkansen from Tokyo station and ride as far as Shizuoka (p134), perhaps stopping along the way for a short pilgrimage to the grave of poor Toby (p113). Spend the afternoon in Shizuoka visiting the hill-top Kunozan Toshogu Shrine.

Day 2 After an overnight stay in Shizuoka, pick up a Kodama shinkansen as far as Kakegawa. From here, backtrack two stops along the conventional JR Tokaido line to Kanaya, starting point for a side trip on the Oigawa steam railway (p114). Finally return to Kakegawa, connect up once again with the shinkansen and continue to Nagoya (p139) for the night.

Day 3 At least two side trips can easily be made from Nagoya; both affording excellent views of the surrounding countryside. The Wide View Shinano LEX runs on the JR Chuo line to the Olympic city of Nagano (p145), with stops along the way at the traditional post towns of Narai (p119) and Tsumago (p121) as well as the castle town of Matsumoto (p150). Alternatively the Wide View Hida LEX runs along the JR Takayama line to picturesque Takayama (p155). Either side trip can be made at a push in a day, but it would be more relaxing to stay overnight somewhere along the way.

Day 4 Return to Nagoya and spend the day seeing some of the city sights or take a short side trip by private Meitetsu Railway to nearby Inuyama (p145).

Day 5 From Nagoya board the Mie rapid train which heads around Ise Bay to Ise (p172), spiritual centre of Japan's indigenous religion, Shinto.

Day 6 After an overnight stay in Ise, pick up the Mie rapid train heading back towards Nagoya but get off at Taki (p171), from where you can transfer on to the Wide View Nanki LEX which heads south towards the Kii Peninsula. By getting off at Shingu (p172), it's possible to take a side trip by JR bus inland to Doro-Kyo Gorge. Overnight in Shingu.

Day 7 From Shingu pick up the Ocean Arrow LEX which follows a coastal route all the way to Shin-Osaka, from where you can begin a rail tour of western Honshu (p204), or visit Kyoto (p180). Jumping on an eastbound Tokaido shinkansen from Shin-Osaka or Kyoto will deposit you back in Tokyo.

Northern Honshu (see pp242-80)

Day 1 From Tokyo, take a Tohoku shinkansen north to Sendai (p265), from where you could take a side trip to Matsushima Bay (p246), considered one of the top three scenic spots in Japan. Return to Sendai for the night.

Day 2 Pick up the shinkansen and travel the short distance to Ichinoseki (p249), from where local trains run along the Tohoku line to the temple town of

Hiraizumi (p250). Stay overnight in a temple with the option in the summer months of taking part in an early morning session of *zazen* (Zen meditation).

Day 3 Retrace your steps to Ichinoseki and continue on the shinkansen to the terminus in Morioka (p251). Change trains here and pick up the Hatsukari LEX to Aomori (p271), Honshu's northernmost city and the rail gateway to Hokkaido (p281).

Day 4 Spend day in Aomori and include a side trip to nearby Nebuta no Sato (p275), a vast exhibition space which displays some of the colourful floats used during the city's Nebuta Festival in August.

Day 5 From Aomori, board the JR bus south to Lake Towada (box p258), formed from a volcanic crater. Spend the afternoon by the lake before picking up another JR bus to Towada-Minami station. From here pick up a local west-bound train on the Hanawa line to Odate (p259). Transfer to the Ou line and head south towards Akita (p260), a useful overnight base.

Day 6 From Akita, pick up the Inaho LEX which runs south to Niigata (p275). Possible stops along the way include Sakata (p262), home to an art museum and traditional Japanese garden, and Tsuruoka (p263), access point for the Dewa-Sanzan mountain chain. Overnight in Niigata.

Day 7 Spend the morning in Niigata before completing the rail loop around northern Japan by picking up a Joetsu shinkansen back to Tokyo.

Western Honshu (see pp202-42)

Day 1 Starting in Osaka (Shin-Osaka) take a westbound shinkansen as far as Hiroshima (p230). Overnight here.

Day 2 Spend day in Hiroshima before picking up the shinkansen and continuing west to Ogori (p211), access point for an excursion across Honshu. Overnight in Ogori.

Day 3 In the morning, take the Oki LEX (at weekends and in summer a steam locomotive operates on this route, see p211) which runs inland along the Yamaguchi line to Yamaguchi (p212).

Day 4 Make an early start by taking the JR bus to the limestone cave at Akiyoshi-do (box p213). Return to Yamaguchi, pick up the Oki and continue north to the picturesque town of Tsuwano (p214), where you'll find plenty of inexpensive *minshuku* and *ryokan*.

Day 5 Spend day in Tsuwano before picking up the Oki once again. From here, the train heads east following the San-in coast to Matsue (p237), known as the 'city of water'. Two possible places to stop en route are the new aquarium in Hamada (p217) and Nima (p217), home to the unusual Sand Museum. Overnight in Matsue.

Day 6 Spend day visiting Matsue Castle and the old haunts of Irish writer Lafcadio Hearn before taking a leisurely sunset cruise around Lake Shinji (p241). Spend a second night in Matsue.

Day 7 From Matsue, pick up the Super Yakumo LEX which cuts across Honshu to Okayama (p225) on the Sanyo coast. There should be enough time to visit the city's stroll garden before taking the shinkansen back to Osaka.

Hokkaido (see pp281-319)

Day 1 Starting from Aomori on the northern tip of Honshu (p282), take the Hatsukari LEX and head through the Seikan tunnel to the port city of Hakodate (p304); spend the night here.

Day 2 From Hakodate, take the Super Hokuto LEX to Sapporo (p309), perhaps stopping for a couple of hours at Onuma-koen (p285) to visit the lakes which overlook Mt Komagatake. Overnight in Sapporo.

Day 3 Spend day visiting the island's capital and find out what the city was like in the 19th century by taking a side trip by JR bus to the Historical Village of Hokkaido (p314). By evening take the Super White Arrow LEX along the Hakodate line to Asahikawa (p315) and overnight here.

Day 4 In the morning take the free bus from Asahikawa to the foot of Mt Asahi (p319). A ropeway (cable car) runs part of the way up the mountain or you could opt to take one of the hiking trails to the top. Overnight in the small village at the foot of the mountain.

Day 5 Return by bus to Asahikawa and transfer to a local Furano line train to Furano (p302), known in Japan for its fields of lavender in summer and thick blankets of snow in winter. Overnight here or in nearby Bibaushi (p303).

Day 6 Spend day in Furano before returning to Asahikawa and boarding the Super White Arrow back to Sapporo in time for a final overnight stay.

Day 7 From Sapporo pick up the Super Hokuto, return to Hakodate, transfer to the Hatsukari and head back to Honshu.

Kyushu (see pp320-61)

Day 1 Starting from the capital, Hakata/Fukuoka (p324), take the Kamome LEX west to Nagasaki (p327). Spend day and overnight here.

Day 2 Spend the morning in Nagasaki and then return in the direction of Hakata/Fukuoka as far as Tosu (p327), from where you can transfer to the Tsubame LEX which heads down the west side of the island. Continue as far as the city of Kumamoto (p328), where there should be time to pay a visit to the city's castle before finding somewhere to stay overnight.

Day 3 Take a side trip from Kumamoto inland to the Aso tableland (p334). It's a three-hour journey to Aso (in summer the Aso Boy steam locomotive operates along this route, see p336), from where a bus and ropeway whisk you up to the Nakadake crater. Peer over the side of this active volcano before deciding whether you want to stay overnight in Aso or return in time to stay a second night in Kumamoto.

Day 4 Spend day at leisure in Kumamoto before picking up the Tsubame and continuing south to the terminus in Kagoshima, Kyushu's southernmost city.

Day 5 Spend day and second overnight in Kagoshima.

Day 6 Take the ferry to Sakurajima Island (p361), rent a cycle and spend the day biking around the brooding Sakurajima volcano. Overnight here or take the ferry back to Kagoshima.

Day 7 Retrace your steps by taking the Tsubame back to Hakata/Fukuoka, from where you can take a shinkansen back to Honshu.

Shikoku (see pp362-390)

Day 1 Starting from Okayama (p364) on Honshu, board the Marine Liner rapid train which crosses the Inland Sea before heading to Takamatsu (p365). Visit Ritsurin Park or take a side trip by rail to the nearby roof-top plateau of Yashima (p380) before spending the night in Takamatsu.

Day 2 From Takamatsu pick up the Shimanto LEX and continue south along the Dosan line to Kochi (p365), stopping along the way to visit the mountain-top shrine at Kotohira (p366) and/or Oboke Gorge (p368). Overnight in Kochi.

Day 3 Spend the morning in Kochi before picking up the Nanpu LEX which continues along the Dosan line to Kubokawa. Connect here with a local Yodo line train which chugs slowly west to the bull-fighting city of Uwajima (p371).

Day 4 Spend day and second overnight in Uwajima.

Day 5 From Uwajima take a limited express north along the Uchiko line to Matsuyama (p372), perhaps stopping off briefly in the small town of Uchiko (p372), which contains a well-preserved historical quarter and small Noh theatre. Spend rest of the day and overnight in Matsuyama.

Day 6 Take a side trip by tram from Matsuyama to the hot springs at Dogo Onsen (p386) and relax in the 100-year-old bath house.

Day 7 From Matsuyama board a Shiokaze LEX heading back to Okayama, perhaps stopping along the way in Utazu (p374) to visit the Gold Tower and adjacent World Toilet Museum (see box p375).

Getting to Japan

The travel agencies listed below sell the Japan Rail Pass; most also book flights and accommodation, and can organize itineraries. Enquire also about tailor-made package tours. Please note that the list is not comprehensive; contact a JNTO office (see box opposite) for full details.

FROM THE UK AND IRELAND

All Nippon Airways (☎ 0345-262262, 🖳 www.ana-europe.com) operates daily flights from London Heathrow to Tokyo. ANA's 'Visit Japan Fare' offers discounts to foreign visitors on domestic flights within Japan. A minimum of two coupons and a maximum of five must be purchased; a coupon costs ¥12,600 and is valid for any of 138 routes across Japan. If you're in a hurry and want to see as much of Japan as possible, use these coupons in conjunction with a rail pass.

Both **Virgin Atlantic** (☎ 01293-747747, 🖳 www.virgin-atlantic.com) and **British Airways** (☎ 0845-773 3377, 🖳 www.britishairways.com) operate daily flights to Tokyo and have courier services (see below), the cheapest way to fly to Japan on a direct service. **Japan Airlines** (☎ 0845-774 7700, 🖳 www.jal-europe.com) flies daily to Tokyo and Osaka, and twice-weekly to Nagoya. Fares

⛩ **Japan National Tourist Organization (JNTO)**
The best source of tourist information prior to arrival in Japan is the **Japan National Tourist Organization**. Branches around the world are well stocked with leaflets and staff can answer almost any question you have about Japan on the spot. The offices are information centres only; they do not sell any tickets or rail passes. Their website, **www.jnto.go.jp**, has regular travel updates; alternatively contact the main overseas offices.

● **UK** (☎ 020-7734 9638, 💻 www.seejapan.co.uk, info@jnto.co.uk) Heathcoat House, 20 Savile Row, London W1X 1AE.
● **France** (☎ 01 42 96 20 29) 4, rue de Ventadour, 75001 Paris.
● **Germany** (☎ 069-20353) Kaiserstrasse 11, 60311 Frankfurt am Main.
● **USA** (☎ 212-757 5640, 💻 www.japantravelinfo.com), One Rockefeller Plaza, Suite 1250, **New York**, NY 10020; (☎ 312-222 0874) 401 North Michigan Ave, Suite 770, **Chicago**, IL 60611; (☎ 415-292 5686) 1 Daniel Burnham Court, Suite 250C **San Francisco**, CA 94109; (☎ 213-623 1952) 515 South Figueroa St, Suite 1470, **Los Angeles**, CA 90071.
● **Canada** (☎ 416-366 7140) 165 University Ave, Toronto, Ontario M5H 3B8.
● **Australia** (☎ 02-9232 4522) Level 33, The Chifley Tower, 2 Chifley Square, Sydney, NSW 2000.
● **Thailand** (☎ 02-233 5108) 19th Fl, Ramaland Bldg, No 952 Rama 4 Rd, Bangrak District, Bangkok 10500.
● **Hong Kong** (☎ 2968-5688) Suite 3704-05, 37/F, Dorset House, Taikoo Place, Quarry Bay.
● **Korea** (☎ 02-732 7525) 10th Floor, Press Center Bldg, 25 Taepyongno 1-ga, Chung-gu, Seoul.

from UK to Japan bought direct from airlines start at around £650 for an APEX return. There are no direct flights from Ireland.

If you are travelling on your own and want a direct flight, consider being a courier; for further details contact **British Airways Travel Shops** (☎ 0870 606 1133) or **ACP** (☎ 020-8897 5130), the agent for courier services on Virgin Atlantic. Expect to pay between £350 and £700 depending on the time of year.

The cheapest fares are, however, on indirect routes. Discounted fares are offered through most of the travel agencies listed below; Lufthansa offers the possibility of flying into Tokyo and out of Kansai (Osaka) so it is worth asking about fares on that airline.

● **Japan Travel Centre** (☎ 020-7255 8283, 💻 www.japantravel.co.uk), 212 Piccadilly, London W1V 9LD, has a very useful book store on the ground floor and a small Japanese food section.
● **JTB Corp** (formerly Japan Travel Bureau; ☎ 020-7663 6148, 💻 www.jtb.co.jp/eng/index.html), 95 Cromwell Rd, London SW7 4JT.
● **ANA World Tours** (☎ 020-7478 1900, 💻 www.anatours.co.uk), 3rd Floor, Nuffield House, 41/46 Piccadilly, London W1V 9AJ.
● **Tokyu Travel** (☎ 020-7493 0468, 7493 2456, 💻 tte@JapanGlobe.net), 295 Regent St, London W1B 2HL.

- **Creative Tours** (☎ 020-7495 1775, 💻 www.jaltour.co.uk), Hanover Court, 5 Hanover Square, London W1S 1HE.
- **Leisurail** (☎ 0870-750 0222, 💻 www.leisurail.co.uk), PO Box 5, 12 Coningsby Rd, Peterborough PE3 8HY. Rail pass only.
- **HIS UK Ltd** (☎ 020-7439 3311, 💻 sales@his-euro.co.uk), 25/28 Old Burlington St, London W1X 1RJ.
- **usit Campus** (☎ 020-7730 7285), 52 Grosvenor Gardens, London SW1W 0AG. usit has branches throughout the UK.
- **AWL Travel Ltd** (☎ 020-7222 1144), 1 Artillery Row, London SW1P 1RH. Branch also in **Dublin** (☎ 01-679 5340), 2nd Fl, 42 Dawson St, Dublin 2.

The operators listed below organize package tours to Japan:
- **ANA World Tours** (contact details as above).
- **Jaltour** (operated by Creative Tours, ☎ 020-7462 5577, address as above).
- **JTB Corp** (Sunrise Tours, ☎ 020-7663 6148, address as for JTB Corp).
- **Explore Worldwide** (☎ 01252-760000, 💻 info@exploreworldwide.com), 1 Frederick St, Aldershot, Hants GU11 1LQ.
- **Audley Travel** (☎ 01869-276200, 💻 www.audleytravel.com).
- **Inside Japan Tours** (☎ 0870-7461044, 📠 0870-7461047, 💻 info@inside-japantours.com, www.insidejapantours.com) is an independent travel company which offers tour packages and tailored holidays around Japan.
- **Travel Bureau** Rail Tours (☎ 01902-324343, 💻 www.The TravelBureau.co.uk, leerailtours@TheTravelBureau.co.uk), The Cottage, High St, Wombourne, Wolverhampton WV5 9DN, organizes a bi-annual rail tour in conjunction with the Japanese Railway Society (see box, p69).

FROM CONTINENTAL EUROPE

All Nippon Airways (☎ 08 02 80 32 12 France; ☎ 01-7956 7360 Austria, ☎ 0180-300 0309 Germany) operates direct flights to Tokyo from Paris, and to Tokyo and Osaka from Vienna and Frankfurt. **Lufthansa** in Germany (☎ 01803-803803) and **KLM** in the Netherlands (☎ 0204-747747) are both major carriers to Japan.

From Austria
- **Creative Tours** (☎ 01-502 7580), Kartnerstr 11, Weihburggasse 2, 1010 Wien.

From Belgium
- **Creative Tours** (☎ 02-639 0910), Ave Louise 283, Box 17, 1050 Brussels.

From Denmark
- **Net Travel** (☎ 3332-1616), Vester Voldgade 94, 1552 Copenhagen.

From France
- **Japon Sans Frontière** (☎ 01 40 20 03 33), 12 rue du Marché, St Honoré, 75001 Paris.
- **JCT International** (☎ 01 44 55 15 30), 4 rue Ventadour, 75001 Paris.

From Germany
• **JAL Tour GmbH** (☎ 030-2655 1223), Europa-Centre Hochhaus 10th Fl, Tauentzien Str 9, 10789 Berlin.
• **JTB Corp** (☎ 069-2998 7823), Grosse Friedberger Str 23, 60313 Frankfurt.
• **Intra Express Hobby-und Studienreisen GmbH** (☎ 030-785 3391, 💻 intraex@t-online.de), Burgherrenstr 2, 12101 Berlin. Organizes specialist rail tours worldwide, including in Japan.

From Italy
• **Creative Tours** (☎ 06-481 9417), Via L Bissolati 76, 00187, Rome.
• **Alviaggi Tour Operation SRL** (☎ 02-481 6551), Piazza Po 6, 20144 Milan.

From the Netherlands
• **Tozai Travel** (☎ 020-626 2272), NZ, Voorburgwal 175-177, 1012 RK Amsterdam.

From Spain
• **Creative Tours** (☎ 91-593 3819), C/Luchana 23-6-1A, 28010 Madrid.

From Switzerland
• **JTB Corp** (☎ 022-738 4541), 45-47 rue de Lausanne, 1201 Geneva.

FROM NORTH AMERICA

All Nippon Airways (☎ 1-800 235 9262) and **Japan Airlines** (☎ 1-800 525 3663) have connections from all over North America to Tokyo, Osaka and Nagoya. Major US carriers to Japan include **United** (☎ 1-800 241 6522), **Delta** (☎ 1-800 241 4141) and **American** (☎ 1-800 433 7300).

From the USA
• **Kintetsu International Express** (☎ 212-259-9640), 1325 Ave of the Americas, Suite 2001, New York, NY 10019. Branches also in Chicago (☎ 630-250-8840; 1 Pierce Pl), Los Angeles (☎ 213-622-5600; 611 West Sixth St), and San Francisco (☎ 415-922-7171; Kintetsu Bldg, 1737 Post St).
• **JTB Corp** (☎ 212-698 4900), 810 Seventh Ave, 34th Fl, New York NY 10019. Branches also in Chicago (☎ 847-698-9090; 5600 North River Rd, Suite 190, Rosamont, Il 60018) and San Francisco (☎ 415-986-4764; 360 Post St, Suite 305, CA 94108).
• **Tokyu Travel America** (☎ 212-867-4011, 💻 www.tokyutravel.com), 11th Floor, 489 Fifth Ave, New York, NY 10017.

From Canada
• **JTB International** (☎ 800-268-5942 or 416-367 5824), 77 King St, West Toronto, Ontario M5K 1E7.
• **Pacifico Creative Service Inc** (☎ 604-689 5228), 1030 W Georgia St, Vancouver, BC V6E 2Y3.

FROM ASIA

Singapore Airlines (Singapore ☎ 65-223 8888) operates flights to Tokyo, Osaka, Nagoya, Hiroshima and Fukuoka and has connections with cities around the world from its hub in Singapore. **Cathay Pacific** (Hong Kong ☎ 2747-1888) flies from Hong Kong to Tokyo, Osaka and Fukuoka, while subsidiary **Dragon Air** (Hong Kong ☎ 3193-3888) serves Hiroshima and Sendai.

Hong Kong
● **Package Tours (Hong Kong) Ltd** (☎ 2722-1692), Rm 803, Prestige Tower, 23-25 Nathan Rd, Tsimshatsui East, Kowloon.
● **JTB Corp** (☎ 2734 9288) UG 305, Chinachem Golden Plaza, 77 Mody Rd, Tsimshatsui, Kowloon.

Malaysia
● **Orient Network Tours and Travel** (☎ 03-261 0922), Suite 20.01A, Level 20, Menara Lion, 165 Jalan Ampang, 50450 Kuala Lumpur.

From Singapore
● **JTB Corp** (☎ 65-434 1298), 9 Temasek Blvd 07-01, Suntec Tower 2, Singapore 038989.

FROM SOUTH AFRICA

South African Airways (☎ 0861-359 722, 💻 www.flysaa.com) operates a code-share flight with Cathay Pacific four times a week from Johannesburg to Hong Kong, from where onward connections can be made to Japan The cheapest return fare from Jo'burg to Hong Kong is ZAR5500.

● **AWL Travel** (☎ 011-884 5175, 💻 www.awlt.com), 2nd Floor, Export House, 71 Maude St, Sandton 2146, Johannesburg.

FROM AUSTRALASIA

Qantas (Australia ☎ 13 13 13) operates flights from Sydney to Tokyo.
  Air New Zealand (☎ 0800-737 000) operates flights from Auckland and Christchurch to Tokyo and Osaka. Return fares start from around NZ$1900.

From Australia
● **JALPAK International** (☎ 02-9285 6666), Level 14, Darling Park, 201 Sussex St, Sydney, NSW 2000.
● **Kintetsu International Express** (☎ 03-9654 3320), 9th Fl, 257 Collins St, Melbourne, VIC 3000.

From New Zealand
● **Gullivers** (☎ 09-307 1888), PO Box 505, Auckland.
● **JTB Corp** (☎ 03-365 6929), 78 Worcester St, Christchurch.

Before you go

PASSPORTS AND VISAS

All visitors to Japan must be in possession of a valid passport. Japan has signed agreements with over 50 countries exempting their citizens from applying for a visa if they are visiting for the purposes of tourism. Amongst other countries, citizens of the UK, Austria, Belgium, France, Germany, Ireland, Italy, Netherlands, Singapore, Spain, Switzerland, the USA, Canada, Australia and New Zealand can enter Japan for a period of up to 90 days under the 'reciprocal visa exemption' scheme. Citizens of the UK, Austria, Germany, Ireland and Switzerland can apply for a further 90-day extension while in Japan.

Citizens of all other countries, including Hong Kong and Malaysia, need to apply for a tourist visa from the Japanese embassy or consulate in their home country (see box, p28).

Visa requirements change periodically, so before making travel arrangements check with the Japanese embassy in your home country.

HEALTH AND INSURANCE

No vaccinations or health certificates are required to enter the country and there's no need to worry about diseases such as malaria, which are not endemic in Japan. Tap water is safe to drink even in big cities like Tokyo, but bottled water is readily available in convenience stores (sparkling water is harder to find than still).

Don't arrive in Japan without a comprehensive travel insurance policy. Japanese hospitals invariably offer high standards of care and most doctors speak either English or German, but diagnosis, treatment and prescriptions can be prohibitively expensive.

If you're on medication, bring a copy of your prescription. This may be needed if Customs inspect your bags but will also be useful if you need a repeat prescription. Note that many international drugs are sold under different brand names in Japan.

WHAT TO TAKE

Long staircases are the norm at railway stations (escalators and lifts are rarely available in small stations) and porters are practically unheard of, so the best advice is to pack as little as possible. Travelling light also means you'll have no problem fitting your luggage into a coin locker (see p81) at the station.

A few other tips on what to bring are: if planning to stay mostly in Japanese-style accommodation it's worth bringing slip-on shoes as you're

❏ **Embassies and consulates**
- **Australia** (☎ 02-6273 3244, 🖳 www.japan.org.au), 112 Empire Circuit, Yarralumla, Canberra ACT 2600.
- **Austria** (☎ 01-531920, 🖳 www.embjapan.at/embjapan/), Hessgasse 6, 1010 Wien.
- **Belgium** (☎ 02-513 2340), ave des Arts 58, 1000 Bruxelles.
- **Canada** (☎ 613-241 8541, 🖳 www.embassyjapancanada.org), 255 Sussex Drive, Ottawa, Ontario K1N 9E6. Consulate-General offices in Edmonton (☎ 403-422 3752), Montreal (☎ 514-866 3429), Toronto (☎ 416-363 7038) and Vancouver (☎ 604-684 5868).
- **Denmark** (☎ 3311-3344, 🖳 www.embjapan.dk), Pilestraede 61, 1112 Copenhagen K.
- **France** (☎ 01 48 88 62 00, 🖳 www.amb-japon.fr), 7 ave Hoche, 75008 Paris.
- **Germany** (☎ 030-210940, 🖳 www.embjapan.de), Kleiststrasse 23-26, 10787 Berlin.
- **Hong Kong** Consulate-General (☎ 2522-1184, 🖳 www.hk-japan.org), One Exchange Square, 8 Connaught Place, Central, Hong Kong.
- **Ireland** (☎ 01-269 4244, 🖳 www.mofa.go.jp/embjapan/ireland/), Nutley Building, Merrion Centre, Nutley lane, Dublin 4.
- **Italy** (☎ 06-487 991, 🖳 www.ambasciatajp.it), Via Quintino Sella, 60 00187 Rome.
- **Malaysia** (☎ 03-242 7044), 11 Pesiaran Stonor, 50450 Kuala Lumpur.
- **Netherlands** (☎ 070-346 9544, 🖳 www.emb-japan.nl), Tobias Asserlaan 2, 2517 KC, The Hague.
- **New Zealand** (☎ 04-473 1540, 🖳 www.japan.org.nz), Level 18, Majestic Centre, 100 Willis St, Wellington 1.
- **Singapore** (☎ 65-235 8855, 🖳 www.japan-emb.org.sg), 16 Nassim Rd, Singapore, 258390.
- **South Korea** (☎ 02-733 5626, 🖳 www.japanem.or.kr), 9th Fl, Kyobo Bldg, Jongro-1Ka, Jongro-ku, Seoul.
- **Spain** (☎ 91-590 7600), Calle Serrano 109, 28006 Madrid.
- **Switzerland** (☎ 031-300 2222, 🖳 www.embjapan.ch), Engestrasse 53, 3026 Berne.
- **UK** (☎ 020-7465 6500, 🖳 www.embjapan.org.uk), 101-104 Piccadilly, London W1V 9FN. A Consulate-General (☎ 0131-225 4777) is at 2 Melville Crescent, Edinburgh EH3 7HW.
- **USA** (202-238-6700, 🖳 www.embjapan.org), 2520 Massachusetts Ave NW, Washington DC 20008-2869. There are Consulate-General offices all over the States, including Chicago (☎ 312-280-0400), Los Angeles (☎ 213-617 6700), Miami (☎ 305-530-9090), New York (☎ 212-371-8222), San Francisco (☎ 415-777-3533) and Seattle (☎ 206-682-9107).

expected to take your shoes off in the entrance hall (*genkan*). Guests walk around either in the slippers provided or, if these are too small, just in socks (pack a few pairs without holes!). Guests in Japanese-style accommodation are also usually provided with a small towel which doubles as a flannel; if you prefer a large towel it might be better to bring one.

Nightwear is not essential as guests in most forms of accommodation, apart from hostels, are provided with a *yukata* (a cotton robe tied with a belt) that can be worn in bed and which is used as a dressing gown to go between your room and the bathroom. Yukata (and Japanese-style towels) can often be rented or purchased from the front desk if they are not provided.

Pack according to the season and the region in which you're likely to be travelling (see p11). As a general rule, shorts and T-shirts are fine in the summer, though you'll probably need a sweater or two in the spring and autumn. Take warm clothes for the winter, especially if travelling in northern Japan.

At any time of the year, it's worth packing a few smart clothes – older Japanese in particular are generally well-dressed (even when on holiday themselves) and smart clothes could be useful if you expect to socialize with any Japanese. If you forget anything, clothes and shoes are relatively cheap as long as you avoid the designer-label boutiques, but note that it's not always easy to find large sizes.

Don't bother packing an umbrella as disposable ones are readily and cheaply available in convenience stores. Tourist attractions which involve walking around outside usually have a supply of umbrellas for visitors to borrow.

If you want an unusual souvenir of your trip, take a notebook (see box, p84).

MONEY – see also p56

Japan is a cash-based economy so when travelling around it's best to ensure you always have a supply of cash. Travellers' cheques (in ¥ or US$ only) are possibly the most useful way to take money but ensure you cash them before heading off the beaten track. Also be prepared for a long wait when you go to a bank to exchange them.

Credit cards are accepted in most major tourist places but don't rely on this. Upmarket hotels tend to accept credit cards but cash is the preferred currency in youth hostels, minshuku, budget ryokan and business hotels. Some cities have an ATM that will accept cards issued abroad; these are listed in the respective city guides.

SUGGESTED READING

History

A History of Japan: From Stone Age to Superpower Kenneth Henshall (Macmillan, 1999). A scholarly but very readable book.

A Traveller's History of Japan Richard Tames (Windrush Press, 1993). A great, pocket-sized book that's ideal to dip into as you travel around.

Embracing Defeat: Japan in the Aftermath of World War II John Dower (Penguin, 1999).

Shogun James Clavell (Flame, 1999). Billed as an epic tale of 17th-century Japan, Clavell's novel is based on the story of Will Adams, the first Englishman to arrive in Japan. Hard going at first but worth the effort.

Hiroshima John Hersey (Penguin, 1986). Originally written in the 1960s this remains one of the most authoritative accounts of the A-Bomb's devastation of Hiroshima. The narrative is told from the point of view of different survivors in the moments before, and minutes, hours, days and years after the explosion.

Travel narratives

Hokkaido Highway Blues Will Ferguson (Canongate, 2000). Ferguson travels from southern Kyushu north to Hokkaido following the path of the cherry blossom; an irreverent account of life on the open road.

Japan: True stories of life on the road Edited by Donald George and Amy Carlson (Travelers' Tales, 1999). A superb selection of travel narratives; perfect for dipping into on long train journeys.

The Roads to Sata Alan Booth (Kodansha, 1985). The late Alan Booth walked the length of Japan, from Hokkaido to Kyushu, looking for beer. Equally absorbing is his *Looking for the Lost: Journeys Through a Vanishing Japan* (Kodansha, 1995), a series of travel narratives taking in parts of Japan that most foreigners never see.

Dave Barry Does Japan Dave Barry (Ballantine Books, 1992). Humourist Dave Barry takes a family holiday in Japan, all expenses paid by his publisher. In Japan, look out for his syndicated column from the States which appears weekly in the *Daily Yomiuri*. (See also p81).

A Ride in the Neon Sun Josie Dew (Warner Books 2000). Josie Dew pedals around Japan and writes entertainingly about her encounters and experiences.

Rediscovering the old Tokaido: In the footsteps of Hiroshige Patrick Carey (Global Oriental, 2000). The story of a nostalgic journey on foot along what remains of the road that linked Edo and Kyoto in the days before the Tokaido line.

Life in Japan

Kokoro: Hints and Echoes of Japanese Inner Life Lafcadio Hearn (Tuttle, 1972). The best introduction to Irish writer Lafcadio Hearn's experiences of life in Meiji-era Japan (see p35).

The Japanese Joe Joseph (Penguin, 1994). Written by a former *Times* correspondent in Tokyo, Joseph surveys life in Japan at the height of the bubble economy. Includes the revelation that Sylvester Stallone once advertised a brand of Japanese ham using the slogan: 'It's so delicious, it's a gift of love'.

Angry White Pyjamas: An Oxford Poet Trains With The Tokyo Riot Police Robert Twigger (Indigo, 1997). Brit Robert Twigger abandons an English-teaching career going nowhere fast in Tokyo and takes up *aikido*.

Xenophobe's Guide to the Japanese Sahoko Kaji, Noriko Hama and Jonathan Rice (Oval Books, 1999). A pocket-sized humorous guide to what makes the Japanese tick.

100 Unuseless Japanese Inventions Kenji Kawakami and Dan Papia (HarperCollins, 1995). Kawakami is the wacky inventor of *chindogu*, bizarre gadgets such as the 'cockroach swatting slippers' and 'umbrella head belt'. See also the follow-up book, *99 More Unuseless Japanese Inventions* (HarperCollins, 1997).

Memoirs of a Geisha Arthur Golden (Random House, 1997). Golden's novel about a trainee *geisha*'s life has become a modern classic. Sayuri is born in a fishing village but she is sold to a Kyoto geisha house from where she rises to become one of the city's most famous and sought-after geisha.

Geisha Lesley Downer (Headline, 2000) This is a personal account of the months Downer spent in the Gion tea houses, befriending the *mama-san* who hold the purse strings and manage the careers of trainee geisha. She gets closer than any commentator to a revelation of life behind the enigmatic smiles and painted faces of geisha in Kyoto.

Reading Zen In The Rocks: The Japanese Landscape Garden François Berthier (University of Chicago, 2000, translated by Graham Parkes).

The railway

Japanese Railways in the Meiji Period 1868-1912 Tom Richards and Charles Rudd (Brunel, 1991). The authors provide a detailed account of the railway's early days.

High Speed in Japan Peter Semmens (Platform 5, 2000). The most thorough and engaging account of the shinkansen age.

Both books are available through the Japanese Railway Society (see box p69).

Guidebooks

Lonely Planet's *Japan* (7th edition, October 2000) is one of the most comprehensive general guides to the country. Jan Dodd and Simon Richmond's *The Rough Guide to Japan* (Rough Guides, June 2001) is also good.

⛩ Stamping around Japan

Stamp collecting is a popular pastime in Japan, though the most popular stamps are not of the postage kind. Virtually every tourist attraction here has its own stamp and ink pad at the entrance. Some towns organize seasonal 'stamp rallies', when tourists are invited to follow a trail from one attraction to another, collecting stamps as they go. Small souvenir prizes are sometimes doled out to those who completely fill their 'stamp cards' (a gesture of thanks for contributing to the local tourism industry). In Japan, it's almost as if you only know you've really been somewhere when you can bring back the stamp to prove it.

Stamps are particularly popular on the railway. Even the tiniest rural station will more than likely have a stamp in the waiting room or by the ticket desk. Pack a blank notebook in your luggage, try to forget your image of the nerdy stamp collector, and by collecting stamps as you go you'll have an instant souvenir of your rail trip around Japan, as well as a useful record of your personal itinerary.

Facts about the country

GEOGRAPHY

Japan is made up of over 3000 islands, a total land mass almost as large as the state of California. The four main islands are **Honshu**, the largest, followed by **Hokkaido**, the most northern and also the least populated, then **Kyushu**, the southernmost, and **Shikoku**. Stretching 3000km from north to south, the northernmost regions of Japan are subarctic, while the extreme south is subtropical.

Four-fifths of the land surface is mountainous and rural; most of the 127 million people who live on the four main islands are packed into the coastal plains. This has led to so-called 'urban corridors', the longest of which, and perhaps the most densely inhabited in the world, is the Tokaido belt which runs between Tokyo and Osaka.

HISTORY

Space permits only a condensed 'bullet points' history of Japan. For recommended books on the history of Japan, see p29.

蝶
の
空
七
堂
伽
藍
さ
か
し
ま
に

Birth of a nation: myth and reality

Nobody knows exactly when Japan was first inhabited by humans but estimates range from between 500,000 and 100,000 years ago. The **Jomon period**, named after a rope pattern found on the oldest form of pottery in the world, began around 10,000BC but the country was not unified until the 4th century, when the Yamato dynasty was established and the title of Emperor first used.

A capital is established: 710-794

Up until the 7th century, tradition dictated that the capital was changed every time a new Emperor ascended to the throne. But in 710, the Imperial Court decided to settle in Nara (see p195), a city still proud that it was the capital of Japan and the home of seven Emperors in just 77 years before the court was moved to Kyoto in 794.

To the butterfly in the sky
all buildings on the temple ground
are upside down
(BOSHA KAWABATA)

The **Nara period** was marked by influences from China and the growing popularity of its imported religion, Buddhism. The main Chinese influence is visible today in Todai-ji (see p196), the largest wooden building in the world which contains the biggest statue of Buddha in Japan, a bronze image cast in 752. Religious riches and treasure aside, hunger and poverty were commonplace outside the Imperial Court, though there was worse to come in later centuries.

Flourishing of the arts but rivalry outside the court: 794-1192

Nara was soon over-run with Buddhist temples and Shinto shrines, and Emperor Kammu could no longer bear being closeted there. So, a new capital was established, in 794, in Heian (present-day Kyoto) where it was to remain until 1868. A symbolic fresh start was assured by a complete reconstruction of the city on a grid layout.

Japan's most famous literary work, *The Tale of Genji* by Murasaki Shikibu, was written during this period (the **Heian period**), as was *The Pillow Book*, a revealing account of life at the Imperial court by a woman very much on the inside, Lady-in-Waiting Sei Shonagon. It was not just literature that flourished, but painting, sculpture and poetry; the Emperor hosted outdoor parties where guests would be invited to compose haiku over cups of saké.

Outside the walls of the Imperial Court, far from the parties and poetry gatherings, a new warrior class was emerging: the samurai. The bloodiest military campaign of all for national supremacy raged between the rival Minamoto (also known as Genji) and Taira (also known as Heike) clans. The epic war, now steeped in as much legend as historical fact, swung between the two clans, before a decisive sea battle in 1185 routed the Tairas. But peace was short-lived and the feudal era had begun.

The first shogun: 1185-1333

The bloody corpses of the defeated Taira had hardly washed away before Minamoto no Yoritomo, victorious leader of the Minamoto clan, moved the capital to Kamakura and was sworn in as the country's first shogun. The Imperial Court remained in Kyoto but real power had shifted geographically and politically to the samurai. Government of the country remained in the hands of successive shoguns for the next 700 years, until the Meiji Restoration of 1868.

The popularity of Buddhism grew during the **Kamakura period**. The Zen sect in particular, with its emphasis on a life of simplicity and austerity, appealed to the warrior class who had always been ill at ease with the effete world of culture and arts during the Heian period. Instead of ushering in a new era, Yoritomo's death in 1199 prompted his widow and her family to assume control. The political capital remained in Kamakura until 1333, when Emperor Go-Daigo succeeded in overthrowing the shogunate.

Eruption of civil war, West and East meet: 1336-1575

The Emperor's moment of triumph turned out to be unexpectedly brief. He was soon booted out of Kyoto by Takauji Ashikaga, the military turncoat who had defected from the Kamakura court in time to become the Emperor's right-hand military man and assist in the rebellion against the Kamakura shogunate. Rightly or wrongly expecting credit for this assistance and anticipating the title of shogun as due reward, Ashikaga was aggrieved when Go-Daigo completely overlooked him. Seeking revenge, Ashikaga forced Go-Daigo into mountain exile and appointed a new Emperor who was gracious enough to name him shogun. From his hideaway, Go-Daigo made another attempt to retain direct rule but he died soon after, in 1339, and the rival Imperial Court he established was never a serious threat to the Kyoto government.

The Golden and Silver pavilions, two of Kyoto's major tourist draws, were constructed as villas for the shoguns during this period. As in the Heian period, culture and arts took centre stage, with Noh theatre, tea ceremony and flower arranging all being established in the latter half of the **Muromachi period**. But war was also becoming commonplace as rival feudal lords clashed over territory and isolated skirmishes spiralled into full-scale civil war.

As the nation fought with itself, Christianity made its first appearance in Japan when the missionary Francis Xavier sailed into Kagoshima in 1549, carrying with him enormous ambition: to convert Emperor and shogun alike. He failed, but relations with the West developed further in Nagasaki, where the port was opened to trade with the Portuguese.

Reunification: 1575-1600

The long road to reunification began in 1568 when Nobunaga Oda descended on Kyoto. Nobunaga soon cemented his authority by building the first castle stronghold and, unknowingly, setting a trend to be repeated by feudal lords all over Japan.

Castles, each one grander and its defences safer than the last, became a must-have for every lord needing to prove his power over the people he ruled. Sadly, in the centuries since, most of the castles have been destroyed by war and fire. Only a few original examples, such as the castles of Himeji (see p205) and Matsumoto (see p150), remain intact today.

Nobunaga hardly had time to settle into his own castle before he was assassinated in 1582. His successor, Hideyoshi Toyotomi, picked up where Nobunaga had left off and continued with efforts to reunite the country, a task largely completed by 1590. Flushed with success at home, Hideyoshi rebranded himself as an international warrior during two ill-fated attempts to capture Korea. After his death, his son and heir, Hideyori, was swept aside by the warlord Tokugawa Ieyasu, who went on to establish his own government in Edo (present-day Tokyo).

Closing down on the outside world: 1600-1853

Ieyasu knew that the lessons of history were there to be learnt. The Kamakura shogunate had shown itself open to attack from rival clans but Ieyasu and his successors tolerated no intruders. Some 300 feudal clans across Japan were forced to travel to Edo for regular audiences with the shogun. The expense and length of such journeys, nearly three centuries before the rail network would shuttle anyone to Tokyo within a day, ensured that feudal lords were never able to build up the power or finances to mount a challenge to the Tokugawa shogunate.

Strict laws of personal conduct were enforced and a social hierarchy developed with the shogun at the top and peasants and merchants at the bottom. Sandwiched in between were the samurai, though they too were restricted in movement and activity by their own code of conduct. In 1639, Japan suddenly closed all its ports to international trade, with the exception of a tiny Dutch enclave in Nagasaki. The policy of self-seclusion also prohibited all Japanese from leaving the country. Despite, or perhaps because of, the 'no vacancies' sign held up to the outside world, the **Edo period** was one of the most peaceful in Japanese history. Once again, the arts flourished, kabuki theatres opened and merchants traded in lacquerware and silk. But peace and prosperity at the price of national isolation could not last forever; by the middle of the 19th century, the feudal system was looking increasingly outdated. Not for much longer could the shogun keep the outside world at bay.

The era of modernization: 1853 to the present

Commodore Perry's arrival in 1853 accompanied by the 'Black Ships' of the US Navy was to alter the course of Japan's history for ever. The ships were laden with gifts but Perry's visit was anything but a social call. The Americans demanded that the ports be opened to trade and it became increasingly clear that the authorities would not be able to resist the influx of technology from the outside world. The Tokugawa shogunate clung desperately to power for another decade but was finally overthrown in 1867. In the following year, Emperor Meiji was restored to the throne, though he remained politically powerless. Edo, by now renamed Tokyo, became the official capital and Japan embarked on its long period of modernization. One of the most notable achievements was the building of a national railway, an account of which begins on p66.

As the country began to catch up with the rest of the world, the last remnants of the ancien régime were cast away. The land owned by feudal lords was carved up into prefectures which still exist today. Swordless samurai were deprived of their status and forced to find work elsewhere – even their trademark top-knot hairstyle had to go. A new, Western-style, constitution was instituted in 1889 and compulsory education introduced. Wealthy Japanese parents sent their children to Oxford or Cambridge university, while engineers from the West were drafted in to provide the initial technology which would one day turn Japan into an economic superpower.

However, by the end of the first decade of the 20th century, British and other foreign engineers had all but disappeared (the Japanese learned the skills, then learned how to do better themselves). An increasingly confident Japan sought to gain a foothold in Asia; by the time of Emperor Meiji's death in 1912, the country had already engaged in wars with China and Russia. Elsewhere in the world, Japan was keen to promote its culture and traditions; for six months in 1910, the new international face of Japan was displayed to an intrigued British public at White City in west London, on the site occupied today by BBC Television Centre. Over 8,000,000 visitors caught a glimpse of a country in transition. There were demonstrations of judo, kendo, karate and sumo. A tea house, replica Japanese gardens and Ainu village were constructed. But the star attraction was a white-knuckle ride which gave visitors a bird's eye view of London:

To amuse the masses, the exhibition devised and operated a contraption called the 'Flip-Flap', the sight and sound of which ... caused a terrifying impact on my childhood mind: a pair of great mobile steel towers arranged scissor-like each with an observation cage swinging from its peak ... passengers were loaded into the cages and then, with loud clanging sounds of the steam engine that worked the towers, they slowly rose to what seemed to be a tremendous height, then criss-crossed and eventually the passengers in each cage were lowered to the ground at the opposite side. It seems that always, down to the days of the inauguration of Tokyo Tower, promoters have never failed to make money by simply hauling groups of the populace by mechanical means to points of observation at unaccustomed altitudes. (Ian Mutsu, *Japan Times Weekly*, October 2nd 1971)

The end of the first half of the 20th century was dominated by Japan's involvement in WWII, culminating in the devastating atomic bomb attacks on the cities of Hiroshima and Nagasaki in August 1945. Shortly afterwards, Emperor Hirohito, who had ascended to the throne in 1926, announced Japan's surrender.

Under American occupation after the war, the country embarked upon another period of sweeping reform. By the time the Tokyo Olympics opened in 1964, and the bullet train was speeding between Tokyo and Osaka, Japan's rise to economic superpower was complete.

Over the next two decades, the rest of the world could only watch in amazement as the country that had been closed to outsiders for more than two centuries became the fastest growing economy in the world.

The economic downturn of the late 1990s worried the Japanese and put pressure on the ruling Liberal Democratic Party to produce a magic formula and wipe away the lingering recession in an instant. But nobody's betting that the days of Japan Inc are over.

POLITICS

For almost 50 years Japanese politics has been dominated by the ruling Liberal Democratic Party (LDP), founded in 1955 and still in power today. Though the LDP has been widely credited for Japan's economic success, it has also been dogged by accusations of cronyism and corruption.

Kakuei Tanaka, prime minister in the 1970s, has been dubbed the LDP 'kingmaker' and the country's political powerbroker. Few would argue he was also one of the most corrupt politicians of modern times; his greatest achievement, having a shinkansen line built from Tokyo to Niigata solely because Niigata (see p275) was his constituency, bankrupted the entire national railway.

By the 1990s, as the country was searching for a way out of the economic doldrums, the LDP still showed no signs of reforming itself. When Prime Minister Keizo Obuchi (unflatteringly dubbed 'Cold Pizza' by the media) died in office in 2000, he was replaced by the gaffe-prone Yoshiro Mori, who rapid-

🏯 **Imperial paparazzi**
   The death of Emperor Hirohito in January 1989 was a pivotal moment in Japan's modern history. Once exalted as the divine leader of the nation and later reinvented as a constitutional monarch following American occupation after WWII, Hirohito's death marked the end of an era. His successor and the current Emperor, Akihito, seemed to breathe new life into a monarchy which had ruled for at least 1600 years.

   Ever since Akihito's son, Crown Prince Naruhito, married a career woman and Oxford graduate, Masako Owada, the media has periodically indulged in some light relief from the economic doom and gloom by speculating on when the couple would produce a child.

   Though a far cry from the paparazzi famous for hounding members of the British royal family, Japanese media still erupts into a frenzy whenever a rumour surfaces that Princess Masako may be pregnant. The announcement in May 2001 that she was pregnant gave the Japanese media another opportunity to speculate about a future heir.

   No males have been born into the Imperial family since the crown prince's younger brother, Akishino, in 1965. Under Japanese law, only a male child is eligible to inherit the throne. Thus attention is also focusing on the governing Liberal Democratic Party, which is reported to be considering changes to the law to allow abdication and female succession to the imperial throne: a woman last sat on the Japanese throne over 1300 years ago. Calls for a change in the law are likely to intensify if Princess Masako gives birth to a girl.

ly became one of Japan's most unpopular prime ministers. Mori was barely out of the headlines for the 11 months he was in office, though for all the wrong reasons. One of his most notable gaffes, for which he was forced to make an embarrassing public apology, came when he described Japan as a 'divine country' with the Emperor at its centre. He caused another public outcry shortly before an election when he suggested that wavering voters should 'stay in bed' rather than vote against him on polling day.

Mori was succeeded in 2001 by the maverick Junichiro Koizumi, Japan's 11th prime minister in just 13 years. Koizumi caused a stir after his election when he appointed five women to his cabinet. Considered an outsider and someone who would not shy away from taking genuine economic reform, voters seemed just as impressed by his appearance. Japanese media seemed to speculate more on how Koizumi gained his 'distinctive silvery mane' than on his political manifesto. His own foreign minister, Makiko Tanaka (daughter of former prime minister Kakuei Tanaka), was less complimentary, famously dubbing Koizumi 'a weirdo with a hair cut from the *Lion King*'. Japanese politics, it would seem, are always destined to be just as much about outward appearance as party policy.

Though the LDP appears to be a single, united political force, just beneath the surface lie a number of rival factions, each with its own power base and supporters. Whenever an LDP leadership election is announced, the party's political machine cranks up as each faction vies to put forward the successful candidate. With so much attention focused by the press on the political machinations of the LDP, you'd be forgiven for thinking that politics in Japan is a one-horse race. But there are a number of opposition parties, including the Socialists, who briefly came to power in 1993 as part of an eight-party anti-LDP coalition before joining with the LDP to form an alliance in 1994.

ECONOMY

When Japan's bubble economy finally burst in the early 1990s, the nation and world reeled in shock. Throughout the previous decade, the country's economy had seemed unstoppable. At 2.5%, interest rates were the lowest in the world, making money easy to borrow. Banks assisted in pumping up the bubble by offering loans to virtually anybody with little or no scrutiny of their personal finances. As a piece of real estate, Japan was worth the whole of the US seven times over. The value of land was pumped artificially high and companies staked their livelihood solely on the soaring price of the square feet they owned. This made them profitable on paper but bankrupt the moment the bottom fell out of the property market.

The bubble may have burst long ago but the gloomy economic outlook has extended into the 21st century. Companies are dreaming up ever more bizarre ways to stimulate profits. In summer 2000, employees at Mitsukoshi department store in Tokyo were dressed up in sports uniforms and told to emulate the fighting spirit of Olympic athletes to win 'gold medals' in the campaign against rival department stores.

RELIGION

The two main religions in Japan are **Buddhism**, imported from China, and **Shinto** (literally, 'the way of the gods'), Japan's indigenous religion. Shinto's origins extend as far back as Japanese mythology, to the belief that all aspects of nature (water, rocks, trees and wind, for example) have their own god. Shinto was the official state religion until 1945, up to which time the Emperor himself was considered to be a divine being. Buddhist places of worship are temples, the names of which in Japanese always end with the suffix *–ji*. In Shinto, places of worship are shrines and are much plainer in design than the often brightly-coloured temples. Shinto shrines are most obviously distinguished from temples by the red *torii* (gate) which marks the entrance to the shrine precinct. Despite numerous attempts by foreign missionaries over the centuries, **Christianity** has made few inroads into Japan, though the Western white wedding (see box, p139) is becoming the fashionable way to tie the knot.

For a good introduction to religion in Japan, see the relevant chapter in Ninian Smart's *The World's Religions* (Cambridge University Press, 1989).

THE PEOPLE

Of the 127 million people living in Japan, the vast majority are born Japanese. Commentators liken Japan to an exclusive club; only rarely is anyone from outside the circle given the much sought-after membership card – a Japanese passport. History disputes the much-touted fact that the Japanese are an entirely homogenous people since the country is said to have been first settled by migrants from various parts of mainland Asia. The Ainu, an ethnic minority who are culturally and physically distinct from the Japanese, are further proof that Japan is much more multicultural than it may at first seem. Believed to have inhabited northern Honshu and Hokkaido since the 7th century, the number of Ainu began to dwindle as the Japanese colonized the north of the country. For more details on the Ainu, their cultural heritage and battle for survival, see the box on p316.

It would be wrong to assume that the 'closed shop' nature of Japanese nationality means the people are unwelcoming. On the contrary, it would be hard to find a more friendly and welcoming country. The traditional image of the polite but formal, hard-working Japanese is only partially accurate. Indeed, any generalizations about the Japanese as a whole are unfair. Even the briefest (rail!) journey here proves that the people are as diverse as the landscape is varied.

SPORT

Traditional sports

Perhaps the best-known traditional Japanese sport is **sumo wrestling**. Two wrestlers (who usually weigh between 90 and 160kg each) attempt to push each other out of a 4.55m-diameter clay circle; the winner is decided when any part of a wrestler's body apart from the soles of his feet touches the ground, or if he steps or is pushed out of the ring. Sumo wrestlers are divided into six divisions, the highest rank being that of *yokozuna* (grand champion). There are six sumo tournaments (known as *basho*) every year and each lasts for 15 days. Tickets for ringside seats are expensive and usually sell out weeks in advance and the public broadcaster NHK provides live coverage of the tournaments. Basho are held in Tokyo (January, May and September), Osaka (March), Nagoya (July) and Fukuoka (November).

Of all the martial arts, **aikido** is perhaps the one most steeped in religion. Created in Japan by Morihei Ueshiba (1883-1970; see p177), aikido combines the disciplines of judo, karate and kendo. Practitioners of aikido attempt to harness an opponent's 'ki' (spiritual power) which in turn is said to enable them to throw him or her to the ground with little effort. **Judo** follows a similar principle though the techniques are very different. Much of the basic judo training involves throwing your opponent to the floor and holding him or her down. Judo has been a regular Olympic event since the Tokyo Olympic Games in 1964 and is now practised worldwide. There are ten ranks, called *dan*, which are internationally recognized.

Karate originated in China and only reached mainland Japan in the early 1920s; today it exists in many different styles. **Kendo** (literally, 'the way of the sword') is sometimes known as Japanese fencing. Opponents wear protective masks, chest gear and gloves while using a bamboo stick *(shinai)* or metal sword *(katana)* to strike each other. **Kyudo**, or Japanese archery, is one of the oldest martial arts and can be performed on the ground as well as on horseback, when it is known as **yabusame**.

JNTO (see p23) publishes a *Traditional Sports* leaflet which has details of where and when it's possible to observe practice sessions for the sports mentioned above, as well as information on how to apply for sumo tournament tickets.

Modern sports

Baseball is taken as seriously as it is in the USA, with professional teams divided into Central and Pacific leagues. All major cities have a professional team but the sport also attracts large numbers of students at school and university clubs. **Rugby** has a smaller following and is more of a niche market; the rising star is **soccer**, which has taken off in a big way since the launch of the J-League in 1993. The sport initially received a publicity boost from the signing of foreign players such as England's Gary Lineker, who played out the twilight of his career at Nagoya's Grampus 8. A measure of the sport's success came when Japan was selected to co-host the 2002 World Cup with South Korea.

CULTURE

Japan is known as much for its ancient traditions as its futuristic technology. The following is a brief guide to the country's highly distinctive culture.

Traditional culture

● **Ikebana** Perhaps the most celebrated of Japan's ancient cultural traditions is ikebana, or the art of flower arranging. Ikebana was once synonymous with the formality of the tea ceremony, when participants would contemplate the beauty and careful positioning of the flowers decorating the tea room. Just as there are different schools of judo and karate, so too there are a number of officially recognized schools of ikebana in Japan. Both men and women practise ikebana; indeed, it was even considered an appropriate pastime for the samurai. Foreign visitors interested in attending an introductory class can contact Ikebana International in Tokyo (☎ 03-3293 8188, 🖳 www1.biz.biglobe.ne. jp/~ikebana).

● **Chanoyu** Commonly known as the tea ceremony, chanoyu is one of the country's most highly regarded aesthetic pursuits. Considered to be a form of mental training as well as a means of learning elegant manners and etiquette, *sado* ('the way of the tea') is much more than just an elaborate way of pouring a cup of tea. While the powdered green tea is whipped up with boiling water using a special bamboo whisk and poured into the serving bowl, guests are offered a small cake or sweetmeat to prepare themselves for the bitter taste of the tea. The ceremony, which can last up to a couple of hours, is held in a simple tatami-mat room decorated with hanging scrolls and discretely positioned flowers. Some top-class hotels in cities such as Tokyo and Kyoto offer tea-ceremony demonstrations and even provide stools for guests who aren't used to sitting on their knees for long.

● **Kabuki, Bunraku and Noh** Probably the most accessible of traditional dramatic forms in Japan is **kabuki**, a theatrical art which dates back to the 17th century. A knowledge of Japanese is not necessary to enjoy the colourful performances, where men dress as women, the make-up is as bright as the costumes are lavish, and members of the audience frequently shout out their appreciation when actors take to the stage, strike a dramatic pose or deliver a famous line. The kabuki theatre comes equipped with a *seridashi*, a trap door in the floor which allows actors to enter the stage from below, as well as a gangway through the audience which lets the actors make a dramatic, sweeping entrance, their silk costumes rustling behind them as they step gracefully towards the stage. It would be hard to find a more lively or entertaining theatrical experience in Japan. The best place to sample a performance is at the Kabuki-za theatre in Tokyo (see p92).

Also originating in the 17th century and closely related to kabuki, is **bunraku** (puppet play). Puppets up to two-thirds the size of humans are dressed in costumes which are just as elaborate as those worn by actors on the kabuki stage. The puppets are operated by three stage hands while a fourth narrates the story to the tune of the traditional *shamisen* (wood instrument covered in cat skin with three strings made of silk).

Less immediately accessible than kabuki is **Noh**, a classical form of theatre which dates back more than 600 years. Performances of Noh are a combination of music and dance, but the style of movement is much more formalized than kabuki, while the dancing is stylized to represent actions such as crying and laughing and is accompanied by flutes and drums. Most of the actors wear stylized masks which depict a wide range of facial expressions and emotions. Performances, on a special raised stage with a roof and a sparse set, often take place by firelight during the summer months in the precincts of Shinto shrines.

● **Shamisen, koto and taiko** Proficiency on traditional Japanese instruments such as the **shamisen** (see above) and the **koto** (Japanese harp) was once as much a test of a geisha's talent as her ability to dance. Partly because of the cost of purchasing and maintaining such instruments, their popularity has faded. But one traditional instrument that remains popular for its infectious rhythm is the **taiko** drum. Bare-chested taiko drummers beating a furious rhythm while drenching themselves and their instruments in sweat are a staple sight and sound at most Japanese festivals, where the noise is the perfect accompaniment to a summer parade through the streets. Shaped like a cylinder, the body of the taiko drum is hollow and covered at both ends with leather. Smaller hand drums, known as *tsuzumi*, are often used in Noh and kabuki.

⛩ **Geisha in the 21st century**
   Maiko, apprentice geisha, train for up to six years for the right to be called
a geisha. During this time the maiko-san will learn how to play traditional instruments, such as the shamisen and koto (see p41), how to dance and how to dress in a kimono. Above all the trainee is required to become skilled in the manners and comportment associated with the geisha world, since every one of them will be judged by the customers to whom they are sent in the evenings to entertain.
   In the 1920s, there were about 80,000 geisha and a steady flow of new applicants. Today, one estimate suggests that there are probably no more than 4-5000 throughout Japan. Given the long hours and difficult working conditions, it's not surprising that there are few new applicants. However, a new breed of geisha is shunning the long training programme and opting for a fast-track approach to the profession. More and more young professional women, dressed in platform heels and forever chatting on their Hello Kitty mobile phones by day, are now moonlighting as geisha after only the briefest crash course in technique. Customers unwilling or unable to pay for an evening with a traditional geisha can opt instead for one of the new breeds who charge a fraction of the price.

Popular culture

Manga (comics) are big business in Japan, with an annual turnover of nearly ¥570 billion. Look out for everyone from school children to businessmen reading comic books on the train or subway. Live animation on television has been no less successful.

At the time of writing, the jury was out on whether **Pokemon** was only a passing craze or whether it would become a permanent fixture and join the elite rank of other long-life characters such as **Hello Kitty**, the cat with no mouth, Doraemon, a blue robot from the 21st century, and Miffy the rabbit. The secret to their longevity is a successful career beyond the media for which they were originally created: one manufacturer launched a limited edition Hello Kitty car, complete with Kitty steering wheel, seat covers and paintwork. For the past few years, **Doraemon** has become the undersea face of JR Hokkaido with a 'Doraemon Event' inside the Seikan Tunnel (see box p282) linking Honshu with Hokkaido, and All Nippon Airways proved that the sky was far from the marketing limit when it turned one of its 747s into a 'Pokemon Jet'.

Another popular form of entertainment is a trip to the **pachinko parlour**. Pachinko players sit in front of upright pinball machines and feed them with tiny silver ball bearings. The machines then rattle a lot and, with luck (little skill seems to be involved), more silver balls pour out through the slot into a tray; these can be exchanged for prizes like washing powder and tins of ham. These unglamorous prizes are then traded in for cash at a semi-hidden booth outside. It's illegal to play for cash in the pachinko parlours, so owners get around the law by allowing customers to exchange the prizes for money off the premises.

In big cities you're never far from a video game arcade; the best ones are the **Sega Joypolis**. Here you'll find the latest virtual reality games and hi-tech simulators, as well as more unusual slot machines. One game unlikely to be a hit outside Japan is the Sub Marine Catcher; instead of trying to manoeuvre an electronic arm to grab a prize such as a teddy bear, this version has a tank full of live lobsters. If the player is successful, the arm picks up the lobster and it falls through the slot and straight into his/her hands (plastic bags are provided to carry your winnings home).

● **Television** Japanese television is known for its weird game shows, such as the now defunct *Endurance* which, at its most extreme, challenged contestants to plunge into scorpion pits or sit for as long as possible in tanks of ice. The trend continues with shows such as *Muscle Ranking* and *Super Human Coliseum*.

Travel documentaries are popular, even more so if they are dressed up as game shows. *Experience the World* sends a celebrity to a far-flung corner of the globe to complete a series of challenges, while yet more celebrities compete to answer questions about the tasks back in the studio.

Cookery programmes, drama serials and love stories are also a mainstay of TV schedules. Many people wake up to NHK's 15-minute drama broadcast every weekday at 8:15am (see the box on p292).

● **Music** There is no greater music phenomenon in Japan than **J-Pop**. Most pop artists disappear as quickly as they rise to fame; longevity is counted in months not years. Those who have survived longer than most include the kings of pop, Tsuyoshi and Koichi Dohmoto, better known as the Kinki Kids, and the five-member boy band, SMAP.

Girl-band Morning Musume ('Morning Daughters'), known simply as MoMusu, was formed when producer Tsunku trawled round search-for-a-star contests, literally picking out losers as he went. The group quickly proved that lack of talent was no impediment to commercial success. Whenever one member of the group faded in the popularity stakes, she was simply replaced by another person from the bottomless talent pool. Flushed with success, Tsunku went on to create a whole stable of girl groups, including the all-foreigner 'Coconuts Musume', 'Country Musume' (members of which were drawn from rural areas of Japan), and 'World of Kiss' who were four female professional wrestlers.

Celebrity spotting in the commercial break
Ever since Roger Moore, the suave, sophisticated TV *Saint*, came over to Japan to become the face for Lark Cigarettes (slogan: 'Speak Lark'), there's been no shortage of foreign celebrities happy to be flown here first class to lend their name to a range of products – in exchange for a handsome fee and an assurance that their endorsements would not be seen outside Japan.

In recent years, celebrities drafted in to give that glamorous edge to household products include Bart Simpson (advertising soft drink CC Lemon), Tiger Woods (Wonda Coffee, slogan: 'It's wonderful Wonda'), Brad Pitt (Levi's 501 jeans), doctored footage of Elvis Presley and John Lennon (cup noodles), and Leonardo DiCaprio (Orico credit card and Suzuki).

Artists with longer staying power also include R&B pop sensation Utada Hikaru, who has enjoyed success in the States under the name Cubic U but is known in Japan as 'Hikki'. Pop diva Namie Amuro made the mistake of taking a year off to have a baby and has since struggled to make a comeback.

If you're in Japan on New Year's Eve, NHK broadcasts its *Red and White Song Contest*, where the biggest music stars from the last year perform live in a competition between male and female artists.

Practical information for the visitor

ARRIVING IN JAPAN

Japan has two major international gateways, Narita Airport, east of Tokyo, and Kansai Airport, built on a man-made island off the coast in Osaka Bay. Immigration and Customs are efficient at both but don't expect to rush through the formalities.

If you can choose to fly into either Narita or Kansai opt for the latter, since the airport is more modern and offers a wider range of facilities. If you're planning to travel around the Kansai region (which includes Kyoto) it makes sense anyway to fly into Kansai rather than Narita. Both airports offer ample facilities for changing money and both are connected to the Japan Rail network, so you can exchange your rail pass and begin your journey soon after touching down.

Tokyo

New Tokyo International Airport, known as **Narita** (🖳 www.narita-airport.or.jp/airport), is Japan's major international gateway. Despite the name, it's not really in Tokyo, being almost 70km outside the city, and it's not new at all since it opened in 1978. With landing slots filled to capacity, delays are common; local objections to a planned new runway mean that congestion is not likely to ease in the near future. Tokyo's second airport is **Haneda** but you'll only pass through here if you're taking a domestic flight or if you're on a China Airlines flight to/from Taiwan. Haneda is closer to the centre of Tokyo than Narita and is accessible via a monorail which runs from Hamamatsucho station on the JR Yamanote line (see p87).

Narita has **two terminals** connected by a free shuttle bus. In the arrivals lobby of both is a **tourist information desk** (☎ 0476-34 6251 or 30 3383, daily, 9am-8pm), where accommodation bookings can be made through the **Welcome Inn Reservation Center** (daily, 9am-7:30pm). The **money exchange counter** (daily, 6:30am-11pm) is a good place to change travellers' cheques or foreign currency, particularly at the weekend when banks are closed.

Japan Rail and the private Keisei Railway also have ticket desks in the arrival lobbies but to convert an exchange order you have to go to the rail station level on B1 (one floor below the arrivals hall). **Rail-pass exchange orders** can be converted to the relevant pass at the View Plaza travel agency (11:30am-7pm), or at the normal JR ticket office outside these times. Seat reservations can also be made if you've already planned your itinerary.

See p95 for notes about getting to Tokyo from Narita.

Osaka

International flights land at **Kansai International Airport** (🖳 www.kansai-airport.or.jp/index-e.html). Kansai Airport (opened in 1994) is a more impressive gateway to Japan than Narita but has its own share of problems. Conceived before Japan's economic bubble burst, the airport is now hugely in debt; airlines are objecting to the exorbitant landing fees and the island it's built on has been sinking at such an alarming rate that a moat is to be built around it.

International arrivals are on the first floor and departures are on the fourth. Staff at **Kansai TIC** (☎ 0724-56 6025, daily, 9am-9pm), in the arrivals lobby, can advise on travel throughout the Kansai region and will book accommodation anywhere in Japan through the Welcome Inn reservation network (see p48). The office is not usually busy (partly because it's slightly hidden) and staff are only too pleased to help anyone who can find them. Changing money or cashing travellers' cheques is easy as there are branches of nine banks; at least one is open between 6am and 11pm. There are also ATMs in the arrivals lobby which accept foreign-issued credit cards.

Rail pass exchange orders can be converted either at the small JR West Information Counter (daily, 9:30am-7pm) in the arrivals lobby, or at the JR Travel Center (daily, 10am-6pm) or ticket office (daily, 5:30am-11pm) at Kansai Airport station. Most people don't notice the information counter and go straight to the station but you might save time by stopping here first.

Note that departing international passengers must pay a **Passenger Service Facilities Charge** (¥2650, 2-12 years ¥1330). This charge is not included in air fares and is paid directly at the airport before you leave; most credit cards are accepted but if you do not have one make sure you have enough yen.

See p106 for notes about getting to Osaka/Kyoto from Kansai airport.

TOURIST INFORMATION

The staff in the main **tourist information centres (TICs)** at Narita and Kansai (see above) and in Tokyo and Kyoto (see the relevant city guides for details) speak English and can provide information on onward travel throughout Japan. Most towns and cities have a tourist information office (look for the 'i' logo).

鳥居 Japan Travel Phone
If you're stuck anywhere in Japan and need assistance in English, call the toll-free Japan Travel Phone (☎ 0088-22 4800, daily 9am-5pm) from any phone. Operators are very knowledgeable and will help with any travel or tourism enquiry. The toll-free number works everywhere except in Tokyo (☎ 3201-3331) and Kyoto (☎ 371-5649), where calls are charged at ¥10 per minute.

> ⛩ **Welcome cards**
> Welcome cards, which are free, offer discounts of at least 10% on a number of hotels, restaurants, museums and tourist attractions in many parts of Japan (eg the Inland Sea area, Aomori, Kitakyushu, Fukuoka, and Kagawa). Welcome cards are available from the tourist information offices in these areas; just show your passport with a 'temporary visitor' stamp. The card comes with a guide which lists all the places where discounts are offered.

Though staff at the smaller offices do not always speak English they can usually provide maps and town guides in English.

A network of **goodwill guides** operates in a number of towns and cities. These are English-speaking volunteers who guide foreign tourists around local sights. They can usually be contacted via the local tourist information office.

GETTING AROUND

By rail (see pp72-84)

By air

Japan's three major airlines operate a comprehensive network of domestic flights. Of the three, All Nippon Airways (ANA, ☎ 0120-029222) operates the largest number of domestic routes, followed closely by Japan Airlines (JAL, ☎ 0120-255971) and Japan Air System (JAS, ☎ 0120-511283). Following the deregulation of the airline market a number of smaller airlines have begun operating selected routes: Hokkaido International Airlines (ADO, known as Air Do, ☎ 03-5350 7333) flies between Tokyo and Sapporo, while Skymark Airlines (SKY, ☎ 03-3433 7670) operates between Tokyo and Fukuoka. Skymark has a dedicated women-only cabin; the airline boasts that its new service is designed to 'accommodate those who do not enjoy sitting next to men'.

If you're pushed for time and are planning to travel long distances it can make sense to combine use of the rail pass with a domestic flight. However, do a bit of research because it may work out quicker to take a shinkansen if you add on the time it takes to get to/from the airports.

Domestic flights are also expensive: a one-way economy-class fare from Tokyo to Osaka costs ¥16,250; to Sapporo ¥24,700 and to Nagasaki ¥29,100, whereas a one-week rail pass costs ¥28,300. Discounts are available if you book two months ahead but the best deal on flights for foreign visitors are the discount tickets offered by ANA and JAL, see p22.

> ☐ **Cable cars and ropeways**
> An important point to note is that a **cable car** in Japan is a funicular/mountain railway and a **ropeway** is what many others consider a cable car (ie carriages suspended from a cable).

> 开 **JR bus/ferry services**
>   In addition to its rail services, JR also operates a network of **local buses** and
> some **Highway Bus** routes, though they hardly compete with the trains in terms of
> speed and are prone to getting snarled up in traffic. They are also less user-friendly
> than the trains since announcements are usually in Japanese only. The main JR
> Highway Bus route, for which rail passes are valid, runs from Tokyo railway station
> to Nagoya, Kyoto and Osaka railway stations. Seats for this service should be
> booked in advance at the JR bus ticket office at the relevant train station. Further
> details are not included because it's faster and more convenient to travel by train.
> However, JR bus services to places of interest not accessible by rail are included in
> the route guides.
>   Rail passes are also valid for the JR **ferry service** which operates between
> Miyajima-guchi (near Hiroshima) and Miyajima Island (see p235).

By bus or tram

The **bus** service in Japan is almost as efficient as the rail service; a novel experience for anyone who comes from a country where bus timetables are largely fictional. (See also box above). On most intra-urban buses, you enter at the back and take a ticket from the machine by the door. To work out how much the fare is, just before your stop, match the number on the ticket with the fare underneath the corresponding number on the board at the front of the bus. Leave the bus at the front, throwing the fare into the box by the driver (there are change machines at the front but only put the exact fare into the box).

Several cities and large towns still have a **tram** service. On most trams fares are collected in the same way as on buses.

By taxi

Taxis are usually available outside even the tiniest stations but it's also fine to flag one down in the street if the red light in the lower right-hand corner of the windscreen is on. The starting fare is around ¥660 for the first 2km plus ¥80 for each additional 280m thereafter; a surcharge (up to 30%) is added between 11pm and 5am. Thus, taxis are not cheap but you pay for the service. The drivers wear white gloves and peaked caps, and you don't even have to open the door yourself because the left-side passenger door opens and closes automatically (don't try to open or close it yourself as this may upset your driver!).

By bicycle

It is possible to rent a bike at many stations; see p84.

ACCOMMODATION

There is a wide range of possibilities and accommodation is almost always of a high standard. Unless stated otherwise, rates quoted are generally the lowest you should expect to pay. Note that for most accommodation **check-in** starts **from 4pm** on the day of arrival and **check-out** is **by 11am**. In most business hotels, guests are asked to vacate their rooms by 10am.

⛩ **Booking accommodation**
It's wise though not essential to book your first couple of nights' accommodation before you arrive in Japan. If booking directly from overseas, it's best to **fax or email** your reservation, clearly stating dates and specific requests. Communicating your request on the phone may be complicated and hoteliers much prefer to have written confirmation.

If you do turn up without a place to stay, most tourist information offices can assist with hotel reservations. Before you leave for Japan, ask JNTO (see p23) for information on/copies of the following:

● *Directory of Welcome Inns* – a directory of budget to mid-range hostels, hotels and ryokan which can be booked free of charge through the Welcome Inn Reservation Center (WIRC). Many of the places featured can be booked on-line at 🖳 www.itcj.or.jp or via JNTO's website 🖳 www.jnto.go.jp. A directory which lists all Welcome Inn properties nationwide is available from JNTO offices before you leave for Japan. Note that the staff at JNTO offices cannot book accommodation. In Japan, bookings are accepted if you go in person to WIRC counters at the tourist information offices in Tokyo (see p96), Kyoto (see p188), and at Kansai and Narita airports.
● *Youth Hostels Map of Japan* – includes contact numbers for hostels across Japan. For general information in English check 🖳 www.jyh.or.jp.
● *Japanese Inn Group* – a nationwide directory of ryokan (not a chain of inns) which are used to dealing with foreign guests. Traditionally, ryokan rates in Japan include two meals but Japanese Inn Group members also offer room-only rates. Some of the inns in the group can be booked on-line and most accept credit cards. See the directory for a booking form and for details of each member inn, or check 🖳 http://members.aol.com/jinngroup/.
● *Japan Economy Hotel Group* – the leaflet has details of Western-style hotels which offer reasonable rates and convenient locations (generally within a short walk from the station). The leaflet includes a 'reservation request form' if you wish to book direct.

Japan has not been as quick as other countries to develop on-line reservation systems but this is beginning to change. E-Ryokan is a new web-based booking service for Japanese inns nationwide. On-line booking in English is available at 🖳 www.eryokan.co.jp. Two good resources if you're looking for budget hotels are 🖳 www.japanhotel.net and 🖳 http://e-hoteljapan.com, both of which include pictures and descriptions of properties and an on-line reservation service.

Hostels/temples

The cheapest places tend to be **youth hostels**, which get crowded out with young Japanese during Golden Week (see p11) and in the summer. These are great place to stay if you want to meet and socialize with other travellers as many of the hostels organize a programme of events, evening sing-songs and the like. Some of the most atmospheric hostels are found in rural areas; Hokkaido in particular has a number of excellent hostels.

There are two kinds of hostel: a small number are operated by local authorities but the majority are privately run and belong to the Association of Japan Youth Hostels (JYH). The municipal hostels tend to be marginally cheaper

⛩ **The JR Hotel group**
　Japan Rail pass-holders will receive a list of JR-run hotels which offer small discounts (usually around 10% off the rack rate). The hotels are all Western style and are convenient since they're nearly always right outside the station (or in some cases, above the station). They range from standard business to top-class luxury hotels. They're rarely the cheapest overnight option but may be useful as an overnight base if planning an early rail journey the next day. See the city guides for individual hotel details.

though both charge around ¥2500-3500 per person. Two rates are generally offered: the lower one is for YH(HI) members (bring a YH/HI card) while non-members pay about ¥1000 extra. A few hostels will only accept YH(HI) members but you should be able to buy a membership card on the spot.

All hostels provide dormitory accommodation while some also offer private rooms (ideal for families travelling together) for an additional charge. At most hostels breakfast and dinner are included and almost always excellent value but it's usually possible to ask for the 'no meals' rate. Some hostels have communal kitchen facilities. It's wise to call ahead and make a booking since managers may not appreciate it if you turn up unannounced.

A few hostels, such as the ones in Takayama (see p159) and Nagano (see p147), are attached to, or in, **temples**. At these places it may be possible (if you ask!) to join early-morning prayers or participate in a session of zazen with resident monks. A few temples which are not hostels also open their doors to paying guests; these too are an excellent opportunity to experience a part of Japanese culture close up. Two places worth seeking out are Koya-san, deep in the mountains in Kansai (see box p200), and Motsu-ji in Hiraizumi (see box p250).

Camping

JNTO publishes a leaflet, *Camping in Japan*, with a region-by-region guide to some of the most popular camp-sites in the country, access details and overnight charges. A drawback for rail travellers is that nearly all camp-sites are a long way from stations.

Minshuku

Minshuku are small, family-run inns where the rates usually include supper and breakfast; expect to pay around ¥6000 per person; reduced rates are usually offered for children. However, room-only rates are available in some minshuku. JNTO publishes a useful booklet, *Minshukus in Japan*, listing over 250 minshuku nationwide.

Urban minshuku are usually fine but are often less personal and characterful than rural ones which might be in old farmhouses and thus offer a great experience of being in a traditional Japanese home. Rooms are Japanese style (tatami mats and futons); see box p50. There are no private bathrooms and you may not be provided with a towel or yukata, but most have a TV in the room.

⛩ **Ryokan and minshuku etiquette**
A stay in a Japanese inn is a wonderful experience and thoroughly recommended, but it's worth bearing in mind a few golden rules:

You'll find a row of **slippers** waiting in the entrance hall; this is where you're expected to leave your outdoor shoes. The slippers can be worn anywhere except on the tatami floor of your room and in the toilet/bathroom (see below). If you're heading out for a stroll around the local area, *geta* (wooden clogs) are usually provided as an alternative to putting on your outdoor shoes.

Before you enter the toilet or bathroom make sure you take off the house slippers because toilets in particular have their own (plastic) slippers. These are hard to miss as they usually come in bright blue or pink and have 'toilet' written on them. Don't forget to switch back to your other slippers when you leave.

The **bedding** is stored in cupboards in the rooms; at most ryokan, staff lay your futon out each night and put it away in the morning, while at minshuku you're expected to do it yourself. Don't be surprised to find that the pillow is very hard – traditionally pillows are filled with rice husks – and, in winter, that a blanket is put below the duvet part of the futon. Also in the room you'll find a hand towel and a yukata (a dressing gown/pyjama combo). Remember to cross the yukata left over right (the opposite way is for the deceased).

The golden rules for **having a bath** are: wash outside the tub, only climb in once you're clean, and never let the bathwater out! When you enter the bathroom you will find bowls, stools and taps; pick up a bowl and a stool and sit in front of a tap. Soap and shampoo are usually provided; use your small towel (if provided) as a flannel and scrub as hard as you can! Expect the water in the bath to be fairly hot. Bathrooms are nearly always communal but this doesn't necessarily mean you have to share your bath time with complete strangers. In the majority of places used to foreign guests the bathroom can be locked from the inside. The bath is often large enough to accommodate two or three and may be made of cedar-wood and the water scented with pine or mint.

Tipping is not encouraged but if you've enjoyed exceptional service you might want to leave a small amount of money (notes only) in an envelope or wrapped in tissue paper in your room.

Meals are eaten at set times (usually 6 or 6.30pm for supper and about 7.30am for breakfast), occasionally with the family. Invariably the food is Japanese, so be prepared for fish and miso soup at breakfast! Also be aware that if you are offered an egg at breakfast time it is likely to be raw.

Pensions

Pensions are the Western-style equivalent of minshuku and are becoming increasingly popular with Japanese. Like minshuku, pensions are usually small, family-run affairs but they offer beds rather than futons. Rates start from around ¥6000 and usually include a Western breakfast but not dinner.

Business hotels

A little more expensive but with less character are business hotels, used as the name suggests by businessmen looking for a place to crash. Business hotels are

> **⛩ The personal touch**
> In one ryokan we were lucky enough to get a ground-floor room with access onto a teeny Japanese garden. The grandmother staff member spoke no English but was very chatty. She frequently gave us tea and sweets if we were hanging around and insisted on giving us little presents when we left! It was a bit scary when she burst into the bathroom while we were in the bath to explain (in Japanese) how to keep the water hot, but it was all part of the rich experience!
>
> **Froniga Lambert (UK)**

not to be confused with Japan's infamous capsule hotels (see p52), since you get a proper room rather than a sleeping compartment. Most rooms are singles though virtually all business hotels have some twins and doubles. Facilities include a café where you can get evening meals and breakfast (not included in the room rate) and vending machines (soft drinks, beer, saké, and perhaps pot noodle and ice cream). Rooms are clean but tidy, with cramped toilet/bath units and rarely much space to hang your clothes. Rates vary from around ¥4500 for the most basic singles up to ¥9000 for a room with slightly more breathing space. A towel, yukata, TV, and Japanese tea are usually provided.

There is invariably a cluster of business hotels outside main stations. Some of the newer ones offer a no-smoking floor and a few have women-only floors. The newest even boast an automatic check-in where you feed your money into a slot and receive an electronic key card in return. Many business hotel chains operate nationwide; names to look out for are Green Hotels, Tokyu Inns, Washington Hotels and Sunroute. Two new chains, Hyper Hotel and Super Hotel, are expanding rapidly and are worth seeking out since the rates at both include breakfast.

Ryokan

Ryokan are more upmarket and have better amenities than minshuku (see p49) and you really should plan to stay at least one night in one. In luxury ryokan particularly, where per person rates start from around ¥20,000, every guest is a VIP. From the moment you arrive, you're waited on by your own kimono-clad maid who will pour tea as you settle in, serve you meals (usually in your room) and lay out your futon. But you don't have to stay in a luxury property to enjoy first-class service. Most ryokan charge more affordable rates averaging ¥7000-10,000 per person including two meals. Rooms are more spacious than those found in business hotels and may include *shoji* (sliding paper screens) and an alcove or two containing a Japanese fan, vase or scroll.

Most ryokan have a garden and some have their own hot spring which may or may not include a *rotemburo* (hot outdoor bath), the perfect place to unwind after a hard day's sightseeing.

Meals are nearly always Japanese and the dishes are prepared so that they are as much a visual treat as a gastronomic one and will often feature local produce/specialities. A typical meal might include some tempura, sashimi/sushi, a meat dish, vegetable dishes and pickles, and will always include miso soup and rice; dessert is likely to be slices of fresh fruit. All this can be washed down with beer, saké and/or Japanese tea. Some ryokan offer a choice of Japanese- or Western-style breakfast.

Other accommodation options

Also at the top end of the market are luxury **Western hotels**, including international chains such as the Hyatt and Marriott, where rates start from around ¥20,000 for a standard twin.

If all else fails and you're stuck for accommodation in a city, find out the location of the nearest **capsule hotel**, good for a one-off novelty but not recommended for claustrophobics. The majority of capsule hotels are for men only.

A final option might be a night in a Japanese **love hotel** where, during the day, rooms are available at an hourly rate for a euphemistic 'stay', but in the evening (from around 10pm) can be booked for an overnight stay. Rates are about the same as, or slightly cheaper than, business hotels. Like capsule hotels, you'll find love hotels in big cities and primarily in areas around mainline stations. They're easy to spot because the exteriors are usually bright and garish. The over-the-top design continues inside with a variety of themed rooms which sometimes contain bizarre optional extras like rotating beds, tropical plants and waterfalls. The service in these places, by contrast, tends to be very discrete and you are unlikely ever to see a staff member. A display board at the entrance lights up to inform guests what rooms are available. You then go to pay at a counter after which a mysterious hand passes you the key to your room. The whole experience is not as seedy as it might sound; the arrival process is designed to protect the customers' anonymity and a night here is just as much an experience of Japan as is a stay in a traditional ryokan.

WHERE TO EAT

Eating out in Japan can seem a daunting prospect but with so much on offer it's also a great opportunity to try a variety of cuisines.

Japanese restaurants tend to specialize in a particular kind of food, so it's more common to find a *sushi* restaurant or *soba* shop than a generic 'Japanese restaurant'. It's also worth bearing in mind that many restaurants close early, often by 10pm. For late-night eating try bars or *izakaya* (see p55).

🏮 Vegetarians

Vegetarians are rare in Japan, so foreign visitors need to make their dietary requirements clear to restaurant staff. It may be assumed, for example, that as a vegetarian you eat fish or even chicken. To avoid being given something you don't want, it's far better to explain exactly what you can eat rather than simply say you're a vegetarian. The best place for a truly vegetarian meal is a Buddhist temple. The superbly crafted *shojin ryori* prepared by monks can be tried in some places, such as the temple town of Koya-san (see box p200).

冊 Vending machines

Vending machines (*jidohan-baiki*) are on every street corner, as well as in unexpected places such as mountain tops, temple precincts and remote villages. Few sell food, except ice cream, but many sell hot and cold drinks. Hot, and cold, cans of tea and coffee come in a variety of formats. Check that fruit juices say '100% juice' or you might get a sweet syrupy concoction. Note that beer and saké vending machines close at 11pm.

Japanese food

For details of Japanese food and drink, see Appendix A, p390.

● **Budget** A quick and cheap breakfast is served in coffee shops advertising 'morning service' – usually coffee, toast and boiled egg. Two chains to look out for are Pronto and Doutor; Starbucks is also spreading across Japan. There seem to be branches of Mister Donut everywhere – the doughnuts are good but of more interest is the bottomless coffee cup.

To save time and money for lunch, convenience stores (known as *conbini*) are a good bet; all stock sandwiches, rolls, noodles and the like, and nearly all are open 24 hours. Major convenience-store chains include Lawson, 7-Eleven and Family Mart; in Hokkaido, look out for Seicomart covenience stores. Other good places for snack-style food are bakeries (every large station has at least one) and the food halls, usually in the basement, of department stores. Here, as well as in stations, you'll find take-out lunch boxes which are cheaper than eating at a restaurant. For details on the *ekiben* (rail station lunch box), see p82.

The cheapest sit-down meals are at counter-service *ramen*, soba and *udon* shops. A bowl of ramen costs about ¥400. Alternatively, try a *shokudo*, a restaurant which serves a variety of economical dishes. Shokudo, popular with young people and students, always have plastic models of food outside and there are usually several in and around station areas.

Two other places to consider when eating on the cheap are canteens on university campuses (if you can find them) and in city halls. The latter are probably the easiest to locate. Canteens in city halls are subsidized and meant for the staff but are open to anyone. They're often on the top floor which means you get a cheap meal and a decent view thrown in to the bargain.

Look out for stalls in the evenings and at festivals (see p60) which sell snacks such as *yakitori*, *yaki-imo*, *takoyaki*, as well as hearty bowls of noodles and steaming hot plates of *yakisoba*.

● **More upmarket** Japan's best known culinary export is sushi; the cheapest sushi restaurants are *kaiten-zushiya*, where you sit around a revolving counter and help yourself to plates of sushi (different colour plates denote different price bands). At the end of the meal the restaurant staff count how many plates you've taken and tell you how much to pay. It's usually possible to eat your fill for under ¥1500. Restaurants specializing in *tonkatsu* are also a culinary mainstay;

⛩ **Eating out and how to order**

Most restaurants hang a *noren* (split curtain) at the entrance whenever they are open. In the evenings, bars show they are open by hanging or illuminating a red lantern outside.

Before entering the restaurant take a look at the food display in the window outside. Here you'll find plastic models of the dishes on offer; make a mental note of what you think looks good before heading inside.

As you go in, don't be alarmed by the loud greeting that is often shouted not just by the waiter or waitress but by the entire kitchen staff. After the chorus of 'Irasshaimase' ('Welcome') dies down you'll be taken to a table and handed the menu along with hot towels and glasses of ice cold water or Japanese tea (all part of the service). If you're lucky, the menu will contain pictures of what's on offer. If not, your earlier preparation will pay off. Staff are usually more than happy to come outside with you to see what 'model' you want rather than risk bringing something you didn't order or can't eat.

At some (noodle) places you choose what you want from a list on a machine at the entrance, buy a ticket, hand it to the person behind the counter and then take a seat.

there are usually one or two in large stations. *Tempura* restaurants tend to be a bit more expensive than sushi places.

All department stores have at least one 'restaurant floor' where you'll find a variety of cheap Western and Japanese eateries; most offer a daily set lunch which can be very good value. Restaurant floors tend to stay open until 10pm, though the department stores themselves close earlier.

Other foods

In major cities you'll rarely be far from restaurants serving ethnic cuisine, the most popular being Chinese, Indian, Italian and French. Italian places tend to be cheap but bland, while Indian restaurants serve relatively authentic curries. Cheap Japanese restaurants often serve their own version of the Indian dish, a comfort food known as *curry rice* (see p390).

French food is considered classy and therefore is expensive. Luxury hotels invariably have at least one French restaurant, where a bottle of imported Perrier costs nearly as many yen as it has bubbles. Malaysian and Thai restaurants are becoming increasingly popular, though the spiciness you might expect is often toned down to suit the Japanese palate.

For fast food, McDonald's is everywhere, but look out too for the Japanese chain Mos Burger. In big cities you'll find branches of Pizza Hut, Wendy's, Lotteria and KFC. Don't reject out of hand the large number of so-called 'family restaurants' that seem to be everywhere. The menu at these places is mostly a mix of spaghetti, steaks, pizza and noodles. Some places also offer a salad bar and all-you-can-drink soft drinks bar. Popular family restaurant chains include Royal Host, Denny's, Gusto and Ringer Hut. An advantage of family restaurants is that they have picture menus which makes ordering easy.

NIGHTLIFE/ENTERTAINMENT

Japan has its fair share of clubs, discos and bars. Some are ultra-exclusive and expect you to part with a wad of cash in the form of a cover charge before you even see the drinks menu but many more offer good value for money. Every town and city has its own entertainment district which often radiates out from the area around the main railway station. To find the nightlife look for the large numbers of businessmen staggering about at dusk in search of their favourite karaoke bar or izakaya. For details of traditional Japanese entertainment see pp40-41.

● **Karaoke bars** Some people have never forgiven Japan for inventing karaoke but its presence in every town and city is unavoidable. You'll know you've stumbled into a karaoke bar if you see television screens strategically placed around the room and rows of whisky bottles stacked up behind the bar (most bars operate a 'bottle keep' system for regulars). If you do visit a karaoke bar, sooner or later you'll be invited to sing. Protest in these situations is futile and it's at least reassuring to know that virtually all karaoke machines have some English songs programmed into them (usually a mixture of Beatles, Carpenters and Bob Dylan).

● **Izakaya and robotayaki** **Izakaya** are small atmospheric Japanese-style pubs. They are often filled with locals who go along after work for a few beers and an evening meal. A typical izakaya consists of seating along a counter, with tables squeezed into any other space available. The menu changes according to what the owner (known as the 'master') has bought in from the market but there's nearly always a choice of fresh fish and meat. Don't worry about not being able to read Japanese as you can always point to what's in the chilled cabinet on the counter. Izakaya are great places to meet people and it will probably not be long before someone strikes up a conversation with you. These places don't tend to open much before 6pm and close around 1am; to find them, look for the tell-tale red lanterns hanging outside. **Robotayaki** offer similar food and drink; the main difference is that the food is cooked in front of you.

● **Beer gardens** The name is a bit of a misnomer because beer gardens are almost always on the roof of department stores and large hotels rather than on the ground. For a fixed price (¥3000-4000) most places offer an all-you-can-eat-and-drink beer-and-buffet deal for a set time (90-120 minutes). Beer gardens are open only from the end of May to early September and are highly recommended as places from which to escape the summer humidity.

● **Cinema** The multiplex rules in Japan so you're rarely more than a short walk from a cinema. The good news is that films are shown in their original language and subtitled in Japanese. The downside is that tickets tend to be expensive. Avoid the high prices by going in the afternoon or early evening or try showing a student card. Most cinemas also offer reduced prices once a month on 'movie day' and women can take advantage of half-price tickets on the weekly 'ladies day' (often a Wednesday).

MEDIA

Four English-language daily **newspapers** are published in Japan but the best are the *Japan Times* and the *Daily Yomiuri* – you can find copies at kiosks in most large stations. Outside the Tokyo metropolitan and Kansai areas, they're usually a day late.

The main national broadcaster of **television** programmes is NHK (Nippon Hoso Kyokai), the Japanese equivalent of the BBC. NHK operates two analogue channels, NHK-G (the main channel) and NHK-E, which broadcasts mainly educational programmes. The nightly news programme on NHK-G at 7pm is simultaneously broadcast in English and Japanese but you can pick up the English only if the TV in your hotel has a 'bilingual' button. Private broadcasters like TBS, Fuji and TV Asahi fill the rest of the airwaves with unashamedly ratings-driven shows (see Popular culture, p43). Both the *Daily Yomiuri* and *Japan Times* carry TV listings in English.

Radio is not as popular as TV and most programmes are broadcast only in Japanese. A few cities produce selected pop music shows in English; FM Co Co Ro (76.5KHz) in the Kansai area is one example.

ELECTRICITY

The electric current in Japan is mostly 100 volts AC, but there are two different cycles: 50Mhz in eastern Japan (including Tokyo) and 60Mhz in western Japan.

TIME

Japan is GMT + 9 hours so at 9pm in Tokyo it is 12 noon in London, 7am in New York, 4am in California and 11pm in Sydney (all same-day times).

BANKS AND MONEY MATTERS

The unit of currency is the Japanese yen (¥). Bank notes are issued in denominations of ¥10,000, ¥5000, ¥2000 and ¥1000. Coins are ¥500, ¥100, ¥50, ¥10, ¥5 and ¥1; ¥50 and ¥5 coins have a hole in the middle.

For such a sophisticated economy banking practices are archaic. Banks are open Monday to Friday from 9am to 3pm only. The section dealing with currency exchange (travellers' cheques) often operates limited hours and the staff

---

⛩ Taxes and tipping

A **5% consumption tax** (called *shohizei*) is levied on nearly all goods and services in Japan but this is not normally added until you reach the till. Hotel rate-cards also exclude the tax, so expect 5% to be added to your bill.

Additionally, upmarket hotels levy a **service tax** of between 10 and 20% in addition to the 5% consumption tax. Room rates quoted in this guide are mostly on a per room basis and do not include taxes unless otherwise stated.

The good news is that there is no culture of **tipping** in Japan but see box, p50.

may not exchange money until they have received that day's rates from head office. Always take a passport along and expect to wait at least 30 minutes for the transaction to be completed.

Japan has always been a cash-based society and credit cards are nothing like as popular as they are in many other countries so check that any hotel, restaurant or shop accepts credit cards before you go in.

The good news is that 26,000 ATMs in post offices nationwide should now accept Visa, Mastercard and Cirrus cards issued outside Japan. Don't rely on this, though, as it has only recently been introduced and not all post offices may be geared up for the service. Note also that with very few exceptions, ATMs in Japan are not open 24 hours. The normal operating hours are 9am-7pm on weekdays and 9am-5pm on Saturday. Most ATMs are closed on Sunday and public holidays.

The ATMs at branches of Citibank in Tokyo, Osaka, Kyoto and a few other cities definitely accept foreign Visa cards and have the added bonus of being open 24 hours. Alternatively, try the main branches of banks in towns and cities. Some will agree to give you a cash advance over the counter (bring your passport), though this procedure can take time (anything from 15 to 45 minutes!) while phone calls are made to your card issuer.

❏ Exchange rates	
£1	¥173
Euro1	¥107
US$1	¥119
Can$1	¥77
Aus$1	¥62
NZ$1	¥52

To get the latest rates of exchange visit 💻 www.oanda.com/convert/classic or www.xe.net/currency/.

POST AND TELECOMMUNICATIONS

Post
Post offices open Monday to Friday 9am-5pm; main branches also offer a limited service in the evening and at weekends. Post offices in Japan are identifiable by a red T sign outside. A poste-restante facility is available only in main city post offices.

Japan's postal service is fast and very efficient but not all that cheap. Postcards cost ¥70 to send abroad and ¥50 within Japan. Aerograms cost ¥90 anywhere in the world. For airmail letters the price depends on the destination; letters up to 25g cost ¥90 within Asia, ¥110 to North America, Oceania, Europe and the Middle East and ¥130 to Africa and South America. For letters up to 50g, the prices increase to ¥160, ¥190 and ¥230 respectively.

The location of the main post office in a particular city is marked on the city map but details, such as specific opening hours, are not provided in the text.

Email
Japan has not been as quick as the United States in rolling out Internet access but is catching up fast. Every city and town has at least one Internet café, some have dozens, and the going rate is around ¥200 per hour. In some places you

may be expected to buy a drink or pay a one-off membership fee of ¥500 to 'join' the café. See the individual city guides for information on the location of Internet cafés.

If you're bringing your laptop and are looking for email/web access without having to pay hotel call charges, try any grey (international) phone box as these come equipped with analogue and ISDN jacks which you can connect to your modem cable and use to call a local or international dial-up number for your ISP.

Phone

In the last five years **mobile phones** have become the ultimate everyday accessory in Japan as around the world. If you're only visiting Japan but want to stay in touch while on the move it might be worth getting a *puree-koru* (Pre Call) mobile phone from an NTT DoCoMo store. Pre Call mobiles are sold along the lines of the pay-as-you-go tariffs in the UK; you purchase the handset and can then buy 'pre-call' cards to charge your phone with credit. Expect to pay ¥8-10,000 (£45-60, $65-80) for the cheapest Pre Call mobile phone. You'll need to provide proof of identity and an address at the time of purchase.

The proliferation of mobile phones has not yet led to a decrease in the number of **public telephones**. Green phones and the newer grey boxes accept both ¥10 and ¥100 coins and/or telephone cards. It's best to use only ¥10 coins for local calls since no change is given in return for partially used ¥100 coins. Local calls cost ¥10 per minute. The old red phones are now quite rare but accept ¥10 coins only. Public telephones are also installed on all shinkansen and some limited express services, though a surcharge is levied and you may get cut off if the train heads into a tunnel. Numbers with the prefixes 0120 or 0088 are toll free.

To make **international calls**, look for the grey (ISDN) phone boxes; it's best to purchase a prepaid telephone card from a shop or kiosk or from the vending machine inside the phone box. Many cities and individual tourist attractions sell their own souvenir phone cards which are great to collect as well as use. Both green and grey phones accept the cards, which are sold in units of 50 (¥500) and 105 (¥1000). A one-minute local call 'costs' one unit.

Making a call When calling **city-to-city** in Japan dial the area code first (all telephone numbers in this guide include the area code). The area code can be omitted if calling a local number (for example, if you call a Tokyo number from within Tokyo omit the prefix 03).

While Nippon Telecom (NTT) is the company responsible for national telecommunications, three operators provide **international services**. Though the three are competing with each other for business, their rates do not vary a great deal. The three companies and their respective access codes are Japan Telecom (0041), IDC (0061) and KDD (001).

To make an international call, dial any of the three access codes, followed by the country code, area code (minus the initial '0') and telephone number. The best time to call overseas is between the hours of 11pm and 8am, when a late-

⛩ Female travellers

Japan is one of the safest countries in the world and it's unlikely females travelling alone will have any problems. If someone does approach you in the dark the chances are that all he wants to do is practise his English. However, in crowded commuter trains women might find themselves being groped. The best thing to do is shout out – the offender will be embarrassed – or try to move away.

The best advice for safe travel is the same as for anywhere else in the world: don't take unnecessary risks, know where you're going if someone invites you out, and always arrange to meet in a public place.

night discount of between 25 and 40% applies. A 20% discount applies for calls made between 7 and 11pm Monday to Friday, and from 8am to 11pm on weekends and public holidays.

Two alternative but expensive options are to place a direct-dial call from your hotel room or to look for one of the public phones in major cities which accept credit cards, though these are as yet few and far between.

Fax

Most hotels will send faxes for you but there is usually a hefty surcharge. A cheaper alternative is to go to a convenience store; most have a coin-operated fax machine next to the photocopier. Many mainline railway stations also have a public fax machine somewhere on the concourse.

MUSEUMS AND TOURIST ATTRACTIONS

Most museums and tourist attractions are open on Sunday and national holidays but closed on Monday. If a public holiday falls on a Monday, museums are closed on Tuesday instead. Typical opening hours are 9:30am-5pm but last admission is usually 30 minutes before the official closing time.

Admission prices quoted in this guide are for standard adult tickets. The child rate (up to age 16) is usually 50% of the adult rate. University students sometimes qualify for small savings so it's worth showing an ISIC card at the entrance to find out if a discount is available.

NATIONAL HOLIDAYS

Japan observes 15 national holidays, when all banks and most shops are closed. Museums and tourist attractions are usually open. Note that nearly everything closes for the New Year holiday, from December 31st to January 3rd. If a holiday falls on a Sunday, the following day is treated as a holiday.

● **January 1st** New Year's Day
● **2nd Monday in January** Coming of Age Day – girls who have reached the age of majority (20) mark the occasion by dressing up in gorgeous kimono and visiting their local shrine.

- **February 11th** National Foundation Day – commemoration of the legendary enthronement of Japan's first Emperor (Jimmu)
- **March 20th** Vernal Equinox Day
- **April 29th** Greenery Day
- **May 3rd/4th** Constitution Memorial Day and an additional day
- **May 5th** Children's Day
- **July 20th** Maritime Day
- **September 15th** Respect-for-the-aged Day
- **September 23rd** Autumnal Equinox Day
- **2nd Monday in October** Sports Day
- **November 3rd** Culture Day
- **November 23rd** Labour Thanksgiving Day
- **December 23rd** The Emperor's Birthday

FESTIVALS

Japan is truly a land of festivals; hardly a day goes by when there is not a celebration taking place somewhere in the country. These can be huge, rowdy events attracting thousands of visitors, such as Sapporo's Ice Festival (see p312), Aomori's Nebuta Festival (see p274) or Kyoto's world-famous Gion Festival (see p189), or local festivals in small towns and villages which are little known outside the area.

Parades of large floats, street processions to the tune of taiko drummers and colourful costumes are all part of the festival experience. Eating while walking around in public is generally frowned upon but this rule is broken at festival time; street stalls serve yakisoba, takoyaki, kakigori (crushed ice served with different fruit flavours, similar to Slush Puppy), candy floss, beer and cups of hot saké.

The busiest month in the festival calendar is August; for information on specific festivals, see the relevant city guides. JNTO (see p23) publishes a comprehensive month-by-month list of festivals which is useful if you want to plan your itinerary to include one or more.

LANGUAGE

Japanese is one of the most difficult languages to learn to read/write, mixing as it does Chinese characters, known as *kanji*, with two different syllabaries, *hiragana* and *katakana* (the latter is used exclusively for writing words which the Japanese have borrowed from other languages); see Appendix B, p393.

That said, basic greetings and phrases are not difficult to remember and any efforts to speak Japanese will be welcome. The Japanese always seem amazed and impressed that foreigners can speak their language, especially given the various levels and subtle nuances that need to be used in certain situations. Foreigners are not expected to know the intricacies of the language so there's no need to worry about making a linguistic faux-pas. Basic phrases such as those listed in Appendix B should help.

⛩ **English or Japlish?**
'English' is everywhere you look in Japan, on vending machines, advertising hoardings, in shops and on television, though it doesn't take long to realize that this is not the English you may know from back home. The Japanese use of English to sell products or simply look trendy on T-shirts has been dubbed 'Japlish'; books of examples are available in Tokyo. Here is a selection of signs I spotted around the country:

● On a plastic bag with a picture of a frog: 'Through thick and thin, whether green skin's out or in, just say "ribbit" and you'll be OK!'

● On a T-shirt: 'It is man made. It is supposed to break down.'

● At a market stall selling dried fish in Saga station: 'When a fish slip, a fish start to walk."

● In the books section of a Tokyo department store: 'A good heavy book holds you down. It keeps you from getting up and having another gin and tonic.'

A misunderstanding sometimes arises over the meaning of the Japanese word 'hai' which is translated into English as 'yes'. Anyone who has had contact with the Japanese business world knows that the Japanese do not like to commit immediately to a straightforward 'yes' or 'no' answer to a proposal, at least during a first meeting. Thus, 'hai' can often mean 'yes, I am listening' (this also applies when talking on the phone) rather than 'yes, I agree'.

Although nearly everyone in Japan learnt English at school, this does not mean they can speak it. Despite efforts to bring more native English speakers into Japanese schools as 'assistant language teachers', the classroom emphasis continues to be on written English and grammar, rather than spoken skills. If you need help, try talking to school or university students. If you can't make yourself understood, try writing your question down; many Japanese find reading English much easier than listening to, or speaking, it.

ASSISTANCE

Even if you don't immediately find someone who speaks English, it's unlikely you'll find anyone unwilling to help if you ask. I once asked for directions to an ATM; instead of just being pointed the right way I was accompanied on the 20-minute journey to the cashpoint. This is not an exception to the rule; you'll almost certainly find that the Japanese are delighted to go out of their way to help you.

Though few police officers outside large cities speak English, all are invariably polite and helpful. In even the smallest village you're likely to find a street corner *koban* (police box), where officers are only too pleased to give you directions if you're lost.

Pharmacies are everywhere in Japan and can be recognized by the green cross outside the store. Few pharmacists speak much English but gestures will generally do the trick.

Cultural tips

Perhaps the most important piece of advice to remember when visiting Japan is that foreigners are not expected to know the conventions that dictate how the Japanese behave in public. Nobody's going to care, for example, if you haven't mastered the art of bowing. Indeed, people would probably be more concerned if you did know exactly how low to bow on every occasion since it might suggest you know more about the culture than the Japanese themselves (which is a far greater sin). There are a few cultural tips worth knowing about, though the best advice if in doubt is to copy what everyone else around you is doing.

● The Japanese prefer consensus over disagreement and rarely show strong emotions. Flaring into a temper if your hotel room is not ready, for example, would be considered inappropriate behaviour and people might not know how to react.

● Avoid blowing your nose in public as this is considered rude; sniffing, however, is seen as a demonstration of your ability to resist temptation.

● It's understood that foreigners are unable to sit on their knees for long periods of time so if you have to sit on the floor it's fine to sit cross-legged, but don't point your legs towards anyone.

● Take your shoes off as you enter a minshuku, ryokan, temple, or someone's home; shoes and slippers are never worn on tatami mats.

● Chopstick etiquette is important to the Japanese. Pitfalls to avoid include 'spearing' food with chopsticks or using them to rummage through dishes. Avoid passing food between pairs of chopsticks and never stick them upright in a bowl of rice as these are associated with death.

● Slurping noodles is supposed to improve the flavour and is encouraged; it's also common to bring the bowl up to your mouth to ensure you don't spill the liquid.

● If drinking beer or saké with a group it's polite to pour someone else's glass and wait for yours to be filled.

● Except at a festival (see p60), it's not customary to eat while walking along the street, though at most you might receive a few bemused stares.

● Punctuality is sacred; the Japanese seem to abide by the 'five minutes early' rule for meetings and appointments.

● Business cards (known as *meishi*) are also sacred. Though tourists are not expected to carry a supply it's a good idea to bring some if you have any; at the very least it will save you writing out your details every time anyone asks for your address. If you are offered a business card, it's considered very bad form to put it straight in your pocket and even worse if you get out a pen and scrawl notes on it. It's best to look at it for a while before putting it away.

● If you're expecting to visit someone's home bring a souvenir from your home country as a gift; otherwise bottles of whisky, chocolates, flowers or tea towels are perfect.

For details of etiquette in a ryokan/minshuku, see the box on p50.

SHOPPING

Department stores open daily from 10am to around 7 or 8pm, but are closed one day a month (usually Wednesday or Thursday but rarely Sunday).

If you arrive when the store opens dozens of eager staff members will be standing in position to greet and bow to you. The bowing and welcoming does not stop when you step inside as dozens more staff wait at the foot and top of each escalator (and in the lifts) to welcome you personally to each floor.

卅 Hi-tech attention to the call of nature
Most toilets in Japan are Western style, though on some older trains and in public loos you'll still find Asian squat toilets. Note that toilet paper is rarely found in public loos.

Big hotels constantly try to outdo their rivals by fitting guest rooms with futuristic lavatories. The facilities on some top-class models include a choice of background music (to hide your own natural noises), heated seats with adjustable temperature gauge, a built-in bidet and a device that measures your blood pressure while you wait. On even the most basic models there are at least two buttons to press: one is for the flush and the other activates a vertical hot water jet – you really don't want to get these two mixed up. On some toilets there are two levels of flush though the effect of using the wrong one is not so dramatic.

Don't be surprised if you catch sight in the evening of drunk businessmen relieving themselves in the street or on station platforms – a reminder, perhaps, that however hi-tech the Japanese make their toilets, there are never enough of them.

Real enthusiasts will want to pay a visit to the World Toilet Museum (see p375) in Utazu.

If you can negotiate your way through the hordes of staff (realizing as you go that this is how Japan achieves its low unemployment figures) you'll eventually find departments that sell everything from furniture to food, from digital cameras to kimonos. The sheer variety of goods can be overwhelming but if you have time department stores are a great place to explore and discover Japan's latest fashions and craziest inventions. Souvenir hunters will certainly not be disappointed: watches, silks, bamboo and lacquerware, pottery, woodblock prints, Japanese fans, dolls, kimonos, chopsticks and the ubiquitous *tamagotchi* can all be found under one roof. As if selling goods were not enough, department stores also stage exhibitions of art or ikebana and sometimes even fashion shows. Some have playgrounds and amusement arcades; these are often on the roof.

Finding your way around a department store is not always easy because many are made up of several buildings and annexes all of which interconnect. Also, a point of confusion, particularly for the British, is the way floors are numbered. '1F' means the ground floor, and is not the same as the 'first floor' (which is really the second floor). 'BF' indicates the basement. Some of the larger stores produce their own guide books to help visitors get around.

If you prefer to stay on ground level Japan also boasts a wide range of **speciality shops** and stores. Every town or city has its own shopping area often identified by plastic flowers, the colour of which varies according to the season, suspended from lamp posts; many such areas are pedestrianized and provide covered walkways. Shopaholics will not be disappointed.

Another great shopping experience are the many **open-air markets** which sell locally-made goods, traditional handicraft and fresh produce. Tourist information offices can provide details of the market day(s) in a particular town or city. Fresh fruit and vegetables are inevitably good buys. Melons, for example, are one of the most expensive kinds of fruit in Japan, but you'll often be able to

---

🏯 **Volcanoes, earthquakes and typhoons**
Japan is a hotbed of **volcanic activity**; even world-famous Mt Fuji, which last erupted in 1707, has recently shown renewed signs of life. Hokkaido in particular has several active volcanoes but there's no need to panic as the island's hiking routes and paths are always closed at the first sign of smoke.

Earthquakes of course are not seasonal, nor can they be accurately predicted. They are, however, a fact of life in Japan and most cities have an earthquake centre equipped with a simulator room where Japanese can prepare for any eventuality by experiencing the full force of the Richter scale. Minor quakes/tremors are very common but unless you're particularly sensitive you'll probably only hear about them the next day. In the very unlikely event you find yourself waking up to a sizeable quake, the best thing to do is to get under something solid, such as a table. Major quakes are extremely rare and not worth becoming paranoid about.

Typhoons (*tsunami*) strike coastal regions, particularly in Shikoku and Kyushu, in late summer. Fortunately these are usually predicted a day or two before they hit the coast so it's unlikely you will be taken unawares.

---

buy one for a quarter of the price you'd pay in a department store (though you have to forego the fancy wrapping paper, beautifully packaged box and gold ribbons).

ACTIVITIES

Hiking

Since four-fifths of Japan is mountainous there are some excellent hiking opportunities; routes and paths are nearly always well signposted and almost always well trodden. The Japanese Alps (see Central Honshu pp109-65) and Hokkaido (see pp281-319) are the places to head for the most spectacular hiking. For more information on the great outdoors, see the regularly updated 🖳 www.outdoorjapan.com.

Skiing

It's worth trying skiing in Japan, if only for half a day – where else in the world can you get bowed off a chair lift?

There are skiing opportunities throughout the Japanese Alps; anyone visiting the country for a skiing holiday should get hold of T R Reid's *Ski Japan!* (Kodansha, 1994), still the only guide in English dedicated to the ski slopes of Japan, with reviews of over 100 ski areas.

For the latest snow reports in English, resort reviews and even information on how to find an English-speaking ski instructor and where to buy the most

---

Opposite: Ancient and modern: kimono-clad geisha head towards Kyoto's futuristic station. (Photo © Richard Brasher).

fashionable snowboard, check 💻 www.skijapanguide.com. JNTO publishes a mini-guide called *Skiing in Japan* which provides details of 20 of the best ski resorts in the country.

Relaxing in a hot spring

Hot springs, known as *onsen*, are hugely popular among Japanese who consider the chance to relax in a hot tub the perfect escape from the stress of life. Hokkaido in particular is full of natural hot springs where the water is often pumped direct from a bubbling pool of volcanic rock. Diehard onsen lovers travel the country in search of the perfect hot spring. Open-air baths in rural areas are often the least accessible since they're usually high in the mountains. They also lack facilities such as changing areas and are rarely segregated, though they are nearly always free of charge. At the other extreme are Japan's infamously gaudy onsen resorts, such as Beppu in Kyushu (see p330), where luxury hotels operate themed bath houses and the water is really only a sideshow. Somewhere in between these two extremes are public bath houses and small-scale hot springs. These generally include several indoor baths of varying temperatures, a sauna, plunge pool and at least one outdoor bath called a rotemburo. If you're lucky with the location, the outdoor bath will afford sweeping views of the mountains and surrounding countryside.

The usual procedure at any bath house after buying a ticket at the entrance (from the counter or from a vending machine) is to head directly for the changing rooms. To avoid stumbling into the wrong room, memorize the Japanese characters for male and female (see p395). As when taking a bath in a minshuku or ryokan, you're expected to wash before entering the water (see box on p50). Swimming costumes are not worn but small towels are provided to protect your modesty when walking around. The onsen experience does not end the moment you step out of the bath. Changing rooms are often equipped with exercise bikes, massage chairs, weighing machines, combs, brushes, aftershaves, scents, industrial-size fans to help you dry off, and vending machines.

With so many hot springs scattered around Japan, it's hard to know where to start, though JNTO's leaflet *Japanese Hot Springs* contains a useful region-by-region guide to the country's best-known onsen.

However, a place on Shikoku that is definitely worth considering, because it is both traditional and easily accessible, is Dogo Onsen (see p386). For an unusual bathing experience in a holy hot spring by the ocean, take a trip to the island of Sakurajima on Kyushu (see p361). Rail enthusiasts might prefer to head for the Kansai area where there's a chance to soak in a tub which affords views of a railway track (see p174).

Opposite: Top: A Nozomi shinkansen prepares to glide out of the station and race further down the line. **Bottom:** Steam locomotives are making a comeback in Japan; one of the most accessible is the Oigawa Steam Railway (see box, p114). (Photos © Richard Brasher).

Railway history

When Commodore Perry appeared off the coast of Japan in 1853 with the US Navy's 'Black Ships' (see p35), the country, like many others, had no railway whatsoever. In the years since the end of Japan's policy of self-isolation, its rail network has become the envy of the world. This transformation, given the country's natural topography and history of devastating earthquakes, is nothing short of extraordinary.

PIONEERING EARLY DAYS

One of Perry's gifts on his second trip to Japan in 1854 was a quarter-size steam locomotive and accompanying track. However astonishing the sight of this miniature railway set up on the beach must have been, it would be a mistake to believe that the Tokugawa shogunate was entirely ignorant of technological developments outside Japan. From the tiny Dutch enclave in Nagasaki, the only point of contact with the outside world in 265 years of self-imposed isolation, the Shogun had received an annual report on developments in the rest of the world. But it was not until the Meiji Restoration of 1868 (see p35) that the idea of constructing a railway in Japan began to take root.

Given the lamentable state of Britain's railways today, it comes as something of a surprise to discover that the Japanese government employed a number of British engineers and pioneering railwaymen to assist in the development of the country's rail network, notably Edmund Morel (1841-71); Morel was appointed chief engineer but died a year before the opening of Japan's first railway line, between Tokyo and Yokohama, on 12th October 1872. Ninety-two years before the inauguration of the Tokaido shinkansen between Tokyo and Osaka, Emperor Meiji and his entourage set off on the country's first official train ride, a 30-km journey from Shimbashi, in Tokyo, to Yokohama. The driver for this historic journey was British and the coach the Emperor rode in was made in Birmingham. Some Japanese guests, it is reported, kept to tradition (see p62) by taking off their shoes before boarding and so travelled to Yokohama in their socks.

蒸気機関車マリゴールドの野を過ぎる

The steaming locomotive passing across the field full of marigold at night (KAZUKO KONAGAI)

The use of foreign engineers was not without its complications, not least of which was the language barrier. British railwaymen accus-

> ## ⛩ The Golden Age of steam?
> The JR network may now be the envy of the rest of the world but it would appear from Kelly and Walsh's *Handbook of the Japanese Language* (Yokohama, 1898) that rail travel in Japan used to be far from trouble-free. The following phrases appear (together with their Japanese equivalent) in a section entitled 'A Journey By Railway' and are a useful gauge of the state of the nation's railway in its early days:
>
> *When will the train start?*
>   *Immediately, Sir.*
> *Didn't you tell me 'immediately' half an hour ago?*
>
> *The Railroad Department seems to be asleep!*
> *The whole railroad system is disorganised and upset.*
> *The Railroad Department doesn't seem to care the least for the convenience of the Public.*
>
> *They don't yet realise the value of time.*
> *Are we not behind time?*
>   *That is the usual thing in Japan.*
>
> *We are now at last at our destination.*
> *We are three hours late*

tomed to grey skies and drizzle also found it hard to adapt to Japan's hot and humid climate. Edmund Holtham, writing about his time as a railway engineer, describes how the summer heat made work 'rather a burden for me ... in spite of running down to Kobe for a game of cricket and a plunge in the sea, I fell out of condition' (*Eight Years in Japan*, 1883).

A significant turning point came in the spring of 1879 when Japanese drivers were allowed to operate the trains between Tokyo and Yokohama – though on about one-sixth of the salary. It wasn't long before the Japanese were taking over from the British and other Western engineers. By 1904, as the last British railwayman set off for home, the country had embarked on an unprecedented expansion of the railway network.

NATIONALIZATION AND EXPANSION

As the railway expanded, people began to move around at previously unimaginable speeds. The old Tokaido road, for centuries the only way of getting between Edo (Tokyo) and Kyoto, was quickly abandoned after the opening of the Tokaido line in July 1889. A journey which had taken 12 or 13 days could now be completed in just 20 hours. By 1906, when a 'super express' was introduced, the journey time was cut still further to 13 hours 40 minutes.

The year 1906 was significant in another way; 8000km (5000 miles) of track had been laid in just 34 years, though the majority of this was in the hands of private rail companies. Under pressure from the military, who were finding it increasingly difficult to move around the country at any speed when they had to wait for connections between the private railways, the government passed the 1906 Railway Nationalization Act, giving itself the authority to purchase the 'trunk' lines, while allowing private railways to own local lines. The railway was to remain a nationalized industry until 1987.

ARRIVAL OF THE 'BULLET TRAIN'

Electrification

A nationwide network of trunk lines was well on its way to completion by 1910 but major electrification of the railway had to wait until after WWII, during which many lines sustained severe damage from bombing raids. In the early 1950s the journey by train between Tokyo and Osaka took most of a day and there was an observation car at the back with armchairs for passengers to enjoy the view down the line. The Tokaido line, running through what had become Japan's major industrial corridor, was electrified in 1956. It was also in the mid-1950s that the idea began to surface for a new, high-speed link between Tokyo and Osaka. The proposal was not just for an upgrade of the existing Tokaido line but for a completely new railway that would allow a top speed of 250kph. Crucially, businessmen in Tokyo and Osaka would be able to commute between each city and return home the same day.

Picking up speed

There is no more instantly recognizable symbol of modern Japan than the *shinkansen* (literally 'new main line'), known throughout the world as the bullet train. When the government finally gave its approval for the project in 1958, Japan National Railways (JNR) had six years to prepare the line in time for the opening ceremony of the 1964 Tokyo Olympics. The deadline was made and the ribbon cut at precisely 6am on October 1st 1964, but the construction bill had spiralled from an original estimate of ¥200 billion to ¥380 billion. Initial design faults also meant passengers experienced ear pain whenever the train darted into a tunnel and, more alarmingly, gusts of wind blowing up through the toilets.

The foreign press corps was taken for a test run, however, and appeared suitably thrilled. A *Times* journalist gushed on cue to his readers, remarking that the shinkansen fully lived up to the boast of a 'new dimension in train travel': 'In the airliner-style seats one groped subconsciously, but in vain, for the safety belt as the train hummed out of Tokyo, rather like a jet taking off in a narrow street. Bridges, tunnels, even passing trains flash by, thanks to the air-tight doors, as in a silent film. It is uncannily smooth…So much tends to the vulgar in modern Japan that it is pleasant to report the superb fittings and finishing in this train…Ablution facilities dazzle, with winged mirrors, and three lavatories per car set, one of them Western-style…' (*The Times*, September 28th 1964).

Two services began operation in 1964, the *Hikari* ('light'), which initially took four hours and stopped only in Nagoya and Kyoto, and the stopping

Kodama ('echo'), which took five hours. The new line was an instant success and tickets sold out weeks in advance; Queen Elizabeth II and Prince Philip went for a ride during their 1975 state visit to Japan – though only after a railway strike was called off at the last minute. The construction deficit was overturned and the line was soon extended west to Okayama in 1972, and on to Hakata in 1975. Expansion east of Tokyo on the Tohoku shinkansen quickly followed.

Out of control

As the shinkansen spread further and sped faster, JNR's debt loomed larger. Though the Tokaido shinkansen was a financial success, the rest of the network was in meltdown. The railway's total deficit year on year throughout the 1970s and 80s spiralled into thousands of billions of yen. Fares became daylight robbery, particularly in comparison with those offered by private railways, the network was grossly over-staffed, labour relations were poor and morale low. Some pointed the finger at greedy politicians. Such was the glamour of the shinkansen, reported *The Times* in January 1987 (23 years after it had enjoyed that free test ride), that 'every politician of note feels he needs a shinkansen station in his district': 'Over the years, promises of shinkansen services have brought in innumerable votes for the ruling Liberal Democratic Party. And with every new shinkansen put on to a marginal or loss-making line, JNR's deficit has increased.'

At midnight on April 1st 1987, the whistle was finally and literally blown on all this by the president of JNR, who rode a steam locomotive back and forth near Shimbashi in Tokyo (the starting point for Japan's first railway in 1872) on a symbolic last journey for the nationalized industry. JNR, undeniably the ultimate political pork barrel in Japan, had not made money for 20 years. Its liabilities on that April Fool's Day stood at ¥37 trillion (£160 billion), more than the combined debts of Brazil and Mexico, and £12 billion more than the US budget deficit of the previous year.

Privatization of the railway was achieved by carving up the network into six regional passenger railway companies and one nationwide freight company, to be known collectively as the JR Group. In a bid to reduce some of the debt, unprofitable lines were closed, railway land was sold and staffing levels reduced. No longer constricted by the rules governing a nationalized company, the JR companies have since diversified into everything from department stores

---

The Japanese Railway Society

Rail enthusiasts might be interested in joining the Japanese Railway Society, which has members all over the world. The society takes an interest not just in the old steam days but in the state of Japan's railway today as well as how it might look in the future. Members receive a quarterly journal, *Bullet-In*, and the society organizes bi-annual rail trips to Japan. For details, see the JRS website at **www.japaneserailwaysociety.org**, which includes details of steam operations in Japan.

┌───┐

🏮 **Rail museums**

Rail museums of varying size and interest are spread throughout the country but space does not permit a nationwide listing. Three of the best-known are the **Transportation Museum** in Tokyo (see p92), the **Modern Transportation Museum** in Osaka (see p104) and the **Umekoji Steam Locomotive Museum** in Kyoto (see p182). See the appropriate city guides for full details.

Keen rail buffs should also consider heading for Hokkaido (see p281). The island boasts some of Japan's most scenic rural railway lines and is also home to an excellent open-air transport museum in the port city of Otaru. Although not included in the route guide around Hokkaido, Otaru is easily reached in 30 minutes by rapid train along the Hakodate line from Sapporo (see p315). **Otaru Transportation Museum** (☎ 0134-33 2523; daily, 9am-5/6pm, ¥940 Apr 10th to Nov 3rd, ¥470 Nov 4th to Apr 9th) is built on the site of Hokkaido's first railway station and is filled with locomotives and carriages. There's even the chance to take a 400m ride on a steam locomotive from one end of the ground to the other. To reach the museum take a bus from stop No 6 outside Otaru station and get off at 'Kotsu kinenkan mae'.

Elsewhere in Japan, the outdoor **Sakuma Rail Park** (see box p116) in central Honshu is worth visiting as much for the train journey out to it along the rural Iida line as for the museum itself. And if you're heading towards Nagano by shinkansen from Tokyo stop off at Karuizawa (see p117). Next to the sleek new shinkansen station is the former JR station now restored to its former glory and open to the public as a reminder of the railway's heyday.

There's another good **railway museum** in Yokokawa, accessible by JR Shinetsu line from Takasaki (see p116). This line used to continue beyond Yokokawa to the mountain resort of Karuizawa, but when the Hokuriku shinkansen to Nagano was completed the route between Yokokawa and Karuizawa was closed since it was expensive to operate. The museum (daily except Tue, 10am-4/4:30pm, ¥500) is built on the site of the old Yokokawa depot and has a good collection of rolling stock. A small discount is available if you buy a ticket from the JR counter in Yokokawa station rather than at the museum's ticket office. The museum is a short walk from the station (ask JR staff to point you in the right direction).

└───┘

to hotels, hospitals and helicopters. JR Central, the company in charge of the Tokaido shinkansen line, even owns an upmarket Japanese restaurant, called Matsuri (🖥 www.matsuri-restaurant.com), in central London, UK.

MAGLEV: THE FUTURE?

The future of the railway is brighter and its operating companies healthier than could ever have been imagined prior to 1987 but many grand projects are still on hold. Aspirations that shinkansen lines would one day stretch to Nagasaki and Kagoshima in Kyushu, as far north as Aomori and beyond that through the Seikan Tunnel to Hokkaido, remain just that. Fierce competition from an airline industry just beginning to reap the benefits of increased deregulation has put pressure on the rail companies to answer back with discounts and value for money. But in fast-paced Japan, where nobody ever waits for a train, there will always be demand for yet more speed. That demand is now being met with test runs of the Maglev, or the 'superconducting magnetically-levitated linear motor car'. The Maglev, it is hoped, will one day travel at over 500kph along an as yet unconstructed Chuo shinkansen line, bringing Tokyo and Osaka to within 60 minutes of each other.

In the meantime, railway history continues to be made. A small but significant milestone was reached in August 2000 when two women were appointed shinkansen drivers, operating JR West shinkansen between Shin-Osaka and Hiroshima. The trouble is, the driver's cabin speeds by so fast that you'll almost certainly never see either of them.

STEAM RAILWAYS

In 1936 around 8700 steam locomotives were in operation across Japan. Complaints about the emission of black smoke and technological advances brought about the demise of the commercial steam railway, as more efficient diesel and electric trains were brought into service after the war. By 1976, steam had all but disappeared.

For years, many steam locomotives (known in Japan as SLs) were left to rust away in museums, or were shunted into corners of public parks and quietly forgotten. Perhaps because the Japanese now have the psychological room to look back on the nation's history of modernization, restored SLs have made a comeback.

⛩ Steam locomotive (SL) operations

The following is a list of major preserved steam operations in Japan. Listings show the name, type of engine, operating route, and railway company. Rail passes are valid for SL journeys on JR Group lines but seats should be reserved in advance. Schedules change annually but as a rule of thumb trains run at the weekend between March and November and daily during the summer season. For up-to-date information in English, contact JR's information line (☎ 03-3423 0111).

● **SL Suzuran** (C11 171) Fukagawa to Rumoi on the Rumoi line. Run by JR Hokkaido. See p291.

● **SL Banetsu-Monogatari** (C57 180, nickname Lady of Rank) Niitsu to Aizu-Wakamatsu on the Banetsu-Sei line. Run by JR East. See box p2165.

● **SL Kita-Biwako** (C56 160) Maibara to Kinomoto on the Hokuriku line. Run by JR West. See p168.

● **SL Yamaguchi** (C57 1) Ogori to Tsuwano on the Yamaguchi line. Run by JR West. See p211.

● **SL Aso Boy** (58654) Kumamoto to Miyaji via Aso on the Hohi line. Run by JR Kyushu. This is the oldest operating mainline steam locomotive in Japan, built in 1922 and in operation until 1975. It restarted as the Aso Boy in 1988. See p336.

● **Oigawa Railway** Kanaya to Senzu on the Oigawa line. Operated by the private Oigawa Railway (☎ 0547-45 4113; rail passes not valid), this is one of the busiest preserved steam operations in the country, with services throughout the year. Several locomotives, including the C12 164, which was restored thanks to a ¥50 million funding initiative by the Japan National Trust, are run. See p114.

🏯 **Thomas and friends**
No railway history would be complete without a mention of Thomas The Tank Engine. Thomas and his steam-engine friends have enjoyed huge success in Japan, ever since the British animation series was first broadcast on Japanese television in October 1990. At first airing once a week, the series was such a hit that it eventually got its own daily slot. Thomas survived the cultural leap from Britain to Japan almost entirely intact, except that British narrator Ringo Starr was replaced by Leo Morimoto, a Japanese TV and feature film actor. The Japanese love of old-fashioned steam engines, coupled with the importance of the railway to daily life in Japan, partly explains why the series has been so successful. But much of the credit goes to narrator Leo Morimoto: 'Thomas was so different to anything Japanese children had seen until then and could look scary,' say the series creators, but Morimoto sounds like a 'kind father reading to his children, so they could watch without fear'.

But Thomas in Japan was always going to be much more than just a small-screen little blue engine. Thomas Land, the first theme park in the world devoted to the character, opened here in 1997. Thomas merchandise unique to the Japanese market includes chopsticks, rice and noodle bowls, toilet rolls, disposable bibs and car seatbelt covers. All of which leaves you wondering what Rev Wilbert Awdry, the Anglican clergyman and railway enthusiast who wrote the original stories in the 1940s and who died in 1997, would have made of the phenomenon of Thomas and the Fat Controller in the land of the bullet train.

In the late 1980s and 90s, with the vocal and financial support of nostalgic rail fans and local authorities, steam trains began to reappear as tourist attractions. At precisely the time Thomas the Tank Engine was building up a nationwide fan base (see box above), so too real-life steam engines were once again gathering speed on rural lines. No longer the exclusive preserve of *tetsudo maniaku* (rail enthusiasts), of which there are thousands in Japan, preserved steam operations now cater to the tourist trade. But some experts warn that the current nostalgia boom will be short-lived. Railway-equipment manufacturers are no longer geared up to supply spare parts for old locomotives and it may only be a matter of time before the SLs are once again shunted away into the sidings.

The railway

JAPAN RAIL TODAY

The railway in Japan is widely considered to be one of the most efficient in the world and reaches nearly all parts of the four main islands. Private railways provide additional coverage but the bulk of the railway network is operated by six regional companies known collectively as the JR Group (hereafter known as JR). For the Japan Rail pass-holder, the six companies can be considered one

> ⛩ **Rail information in English**
> For information in English on all JR services once you're in Japan, call the **JR East Infoline** (☎ 03-3423 0111, Mon-Fri, 10am-6pm). Operators can provide information on timetables and fares, and advise on routes. Seat reservations are not accepted by phone. This service is provided by JR East, but information is available for all services operated by the JR Group.

national company because the pass is valid on virtually all trains across the entire JR network.

Every day, 26,000 JR trains travel on a network which stretches for 20,000km. These range from some of the fastest trains in the world shuttling businessmen from one meeting to another, to one-carriage diesel trains on remote rural lines. JR well deserves its reputation for punctuality and efficiency on all its lines; it is extremely rare for services to run late. While in Japan, I ended up on a delayed train on average once every three months – but even these delays were never more than a few minutes and staff made frequent apologies.

The only time when there is a risk of major disruption is after a serious earthquake or in the event of really extreme weather conditions. Warm water is sprayed on to the tracks on the Tohoku shinkansen east of Tokyo to ensure that snow does not disrupt service, but in northern Honshu and Hokkaido severe snow in winter occasionally causes disruption.

Rail companies around the world must envy JR's track record: not a single derailment on the shinkansen since services began in 1964. After midnight, when the shinkansen closes down for the night, a small army of engineers inspect and repair the track on a special shinkansen nicknamed the 'Dr Yellow'. They have only six hours each night to carry out essential track maintenance.

Not only is JR the most efficient rail network in the world, the trains are also some of the best maintained. It's worth turning up early for your shinkansen to see the army of uniformed cleaning staff who have only a few minutes to ensure the carriages are swept, the toilets cleaned and all the seats turned around to face the correct way. At stations, platforms are always spotless, floors are constantly swept, wiped and disinfected, dustbins emptied before they are ever full and escalator rails wiped (staff seem to be employed exclusively for this task).

THE TRAINS

Shinkansen

JR's flagship trains are, of course, the shinkansen, better known as the bullet train. All shinkansen can be used with the rail pass except for the new Nozomi ('Hope') super express, which runs on the Tokaido and Sanyo shinkansen lines between Tokyo and Hakata and is the fastest of all the bullet trains. Seats on the Nozomi are by reservation only. If you take a Nozomi you'll have to pay the full

---

♯ **Japan by rail on the Internet**
www.bijapan.com/cgi-bin/expwww/exp.cgi Input your origin and destination points for anywhere on Japan's rail network and this site will come up with
an itinerary, including transfers, journey time and fare.
www.geocities.com/TheTropics/Cove/5750/tips.html One of the best resources
on the web, run by a rail enthusiast with regularly updated information on rail travel in Japan with maps and travel advice pages.
www.h2.dion.ne.jp/~dajf/byunbyun/index.htm Anything you could ever want to
know about the shinkansen, written by a rail enthusiast.
www.jnto.go.jp/db/traffic/ JNTO's page devoted to rail and air travel around
Japan includes an on-line train timetable and colour diagrams showing the layout
of major JR stations.

All the companies in the JR Group have a presence on the web:
JR Hokkaido: www.jrhokkaido.co.jp (Japanese only).
JR East: www.jreast.co.jp/e/ Excellent source of information in English, includ-
ing fares and details about JR East rail passes (see p14).
JR Central: www.jr-central.co.jp Corporate information only is available in
English.
JR West: www.westjr.co.jp/english/ Good English information on JR West's net-
work and rail passes (see p14).
JR Shikoku: www.jr-shikoku.co.jp (Japanese only).
JR Kyushu: www.jrkyushu.co.jp (Japanese only).
JR Group: www.japanrail.com This site is maintained by the JR East New York
office, representing the JR Group. The office (US ☎ 212-332 8686, 🖷 332 8690, 🖳
info@japanrail.com, Mon-Fri, 9am-5pm) provides rail-related information but does
not sell tickets/rail passes. The address is: One Rockefeller Plaza, Suite 1622, New
York, NY10020, USA.

---

fare, including the super express supplement, so make sure that if you're travelling west of Tokyo to Kyoto/Osaka, you take only a Hikari or Kodama
shinkansen (see route guide on p111).

The shinkansen offers what is almost certainly the smoothest train ride in
the world, as the train appears to glide effortlessly along the line; all shinkansen
run on special tracks. The seating configuration is usually 3x2 and, as with all
shinkansen and limited express services, seats can be turned around so that a
group travelling together can face each other.

Facilities on board include telephones, Japanese and Western-style toilets,
and a nappy-changing room which can be used as a 'sick bay' by anyone who
is not feeling well – the key is available from the train conductor. Mini-shops
and trolley services selling sandwiches, bentos, pastries and hot/cold drinks are
found on most services though Nozomi trains have vending machines only.
Whichever train you take, it's far cheaper to stock up at a station kiosk or convenience store before you travel. The culture of enjoying a meal in a dining car
appears to be dying out. The last dining cars on Grand Hikari bullet trains running west of Tokyo were closed in 2000. Dining cars remain on only a few of

---

---

the luxury overnight sleeper services, notably the Cassiopeia (between Ueno, in Tokyo, and Sapporo) and the Twilight Express (between Osaka and Sapporo). The rail pass is not valid on either of these services (see box, p77).

JR East has recently introduced a massage service on selected Tohoku shinkansen. A 15-minute massage in a private booth, on the lower floor of car No 9, costs ¥1600. Designed to appeal to tired, stressed businessmen, the service is likely to be extended to other shinkansen if it proves a success. Massages are currently only available on three trains a day from Tokyo to Sendai/Morioka, so if you want to sort out your itinerary to take advantage of the service, call the JR English infoline (☎ 03-3423 0111) to check timetables. There is speculation also that the world's first on-board bidets are soon to be introduced on selected Tohoku shinkansen services!

Limited expresses

Next step down are limited expresses (LEX; called *tokkyu*), which run on the same tracks as ordinary trains (see below) but stop only at major stations. The standard of comfort and range of facilities on board varies considerably. Most limited expresses are modern and offer almost as smooth a ride as the shinkansen but a few (mainly diesel-powered ones) are not quite as glamorous or hi-tech. The JR companies constantly try to outdo each other by rolling out ever more space-age-style interiors whenever they upgrade their limited express services. Many trains have on-board vending machines and telephones (though expect to pay a premium rate). The seating configuration varies but is very often 2x2 and as with the shinkansen all seats can be turned around to face the other way. Few limited expresses have a buffet car though virtually all offer a refreshments trolley. There is usually a mixture of Japanese and Western-style toilets though on the oldest trains you may find Japanese toilets only.

Express, rapid and local trains

Despite their names, **express** (*kyuko*) and **rapid** trains (*kaisoku*), are much slower than limited expresses and boast few facilities; they are also increasingly rare. Seating is usually 2x2 though on some local trains there are long rows of bench-style seats on either side of the train which leaves plenty of standing room in the middle. Don't expect to find a buffet car or trolley service but most of these trains have at least one toilet, though (particularly on local trains) this is likely to be Japanese style.

> **Luggage space**
> On all shinkansen and most limited express trains there are luggage racks at either end of each compartment which are wide enough to store rucksacks and suitcases. On some of the more modern trains you'll also find airline-style overhead storage bins. Local trains do not have dedicated storage areas but as long as you're not travelling during the rush hour, there's always space to leave your luggage by the door, on a seat or in the aisle.

Slowest of all are the **local trains** (*futsu*) which stop at every station. The smallest trains with just a single carriage are called 'one-man cars'. A few lines in rural areas, particularly in Hokkaido (see p281), are served by local trains only. In all other places the only reason for taking the local train is if you plan to stop at a station not served by limited express.

One of the pleasures of a ride on a local train is the chance to stand right at the front next to the driver's compartment; here you'll see close-up how and why the Japanese rail network is so efficient. Wearing a suit, cap and regulation white gloves the driver of the smallest local train seems just as meticulous as the driver of a 16-carriage shinkansen. Before the train pulls away from each stop the driver points at the clock as if to confirm the train is indeed leaving on time, then points ahead to check the signals have given him (or her) the all clear to go.

Seat reservations can be made on shinkansen, limited express and express services, but rapid and local trains are all non-reserved.

Sleeper trains

In addition to the trains mentioned above, JR operates a number of sleeper services. On services which are all berths and do not have a reserved seat section, rail-pass holders have to pay both the limited express charge and a hefty supplement for use of a berth. This can be anything from ¥6300 for a bed in a compartment to ¥17,180 for an 'A' class bed on the Twilight Express (see below); supplements vary according to the distance travelled.

The type of berth available varies from train to train so check when making a reservation what the accommodation choice is. A reserved seat is the cheapest option though some trains are 'all bed' (couchette or semi/private compartment). The de luxe sleepers (Cassiopeia and Twilight Express) which run between Osaka/Tokyo and Hakodate/Sapporo have luxuries such as on-board showers and dining cars, but don't expect great facilities on other services. Slippers and a yukata are often provided but, surprisingly, buffet cars/vending machines are rare. The best advice is to pick up some snacks and drink before you set off.

Other overnight services have either reclining seats or carpet space where you can lie down on the floor; these are free to rail-pass holders but places should be reserved in advance.

❏ Major sleeper services

Name of train	To/from	To/from
*Akatsuki	Kyoto	Nagasaki
Akebono	Ueno (Tokyo)	Aomori
Asakaze	Tokyo	Shimonoseki
Cassiopeia	Ueno (Tokyo)	Sapporo
*Chikuma	Osaka	Nagano
*Daisen	Osaka	Yonago (near Matsue)
*Dream Nichirin	Hakata	Minami-Miyazaki
*Dream Tsubame	Hakata	Nishi-Kagoshima
Fuji	Tokyo	Oita
Hakutsuru	Ueno (Tokyo)	Aomori
*Hamanasu	Aomori	Sapporo
Hayabusa	Tokyo	Kumamoto
Hokuriku	Ueno (Tokyo)	Kanazawa
Hokutosei	Ueno (Tokyo)	Sapporo
Izumo	Tokyo	Izumo-shi
*Midnight	Hakodate	Sapporo
*Moonlight Echigo	Shinjuku (Tokyo)	Murakami (near Niigata)
*Moonlight Nagara	Tokyo	Ogaki (near Nagoya)
*Naha	Shin-Osaka	Nishi-Kagoshima
Nihonkai	Osaka	Hakodate
*Okhotsk	Sapporo	Abashiri
Sakura	Tokyo	Nagasaki
Suisei	Shin-Osaka	Minami-Miyazaki
**Sunrise-Izumo	Tokyo	Izumo-shi
**Sunrise-Seto	Tokyo	Matsuyama/Takamatsu
Twilight Express	Osaka	Sapporo

* Reserved seating is available to rail-pass holders without supplement.
** Reserved carpet space (called *nobi-nobi zaseki*) is available to rail-pass holders without supplement.

ALTERNATIVES TO A JAPAN RAIL PASS

If you arrive in Japan without a rail pass there are other ticket options, though none is quite such a good deal.

A 7-day **JR Hokkaido Free Pass** is available to both Japanese and foreigners and is valid for rail travel throughout the island of Hokkaido (see p281). The price is ¥23,750 for standard class and ¥34,860 for Green (first) class. Alternatively, a 7-day **JR Hokkaido Pair Pass**, valid for two people travelling together, costs ¥43,220 (standard) or ¥63,200 (Green). Both passes can be purchased at mainline JR stations in Hokkaido or from JR Hokkaido's office at Tokyo station (Mon-Fri 9am-7pm, Sat/Sun 9:30am-5pm) by the Central Marunouchi exit.

The JR group companies offer seasonal excursion tickets which allow unlimited travel in selected areas over a set number of days. The validity and

---

鳥 Full Moon passes
Couples (husband and wife) whose combined age is over 88 might be interested in the **Full Moon Green Pass**. This 'double ticket' entitles the bearers to travel in the Green car (first class) on any JR line and is also valid for B-class sleeping berths on overnight rail services. The pass is available for periods of five days (¥80,500), seven days (¥99,900) or twelve days (¥124,400) and is sold between September 1st and May 31st for travel between October 1st and June 30th. The pass cannot be used during peak holiday periods (Dec 21st-Jan 6th, Mar 21st-Apr 5th, Apr 27th-May 6th).

A **Silver Full Moon Green Pass** is available where at least one person is aged 70 or over. The pass is valid for the same periods of five, seven and twelve days and costs ¥75,500, ¥94,900 and ¥119,400 respectively.

Unlike the normal rail passes (see p12), these can only be purchased in Japan. Both Full Moon passes are available at major stations and travel agents such as JTB. You need to show proof of age and, for the Full Moon Green pass, marriage (ie same surname), in the form of a health insurance card or passport. Note that like regular rail passes, the Full Moon pass cannot be used on Nozomi shinkansen.

---

type of these tickets changes regularly, so enquire at any tourist information centre or JR ticket office for details. Probably the best buy is the budget **Seishin Juhachi Kippu** ('Youth 18 ticket'); this is a seasonal ticket aimed at young people travelling around in holiday time, but there is no upper age limit.

The ticket costs ¥11,500 and what you receive is actually a set of five tickets which can be used for travel on local trains only. The five tickets can be used by five people travelling together on one day (which works out at ¥2300 per person), or by one person travelling on any five days within the period of validity. The ticket can be purchased from any JR ticket office between July 1st and August 31st and is valid for travel between July 20th and September 10th. It is also sold during the following periods: February 20th to March 31st, for travel between March 1st and April 10th, and December 1st to January 10th for travel between December 10th and January 20th.

BUYING A TICKET

This is the most expensive way of travelling and is not really recommended if you can purchase a rail pass. The fare structure in Japan is straightforward. First there is a **basic fare** which corresponds to the kilometre distance you travel. This ticket is valid only on local and rapid trains. **Supplements** have to be paid if using any other train. The fare for a **return trip** by rail is discounted by 20% if the one-way distance exceeds 600km.

Tickets can be purchased from ticket machines or at JR ticket offices. If buying from a machine and unsure of the fare to your destination, the best advice is to buy the cheapest ticket and then pay the difference to the train conductor or at a 'fare-adjustment machine' at your arrival station. Note that if travelling in a group, most ticket machines have an option to purchase several tickets for the same journey in one go – push the button which indicates the appropriate group size.

Some ticket counters at Tokyo station accept credit cards issued overseas but in most other places you'll need to pay in cash. Tables of the basic per kilometre fares and limited express/super express (shinkansen) supplements are printed in the condensed English-language timetable; a few sample fares are provided in the box.

❑ **Sample single fares from Tokyo**

To	Fare	Supple-ment
Aomori (739km)	¥10,190	¥6850*
Hakata (1176km)	¥13,440	¥8280
Hiroshima (894km)	¥11,340	¥6710
Kyoto (514km)	¥7980	¥5240
Nagano (222km)	¥3890	¥4080
Nagasaki (1330km)	¥14,810	¥9370*
Sapporo (1212km)	¥14,070	¥8300*
Takayama (533km)	¥8510	¥5790*

* Includes both the shinkansen and limited express surcharge.

TIMETABLES

This guide contains timetables (see Appendix C, p396) for the main routes described. JNTO publishes annually a condensed JR timetable (*Railway Timetable*) in English which contains details of the major shinkansen and limited express services. If you are intending to stick only to main rail routes, this is all the information you will need. Bear in mind, however, that timetables change so you should not rely on either of these sources. Double check through the English infoline (see box, p73) or at a rail station before you travel.

Alternatively, if you can read Japanese, or even if you can't but are up for the challenge, get a copy of the Japanese timetable (*Jikokuhyo*/¥1050). The huge volume, which lists everything that moves in Japan (trains, buses, ropeways, cable cars, ferry services, chair lifts) is published monthly. You'll find a well-thumbed copy in every JR ticket office. Much easier to carry around is the pocket-sized version (Pocket *Jikokuhyo*/¥500), also published monthly; this condensed volume still contains much more information than JNTO's *Railway Timetable* or the timetables in this guide. Both versions of the Japanese timetable are available from any bookstore in Japan.

For a guide to using the Japanese timetable, see Appendix C, p396.

Midori no Madoguchi
(Green Window)
reservation
office

MAKING SEAT RESERVATIONS

Seat reservations can be made up to one month before the date of travel but only in Japan. To make a reservation either find the ticket office, known as '**Midori no Madoguchi**', at any JR station or if there are long queues, try a **Travel Service Center** (**TSC**). TSCs are JR-run travel agencies which also handle seat reservations; they are found in larger stations – look for the racks of holiday brochures outside.

The regional JR companies call their TSCs by different names but they all offer the same service. The names to look out for are **JR Tokai Tours** (in the JR Central area), **View Plaza**

❏ **Last-minute booking**
Thanks to JR's computerized seat-reservation system, you can book seats up to the very last minute and even as the train is waiting in the station. Only at peak travel times, such as the Golden Week holiday, are seats booked weeks in advance.

(JR East), **Travel Information Satellite (TiS)** – not to be confused with tourist information offices – (JR West), **Warp Navi** (JR Shikoku), **Joyroad** (JR Kyushu) and **Twinkle Plaza** (JR Hokkaido).

Seat reservations on all shinkansen (except the Nozomi super-express) and limited express trains cost nothing if you have a rail pass so it's always worth making a reservation, particularly if travelling at peak times. (All other passengers have to pay a supplement for a reserved seat).

Remember that if you board a train without a seat reservation and sit in a reserved carriage, the conductor will charge you the appropriate supplement for the distance you're travelling, even if you have a rail pass. Pass holders, however, are not penalized for not using a seat reservation, so it doesn't matter if you miss the train (see box above) or change your plans – just cancel your reservation by handing in your seat reservation ticket and then make another one.

At the time of reservation you can usually choose on which side of the train you want to sit. For the classic view of Mt Fuji from the shinkansen, ask for a seat on the right side coming from Tokyo, and on the left side from Kyoto. You can also choose if you want to be in a smoking or non-smoking car. Smoking is not permitted on local trains, but on limited express and shinkansen trains there is a choice of both reserved and unreserved smoking and non-smoking cars. Note that on most limited expresses there is only one Green Car and it is usually non-smoking.

In all ticket offices you'll find reservation request forms that are supposed to be filled out before going to the ticket desk. Almost always, however, staff are happy to issue seat reservations without a form, so just head to the desk and tell them where and when you want to go (or at least write the basic information down on a piece of paper). Even if the staff do want you to complete a form it is not difficult as some forms have English on them.

JR has plans for an online seat reservation system in English and Japanese at some time in 2002-3; contact JNTO to find out if it is now operational.

For details of how to read your seat reservation ticket, see the sample in Appendix B on p395.

The Japanese calendar
Traditionally the Japanese have named and counted their years by the length of an Emperor's reign. The count starts with each new Emperor. The year 2000, for example, was known as Heisei 12; Heisei being the name that refers to the current Emperor's era, and 12 being the number of years that have elapsed since he ascended to the throne; the year 2002 is Heisei 14. While the Western system of counting years is widely used, the Japanese system is often found on official documentation (eg train and seat reservation tickets).

> ⛩ **Information overload**
>   'Usually we had reserved-seat tickets, which meant we'd have to get to the
> right station, then get to the right platform, then get to the right position on the plat-
> form, then get into the right car, then find the right seats...So we'd be lugging our
> luggage through a crowded, bustling station, with me leading the way, frowning at
> the tickets, trying to decide whether we wanted Car 9 of Train 17 on Track 3, or Car
> 3 of Train 9 on Track 17, or possibly even Car 17 on March 9, and I'd announce, "Up
> this stairway!" And Beth would say, "Are you sure?" And I'd say "Of COURSE I'm
> sure," in the irritated, superior manner characteristic of a guy who is lost.'
>   **Dave Barry**, *Dave Barry Does Japan* (Ballantine Books, 1992)

RAILWAY STAFF

JR staff are always impeccably dressed in company uniforms which differ
slightly in design from one region to another. Suits are the norm but short-
sleeve shirts are worn in summer. JR Central's conductors on the shinkansen
are given a new tie once a month. The female staff who serve refreshments on
board JR Hokkaido trains wear badges announcing themselves as 'Twinkle
Ladies'.

Don't expect all JR staff to speak English, though basic questions concerning platform and destination are usually no problem. At the ticket offices in
major stations (such as Tokyo and Kyoto), you'll find someone who speaks
English. Some train conductors on the bullet train also speak some English. All
carry pocket timetables and can advise on connection times and even tell you
from which platform your next train will be departing.

STATION FACILITIES

Coin lockers

All large stations and most smaller stations have coin lockers which range in
price from ¥300 to ¥600; ¥300 lockers are big enough for day packs only, while
all but the biggest ruck sacks should fit comfortably into a ¥500 locker. Lockers
take ¥100 coins, so if you need change ask at a station kiosk. The fee is charged
on a midnight to midnight basis, so if you store your luggage at 6pm and leave
it there until the following morning or afternoon, you have to pay the same fee
again to retrieve it.

If there are no lockers, or your luggage is too big to fit inside one, ask a
member of JR staff. Bags can sometimes be kept in the station office for ¥410
per item. If all else fails, you may feel that Japan is safe enough to risk leaving
your belongings in a quiet corner of the station.

Note that though check-in time in Japan is not usually until late afternoon,
the majority of hotels, ryokan and hostels are happy to keep your luggage for
free during the day before you check in, so you don't have to fork out for coin
lockers every time you arrive somewhere.

⛩ **Standing in line**
The British may be known for queuing but the Japanese have turned standing in line into an art form. At mainline stations, including all shinkansen stops, locator maps of trains are found on each platform. These show the layout and configuration of your train and indicate precisely where you should wait on the platform. Look

out along the edge of the platform for numbered signs which indicate the stopping point for each carriage. You can be sure that the train will stop where it should and the doors of each carriage will open opposite the appropriate platform markers.

At busy stations there are often a bewildering number of signs telling you where to stand for particular trains. If you've got a seat reservation ticket, you could show it to someone on the platform and ask them to point you in the direction of the right queue. But don't get unduly stressed about standing in the right line: all the carriages are interconnected and you can easily find the way to the right compartment once you're on board.

Food

The cheapest places to look for food are in station bakeries and coffee shops, open from around 7am to 9pm. If you just want to pick up a snack or a drink, look either for a convenience store outside the station or for kiosks inside the station. Stations of all sizes have at least one noodle stall, where you can get a filling bowl of udon or soba for around ¥300-400; see also p52.

The most popular railway food is the ekiben, or station lunch box. 'Bento' is a generic term for a packed lunch, but the ekiben is a cut above the rest. There's an ekiben stall (or several) in every station; the boxes feature local ingredients which give you a taste of the place you are passing through. The boxes are also sold on shinkansen and limited express trains, but it's much cheaper to buy one at the station before you leave. A JR website 🖳

⛩ **Let's Kiosk!**
Japan's first station stall opened in 1872, when a British resident of Yokohama started selling newspapers at the city's train station. The 'kiosk' brand name was introduced a century later in 1973, after a nationwide competition to find the most appropriate word for the stalls. Kiosk (pronounced *kiyosuku*) was chosen because it incorporates the Japanese words *kiyoku* (cleanliness) and *kiyasuku* (feeling free). The slogan displayed on many station stalls reads 'Let's Kiosk', but a sign at Hakata station reveals the true spirit of the railway stall: 'People come and go through the station. Their destinations may be different, but all of them can meet and shop at KIOSK along the way. That's the reason we're here.'

⛩ **Railway fare**
Crucial to the success of an ekiben (station lunch box) is the shape of the box and whether the contents are pleasing to the eye as the the lid is uncovered. Most are priced at around ¥1000 but Kanazawa station has a ¥10,000 bento box, shaped like a chest of drawers – you pull out each drawer to reveal another layer or course of your meal.

Though ekiben are quintessentially Japanese, their contents are not always so. A catering company in Sendai recently introduced cuisine from Brittany in its international lunch box – beef tongue in apple sauce with lentils, followed by a cooked apple dessert. This ekiben was even taste-tested by residents of Rennes, Sendai's sister city in France. An official from Rennes marked the occasion with a goodwill message to the people of Sendai: 'It makes us happy that cultural exchange can take place through ekiben'.

Careful research also went in to the creation of the 500 pack a day 'limited-edition' paella lunchbox, which made its debut at Tokyo station in 1994. The Japanese caterers first went on a study trip to Europe before spending three months turning the concept into a culinary reality. Members of the Spanish Association in Japan were even brought in to dispense advice and fine tune the lunchbox. The whole process, from idea through to its appearance at station kiosks, took eight months, twice as long as it usually takes to develop an ekiben.

However, like all institutions, the press delights in reporting on the ekiben's imminent demise (why pay for a fancy lunch box when you can grab a cheap burger?). Statistics suggest that sales of ekiben are nearly half what they were several years ago. This is partly because of faster train services (by the time you've unwrapped the box, you're nearly at your destination) but also an indication of the lingering recession, which has forced many people to cut back on travel.

www.jr.odekake.net (Japanese only) lists train times but also allows you to check the ekiben available at a station and pre-book one, so food fanatics can plot their journey according to their taste buds.

Facilities for the disabled

In large stations there are adequate facilities for disabled passengers, including elevators, ramps or stair lifts from platform to concourse level. Unfortunately, in most smaller stations there are no special facilities and often only stairs and overhead walkways. Rail travel in Japan for disabled travellers is far from ideal and it seems that stations have been designed solely with able-bodied passengers in mind. The situation is changing slowly; new stations with improved facilities are being built but don't expect your image of hi-tech Japan to ring true in terms of wheelchair accessibility.

Where there are no special facilities, JR staff are happy to provide assistance to disabled passengers. Enquire at the JR ticket office at least 30 minutes before the departure of your train. Train conductors and/or station staff will also help with boarding and exiting carriages. On older trains, aisles are narrow and not designed for wheelchair use. Unless facilities are specifically referred to in the route and city guides, seek assistance from station staff.

BICYCLES

JR does not generally allow cycles to be carried on trains unless they can be folded up or dismantled and carried in a special bag. Cycles, however, can be rented from many JR stations (enquire at the ticket counter); rates are about ¥200 per hour or ¥1000 for the day.

⛩ **Using the rail route guides in this book**
　　The route guides cover all four main islands. Each route has at least one point of connection with other routes described. Thus, if you are following the route round Western Honshu (see p202) you will pass through Okayama (see p205), the starting point for the route guide around Shikoku (see p364). Each route guide begins with an introduction to the area, with information on regional highlights and suggested stopping-off points. Routes can be followed in reverse but in this case all points of interest from the train will be on the opposite side.

　　Though it's possible to travel every route by local train, it's assumed that most travellers will have a rail pass so will use the shinkansen and/or limited express (LEX) services. It is not possible to mention every station so, as a rule of thumb, only stops served by limited expresses (or by shinkansen if the route follows a shinkansen line) are included. Stations served solely by local trains are listed if they, or the area around them, are of particular interest.

　　When a route includes a stop in a large town or city, a cross reference is given to that place's entry in the city guides section which appears immediately after the respective route guide.

　　The fastest point-to-point journey times are provided for each section of the route. Even though each route has been divided into different sections it may not be necessary to change trains as you go from one section to the next. Occasionally, however, it is essential to change train in order to complete the route described. Such instances are denoted by the following symbol ▲. Places which are served by local trains only are marked ◆.

Tokyo

INTRODUCTION

It will come as no surprise to first-time visitors that Tokyo is the most populous city in the world – it even has an entry in the *Guinness Book of Records* to prove it; 26.4 million people are packed into the city and suburbs. There's no denying this makes Tokyo seriously overcrowded. Rumours that staff are employed at some stations to push people on to trains are true, at least during peak rush-hour times. But if you avoid the morning and evening rush hours, it's possible to travel around Tokyo in comfort. And whatever the time of day, the trains run according to the timetable.

More surprising than the mass of people is the fact that Tokyo became Japan's official capital only in 1868, when Emperor Meiji was restored to the throne (see p35). For centuries before, it was an undiscovered backwater and might have remained so had Tokugawa Ieyasu not decided to settle there.

In 1603 Ieyasu chose Edo (called Tokyo since 1868) as the seat of government for the Tokugawa shogunate. Right up until the collapse of the shogunate in 1867, Japan's official capital remained Kyoto but the Emperor who resided there exercised no real power.

In the years since Edo was renamed Tokyo and snatched the capital prize from Kyoto, the small town has become a thriving city of commerce, industry, entertainment and luxury. Little of the old Tokyo remains but one area worth seeking out for its atmosphere is Asakusa (see p93), home to one of Japan's most vibrant temples and packed with narrow streets which are a world and at least a century away from the skyscrapers of Shinjuku (see p87).

Some arrive in Tokyo and never leave, captivated by the neon, designer stores and relentless energy of the place. Others arrive and never leave their hotel rooms, terrified of the noise and sheer number of people who fill the streets day and night.

The answer is somewhere between these two extremes. Stay just long enough to get a feel for the city but get out in time to make full use of the rail pass and discover how much lies beyond this metropolis.

さまざまの事おもひ出す櫻かな

Ah! what memories!
Myriad thoughts evoked
by those cherry trees!
(Matsuo Basho)

WHAT TO SEE AND DO

JR's Yamanote line runs in a loop around Tokyo; the text below suggests stopping-off points both on and off the line. The route begins and ends at Tokyo station, the main arrival/departure point by shinkansen.

On the Yamanote line

Tokyo The Marunouchi side of Tokyo station is the old half and has a traditional red-brick frontage which houses an expensive hotel and **Tokyo Station Gallery** (daily except Mon 10am-7pm, Sat/Sun to 6pm; usually ¥800 but it depends on the exhibition); this gallery could be a good place to kill time if you're waiting for a train. The entrance is just outside Marunouchi north exit.

A short walk north-west from the Marunouchi exit brings you to the imposing **Imperial Palace**, surrounded by a stone-wall moat. Home to the Emperor and his family, this is a quiet oasis of green but is mostly off-limits to the public except on two days of the year (December 23rd and January 2nd), when the Emperor and his wife wave from the balcony to thousands of flag-waving patriots and tourists. The **East Garden** (Higashi Gyoen) is open to the public (9am-3pm Dec-Feb, 9am-4pm Mar-Nov, daily except Mon/Fri, free), as is **Hibiya Park**, adjacent to Palace Plaza.

Yurakucho Alight here for the tourist information centre (see p96); it's in Tokyo International Forum Building, which is right outside the station.

Shimbashi In the square outside the station is a replica of Japan's first-ever steam locomotive (see p66).

Shimbashi is the birthplace of the railway in Japan and it remains a centre of rail innovation as the starting point for the Tokyo Waterfront New Transit Line, a monorail better known as the **Yurikamome**. The driverless Yurikamome whisks passengers to **Odaiba**, an island of reclaimed land in Tokyo Bay. A highlight is when the train crosses the spectacular Rainbow Bridge. Look out on the Tokyo Bay side for **Telecom Tower**, which resembles the Grande Arche de la Défense in Paris.

The chance to see Tokyo from another angle makes this trip worthwhile in itself but the monorail calls at plenty of tourist attractions along the way, including **Sega Joypolis** with the latest virtual reality attractions, the **Museum of Maritime Science** (built in the shape of a cruise ship), and **Palette Town**, which includes the **Mega Web** theme park, a showcase for Toyota with paid attractions such as a 3D motion theatre and the 'E-com Ride' where you can go for a spin in a car which drives itself. Fuji Television Network has its studios on Odaiba (look for the space-age metallic building with a sphere suspended in the middle). There is no charge to visit the studios (10am-8pm) but you have to pay to go in the spherical observatory (daily except Mon, 10am-8pm; ¥500).

A one-day pass for the Yurikamome costs ¥800, valid for unlimited travel between Shimbashi and the monorail terminus at Ariake. Sit in the front carriage (where the driver should be) for the best views. As an alternative route back to Tokyo, get off at **Hinode**, two stops before the terminus, and walk a couple of minutes to the passenger ferry terminal. From here you can catch a ferry (daily, 9am-6pm, dep every 40 mins, approx 40 mins; ¥660) up Sumida-gawa to **Asakusa** (see p93). This is another great way of seeing Tokyo; an on-board commentary is provided in English and Japanese.

Hamamatsucho The Tokyo Monorail to **Haneda Airport** (p44) starts here.

Shinagawa A new state-of-the-art shinkansen station is scheduled to open here in autumn 2003. When it opens, some Tokaido shinkansen trains will arrive and leave from here instead of Tokyo station.

Meguro Meguro is an upmarket area that's home to some of Japan's TV celebrities since it's convenient for Shibuya (home to NHK, the Japanese equivalent of the BBC) and Akasaka (home to the more commercial and ratings-driven TBS).

Ebisu From the station, follow the signs for Yebisu Garden Palace, accessed via a series of moving walkways. Here you'll find shops, a cinema, restaurants, hotel and **Beer Museum Yebisu** (daily except Mon, 10am-5pm; free). Located behind Mitsukoshi department store, the museum was opened by Sapporo Breweries and is dedicated to the 'history, science and culture of the beloved beverage'. No beer is brewed here but there is a chance to tour a 'virtual brewery'. There is a tasting lounge at the end (¥400 to taste four different beers). A leaflet in English is provided at the entrance but signs are mostly in Japanese. This museum is worth a look if you're not visiting Sapporo, where you can tour a working brewery and get a free can of beer at the end (see p310).

Shibuya Follow the signs for the Hachiko Exit, which will lead you to the main shopping area. The zebra crossing in front of the station is always packed with people making a beeline for the big names and high-street retailers crammed into this area. Head up the main street away from the station to find Tower Records (foreign books are on the seventh floor), Häagen Dazs and all the top fashion department stores. Come here to see where and how young Japanese spend their pocket money and look in vain for anyone over the age of 40.

Harajuku Opposite Harajuku station is Yoyogi Park, home to **Meiji Jingu**, Tokyo's best-known shrine. Dedicated to the Emperor Meiji and his consort, the shrine is divided into Outer and Inner gardens. Busy throughout the year, the shrine is invaded by thousands on New Year's Eve and New Year's Day.

Harajuku is just as hip as nearby Shibuya and there are plenty of restaurants and cafés in the streets around the station.

Yoyogi The huge skyscraper you can see looming over Yoyogi station is Nippon Telecom's DoCoMo Tower.

Shinjuku Probably the busiest station in the world – 1.52 million passengers pass through every day – Shinjuku is home not only to JR but also to the private

Odakyu and Keio railways. Tokyo TIC (Mon-Sat, 9am-6pm) is on the ground floor of the east exit and has English-speaking staff.

If you were to follow any of the mass of commuters (taking the west exit) between 6 and 8.30am, you would probably end up heading directly for the **Tokyo Metropolitan Government Building**, completed in 1991 and the work-place of 13,000 bureaucrats. The best reason for visiting here is the free, bird's eye, view of Tokyo. Take the direct elevator inside the No 1 Building up to one of two 202m-high observatories (daily except Mon, 9:30am-5pm, longer in summer, free) on the 45th floor. The cafés on the 45th floor are overpriced but there's a cheap cafeteria on the 32nd floor; it's meant for government employ-ees but is open to anybody – take one of the ordinary lifts to reach this floor.

Shinjuku Gyoen (daily except Mon 9am-4:30pm, ¥200) is a complete sur-prise in amongst Shinjuku's skyscrapers. Built in 1906 as an Imperial Garden, all 58.3 hectares are open to the public and the site includes an English land-scape garden, French garden and traditional Japanese garden. A couple of tra-ditional tea houses serve green tea and Japanese sweetmeats for ¥700. People come here to escape the busy city that surrounds the park; though you never quite feel you've left the metropolis, this is a pleasant temporary escape. Take the east exit from Shinjuku station and walk south-east for about 10 minutes.

For somewhere to eat, head for one of the 28 restaurants on the 12th-14th floors of Takashimaya department store in Times Square, on the south side of Shinjuku station (it's connected to the station by a walkway). Times Square also contains an I-MAX cinema, a huge branch of Kinokuniya Books (foreign books are on the sixth floor) and the entertainment arcade, Shinjuku Joypolis.

There's a certain Jekyll and Hyde character to Shinjuku. While the west side of the station is a sea of grey suits and immaculately turned-out businessmen, conformity is abandoned over on the east side. The streets around **Kabukicho**, a few minutes walk north of the east exit, fill up as the sun sets and the neon is switched on. Cinemas, clubs, restaurants, pubs and hostess bars all compete for business.

Shin-Okubo Years before the Bankside Globe opened in London, the Japanese had built their own reproduction of Shakespeare's playhouse, the **Tokyo Globe**. Most of the performances are in Japanese, though the RSC per-forms here when touring in Asia. Turn left out of the station and then right at the first junction (look for a McDonald's). Continue straight along this street for 5-10 minutes until you reach the Globe. On the adjacent 'Shakespeare Alley' is the Globe Tavern, serving evening meals and beer on tap for an authentic Elizabethan experience. For more of the Bard on location in Japan, see p100.

Takadanobaba Bus No 2 runs from outside this station to Waseda University campus, home to the **Tsubouchi Memorial Theatre Museum** (Mon, Wed, Thur, Sat, Sun 10am-5pm, Tue and Fri 10am-7pm, closed during university hol-idays; free). The museum is right in the middle of the campus and is dedicated to Shoyo Tsubouchi (1859-1935), founder of Waseda's Department of

Literature and the first person to translate the complete works of Shakespeare into Japanese. The museum was built in 1928 and is modelled on the 17th-century Fortune Theatre, which once stood in London. Pick up the excellent pamphlet, from the library on the ground floor, and then explore the three floors dedicated to the performing arts, with exhibitions on Shakespeare, Noh (try on a Noh mask and have a go at walking like a Noh actor) and Kabuki. If you get lost on your way to the museum, ask any student for the 'Waseda-daigaku Tsubouchi-kinenkan Engeki-hakubutsukan' – it's easier to find than it is to say.

Ikebukuro On either side of Ikebukuro station are two enormous department stores; **Seibu** is on the east side and its rival **Tobu** is on the west. An underground passageway links both sides of the station. Both Seibu and Tobu have restaurant floors and food halls.

Otsuka Transfer here for the Arakawa tram line (see p93).

Nippori Nippori is a point of transfer for the private Keisei Railway line to Narita Airport (see p95).

Uguisudani Up until WWII, Uguisudani was a popular geisha quarter but it is now better known as a night-time pleasure area full of love hotels.

Ueno A major rail junction and the second stop after Tokyo for shinkansen services to the north. Right outside the station is **Ueno Park**, Japan's oldest public park and the largest in Tokyo. During the cherry blossom season in April, thousands of Tokyo residents descend on Ueno Park armed with portable karaoke machines, picnic hampers and crates of beer.

The park is home to a number of big museums, including **Tokyo National Museum** (daily except Mon 9:30am-5pm, ¥420), the country's largest museum with exhibits on the history and fine arts of Japan, China and India. Also here are the **National Museum of Western Art** (daily except Mon 9:30am-5pm, Fri to 8pm; ¥420), which displays masterpieces collected by a Japanese business magnate while travelling around Europe in the early 1900s, and **Ueno Zoo** (daily except Mon 9:30am-5pm, ¥500), which opened in 1882 and is known in particular for its giant panda.

Aside from the park, another good reason for visiting Ueno is to wander around **Ameyokocho Market**. Take the Shinobazu exit at Ueno station and head for Ameya-dori, a long shopping arcade that extends out beneath the elevated rail tracks. Stallholders call out loudly to passers-by and this is one of the few places in Japan where you are expected to haggle. You can buy almost anything here, including (fake?) Prada handbags, Rolex watches, clothes, fresh fish, meat, fruit and vegetables.

Okachi-machi Okachi-machi is known for its cheap jewellery stores.

Akihabara Akihabara is the discount electrical goods district of Tokyo and is worth visiting if you want a chance to see the latest gadgets months before they hit the worldwide market. Digital cameras, TVs, CDs, DVDs, PCs and other

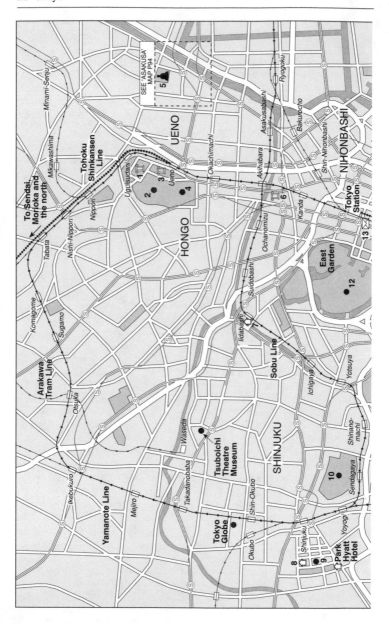

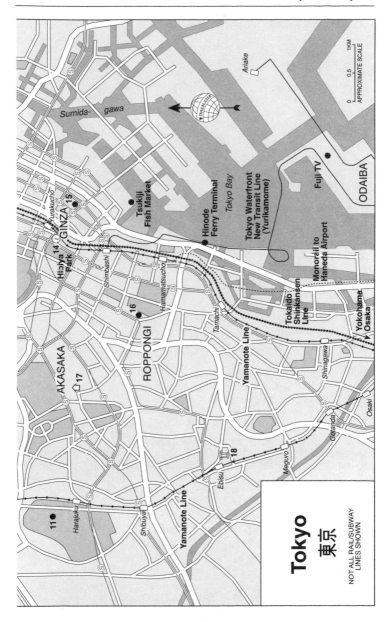

Tokyo
東京

NOT ALL RAIL/SUBWAY
LINES SHOWN

TOKYO 東京

Where to stay

7	Tokyo International Youth Hostel	7 東京国際ユースホステル
8	Hotel Century Hyatt	8 ホテル センチュリーハイアット
17	Asia Center of Japan	17 アジア会館

Other

1	Tokyo National Museum	1 東京国立博物館
2	Ueno Park	2 上野公園
3	National Museum of Western Art	3 国立西洋美術館
4	Ueno Zoo	4 上野動物園
5	Senso-ji	5 浅草寺
6	Transportation Museum	6 交通博物館
9	Tokyo Metropolitan Government Bldg	9 東京都庁
10	Shinjuku Gyoen	10 新宿御苑
11	Yoyogi Park/Meiji Jingu	11 代々木公園／明治神宮
12	Imperial Palace	12 皇居
13	Central Post Office	13 中央郵便局
14	Tourist Information Centre	14 観光案内センター
15	Kabuki-za (theatre)	15 歌舞伎座
16	Tokyo Tower	16 東京タワー
18	Beer Museum Yebisu	18 恵比寿麦酒記念館

abbreviations that will soon be part of the global electronic vocabulary are all on display and available for purchase. If you're planning to buy, check first whether the guarantee is valid overseas and if the equipment is compatible with the electrical current in your home country.

It is also home to the JR-run **Transportation Museum** (daily except Mon, 9:30am-5pm, ¥310). Most forms of transport are given space here but trains are the priority. On display is one of the locomotives used on Japan's first rail line (see p66), as well as a carriage used by Emperor Meiji during a ceremony to mark the opening of the railway line between Kyoto and Kobe in 1877. The shinkansen and trains of the future are also given exhibition space. To find the museum, take the 'Electric Town' exit at Akihabara station and then look for a sign pointing towards the museum. If you miss the sign, the museum is situated next to, and slightly to the right of, the railway bridge that runs over Chuo-dori.

Tokyo This completes the loop around the Yamanote line.

Off the Yamanote line

Ginza One stop on the Marunouchi subway line from Tokyo, Ginza is billed in tourist literature as the 'most fashionable shopping paradise in Japan'; the main thoroughfare, Chuo-dori, is lined with upmarket department stores and designer label boutiques.

Apart from shopping, Ginza's best-known entertainment is kabuki (see p41); performances are staged at **Kabuki-za**, 10 minutes south-east of central

Ginza on a corner of Harumi-dori. Tickets for most performances range from ¥2500 to ¥10,000 but if you don't want to sit through a whole performance (four to five hours), tickets for the fourth floor (around ¥1000; unreserved seats) are valid for one hour but are only available half an hour before the performance. Headphones for an English translation can be rented for the first, second and third floors. The programme changes every month; performance schedules are available from the tourist information centre (see p96) or by contacting Kabuki-za (☎ 03-3541 3131).

Tsukiji Tsukiji, two stops from Ginza on the Hibiya subway line, is Japan's biggest fish market (90% of all fish sold in Tokyo comes from here). The market kicks into life at 5am with the fish auction (you can get a cheap sushi breakfast if you wake up early enough) and runs through until 12 noon. The market is closed on Sunday, national holidays and the second and fourth Wednesday of the month.

Roppongi Also on the Hibiya subway line (transfer from the Yamanote line at Ebisu), Roppongi comes alive at night, when the neon goes on and clubs and bars throw open their doors. The only reason for visiting here by day is to climb the landmark, 333m-high, **Tokyo Tower** (daily, 9am-7/8/9pm depending on season), which opened in 1958; it is 13m higher than the Eiffel Tower (320m) in Paris. Entry to the 150m-high observatory costs ¥820; an additional ¥600 gets you up to the 250m 'special observatory'. Mt Fuji can sometimes be seen from here.

Arakawa tram line Tokyo's only surviving tram line runs between Waseda and Minowa-bashi; the complete journey (29 stops) takes around 50 minutes. The line passes through some of Tokyo's oldest neighbourhoods and the best place to join it is outside **Otsuka station** on the Yamanote line (see p89). For part of the journey through the back streets, it hardly feels as if you're in Tokyo at all. The flat fare is ¥160 (throw the money in the box as you enter). Bilingual area maps are located at each tram stop.

Asakusa (See map, p94) The best-known landmark in Asakusa, the last stop on the Ginza subway line, is lively **Senso-ji**, also known as Asakusa Kannon-ji. The temple is said to have been founded in the 7th century and was named after Kannon, goddess of mercy. The present main hall was rebuilt in 1958. The temple is reached through Kaminarimon Gate and along a street lined with stalls selling everything from lucky charms to Japanese rice crackers. Across the street from Kaminarimon Gate is a tourist information office (daily, 10am-5pm) staffed by English-speaking volunteers. On Sunday, free tours of Senso-ji are offered at 1:30 and 3pm, starting from the office.

Asakusa is also home to a couple of quirky museums. The **Drum Museum** (daily except Mon/Tue, 10am-5pm, ¥300) is in the Miyamoto Japanese Percussion and Festival Store, close to Taito Ryokan (see p97). Packed into one floor are drums of all shapes and sizes from around the world – the best part is that you're allowed to play some of them.

ASAKUSA 浅草

Where to stay
1 Sukeroku no Yado Sadachiyo Ryokan
2 Asakusa View Hotel
4 Taito Ryokan
6 Ryokan Asakusa Shigetsu
7 Dormy Inn Asakusa
8 Hotel Skycourt Asakusa

1 助六の宿 貞千代旅館
2 浅草ビューホテル
4 台東旅館
6 旅館浅草指月
7 ドーミーイン浅草
8 ホテルスカイコート浅草

Other
3 Senso-ji
5 Drum Museum
9 Toy Museum

3 浅草寺
5 太鼓館
9 日本玩具博物館

> ⛩ **The 'Object of Flame'**
> Visible across Sumida-gawa from Asakusa, the Object of Flame sculpture sits atop Asahi Breweries' Super Dry Hall. During its annual cleaning, three men with rock-climbing experience spend two weeks polishing the steel flame. They are tethered to the top of the sculpture about 50m above ground and gently wipe its surface with dust cloths.
>
> In the evening, various Asahi Beer restaurants open around Super Dry Hall. All offer freshly-brewed beer but the food menus differ in each one; only the *Flamme d'Or* restaurant is directly underneath the sculpture.

The **Japan Toy Museum** (daily except Mon, Tue, 3rd Wed, 9:30am-5pm, ¥200), further north up Sumida-gawa, is on the ninth floor of the Tsukuda toy company building. Buy a ticket from the vending machine on the ground floor and take the lift up to the ninth floor. Some of the more unusual items on display include 'Suzette the Eating Monkey', various original Nintendo games, a small collection of Japanese kites, cabbage patch kids and limited edition batmobiles. The museum is hard to find and is not obviously marked from the outside. Ask the staff at the tourist information office opposite Senso-ji for a map. From Asakusa station, take a Toei bus bound for Minami-Senju and get off at 'Kiyokawa 1-chome'.

A good way of moving from traditional to futuristic Tokyo is to take a boat cruise from Asakusa ferry terminal to the Tokyo Bay area. The **Sumida-gawa Line** runs between Asakusa and Hinode Pier (see p87). Hinode is linked with the Yurikamome monorail (see p86).

PRACTICAL INFORMATION
Arrival and departure
Getting to and from Narita Airport
The quickest and most efficient way between Narita and downtown Tokyo is by train. Japan Rail operates the **Narita Express** (N'EX; see table 1, p397) service which takes an hour to downtown Tokyo (¥2940 to Tokyo station, ¥3110 to Shinjuku/Ikebukuro); this is the best option for those using rail passes. All seats on the N'EX are reserved (reservations are free to rail-pass holders); since the trains often get booked up it is worth making a reservation for your journey back to the airport as soon as possible. JR also operates a 'rapid' service which is slower than N'EX but cheaper (¥1280; 80 mins to Tokyo station).

The privately-operated Keisei Railway also offers a service to Tokyo, worth considering if you don't have a rail pass as this is also cheaper than the N'EX. The fastest service is the **Keisei Skyliner** (¥1920; 55 mins to Nippori) which stops at Nippori station on the JR Yamanote line, from where connections can be made to other areas of Tokyo, before terminating at Keisei Ueno station. A slower but cheaper **Keisei rapid** train is convenient for going direct to **Asakusa** (see p93 and p97) from Narita (¥1060, 71 mins).

The **Friendly Airport Limousine Bus service** (☎ 03-3665 7220 for reservations) connects Narita with major hotels in downtown Tokyo in 80-100 minutes. The one-way fare to Tokyo station costs ¥3000. Tickets are available from the Limousine bus counters in the arrival lobbies at Narita.

Don't even consider taking a **taxi** from Narita to Tokyo unless you want to part with ¥20,000 before you've even really arrived.

Note that when coming to Narita by train, Terminal 2 is the first stop, followed by Terminal 1; check which terminal your airline operates from before heading out to the airport.

Tokyo station Tokyo station is a terminus for all shinkansen services as well as conventional JR lines. The station is divided into **Marunouchi** and **Yaesu** sides. There are places to eat everywhere, as well as several areas of coin lockers (all sizes), particularly on the Yaesu side.

The main exit is on the Yaesu side. From the platforms, head for the Yaesu Central Exit, which will bring you out in the middle of the main concourse, known as Yaesu Central Hall. To your right is the main JR ticket office (daily, 5:30am-11pm), where you can convert exchange orders and make seat reservations.

Tourist information

The main **tourist information centre** (☎ 03-3201 3331, Mon-Fri, 9am-5pm, Sat 9am-12pm) is in the basement of the Tokyo International Forum, an enormous glass building outside Yurakucho station, one stop on the Yamanote line from Tokyo station. Take the International Forum exit and head down to the basement level. It's not the easiest place to find and you should phone ahead before trying to come here since it may be moving soon. It's worth hunting out as staff are clued up about travel all over Japan and have leaflets on virtually everything. There's also a noticeboard with information on current events (or call the 24-hour recorded information line, ☎ 03-3201 2911).

If you want to book accommodation make use of the free **Welcome Inn Reservation Center** (Mon-Fri 9:15-11:30am and 1-4:45pm) in the tourist information office. Staff can help make bookings at hotels, hostels and ryokans in Tokyo and throughout Japan.

If you plan to be in Tokyo for a while, it's worth investing in a city guide book.

Both Lonely Planet and Rough Guide publish *Tokyo* city guides, but an off-beat alternative is Rick Kennedy's *Little Adventures in Tokyo* (Stone Bridge Press, 1998). This is recommended if you want to explore the side streets rather than the tourist traps. Kennedy is also the man behind one of the best web sites dedicated to the capital, 🖥 **www.tokyoq.com**; this is constantly updated and has information on events, restaurants, bars and clubs in the capital.

Getting around

For rail-pass holders the free and most convenient way of getting around is on the JR **Yamanote Line** which runs in a loop around the city stopping at virtually all the major points. The subway will get you everywhere else. There are 12 subway lines: eight are run by the Teito Rapid Transit Authority (TRTA) and four by a company called TOEI. All lines operate from 5am to shortly after midnight and fares are based on distance.

If in doubt about how much to pay, buy a ticket from a machine for the minimum amount, take the ticket and 'fare adjust' when you arrive at your destination. Fare Adjustment machines are located by the exit barriers at all stations. Insert the ticket and the machine calculates how much extra you have to pay; the machines give change.

A one-day ticket for use on TRTA subway lines costs ¥710. A 'Tokyo Combination Ticket' is ¥1580 and can be used on all subway lines, Toei buses, Tokyo's tram line and on JR trains in the metropolitan area. If in Tokyo for a month or more, consider the 'One-Month Open Pass' (¥16,820), valid on all TRTA lines.

Internet

There are plenty of Internet cafés around the city, though the turnover rate is high. Tokyo TIC publishes an up-to-date list of Internet cafés.

Opposite: Top: The main entrance to Senso-ji (see p93) in Asakusa, Tokyo, marks the start of a long parade of stalls which leads towards the main temple compound. **Bottom:** No need for street lamps in Osaka: neon lights the way from dusk till dawn. (Photos © Ramsey Zarifeh).

❑ **Embassies in Tokyo**
● **Australia** (☎ 03-5232 4111) 2-1-14 Mita, Minato-ku.
● **Austria** (☎ 03-3451 8281) 1-1-20 Moto-Azabu, Minato-ku.
● **Canada** (☎ 03-3408 2101) 7-3-38 Akasaka, Minato-ku.
● **France** (☎ 03-5420 8800) 4-11-44 Minami-Azabu, Minato-ku.
● **Germany** (☎ 03-3473 2350) 4-5-10 Minami-Azabu, Minato-ku.
● **Holland** (☎ 03-5401 0411) 3-6-3 Shibakoen, Minato-ku.
● **Republic of Ireland** (☎ 03-3263 0695) 2-10-7 Kojimachi, Chiyoda-ku.
● **Italy** (☎ 03-3453 5291) 2-5-4 Mita, Minato-ku.
● **New Zealand** (☎ 03-3467 2271) 20-40 Kamiyamacho, Shibuya-ku.
● **Spain** (☎ 03-3583 8531) 1-3-29 Roppongi, Minato-ku.
● **Switzerland** (☎ 03-3473 0121) 5-9-12 Minami-Azabu, Minato-ku.
● **UK** (☎ 03-3265 5511) 1 Ichibancho, Chiyoda-ku.
● **USA** (☎ 03-3224 5000) 1-10-5 Akasaka, Minato-ku.

Money
There are several branches of Citibank with 24 hour ATMs which accept foreign-issued Visa cards and where staff speak some English. For a list of banks in the Tokyo metropolitan area, visit Tokyo TIC (see p96).

Where to stay
Accommodation is available all over Tokyo but this guide focuses on the Asakusa district. Apart from being a very atmospheric area to stay, there are places to suit all budgets and the location is good for exploring the city. From Tokyo station, take the Yamanote line one stop to Kanda. Change to the Ginza subway line and get off at Asakusa (the last stop).

● **Accommodation in Asakusa** (see map, p94) *Taito Ryokan* (☎ 03-3843 2822, 💻 www.libertyhouse.gr.jp) has only a few tatami rooms (with common bath) in an old building but it is centrally located. The manager is extremely friendly and will help you get the most out of your stay in Tokyo. A nightly rate of ¥3000 (no meals) makes this one of Tokyo's real bargains. Single guests may be asked to share rooms. More expensive is *Ryokan Shigetsu* (☎ 03-3843 2345,

📠 3843 2348, 💻 shigetsu@roy.hi-ho.ne.jp), just off the arcade which leads up to Senso-ji. The top floor public bath has a view of the temple's five-storey pagoda. Western singles go from ¥7300, with tatami rooms for two at ¥16,000 (no meals).

If you're looking for a mid-range Western hotel, *Dormy Inn Asakusa* (☎ 03-3845 1122, 📠 3845 1123) has comfortable rooms, each equipped with a mini-kitchen. There's also a coin laundry and a (men-only) hot spring/sauna. Standard singles cost ¥8500, while executive singles, spacious enough to sleep two, are ¥14,000. A cheaper option is *Hotel Skycourt Asakusa* (☎ 03-3875 4411, 📠 3875 4941, 💻 asakusa@skycourt.co.jp; ¥7000/S, ¥10,500/D, ¥13,000/Tw); YH(HI) members get a special rate of ¥5000 per person. Take bus No 42 from outside Matsuya department store and get off at 'Asakusa 7-chome', right outside the hotel. Western luxury in Asakusa is represented by *Asakusa View Hotel* (☎ 03-3847 1111, 📠 3847 2117; ¥13,000/S, ¥21,000/D).

Finally, for an authentic Edo experience try *Sukeroku no Yado Sadachiyo Ryokan* (☎ 03-3842 6431, 📠 3842 6433, 💻 front@sadachiyo.co.jp). The ryokan is

---

Opposite: Impressive from the outside, it's also worth taking the lift inside Osaka's Umeda Sky Building up to the Floating Garden Observatory (see p105). (Photo © Ramsey Zarifeh).

everything you imagine a Japanese inn to be. Tatami rooms have attached bath and toilet and are decorated with antiques from the Edo period. Prices are per person, with two people paying a minimum of ¥9700 each for a standard room; add another ¥8500/pp for two meals. Look out for the rickshaw parked outside.

● **Accommodation in other areas** (see map, p90) Shinjuku has several world-class hotels. One of the best is *Hotel Century Hyatt* (☎ 03-3349 0111, 🖹 3344 5575, 💻 www.hyatt.com; rooms from ¥32,000, check website for packages), nine minutes on foot from the west exit of Shinjuku station. A free shuttle bus operates between the hotel and the west exit. Rooms are spacious and facilities include several restaurants and a top-floor pool.

Tokyo International Youth Hostel (☎ 03-3235 1107; ¥3100/pp), on the 18th and 19th floors of the Iidabashi Central Plaza, right outside the west exit of Iidabashi station on the JR Sobu line (transfer from Yoyogi or Akihabara on the Yamanote line), has mostly bunk-bed dorms. Breakfast costs ¥400 and dinner ¥800. There's a maximum stay of three consecutive nights and a 10:30pm curfew.

Asia Center of Japan (☎ 03-3402 6111, 🖹 3402 0738) in Akasaka (not to be confused with Asakusa) has moderately-priced Western rooms. Singles/twins without bath cost ¥5100/¥6800 (¥10,500 with bath). Facilities include a coin laundry and an inexpensive restaurant. Take Exit No 2 of Nogizaka station on the Chiyoda subway line.

There's no shortage of hotels in the airport vicinity, though most are overpriced. The best deal, particularly if you're a Youth Hostel (YH/HI) member, is *Hotel Skycourt Narita* (☎ 0478-73 6211, 🖹 73 6212; ¥4000 YH/HI; others ¥5000). It's a business hotel, so all rooms are private with attached bath. A free shuttle bus operates to and from Narita. Note that though this hotel is near the airport, there are no amenities in its immediate vicinity, so bring food with you if arriving late.

Where to eat

Tokyo has some of the best and most expensive restaurants in Japan, many of which are in the top hotels. Tokyo, Shinjuku and Ikebukuro stations all have attached department stores with restaurant floors which are usually open until 10pm. Ginza, Harajuku and Shibuya are good areas to wander around in search of cafés and restaurants.

If you're staying in Asakusa (see p97), there are plenty of small, atmospheric, ramen restaurants and pubs that serve yaki-tori, fried fish and draught beer. Finally, it's hard to look anywhere in Tokyo without seeing a branch of a fast-food chain, such as McDonald's, KFC, Mos Burger and Mister Donut.

Nightlife

Tokyo is very much a 24-hour city, though there are certain areas which really only come alive after dark. You'll never be far from a bar or club in downtown Roppongi (see p93), or in Kabukicho (see p88). In the summer many hotels and department stores open rooftop beer gardens which offer two-hour all-you-can-eat-and-drink deals for around ¥3000.

If you fancy an end of holiday splurge, head for the *New York Bar* of the Park Hyatt Hotel in west Shinjuku (adjacent to the Tokyo Metropolitan Government Buildings, see p88). Recently voted one of the world's best rooftop bars, the gin and tonics don't come cheap but they have great live jazz and if you can secure a window table you'll get a breathtaking view of Tokyo by night.

Festivals

Senso-ji (see p93) has one of the busiest festival calendars in Japan. One of the more unusual events is the **Asakusa Samba Carnival** in early September. First organized 19 years ago, the festival combines the Japanese culture of carrying *mikoshi* (portable shrines) with the rhythm of samba. Dancers from Brazil join in the street party.

SIDE TRIPS FROM TOKYO

Kamakura

Kamakura, a small town by the sea one hour south of Tokyo, is packed with temples and shrines and makes for a relaxed escape from the nearby city. It became the seat of feudal government in the 12th century after the struggle for power between the rival Taira and Minamoto clans was won by Minamoto Yoritomo (see p33). Although its importance as a national power base faded many centuries ago, Kamakura is known for its Daibutsu, an 11.4m-high bronze statue of the Buddha built in 1252, the second largest in Japan after the one in Nara (see p196). Kamakura's manageable size, open spaces, variety of temples and nearby beaches make it one of the best side trips from Tokyo.

To reach Kamakura by JR take a local train along the Yokosuka line from Tokyo station (five/hour; 60 mins; ¥1780 return). Direct services also run between Kamakura and Narita Airport (see p44) in 2 hours 30 minutes. The private Odakyu railway runs services from Shinjuku (see p87) to Fujisawa, where you change on to the Enoden line to reach Kamakura (¥1430 return).

Tokyo Disneyland

Only a short journey by train from Tokyo station but a world away from the commuter belt which surrounds it, is Tokyo Disneyland. It's almost an exact copy of the original California theme park. A one-day passport costs ¥5500 (12-17 years ¥4800, 4-11 ¥3700). The After 6 Passport (¥2900) offers reduced price entry on week nights after 6pm and the Starlight Passport (¥4500, 12-17 years ¥3900, 4-11 ¥3000) is available at weekends/holidays for admission after 5pm.

Hotel MiraCosta is the focal point of Tokyo DisneySea Park, a Disney resort which opened here in September 2001; the site also includes Ikspiari, a shopping and entertainment town with a 16-screen cinema complex. The nearest train station is Maihama on the JR Keiyo line (take the train direct from Tokyo station). For opening hours, call ☎ 0473-54 0001, or check the web site 🖳 www.tokyodisneyresort.co.jp.

Hakone

The private Odakyu Railway (🖳 www.odakyu-group.co.jp/english) runs services from Odakyu Shinjuku station (connected to JR Shinjuku) to Hakone, an area of lakes and mountains 90km west of Tokyo, between Mt Fuji and the Izu Peninsula. Rail tickets, accommodation and one-/two-day package tours of the region can be booked at the Odakyu Sightseeing Service Center (☎ 03-5321 7887, daily, 8am-6pm), on the ground floor concourse by the west exit of Odakyu Shinjuku station. This centre is designed for foreign visitors to Japan and staff speak English. Best value is the Hakone Free Pass, a package ticket which includes return rail travel from Shinjuku to Hakone. The pass is valid for three days and for a variety of modes of transport in Hakone. The trip doesn't have to be particularly strenuous since you get to make a loop of the area via a mountain railway, funicular and ropeway, from which there are excellent views of Mt Fuji if the weather cooperates. Apart from the scenery, one of the high-

⛩ **The Bard on tour**

Maruyama, 145km south-east of Tokyo, is dotted with rice fields and small Shinto shrines but is also home to Shakespeare Country Park (daily, 9am-5pm, ¥800), a re-creation of Stratford-upon-Avon just yards from the Pacific Ocean and a mere 15,600km from London according to the sign at the park entrance. Visitors can take a look inside the wooden theatre, wander around the thatched house where Shakespeare was born, buy lavender ice cream from staff dressed in period costume and even put their heads in the stocks on the village green.

This is a truncated, easily digestible, slightly ludicrous glance at Elizabethan England; at the flick of a switch, waxwork models of Shakespeare and his characters burst into life. The orchard, fountains and Greek statues of Rosemary Garden appear to have been lifted from the set of a lavish production of *Much Ado About Nothing*, while the village hall, with its stained-glass windows and tall spire, could easily be mistaken for an Anglican church. There's even a replica Elizabethan toilet in one of the upstairs rooms.

A reality check lies just a couple of minutes' walk from the park exit, where surfers take advantage of the crashing waves of the Pacific Ocean. Not even Shakespeare, perhaps, could have dreamed up a stage location as extraordinary as this.

Don't head for Maruyama expecting to find too much authenticity; the park is really geared to domestic visitors who don't have the time, money or inclination to visit the real Stratford. But it may be of interest to anyone keen to experience a quintessentially Japanese day out. To reach Maruyama from Tokyo station, take a View Sazanami LEX along the Uchibo line to Chikura (120 mins). At Chikura, change to a local train for the eight-minute journey to Minamihara, the closest station to Shakespeare Country Park. JR staff at Minamihara have a supply of maps showing the direction on foot from the station to the park; it's about a 15-minute walk.

lights is a trip on board the kitsch but fun 'Hakone Sightseeing Ship', a Spanish galleon replica which whisks you across Lake Ashi; the lake was formed by the eruption of a volcano and is surrounded by thick forest. It's just about possible to do all this in a day if you make an early start from Shinjuku but an overnight stay would be more relaxing.

From Shinjuku, the Hakone Free Pass costs ¥5500 (children ¥2750). Railpass holders can save over ¥1000 by taking a shinkansen from Tokyo west along the Tokaido line as far as Odawara (see p112) and then transferring to the Odakyu railway for the rest of the journey to Hakone. From Odawara, the pass costs ¥4130 (children ¥2070). It's even cheaper if you travel between Monday and Friday, though in this case the pass is only valid for two days (from Shinjuku: adults ¥4700, children ¥2350; from Odawara: adults ¥3410, children ¥1700). The weekday pass is not sold during peak holiday times (May 19th-Apr 10th, Apr 28th-May 5th, Jul 19th-Aug 31st, Dec 29th-Jan 3rd). The pass includes the journey by regular Odakyu trains from Shinjuku to Hakone-Yumoto (change trains in Odawara) but for an ¥870 supplement each way you can take the more luxurious Romance Car LEX which is slightly faster and runs direct to Hakone-Yumoto.

Nikko

Some 150km by rail north of Tokyo lies the temple and shrine town of Nikko, where the star attraction is the grand Toshogu Shrine, originally built in 1616 as a mausoleum for Tokugawa Ieyasu, founder of the Tokugawa shogunate. The first shrine was rebuilt a few years later in 1636 on the orders of Ieyasu's grandson, Iemitsu, who wanted an even more grand and everlasting memorial to his grandfather. As much as the colourful opulence of the shrine complex, it's Nikko's location, in the mountains and surrounded by lakes and waterfalls, which attracts the crowds.

By JR, the best way of reaching Nikko is to take a Tohoku shinkansen as far as Utsunomiya (see p245) and then transfer to a local, Nikko-line train for the 50-minute journey to Nikko (at least one service an hour). Without a rail pass, the best way of reaching Nikko is by private Tobu Railway (🖳 www.tobu.co.jp/english) direct from Asakusa station to Tobu Nikko station (two hours, ¥1320). Even though it is possible to visit Nikko in a day it is worth considering spending a night there, particularly if you are visiting in the autumn as the colour of the leaves is spectacular. However Nikko's main drawback is its proximity to Tokyo which means it attracts lar   ·ds year-round.

Osaka

INTRODUCTION

Osaka is the commercial and industrial centre of western Japan; a   more appeal to the businessman than the tourist. With the ancient   Kyoto (see p180) and Nara (see p195) so close, there's no great incentive   in Osaka for very long. But with an international airport close by, Japan's th   largest city functions as a useful gateway to the Kansai area and is only three hours by shinkansen from Tokyo.

The city's big historical draw is Osaka Castle but as a modern reconstruction it's nowhere near as impressive as nearby Himeji (see p204). Like everywhere else in Japan, Osaka has suffered from the economic downturn of the last decade but local tourism has received a massive boost with the opening of the new Universal Studios Japan theme park on Osaka Bay (see box, p105).

WHAT TO SEE AND DO

Open Air Farmhouse Museum

The Open Air Farmhouse Museum (daily except Mon 10am-5pm Apr-Oct, 10am-4pm Nov-Mar, ¥500) is three stops north of Shin-Osaka by subway. You can walk around this quiet wooded area and look inside 11 farmhouses collected and reassembled from all over Japan. In the houses are displays of craft and

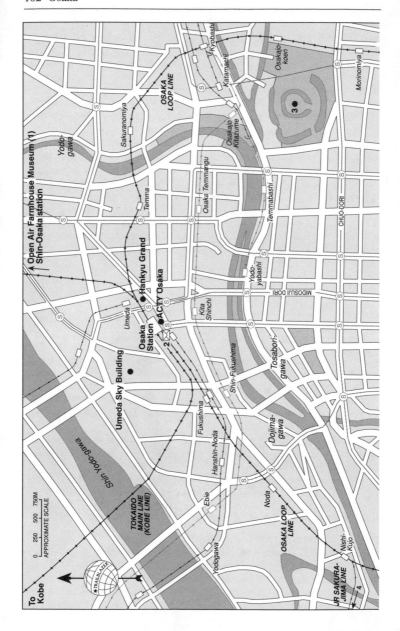

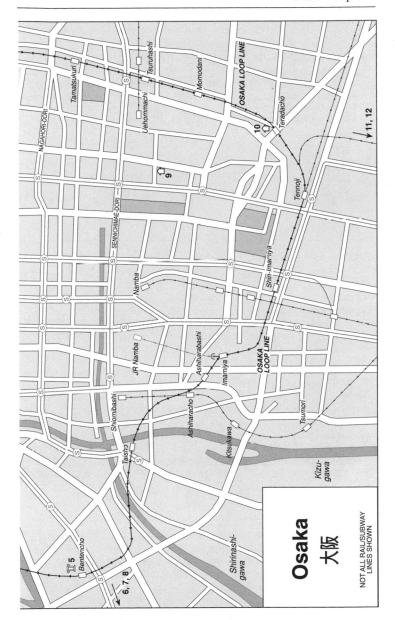

OSAKA 大阪

Where to stay

6	Hyatt Regency Osaka	6	ハイアットリージェンシーオーサカ
9	Osaka International House Hotel	9	大阪国際交流センターホテル
10	Hyper Hotel Tennoji	10	ハイパーホテル天王寺
11	Osaka International YH	11	大阪国際ユースホステル
12	Osaka Municipal Nagai YH	12	大阪市立長居ユースホステル

Other

1	Open Air Farmhouse Museum	1	日本民家集落博物館
2	Central Post Office	2	中央郵便局
3	Osaka Castle	3	大阪城
4	Universal Studios Japan	4	ユニバーサル・スタジオ・ジャパン
5	Modern Transportation Museum	5	交通科学博物館
7	Osaka Aquarium	7	海遊館
8	Osaka Maritime Museum	8	なにわの海の時空館

farm implements; there are bilingual signs but it's worth picking up a pamphlet at the entrance. This is a great opportunity to see something of rural Japan without having to leave the sprawling metropolis of Osaka. It's an amazingly peaceful retreat – from inside the grounds of the museum it's hard to tell you're less than ten minutes from the city. Take the Midosuji subway line from Shin-Osaka to Ryokuchi-koen station and head for the west exit which leads into Ryokuchi koen (park). The museum is on the north side of the park, about 15 minutes on foot from the station (follow the signs).

Osaka Castle

This castle (daily, 9am-5pm, ¥600) was originally built in 1586 by Toyotomi Hideyoshi but was destroyed by fire only a few years later in 1615. It was completely reconstructed in 1629, only for the main tower to be struck by lightning and once again burnt to the ground. A further reconstruction in the 1930s suffered aerial bombardment during WWII. The *donjon* has been fully restored and is worth climbing for the views of Osaka but the displays inside are less impressive. The castle is a short walk from Osakajo-koen station on the Osaka Loop line. Taking the central exit, you'll see the castle in front of you in the distance. Renovation work was carried out in 1997 and the castle tower has an elevator for wheelchair access.

Modern Transportation Museum

The Modern Transportation Museum (daily except Mon, 10am-5:30pm, ¥400) is underneath Bentencho station on the Osaka Loop line. It's one of the best-organized transport museums in Japan with exhibits on the history of the railway from steam age to the future. Boats, planes, buses and cars are given a little space, but the focus is on rail. A huge model railway periodically bursts into

> ## ⛩ Universal Studios Japan
> Osaka's big new tourist draw for the 21st century is Universal Studios Japan, opened in spring 2001 on a 54-hectare site in Osaka Bay. Modelled on the Universal Studios theme park in Florida, visitors are offered a similar mix of attractions and can expect long queues though it is possible to get timed tickets for the major attractions. The park also has a working TV studio, and backstage production tours let visitors see behind the scenes at Japanese drama and variety shows.
>
> A one-day passport costs ¥5500. Tickets can be purchased at the park entrance but also in advance at JR ticket offices, Lawson convenience stores, and on the Internet (see below). Park operating hours vary according to the season (extended opening hours in summer), so call the information line ☎ 06-4790 7000 or check 💻 www.universalstudios.com or www.usj.co.jp. The park is about 250m on foot from Universal City station on the JR Sakurajima line, which starts from Nishi-Kujo station on the Osaka Loop line. The journey (from Osaka station) takes 15 minutes.

life, while outside there's a collection of full-size locomotives and passenger carriages. Ask for the excellent English brochure at the entrance, since nearly all signs are in Japanese only.

Umeda Sky Building
JR Osaka station is in the Umeda area of the city. There is little here in the way of sights but it's a great place to shop and eat. Umeda Sky Building behind the station is one of Japan's most imaginative skyscrapers, with a 'Floating Garden', and a rooftop gallery which affords a panoramic view of the city (daily 10am-10pm, ¥700).

Bayside Osaka
Osaka Aquarium (daily, 10am-8pm, ¥2000) is part of Tempozan Harbor Village on Osaka Bay; in the 10 years it's been open it has become one of the most popular attractions in the Kansai area, receiving more than 2.5 million visitors a year. Riding an escalator to the top of the building, you begin a journey down to the depths of the ocean, passing every conceivable fish along the way. Some visitors seem to take more interest in the scuba-diving cleaning staff who scrub the inside of the tanks, but the real stars are the sharks, crabs, dolphins and penguins. A highlight is the main 'Pacific Ocean' tank which extends down several floors, but there's also a surprise right at the end with the tanks of fluorescent floating jelly fish: 'the world of the floating jelly fish, whose transparent body consists mostly of water, is extremely fantastic'. And it really is – this is one attraction that's worth the expense. From Bentencho on the Osaka Loop line, transfer to the Chuo subway line and get off at Osaka-ko station.

The aquatic theme continues at the new **Osaka Maritime Museum** (daily, 10am-6pm, ¥600), in a huge glass dome and accessed through a tunnel under Osaka Port. The museum shows how ships and ports developed in Osaka and around the world – a celebration of man's triumph on the high seas. The muse-

---

⛩ **Osaka's comic heritage**
Osaka has always been a breeding ground for Japanese comedians and the most successful TV funnymen all speak a version of the local dialect, Osaka-ben. Tokyo may be in the *Guinness Book of Records 2001* for its population size, but Osaka also makes an appearance in the shape of comedian Akashiya Sanma (universally known as Sanma-san), who is officially recorded as the most popular personality on Japanese TV.

The people of Osaka even voted a stand-up comedian as their city governor (with a record number of votes), but the political career of 'Knock' Yokoyama was not destined to last very long – he resigned in disgrace after pleading guilty to charges of molesting a female assistant during a re-election campaign in 1999.

---

um centrepiece is a full-scale reproduction of the *Naniwamaru*, an Edo-period cargo vessel. Four floors of exhibits are built around the 30m-long ship; one of the most popular attractions is a virtual Venetian gondola ride. Take the Chuo subway to Osaka-ko then transfer to the OTS line and go one stop to Cosmosquare.

PRACTICAL INFORMATION
Arrival and departure
● **Getting to and from Kansai Airport**
The fastest way of accessing Osaka and Kyoto from Kansai is **by rail**. Kansai Airport station is directly connected to the terminal building. The blue half of the station is run by Japan Rail; the red half by the private Nankai Railway. JR's Haruka LEX (see table 2, p397) takes 73 minutes to Kyoto (¥3490) and stops on the way at Tennoji (¥2270, 30 mins) and Shin-Osaka (¥2980, 45 mins). A 'rapid' service (slower than the Haruka) also operates to Osaka station (¥1160, 65 mins). Nankai operates the limited express 'rapi:t' train from Kansai to Osaka Namba station (¥1400, 29 mins) where you can transfer to the Osaka subway. Rail passes are not valid on the rapi:t.

A high-speed **jetfoil** (¥2200, 25 mins) links Kansai Airport with Port Island in Kobe (see p223), from where a shuttle bus runs to Sannomiya and Shin-Kobe stations. **Limousine bus** services also run to various destinations in the Kansai region, including Osaka, Kyoto and Nara.

Tourist information
There are tourist information desks at four stations in Osaka: at Shin-Osaka (☎ 06-6305 3311), Osaka (☎ 06-6345 2189), Tennoji (☎ 06-6774 3077) and JR Namba (☎ 06-6643 2125); all are open daily 8am-8pm). The office at JR Osaka station is badly signposted but is tucked away in a corner by Midosuji Gate, close to Hankyu department store. All the tourist offices are staffed by English speakers who can provide you with a city map and subway plan. If you need information on travel outside Osaka, it's better to visit Kansai TIC at the airport (see p45).

Getting around
The main railway junctions are **Shin-Osaka**, the shinkansen station to the north of the city, **Osaka**, further south in Umeda, and **Tennoji**. Osaka and Tennoji stations are both on the Osaka Loop line. The **Osaka Loop line** (orange colour trains) is the most useful means of getting around the city with a rail pass.

The **subway** is convenient for reaching places off the Loop line. A one-day pass costs ¥850; it allows unlimited use of the subway and also gives discounts at some of the city's attractions. On the 20th of every month as well as every Friday you can purchase a 'No My Car Day Pass' for ¥600; this is valid for unlimited subway travel.

If you arrive at Shin-Osaka by shinkansen, transfer to a local train for the short ride to Osaka station. Osaka station is large and confusing but there are plenty of coin lockers in the main concourse areas and a JR information desk by the main ticket barrier. The platforms are as follows: 5 and 6 for Sannomiya (Kobe) and Himeji; 7 and 8 for Shin-Osaka and Kyoto; 11 for Fukui, Kanazawa and Toyama. The platforms for the Osaka Loop line are not numbered.

Internet
Bean's B:t Café (6-2-29 Uehonmachi, Tennoji-ku, ☎ 06-6766 3566, 🖳 bbc@inter farm.co.jp, daily except 1st/3rd Sun, 8:30am-9pm) in Tennoji charges foreign visitors ¥400 for 30 minutes' surfing. They also have a good selection of drinks and set breakfast/lunch deals. The nearest station is Tanimachi 9-chome on the Tanimachi subway line.

Money
Most banks in Osaka will cash travellers' cheques and give over-the-counter credit card advances. For ATMs, try the central post office outside JR Osaka station or any branch of Citibank.

Where to stay
For luxury accommodation, try the *Hyatt Regency Osaka* (☎ 06-6612 1234, 🖹 6614 7800, 🖳 www.hyattregencyosaka.com) on Osaka Bay. It has all the facilities you would expect of a world-class hotel; indoor and outdoor pools, a state-of-the-art health/fitness centre and a choice of restaurants.

The Hyatt Regency has been designated the 'official five-star hotel' of the nearby Universal Studios Japan theme park (see box p105) and the hotel has special packages which include an overnight stay and one-day passports for the park (midweek: ¥15,000 per person, w/end: ¥19,000 per person; minimum of two people sharing a room). Standard room rates (not including park entry) start at ¥26,000 but enquire about special offers/package deals.

A limousine bus for Kansai Airport (¥1300) stops right outside the hotel. Or

from Bentencho on the Osaka Loop line, take the Chuo subway line to Osaka-ko and transfer to the New Tram line to Nakafuto, from where the hotel is a two-minute walk.
Osaka International House Hotel (2-6 Uehonmachi 8-chome, ☎ 06-6773 8181, 🖹 6773 0777) has good-value, spacious singles for ¥7000 with attached bath, aircon and bilingual TV. There's a restaurant, and an information centre staffed by English speakers. The hotel is a 10-minute walk south from Tanimachi 9-chome station on the Tanimachi subway line.

A good budget choice is *Hyper Hotel Tennoji* (☎ 06-6770 2345, 🖹 6770 2333), which has clean, compact singles with attached bath for ¥4900. The rate for two adults sharing a room is ¥5900, and two adults plus one child is ¥6900. All rates include breakfast. Take the Osaka Loop line to Teradacho. Leave the station, cross to the other side of the road (McDonald's is opposite the exit) and turn left. The hotel is a minute's walk up the road, the third street on your right.
Osaka International Youth Hostel (☎ 0722-65 8539, 🖹 67 3682) is on the south side of Hamadera Park, south of Osaka city. It's a large, modern hostel with excellent facilities. YH(HI) members pay ¥3150 (¥3750 for non-members) for dormitory accommodation, with breakfast at ¥600 and dinner at ¥1000. Take the Loop line to Tennoji and transfer to the JR Hanwa line to Otori. From here, transfer to the Higashi-Hagoromo line and go one stop to the terminus at Higashi-Hagoromo. From here, walk towards Hamadera Park and follow signs to the hostel.
Osaka Municipal Nagai Youth Hostel (☎ 06-6699 5631) is in Nagai Park south of the city. It's another modern hostel, built on the side of Nagai Stadium, home to Osaka's J-League soccer team. The nightly rate of ¥2700 rises to ¥2950 from July to September and December to March. Breakfast costs ¥500 and dinner ¥1000. The hostel closes occasionally, so call ahead. From Shin-Osaka, take the Midosuji subway line to Nagai (exit No 1). Alternatively, take the JR Hanwa line to Nagai station.

Head for the stadium and walk around it until you reach the hostel entrance.

If you need to stay near Kansai Airport, *Kanku Hineno Station Hotel* (☎ 0724-60 1911, 🖺 60-1921, 🖥 www.hot wire.co.jp/hineno/index_e.html; ¥7500/S, ¥13,000/D, and ¥15,000/Tw) is right outside JR Hineno station, ten minutes by local train from the airport. It's a new place with comfortable rooms that include bilingual TV. A free hotel shuttle bus runs in the morning to the airport.

Where to eat
There's endless choice in the area around JR Osaka station in Umeda, particularly for lunch-time deals. The best place to hunt around is ACTY Osaka, in the same building as Daimaru department store in front of the Midosuji side of Osaka station. The **Sky Restaurant Floor** (the 27th floor) has a choice of restaurants and (free) views of Osaka. On the 16th is the **World Restaurant Floor**, with a wide variety of places to eat including Russian, Chinese, Japanese, Mexican and Italian. The Hankyu Grand Building, also close to Osaka station, has two floors of **restaurants** (28th and 29th floors).

In the Osaka Bay area, the *Hyatt Regency Hotel* (see p107) has a good choice of restaurants, and does an all-you-can-eat barbecue deal in the summer. Finally, there's a cheap **restaurant** which serves Western and Japanese meals at Osaka International House Hotel (see p107).

Nightlife
The Kita area, around JR Osaka station, is busy after dark and packed with restaurants and bars.

However, the main centre for nightlife is Dotombori, on the southern side of Dotombori Canal in the Minami (southern) district of the city. A useful point of reference and a good place to start a night out is Ebisu-bashi, a bridge which spans Dotombori Canal. From here, the canal is brightly lit up by competing neon signs and the streets surrounding it are packed with cinemas, cheap eateries, clubs and bars.

Festivals
The biggest event in Osaka's busy festival calendar is the **Tenjin Matsuri** which takes place from July 24th to 25th. The highlight is a procession of more than 100 brightly-coloured boats down Dojima-gawa on the evening of the 25th. Also, performances of traditional dance and music are staged on a boat lit by lanterns and moored in the middle of the river.

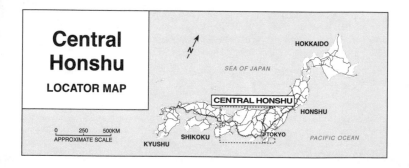

Central Honshu

LOCATOR MAP

0   250   500KM
APPROXIMATE SCALE

N

SEA OF JAPAN

HOKKAIDO

CENTRAL HONSHU

HONSHU

TOKYO

PACIFIC OCEAN

KYUSHU   SHIKOKU

Central Honshu – route guide

INTRODUCTION

Culturally rich and geographically diverse, central Honshu is a vast land area stretching from the Pacific Ocean in the south to the Sea of Japan in the north. If this region is Japan's beating heart, the Tokaido line which runs along the southern coast is the country's transportation artery. It is above all a functional rail line – perhaps the most functional in the world, transporting thousands of passengers every day between the business and industrial hubs of Tokyo, Nagoya and Osaka.

But it would be a great shame to restrict your travel by rail only to the Tokaido shinkansen. Much of the area along the Tokaido line is heavily built up and polluted by factories and heavy industry so, in its own way, a journey along this line offers a real taste of Japan; concrete proof that nature has indeed been spectacularly sacrificed for the industrial revolution. For many visitors who only just have the time to rush between Tokyo and Kyoto, this is all they see of the country. But just a short distance from the industrialized southern coast lie the majestic Japanese Alps.

The easiest way of reaching the region and the Alps is to take a shinkansen from Tokyo to Nagano, home of the 1998 Winter Olympics. The Central Japan rail network is fast, efficient and even in the winter months of heavy snowfall almost invariably on time.

Highlights of a tour around this region include **Takayama** (see p155), a mini-Kyoto in the mountains, the preserved Edo-period 'post towns' of **Narai** (see p119) and **Tsumago** (see p121), and **Kanazawa** (see p159), a city on the Japan Sea coast which is home to one of Japan's most celebrated gardens.

Finally, between April and November, the **Tateyama-Kurobe Alpine Route** (see p126) offers a unique opportunity to appreciate the region's astonishing beauty in a day-long journey from the Japan Sea coast to the Japanese Alps, involving as it does a variety of modes of transport.

A one-week tour would be enough to see a couple of the highlights; two or three weeks would give you time to take in the views and explore more of what the region has to offer.

霧雨や富士を見ぬ日ぞ面白き

Foggy drizzle!
Intriguing is the day
we can't see Mt Fuji
(MATSUO BASHO)

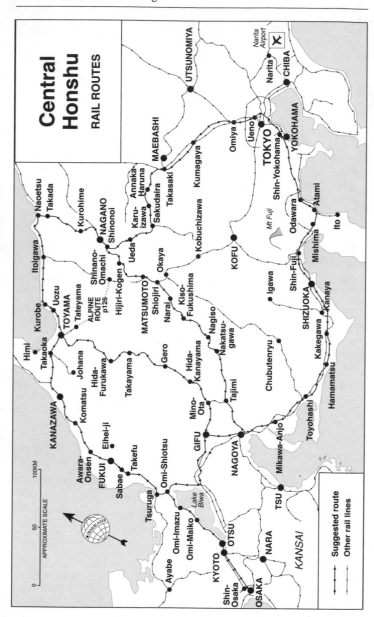

TOKYO TO NAGOYA BY SHINKANSEN
[Table 3, p400]

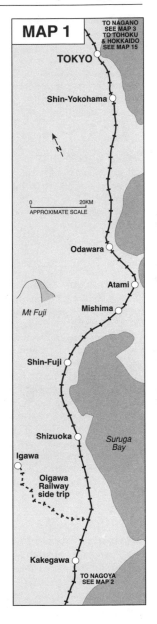

Distances by shinkansen from Tokyo. Fastest journey time: 2 hours.

Tokyo to Atami   [Map 1]
Tokyo   [see pp85-101]

Take a Hikari or Grand Hikari from Tokyo west towards Nagoya, Kyoto and Osaka; some services continue all the way to Hakata. Rail passes are also valid for the slower Kodama but these should be avoided if at all possible because they are the oldest bullet trains in service and stop at every station along the way. Green Car rail-pass holders should try to use the Grand Hikari because compartments are on the top deck and there's lots of space for luggage. When making a reservation, request a seat on the top deck.

Shin-Yokohama (29km) First station after Tokyo but not all Hikari stop here so check schedules before setting off.

The tourist information office (daily 10am-6pm, closed 1-2pm) is behind the shinkansen ticket barrier. Coin lockers (¥300-600) are next to this office. Shinkansen and ordinary train lines run from this station.

Shin-Yokohama's main tourist sight is the unusual **Ramen Museum** (daily except Tue 11am-11pm, ¥300), five minutes on foot northeast of the station – take the exit by the tourist information office (but first pick up a sketch map of the route from tourist information). The ground floor museum tells the story of how noodles rose from a humble beginning to embrace the global market. The main reason the place gets packed out is the re-created ramen village in the basement; a collection of traditional ramen shops from around Japan. The most popular are ones from Sapporo (see p309) in Hokkaido and Hakata (see p336) in Kyushu, the two best-known centres for ramen in Japan. The souvenir shop could be the place to pick up a few unusual mementos.

The area around Shin-Yokohama has seen development in the shape of the enormous **Yokohama International Stadium**, venue for the 2002 World Cup final. For a glimpse of what Japan might look like in the future, take a Yokohama line train (from platform five at Shin-Yokohama) to Sakuragicho. The journey takes about 20 minutes and the train stops on the way at Yokohama station, the main department store area. **Sakuragicho** is home to Minato Mirai 21 (MM21), a city within a city featuring hotels, restaurants, shopping complexes and museums. It all looks very different to how the area around Sakuragicho must have been in 1872, when it opened as a terminus for Japan's first rail line between Tokyo and Yokohama.

Odawara (84km) A few Hikari stop here. In March 1886, the Zuso Jinsha Railway ('human railway') was opened between Odawara and Atami (the next stop along the Tokaido shinkansen line), a distance of 25km. It took more than four hours to go between the two towns. The eight-seater coach, carried by three people, was used for 12 years until the introduction of steam locomotives.

Once an important castle town, Odawara is now a major junction on both the shinkansen and Tokaido mainlines, as well as a terminus for the private Odakyu line from Shinjuku. It's also a gateway to **Hakone**, an area of lakes and mountains accessible as a day trip from Tokyo (see p99).

Atami (105km) A few Hikari stop here. Atami is a famous spa town but, due to its proximity to Tokyo, it often gets unpleasantly crowded. British travellers might want to make a pilgrimage here to the grave of 'poor Toby', a Scottish terrier whose life was tragically cut short after a visit to Atami (see box opposite). There is no tourist information office as such but you can pick up a map which lists the main sightseeing points at the View Plaza travel agency in the station. Coin lockers (¥300) are available.

Hot springs abound, with a choice of seven spas; you can pick up a stamp card and trek around the town visiting them all. A well-known sightseeing spot is **Oyu geyser** (see box opposite), which claims to be one of the three largest geysers in the world, along with the Great Caesar in Iceland and the Old Faithful in Yellowstone National Park, USA. The other main tourist draw is **MOA Museum of Art** (daily except Thu, 9:30am-5pm, ¥1600), on a hillside overlooking Atami; accessible by bus (10 mins) from the station. It contains a large collection of woodblock prints, ceramics and gold and silver lacquerware.

In 1604, the shogun Tokugawa Ieyasu visited Atami to bathe in the hot springs. From that time on, hot spring water was dedicated to the shoguns and transported annually from Atami to Edo Castle. Celebrations are still held in commemoration of this on February 10th and October 10th.

● **Side trip – Atami to Shimoda** Atami is the starting point for the Ito line to **Ito**, where William Adams, the first Englishman to set foot in Japan, spent much of his life after a shipwreck off the coast of Kyushu in 1600. He became known as Anjin-san and his arrival is celebrated during the Anjin Matsuri in August. Beyond Ito, the line continues to **Shimoda** but this section of track is

⛩ **Sir Rutherford Alcock and 'Poor Toby'**
Sir Rutherford Alcock, a British minister, visited Japan in 1859 and the following year climbed Mt Fuji. Clearly not a man used to modesty, Alcock stopped in Atami on his return from Fuji and had a monument built here with the inscription: 'I am the first non-Japanese to have climbed Mt Fuji and visited Atami'. It stands next to the Oyu geyser, alongside a monument to Alcock's faithful Scottish terrier Toby. Having survived the journey from Britain, Toby suffered the misfortune of standing on the piece of ground from where the geyser used to periodically erupt. The inevitable happened; the unsuspecting dog was blasted into the air by the force of the boiling water shooting out from the earth.

A distraught Alcock organized a funeral for his pet in Atami, an event which was almost certainly the origin of Britain's reputation in Japan as a nation of eccentrics. Toby was buried beside the geyser, perhaps as a warning to other mad dogs and Englishmen to beware of the danger that lurks close by. His tombstone reads simply: 'Poor Toby, 23 September 1860'. If the sign at the geyser is to be believed, the dog did not die in vain. 'At that time, Japan had a bad impression of the British people,' reads the sign. Alcock reported back to Britain that the Japanese had been very kind to him during his period of mourning and advised his country that they should not look upon Japan as an enemy. 'Thanks to his report and advice,' continues the sign, 'Great Britain's public opinion towards Japan turned favourable'.

In Toby's day the spring gushed hot water and steam six times a day, 'shaking the earth with its vigorous blasts'. During the 100 years since Alcock's visit to Atami the geyser gradually gave up and died. In 1962 it was given a new lease of (artificial) life and now goes off for three minutes with four-minute intervals.

operated by the private Izukyu Railway so rail passes are not valid. Shimoda is the place to gaze out over the sea and imagine what it must have been like to behold Commodore Perry's 'Black Ships' in 1854 (see p35). Shimoda is the southernmost town on the Izu Peninsula; apart from Commodore Perry, it is known for its beaches and surfing.

Limited expresses depart Atami at 10:23am, 10:56am, 11:24am, 11:54am, 12:20pm, 1:23pm, 2:22pm and 4:46pm, arriving in Ito 20 minutes later and in Shimoda approximately 80 minutes after leaving Ito. Rail passes are valid only as far as Ito. From Shimoda to Atami, limited expresses depart at 9am, 9:55am, 12pm, 12:27pm, 2pm, 3pm and 4pm.

Local trains run roughly half hourly from 5:03am to 11:04pm between Atami and Shimoda, thought some of these require a change in Ito. Local trains take 24 minutes from Atami to Ito and 60 minutes from Ito to Shimoda.

Atami to Nagoya   [Map 1, p111; Map 2, p115]
Mishima (121km) A few Hikari stop here. Mishima is an access point for **Mt Fuji**. If intending to climb Mt Fuji, change here for a local JR train to Numazu (one stop along the Tokaido mainline towards Kyoto). Change at Numazu for the Gotemba line to Gotemba (30 mins), from where you can pick up a Fuji-kyu bus (¥1080; 45 mins) to the fifth station on Mt Fuji. It's then 6½ hours on foot

⛩ **Oigawa Steam Railway**   [see Map 1, p111]
The Oigawa Railway began operations in 1927 to transport timber, freight and tea from the mountains along Oigawa River. During the 1960s, revenue from freight began to fall as did the number of people living in the mountainous areas, so the railway turned to tourism for revenue. The preserved steam operation (top speed 65kph) runs at least once a day (more departures in high season) from Shin-Kanaya station to the terminus at Senzu. Taking the steam train really is like stepping back in time. The train conductor sings old railway songs over the loudspeaker as you pass through the Oigawa tea fields. Sit on the right for views of the river.

To reach the start point for the Oigawa Railway (☎ 0547-45 4113), take a local JR train from Kakegawa two stops east to Kanaya; there are coin lockers (¥300) in the station. The entrance to Oigawa Kanaya station is on your right as you leave JR Kanaya station. Purchase tickets for the steam railway from here, board the train and go one stop along the Oigawa line to Shin-Kanaya station, where you transfer on to the steam locomotive for the journey to Senzu.

With time to kill waiting for the SL departure at Shin-Kanaya, there's a small steam museum (9am-5pm) with a few model railways, as well as a gift shop selling Oigawa tea. There's another small rail museum (10am-4pm, ¥100) at the Senzu terminus. Opposite Shin-Kanaya station is a café called ***Warau Neko*** (daily, 10am-8pm), easy to find as it's the only place full of good luck pottery cats, which according to the owner are supposed to bring in customers – if you're there, it's clearly worked. Alternatively, ekiben – in the shape of a steam train, of course – are sold before you get on the train.

At the end of the main rail line (40km) is a light railway that travels higher up into the mountains (25km) to the very end of the line at Igawa. Only a few families live along the light railway line (the average number of people who get on and off each stop is 0.5). Domoto station is named after the tea-producing family who live there. Look out also for Hirata station, where the 'fairy' lives. When a dam was constructed over 15 years ago in the area the train passes through, around 100 residents were forced to move away as villages were flooded. One man refused to be moved and rebuilt his own home. He still lives here today, without electricity or running water, and has been dubbed the 'fairy' – someone who lives by moisture alone.

Trains depart Kanaya at 10am, 11:50am and 12:45pm (goes first to Shin-Kanaya, where the journey proper commences); they arrive in Senzu at 11:17am, 1:07pm, 2:09pm. Trains depart Senzu at 1:20pm, 2:55pm, 3:30pm and arrive in Kanaya at 2:45pm, 4:09pm, 4:49pm. Note that these times are subject to change.

Kanaya to Senzu costs ¥1810 one-way (¥560 supplement to ride in the steam locomotive); Senzu to Igawa (light railway) is ¥1280 one-way.

to the summit. Note that this bus runs only during the official climbing season (Jul 1st-Aug 31st). For information on climbing Mt Fuji, see the JNTO leaflet *Mt Fuji and Fuji Five Lakes*.

A 35-minute side trip by rail can be made on the private Izu-Hakone line (¥500, rail passes not accepted) which runs some 20km south of Mishima to **Shuzenji**, another popular hot-spring town. The star attraction here is the temple, Shuzen-ji, founded in 807 by Kobo Daishi, the Buddhist monk who now lies in eternal meditation on Koya-san (see pp200-2).

Shin-Fuji (146km) Only Kodama stop here. There are hideous smoke stacks everywhere you look as you pass through Shin-Fuji, which is a shame since you expect a place with this name to afford picture-postcard views of Japan's most famous natural wonder. Sit on the left side of the train (to Tokyo) or on the right side (from Tokyo) for views of Mt Fuji (if you're lucky).

Shizuoka (180km) [see p134-9]
It's worth including a brief stop in Shizuoka on your itinerary.

Kakegawa (229km) Only Kodama stop here, the nearest point of access for Oigawa (see box opposite), home to one of Japan's most spectacular steam railway lines.

Hamamatsu (257km) Home to such world-famous companies as Yamaha, Suzuki and Honda. Hamamatsu is known as the 'music city', partly because of Yamaha's presence (it's said that every piano made in Japan is built here) but also because of the number of music festivals/concerts staged here. The biggest annual festival is the Hamamatsu Matsuri (May 3rd-5th).

The view as the train heads towards Toyohashi may discourage you from stopping there but it has a few attractions and – for rail enthusiasts – connects with the Iida line that runs out to Sakuma Rail Park (see box p116) where old rolling stock is displayed.

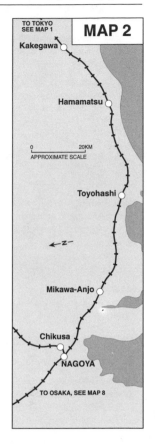

Toyohashi (294km) Take the east exit for the main part of the city and the tram line. The station is equipped with elevators from platform to concourse and street level. Toyohashi Information Plaza (daily, 9am-7pm) on the main concourse has maps which include sightseeing details and corresponding tram stops. Close to the tourist information counter are coin lockers (up to ¥600).

A single tram line runs through the city (¥150 flat fare) and out to **Toyohashi Park**, where you'll find the reconstructed Yoshida Castle, City Art museum, Sannomaru Tea Ceremony Hall (where you can try a bowl of green tea for ¥350), and a small Russian Orthodox church.

Toyotetsu Terminal Hotel (☎ 0532-56 1100, 🖨 56 1110; ¥5200/S, ¥10,000/D, ¥11,000/Tw) is outside the station's east exit. Rooms are small but

---

⛩ **Sakuma Rail Park**
This is not the largest or most convenient open-air railway museum in Japan as it's way out along the JR Iida line but it has enough exhibits, including the driver's cab of a first series shinkansen and a simulator for a local train, to impress the enthusiast. The journey here, through some of the most rural parts of Honshu, is an enjoyable diversion from the Tokaido mainline.

Sakuma Rail Park (☎ 0539-65 0003, 10am-4pm Sat/Sun and daily during Golden Week and August, ¥140) is at Chubutenryu station, some 62km along the Iida line from Toyohashi. It takes just under two hours by local train but twice a day (dep 09:05 arr 10:13 and dep 12:40 arr 13:48) there's a more comfortable limited express (Inaji LEX) that takes just over an hour. Limited express services depart from Chubutenryu at 15:00 (arr Toyohashi 16:10) and 17:04 (arr 18:10).

---

clean. Facilities include a coin laundry and a top floor restaurant which serves set meals in the evening. *Flying Mug Café* in the station does morning sets. A couple of minutes from the east exit is a *Vie de France* bakery with a café on the second floor.

After Toyohashi, Kodama call at **Mikawa-Anjo (336km)** but all other services run fast to Nagoya.

Nagoya (366km)   [see pp139-45]

If continuing to Kyoto, stay on the shinkansen and connect with the route guide starting on p166.

TOKYO TO NAGANO BY SHINKANSEN   [Map 3, p117; Table 4, p402]

Distances from Tokyo. Fastest journey time: 1 hour 21 minutes.

Tokyo (0km)   [see pp85-101]

Pick up the Asama shinkansen bound for Nagano, which departs from platforms 20-24. Note that the Asama has only six carriages and fills up quickly, so reserve a seat if possible. There are luggage storage areas between the carriages.

Ueno (3.6km) Most trains make a brief stop here, though reserve a seat in advance if you're joining the train at Ueno – unreserved cars can fill up before the train leaves Tokyo station.

Omiya (30km) After Omiya(see p245) , a few shinkansen call at **Kumagaya (65km)**.

Takasaki (105km) Takasaki is the point at which the Joetsu shinkansen to Niigata and the Nagano shinkansen lines divide. There's no reason to get out here when the far more attractive surroundings of the Japan Alps are so close.

Takasaki is an important production centre for Daruma dolls, modelled on the founder of Zen Buddhism in China and popular as lucky charms. The idea is that the purchaser of a Daruma paints in one of the eyes at the time of buying it but paints in the other eye only if his/her wish comes true. Daruma craftsmen receive a rush on orders for the dolls during general election campaigns from candidates trying to buy themselves some luck.

After Takasaki, a few shinkansen call at **Annaka-Haruna (124km)** but the majority stop next at Karuizawa. This section includes a number of tunnels, proof enough that this is now mountain territory, as the train heads towards its namesake, Mt Asama.

Karuizawa (147km)

The turn-of-the-century Karuizawa known to Mary Crawford Fraser (see box below), wife of a former British ambassador to Tokyo, is now a thriving mountain resort with top-notch hotels, golf courses and villas for diplomats and celebrities.

Once also a favourite haunt of John Lennon and Yoko Ono, more international recognition came when Karuizawa hosted an equestrian event at the 1964 Tokyo Olympics and the inaugural curling event at the 1998 Nagano Winter Olympics.

Karuizawa station was rebuilt for the Nagano Olympics. From the platforms, follow signs for the north exit to find the Visitors' Information Office (☎ 0267-42 2491, daily, 9am-5pm) on the right after the ticket barrier. Coin lockers are available on the ground floor (mostly ¥300 but a limited number of ¥500 size). The original station, dating from 1910, has been fully restored and is open to the public (daily except Mon, 9am-5pm, ¥200). It's to the left as you leave the station.

> *Poor old Karuizawa was a grand place once...now only mountain pilgrims and crazy foreigners like ourselves go near it. The place has become so poor that it has not even a public bath!*
> **Mary Crawford Fraser**, *A Diplomat's Wife in Japan: Sketches at the turn of the century*, edited by Sir Hugh Cortazzi, Weatherhill, 1982

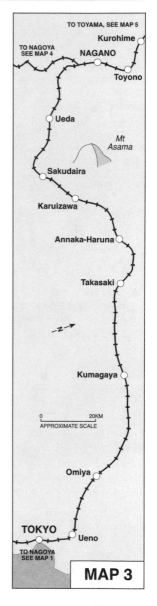

TO TOYAMA, SEE MAP 5

Kurohime

TO NAGOYA SEE MAP 4

NAGANO

Toyono

Ueda

Mt Asama

Sakudaira

Karuizawa

Annaka-Haruna

Takasaki

Kumagaya

0   20KM
APPROXIMATE SCALE

Omiya

TOKYO   Ueno

TO NAGOYA SEE MAP 1

MAP 3

The resort is not much more than a tacky array of gift shops selling mountain honey, jam and pot pourri, and places to eat with names like the 'Domestic Sausage Restaurant'.

The main reason for stopping in Karuizawa is to take a bus ride 21km north to **Onioshidashi-en**, an area of volcanic rock on the northern side of Mt Asama (2560m), a still active volcano. Onioshidashi-en (daily, 7am-6pm May-Sept, 8am-5pm Oct-Apr, ¥400) was formed after Mt Asama erupted spectacularly on August 5th 1783, spewing out enough lava to fill Tokyo Dome 161 times. Lava on the north slope cooled and solidified to become an eerie but magnificent place to walk around. Heavy snowfall means that some of the paths are closed in winter. Take a bus (¥1180 one-way; 35 mins) from stop No 1 outside the station. Services are infrequent, so check at the information office in the station.

Unless you're on a budget-free trip, don't even think about staying the night in Karuizawa. The rich and/or famous stay at *Mampei Hotel* (☎ 0267-42 1234, 🖺 42 7766), where backpacks will not impress the concierge and where if you have to ask the price you should be looking elsewhere.

Sakudaira (164km)

The town of Saku is a case study for the legacy left by the Olympic Games. With the opening of the Nagano shinkansen, the small town boomed. Before, it took over 3½ hours to Tokyo. Now the journey is less than an hour, turning Saku into a satellite commuter town for the capital.

Ueda (189km)

Last stop before the Nagano terminus, Ueda is a former castle town. After Ueda, the train dives into a long tunnel, shutting out the countryside until you finally pull into the Olympic city of Nagano.

Nagano (222km)   [see pp145-50]

Terminus of the shinkansen line, Nagano is a major gateway to the Japanese Alps.

NAGANO TO NAGOYA VIA MATSUMOTO [Map 4, p119; Table 5, p402]

Distances by JR from Nagano. Fastest journey time: 3 hours.

Nagano (0km)   From Nagano, pick up the Wide View Shinano LEX which runs along the Shinonoi line towards Nagoya. The Shinano is a modern train with Western-style toilets and large panoramic windows.

Shinonoi (9km)   The first stop after Nagano by limited express, this is the nearest train station to the Nagano Olympic Stadium, 15 minutes away by taxi (no bus). The stadium is open to the public for special events only, so check the schedule with tourist information in Nagano. Baseball tournaments are held here periodically.

From here, the Shinonoi line becomes the Chuo line, though there's no need to change trains as limited expresses run direct to Nagoya. After Shinonoi, there are views out to the left of the valley and towns below the rail line.

A few limited expresses call at **Hijiri-Kogen (31km)**. There's one very long tunnel shortly before arriving in Matsumoto.

Matsumoto (63km) [see pp150-55]
To return **to Tokyo** from Matsumoto, pick up
the Azusa LEX which takes just under three
hours to the capital. Matsumoto is also a terminus for the JR Oito line to Itoigawa (see
p124 and p154) via the ski resort of Hakuba.

Shiojiri (76km) If planning to visit Narai
(see below), you'll need to change from a limited express to a local train here. The line is
now running through the beautiful Kiso Valley,
surrounded by the Central Alps to the east and
the Northern Alps to the west.

♦ **Narai (97km)** Narai is the first in a series
of 'post towns' along this route that were once
used as stepping stones on the journey to Edo
(Tokyo). In the days before the railway, a total
of 69 post stations lined the Nakasendo highway, a trunk road connecting Edo with Kyoto.
Not all the post towns have survived but a
handful, including the one here in Narai and
two more further down the line, have been preserved. Here you'll find a 1km stretch of road
lined with Edo-period houses. Narai was 34th
of the 69 towns on the highway and the most
prosperous in the Kiso Valley. Steep slopes and
thick forest made this section of the highway
the most challenging (it took three days to
cross the valley), so Narai became an important stop for weary travellers to rest and stock
up on supplies.

There are no coin lockers at Narai station
though it seems safe enough to leave luggage
here for a couple of hours. The old wooden station sets the tone for what to expect along the
main road. Even the benches in the waiting
room are fitted with mini tatami mats. More
unusually, the station is run not by JR staff but
by a local senior citizens club – members take
it in turns to be at the station to meet trains.

Turn left out of the station and the main
street is straight in front of you. Look out for
the odd saké shop (a hangover from the drinking houses that provided travellers with some

liquid relief on their journey to/from Edo) and craft shops, many of which sell locally-made *nurigushi* (lacquered combs).

Several of the old buildings contain small restaurants serving soba. One is immediately on your left as you leave the station. Alternatively, walk down the street for about five minutes and look out on the right for a shop displaying an ice-cream sign. Go in here and at the back are a few tables and a small tatami area where soba is served. Ask for the ¥1400 'ososume menu' (recommended menu), which is huge and includes mountain potatoes and pickles.

The local train service from Shiojiri to Narai (20 mins) and then to Kiso-Fukushima (20 mins), from where it's possible to rejoin the limited express, operates irregularly but approximately once an hour. There is one very long tunnel just after leaving Narai station.

Kiso-Fukushima (118km)   Kiso-Fukushima was once a checkpoint on the highway between Edo and Kyoto and has a few sights scattered around including a temple and rock garden, and the former residence of a local governor who managed the checkpoint in the Edo period. It's also the main rail access point for a visit to Mt Ontake, a 3067m volcano, popular with hikers in summer and skiers in winter.

The station here is small and has no coin lockers. Exit the station and turn to the left for the tourist information counter (☎ 0264-22 4144, daily, 9am-5pm), which can supply basic maps of the area around the station. Cycles can be rented (up to four hours ¥500, one day ¥1000) from the JR ticket office in the station. Buses to Mt Ontake (¥2200 return) take just over 50 minutes but only run three times a day (check with the information counter for departure times). The bus drops you at Ontake Ropeway, from where gondolas climb to 2150m (daily, 8:45am-5:30pm, ¥2400 return). It's then a 3½-hour hike to the summit. A combined ropeway and bus return ticket costs ¥3800. The ticket office is across the street from Kiso-Fukushima station.

This is the nearest station to *Kiso Ryojoan Youth Hostel* (☎ 0264-23 7716, 🖹 23 7773; 🖳 ryojyouan@oct.zaq.ne.jp; ¥2900/YH(HI), ¥3900/non-members), an atmospheric hostel in an old wooden building. Breakfast costs ¥600 and dinner ¥1000. If you haven't made a booking, ask the assistant at the tourist office

---

⛩ **Tsumago – a ghost town comes back to life**
The opening of the Chuo railway line in 1911 along Kiso-gawa effectively robbed the post towns of their purpose, as the old highway was abandoned in favour of the locomotive. For decades in the last century, Tsumago stood forgotten, left behind by the age of the train. But in 1968, a century after the beginning of the Meiji era, a renovation programme began on Tsumago's houses which had by then fallen into a state of disrepair. Now the old post town has been reconstructed and survives, as it did before, thanks to a steady influx of visitors. It's ironic, therefore, that the train – the modern invention that killed off the post towns – now brings visitors to spend money here and keeps the tourism industry alive.

🏯 **Edo highlights in two days**
A possible **two-day itinerary**, starting in Matsumoto and ending in Nagoya, might be as follows: On the first day, leave Matsumoto and travel by train to Narai. Spend the morning in Narai before picking up the train to Nagiso. Take the bus to nearby Tsumago and overnight at a minshuku. Next day, leave Tsumago early and begin the hike to Magome. Spend some time in Magome, then pick up the bus to Nakatsugawa, from where you can connect with the train to Nagoya.

to call ahead and see if there's space. To reach the hostel, take a bus from right outside the station to Ohara, the last stop (20 mins).

Nagiso (152km) Not all limited expresses stop here, the nearest station to the post town of **Tsumago (see box opposite)**. Buses run from outside the station to Tsumago (once every 2 hours, 7 mins, ¥270) or take a taxi (¥1100). Luggage can be left for the day at the station for ¥410 per item (ask JR staff). Cycles can be rented (up to 4 hours/¥500) from the JR ticket office. Inside the station is a tourist information counter (daily, 8:30am-5pm), with guides to Tsumago.

Buses from Nagiso station pull in at the terminal just below Tsumago's main street, from where you head up a path to a side entrance as if walking onto an Edo-period film set. Most of the houses are now craft shops, inns and restaurants. This doesn't mean that the area is tacky or full of souvenir kitsch but it does feel more commercial than nearby Narai (see p119).

A great way to fully experience post-town life is to do what those who once travelled the road between Edo and Kyoto did – stay overnight. In the early evening, once the day crowds have gone, Tsumago feels much less like a Universal Studios Edo theme park. All the minshuku offer the same rates (¥7500 inc two meals); ask at the tourist office (☎ 0264-57 3123, daily, 9am-5pm) along the main street about which have vacancies.

Tsumago is at one end of a popular hiking route through the Kiso Valley to the southernmost post town, **Magome**. The three-hour walk between the two is not particularly strenuous, though you'd need proper hiking boots in winter when snow can be half a metre deep. A luggage delivery service (daily Jul 20th-Aug 31st, Sat/Sun Apr 1st-Jul 19th and Sep 1st-Nov 23rd, ¥500 per piece) is available at the tourist information offices in both Tsumago and Magome. Drop off your luggage by 9am in either town and it will be waiting for you at the other end. To rejoin the rail route after the hike, take a bus from Magome to Nakatsugawa, the next limited express stop along the Chuo line to Nagoya (see below).

Nakatsugawa (171km) Nakatsugawa is only 10 minutes down the line by limited express from Nagiso but it feels much further away. Business hotels, concrete, the odd factory smoke stack ... here are the realities of post-Edo life, an unpleasant warning that you are less than an hour from the industrial heartland of Nagoya. The only reason for stopping here is to take a bus to the post town of Magome (see above).

A tourist information counter (daily, 9am-5pm) is on the left as you leave the station, as are coin lockers (mostly ¥300 but one ¥600). Buses to Magome (¥540) depart from stop No 3 outside the station (operated by Nohi Bus).

Tajimi (215km) Tajimi is a terminus for the local Taita line that takes 30 minutes (two services an hour) to reach Mino-Ota station on the Takayama line. If planning to visit Takayama (see p155), instead of going all the way to Nagoya to change lines, cross via the Taita line here to Mino-Ota and pick up the route to Takayama from p128.

The Japanese Alps are by now a distant memory, replaced by chimney stacks and pachinko parlours for the last 20 minutes into Nagoya.

Chikusa (244km) This is the final stop on the limited express, just a few minutes out of Nagoya.

Nagoya (251km)   [see pp139-45]
From Nagoya, connect up with the Kansai route guide beginning on p166.

NAGANO TO NAGOYA VIA TOYAMA/TAKAYAMA

Distances by JR from Nagano. Fastest journey time: 6¼ hours.

Nagano to Naoetsu   [Map 5, p123; Table 6a/d, p403]
Nagano (0km)   [see pp145-50]
Pick up a local train or the Minori LEX (once a day), along the Shinetsu line heading for Naoetsu. The Minori is an old limited express with only Japanese-style toilets on board. Local trains operate irregularly but approximately hourly; the journey to Naoetsu takes about 90 minutes.

Toyono (11km) If on a local train from Nagano, you may have to change here for another local train. After Toyono, the limited express also calls at **Kurohime (29km)**.

Myoko-Kogen (37km) Again, a few local trains from Nagano terminate here, so you may have to change trains here as well. After Myoko most services stop at **Sekiyama (44km)**.

Nihongi (52km) On either side of the train there are spectacular views of the surrounding mountains. On leaving Nihongi station, the train reverses first before continuing along the line.

Arai (58km) By the time you leave this station, the mountain scenery is beginning to recede. As the line heads towards the coast you can see the height of the mountains gradually drop.

Takada (68km) The old castle town of Takada merged with the port town of Naoetsu in 1971 to become, for administrative purposes, Joetsu City. Joetsu has

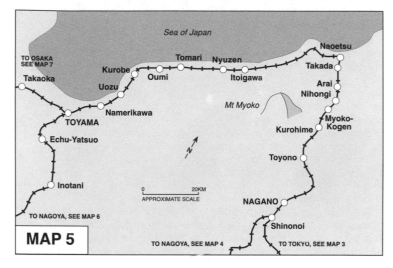

been named 'the birthplace of modern skiing in Japan' after an Austrian officer, Major Theodor Von Lerch (1869-1945), was posted to Japan and asked to teach skiing to the Takada 58th Infantry Regiment. Joetsu's history books record that January 12th 1911 was the day skiing was taught in Japan for the first time. Lerch used only one stick while skiing; his technique is demonstrated every year at the Lerch Festival in early February, when a local ski group takes to the slopes with a pair of wooden skis and a long bamboo stick.

Takada Castle was originally built as a stronghold to maintain peace throughout east and west Japan. A **Lotus Festival** is held in the first half of August along the moats of Takada Park, the former site of Takada Castle. During the festival, tea ceremony parties and haiku poetry gatherings are held in the park, and the moats are completely covered in thick, green lotus leaves.

It takes 15-20 minutes on foot to reach Takada Park. Go straight ahead as you leave the station, over the crossroads by Nagasakiya department store and Manten Hotel. You'll pass Duo Cerezo (a big wedding hall) on your left, after which you'll come to a main road with a Lawson convenience store on one corner. Turn right and keep going down the main road, passing Takada Catholic church on your right. A little further on there's a footbridge and crossroads, with a shrine on one corner. Turn left here and you'll see the moat – the park is on the other side of the moat. If you get lost, going into the Catholic church is a good idea because the priest, Father Mario, speaks excellent English.

Naoetsu (75km) Fittingly for a place where land meets the sea, newly rebuilt Naoetsu station is a replica of a cruiser ship with round portholes for windows. There is no tourist information office but there's a decent hotel opposite the main station exit; *Hotel Century Ikaya* (☎ 0255-45 3111, 🖹 45 3123; ¥6800/S, ¥13,000/D, ¥12,000/Tw).

In December 1942 an old salt warehouse here became a prisoner-of-war camp for 300 Australian soldiers, many of whom died from the cold and sickness. In 1995, a Peace Memorial Park was constructed on the site of the old POW camp, which is now home to Naoetsu Peace Memorial Museum. To visit the museum (admission free), contact Mr Hosaka (☎ 0255-45 4878). To reach the park, go straight out of the station and take the road on the left of the taxi office. It bears right but keep following it. Go over the bridge and then turn left. Go straight ahead and the park is on your left, just before another bridge. If you keep going straight without turning into the park, you will see Naoetsu port.

From Naoetsu there are ferry connections to Sado Island (2 to 4/day; 2¹/₂ hours, ¥2920). Overnight ferries also run year-round between Naoetsu and Hakata in Kyushu (¥11,260 one-way), and Muroran in Hokkaido (¥5250 one-way). For information, contact Joetsu International Network Office (☎ 0255-26 5446).

▲ From here, the Minori LEX turns east and runs along the coast towards Niigata (see p275). To follow the route below, change trains here and join the Hakutaka LEX which runs west along the Hokuriku line towards Toyama.

Naoetsu marks the end of JR East territory. The line and stations west of here are run by JR West (a subtle change in colour of the JR logo from green to blue). Note that JR East passes are not valid for the journey west from Naoetsu.

Don't expect views of the coastline as you hurtle through a series of tunnels. There are occasional sightings of the Japan Sea on the right but mostly the track runs slightly inland past buildings that obscure the coastline.

Naoetsu to Toyama   [Map 5, p123; Table 6b/c, p403]
Itoigawa (114km) A terminus for the Oito line from Matsumoto (see p150). After Itoigawa some trains stop at **Oumi (121km)**, **Tomari (139km)** and **Nyuzen (144km)**.

Kurobe (161km) Most limited expresses stop at Kurobe, from where there's a possible side trip by private railway to **Kurobe Gorge**. The route is as follows: next to JR Kurobe is a station on the private Toyama Chiho Railway line to Unazuki-Onsen (30 mins, irregular service but roughly hourly). A five-minute walk from here (follow the crowds) takes you to Unazaki station, starting point for the private Kurobe Kyokoku Railway line. A 'torocco' train with open-air carriages pulled by a tramcar runs on the 75-minute journey through the gorge to the terminus at Keyaki-Daira (¥1440 one-way).

Anyone into Japan's *onsen* culture should consider taking this side trip as the line passes a number of open-air hot springs. For rail enthusiasts, this is a chance to travel on a narrow-gauge railway which affords sweeping views of the northern Japanese Alps. The Kurobe Kyokoku Railway runs daily, approximately twice an hour, from late April to late November and is very busy during the summer and in late October for autumn leaves viewing.

Uozu (167km) The private Toyama Chiho Railway also has a station here linking Uozu with Kurobe and Unazuki-Onsen (see above) and with Toyama (see below). After Uozu, some limited expresses also call at **Namerikawa (176km)**.

Toyama (193km) Toyama is a major business city and not really a tourist destination. The main reason for stopping here is to begin the **Tateyama-Kurobe Alpine Route** (see box, p126).

Large size (¥600) lockers are available at Toyama station and there's a restaurant on the third floor. There are also department stores, restaurants and cafés in the station area. Take the central exit for the tourist information booth (☎ 0764-32 9751, daily 8:30 am-8pm), in a small hut to the left as you go out. The staff speak some English.

To the left as you exit the JR station is the private Toyama Chiho Railway station, from where services depart to Tateyama (for the start of the Alpine Route) and to Unazuki-Onsen (see p124). Toyama Airport (☎ 0764-95 3100) handles domestic flights and a few international routes to Seoul, Taipei and Vladivostok (for connection with the Trans-Siberian Railway).

If beginning the Alpine Route early in the morning it may be necessary to overnight in Toyama. The cheapest deal is at *Toyama Youth Hostel* (☎/🖹 0764-37 9010), where the rates are ¥2200 for all guests (¥2350 in Jul/Aug and Nov). Breakfast costs ¥500 and dinner ¥900. The hostel is north of the city centre on the coast overlooking Toyama Bay. Buses from Toyama station take 45 minutes (get off at 'Youth Hostel mae'), or take a local train on the JR Toyamako line to the terminus at Iwasehama (20 mins). The tourist information desk outside Toyama station can provide details of other accommodation.

Toyama to Nagoya [Map 5, p123; Map 6, p127; Table 7, p403]
Note that for the next part of the journey, distances quoted are from Toyama.

Toyama (0km) At Toyama, change to the Takayama line and take the Wide View Hida LEX (four a day). Green Car passengers can rent headphones on board (¥290) for the in-seat audio channels. The panoramic windows are great for the views though, because of the mountainous terrain, tunnels frequently block out the scenery. All the same, the line to Takayama remains one of the great rail journeys in Japan, as the train runs south from the coast deep into the Hida mountain range.

The train calls at **Hayahoshi (8km)**, **Echu-Yatsuo (17km)** and **Inotani (37km)** but there's nothing to stop off for until Hida-Furukawa, around 80 minutes after Toyama.

Hida-Furukawa (75km)
If nearby Takayama is a miniature Kyoto, Furukawa is an even smaller version of Takayama and is certainly less crowded.

Furukawa is an ancient town and though it has suffered several serious fires, it retains its historic street plan, its pleasant domestic scale, and most importantly its traditions and identity.
HRH Prince Charles, (1989) in a letter to the Japan National Trust.

⛩ Tateyama-Kurobe Alpine Route

Toyama is a gateway for the 90km Tateyama-Kurobe Alpine Route, a five-hour journey from Toyama on the coast through the Japanese Alps to Omachi. More than a million people every year follow this route, which involves a combination of train, cable car, bus, ropeway and a bit of legwork. The route is accessed by taking a train on the private Toyama Chiho Railway from Toyama to the cable car station at Tateyama; services operate roughly hourly throughout the day though not at regular times.

First opened in 1971, the highest point on the route is 2450m but the most spectacular part is the 23km bus journey from Bijodaira to Murodo; in April/May this usually means going through a corridor of ice. It takes nearly two months of bulldozing to carve out this corridor and remove around 20m of snow.

If any journey in Japan is proof of the Japanese desire to conquer the elements, it must be this one. The route is impassable in winter, when Siberian winds sweep south across the Japan Sea, dumping snow in blizzards across the Tateyama mountain range that doesn't melt away until well into July. The only section of the entire route which requires any footwork is the 20-minute walk across Kurobe Dam, completed in 1963. The route ends with a bus journey to Shinano-Omachi, from where you can pick up a limited express (35 mins) or local train (65 mins) on the JR Oito line to Matsumoto (see p150).

The route is open from around April 25th to the end of November (heavy snowfall can delay the opening). The journey can be completed in either direction and a **one-way package ticket** covering all stages between Toyama and Shinano-Omachi costs ¥10,320. Allow a full day (6-8 hours) to complete the journey; when you buy the ticket the travel agent should provide you with an itinerary showing connection times for the different modes of transport on the route – if not, ask for one.

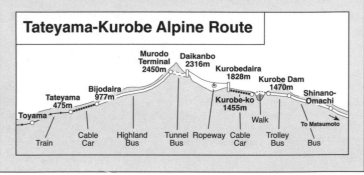

Pick up a map and guide from the tourist information booth (daily, 9am-5:30pm; no English spoken) outside the station. Cycles can be rented (4 hours, ¥500) from the JR ticket office in the station, though the town is manageable on foot.

Every year on April 19th-20th the peace of Furukawa is shattered by the town's annual festival, the highlight of which is a parade of floats and a big drum, carried by a team of men dressed in white loincloths. Throughout the year, a few of the floats are on display in the centre of town (10 mins west of the station) at **Hida-Furukawa Festival Hall** (daily, 9am-5pm, ¥800), where you can also watch a 3D film of the festival parade. Across the street is **Hida-no-takumi Bunkakan** (daily except Tue, 9am-4:30pm, ¥200), a new heritage centre which displays techniques and tools used by Furukawa craftsmen. Prince Charles' letter of commendation (see box p125) hangs on the wall inside. To visit both places, buy the ¥900 combination ticket.

Hida Furukawa Youth Hostel (☎/🖳 0577-75 2979) is in a modern wood building and charges ¥3100 to YH/HI members (¥4100 to others) plus ¥1000 for dinner and ¥500 for breakfast. The hostel is actually closer to **Hida-Hosoe (70km)**, two stops back by local train towards Toyama. It's a 15-minute walk west of the station, opposite Shinrin Park. Alternatively, take a bus from Hida-Furukawa station (15 mins) and get off at 'Shinrin-Koen guchi'. It's a good idea to reserve here as it only sleeps 22. The hostel is closed March 30th-April 10th.

Takayama (89km) [see pp155-9]

From Takayama, the line continues to follow roughly the course of Hida-gawa. The best part of the journey is the next 50km to Gero, with stunning river and mountain scenery on both sides of the track.

Some of the Wide View Hida services that start in Takayama also stop at **Kuguno (103km)**, **Hida-Osaka (117km)**, and **Hida-Hagiwara (129km)**.

Gero (138km) Gero is one of the best-known spa towns in Japan. This onsen resort dates back over 1000 years and is mainly popular with elderly Japanese holidaymakers. The town is also known for its tomato juice, considered to be a healthy tonic after a day wallowing in a hot tub.

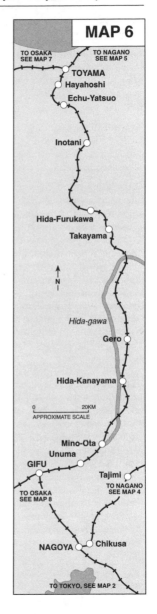

MAP 6

TO OSAKA SEE MAP 7
TO NAGANO SEE MAP 5
TOYAMA
Hayahoshi
Echu-Yatsuo
Inotani
Hida-Furukawa
Takayama
N
Hida-gawa
Gero
Hida-Kanayama
0   20KM
APPROXIMATE SCALE
Mino-Ota
Unuma
GIFU
Tajimi
TO OSAKA SEE MAP 8
TO NAGANO SEE MAP 4
NAGOYA   Chikusa
TO TOKYO, SEE MAP 2

After Gero, a few limited expresses call at **Hida-Kanayama (159km)** and **Shirakawaguchi (193km)**.

Mino-Ota (199km) Situated on Kiso-gawa, Mino-Ota is a terminus for the local Taita line that takes 30 minutes to reach Tajimi on the Chuo line. If planning to visit Matsumoto (see p150), instead of going all the way to Nagoya to change lines, cross via the Taita line here to Tajimi and pick up the route to Matsumoto from p122.

Unuma (209km) Only limited expresses that start in Takayama stop here, the nearest JR station to Inuyama, a popular side trip from Nagoya (see p145). Local trains to Inuyama can be caught from the private Meitetsu Railway's Shin-Unuma station on the other side of Kiso-gawa, across the bridge.

Gifu (226km) Gifu is more of a political and administrative centre than a tourist destination. The city suffered heavy air raids during WWII. A couple of attractions which remain are cormorant fishing on Nagara-gawa, and Gifu Castle, a 1956 reconstruction and therefore not a high priority.

Gifu station is a terminus for the Takayama line and a stop on the Tokaido mainline. There are two sides to the station but the main exit is the Nagara side, outside which the main road heads north towards Nagara-gawa. There are a few coin lockers in a corner of the ticket barrier level but not as many as you would expect in such a large station. A lift for wheelchair users operates from arrival to street level. There aren't many places to eat in the station but at basement level you'll find a branch of the *Vie de France* bakery which includes a café. Gifu City tourist information centre (☎ 058-262 4415, daily, 9am-7pm) is on the same floor as the ticket barrier. Maps are available and staff will help book accommodation.

Gifu Castle is perched on top of Mt Kinka (329m) overlooking Nagara-gawa and accessed via ropeway from Gifu Park. The concrete reconstructed castle (daily, 9am-4:30/5:30pm, ¥200) has little to recommend inside – a video of cormorant fishing and some photos of other castles in Japan. The best part of the visit is the ropeway, which on a clear day affords views of the city and the river. To reach the castle from the station (east exit), take a City Bus from stop No 11 marked 'Nagarasagiyama-mawari' and get off at the Gifukoen-mae stop. From there, take the ropeway (3 mins, ¥1050 return) to the castle.

Cormorant fishing (nightly, May 11th-October 15th, ¥3300) takes place on Nagara-gawa, 2km north of the station. Fishermen dressed in traditional costume of straw skirt, sandals and black kimono use cormorant birds to fish for *ayu* (sweetfish). The birds, tied to reins and steered by fishermen standing inside the boats, dive down and catch the fish in their beaks. The rein around each bird's neck prevents it from swallowing any of the catch. Today, the event is

---

Opposite Top: Forget pot noodles: in Japan the real thing is prepared right in front of you. **Bottom:** A local train in Oigawa (see box p114) runs through tea fields that are still cultivated today as they were a century ago. (Photos © Richard Brasher).

geared towards the tourist trade, but when the river is lit up by fire and the cormorants set to work, it's an impressive sight. If you don't want to pay to watch from a boat, there's no charge for standing along the river bank.

For fishing schedules and ticket information, contact the tourist information office in Gifu station or the boat office by Nagara-gawa (☎ 058-262 0104).

After Gifu, some services stop at **Owari-Ichinomiya (239km)**.

Nagoya (256km)   [see pp139-45]
To link with the Kansai route guide, see p166 or p170.

NAGANO TO NAGOYA/OSAKA VIA TOYAMA AND KANAZAWA

Nagano to Toyama   [Map 5, p123; Table 6, p403]
From **Nagano (0km)**, follow the route guide starting on p122 as far as **Toyama (193km)**, then pick up the route below.

Distances by JR from Toyama. Fastest journey time: (to Nagoya) 3 hours 35 minutes; (to Osaka) 3 hours 10 minutes.

Toyama to Fukui   [Map 7, p130; Table 8, p404]
Toyama (0km) From Toyama, continue along the Hokuriku line towards Kanazawa. The gleaming Thunderbird LEX runs to Kyoto/Osaka via Kanazawa. This train has vending machines and all Green Car seats are fitted with TV (a choice of three satellite stations as well as music and radio programmes). Even those roughing it in the ordinary seats can tune in to the music channels if carrying their own portable radio; FM frequencies are displayed on the screen at the front of each car. The older Shirasagi LEX runs to Nagoya via Kanazawa. The Hakutaka LEX terminates at Kanazawa.

Takaoka (19km) Takaoka feels quiet and uncosmopolitan after Toyama but it does have a seasonal ferry connection with Vladivostok in Russia (see box, p131). It also has the distinction of being the smallest city in Japan to boast its own tram line! A tourist information desk (daily 9:30am-5:30pm) is in the station. Maps are available but the staff do not speak English. A few ¥600 large lockers are on your left as you go out of the station.

Takaoka is known as a centre for bronze production; the biggest bit of bronze in town is the **Daibutsu**, a 15.85m-high bronze Buddha statue weighing 65 tons, the third largest in Japan. The statue is five minutes on foot from the station's north exit; turn right on to the main road (Sakurababa-dori), go straight to the fourth road on your left (Daibutsu-dori), turn left and go straight until you reach the Daibutsu.

In mid-January, a **Nabe Festival** is held here. The nabe, a stew made with cod, crab and other winter seafood, is cooked in a giant cauldron with a capacity

---

Opposite: Wearing standard-issue white gloves the conductor of a Kodama shinkansen ensures it is safe for the train to leave. (Photo © Ramsey Zarifeh).

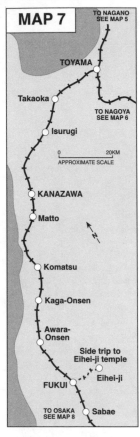

TO NAGANO
SEE MAP 5

TO NAGOYA
SEE MAP 6

TO OSAKA
SEE MAP 8

MAP 7

TOYAMA

Takaoka

Isurugi

0   20KM
APPROXIMATE SCALE

KANAZAWA

Matto

Komatsu

Kaga-Onsen

Awara-
Onsen

Side trip to
Eihei-ji temple

Eihei-ji

FUKUI

Sabae

of 1200 litres. The cauldron is displayed at Takaoka station.

Takaoka is a terminus for two local JR lines, the Johana line which runs south to Johana and the Himi line which runs along the coast to Himi. Both are possible side trips by rail, though neither is a top priority.

On the **Johana line**, two-car, one-man trains run on a 29.9km journey through vast rice paddies dotted with houses which are surrounded by trees to block the wind. The service started in 1897 as the Chuetsu Railway and in 1912 was extended beyond Takaoka station to Himi, on the coast of the Japan Sea. The line was cut down to its current stretch after the Himi line was laid between Takaoka and Himi stations. In the country where even taxi doors are automated, it's a novelty to discover that passengers on Johana line trains have to open and close the doors themselves.

The **Himi line** extends only 16.5km up the coast but there are good (if brief) views of Toyama Bay out to the right. Close to the Himi terminus you'll find Himi Fisherman's Wharf (daily except Wed, 7am-6pm), where you can see the early morning catch of fish before having a sushi breakfast.

Daibutsu Ryokan (Daibutsu-machi 75, ☎ 0766-21 0075, 🖷 22 0075, 🖳 buddha@pl.coral net.or.jp) is almost opposite the Daibutsu and has spacious if slightly faded tatami rooms. Rates are ¥4600 for one, ¥9000 for two or ¥13,200 for three people sharing a room.

Tontei (daily except Tue 11:30am-2:30pm and 5-9:30pm), across the street from the station, serves excellent tonkatsu, prepared and fried in front of you. Set meals cost ¥900-1000.

After Takaoka a few services stop at **Isurugi (35km)**.

Kanazawa (60km)   [see pp159-65]
After Kanazawa a few services stop at **Matto (69km)**.

Komatsu (88km)
Some Thunderbird LEXs do not stop here. Komatsu is not really a sightseeing destination, but it does have a great hotel perfect for rail travellers; since the town is midway between Kanazawa and Fukui it would make a convenient base for visiting both places.

⛩ **Takaoka to Vladivostok**

The frequency of sailings between Fushiki Port in Takaoka and Vladivostok changes every year but there are approximately 20 from early July to December, departing once a week on Thursday (about 38 hours; ¥25,000 one-way and ¥38,000 return). For up-to-date schedules and fares, contact FKK Air Service Ltd (Shimozeki-machi 4-56, Takaoka City, Toyama, ☎ 0766-22 2212, 🖷 22 7456). To reach Fushiki Port, take a local train from Takaoka three stops on the Himi line to Fushiki.

Hyper Hotel Komatsu (☎ 0761-23 3000, 🖷 23 3553; ¥4800/S, ¥5800/Tw, ¥6800/Fam) is brand new and right opposite the station. Breakfast is included in the room rate. Even if you don't stay here, it's worth visiting the Japanese restaurant on the second floor. *Kamado* is a modern izakaya mixing traditional Japanese service with a stylish, modern décor. The menu is only in Japanese but don't let this put you off. As well as fresh fish, there are steaks, cheese fondues, salads and garlic bread. Count on spending ¥2000-4000 per person. Mugs of beer are ¥450.

Kaga-Onsen (102km) Not all limited express trains stop here. Look up to the right just before the train pulls into this station (10 mins after leaving Komatsu) and you'll see a giant gold Kannon statue looking down on the station below.

After Kaga-Onsen, some limited expresses make an additional stop at **Awara-Onsen (119km)**.

Fukui (136km) History has not been kind to Fukui; the city has been completely destroyed twice, once by war and soon after by an earthquake. The main reason for stopping here is to take a side trip to nearby Eihei-ji (see box, p132).

When I visited Fukui, the assistant at the tourist information booth (☎ 0776-63 3102, daily, 8:30am-5pm), to the left of the central ticket barrier, handed me a map but did not seem to want to answer any questions. Coin lockers (all sizes) are in a room to your right immediately after going through the ticket barrier.

Buses go from in front of the station to **Daianzen-ji** (daily except Tue 9am-5pm), founded in 1658. The main attraction here is an 11-faced statue of the Bodhisattva of compassion. The image is celebrated for its matchmaking powers. The best place to sit – where the love vibes are strongest – is immediately under the large, sparkling gold lamp shade. Say a prayer here, it is said, and you may not be walking alone for much longer.

Zazen training sessions are held here twice a month on Friday evenings. The Head Priest is said to be a humorous raconteur. Three-hour sessions (¥400) offer a gentle introduction to Zen meditation. Foreign visitors are welcome but reservations (☎ 0776-59 1014) are required. From the station, take Keifuku bus No 16 (¥400) from stop No 7 bound for Kawanishi and get off at the Daianzen-ji Monzen stop.

> ⛩ **Side trip to Eihei-ji**
>
> Eihei-ji, built onto a mountainside to the east of Fukui, was founded in 1244 by the Buddhist priest Dogen as a centre for Zen training. The name means 'temple of eternal peace', though with so many tour groups piling through it's best to arrive as early as possible to appreciate the tranquillity.
>
> The most sacred building inside the compound is the Joyoden (Founder's Hall), in which Dogen's ashes are kept along with those of his successors. Just as impressive as the fine buildings and beautiful setting is the feeling of how busy and alive the temple remains over 750 years after its foundation. As you walk around you'll almost certainly see priests at work, perhaps practising how to move sacred objects, or a trainee priest reciting a sutra.
>
> Eihei-ji is open daily from dawn except on certain festival days and when there are private ceremonies. Buy a ticket (¥400) from the vending machine at the main entrance. A booklet is available inside the temple (not at the ticket booth).
>
> Rail services to Eihei-ji (¥720; no rail passes) start from the private Keifuku Denki Railway station outside the east exit of JR Fukui station. Change trains at Higashi-Furuichi, where there's either a connecting train or bus (both run by Keifuku Denki) to Eihei-ji. If you take the bus, you'll probably be dropped off right outside the temple. Arriving by train, you'll have to walk up the road lined with the usual tourist goodies for about 10 minutes to find the main temple entrance.

An overnight option in Fukui is *Hotel Riverge Akebono* (3-10-12 Chuo, ☎ 0776-22 1000, 🖷 22 8023, 🖳 www.riverge.com) with good value rooms, a coin laundry, decent restaurant and a hot spring. In the main building, singles cost ¥6200, twins ¥11,000 and doubles ¥12,000. In the newer annex, twins go from ¥14,000 and doubles from ¥16,000. Across the street, the hotel also operates *Akebono Bekkan*, an old Japanese inn with tatami rooms (¥4000/S). The hotel is a 10-minute walk from the station's central exit. Go straight up Ekimae-odori, turn left at the fourth intersection and walk for 50m up this road to the hotel.

Fukui to Tsuruga   [Map 8, p133; Table 8, p404]
The route from Fukui heading south towards Kansai has a number of tunnels so the views are never as impressive as you might think.

Sabae (150km) Some limited expresses make a brief stop at Sabae, which hosted the 1995 World Gymnastic Championships.

After Sabae, some trains also call at **Takefu (155km)**. There's one very long tunnel that lasts around 10 minutes shortly before Tsuruga, just north of Lake Biwa, the largest lake in Japan.

Tsuruga (190km) Tsuruga is one of the largest ports on the Japan Sea coast and is also a major rail junction, marking the end of the Hokuriku line. This is the last chance to change between the Shirasagi LEX for Nagoya and the Thunderbird LEX for Osaka/Kyoto.

Note that the Thunderbird does not always stop at Tsuruga. Fifteen kilometres after Tsuruga, the track divides into two lines which run down either side

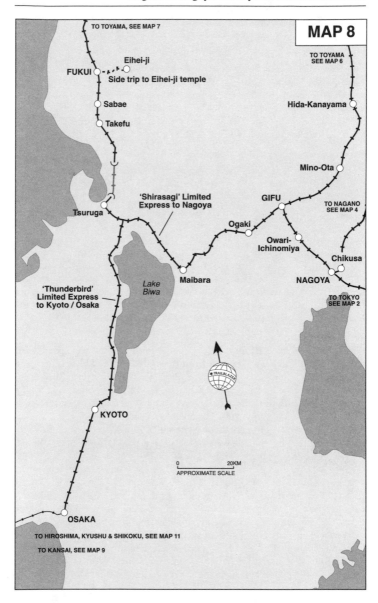

MAP 8

TO TOYAMA, SEE MAP 7

TO TOYAMA
SEE MAP 6

Eihei-ji

FUKUI

Side trip to Eihei-ji temple

Hida-Kanayama

Sabae

Takefu

Mino-Ota

'Shirasagi' Limited
Express to Nagoya

GIFU

TO NAGANO
SEE MAP 4

Tsuruga

Ogaki

Owari-
Ichinomiya

Chikusa

Maibara

NAGOYA

Lake
Biwa

'Thunderbird'
Limited Express
to Kyoto / Osaka

TO TOKYO
SEE MAP 2

TRAILBLAZER

KYOTO

0   20KM
APPROXIMATE SCALE

OSAKA

TO HIROSHIMA, KYUSHU & SHIKOKU, SEE MAP 11

TO KANSAI, SEE MAP 9

of Lake Biwa. There are better views of the lake (on the left) on the journey to Kyoto/Osaka but even so trees and tunnels often block the view.

Moving on from Tsuruga [Map 8, p133]
The Thunderbird LEX heads down the west side of the lake, before joining the Tokaido line westbound to Kyoto (284km; p180), Shin-Osaka (323km; p101) and Osaka (327km; p101).

The Shirasagi LEX runs down the east side of the lake to Maibara (236km; p166), then joins the Tokaido line eastbound to Ogaki (272km), Gifu (286km; p128), Owari-Ichinomiya (299km) and Nagoya (316km; p139).

Central Honshu – city guides

SHIZUOKA

Often overlooked as being too soon after Tokyo to make it a destination in its own right, Shizuoka has a couple of attractions that make an overnight stay worthwhile. Capital of Shizuoka prefecture, a well-known tea-producing area, the city was chosen by the first Tokugawa shogun, Ieyasu, as his retirement home. There's an excellent selection of restaurants and the place feels much more manageable than Tokyo. It's also a good staging post for a visit to the Oigawa Railway (see p114), just a little further down the Tokaido Line.

What to see and do
Don't be put off by signs for the 'incineration plant' and 'sewage plant' marked on the map to Shizuoka available from the tourist office. The two main sights you could pack into one day are the Prefectural Art Museum, which has a superb annex filled with reproductions of Rodin's sculptures, and Kunozan Toshogu Shrine, the journey to which via a winding bus route and ropeway is as impressive as the shrine complex itself.

Before setting off to visit these places, get a bird's eye view of the city and surrounding area by walking over to the **Prefectural Office**, about 10 minutes on foot north of the station. The office is made up of several buildings but the one you want is the tall building to the right as you face the Prefectural Office complex. This is the East Building, connected to the *Bekkan* (annex building). From the second floor, take the passageway through to the Bekkan, where you can ride the elevator up to the 21st floor observation platform. There's a small tea room here. On a (rare) clear day, you can see Mt Fuji.

Immediately behind the offices is **Sumpu Park** (daily, 6am-10pm). There's little left of Sumpu Castle, where Tokugawa Ieyasu spent the last 11 years of his life until his death in 1616, but at least the park is an open space. The reconstructed south-east tower is open to the public (daily except Mon, 9am-4:30pm, ¥200).

Top of the visitor's list should be the excellent **Prefectural Art Museum** (daily except Mon 9:30am-5pm, until 7:30pm on Fri, May-Sept); a combined tempo-rary/permanent exhibition ticket costs around ¥1000 but it depends on the exhi-bition). Find out what the temporary exhibition is, but the real reason for com-ing is to check out the Rodin Wing. This new part of the museum is spacious, well organized and boasts an impressive collection of bronze Rodin casts, including his famous *Thinker* and the *Gates of Hell*. A handset can be rented for an informative and amusing commentary in English on all the sculptures. Outside, a promenade offers excellent views of the mountains – it's hard to believe you're only an hour away from Tokyo by shinkansen. To get here, take bus No 44 (¥350) from stop No 13, which is across the road from Shizuoka sta-tion (take the north exit and cross the road by Hotel Associa Shizuoka). The bus takes 25 minutes and is marked 'Kenritsu Bijutsukan'.

Consider fitting in a visit to **Kunozan Toshogu Shrine**, way out of the city centre but accessible via a scenic road and ropeway. The shrine is a mausoleum to Tokugawa Ieyasu, who spent the last years of his life in Shizuoka. To reach Nihondaira Ropeway station from Shizuoka station, take bus No 42 (35 mins; ¥670) from stop No 13 and get off at 'Nihondaira' (the last stop). The short ride by ropeway (daily, 9:10am-4pm, ¥550 one-way, ¥1000 return) terminates by the entrance to the shrine. Buy the combination ticket here (¥650) that allows entrance to the shrine and the small museum that contains a number of Tokugawa Ieyasu's personal artefacts.

Behind the main shrine, surprisingly ornate and colourful and looking more like a Buddhist temple than an austere Shinto shrine, is the simple mausoleum, surrounded by trees. The reason for the mix of Buddhism and Shinto, evident when you see the main shrine, is that Kunozan Toshogu was originally built as a blend of the two. This coexistence was brought to an end when the Emperor prohibited simultaneous worship of the two religions. Buddhist decoration was torn down. The Bell Tower became the rather more solemn Drum Tower and a five-storey pagoda that once stood here was bulldozed. By contrast, the small museum is a colourful treasure trove of Tokugawa Ieyasu's possessions. A col-lection of glittering swords, hanging scrolls, samurai armour and an antique table clock from Madrid make this a fascinating diversion and alone worth the visit to the shrine.

⛩ Tokugawa Ieyasu – where does he lie?

If you ask most people where Tokugawa Ieyasu is buried you will almost certainly be told that his mausoleum is in Nikko (see p101), the famous temple and shrine town north of Tokyo. But anybody from Shizuoka will tell you that the man is in Kunozan Toshogu Shrine, just outside their city. Once pressed a little, howev-er, the typical citizen of Shizuoka will cave in and admit that his body was actual-ly moved to Nikko – though they'll point out that Kunozan Toshogu was the origi-nal mausoleum.

There are two ways back to the shrine from Shizuoka. One way is to take the ropeway back to Nihondaira and then pick up the bus back to the station. A combined return ropeway, shrine and museum ticket (available only at the top ropeway station) costs ¥1550; this represents the best value if you intend to return to Shizuoka city by bus from Nihondaira.

The alternative is to walk down the 1159 steps from the shrine to the coast and pick up a bus from there. The steps, the traditional entry point to the shrine, are much more manageable going down so it's far better to do it this way round. There's the added attraction of a number of strawberry farms at the bottom. Even if you're not here in the strawberry season, there are shops at the foot of the steps where strawberries are big business year-round – strawberry juice, ice cream and jam are there in abundance. Turn left when you reach the foot of the steps (don't go as far as the main road in front of you) and walk 150 metres to the bus stop, where you can pick up a bus (No 14; ¥470) back to Shizuoka station. If you really want to climb the 1159 steps up to the shrine you can catch this bus from stop No 4 outside Shizuoka station.

PRACTICAL INFORMATION
Station guide
Shizuoka has both north and south sides but the main exit for the city (where all the buses arrive and depart) is the north side. In the middle of the station concourse is the entrance to ASTY, a restaurant complex with a variety of reasonably priced if rather unexciting options. On both sides of the north exit are entrances to the Parche shopping complex.

For coin lockers (up to ¥600) look down the passageways that run off from the main concourse.

Tourist information
There is normally an English speaker on hand at the tourist information office (☎ 054-252 4247, daily 8:30am-6pm), along a passageway behind the JR ticket gate.

The guide to the city bus service tells you how to get to the main sights, what bus to catch, how much the fare is, how long it will take and which bus stop to wait at. Maps are also available. However, staff here can't help with accommodation bookings aside from giving you a list of hotels/ryokans.

SHIZUOKA 静岡

Where to stay

6 Hotel ECC Shizuoka	6 ホテルエックシズオカ
7 Crescent Hotel	7 クレセントホテル
16 Hotel Associa Shizuoka Terminal	16 ホテル アソシア 静岡 ターミナル
18 Shizuoka Station Hotel	18 静岡ステーションホテル
19 Ryokan Kagetsu	19 旅館花月

Where to eat

3 Café Ciccio	3 Cafe Ciccio
4 Kushiko	4 串幸
5 El Pollito	5 エルポジート
7 Ninnikuya	7 にんにくや
8 Sabaai Diiru	8 サバーイデイール

Where to eat (cont'd)
   9 Jenbatan Merah
  10 Undercover
  13 The Lockup
  17 Baskin-Robbins/Revolving sushi
      restaurant

Other
   1 Sumpu Park
   2 Prefectural Office
  11 Shin-Shizuoka Center
  12 Central Post Office
  14 Prefectural Art Museum
  15 Kunozan Toshogu Shrine

   9 ジェンバタンメラ
  10 Undercover
  13 The Lockup
  17 バスキンロビンス
      /回転ずし屋

   1 駿府公園
   2 県庁
  11 新静岡センター
  12 中央郵便局
  14 県立美術間
  15 久能山東照宮

Getting around

To get a feel for the city, jump on the Shizuoka sightseeing bus that, for a flat fare of ¥100, does a 40-minute loop of the city. The old-fashioned retro bus departs from stop No 1 outside the north exit and calls at Sumpu Park, convenient for the Prefectural Office.

Internet

Free Internet access is available on the second floor of the Prefectural Office East Building (see p134). Head for the Kenmin Service Center (Mon-Fri, 8:30am-5pm). Sign your name at the desk and you'll be told which computer to use; a maximum of 30-60 minutes, depending on how busy it is.

Money

Visa/Mastercard/Cirrus cards issued overseas can be used for cash withdrawals at the ATM corner on the ground floor of the central post office outside Shizuoka station.

Where to stay

The most convenient place is *Hotel Associa Shizuoka Terminal* (☎ 054-254 4141, 🖺 255 3721, 🖵 www.associa.com/english; ¥8700/S, ¥13,200/D, ¥16,200/Tw), immediately on your right as you take the north exit from Shizuoka station. The reception staff speak English and the rooms are bright and furnished with a minibar and bilingual TV. There's a top-floor French restaurant, *Belle Vue*, and a good second-floor coffee shop. This hotel offers affordable luxury in a central location (10% discount with rail pass).

If you're looking for a night in a Japanese inn, *Ryokan Kagetsu* (☎ 054-281 0034, 🖺 281 0759; ¥5000/pp) has modern tatami rooms and there's a large communal bath. Staff are friendly and speak a little English. It's a seven-minute walk from the south exit of Shizuoka station. Take the main road in front of you until you come to a road that leads off diagonally to the right. Go up this road to the end, then bear left and carry on straight until you come to a small driveway on the right, at the end of which is the ryokan. If you get to a petrol station on your left, you've gone too far.

Also on the south side of the station, just a couple of minutes from the exit, is *Shizuoka Station Hotel* (☎ 054-281 7300, 🖺 281 5320; ¥7200/S, ¥12,000/Tw/D). Good value, smart rooms and the usual small bathrooms but bilingual TV is a surprise in this category.

Over on the north side of the city, a bit further from the station, are a couple of good mid-range hotels. *Hotel ECC Shizuoka* (☎ 054-251 1741, 🖺 251 6797) has small but clean rooms and offers free coffee/bread for breakfast. Singles are ¥6700 (or squeeze two people in for ¥9000) and twins ¥12,000. *Crescent Hotel* (☎ 054-251 7911, 🖺 273 2334; ¥7600/S, ¥12,800/D, ¥15,200/Tw) feels like an upmarket boutique hotel but doesn't come with the expected high charges.

Where to eat

For budget food, head for the Prefectural Office. In a corridor inside the main building (the old building in the centre as you stand facing the prefectural office complex) is a highly recommended *onigiri stall* (Mon-Fri, 9am-12pm). They sell over 100 types of onigiri (from ¥900; the onigiri are so popular that they're usually sold out by 11:30 am. Stock up here and have lunch in adjacent Sumpu Park.

There's a good choice of bars and restaurants in Shizuoka. A good place for lunch is *Café Ciccio*, an Italian café that opens out on to the street. It's open all day but the best time to stop here is 11am-3pm when they do a panini lunch-set with your choice of filling, including a salad and coffee for ¥800.

In Parche department store, just across from the Associa Hotel outside the station's north exit, is a conveyor-belt sushi restaurant (kaiten-zushiya) that is often packed out, since it's cheap and the sushi is fresh and delicious. Also here is a branch of *Baskin-Robbins* ice cream. The ASTY food complex inside the station also has a selection of casual restaurants at their busiest in the early evening.

Shizuoka is also very much into ethnic cuisine, with a great Indonesian place called *Jenbatan Merah* that's closed on Monday. If you prefer Thai food, *Sabaai Diiru* is absolutely authentic – right down to extreme spiciness. Mexican food is also no problem here with *El Pollito*. There's a menu in English and a selection of Mexican beers (not just Corona) from ¥600.

Fun to try in the evening is *Kushiko*, a robatayaki place where you sit at the counter and order huge chunks of meat on big metal sticks (like giant kebabs). The friendly owners have an unusual speciality house drink called *shochu-ochaiwari* – a mix of green tea and shochu.

An unusual place to head for an evening drink and some food is the *Lockup*. The prison theme is obvious from the out-side, to get in you have to put your hand in a guillotine, you're 'handcuffed' and led to your seat by prison warders … you get the idea. Fun if that's your kind of thing. In a basement across the street from the Shin-Shizuoka Center, *Undercover* is run by two Aussies who serve a range of beers (from ¥400) and hearty pub food. Garlic lovers should make a beeline for the basement of the Crescent Hotel, where you'll find a branch of the popular garlic-with-every-thing *Ninnikuya* chain. This place gets busy on weekend evenings.

In summer, the *Associa Hotel Beer Garden* is a good place to head in the evening for an all you can eat/drink deal during a set time.

NAGOYA

Just over a century ago, Nagoya had a population of 157,000. Today, over two million people live in what has become the fourth largest city in Japan. Much of the city was flattened by WWII air raids, and in 1959 a typhoon struck the southern part of Nagoya flooding the entire area and destroying over 100,000 buildings. But the city has bounced back to become a major industrial centre with the headquarters and production plants of Toyota, Honda and Mitsubishi all in the area. Though not an attractive city, Nagoya functions as a rail gateway to the Japanese Alps and to Kansai, which means that most rail travellers will pass through at some stage. Osaka and Tokyo may be better known but Nagoya feels more relaxed and easier to manage than either of them.

> ### ⛩ White weddings
> Weddings have always been big business in Japan. Most of the large hotels have their own chapels, Shinto shrines and reception rooms, but Nagoya has taken the lead in building 'wedding halls' that offer a one-stop package including reception and even a fake priest to preside over a Western white wedding ceremony in an unconsecrated chapel. The popularity of films such as *Four Weddings and a Funeral* has led to the boom in Western white weddings.
>
> Newly-weds in the Tokai region which includes Nagoya spend more money on weddings than anywhere else in the country: recent figures suggest couples spend on average ¥7 million on their big day. Couples in Tokyo, by contrast, spent only ¥5.93 million on the event.
>
> Foreign residents in Japan able to project enough gravitas are donning cassock and dog collar at weekends and becoming part-time priests to fulfil demand, often turning over several weddings in one day. Genuine clergy in Japan have complained that business is being taken away from them. But in the country where appearances are everything, it's not so important that you are a priest, just that you should look and sound like one.

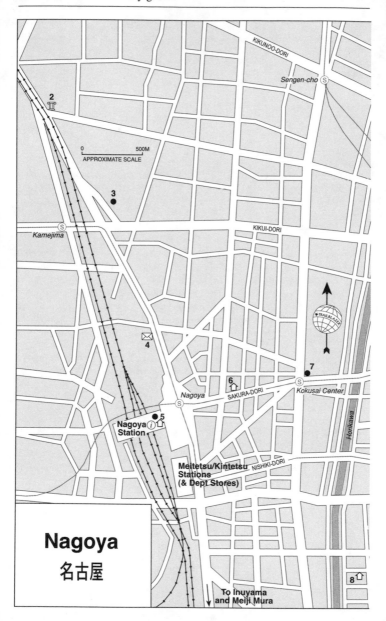

KIKUNOO-DORI

Sengen-cho Ⓢ

2

0   500M
APPROXIMATE SCALE

3

Kamejima Ⓢ

KIKUI-DORI

TRAILBLAZER

4

7

6 Ⓢ

Nagoya Ⓢ   SAKURA-DORI   Kokusai Center

Horikawa

5
Nagoya
Station

Meitetsu/Kintetsu
Stations
(& Dept Stores)   NISHIKI-DORI

Nagoya
名古屋

8

To Inuyama
and Meiji Mura

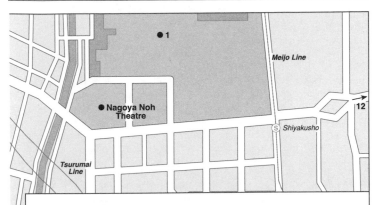

NAGOYA 名古屋

Where to stay

5	Nagoya Marriott Associa Hotel	5	名古屋マリオットアソシアホテル
6	Fitness Hotel 330 Nagoya	6	フィットネスホテル330名古屋
8	Aichi-ken Seinen Kaikan YH	8	愛知県青年会館YH
10	Ryokan Meiryu	10	旅館名龍

Other

1	Nagoya Castle	1	名古屋城
2	Commemorative Museum of Industry and Technology	2	産業技術記念館
3	Noritake Craft Center	3	ノリタケクラフトセンター
4	Central Post Office	4	中央郵便局
5	JR Takashimaya Dept Store	5	JR名古屋高島屋
7	Nagoya International Center	7	名古屋国際センター
9	Buttsu Trick Bar	9	ブッツトリックバー
11	Nagoya Port Area	11	名古屋港
12	Tokugawa Art Museum	12	徳川美術館

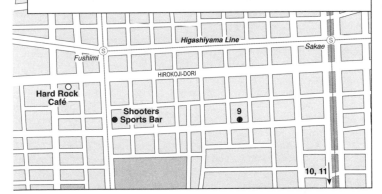

What to see and do

For a bird's eye view of Nagoya, take the express elevator from the 2nd floor of Nagoya station to the 15th, the entrance to Marriott Associa Hotel. What you'll see is a sprawling city, most spectacular when lit up at night. Don't bother with the Panorama House (¥1000), a viewing platform accessed from the 12th floor.

Nagoya Castle (daily, 9am-4:30pm, ¥500) was built in 1612 on the orders of Tokugawa Ieyasu to be a secure base along the main Tokaido Highway. The castle was razed to the ground during a WWII air raid and only three corner towers and gates survived. The donjon was reconstructed in 1959 and is known for the pair of gold dolphins on the roof. Though hard to tell from the ground, the dolphin on the north side is male and the one on the south side is female. It's worth climbing up the tower to reach the seventh floor observatory. To reach the castle, take the Meijo subway line to Shiyakusho.

After visiting the castle, look in on the 630-seat **Nagoya Noh Theater** (same times as castle; free), built in 1997. It's open to the public when there are no performances.

Tokugawa Art Museum (daily except Mon 10am-5pm, ¥1200) exhibits treasures that belonged to the Owari branch of the ruling Tokugawa family as well as sections of a 12th-century illustrated scroll of *The Tale of Genji* – though the pieces are too fragile to be kept on permanent display. The gorgeous contents of the museum are matched by an equally extravagant entry fee. Take a local train from JR Nagoya station along the Chuo line four stops to Ozone station. The museum is 10 minutes on foot from the south exit.

In the former headquarters of the Toyoda Spinning & Weaving Company is the **Toyota Commemorative Museum of Industry and Technology** (daily except Mon 9:30am-5pm, ¥500), much more interesting than it sounds. The Toyota Group was founded by Sakichi Toyoda, inventor of the automatic loom. Automobiles were only added later, by Kiichiro, Sakichi's eldest son. In the museum, the Textile and Automobile Pavilions are interactive in parts, and exhibits are informative about how prototype ideas are turned into reality.

The name 'Toyoda', incidentally, didn't change to 'Toyota' until 1935, when it was used as a brand name for export cars. It was thought that Toyota would be easier for foreigners to pronounce. The new spelling also brought the number of katakana strokes in the word to eight, which is considered lucky in Japan; Toyoda had 10 strokes. The museum is a 15-minute walk north from the Sakura-dori exit of JR Nagoya station.

Just before the Toyota Museum, on the same side of the road, is **Noritake Craft Center**. This porcelain company runs guided tours of its production line. After watching a short company promo, you walk through the factory, following the process from creation and decoration to final inspection. On one floor you'll see hand decoration on some of the special order vases, with price tags of up to ¥10 million. The tour ends in the 'tabletop gallery' – a shop window of lavish dinner sets produced for the export market (pick one up if you've got the cash!). Tours in Japanese or English run Monday-Friday at 10am and 1pm and last 90 minutes. Admission is free but call in advance (☎ 052-561 7114) to reserve a place.

● **Nagoya Port Area** South of Nagoya city, Nagoya Port has been redeveloped as a 'Leisure Zone' with a number of attractions including the **Fuji Antarctic Museum** (daily except Mon 9:30am-5pm, ¥300), on board the *Fuji*. *Fuji* was used for 18 Antarctic expeditions until its retirement to Nagoya Port in 1983. Inside are crew quarters, including kitchen, dentist surgery and barber shop, as well as operation rooms. On the top deck is a small museum about the Antarctic expeditions.

The Antarctic theme continues at **Nagoya Public Aquarium** (daily except Mon 9:30am-5/5:30pm, ¥1500), where the penguin tank recreates extreme weather conditions to make the birds feel at home. A new stadium for shark and dolphin shows opened next to the aquarium in 2001. Least interesting is the **Port Building**, which contains a Maritime Museum (daily except Mon, 9:30am-5pm, ¥300) and observation platform (daily except 3rd Mon, 9:30am-9pm, ¥300). A combination ticket for all the above costs ¥2000.

To save a few yen on the subway fare to Nagoya Port, first take a local train from JR Nagoya station one stop on the Chuo line to Kanayama station, from where you can connect up with the Meijo subway line to the terminus at Nagoyako (Nagoya Port) (¥230).

PRACTICAL INFORMATION
Station guide
Nagoya station officially welcomed in the new century with the opening of the spectacular Twin Towers immediately above the station concourse, home to Nagoya's newest luxury hotel and the JR-Takashimaya department store. The station has two main sides but for the city centre take the Sakura-dori exit. Sakura-dori is the main road heading away from the station towards Sakae. Within the station, there are plenty of coin lockers (up to ¥600).

JR lines running through or terminating at Nagoya are the **Tokaido line** (platforms 1-6) which heads east to Toyohashi and west to Gifu (see p128), the **Chuo line** (platforms 7-10) for Nakatsugawa and Matsumoto (see p150) and the **Kansai line** (platforms 11-13) for Matsusaka (see p170). The shinkansen tracks (platforms 14-17) have a separate entrance near the Taiko-dori side of the station.

Nagoya is also a junction for two private railways, the Meitetsu and Kintetsu. The stations (first Meitetsu, then Kintetsu) are a couple of minutes' walk from the Sakura-dori side of JR Nagoya. Head out of the station and turn right.

Tourist information
A tourist information office (☎ 052-541 4301, daily, 9am-7pm) is on the first floor concourse of the station. The English-speaking staff can provide city maps and accommodation lists but can't make bookings. In the same office is a JR desk where rail-pass vouchers can be exchanged (daily, 10am-6pm).

For more information, **Nagoya International Center (NIC)** (☎ 052-581 0100, Tue-Sat 9am-8:30pm, Sun 9am-5pm, closed Mon) is a 10-minute walk east from the station along Sakura-dori. The centre has newspapers, magazines, satellite TV, a library and Internet access (30 mins/¥250). If you'd like to visit a Japanese home for the afternoon ask here; bring your passport. This service is free but transport costs must be paid by the visitor.

NIC publishes the monthly *Nagoya Calendar*, which contains listings of city-wide events. *Chubu Weekly* has more articles about the area but also contains film and concert details. Finally, *Nagoya Avenues* is a bi-monthly magazine with features on the city and surrounding area. You can find all of these at NIC and some may be available from the tourist information counter at the station.

Getting around

Nagoya has an efficient subway system with four lines: Higashiyama (yellow), Meijo (purple), Tsurumai (blue) and Sakura-dori (red). Nagoya station is connected with the Higashiyama and Sakura-dori lines. A one-day subway pass costs ¥740, or subway plus bus pass is ¥850.

On the 8th of every month, the price of the subway plus bus pass is reduced to ¥620. The best deal for visitors is the **Ikomai Pass**, billed as 'ecological and economical'. Available from subway ticket offices, this costs ¥1300 and allows unlimited travel on the subway for one day and includes free entry on that day to a number of attractions, including Nagoya Castle (see p142). The pass also gives discounts at other sights, including Tokugawa Art Museum, Toyota Commemorative Museum of Industry and Technology, and Fuji Antarctic Museum. These discounts are valid for one year, so there's no rush to see the lot in one day.

Until a new off-shore airport opens in 2005, Nagoya will continue to be served by Komaki Airport, which has both domestic and international terminals. A limousine bus (30 mins, ¥870) runs from outside JR Nagoya station's Hirokoji exit.

Money

Foreign-issued Visa/MasterCards can be used at an ATM inside Meitetsu department store. From JR Nagoya station, follow signs for the 'Hirokoji exit'. Meitetsu is opposite this exit. The ATM is just inside the doors nearest to you.

Festivals

The biggest festival of the year is **Nagoya Matsuri**, a three-day event in mid-October.

Where to stay

The city's new giant, towering immediately above JR Nagoya station, is the elegant *Nagoya Marriott Associa Hotel* (☎ 052-584 1111, 🖷 584 1112, 🖵 www.associa. com/english). Japan's newest world-class hotel certainly can't be beaten for location – from the station concourse, a sky shuttle whisks you up the twin towers to the gleaming 15th floor lobby. It's hard to see how any hotel could possibly improve on the service, facilities and wall-to-wall luxury. Rooms are beautifully furnished and have spacious bathrooms. Facilities include 24-hour room service, a dedicated concierge floor and a fitness club with an indoor pool and state-of-the-art gym. Rates vary according to season but start from around ¥20,000 for a standard room. It's worth asking if there are any special deals or packages.

A five-minute walk up Sakura-dori from the station is *Fitness Hotel 330 Nagoya* (☎ 052-562 0330, 🖷 562 0331), which according to its publicity operates on 'the concept of "fitness=health" aiming at the life toward the next century'. There's no fitness centre but you do get a grey track suit instead of a dressing gown in your room. Compact but modern singles go from ¥8500. *Aichi Ken Seinen Kaikan* (☎ 052-221 6001, 🖷 204 3508) offers bargain dormitory-style accommodation (¥2992/pp for YH/HI members) and has a few private rooms. It's south-east of the station across Hori-gawa.

Finally, *Ryokan Meiryu* (☎ 052-331 8686, 🖷 321 6119, 🖵 meiryu@japan-net.ne.jp) is a homely Japanese inn with tatami rooms (none en suite). Rates are ¥5000 for one person, ¥8000 for two and ¥10,500 for three. The ryokan is a three-minute walk south-east of Kamimaezu station on the Meijo subway line.

Where to eat

Inside the station, head for Towers Plaza on the 12th and 13th floors of the JR-Takashimaya department store, where you'll find nearly every kind of Japanese food as well as a good selection of others, including Italian, Chinese and a branch of

Starbucks Coffee. The two basement floors are also crammed with food and freshly-made lunch boxes to take out. For more upmarket dining, Nagoya Marriott Associa Hotel above Takashimaya has a wide range of restaurants including *Mikuni Nagoya*, a top-class French restaurant on the 52nd floor with views over the city. *La Jolla* is a California Grill on the 15th floor, also offering panoramic views and inventive cuisine. *Ka-Un* is the hotel's best Japanese restaurant with sushi and tempura bars, as well as table and tatami seating.

After dark, the best place for entertainment is the Sakae district east of Nagoya station across Hori-gawa. *Buttsu Trick Bar* in Sakae is worth a look if only for its giant Buddha but it also does good Asian food and a range of cocktails. It's on the eighth floor of a building very close to the Princess Garden Hotel and is open evenings only from 6pm.

In the Fushimi district just west of Sakae is a *Hard Rock Café*, serving the usual burgers and fries to a young crowd (happy hour Mon-Thu 4-6:30pm). Look for it next to the Hilton Hotel. Also in Fushimi and popular with foreign residents is *Shooter's Sports Bar*, which has draught beer, pool tables, and a lunch menu from ¥790.

Side trips by rail from Nagoya

A popular side trip is to nearby **Inuyama**, known for its **castle** (daily, 9am-5pm, ¥300), perched on a hill overlooking Kiso-gawa. Built in 1537, it was partly destroyed during the division of Japan into prefectures at the beginning of the Meiji era in 1871 and after an earthquake in 1891. Four years later, what was left of the castle was handed back to the Naruse family who had originally owned it – this act of charity was, however, tempered by a condition: the castle had to be repaired. Restoration work on the donjon was completed in 1965.

The other big sight is **Meiji Mura** (daily 9:30am-5pm Mar-Oct, 9:30am-4pm Nov-Feb, ¥1600), an open-air collection of Western-style buildings from the Meiji era, including the 1898 Sapporo Telephone Exchange, St John's Church from Kyoto and a steam locomotive that chugs the short distance between 'Tokyo' and 'Nagoya' stations.

Inuyama can be accessed along the private Meitetsu Inuyama line from Meitetsu Railway's Shin-Nagoya station (¥540, 30 mins), next to the Sakura-dori exit of JR Nagoya. From Inuyama station, a bus service runs to Meiji Mura (¥410, 20 mins). For Inuyama Castle, continue on to Inuyama-Yuen station, one stop after Inuyama.

NAGANO

Situated in the centre of Honshu, Nagano is the junction of the northern, central and southern Japanese Alps, and is often referred to as the 'roof of Japan'. The city has expanded from its original site around Zenko-ji. However, the temple, a 30-minute walk north of the station, remains the focal point of the city. The extension of the shinkansen from Tokyo to Nagano in time for the 1998 Winter Olympics reduced the journey time from the capital to just 95 minutes.

What to see and do

The 1998 Winter Olympics officially began with the ringing of the bell at **Zenko-ji**. The temple is said to have been founded in the 7th century as a place

---

♛ The Olympic flame: lit and extinguished

How long does the Olympic dream last? Perhaps only as long as the athletes and sponsors are in town. Within a day of the 1998 closing ceremony, all the Coca Cola outlets had packed up and closed down, and the international media village stood deserted. What does the city do with its vast arena built for the Games? The stadium built for the opening and closing ceremonies is now used occasionally for pro-baseball and high-school baseball tournaments.

Central Square, on Chuo-dori heading towards Zenko-ji, was the venue for the nightly medal ceremony during the Games. A sign next to the square reads in a variety of languages: 'It is our sincerest hope that in addition to its role as the venue for the official medal award ceremonies for the Olympic Games, that Central Square be used by the public as a place to gather and to enjoy exhibitions and festivals, and that it becomes the core of a growing number of activities in central Nagano'. It is now a disused car park. This is the reality of life after the Olympics, when the athletes, crowds and TV cameras have moved on.

---

to house the golden triad, a sacred image of the Buddha. It is never displayed in public but every seven years an exact copy is brought out as part of the Gokaicho ceremony – the next will be in 2003. Inside the main hall, people gather around the statue of Binzuru, considered to be Buddha's most intelligent follower; by rubbing the statue, they hope their own aches and pains will be rubbed away. Access to the pitch-black passage containing the 'key to paradise' is by ticket from vending machines (daily 9am-4:30pm, ¥500) inside the main hall. Anyone who touches the key is assured eternal salvation. Anyone who doesn't can buy another ticket and try again. Don't go in if you're claustrophobic or afraid of the dark.

To avoid the crowds, arrive in the early evening or better still at dawn, when the high priest and priestess make an appearance to pray for the salvation of visiting pilgrims. The starting time of this daily ceremony depends on the season – in the summer, it's as early as 5:30am, in December at 7am; check the exact times with the tourist office. You can buy a guide for ¥50 at the information office on the left side of the approach to the temple.

Though it's possible to take a bus to the temple from the station, it's easy to walk the 30 minutes north up Chuo-dori. Heading up the main street lined with shops and department stores, look out on the right for **Saiko-ji**, a small temple founded in 1199; a leaflet is available. Much further up the road, just before you reach the start of the main path towards the temple, look out on your right for **Fujiya Ryokan** (see p148). From the street, the building looks more like a Western hotel than a classic Japanese ryokan but step into the entrance hall and the atmosphere immediately changes. The building first opened as an inn for travellers in 1661 and is still in business today. Shops, soba restaurants and stalls line the street leading up to the temple's main gate.

To relive the Olympics, visit the **M-Wave Arena**, speed-skating venue during the Games and now home to the **Nagano Olympic Museum** (daily except

Tue, 10am-4pm, ¥700). On display are Olympic medals, pictures and a digital video database of clips from previous Games. Pride of place is given to Hiroyasu Shimizu's skates. Shimizu became a national hero when he took gold in the 500m speed-skating event and bronze in the 1000m in the M-Wave Arena. A 3D-video theatre shows highlights of the Games, including the opening ceremony and Shimizu's moment of triumph. While you're here, take a look in the vast arena; its suspended wooden roof is supposed to resemble ocean waves. In summer, the arena is used for a variety of events including a sumo tournament. The skating rink is open from October to March (daily, 10am-6pm).

To reach the M-Wave Arena, take a Nagaden bus (¥300, 20 mins) bound for Yashima from bus stop No 1 on the ground floor of the station east exit and get out at 'M-Wave-mae'.

PRACTICAL INFORMATION
Station guide
Rebuilt for the Olympics, Nagano station has two sides, East and Zenko-ji. Take the latter for the city centre and Zenko-ji. Coin lockers (up to ¥500) are near both exits. Shinkansen services depart from platforms 11-14 and have a separate entrance to other JR lines. There are lifts between the main concourse and street level.

Tourist information
Nagano City TIC (☎ 026-226 5626, daily, 9am-6pm) is on the station concourse. English-speaking staff are available most days. Ask for leaflets in English as it's mostly only Japanese brochures on display. Staff will book accommodation for you (Nagano city only) and can advise on the best places to ski/hike. They have bus timetables and information on late-season skiing.

Getting around
The private Nagano Dentetsu Railway, known as 'Nagaden', operates in the Nagano area (see p150). The entrance to the underground station is outside the Zenko-ji exit of JR Nagano station. The main bus terminal is at street level outside the Zenko-ji exit. Stop No 1 is for buses to Zenko-ji.

If you're considering the Tateyama–Kurobe Alpine Route (see p126), highway buses (¥2300 one-way, 100 mins) operate from April to November between Nagano station and Ogisawa, starting point for the Alpine Route west to Toyama.

Money
The ATM on the ground floor of Heiando, the book store opposite the station, accepts foreign Visa cards.

Where to stay
A good business hotel is **Hotel Nagano Avenue** (☎ 026-223 1123, ▤ 223 7690; ¥6000/S, ¥12,000/Tw). Facilities include a restaurant, coin laundry and sauna. **Holiday Inn Express Nagano** (☎ 026-264 6000, ▤ 264 5511; ¥8000/S, ¥14,000/D/Tw), built for the Olympics, has very comfortable rooms.

Zenko-ji Kyojuin Youth Hostel (☎/▤ 026-232 2768; ¥2900 YH(HI), ¥3900 non-members, no meals) is just outside the main temple compound. Bags must be left in the entrance hall lockers so as not to damage the specially hand-made tatami in all the dormitory rooms (the building is over 100 years old). It's 20 minutes on foot from the station up Chuo-dori.

Finally, anyone not on a budget should consider a night at one of the oldest and most atmospheric Japanese inns you're likely to find outside Kyoto.

Fujiya Ryokan (☎ 026-232 1241, ▤ 232 1243; from ¥9000/pp inc two meals) is near the main entrance gate to Zenko-ji, on the right-hand side as you approach the temple. It has wooden floorboards and small hidden gardens.

Where to eat

To the left as you take the Zenko-ji exit of Nagano station are a number of casual restaurants including pizza and pasta chain *Capricciosa* (daily, 11am-10pm), *Pronto coffee shop* (which turns into a bar in the evenings), *McDonald's* and soba and ramen restaurants. All of these are on the second floor (the same level as the station concourse). For take-out lunches, try the food hall in the basement of Tokyu department store outside the Zenko-ji exit.

Opposite the station is *Heiando Books and Café* (daily, 10am-9pm). The café is on the third floor and has fresh juices as well as coffee/cake sets. There are plenty of soba restaurants on the approach to Zenko-ji, including *Fujikian*, along Chuo-dori opposite a small branch post office. The name is written in kanji in grey letters above the front. Seating is on tatami or at wooden tables. The tempura and soba (from ¥1000) are delicious.

A little further up the same road (just before the final approach to Zenko-ji begins), on the corner nearly opposite the Fujiya Ryokan, is *Daimaru,* another soba restaurant with low wooden tables. Look out for the large shop-front window where you can see the owner preparing the noodles. It's a fraction cheaper than Fujikian. Note that most soba restaurants close around 6/7pm.

Suyakame Miso is easy to spot because it's on a corner as you approach the temple and they have a sign in English; it does grilled rice balls with miso (soybean paste) and miso-flavoured ice cream – sounds awful but tastes good.

Monzen Gyoko is an 'International Beer Restaurant' along Chuo-dori, just before the covered Gondo arcade. It's a busy place with long tables and an equally long menu of meat, fish and side dishes like salad and garlic fried potatoes. Despite the Visa sign outside, they will only reluctantly accept foreign-issued Visa cards.

Heading from the station up Chuo-dori, *Café comme Ca* is on the ground floor of the Again department store, shortly after the Howdy Seibu department store on the left-hand side. Good coffee and a wide selection of cakes are served in this gleaming white café.

NAGANO 長野

Where to stay

2	Zenko-ji Kyoju-in YH	2	善光寺教授院 ユース ホステル
5	Fujiya Ryokan	5	藤屋旅館
10	Hotel Nagano Avenue	10	ホテル ナガノ アベニュー
12	Holiday Inn Express Nagano	12	ホリディインエクスプレス長野

Where to eat

3	Suyakame Miso	3	すやかめみそ
4	Daimaru	4	大丸
6	Fujikian	6	藤木庵
7	Monzen Gyoko	7	門前漁港
11	Café Comme Ça	11	Cafe Comme Ca
15	Capricciosa/Pronto	15	カプリチョーザ/プロント

Other

1	Zenko-ji	1	善光寺
8	Central Post Office	8	中央郵便局
9	Saiko-ji	9	西光寺
13	Nagano Tokyu Dept Store	13	東急
14	Heiando/Visa ATM (International)	14	平安堂/Visa ATM(インターナショナル)

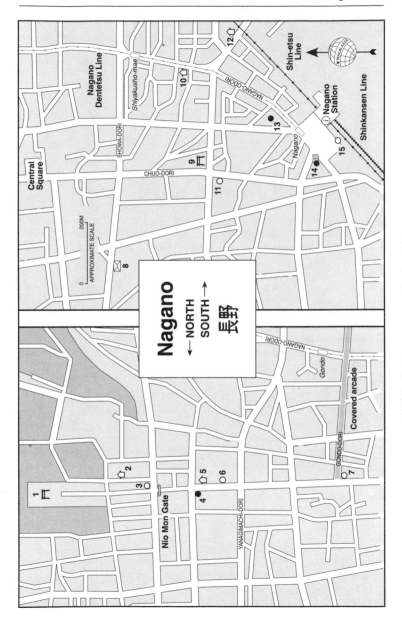

Nagano
← NORTH
SOUTH →
長野

Central Square

Nagano Dentetsu Line

SHOWA-DORI

Shiyakusho-mae

CHUO-DORI

APPROXIMATE SCALE
200M
0

8

9

10

11

12

13

14

15

Nagano Station

Shin-etsu Line

Shinkansen Line

NAGANO-DORI

Nagano

Nio Mon Gate

YANAGIMACHI-DORI

GONDO-DORI

Gondo

NAGANO-DORI

Covered arcade

1

2

3

4

5

6

7

Side trips by rail from Nagano

A possible side trip by private Nagano Dentetsu Railway is to the small town of **Obuse** (20 mins by express train, ¥750 one-way). The town was a stop on the old highway linking the Japan Sea with Edo (Tokyo) and now boasts a number of museums, temples and gardens.

The biggest draw is **Ganshoin Temple** (daily, 9am-5pm Apr-Oct, 9:30am-4:30pm Nov-Mar; closed Wed Dec-Mar, ¥200), which belongs to the same Zen Buddhist sect as Eihei-ji (see p132). The temple is renowned for its ceiling painting of a phoenix 'staring in eight directions' by the artist Katsushika Hokusai (1760-1849). Pick up a map of Obuse from the tourist information office at Nagano station. The lockers (¥300) at Obuse station are suitable for day packs.

From Obuse, it's a further 20 minutes to the rail terminus at **Yudanaka** (¥1230 one-way by express train from Nagano), from where buses take 30 minutes to reach the vast skiing terrain of **Shiga Kogen Heights**, north-east of Nagano in the centre of Joshin-Etsu Kogen National Park. With mountain peaks of over 2000m and 22 ski grounds connected by chair lifts, this is the place to go for late-season skiing (usually until the end of the first week of May) on the slopes that hosted the downhill slalom courses during the Nagano Winter Olympics. A one-day lift pass costs ¥4800. Check with tourist information at Nagano station for ski season dates. Direct buses (¥1800 one-way) also operate during the ski season between Nagano station (east exit, stop No 3 or 4) and Shiga Kogen.

There's more skiing in **Hakuba**, some 30km west of Nagano. 'Highland Express' buses (¥1400 one-way) operate from Nagano station to Hakuba's main ski resort of Happo-One, but the area is best accessed by JR as a side trip by rail from Matsumoto (see p154).

MATSUMOTO

Surrounded by mountains, Matsumoto is an ancient castle town and a gateway to the north-western corner of Nagano prefecture. The 3000m peaks of the Japanese Alps form a backdrop to the west of the city. Locals like to think of Matsumoto as not the heart but the 'navel' of Japan – whichever it is, thousands visit the city every year to see one of the country's best-preserved castles.

What to see and do

Fifteen minutes on foot north of the station is **Matsumoto Castle**, considered to be one of the finest castles in Japan. A small fortress was first built here in 1504 but this was remodelled and expanded in 1593 to become what still stands today. It's a rare example of a Japanese castle which is not a 20th-century concrete reconstruction. The fortification once dominated the city skyline but the view is now obscured by office blocks and the castle remains invisible until the final approach.

The five-storey donjon is known as 'crow castle' because the outside walls are mainly black. The design is unusual because the castle is built on a plain rather than a hill, but it still contains traditional defensive elements: the hidden floor, sunken passageways, specially constructed holes in the wall to drop stones on the enemy below and incredibly steep stairs to make an attack on the castle difficult for intruders. Tacked on to the side is the moon-viewing room, a later addition and the venue for 'moon-viewing parties', when invited guests could stare up at the moon while enjoying a cup or two of saké. Tickets (¥520) for the castle include admission to the nearby **Japan Folklore Museum**. Both are open daily, 8:30am-4:30pm.

Ten minutes on foot north of the castle is **Kaichi Gakko** (daily Mar-Nov but closed on Sun Dec-Feb, 8:30am-4:30pm, ¥310), a former elementary school built in 1876 which looks like something out of little England. The oldest Western-style school building in Japan, it remained open for 90 years. There's proof inside that, contrary to popular belief, the education system in Japan is not all work. The classrooms are open to the public and there's also a room dedicated to extra-curricular activities, which included ice-skating (note the 'geta-skates' that look uncomfortable and dangerous to wear – the geta provided by some ryokans seem comfortable in comparison!). Upstairs, in the main hall, look out for the coil of rope used in *tsunahiki*, a tug-of-war tournament between classes that took place every year at the school athletics festival.

Finally, even if you're not staying at Marumo Ryokan (see p153), it's worth heading over to the **Nakamachi district** along the south side of Metoba-gawa, where you'll find old houses, craft shops and cafés.

PRACTICAL INFORMATION
Station guide
As trains pull into Matsumoto station, a female voice virtually sings the station's name to arriving passengers. From the platforms, follow signs to the Central Exit/Matsumoto Castle.

Passing through the ticket barrier, you arrive at the main concourse on the second floor, where you'll find a revolving model of Matsumoto Castle. Take the stairs down to the ground and turn left at the bottom for coin lockers (all sizes). There is an elevator from concourse to street level but assistance should first be sought from station staff. The bus terminal is beneath Espa department store across the street from the station.

Tourist information
The small tourist information office (☎ 0263-32 2814, daily April-Oct 9:30am-6pm, Nov-March 9am-5:30pm) is to the

right of the station exit at street level. Friendly, English-speaking staff can assist with same-day reservations and will provide travel information.

Getting around
Matsumoto city is compact enough to visit on foot. The private Matsumoto Dentetsu line runs from Matsumoto station to Shin-Shimashima (see p154). Matsumoto Airport has connections with Osaka, Fukuoka, Sapporo and Matsuyama. A shuttle bus operates between the airport and the station.

Internet
You can surf the net at People's Restaurant and Bar (30 mins; ¥200 + one drink), see p154.

Festivals
An outdoor performance of Noh is held in the grounds of Matsumoto Castle on the

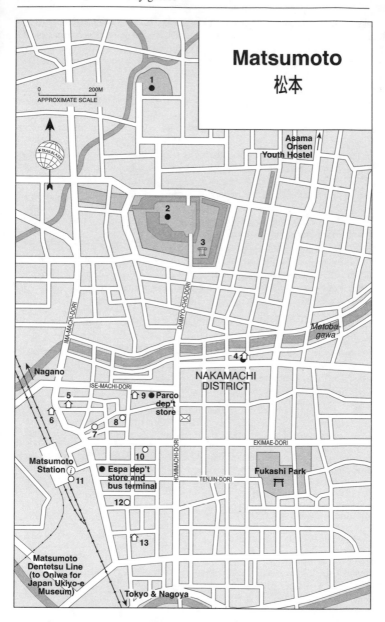

Matsumoto
松本

0   200M
APPROXIMATE SCALE

★TRAILBLAZER★

Asama
Onsen
Youth Hostel

1

2

3

Metoba-
gawa

Nagano

4

NAKAMACHI
DISTRICT

IMA-MACHI-DORI

DAIMYO-CHO-DORI

ISE-MACHI-DORI

5

6

7

8

9 ● Parco
dep't
store

10

Matsumoto
Station ⓘ

11

● Espa dep't
store and
bus terminal

12

13

HOMMACHI-DORI

EKIMAE-DORI

TENJIN-DORI

Fukashi Park

Matsumoto
Dentetsu Line
(to Oniwa for
Japan Ukiyo-e
Museum)

Tokyo & Nagoya

evening of August 8th. The performance is lit by bonfires with the brooding presence of the castle as a backdrop. On November 3rd, Matsumoto Castle Festival features a samurai parade and puppet shows.

Where to stay
Top of the range is *Hotel Buena Vista* (☎ 0263-37 0111, 🖂 37 0666), which is very plush and very expensive. Between July and October singles cost ¥11,000 and twins ¥21,000. Rates are reduced slightly outside this peak season. Opened in late 2001, *Roynet Hotel Matsumoto* (☎ 0263-37 5000, 🖂 37 5505, 🖳 www.roynet.co.jp, ¥9048/S, ¥11,905/D, ¥16,191/Tw, ¥20,000 /Tr) is just a few minutes on foot from the main station exit and next to Parco department store. It's a hyper efficient place with automatic check-in, clean, compact rooms and a coin laundry. A more economical option is *Hotel New Station* (☎ 0263-35 3850, 🖂 35 3851; ¥6800/S, ¥13,600/Tw), only two minutes on foot from the station. The rooms are basic but all have attached bath. Just across the street, a newer business hotel is *Hotel Mor-Schein* (☎ 0263-32

0031, 🖂 32 0328; ¥6700/S, ¥11,000/D, ¥13,000/Tw). *Marumo Ryokan* (☎ 0263-32 0115, 🖂 35 2251; ¥5000/pp), a traditional inn in the Nakamachi district by Metoba-gawa, has tatami rooms (none en suite) with a fantastic wooden bath.

The nearest youth hostel is at Asama-Onsen. Take a bus from stop No 7 (from the terminal under Espa department store) bound for Asama-Onsen and get off at 'Matsumoto Dai-ichi Koko-mae' (20 mins). *Asama-Onsen Youth Hostel* (☎ 0263-46 1335; ¥3200/YH(HI), ¥4200 non-members, no meals) is a bit grey and depressing.

Where to eat
There's a good coffee shop on the station concourse opposite the JR ticket desk. Right next to the tourist information office outside the station is *Café de Pomme*, which is not French at all but a restaurant that specializes in curries – lunch deals including nan bread and salad cost ¥980. Also near the station you'll find branches of *Mister Donut* and *Doutor*.

One of Matsumoto's specialities is *basashi*, raw horsemeat that's also popular

MATSUMOTO 松本

Where to stay
4 Marumo Ryokan	4 まるも旅館
5 Hotel Mor-Schein	5 ホテルモルシャン
6 Hotel New Station	6 ホテルニューステーション
9 Roynet Hotel Matsumoto	9 ロイネットホテル松本
13 Hotel Buena Vista	13 ホテルブエナビスタ

Where to eat
4 Kissa Marumo	4 喫茶まるも
7 Mister Donut	7 ミスタードーナッツ
8 Doutor Coffee	8 ドトールコーヒー
9 Skylark	9 すかいらーく
10 Yoneyoshi	10 米芳
11 Café de Pomme	11 Café de ポム
12 People's Restaurant and Bar	12 People's Restaurant and Bar

Other
1 Kaichi Gakko	1 開智学校
2 Matsumoto Castle	2 松本城
3 Japan Folklore Museum	3 日本民俗資料館

in Kumamoto (see p354). A good place to try it is *Yoneyoshi*, less than five minutes from the station on the right-hand side of Ekimae-dori; look for the white hanging curtain and the glass cabinet outside that contains a bowl and vase with a horse painted on them.It's an izakaya-style place, with seats along the counter and at tables. If you're not sure what to have, go for one of the set meals (teishoku). If you want to try basashi, go for the 'Yoneyoshi Teishoku' (¥1650).

In the evening, a good place to search out is *People's Restaurant and Bar* (daily, 6pm-2/3am), across from the small park area opposite the Buena Vista Hotel.

There's a menu in English, big portions of pasta, and prices are reasonable. This place sometimes has live music. It's on the second floor but look for the English sign on the street outside. *Skylark*, a 24-hour family restaurant on the first floor of Hotel Roynet Matsumoto, is open to anyone (not just hotel guests) in need of some late night sustenance.

If you're in the Nakamachi area, it would be a shame to miss stopping at *Kissa Marumo* (daily, 8am-8pm), a café attached to Marumo Ryokan (see above), which plays classical music and serves good coffee, ice cream and mouthwatering cakes.

Side trips by rail from Matsumoto

On the outskirts of Matsumoto is the **Japan Ukiyo-e Museum** (daily except Mon, 10am-4:30pm, ¥1000), a private museum built by the Sakai Family which houses a collection of over 100,000 Japanese woodblock prints – only a fraction are on display at any one time. The current owner is the 11th generation of the Sakai family and still travels the world looking for new acquisitions. To reach the museum by public transport, take the private Matsumoto Dentetsu Railway from Matsumoto station to tiny Oniwa station. Ask at the Oniwa ticket office for a map with directions to the museum; it is about a 15-minute walk from the station.

Continuing along Matsumoto Dentetsu Railway to the terminus at Shin-Shimashima (¥680) and transferring to a bus (75 mins; ¥2500) brings you to the hiking resort of **Kamikochi**, at an altitude of 1500m right in the centre of the Japanese Alps National Park. Japanese holidaymakers have flocked to Kamikochi ever since British missionary Walter Weston scaled the peaks at the end of the 19th century and popularized mountaineering. Kamikochi is open only from late April to early November, after which heavy snow shuts off road access for the winter.

In winter, the best **skiing** is 60km north-west of Matsumoto in **Hakuba**. Local trains run 60km along the Oito line from Matsumoto to Hakuba in 90-110 minutes. Limited expresses (starting from either Shinjuku or Nagoya) stop in Matsumoto before heading along the Oito line to Hakuba in 60 minutes.

From Hakuba station, buses take five minutes (¥180) to **Happo-One** ski resort, which has a network of fast gondolas and chair lifts up to peaks as high as 1900m – there's a mixture of runs suitable for all ski levels. Skis and boots can be hired from a number of shops in the resort. A one-day lift pass costs ¥4600 or half-day is ¥3300. The ski season lasts from December to April.

Instead of backtracking to Matsumoto, it's possible to continue north along the Oito line from Hakuba to the terminus on the Japan Sea coast at **Itoigawa**, a point of connection with the rail route west to Toyama and beyond (see p124). From Hakuba, trains run as far as Minami-Otari, where it's necessary to change trains for the last leg of the journey to Itoigawa.

TAKAYAMA

Deep in the mountains, in the region known traditionally as Hida, Takayama is deservedly one of the most popular destinations in central Honshu, combining as it does ancient traditions with a stunning natural location. Often referred to as 'little Kyoto', Takayama boasts temples, shrines, small museums, traditional shops and inns. As a result it gets very busy, particularly during the spring and autumn festivals, when 300,000 people come to watch the parade of floats.

The greatest pleasure, however, comes not from the museums or tourist sights but from the chance to wander round the old, narrow streets of wooden houses and discover a part of Japan that has been largely airbrushed out of the big cities. Set aside enough time to forget the 'sights' and enjoy the atmosphere; two or three days would be ideal. Takayama is also a good place to hunt around for souvenirs, particularly lacquerware, wood craft and pottery.

What to see and do

One of Takayama's many highlights is a visit to the daily **morning markets** (6/7am-12pm). One is right outside Takayama Jinya (see p156), the other on the banks of Miya-gawa. Every morning, women from the surrounding area come here to sell vegetables, flowers and locally-made crafts.

During the Edo period, **Takayama Jinya** (daily, 8:45am-4:30pm, ¥420) was used as the government building for Gifu prefecture. It's now open to the public but most of the rooms are empty; tours are sometimes available in English (enquire at the main entrance). One or two of the rooms need little explanation;

⛩ Sukyo Mahikari – a new religious movement

Look out on the bus ride back to Takayama from the Folk Village for the **Main World Shrine** (daily, 9:30am-4pm, free), along Highway 158 at the bottom of the hill and instantly recognizable from its elaborate gold roof with a red sphere perched on top.

You won't find this place on any official maps of Takayama because it is home to Sukyo Mahikari, one of Japan's 'new religions' that have sprung up in the postwar years. Mahikari is described as 'true light, a cleansing energy sent by the Creator God that both spiritually awakens and tunes the soul to its divine purpose'.

The movement began in 1960 when Yoshikazu Okada founded the 'Lucky and Healthy Sunshine Children'. In order to be taken more seriously, the name was changed over the years until in 1974 it became Sukyo Mahikari, and Okada was replaced at the top by a woman called Keishu, who he proclaimed to be his daughter. Anyone is welcome to visit this bizarre shrine; the twin towers at the entrance look like minarets, an enormous fish tank stretches across the inside wall, there's a pipe organ that wouldn't be out of place in a cathedral, and a hall with a seating capacity of 4500. The sheer scale of the place is overwhelming.

the torture room, for example, tells its own story. Look out for the old toilet in one of the rooms, with the helpful 'out of use' sign on it – it would be a desperate visitor who felt the need to relieve him/herself in front of crowds of sightseers.

If you're not here at festival time (see p158) you can see four of the large floats used during the festival at **Takayama Yatai Kaikan** (Float Exhibition Hall), open daily 8:30am-5pm, ¥820; the floats change three times a year, in March, July and November. Each float would cost the equivalent of $4 million to replace. A tape commentary in English is available.

The main temple district is just east of Enako-gawa in **Higashiyama**, which is a little hilly but still a great area to explore on foot. The map available from the tourist information office has a suggested walking tour of the area. The youth hostel (see p159) is part of Tensho-ji.

● **Hida Folk Village area** Twenty minutes out of town along Highway 158, in the hills overlooking Takayama, is **Hida Folk Village** (daily 8:30am-5pm, ¥700). Over 30 traditional farmhouses and merchant cottages from rural areas have been moved here and restored. On a fine day it's a great mini-escape from the town below but since the village is all open air it's not so much fun in the rain. As well as the buildings, traditional crafts like woodcarving and weaving have also been preserved and there are displays inside some of the houses. To reach the Folk Village take a bus from stop No 6 at the terminal outside the station. A ¥900 ticket available from the bus terminal includes return bus ride and entry to the village.

TAKAYAMA 高山

Where to stay

2	Tenshoji Youth Hostel	2	天照寺ユースホステル
10	Best Western Hotel Takayama	10	ベストウェスタンホテル高山
12	Hotel Associa Takayama Resort	12	ホテルアソシア高山リゾート
13	Minshuku Sosuke	13	民宿惣助

Where to eat

3	Arisu	3	ありす
4	Masakatsu Tonkatsu	4	政かつ とんかつ
6	Belgins Bells	6	ベルギンズベル
7	Bistro Mieux	7	ビストロミュー
11	McDonald's	11	マクドナルド

Other

1	Takayama Yatai Kaikan	1	高山屋台会館
5	Morning Markets	5	朝市
8	Central Post Office	8	中央郵便局
9	Takayama Jinya	9	高山陣屋
14	Hida Folk Village	14	飛騨高山民族村

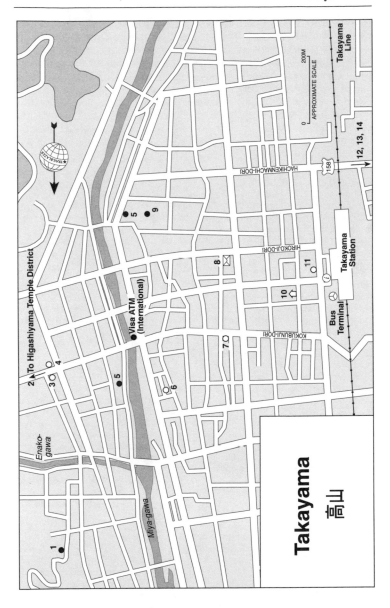

Takayama
高山

To Higashiyama Temple District

Enako-gawa

Miya-gawa

Visa ATM
(International)

TRAILPLAZA

HACHIKENMACHI-DORI

HIROKOJI-DORI

KOKUBUNJI-DORI

Takayama
Station

Takayama
Line

Bus
Terminal

12, 13, 14

158

200M

0

APPROXIMATE SCALE

A short walk down the hill from the Folk Village, very young children might like the **Teddy Bear Eco Village** (daily 10am-6pm, ¥600), a museum full of bears from all over the world, the oldest of which dates back to 1903. In the ecology corner, there's a display of how real bears are suffering as a result of environmental destruction.

Of more interest is **Takayama Museum of Art** (daily 9am-5pm, ¥1300) which has a large collection of glassware from the 16th to 20th centuries. It's in a modern building two minutes further down the road from the Teddy Bear Eco Village. The bus that stops at the Hida Folk Village also stops outside the museum, so you can visit the village, then walk to the art museum and catch a bus back into town from there.

PRACTICAL INFORMATION
Station guide
The small station gives a hint of the scale of Takayama itself. A coin locker room containing large ¥500 lockers is open daily, 7am-9pm. Turn right as you go out of the station and it's on the right.

Tourist information
Hida TIC (☎ 0577-32 5328, daily 8:30am-5/6:30pm) is in a wooden booth outside the station. The English-speaking staff are very knowledgeable and will help book same-day accommodation. Takayama isn't as shamelessly geared towards tourists as Karuizawa (see p117) but you will almost certainly not be alone here. The advantage of this is that there are plenty of signs in English.

Getting around
Takayama is best negotiated on foot, though tourist rickshaws are an emergency standby.

Alternatively, Rent A Cycle (one hour ¥300, ¥200 for every hour thereafter) is to the right as you leave the station.

A bus service operates between Takayama and Matsumoto (90 mins). Since 1999, when a tunnel along the route was opened, the service has operated year-round. There are also highway buses linking Takayama with Shinjuku in Tokyo, and Osaka. For schedules, enquire at the tourist office.

Money
An ATM that accepts foreign Visa cards is up Kokubunji-dori, on the right-hand side, just before you cross Kaji-bashi bridge.

Festivals
Takayama is known for its two annual **float festivals**, when 300-year old floats are paraded through the streets. One is in spring (Apr 14th-15th) and the other in autumn (Oct 9th-10th). Look out around town for signs in English about the different floats. One sign reveals that a float puppet show was prohibited in 1892 because a scene involving an 'exotic woman's dance', during which 'a lion's head suddenly comes out of her mid-section' was deemed immoral. The scene was not reinstated until 1984.

Local records reveal that in 1697 Takayama was home to no fewer than 56 saké breweries. Over 300 years later, the number has shrunk to eight, though the popularity of the drink does not seem to have diminished. Every year in January and February, saké breweries in Takayama open their doors to the public and organize promotions where you can try their products for free – an excellent winter warmer. For further details, enquire at the tourist information office.

Where to stay
Top of the list has to be *Hotel Associa Takayama Resort* (☎ 0577-36 0001, ▤ 36 0188, ☐ www.associa.com/english). JR owned and operated, this is where to head

for first-class luxury in the hills overlooking the town. Expect spacious en-suite rooms, the hotel's own hot spring, two high-quality restaurants and impeccable service. The buffet breakfast is recommended. Standard twins are ¥18,000, deluxe twins are ¥28,000 and triples are ¥30,000 (10% discount with rail pass). A free shuttle bus service runs between Takayama station and the hotel (a 10-minute journey). Next door is **Kur Alp Spa** (daily 10am-9pm), a hot spring leisure complex with 21 different spas and a water slide. It's connected to the hotel by an underground passage and hotel guests receive discounted entry.

One of Takayama's newest hotels is the *Best Western Hotel Takayama* (☎ 0577-37 2000, 🖹 37 2005; ¥6500/S, ¥11,000/D). It's a five-minute walk east of the station and has rooms and facilities you would expect from an international chain.

The best ryokan in Takayama can set you back up to ¥25,000 (inc two meals) but minshuku are a much more affordable option. A very homely minshuku, a short walk behind the station, is *Sosuke* (☎ 0577-32 0818, 🖹 33 5570; 🖳 www.irorisosuke.com), which charges ¥7700 per person with two meals or ¥4700 without.

Cheapest of all and maybe the most atmospheric place to stay is *Tenshoji Youth Hostel* (☎ 0577-32 6345, 🖹 35 2986). Rates are ¥2800 for YH/HI members and ¥3800 for others; an extra ¥1000 will get you your own room. Lights go out at 10pm in the dorms. Cycles can be rented here for ¥800 per day and a map of places to eat around the temple area is available from the front desk. The hostel is 20 minutes on foot east from the station across the Miya-gawa and

Enaka-gawa rivers, at Tensho-ji in Higashiyama.

Where to eat
Masakatsu Tonkatsu (daily except Tue 11am-2pm, 5-8pm) on Yasugawa-dori is a small place that serves large portions of melt-in-the-mouth tonkatsu. Seating is at a few tables or along the counter. This is a great place to go if you're hungry. Almost directly opposite is *Arisu* (daily except Wed, 11am-2pm, 4:30-8pm), which serves a variety of set meals for ¥1000-1800. The cheapest deal is the 'service lunch' for ¥850. The menu is a mixture of Japanese and Western food and there are pictures for easy ordering.

Belgins Bells (daily except Tue, 6pm-12am), a pub restaurant run by a Swiss expat serving a mix of pizza, meat and fish dishes, has become something of a travel guidebook institution – the chances are you'll bump into other foreign travellers here eager for a taste of Switzerland in this small wooden restaurant in a quiet corner of town.

Bistro Mieux (daily except Wed, 11am-1:30pm and 5-9:30pm) is a five-minute walk from the station along Kokubunji St. Creative French food is presented with flair and there's a good selection of wines. Seating is at a high counter, or on tatami mats in the stylish back room, where they've thoughtfully provided space underneath the tables to put your legs. The dinner menu starts from ¥4000 but lunch menus are ¥1500-3500. The three-course ¥1500 set lunch is excellent value.

Anyone desperate for fast food will be glad to know there's a branch of *McDonald's* opposite the station, underneath the Washington Hotel.

KANAZAWA

Though somewhat isolated on the Japan Sea coast, the variety of sights in Kanazawa more than repays the effort of the journey.

In 1580 the Maedas, the second largest clan in feudal-era Japan, settled here. Peace and stability followed and Kanazawa quickly became a prosperous centre for the silk and gold lacquer industries. As its citizens became wealthy,

Kanazawa's arts and culture scene began to flourish. Still today Kanazawa has a reputation for its patronage of 'high-class' arts such as Noh and the tea ceremony.

Apart from the much-hyped Kenrokuen garden there are other surprises, such as well-preserved geisha and samurai districts and a working Noh theatre. The city also functions as a gateway to the Noto Peninsula, a knuckle of land that juts out into the Japan Sea north of the city. And just for good measure, a short train ride away is the intriguing UFO town of Hakui (see p164).

What to see and do

The first major stop on the bus to the city centre is at **Omicho**, a daily indoor market for fish, fruit and vegetables. For the main shopping and eating district called Katamachi, stay on the bus until **Kohrinbo**. Most of the sights described below are within walking distance of Kohrinbo.

● **Kenrokuen and around** Everyone visits Kanazawa to see **Kenrokuen** (daily Mar 1st-Oct 15th 7am-6pm, Oct 16th-Feb 28/29th, 8am-4:30 pm, ¥300), rated as one of the top three gardens in Japan. Inside, professional photographers wait around for the tour groups but if you can find some space away from the crowds, a couple of hours can easily be spent wandering round the grounds.

Constructed 200 years ago as the garden for Kanazawa Castle (of which just one gate remains), Kenrokuen is spread over 11.4 hectares and contains about 12,000 trees. The number six (roku) in the garden name refers to the six attributes of a perfect garden: vastness, seclusion, careful arrangement, antiquity, water and panoramic views. Water features in particular are everywhere – including the first fountain ever placed in a Japanese garden. Kenrokuen is in the city centre, 15 minutes by bus from the station. Maps are available at the entrance.

Close to Kenrokuen is the **Prefectural Art Museum** (daily 9:30am-5pm, ¥350), full of hand-crafted lacquer cabinets, fancy cosmetic boxes, decorated plates, hanging scrolls and shoji screens. Across the street is **Ishikawa Prefectural Noh Theater** (daily except Mon, 9am-5pm, free). Performances (some free) are held on many weekends throughout the year. If there are no performances, it's possible to take a look inside (enquire at the office).

● **Higashiyama, Teramachi and Nagamachi districts** Across Asano-gawa is **Higashiyama**, Kanazawa's former geisha quarter, where you'll find a few streets lined with old geisha houses, instantly recognizable by their wooden latticed windows. Tea and coffee shops are now open in some of the houses but the area still retains a traditional charm and in the early evening there's the chance of spotting a geisha.

Opposite: Top: In their rush to visit Kyoto's Nijo Castle, most people miss the tiny Shinsen-en garden (see p191) which lies just outside. **Bottom left:** Himeji Castle's wooden interior (see p205) is just as striking as its celebrated white exterior. **Bottom right:** The water hasn't yet run dry at this old drinking fountain in Takayama (see p155). (Photos © Richard Brasher).

More than 90% of Japan's gold leaf is produced in Kanazawa, and it's in Higashiyama that you'll find the **Sakuda Gold and Silver Leaf Shop**, where the most expensive item for sale is a pair of gold leaf screens for ¥3 million. At the other end of the scale are gold-leaf boiled sweets and telephone cards, but there's no charge at all for using the gold and platinum toilets on the second floor.

A JR bus heads out to the Higashiyama district (rail passes are accepted). Buses leave from the JR bus stop outside Kanazawa station's east exit. Get off just after crossing Asano-gawa.

Temple lovers should head south of Sai-gawa to the **Teramachi district**. The most famous is Myoryu-ji, better known as **Ninja-dera** (daily, 9am-4pm, ¥700). A defensive stronghold as well as a temple, rooms contain trick doors, false exits, secret tunnels and pits – no wonder you have to go on a guided tour (reservations required; call ☎ 0762-41 2877). Tours are only in Japanese, so ask at the tourist office inside Kanazawa station for an English translation. To reach the temple, take a bus from the station to the Nomachi-Hirokoji stop.

The **Nagamachi district** is an area of narrow cobbled streets with a few preserved samurai houses. It's a pleasant surprise to stumble upon Nagamachi, a few minutes' walk west of the busy Katamachi shopping district. A **samurai house** that belonged to the wealthy Nomura family (daily, 8:30am-4:30/5:30pm, ¥500) is open to the public and contains a shrine, samurai armour and a small but immaculate Japanese garden. For an extra ¥300, tea is served in a room overlooking the garden.

PRACTICAL INFORMATION
Station guide
The station has a west gate and east gate. Take the east gate for the city centre. Look in the corridors off the main concourse for coin lockers (all sizes). The face of the station's east exit changed in autumnn 2001 with the opening of Ishikawa Prefectural Concert Hall.

Tourist information
The tourist information centre (☎ 0762-32 6200, daily 10am-6pm) is just inside a shopping mall off the main station concourse. An English-speaking volunteer will help with reservations and provide information on Kanazawa and the surrounding area.

Another source of information is **Ishikawa Foundation for International Exchange** (☎ 0762-62 5931, Mon-Fri 9am-6pm, Sat/Sun 9am-5pm), on the third floor of the Rifare Building, about a 10-minute walk south-east of the station. Satellite TV, a library, and free Internet access are available. Also pick up from here or the tourist information centre the monthly *Ishikawa International Times* newsletter with local event details and film listings.

Money
For foreign-issued Visa card ATMs, try the first floor of Labbro department store (closed Wed) on Katamachi shopping street.

Festivals
The Hyakumangoku Festival takes place every year around June 14th. The event celebrates the arrival of Lord Maeda into the city and begins at dusk with a procession of floating lanterns down Asano-gawa. Public

Opposite: One of the highlights of a visit to Takayama (see p155) is a trip to the morning market. (Photo © Richard Brasher).

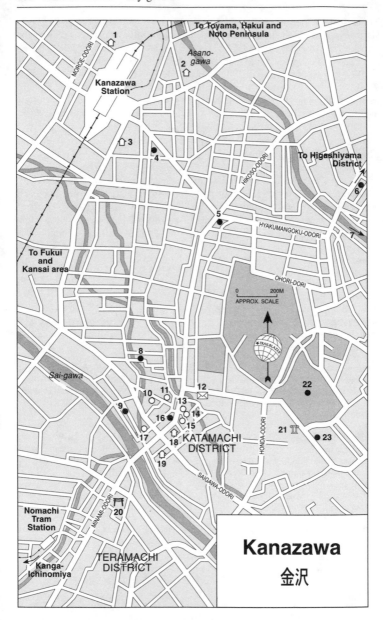

To Toyama, Hakui and Noto Peninsula

Asano-gawa

1

2

MOROE-ODORI

Kanazawa Station

3

4

To Higashiyama District

6

HIKOSO-ODORI

5

HYAKUMANGOKU-ODORI

7

To Fukui and Kansai area

OHORI-DORI

0   200M
APPROX. SCALE

TRAILBLAZER

8

Sai-gawa

10   11

12

9

13

14

16   15

22

17

18

KATAMACHI DISTRICT

21

23

19

HONDA-ODORI

SAIGAWA-ODORI

MINAMI-ODORI

20

Nomachi Tram Station

TERAMACHI DISTRICT

Kanga-Ichinomiya

Kanazawa
金沢

tea ceremonies are also held in Kenrokuen (see p160) but the highlight of the day is a colourful parade through the streets which mixes acrobatics, horse-riding, period costume and even a 'Miss Hyakumangoku' beauty contest.

Getting around

The city centre is a 10-minute bus ride from the station. Buses leave from stops outside the east exit; take any bus from stop Nos 7, 8 or 9. There's a flat fare of ¥200 within the city centre. Kanazawa Retro Bus (daily, 8:30am-6pm, every 15 mins) runs in a loop around the city; ¥500 one-day passes can be bought at the tourist information office inside the station, at the bus ticket office outside the east exit or from bus drivers.

The pass can only be used on the Retro bus, not on ordinary city buses. The Retro Bus leaves from stop No 0, in front of the ANA Hotel outside the station's east exit.

Rent A Cycle (daily, 7am-8:30pm; 2 hours ¥400) is to the left as you take the station's west exit.

Where to stay

For top-class luxury, head for *Hotel Nikko Kanazawa* (☎ 076-234 1111, ▤ 234 8802; ¥13,000/S, ¥26,000/Tw). It's outside the station's east exit and can hardly be beaten for its friendly staff and service. Less than a five-minute walk east of the east exit is *Kanazawa Central Hotel* (☎ 076-263 5311, ▤ 262 1444; ¥6800/S, ¥13,000/Tw, ¥18,000/Tr). It's a

---

KANAZAWA　金沢

Where to stay
1 Kanazawa Manten Hotel	1 金沢マンテンホテル
2 Kanazawa Central Hotel	2 金沢セントラルホテル
3 Hotel Nikko Kanazawa	3 ホテル日光金沢
7 Kanazawa Youth Hostel	7 金沢ユースホステル
18 Ryokan Murataya	18 旅館村田屋
19 Matsui Youth Hostel	19 松井ユースホステル

Where to eat
10 Hamano	10 浜の
11 Sayur	11 サユル
13 McDonald's	13 マクドナルド
14 Doutor Coffee	14 ドトールコーヒー
15 Capricclosa	15 カプリチョーザ
17 Ninnikuya	17 にんにくや

Other
4 Rifare	4 リファーレ
5 Omicho Market	5 近江町市場
6 Sakuda Gold and Silver Leaf Shop	6 金銀箔工芸さくだ
8 Nomura Family Samurai House	8 武家屋敷野村家
9 Equator Bar Pole Pole	9 Equator Bar Pole Pole
12 Central Post Office	12 中央郵便局
16 Labbro Department Store	16 ラブロ片町
20 Myoryu-ji (Ninja-dera)	20 妙立寺（忍者寺）
21 Ishikawa Prefectural Art Museum	21 石川県立美術館
22 Kenrokuen	22 兼六園
23 Ishikawa Prefectural Noh Theater	23 石川県立能楽堂

good standard business hotel with clean, comfortable rooms.

A three-minute walk from the station's west exit is the new *Kanazawa Manten Hotel* (☎ 076-265 0100, 🖹 265 0120; ¥5500/S, ¥11,000/Tw). Rooms are small but well furnished and all single/twin rooms feature semi-double beds. If you prefer to be in the city centre, a great choice is *Ryokan Murataya* (☎ 076-263 0455, 🖹 263 0456; ¥4500/S, ¥8500/Tw, ¥12,000/Tr). This traditional inn is just set back from the Katamachi shopping district. Some of the rooms overlook a small garden and all are simply decorated with Japanese paper screens and hanging scrolls.

Kanazawa Youth Hostel (☎ 076-252 3414, 🖹 252 8590; ¥2900/YH(HI), ¥3500 non-members) is on a hill above Higashiyama. From the station, take bus No 90 bound for Utatsuyama and get off at Youth Hostel-mae, from where you have to walk the rest of the way uphill. *Matsui Youth Hostel* (☎ 076-221 0275; ¥3100 YH(HI), ¥4100 non-members) is more centrally located but there's a 10pm curfew, so anyone planning a night on the town might prefer to stay at a business hotel.

Where to eat

A good place to stop for lunch is one of the sushi restaurants inside Omicho market as the fish is guaranteed to be fresh. Plenty of shops and restaurants line the streets of the Katamichi shopping district.

Here you'll find the Italian chain Capricciosa, and branches of *McDonald's* and *Doutor* coffee shop. *Capricciosa* is open daily (11am-11pm, last orders 10pm) and has half-size meal deals including salad and a drink for ¥830. Vegetarians don't normally get much of a deal in Japan but *Sayur* is a popular vegetarian restaurant with a friendly manager.

Hamano is the place to head if you like fish; their speciality is local catches from the Noto Peninsula. Seating is along the main counter and there's plenty of saké and beer. Look for the name written outside in black kanji on white. *Ninnikuya* (daily, 5pm-12am) serves garlic in practically all its dishes and is very busy at weekends.

Down by Sai-gawa is the *Equator Bar Pole Pole*, a local *gaijin* hangout. The popularity of this bar seems to rest entirely on the fact that peanut shells are left to pile up on the floor.

Side trips by rail from Kanazawa

A short side trip can be made by taking the private Hokuriku Railway 16km from Nomachi station (just south of the Teramachi district) to the terminus at **Kanga-Ichinomiya** (¥500, 35 mins). On the right across the street from Kanga-Ichinomiya station is an old tofu shop, where tofu has been made in a traditional way for over 70 years. In front of the station is a road that leads up to Shirayama Shrine. There's no charge to enter the shrine which receives a large number of visitors on the first day of the New Year.

The area is very much off the beaten track and there's a real feeling of stepping back in time. The train ride itself, passing through tiny stations as it heads towards the countryside, is also fun. From Nomachi, roughly one train an hour goes to Kanga-Ichinomiya.

From Kanazawa, the JR Nanao line heads north towards the **Noto Peninsula**. An intriguing place to visit lies 40km along the line at **Hakui**, a self-proclaimed 'UFO town'. There's a tourist information desk in Hakui station (☎ 0767-22 7171, daily, 10am-6pm), though they only have Japanese maps and the staff don't speak English. Cycles can be rented from the JR ticket office (2 hours/¥300, 4 hours/¥600).

Little green men
Hakui's connection with UFOs can be traced back to the discovery of a manuscript called 'Kashima Choshi', written before the Edo period; chapter 16 describes the sighting of a mysterious fireball in the sky – an ancient form of UFO? On the strength of this and other local tales a healthy tourism industry has built up; Cosmo Isle Hakui now attracts 70,000 visitors every year. It's all thanks to the museum's director (a former monk turned TV scriptwriter) who persuaded the Ministry of Home Affairs to pay half the construction bill for the dome. Even *Time* magazine picked up on the story of the UFO town on the Noto Peninsula, sending a reporter to ask 'why Hakui?' (Answer: 'The Japanese government is an easy touch for funds that might bring business to fading areas, and Hakui is near the constituency of former Prime Minister Yoshiro Mori').

Cynicism aside, the town is revelling in its UFO status and the boom has even spread to local restaurants, where 'UFO ramen' (noodles mixed with baby octopus, which in Japanese cartoons look like extra terrestrials) has become a hit on the menu. Get there before the aliens do.

Cosmo Isle Hakui (daily except Tue 9am-5pm, ¥800), an enormous dome containing a UFO museum, cost ¥5,260,000,000 to build when it opened in 1996.

On display are assorted space craft, astronaut suits and genuine moon dust. A few of the exhibits, including the Soviet Union's Vostok capsule and a NASA space suit with 24-carat gold helmet, are real. Just to prove the museum isn't all serious, there are items like the prop box used by Tom Hanks to store his space suit during the filming of *Apollo 13*. Video booths show interviews with sober and eccentric professors and scientists connected with SETI (Search for Extra Terrestrial Intelligence) and there's also an extensive UFO database – conspiracy theorists can call up images of UFOs, and zoom in on each photo for a closer look.

Cosmo Isle Hakui is 10 minutes on foot north of Hakui station. It's easy to spot, as it's the only building with a 26m American rocket parked outside. Signs in the museum are in Japanese and English.

Kansai – route guide

INTRODUCTION

All roads lead to Kyoto, at least that's what most tourist brochures and travel documentaries on Japan let you assume. The ancient capital does indeed lie at the heart of the Kansai region but it would be a shame to restrict your travel solely to the well-beaten track. Japan's even more ancient capital, Nara, is less than an hour away by rail and it's easily worth staying a night or two there. Further south, the landscape becomes more rural, the crowds thin out and the views are worth seeking out. Kansai has one of the most extensive networks of rail lines in the country (operated by JR and private railways), which means you

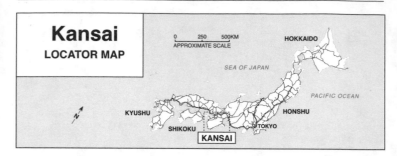

Kansai
LOCATOR MAP

0   250   500KM
APPROXIMATE SCALE

HOKKAIDO

SEA OF JAPAN

PACIFIC OCEAN

KYUSHU   HONSHU

SHIKOKU   TOKYO

KANSAI

can go off the beaten track without the fear of leaving the big city far behind.

The first part of this route guide follows the shinkansen line **from Nagoya to Osaka** via Kyoto – there is relatively little to see en route but it's useful if you're in a hurry. With more time, consider a much longer route to Kyoto **via the rural Kii Peninsula**, easily accessed from Nagoya but very much off the traditional tourist trail. Limited expresses operate around the peninsula so the journey needn't be too time-consuming; the countryside and coastline certainly repay the effort. Taking this longer route also gives you the opportunity to go to **Ise** (see p172), home of the Grand Shrine and spiritual centre of Japan's indigenous religion, Shinto.

Finally, another spiritual centre, the mountain retreat of **Koya-san** (see box, p200) offers a wholly unexpected change of pace. Koya-san can be accessed from Kyoto, Nara or Osaka, or as part of a longer journey around the Kii Peninsula and is ultimately reached by a hair-raising cable car.

If you've arrived in Japan without a rail pass, JR West, which operates services throughout the Kansai area, sells regional passes over the counter. For details, see p14.

TOKYO/NAGOYA TO OSAKA BY SHINKANSEN

Distances from Tokyo. Fastest journey time (from Tokyo): three hours; (from Nagoya): one hour.

Tokyo to Nagoya (366km)   [Map 1, p111 Map 2, p115; Table 3, p400]

▲ Note that some Hikari and all Nozomi run fast from Nagoya to Kyoto.

Nagoya   [see pp139-45]

Nagoya to Osaka   [Map 9, p169]

Gifu-Hashima (396km) Only Kodama stop here. Despite its name, this station is not close to Gifu city (see p128) at all, which is better reached by train from Nagoya and is included as a stop on the route starting on p125.

Maibara (446km) Maibara is a major rail junction on the Tokaido line and Hokuriku line (to/from Kanazawa, see p159) as well as the shinkansen. In sum-

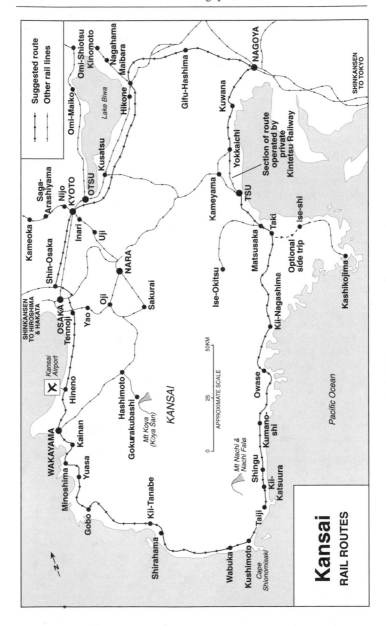

Kansai
RAIL ROUTES

mer, the 'SL Biwako Go' runs 22km along Lake Biwa between Maibara and Kinomoto on the Hokuriku line. A ride on this steam locomotive is worthwhile if you stop along the way at Nagahama, where you'll find an old station building, dating back to the time when passengers changed to a ferry for the journey across Lake Biwa.

Maibara is one stop (approximately four trains per hour) from the castle town of **Hikone**, situated on the eastern shore of Lake Biwa, Japan's largest lake. Hikone is known for its castle (Hikone-jo), about a ten-minute walk up the main street, Ekimae Oshiro-dori, from the station. The castle is not quite as dramatic as the one further down the line at Himeji (see p204) but it benefits from the superb natural backdrop of Lake Biwa. Genkyu-en, a Japanese garden dating back to 1677, is at the foot of the castle. Green tea is served (¥500) in an old guest house that overlooks the garden.

Five minutes by taxi from Hikone station (no bus) is Matsubara Beach on the shore of Lake Biwa, venue for the annual International Birdman Contest (see box below). Near the beach is Hikone Port, from where cruise boats make excursions to a couple of islands on the lake. A tourist information office (☎ 0749-22 2954, daily, 9am-6pm, English spoken) is to your left at the foot of the stairs leading down from Hikone station.

From Hikone, either backtrack to Maibara and pick up the shinkansen to Kyoto/Osaka or continue directly along the Tokaido line from Hikone station (the fastest trains take 50 minutes to Kyoto).

Kyoto (514km)   [see pp180-91]
Japan's ancient capital is the first stop after Maibara. From here, it's only 15 minutes to Shin-Osaka.

⛩ Flying without wings
Every year in late July, the Birdman Contest is held at Matsubara Beach on Lake Biwa. The purpose of this fiercely competitive event is to see how far humans can fly before ditching into the water of Lake Biwa. A giant runway is built for the occasion and teams (individuals and groups) compete to 'fly' off the edge. This may be an eccentric sport but many of the teams are made up of engineering students who spend months designing and building the perfect, streamlined human craft. The record for a human flight without propellers was set in 1998 when the winning team flew 364.08m before crashing into the lake. For a few, the finish is less dignified. In 2000, the 'Flying Turkeys', a team of Tokyo university students, fell into the lake at the moment they took off, leaving their craft to glide on without them. They recorded the following distance: 21.63m (without crew), 0m (with crew). Another contestant in the same year suffered the ultimate humiliation of going less than nowhere by ditching immediately, falling backwards under the runway, and thus clocking up a minus reading on the distance display board.

The contest usually takes place on the last Friday and Saturday in July. Check with Hikone TIC (☎ 0749-22 2954) for exact dates. During the contest, free shuttle buses run between Hikone station and Matsubara beach.

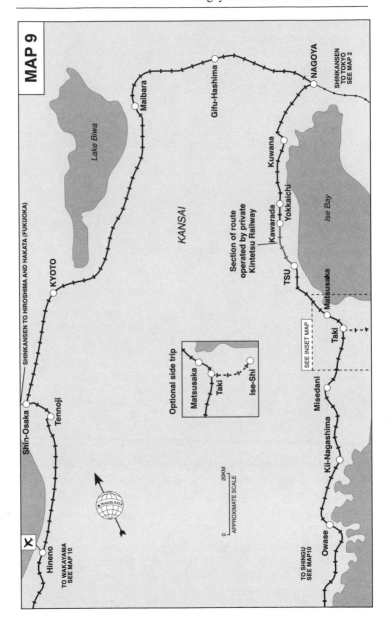

MAP 9

SHINKANSEN TO HIROSHIMA AND HAKATA (FUKUOKA)

Lake Biwa

Maibara

Gifu-Hashima

NAGOYA

SHINKANSEN TO TOKYO SEE MAP 2

Kuwana

KANSAI

Kawarada

Yokkaichi

Ise Bay

Section of route operated by private Kintetsu Railway

TSU

Matsusaka

KYOTO

Taki

SEE INSET MAP

Optional side trip

Matsusaka

Taki

Ise-Shi

Shin-Osaka

Tennoji

Misedani

Kii-Nagashima

20KM

APPROXIMATE SCALE

0

Hineno

TO WAKAYAMA SEE MAP 10

TO SHINGU SEE MAP10

Owase

⛩ **Kintetsu Railway supplement**
Note that a small section of the track between Nagoya and Tsu is owned by Kintetsu Railway. If you have bought a ticket, the fare will include the supplement for the Kintetsu section between Kawarada and Tsu. Rail-pass holders are supposed to pay the conductor on board the train. If travelling on the Nanki LEX this means paying both the standard fare (¥490) and limited express fare (¥310 yen) just for that section (whatever your total journey is).

On the Mie rapid train, only the standard charge (¥490) has to be paid. You could get away without paying the supplement if you are in a non-reserved seat and if the conductor checks tickets only when the train has left Tsu, since there is no way of telling from the rail pass where you joined the train.

Nara lies off the shinkansen route but is accessible by JR Nara line from Kyoto (see p193). Nara city guide begins on p195.

Shin-Osaka (553km)   [see pp101-8]

NAGOYA TO OSAKA VIA THE KII PENINSULA

Fastest journey time from Nagoya to Osaka: 7 hours.

Nagoya to Owase   [Map 9, p169; Table 9, p404]
Distances by JR from Nagoya.

Nagoya (0km)   [see pp139-45]
From Nagoya board a Wide View Nanki LEX or the slower Mie 'rapid' train heading towards Tsu and Shingu. The Nanki has Western/Japanese toilets and a trolley service. Green Car seats have an in-built audio system but there is a charge for headphone rental. If planning to visit the Grand Shrine at Ise (see box p172) it's best to take the Mie train; this is not as luxurious as the Nanki but does run direct from Nagoya to Ise. Both the Nanki and the Mie have reserved and non-reserved cars.

The private Kintetsu Railway also runs services from Nagoya to Ise; this would be the most convenient route for those without a rail pass.

Kuwana (24km) The journey as far as Kuwana is not particularly scenic.

Yokkaichi (37km) After leaving Yokkaichi the industrial landscape starts to clear. Some trains stop at **Suzuka**.

Tsu (75km) Tsu has little worth making a stop for unless you want an ice-cream break; there's a branch of Baskin-Robbins outside the station.

Matsusaka (95km) Matsusaka is known for its locally-bred cows and in particular for their unusual diet which is supposed to make them all the more flavoursome when served up in strips on the table. 'If a cow should lose her appetite', informs a local leaflet, 'she is given beer to drink as a tonic to activate her stomach, along with a gentle, full-body massage. Every cow receives meticulous care'. Some sushi shops in Matsusaka even do a brisk sale in beef sushi, though in restaurants the most popular dish is either steak or *shabu shabu*.

A guide map to Matsusaka is available from the tourist information office (☎ 0598-23 7771, daily except Mon, 9am-4pm), in the glass building next to the police box (koban), on the right as you leave the station. The staff here don't speak English. The main sights are in or around the castle ruins of **Matsusaka Park**, a ten-minute walk north-east of the station. Only a few stone walls are left of Matsusaka Castle, so walk instead through the park and go out the back to find a preserved street that looks as if it has been lifted from the set of a samurai movie. A few of the residents on this street are descendants of the samurai families who once lived in the same buildings. One building, the **Castle Guardman's House**, is open to the public (daily except Mon 10am-4pm). It's first on the right as you walk down the street from the park; admission is free.

For a snack, try *Café comme ça* on the ground floor of the department store attached to the station. To try some of Matsusaka's famous beer-fed beef, head up the main road that runs straight ahead from the station. On the corner at the first set of traffic lights, and on the right, is *Kameya*, a casual restaurant that serves up good-value beef set meals, including shabu-shabu. The entrance is next to a butcher's counter, so you can guarantee that the meat is fresh. It closes at around 6:30pm. Further along the same street but on the left is a Mister Donut.

Taki (102km) In the Edo Period, Taki was a stop along the pilgrim path to Ise Grand Shrine. Today it is home to Sharp's largest Liquid Crystal Display factory but tours are not usually open to the public. Taki has some quiet country lanes which make for good cycling terrain. Cycle rental is available through the station office (daily, 8am-6pm, 4 hours, ¥500; one day ¥1000). If you do go cycling around here, note that there's not much in the way of English signs but if you get stuck or need further information try calling the town office (☎ 05983-81117). There may be someone who can speak English.

▲ Taki is a tiny station but an important rail junction. The track divides here. The Sangu line goes off to Ise-shi (approx hourly, 20 mins by local train). Beyond Ise, JR trains run as far as **Toba**, famous for Mikimoto pearls, but the only way of moving on from Ise to continue the rail route described below is to backtrack to Taki. This route follows the Kisei line south towards Shingu and the Kii Peninsula.

If you took the Nanki LEX from Nagoya but are planning to visit the Grand Shrine at Ise (see box, p172), change here. The limited express does not go to Ise but continues south towards the Kii Peninsula. The Mie rapid train does continue on to Ise.

Leaving Taki sit on the left side of the train for the best views of the small mountain ranges and rivers that pass by, though the train sometimes dives into a tunnel. Some trains stop at **Misedani (127km)**.

Kii-Nagashima (158km) Until now the train has followed an inland course. From here, the track shadows the Pacific coast, albeit at a slight distance. A cou-

📛 **Side trip to the Grand Shrine at Ise**
    Ise Grand Shrine is the centre of Japan's indigenous religion, Shinto. The town receives over six million visitors annually, many of whom are making a once-in-a-lifetime pilgrimage to the place considered to be the spiritual home of the Japanese.
    A visit to the shrine is necessarily in two parts, since the outer and inner shrines are separated by a ten-minute bus ride (¥410). The outer shrine, or **Geku**, is an eight-minute walk from JR Ise-shi station. Turn right as you go out of the JR side of Ise station and take the main road that heads straight up until you reach the entrance to the shrine. Devoid of gaudy decorations, and lacking the gold and red colours you find at Buddhist temples, the shrine is simple to the point of austerity.
    From the Geku, retrace your steps to the entrance where a fleet of taxis waits to take pilgrims and visitors on to the **Naiku**, the Inner Shrine. Board a No 51 or 55 bus (¥410; 10 mins) for the Naiku. The sun goddess Amaterasu Omikami, the Imperial family's ancestral kami (deity), is enshrined here. A sacred mirror, symbol of the kami, is carefully wrapped up and hidden away in the inner sanctuary and never shown in public. Indeed, there's not a great deal to see at all, since the interior of both shrines is off limits. Both the outer and inner shrines, as well as Uji Bridge which you have to cross to reach the inner shrine, are completely rebuilt every 20 years. The last time was in 1993, so the next rebuilding will be in 2013.
    Most coach parties rush off after a lightning tour of both shrines but with more time, and to make up for a lack of 'sights' at the shrines, it's worth visiting at least one of the three museums a short bus ride from the inner shrine. The obvious choice is **Jingu Chokokan Museum**. From the inner shrine, take bus No 51 (¥280) that goes to Uji-Yamada and Ise-shi stations via the Chokokan Museum. It's a Meiji-era building that houses a large-scale model of the inner shrine, allowing you to see all around the compound. This bird's eye view makes you realize how little of the shrine you see for real when standing at the outer gate. Also on display are some elaborate festival costumes, a selection of kagura masks, sacred treasures offered to the deities on the occasion of previous shrine renewals, and a few random paintings of Corsica. (cont'd opposite)

ple of minutes out of Kii-Nagashima is the small Nagashima Shipyard out to the left, followed by great views to the left of clusters of rock and small islands.

Owase (183km) A major junction on the line, but the area is not very attractive. A few minutes from here there are more glimpses of the coast but also a number of tunnels.

Owase to Shingu   [Map 10, p175; Table 9, p404]
Distances by JR from Nagoya.

Kumano-shi (218km) Five minutes by bus from here is **Onigajo**, a series of connecting caves along the shore which according to legend were once used by a pirate called Tagamaru as his secret den.

Shingu (240km) Shingu, in Wakayama, one of Japan's most rural and isolated prefectures, serves as a useful transport hub.

Side trip to Ise (cont'd)

From the Chokokan, go down a flight of steps, and across the road is a modern building that is home to the **Jingu Museum of Fine Arts**, opened in 1993 to commemorate the last rebuilding of the shrine. Inside are works of art offered to the shrine by Japanese artists; fortunately, instead of hiding them away in the inner shrine, they have been put on public display. Finally, back across on the other side of the road is the **Jingu Agricultural Museum**. This is less interesting but does contain a photo of the current Emperor in wellington boots, getting down to a bit of manual labour in a field. After visiting the museums you can pick up the bus at the Chokokan stop and head back either to Ise-shi or Uji-Yamada stations.

Ticket deals for the three museums are as follows: ¥500 to visit just the Museum of Fine Arts, ¥300 to visit the Chokokan and Agricultural Museums, or ¥700 for a package ticket to see all three. Student discounts apply at all three museums (package ticket ¥400). All three museums are open daily except Monday (April-Oct 9am-4:30pm, and Nov-Mar 9am-4pm).

Near the entrance to the outer shrine, and opposite the stop for buses going to the inner shrine, is Ise City TIC (daily, 9am-5pm) which has guide maps and a useful explanatory leaflet about the shrines. The latter is also available at the shrine offices by the entrance to both Geku and Naiku.

A good overnight choice in Ise is the new ***Pearl Pier Hotel*** (☎ 0596-26 1111, 🖹 26 3611), a five-minute walk behind JR Ise station, next to the much older Ise City Hotel. A coin laundry is available. The hotel is easily recognizable – it's the building with a steel lifeboat hanging off one side. Singles start at ¥6500, though for ¥8000 you get a more spacious room. Doubles cost from ¥13,000 and twins from ¥14,000. The hotel has a good Italian restaurant, *Il Mare* (11:30am-2pm and 5-10pm), which does a buffet lunch including a pasta main course for ¥1000. It's a good place to fill up before tackling the Grand Shrine.

The station is very small with a few coin lockers, an ekiben stand and Rent A Car office. A bonus is the small tourist information desk (daily except Thur, 9am-5pm), staffed by a friendly English speaker. It's in the same office as Eki Rent A Car, to the left as you leave the station. You can pick up maps and information about both Shingu and the surrounding area.

Two minutes away, just 100m to the east of Shingu station, a large Chinese gate marks the entrance to small **Jofuku Park**. Bikes can be rented for free (¥2000 deposit required) from the shop inside this park. One sight to head for is **Kamikura Shrine**, 20 minutes on foot over to the east side of town. On the evening of February 6th, there's a 'procession of fire' down the steps from the shrine as participants race to the bottom carrying burning torches.

A day excursion from Shingu can be made inland to **Doro-Kyo Gorge**. Package tickets including return bus and boat trip around the gorge are available but if you have a rail pass the best way of accessing the gorge is to take a JR bus from the bus terminal to the left as you leave Shingu station. The bus journey is 40 minutes to Shiko, from where boat cruises operate (¥3340). The tourist information office at Shingu station has bus timetables.

Shingu has a small number of cheap business hotels, one of which is **Sunshine Hotel** (☎ 0735-23 2580, ≣ 23 2781), seven minutes on foot from JR Shingu station. Go past the tourist office, turn left and walk over the railway track. Follow the road until you reach a set of traffic lights and turn left. Walk along this road until you see a small post office on the corner of a narrow road on the right. Turn on to this road and the hotel is on your right. It has very basic but spacious singles with attached bath at ¥5880 and twins at ¥10,500. For food, try the local speciality, *meharizushi* – literally translated as 'goggle-eyed sushi', so called because each piece is so large that your eyes are supposed to open wide at the sight. **Mehariya**, a restaurant with both counter and tables, is a friendly place serving freshly-made meharizushi with a bowl of soup for about ¥750. Look for it on the street beyond Sunshine Hotel.

Shingu to Osaka/Kyoto   [Map 10, p175; Table 10, p404]
Distances by JR from Shingu.

Shingu (0km) From Shingu, continue along the JR Kisei line towards Tennoji in Osaka. Two limited expresses operate along this stretch of line. The most frequent is the Kuroshio, though the slightly faster Ocean Arrow has the bonus of a small lounge area with seats which face large, panorama windows. Lounge seats are non-reserved and are the best place to sit for views of the Pacific Ocean.

For the most part, the line from Shingu to Nachi follows the coast, though the view is occasionally obscured by trees.

♦ **Nachi (13km)** Limited expresses don't stop here, so take a local train from Shingu (20 mins); the service is irregular but operates approximately once an hour, except in the middle of the day. Buses run from outside the station (15 mins; ¥470) to **Nachi Falls**. Get off at the 'Taki-mae' bus stop, from where you walk under the torii (shrine gate) and down a flight of stone steps towards a 133m-high waterfall, where there's an altar at which visitors pray. The reason for the torii, usually found at the entrance to a shrine, is that this is believed to be a sacred waterfall. Legend has it that Emperor Jimmu arrived here (in the 7th century), after seeing the cascading water from the sea shore, and announced that it was the spiritual embodiment of a kami. A short walk uphill brings you to a Shinto shrine (Kumano Nachi) and adjacent Buddhist temple, (Seiganto-ji).

Though very small, Nachi station does have the unique feature of its own **hot spring** on the second floor, a good place to head if you've got time to kill waiting for a bus to the falls. The onsen is called Nishiki no Yu (daily except Mon, 10am-8pm, ¥600 and ¥200 towel rental); from the bath there are great views out over Nachi Bay and also of the train tracks below, so rail enthusiasts can enjoy the unusual experience of trainspotting from the comfort of a bathtub.

Kii-Katsuura (15km) Katsuura has a number of onsen, the best known is **Boki-do spa**, inside a cave, from where there are views out to sea. The cave is part of **Hotel Urashima**. To reach it, first walk ten minutes from Kii-Katsuura

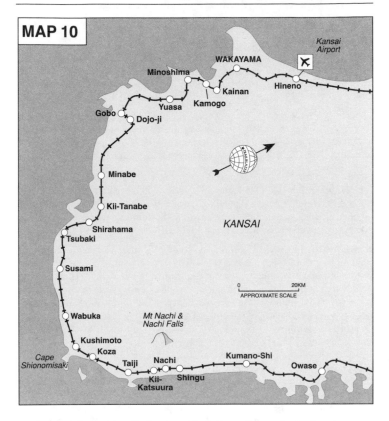

MAP 10

Kansai Airport

WAKAYAMA

Minoshima

Kainan

Hineno

Yuasa   Kamogo

Gobo

Dojo-ji

KANSAI

Minabe

Kii-Tanabe

Shirahama

Tsubaki

Susami

0   20KM
APPROXIMATE SCALE

Wabuka

Mt Nachi & Nachi Falls

Kushimoto

Koza

Kumano-Shi

Cape Shionomisaki

Taiji   Nachi

Owase

Kii-
Katsuura   Shingu

station straight ahead to the boat terminal. From there, take the free ferry service to the hotel. Entrance to the cave spa is through the hotel (¥500, daily, 5am-11pm). Check where the boat is going before boarding, as there's also a ferry service to another hotel, *Hotel Nakanoshima*, which also has a hot spring, though at ¥2000 a go it's much more expensive.

Taiji (20km) Some limited expresses stop here. Despite calls for a worldwide ban on whaling, whale meat still turns up on the menu around this part of the Kii Peninsula. At Shingu station (see p173), for example, you can buy a whale-meat lunch box and further down the line at Kushimoto (p176) one shop serves whale ramen. But it's Taiji that's famous for whaling and it has a number of whale-related attractions. From Taiji station, buses (¥200) run to **Taiji Whale Beach Park** (daily, 8:30am-5pm; ¥1050). Attractions include a Whaling Ships Museum, Whale Museum and Marine Land. The whole

> **⛩ Before the 'Black Ships'**
> Just off the Honshu coast close to Kushimoto is the island of Oshima, a place which challenges the history books over the timing of the end to Japan's period of isolation from the rest of the world.
>
> In April 1791, when the country's doors were still very firmly closed, two American merchant ships laid anchor at Oshima. The *Lady Washington*, commanded by Captain John Kendrick, and the *Grace,* commanded by Captain William Douglas, landed on Oshima to stock up on water and firewood. If this story is to be believed they predated Commodore Perry's better-known arrival in 1854 with a fleet of 'Black Ships' by a full 63 years (see p35).

emphasis on whales as a fun day out is rather offset by international outcry over the continued practice of whaling. The focus of the whale park seems to be more on celebrating man's 'triumph' over the whale than on the creature itself.

For the final part of the journey towards Kushimoto, the train heads inland. After Taiji, some trains stop at **Koza (35km)**.

Kushimoto (42km)   Kushimoto station is the nearest stop to Cape Shionomisaki, a 15-minute bus ride away (¥600 return). There is no tourist information here but the bus stop is right outside the station. There's a small locker area in the station (including one ¥600 large locker!) but it's cheaper to leave large bags in the station master's office (¥300 for the day). This service is not advertised and staff are not obliged to accept luggage.

Cape Shionomisaki is the most southerly point on Honshu and there's a lookout tower (¥300) next to the last stop on the bus route. Nearby is a lighthouse that can be climbed (¥150) for further views of the cape. Besides these official lookout points, there is also an overgrown path at the cape that few people take, leading down to the rocks below. You might see fishermen down here doing battle with the waves.

If you fancy a night at Honshu's most southerly tip, there's a choice of two youth hostels. *Misaki Lodge Youth Hostel* (☎ 07356-21474) and *Shionomisaki Youth Hostel* (☎ 07356-20570) are very close to each other and there's little to tell them apart. It's best to phone ahead since if you arrive in the middle of the day there may not be anybody around. Both charge about ¥2800 excluding meals. Shionomisaki YH is right by the last bus stop and Misaki Lodge is one stop before (the stop is 'Kuroshiomae').

♦ Wabuka (56km)   You'll probably only notice this tiny station if on a local train but it's a good vantage point for views of the Pacific Ocean, with waves crashing over rocks. The latter half of the journey towards the next major stop at Shirahama is mostly inland.

Shirahama (95km)   Shirahama is a popular summer vacation destination; to make sure people know it, JR and tourist information staff wear Hawaian shirts as hula music plays in the background (June to August). The immediate station vicinity hardly blends in with this tropical atmosphere, though a fleet of taxis outside the station and regular buses (¥330, 15 mins) will speed you off to the main Shirahama resort area. The tourist information desk (☎ 0739-42 2900) in the station is open daily, 8:30am-5pm, though there's only a skeleton staff on Thursdays.

Shirahama is not the place to come for deserted, unspoilt beaches. Resort hotels, hot springs, glass-bottom boat rides and a 'laser beam studded dance show' turn the bay area into a summer tourist mecca. One of the closest attractions to the station is **Adventure World** (daily, 9am-5pm, ¥3500). The park is divided into zones, including Safari World, Marine World and Panda Land. One of the two giant pandas on display, Mei Mei, arrived from China in 2000. In the summer, there are extended opening hours and additional attractions such as a night safari tour. May be a good trip for a family with young children but the expense is a major drawback.

Kii-Tanabe (105km) Right in front of the station are love hotels, pachinko parlours and a whole street lined with bars and restaurants. However, there's more to Tanabe than this. The founder of aikido, Morihei Ueshiba (1889-1969), was born here; his statue stands close to the ocean on the other side of town. Tourist information (Japanese only) is available from an office to the right as you exit the station. A good place if you wish to stay the night is *Altier Hotel* (☎ 0739-81 1111, 🖷 81 1112, 🖳 altier@altierhotel.com; ¥5500/S, ¥11,000/Tw inc continental breakfast). Opened in 2000, the rooms are small but have attached bath and wide beds. It's on the right side, five minutes down the main street that runs away from the station.

About 10 minutes out of Kii-Tanabe, there are views of the Pacific as the train runs along an elevated track. Some trains stop at **Minabe (114km)**.

♦ Dojo-ji (145km) Only local trains stop here, from where it's a short walk to **Dojo-ji** temple. If on a limited express, the best plan is to get off at Gobo, the next station along from Dojo-ji, and then backtrack one stop on a local train. Services leave Gobo hourly at anything between 51 and 59 mins past the hour and arrive in Dojo-ji approximately four minutes later. Return services leave on the hour or a minute before/after except for the train at 16.07 and 17.07.

From the station, turn left on to the main road, go to the first junction and turn right. The temple is at the end of the street and is reached by a flight of steps at the end of a row of souvenir shops. Inside the temple is a three-storey pagoda, as well as the main hall. People come here to listen to the monks tell stories with the aid of long, painted scrolls. The best-known story, handed down by successive generations of priests, is about Kiyohime, a girl who falls hopelessly in love with Anchin, a pilgrim monk. It's a tragic tale of unrequited love with an unusual ending: Kiyohime turns into a serpent and burns the one she most desired to death. For the full story, as well as general information about the temple, ask for the *Brief Guide to Dojo-ji Buddhist Temple* at the office in the new building to the left as you enter the temple compound.

There are a couple of places to eat at along the road to the temple but back at the station is a good place that serves noodles and curry rice at reasonable prices. They also do breakfast sets until 11am. The interior is like a log cabin. Look for it on the right just as you leave the station.

Gobo (146km) Rail enthusiasts may want to take a ride on the Kishu Railway that runs the short distance (2.7km) between Gobo and Nishi-Gobo; some say that this is the shortest railway line in Japan. The journey takes eight minutes and costs ¥180. At Gobo station, you can board a Gobo Nankai Bus for **Amerika-Mura** (¥440, 20 mins), a small village of Japanese emigrés. To get you in the mood, platform speakers at Gobo play vaguely American-style music in between announcements. There's no tourist office at the station but ask JR staff for a local map.

Between Gobo and the next limited express stop at **Yuasa (164km)**, the train passes through a number of tunnels. After Yuasa, the scenery is just a line of identikit towns.

Minoshima (175km) Some limited expresses stop at Minoshima, part of Arida city, which is known for its oranges and for cormorant fishing on the Arida-gawa (1 June to early September). Shortly after leaving Minoshima, there's a large and ugly factory complex out to the left, so for once there's good reason to be grateful for the tunnel that follows soon after, blocking out the possibility of a lingering view.

Kainan (190km) Just before the train pulls in here there's a row of industrial plants out to the left, drawing a final line under the rural part of the peninsula.

Wakayama (201km) There's little to see in Wakayama apart from an average castle (¥350 to enter), from the top of which are views out over Kinokawa River. Originally constructed in 1585, the castle followed the fate of so many Japanese fortresses and was destroyed by fire. The present reconstruction dates from 1958. It's a ten-minute bus ride (¥220); buses leave from stop No 1 right outside the station.

⛩ **Laughter Festival**
    Fifteen minutes by taxi from Gobo station (no bus) is Niu Shrine, where an unusual festival takes place every year on the second Sunday in October. The main event of the Laughter Festival is a parade through the streets of participants in bright festival gear, all laughing uncontrollably.

    The event dates back to a time long ago when a princess lived in this area. According to legend, she was due to attend an important meeting in the town of Izumo but overslept. Sad and embarrassed at missing the meeting, she locked herself in her room and refused to speak to anybody. Local citizens proved that laughter really was the best medicine by dancing and cackling outside her room until she cheered up and joined in the general merriment.

⛩ Crying Babies Sumo Festival
Fifteen minutes by taxi (no bus) from Kamogo station, accessible by local train from Minoshima, is Yamaji Oji Shrine where the Crying Babies Sumo Festival takes place on Sports Day (see p59).

This bizarre festival, which dates back 250 years, is open to boys aged 4-5 months. Since they are too young to appreciate what they have been entered for, the nappy-clad competitors are given a helping hand by adults. Not surprisingly, the babies usually cry throughout, which is why the event became known as 'crying sumo'. A crucial element of the contest is that it takes place on the ground, since it's believed that touching the soil will ensure that the babies grow up to be healthy.

The tourist information desk at Wakayama station is on the right as you exit the ticket barrier (☎ 0734-22 5831, daily, 9am-5pm). A bilingual English/Korean guide booklet to the city is available. To find coin lockers (all sizes), turn left out of the station and look for a room on the side of the station building. The station area is a good place to hunt for food. Within the station building there are restaurants on the basement level of VIVO department store and a small bakery on ground level. Another good place to try is the fifth floor 'Gourmet Park' in Kintetsu department store, on your right as you leave the station. Also around the station area you'll find a *Mister Donut* and *McDonald's*.

From Wakayama, trains continue along the JR Hanwa line towards Tennoji and Shin-Osaka. To reach Kansai International Airport, take a train on the Hanwa line and change at Hineno. The JR Wakayama line runs inland from here and goes part of the way to the mountain resort of Koya-san (see box, p200).

Hineno (227km) Change here for the short journey on the Kansai Airport line to Kansai International Airport. The hotel (see p107) outside this station is useful if you need to stay close to the airport. A few trains stop at **Otori (247km)**.

Tennoji (262km) Tennoji is a station on the JR Osaka Loop line (see p106). Change here if going to Osaka station.

Shin-Osaka (277km)   [see pp101-8]
Osaka's shinkansen station. Change here for the route around western Honshu (see p204). A few limited expresses continue on to **Kyoto (316km; see p180)**.

❏ Using the rail route guides
The fastest point-to-point journey times are provided for each section of the route. Even though each route has been divided into different sections it may not be necessary to change trains as you go from one section to the next. Occasionally, however, it is essential to change train in order to complete the route described. Such instances are denoted by the following symbol ▲. Places which are served by local trains only are marked ♦.   **(For more information see p84)**

Kansai – city guides

KYOTO

Arriving in this sleek and bustling JR station, you'd be forgiven for thinking Kyoto was still the nation's capital. Kansai International Airport, opened in the last decade, offers direct access to the ancient city, and easily beats Tokyo's Narita Airport as an attractive gateway to Japan. Even if Kyoto ultimately lost its status as national capital and Imperial home in 1868 at the time of the Meiji Restoration (see p35), nobody could dispute its title of tourist capital. Here you'll find some of the most expensive hotels and luxurious ryokan, the grandest palaces and the most ornate temples.

Yet even in a city with more temples per square kilometre than anywhere on earth (at least that's what you're likely to conclude after a day or two here), Kyoto's ancient traditions and quiet back streets have to be sought out. Arriving by bullet train, the impression is more of a city like so many others: Kyoto has skyscrapers as well as shrines, *Starbucks* as well as wooden tea houses. There's no better way of seeing for real the pace of change in Kyoto than through its dwindling geisha population – nowadays you're more likely to see a Japanese (or a foreigner) who has paid to be dressed up as a geisha for a day than catch a glimpse of a real one (see box below).

Despite fears that Kyoto's ancient traditions, wooden buildings and sacred precincts may one day be swamped by the 21st century demand for more space,

---

⛩ Getting to know geisha

Perhaps the best way of discovering what a geisha (see box, p42) is like is to get yourself invited to an evening party at one of the Gion tea houses. This requires contacts in extremely high places (no amount of money will do unless you know someone) and is not an option for the majority of visitors.

The more likely option is to try and see one walking around but the chances of this depend very much on luck and whether you happen to be standing by the right doorway at the right moment. The best time and place to look for maiko-san (apprentice geisha) is around 5-6:30pm, along Hanami-koji in Gion. Take bus No 100 (¥220) from Kyoto station and get off at Gion.

Anyone with a lot of spare cash might consider dressing up as a maiko/geisha. A number of places around the city will dress you up, daub you with makeup and transform you from bulky foreigner to petite maiko; the cheapest makeovers start at around ¥8000. Shop around, as some places include a free photo as well as the chance to walk/mince around outside. The tourist information centre (see p188) publishes a list of shops offering this service. Most require reservations.

If all else fails, the last means of penetrating the mysterious geisha world is to read up on it (see p31).

it remains a grand and magnificent city. With a superb network of trains radiating out from here, Kyoto would make a ... Kansai and beyond – it's also the perfe... somewhere else waiting to be discovere...

What to see and do

After a day or two in Kyoto, it's easy to get 'templed out'. Quite apart from the fatigue of traipsing around endless numbers of temples and shrines, the cost can quickly add up. With most temples charging ¥400-600 per person, a day of frantic temple ticking-off can easily add up to the cost of a night's accommodation. This applies even more from mid-October to the end of November, when the entrance fee to some temples is hiked up as people pour in to see the falling autumn leaves. A good idea is to home in on a few temples to get a flavour of Kyoto but also save time for a few of Kyoto's museums and other sights.

If you've already started your rail pass before arriving in Kyoto and are planning to stay in the city for more than a couple of days, you'll probably want to use it as much as possible rather than 'waste' days of rail travel you've paid for. With this in mind, the following is a brief description of the area around Kyoto station, a selection of city-wide must-sees, and lastly a couple of suggestions for half-/full-day excursions by rail.

● **Kyoto station area** The station area used to be much maligned as a disappointing gateway to the city but this view has changed since the opening of the new station building. Performances are held most weekends in the event space inside the station and the area outside; this means that the long flights of steps leading up the station atrium has become the place to hang out.

The top of the station is a good vantage point for views of the city, since it's free. **Kyoto Tower Observatory** (daily, 9am-9pm), the eyesore across the street, may be higher but it also costs ¥770 (¥100 discount ticket from the tourist information centre) to take the lift up to the observation gallery. The only advantage to viewing Kyoto from inside Kyoto Tower is that it's the one building you can't see.

On the second floor of Theater 1200, attached to the station building, is **Tezuka Osamu Animation Theater** (daily, 10am-7pm, ¥400). Tezuka Osamu is a famous Japanese animator who created the character Astro Boy. The theatre claims to be the 'only place on earth where you can see Tezuka original cartoon movies'.

A five-minute walk north of the station are two temples, Higashi Hongan-ji and Nishi Hongan-ji (both free entry). These are not a bad place to start to get a feel for Kyoto's size and opulence. The scale of the buildings is unlike anywhere else in Japan and these are just a couple of many. **Higashi Hongan-ji** has an enormous Founder's Hall that boasts 175,967 roof tiles and contains 927 tatami mats. Look for the rope on display made of women's hair; 53 ropes of this kind were used to transport the enormous wooden beams of the two main halls to where they are today when they were rebuilt in 1895. Conventional ropes were not strong enough for the task, so women's hair was used instead.

A short walk east of Higashi Hongan-ji brings you to **Shosei-en** (daily, 9am-4pm, free), a garden belonging to the temple. The Founder's Hall at nearby **Nishi Hongan-ji** is under restoration until 2008; a donation of ¥10,000 entitles you to have your name written on one of the roof tiles.

One more place in the station area that rail enthusiasts will want to seek out is **Umekoji Steam Locomotive Museum** (daily except Mon 9:30am-5pm, ¥400). Fans of the railway's golden age will be in paradise as there are a large number of steam locomotives on display, and some are in working condition. One of the locos runs along a specially constructed track (¥200 for a ride). This short run can't compete with the growing number of preserved steam locomotives running along real lines (see p71) but is fun if you haven't had the chance to ride a steam train before. The journey lasts about ten minutes and operates at 11am, 1:30pm and 3:30pm. The museum is about a 20-minute walk west of Kyoto station, or take a city bus from outside the station to 'Umekoji Koenmae'. Pick up the leaflet available at the entrance.

● **Must sees** **Kiyomizu Temple**, or Kiyomizu-dera (daily, 6am-6pm, ¥300), is always packed with tour groups crowding the wooden observation platform which affords a spectacular view out over Kyoto. Every 33 years the crowds get even bigger when an 11-headed Kannon statue is put on display (the next is in 2033). Visit early in the day, or be prepared for the crowds.

From Kiyomizu-dera, head north towards the Gion District, known as Kyoto's geisha quarter but also the home of **Yasaka Jinja** (free entry), a Shinto shrine dating back to 656. It becomes the focus of the city for the entire month of July during the Gion Festival (see p189).

Standing at the entrance to the shrine, Shijo-dori runs west towards the centre of **Gion**, while Higashioji-dori runs north and south. Head down Shijo-dori for the busy downtown shopping and entertainment district, and look out at the

---

KYOTO – STATION AREA　京都－駅周辺

Where to stay

2	Tour Club	2	旅倶楽部
5	Matsuba-ya Ryokan	5	松葉屋旅館
7	Murakamiya Ryokan	7	村上家旅館
8	Kyoka Ryokan	8	京花旅館
9	El Inn Kyoto	9	エルイン京都
10	Hotel Granvia Kyoto	10	ホテルグランヴィア京都

Other

1	Nishi-Hongan-ji	1	西本願寺
3	Coin Laundry	3	コインランドリー
4	Higashi-Hongan-ji	4	東本願寺
6	Shosei-en	6	渉成園
11	Central Post Office	11	中央郵便局
12	Umekoji Steam Locomotive Museum	12	梅小路蒸気機関車館

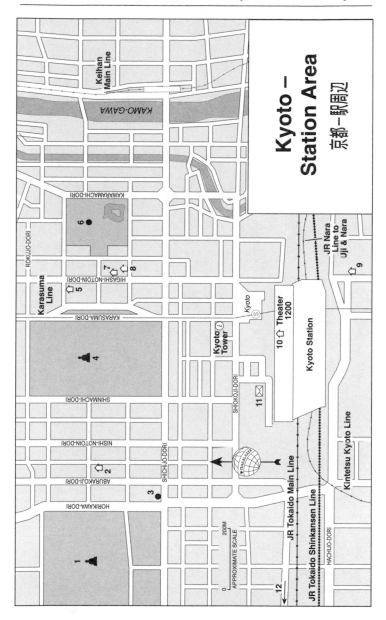

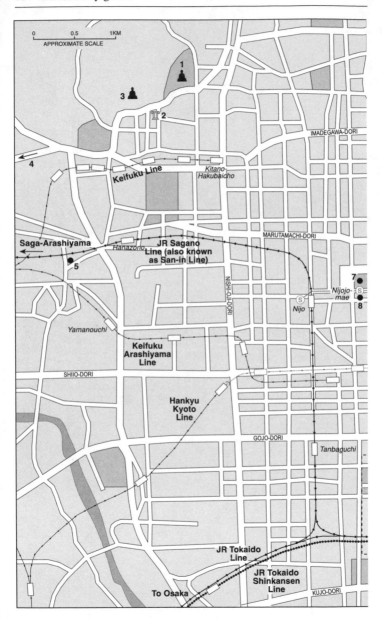

0   0.5   1KM
APPROXIMATE SCALE

1

3

2

4

Keifuku Line

Kitano
Hakubaicho

IMADEGAWA-DORI

MARUTAMACHI-DORI

Saga-Arashiyama

Hanazono

JR Sagano
Line (also known
as San-in Line)

5

NISHI-OJI-DORI

7

Nijojo-
mae

S

Nijo

8

Yamanouchi

Keifuku
Arashiyama
Line

SHIIO-DORI

Hankyu
Kyoto
Line

GOJO-DORI

Tanbaguchi

JR Tokaido
Line

JR Tokaido
Shinkansen
Line

To Osaka

KUJO-DORI

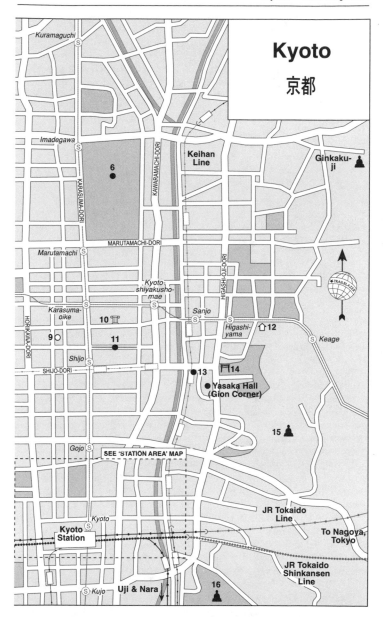

Kyoto

京都

KYOTO 京都

Where to stay
- 4 Kyoto Utano Youth Hostel   4 京都宇多野ユースホステル
- 12 Higashiyama Youth Hostel   12 東山ユースホステル

Where to eat
- 9 Dog Café   9 ドックカフェ京都

Other
- 1 Kinkaku-ji (Golden Pavilion)   1 金閣寺
- 2 Museum for World Peace   2 国際平和ミュージアム
- 3 Ryoan-ji   3 竜安寺
- 5 Toei Uzumasa MovieLand   5 東映太秦映画村
- 6 Kyoto Imperial Palace   6 京都御所
- 7 Nijo Castle   7 二条城
- 8 Shinsen-en   8 神泉苑
- 10 Museum of Kyoto   10 京都文化博物館
- 11 Nishiki Food Market   11 錦市場
- 13 Minami-za   13 南座
- 14 Yasaka Shrine   14 八坂神社
- 15 Kiyomizu-dera   15 清水寺
- 16 Tofuku-ji   16 東福寺

---

western end of the street (just before Shijo Bridge) for **Minami-za**, Kyoto's famous kabuki theatre. There are no tours of the theatre building, so in order to see inside you have to buy a ticket for a performance (see p191). The biggest annual event is in December when some of the country's best-known kabuki actors come here to perform.

Kinkaku-ji (daily, 9am-5pm, ¥400), better known as the **Golden Pavilion**, is perhaps Kyoto's most famous sight. The pavilion, its reflection glittering in the Mirror Pond, is deservedly one of Japan's most photographed buildings – even on an overcast and rainy day, the golden façade sparkles defiantly. Bus loads of tourists make a stop here, so there's little else you can do but follow the crowds along the set path.

From Kinkaku-ji, it's a 15- to 20-minute walk south-west to Ryoan-ji. As you exit, turn right on to the street and go straight. Mid-way between the two temples, look out for a sign pointing towards the 'Museum for World Peace' – not an essential stop but interesting if you have time (see opposite).

Ryoan-ji (daily, 8am-5pm, ¥400) provides a complete contrast to the showy opulence of the Golden Pavilion. Everyone comes here to sit and gaze out over Kyoto's (and probably the world's) best-known rock garden. Assembled sometime between 1499 and 1507 and measuring about 200 sq metres, the garden consists of just 15 rocks, divided into five groups. Visitors are asked to remain silent, though the peace and quiet is regularly interrupted by a recorded history of the temple. For an excellent account of Ryoan-ji's rock garden, and the different ways in which it might be interpreted, read François Berthier's *Reading Zen In The Rocks: The Japanese Landscape Garden* (see p31).

Ryoan-ji and Kinkaku-ji are in north-western Kyoto, some distance from the centre. The good news for rail-pass holders is that a JR bus service runs here roughly once an hour; the buses leave from the three JR bus stops right outside the main side of Kyoto station, before the main bank of city bus platforms. The bus for Kinkaku-ji and Ryoan-ji departs from JR Bus stop No 3. For Kinkaku-ji, get off at the 'Wara-tenjin mae' stop. From here, walk on further up the road until you reach the second set of traffic lights, when you turn left and go straight until you reach the entrance to Kinkaku-ji. For Ryoan-ji, stay on the bus for another five minutes. The bus stops right outside the entrance.

● **Optional stops** The **Museum of Kyoto** (daily except 3rd Wed, 10am-7:30pm, ¥500) is on Sanjo-dori in central Kyoto, a three-minute walk from Karasuma-Oike subway station. The museum traces the history of Kyoto, focusing on its glory days as the nation's capital and then moving on to the period of modernization after power shifted to Edo (Tokyo). There are good model displays that let you see what Kyoto once looked like but otherwise not much of a permanent collection. The redeeming factor is an excellent English volunteer guide service; this is very useful as most of the displays are only in Japanese. On the ground floor is a recreated Kyoto street from the Edo period with shops selling traditional crafts and a couple of restaurants.

Ritsumeikan University's **Museum for World Peace** (daily except Mon, 9:30am-4:30pm, ¥300) is not widely publicized even though it is situated between Ryoan-ji and Kinkaku-ji (see opposite). Perhaps because there are better known peace museums in Hiroshima (see p230) and Nagasaki (see p344), Kyoto's museum seems to attract few visitors but it really is worth fitting into your schedule. Built by Ritsumeikan University to promote the cause of peace, the museum tackles with astonishing candour the subject of Japan's military aggression during WWII and the country's 'unresolved war responsibilities'. It's unlikely you'd find anywhere else a picture of 'schoolchildren beating the portraits of Roosevelt and Churchill with large sticks in 1943'. The displays are well thought-out and informative, and include images of what Kyoto might have looked like had it suffered the fate of Hiroshima and Nagasaki. Originally on the list of possible A-Bomb targets – the planned epicentre was about 1km west of Kyoto station – Kyoto was later removed as a target for nuclear attack. Pick up the excellent brochure at the entrance.

Kyoto Imperial Palace (Mon-Fri and 3rd Sat, tours at 10am and 2pm, free; over 20s only) can only be visited with an official guide; applications to join a tour must be made in advance to the Imperial Household Agency (see over). The palace grounds, which include some picture-postcard Japanese gardens, are interesting enough to make the effort of applying to join a tour worthwhile.

Rooms have to be viewed from a distance but it's just possible to make out the inside of the throne room. When the present Emperor was crowned in Tokyo, the thrones were taken from here and flown by helicopter to the capital.

Even though the palace is no longer home to the Imperial Family, tight security remains; an official carrying a walkie-talkie follows the tour group around to make sure nobody sneaks away. The impression is not so much of grandeur but of how much the grounds feel like a prison – or must have done for the Emperor, who hardly ever left the palace.

To sign up for a tour, go with your passport to the Imperial Household Agency office, in the outer grounds of the palace, at least 20 minutes before the start of the tour (or the day before to be sure of a place). Applications for tours on the third Saturday of each month must be made by Friday. The Imperial Household Agency (☎ 075-211 1215) is open for enquiries/tour applications Mon-Fri, 8:45am-12pm and 1-4pm. To reach the Imperial Palace, take the subway from Kyoto station in the direction of Kokusai Kaikan and get off at Imadegawa station (the fifth stop). The entrance to the palace grounds is on Karasuma-dori.

Over on the east side of Kyoto lies **Ginkaku-ji**, better known as the Silver Pavilion. Originally modelled on its better-known golden counterpart, don't be fooled by this temple's name. The original plan was to cover its outer walls in silver; though the plans were never carried out, the name remained.

PRACTICAL INFORMATION
Station guide

Kyoto station, rebuilt in 1997, is one of Japan's most eye-catching modern buildings. Japanese architect Hiroshi Hara suggests that the 27m-wide, 60m-high and 470m-long concourse lets you feel what it's like 'travelling down the side of a mountain into the valley basin'. Certainly it's an impressive sight either from the main concourse or up on the 12th floor Sky Garden, from where you can look down on to the station atrium and out over the city.

Isetan, the big in-station department store, stretches up both sides of the escalators that run up from the ground floor concourse. On the 7th floor is the 'Eki' museum with changing exhibitions. On the 10th floor is a 'SEGA Joypolis' amusement centre, and on the 11th is the 'Eat Paradise' restaurant floor where you'll find almost every kind of food. Most restaurants have tables either overlooking the station atrium or with window views of the city. See p190 for details of other places to eat in the station.

There are plenty of coin lockers (all sizes) around the station but if you need to keep bags in storage for more than three days, a baggage handling office (daily, 8am-8pm, ¥410/item/day) is on the basement floor next to KCAT.

Kyoto City Air Terminal

Kyoto City Air Terminal (KCAT) is on the basement level of Kyoto station. It's only of use if you're flying from Kansai International Airport (see p45) with JAL or Air France, as you can check your baggage in here up to three hours before flight departure. Departing passengers must have a ticket for the Haruka LEX to Kansai (rail passes OK). KCAT is open daily 6am-5pm.

Tourist information

The main JNTO-run **Kyoto TIC** (☎ 075-371 5649, Mon-Fri 9am-5pm, Sat 9am-12pm) is in the Kyoto Tower building, opposite the station. If this is closed, try **Kyoto City Tourist Office** (daily, 8:30am-7pm), on the second floor of the station building. The staff speak English and will help book same-day accommodation.

Less well known, since it's over on the ground floor of the shinkansen side of the station, is the information desk (daily, 10am-4pm) staffed by volunteers. There's always an English speaker here who will help with any tourism-related questions. Another place that's hidden away and consequently attracts few visitors is **Kyoto Tourism Federation** (daily, 9:30am-6pm) on the ninth floor of Isetan (take the south elevator from the second floor of the store).

The English-speaking staff can advise on travel in Kyoto as well as the surrounding area. Also on the ninth floor is **Kyoto Prefecture International Center** (☎ 075-342 5000, daily except 2nd/4th Tue, 10am-6pm), which doesn't provide tourist information but does have foreign newspapers and magazines, and CNN on TV. Internet access is also available (see below).

The best publication for listings and a guide to what's on in Kyoto is the monthly *Kyoto Visitor's Guide*, available free at all the tourist information counters listed above as well as at major hotels. *Kansai Time Out* is another useful monthly magazine with information on Kyoto, Osaka, Nara and Kobe. Its website, 🖳 www.kto.co.jp, is also worth a look.

Money
Most banks in Kyoto will cash US$ travellers' cheques or foreign currency. The city tourist information office inside Kyoto station has a list of the ATMs in Kyoto where foreign-issued Visa/Master Cards can be used. The nearest to Kyoto station are either on floor B1 of the Kyoto Tower building (daily, 10am-9pm) or on the ground floor of Platz Kintetsu department store (10am-7:30pm; closed Thurs), further along the road from Kyoto Tower.

Internet
Kyoto Prefecture International Center (see above; daily except 2nd and 4th Tue, 10am-6pm) offers Internet access at ¥250/30 mins.

Getting around
Since Kyoto is so spread out, it's not really feasible to walk everywhere. The best plan is to take buses/subways to the different areas and then explore on foot. There's a flat rate of ¥220 on buses within the city but if you're going to be taking more than a couple of buses a day it's worth investing in a bus pass. A one-day city bus pass (valid only within the city centre) costs ¥500. Pick up a transport map from tourist offices which clearly shows how far you can go with the ¥500 pass. Alternatively, a combined subway/city bus ticket costs ¥1200,

or a two-day ticket is ¥2000. Both passes are available from the bus ticket office outside the main side of Kyoto station, near bus stop D1, or from the city tourist information office on the second floor of Kyoto station. Before taking any bus, pick up a copy of the *City Bus Sightseeing Chart* from tourist information; this tells you how to get from the station and between the main sights by bus.

Hajime Hirooka, otherwise known as **Johnnie Hillwalker**, conducts walking tours of Kyoto in English every Mon, Wed and Fri morning Mar 1-Nov 29. The four-hour guided tour (¥2000) starts at 10:15am in front of Kyoto station and ends at 2:30pm near Kiyomizu-dera (see p182). Reservations are not required.

Festivals
In a city packed with temples, there's nearly always a festival going on somewhere. Some are small and not widely publicized, others are known worldwide and attract thousands of visitors. For details of special events, enquire at any tourist office, or check the *Kyoto Visitor's Guide*.

One of the biggest festivals is **Jidai Matsuri**, which takes place in October (check the exact date with the tourist office). The highlight is a huge street procession which traces Kyoto's history from 1868 all the way back to 781, the date of the city's foundation. The festival began in 1895 to revive the city's fortunes after it lost its status as Japanese capital to Tokyo. It's one of the most colourful and vibrant events you'll find anywhere in Japan.

Another big festival is **Gion Matsuri**, which runs through the entire month of July and is the main annual celebration at Yasaka Shrine (see p182). The main events are between July 15th and 17th, when there's a huge procession of floats.

Where to stay
If you arrive without any accommodation, the Welcome Inn Reservation Desk in Kyoto TIC (see opposite) operates a free booking service for member inns and hotels. The centre is not open at the weekend.

Station area Built into JR Kyoto station is the classy *Hotel Granvia Kyoto* (☎ 075-344 4433, 🖷 344 4400; ¥18,000/D, ¥20,000 /Tw), where all the rooms are tastefully furnished and have large bathrooms. It's a luxurious haven from the noise of the station downstairs and an ideal base if you're travelling a lot by rail. The indoor pool has excellent views of the station's atrium and there are a number of restaurants.

Cheaper Western-style accommodation is to be had at *El Inn Kyoto* (☎ 075-672 1100, 🖷 672 9988), a relatively new place just a couple of minutes on foot south-east of the shinkansen side of Kyoto station. Most rooms are singles (¥6800 inc tax), though there are a few twins at ¥12,000. The hotel has wide beds, a coin laundry and a reasonable Western-style restaurant.

There are also a number of good-value Japanese inns in this area. *Matsuba-ya Ryokan* (☎ 075-351 3727, 🖷 351 3505), with very friendly owners, is five minutes east along the main road from the station. It has spacious tatami rooms, some of which overlook a small garden. Rates are ¥4500 for one, ¥9000 for two and ¥12,600 for three; add ¥500 per person for a room overlooking the Japanese garden.

Kyoka Ryokan (☎/🖷 075-371 2709) is a bit faded but offers cheap rates of ¥4000 per person for a tatami room (no attached bath). There are also a couple of newer rooms with attached toilet/bath that are ¥12,000 for two and ¥16,500 for three. Just around the corner is *Murakamiya Ryokan* (☎ 075 371 1260, 🖷 371 7161), a rambling but efficiently-run place that charges ¥4000 per person per night.

The best bargain, and conveniently close to the station, is the new, friendly, spotless *Tour Club* (☎ 075-353 6968, 🖷 353 6978, 🖳 www.kyotojp.com), a very small place with four-bed bunk dorms set around a small rock garden. The overnight charge is ¥2300 with breakfast at ¥290. For a bit more privacy, opt for one of the newly renovated twins (¥7400) or triples (¥8900). Facilities include internet access (¥50/5 mins) and the cheapest bike rental in Kyoto (¥490 per day).

Others YH/HI members might consider staying at *Higashiyama Youth Hostel* (☎ 075-761 8135, 🖷 761 8138; ¥4000) in eastern Kyoto. It has an institutional feel right down to the requirement to eat evening meals at the hostel. Even though overnight and meal rates are published separately in Japan's official YH/HI guide book, the management here insist that all guests must pay for both. If you want to eat out, or just want a more relaxed place to stay, go elsewhere. The hostel is reached by taking a No 5 city bus from Kyoto station (get off at Higashiyama-Sanjo).

More relaxed but less well located is *Kyoto Utano Youth Hostel* (☎ 075-462 2288, 🖷 462 2289), north-west of the city. The nightly rate is ¥2800, with optional dinner at ¥850 and breakfast at ¥500. From Kyoto station, take No 26 City Bus and get off at 'Utano Youth Hostel Mae'. Note that the Tour Club beats both of these hostels for friendliness and price.

Where to eat

At the station, the best place to head for is the 11th floor 'Eat Paradise' in *Isetan* department store; for take-out food, try the food hall in the basement. For more upmarket dining, *Hotel Granvia Kyoto* has several restaurants which tend to be less crowded than those elsewhere in the station. Don't forget the excellent *Vie de France* bakery on level B2 (central side), where you can eat in or take out a range of cakes, sandwiches and pastries.

Otherwise, the best place to hunt for restaurants is in the downtown area. *Nishiki Food Market* in central Kyoto is a covered arcade known as 'Kyoto's kitchen'. It's a good place to wander round and pick up a bite to eat. Look out for the shop that sells tofu ice cream and doughnuts, and for the spices shop where you can buy freshly-made spicy ice cream!

Canine lovers may like to visit Kyoto's *Dog Café* (daily except Mon 11am-8pm), where the sign outside reads 'all good dogs welcome'. Humans are also allowed in (you don't have to be accompanied by a pet) to this old wooden building where there are good cakes and the coffee is freshly ground. There's also a range of doggie treats to eat in or take away and you'll always find a couple of pups inside. It's on Takoyakushi-dori (look for the sign as it's slightly set back from the main street), just south-east of Nijo Castle, so a stop here could be included in the excursion described below.

Evening entertainment

Kabuki is sometimes staged at Minami-za in Gion, though it's not a cheap evening out as reserved seats start from ¥4200.

'Gion Corner' is a nightly performance of traditional Japanese arts catering to tourists. For ¥2800, you get to see a truncated version of the tea ceremony, ikebana (flower arranging), traditional dances as well as excerpts from kyogen (traditional comic plays) and bunraku (puppetry). Performances nightly (Mar 1-Nov 29 only) at 7:40 and 8:40pm on the first floor of Yasaka Hall in Gion, close to Yasaka Shrine (see p182). Tickets can be booked in advance from major travel agencies.

Side trips by rail from Kyoto

The first of the two sample excursions described below can be done as a day trip, while the second is convenient as part of a trip to Nara (see p195).

● **Along the JR Sagano line** A trip along the Sagano line makes an ideal half- or full-day excursion, and there's the bonus of knowing you are making use of the rail pass. The destination is Saga-Arashiyama, which is only 15 minutes away from Kyoto station but offers a complete change of pace and scenery. Take a local train (from track Nos 31-34) to follow the route below (distances are from Kyoto station).

Spend the morning (two hours would be fine) in Nijo Castle, before continuing on to the Arashiyama area. It would be difficult to include a visit to Toei MovieLand on the same day, so plan this as an additional day. It's best to pick up a copy of *Walking Tour Courses In Kyoto* from Kyoto TIC before setting out, as it contains a good map of the Arashiyama area.

Nijo (4.2km) The second stop along the line, Nijo, is the nearest rail station to **Nijo Castle** (daily, 8:45am-5pm, ¥600). Nijo station is a modern building with a large wooden roof (the original station building is preserved at Umekoji Steam Locomotive Museum, see p182). On the ground floor are a convenience store and a few coin lockers.

After leaving the station, head straight up the road in front of you. It takes about 15 minutes to reach **Shinsen-en**, a small Japanese garden that will be on your left. The garden is not well known but it's peaceful and features a red-lacquered bridge. Take the road that leads behind the garden to reach the outer perimeter of Nijo Castle. With the castle grounds in front of you, turn right and follow the perimeter round until you reach the main entrance gate.

The castle is one of Kyoto's best attractions and contains beautiful landscaped gardens in addition to Ninomaru Palace. Originally built in 1603 as an official residence of the first Tokugawa shogun, Ieyasu, it is well preserved and, unlike the former Imperial Palace (see p187), visitors are allowed inside. An unusual feature of Ninomaru Palace is the 'nightingale floor', so called because the floorboards that run along the side of the building 'squeak and creak' when you tread on them. Unfortunately, the squeaks are often drowned out by the recorded commentary or noisy chatter of tour groups hurrying through. On your way out through the gardens, look out for the koi (carp) in the central pond. Despite the tour groups, this castle should rank high on your list of places to see in Kyoto.

Hanozono (6.9km) Toei Uzumasa MovieLand (daily 9am-5pm Mar-Nov, 9:30am-4pm Dec-Feb, closed Dec 21-Jan 1; ¥2200) is about 15 minutes on foot from the station. After a couple of days touring Kyoto's ancient temples, this very in-your-face thrills and spills entertainment park may be a good antidote. If you want to see actors running around dressed as samurai, or enjoy special effects such as collapsing mountains, this is the place to go. The park owners stress that MovieLand is a working film set, so there's a chance to see a real samurai film in production. It's not the most traditional of environments but it's possible to dress up as a maiko (trainee geisha), though it's not cheap at ¥11,000 (on top of the park entrance fee).

Saga-Arashiyama (10.3km) You can tell if somewhere in Japan has sold out to tourists when you see (1) an Orgel Museum, (2) *jinrishika* (rickshaws) lined up to ferry you about, and (3) a monkey park. Arashiyama has all of these but a lot more that is worth visiting as well, so don't be put off by the outward signs of tourist tack. There are ¥300 coin lockers outside the station. The Torokko train station (see box opposite) is to the right as you exit. There is no tourist office. Cycles can be rented from the shop opposite the Torokko station (daily Mar-Dec 9am-4:30pm, ¥500/2 hours).

The best place for a wander in Arashiyama is through the **bamboo forest**, about 10 minutes' walk west of the station. Cool and shady in the summer, the forest also contains the small **Nonomiya Shrine**, where Imperial princesses underwent purification rites for three years as part of their training before being sent to the Grand Shrine at Ise (see p172). Just outside the forest is **Tenryu-ji**, originally built in 1255 as a palace with a view of Mt Arashiyama. Converted into a Zen temple in 1339, the garden is now open to the public (daily, 8:30am-5/5:30pm, ¥500). Near the entrance to the temple, look out for a sign that announces a secret supply of oysters buried underground. 'The function of the human body,' reads the sign, 'is activated by even a small amount of oyster extract…[in the event of an earthquake] this will keep you alive for three days without any help from others, while you wait for official assistance to come'.

North of the station is **Seiryo-ji**, once a country villa and a good place for lunch (no oysters) as there's a tiny restaurant called *Chikusen* (daily except Thur, 10am-4:30pm) within the temple grounds. There are only a few low wooden tables but the service is excellent. The ¥3500 lunch served on a tray is

---

Opposite: Perhaps the most photographed sight in Japan: Kyoto's Golden Pavilion (see p186) shines even on a grey day. (Photo © Ramsey Zarifeh).

> ## ⛩ Riding the Romantic Train
> Expensive but fun is a ride on the Torokko open-air carriage 'romantic train' which runs on a 25-minute journey along the scenic Hozu River. It gets completely booked out in the autumn when crowds descend on Arashiyama to see the leaves fall. It's wise to book tickets in advance (at JR ticket counters or from the TiS travel agency in Kyoto station; ¥600 one-way, ¥1200 return); rail passes are not accepted. Note that there are no services on Wednesday except in peak season (Apr 29th-May 5th, Jul 21st-Aug 31st, Oct 15th-Nov 30th) and the Torokko does not run between December 30th and the end of February.
>
> As an alternative to buying a return ticket, it's possible to take the train one way and then return to Arashiyama by boat. The course from the starting point in Kameoka (shuttle buses run between the Torokko station at Kameoka and the starting point for the boat rides) back down to Arashiyama is 16km and takes about two hours. Accept as hyperbole the description of the journey down the rapids as being the 'most exciting experience not only in Japan but also throughout the world'. It's not the Zambezi but the scenery is still spectacular and the ride makes for a good alternative to taking the train back. Departures are hourly between 9am and 3pm, March-November. Services are less frequent in winter but the boats are heated! Tickets cost ¥3900.

a real visual delight. Tea and a Japanese sweetmeat are also served (¥650). Just north-east of Seiryo-ji is **Daikaku-ji** (daily, 9am-4:30pm, ¥500), which has a viewing platform over adjacent Osawa Pond. Originally part of the country villa of Emperor Saga, the complex became a temple after his death in 876.

● **Along the JR Nara line** If planning to visit Nara and using a rail pass, you'll be taking the route below. The fastest service by JR (rapid train) takes 40 minutes. Trains depart (from track Nos 9 and 10) roughly three times an hour though most services are local and take over an hour. If possible, time your departure to take one of the rapid trains which depart from Kyoto at 51 minutes past the hour and arrive in Nara at 35 minutes past. The first of these departs from Kyoto at 9:51am and the last at 4:51pm. In the opposite direction, the rapid trains leave Nara at 53 minutes past the hour and arrive at 39 minutes past. The first departs from Nara at 9:53am and the last at 4:53pm. If you're not in a hurry, however, take a local train, and consider stopping off along the way at one or more of the places described below.

Tofuku-ji (1.1km) Just one stop along the line and barely out of Kyoto station, it's a few minutes' walk south-east of the station to **Tofuku-ji**, one of Kyoto's largest Zen monasteries and home to a famous five-storey pagoda. Foreign visitors can try *zazen* (Zen meditation); sessions, led by the head of the

Opposite: Top: At weekends, the long flight of steps inside Kyoto's atrium-style station becomes a stage for cultural and musical performances. **Bottom:** In most ryokan you'll find a supply of *geta* (wooden shoes) in the hallway for guests who want to take an evening stroll around the neighbourhood. (Photos © Richard Brasher).

temple complex, are held once a month. Call in advance (☎ 075-561 0087) or enquire at Kyoto TIC. Within the temple compound is an attractive garden (daily, 9am-4pm, ¥300).

Inari (2.7km) Next stop along the line; right outside this station is the first orange-lacquered torii (shrine gate) which marks the entrance to **Fushimi-Inari Shrine**. The station itself is bright orange, giving you a taste of what to expect in the shrine.

Fushimi-Inari is a huge complex and contained within the grounds is a long tunnel of orange shrine gates. Pilgrims dressed in white are a common sight here. It's only a short walk to the main shrine, behind which a path leads off through a 4km tunnel of some 10,000 torii which snakes up Mt Inari. Though the walk is surrounded by trees and mostly in the shade, it's a step up from a gentle stroll, so wear trainers. There are a few tea houses along the way, where you can sit on tatami mats by the window and enjoy views of the mountain on which the shrine complex is built. You are rewarded for your effort when you reach an observation point offering a great view of Kyoto, though from here it's a further walk up to the highest point of 233m (where there are no great views).

Before jumping back on the train, it's worth seeking out the small **Sekiho-ji**, or more precisely the bamboo garden behind it (daily, 9am-5pm, ¥300). Five to ten minutes on foot from Fushimi-Inari, but not easy to find, this small temple has one of the most peaceful gardens in Kyoto. To head in the right direction, turn right out of Inari station and go straight until you reach the rail track. Don't cross the track but turn left up the road and walk up until you reach an area of tombstones on your right. Turn right and go past the tomb stones to find the temple entrance. It's well hidden but this means that few people bother to look for it. The secluded bamboo grove on the hillside behind the main temple building is filled with stone statues of the Buddha and his disciples. The images were created by artist Ito Jakuchu in the late 1700s and are known for their comical facial expressions. The images are supposed to calm the souls of the dead and help relieve the grief of those left behind.

Uji (14.9km) Uji has been a well-known tea-producing area since the Kamakura era (1185-1333) and also features in the last ten chapters of one of Japan's most famous novels, *The Tale of Genji*. Uji Bridge, mentioned in some of the chapter headings, was first built by a Buddhist priest in 646, though the present construction dates from the 1990s. Heading towards Uji-gawa (turn left as you leave the station and go straight), you'll first reach a small tourist information booth, on the corner just before you cross the bridge. Staff can provide you with a map and point you in the right direction of Byodo-In, a five-minute walk south along the river.

Byodo-In (daily, 8:30/9am-4/5pm, ¥500) is a peaceful temple just set back from the west bank of Uji-gawa. It's known for its large Buddha statue in the main hall. The main building is known as Phoenix Hall since its shape, with two wings stretching off either side of the main hall, 'resembles a phoenix spreading its wings'. After visiting the temple, a good place to take a rest is at the river-side **Taiho-an Tea House**, where green tea and Japanese cakes are served (daily 10am-4pm, ¥500, closed Dec 21st-Jan 31st; tickets from the adjacent tourist information office). Both the tea house and tourist information office are just outside the temple complex along Uji-gawa.

Uji to Nara (41.7km) Rapid services fr [   ] Kyoto stop at Uji; [   ] the train up here and continue directly to [   ] [   ] (journey time 30 min).

NARA

Some 40km south of Kyoto, Nara boasts a longer history than its nearby rival. Well before Kyoto rose to pre-eminence, Nara enjoyed the title of national capital. Nara became Japan's first permanent capital in 710 and, even though its time at the top was short-lived (the Imperial court had decamped to Kyoto by 794), the period was marked by the influence of Buddhism from mainland China.

Nara's tremendous collection of temples, particularly enormous Todai-ji, which houses Japan's largest statue of the Buddha, still stand today as proof of that influence, and of the great wealth that once poured into the city. Just outside the centre of Nara, Horyu-ji contains the world's oldest surviving wooden structures (an impressive fact, when you consider how frequently wooden temples burn to the ground in Japan).

Apart from its rich cultural heritage, Nara is known for the harmonious co-habitation of humans and deer. It won't be long before you spot one (they tend to wander in and around the shops along Sanjo-dori in search of food), and it's often not up to you how close you want to get to them. At least this means a picnic in Nara Park will never be lonely.

Nara's compact size makes it much more manageable than Kyoto and its vast park is more attractive than Kyoto's urban sprawl. A lightning-fast day excursion can be made from Kyoto but an overnight stay in Nara would allow you time to enjoy the sights at a more leisurely pace.

What to see and do

With just one day here, devote all your time to covering as much as possible in Nara Park. With more time, you could also take in the Naramachi quarter, visit one or two of the museums, or make the short trip out to nearby Horyu-ji.

Approaching Nara Park from JR Nara station along Sanjo-dori, look out on your left for the three- and five-storeyed pagodas which belong to **Kofuku-ji**. Moved here in 710 when Nara became the capital, at the height of its prosperity this temple boasted as many as 175 buildings but most of them have burnt down in the intervening 1300 years. The three-storeyed pagoda dates from 1143 and the five-storeyed one from 1426. The latter is at its most spectacular when lit up at night (summer only). The Tokondo (Eastern Main Hall) and Treasure House (daily, 9am-5pm, Treasure House ¥500, Tokondo ¥200) display a variety of Buddhist sculptures. Performances of Noh take place in the temple precincts in April. Enquire at the tourist office for dates and times.

The biggest draw in the park is **Todai-ji** (daily, 7:30/8am-4:30/5pm, ¥400), known for its Daibutsu, a 16.2m-high, 15-ton bronze statue known as the 'Great Buddha of Nara'. The main building which houses the Daibutsu is the world's largest wooden structure.

Nara's most important shrine is **Kasuga Taisha**, the pathway to which is lined with lanterns (there are said to be 3000 in the precincts around the shrine). Founded in 768 at the foot of Mt Mikasa, this shrine of the Fujiwara family remained influential throughout the Heian Period (794-1185), after the capital had moved to Kyoto. Inside the shrine compound, fortune sticks are available in English for ¥200. The main shrine's annual festival is held on March 13th.

Nara National Museum (daily except Mon, 9am-4:30pm, Fri until 8pm Apr-Nov, ¥420), inside the park, opened in 1895 as one of three Imperial museums (the other two were in Kyoto and Tokyo). It has now greatly expanded to include separate east and west wings as well as the original building. The permanent collection is entitled 'Masterpieces of Buddhist Art' and is vast (only a part of the museum's holdings can be displayed at one time). Nearly all exhibits have a brief explanation in English but it's difficult to get a perspective on the

---

NARA　奈良

Where to stay

1	Nara Youth Hostel (YH)	1	奈良ユースホステル
2	Nara-ken Seishonen Kaikan YH	2	奈良県青少年会館YH
5	Nara Washington Hotel Plaza	5	奈良ワシントンホテルプラザ
13	Ryokan Seikan-so	13	旅館静観荘
14	Nara Hotel	14	奈良ホテル
19	Nara Kasugano Youth Hostel	19	奈良かすが野ユースホステル

Where to eat

5	Skylark	5	すかいらーく
7	Capricciosa	7	カプリチョーザ
10	Hiten	10	飛天
12	Asuka	12	飛鳥
14	Hanagiku	14	花菊
15	Uma no me	15	馬の目

Other

3	Central Post Office	3	中央郵便局
4	Horyu-ji	4	法隆寺
6	Nara City Information Center	6	奈良市観光案内所
8	Kintetsu Rent-A-Cycle	8	近鉄レンタサイクル
9	Keirindo (CAN)	9	啓林堂　(CAN)
11	Kofuku-ji	11	興福寺
16	Nara National Museum	16	奈良国立博物館
17	Todai-ji	17	東大寺
18	Kasuga Taisha	18	春日大社

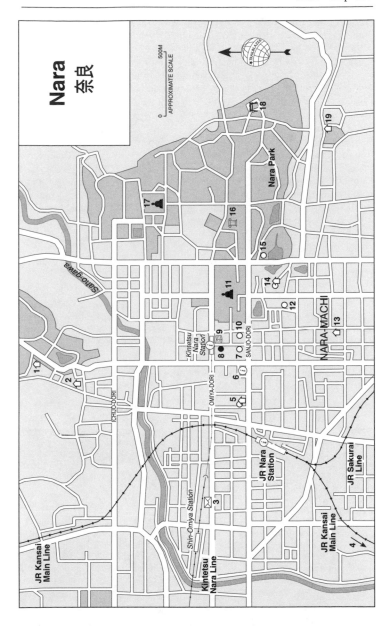

Nara
奈良

APPROXIMATE SCALE

0   500M

Saho-gawa

Nara Park

NARA-MACHI

Kintetsu
Nara
Station

JR Kansai
Main Line

JR Sakurai
Line

JR Nara
Station

JR Kansai
Main Line

Shin-Omiya Station

Kintetsu
Nara Line

ICHIJO-DORI

OMIYA-DORI

SANJO-DORI

1
2
3
4
5
6
7
8
9
10
11
12
13
14
15
16
17
18
19

wealth of ceremonial objects, paintings, scrolls, statues and sutras on display without the help of an English-speaking guide. Though it's easy enough to tour Nara Park without a guide, it may well be worth organizing a guided tour of the museum with one of the volunteer guide groups mentioned below.

If you have time, head south of the city centre for a stroll around the **Naramachi** district. This is a very atmospheric old quarter, filled with traditional houses, narrow streets, craft shops, mini museums and cafés.

Some 12km south-west of Nara lies **Horyu-ji** (daily, 8am-4:30/5pm, ¥1000), founded in 607 and registered by UNESCO in 1993 as a World Heritage Site. The temple grounds are divided into two precincts, the western and eastern compounds. Highlights of the western compound are the Five-storeyed Pagoda and the Main Hall, believed to be the world's oldest surviving wooden structure. In the eastern compound, look out for the Hall of Dreams, built in 739 and housing a statue of the temple's founder, Prince Shotoku. Its octagonal shape is auspicious, since the number eight is considered lucky in Japan.

To reach Horyu-ji, take a local train on the Yamatoji line from JR Nara station (10 mins). Bus No 72 runs from outside Horyu-ji station to the temple (3/hour, 5 mins, ¥170). Get off at 'Horyujimon-mae'. Horyu-ji lies on the Kansai line between Nara and Osaka so could be visited en route to either city.

PRACTICAL INFORMATION
Access
To reach Nara **from Kyoto** follow the route starting on p193. The private Kintetsu Railway also runs services from its station in Kyoto (inside the JR station) to Kintetsu Nara station. Coming **from Osaka,** take a JR Yamatoji line train direct to Nara. A limousine bus operates between Kansai International Airport and JR/Kintetsu Nara stations (¥1800 one way; 90 mins).

Station guide
Anyone with a rail pass is likely to arrive at JR Nara station. The two principal JR lines are the Yamatoji line (to/from Horyuji, Tennoji and Osaka) and the Nara line (to/from Uji and Kyoto). The main concourse is just past the ticket barrier. Coin lockers (almost all ¥300 size only) are outside the main building to the right, which is also where the TiS travel agency is. There are bus stops in front of the main station exit.

Tourist information
There are counters in both JR Nara (☎ 0742-22 9821, daily 9am-5pm) and Kintetsu Nara

(☎ 0742-24 4858, daily 9am-5pm) stations. Both have English speakers and staff can assist with accommodation bookings. The main Nara City Information Center (☎ 0742-22 3900, daily 9am-9pm) is along Sanjo-dori, five minutes from JR Nara station. Here you'll find a scale model of Nara where you can push buttons and get an introduction in English to the city's sights.

Goodwill guides
Nara YMCA organizes free English-speaking guides for tours of Nara. Reservations are preferred (☎ 0742-45 5920, ▤ 47 6459) or enquire at the tourist information counters inside JR/Kintetsu Nara stations. A similar service is provided by Nara Student Guides (☎ 0742-26 4753).

Money
Most banks around the city have signs offering to cash travellers' cheques. To get a cash advance on a foreign-issued Visa/Master Card, there's an ATM in the bus centre opposite Kintetsu Nara station. The ATM is tucked away in a back corner of the ground floor.

Internet

On the second floor of the CAN bookstore (Keirindo) are some computer terminals where you can surf the net/check email for ¥200/30 minutes. CAN is just around the corner from Kintetsu Nara station.

Transport

The best way of seeing Nara is on foot, though renting a cycle is a good option if you're pressed for time.

Cycles can be rented from Kintetsu Rent-A-Cycle (☎ 0742-24 3528, daily, 9am-5pm), near Kintetsu Nara station. The charge is ¥900/four hours or ¥1100/one day. Add ¥100 for weekends. Bikes must be returned by 5pm.

Festivals

As one of Japan's ancient capitals, Nara has many festivals, though one you may wish to avoid is the annual antler-cutting ceremony held for Nara deer in the autumn. July to October is the 'light up' season, when some of Nara's best-known sights, including Kofuku-ji and Todai-ji, are lit up nightly until 10pm.

Where to stay

By far the most atmospheric place to stay is *Nara Hotel* (☎ 0742-26 3300, 🖹 23 5252, 🖳 narah268@gold.ocn.ne.jp). The old wing has enormous rooms with high roofs and spacious bathrooms. Rooms in the new wing may lack the history but are just as comfortable. In the evening the bar is the perfect place to sip a gin and tonic after a hard day's sightseeing and maybe flick through the guest book. Members of the Imperial Family always stay here when visiting Nara (snapshots of their visits line a wall near reception). Singles cost ¥14,000 and twins start at ¥22,000 but special rates are offered to rail-pass holders: ¥9000 for a single and ¥15,100 for a twin.

An excellent mid-range option is the new *Nara Washington Plaza Hotel* (☎ 0742-27 0410, 🖹 27 0484; ¥5975/S, ¥10,390/Tw/D), five minutes from JR Nara station along Sanjo-dori. Rates rise during April/May and October/November.

One of the most appealing areas to stay is Naramachi, an old district full of small lanes and traditional houses. Here you'll find *Ryokan Seikan-so* (☎/🖹 0742-22 2670; ¥4000/pp, Western breakfast ¥450), an old inn built around a traditional Japanese garden. None of the tatami rooms has an attached bath but this is a popular, very reasonably priced place that fills up quickly. It's 15 minutes on foot south of Kintetsu Nara station (part of the way is along a covered arcade) or 25 minutes from JR Nara station.

The best bargain in town is at the new *Nara Kasugano Youth Hostel* (☎ 0742-23 5667, 🖹 23 5679). It doesn't really look like a hostel as it's a small wooden house and takes only 11 people. The rate for YH/HI members is ¥3000, ¥4000 for others; ¥4500 and ¥5500 respectively including two meals. From bus stop No 1 outside JR Nara station, take bus No 2 (city loop bus) and get off at Wara-ishi.

Nara Youth Hostel (☎ 0742-22 1334, 🖹 22 1335) has dormitory accommodation and a nightly rate of ¥3000 for YH/HI members and ¥4000 for others. Breakfast costs ¥600 and dinner ¥1000. From JR Nara station, take bus No 108, 109, 111, 115 or 130 from stop No 9 of the bus terminal outside the station and get off at 'Shieikujou' stop. Nearby *Naraken Seishonen-Kaikan Youth Hostel* (☎/🖹 0742-22 5540) is older but does have the advantage of offering single and twin occupancy rooms if they're not busy (additional charge). The basic nightly rate is ¥2600 for YH/HI members and ¥3600 for others, with breakfast at ¥330 and dinner an additional ¥900. To reach the hostel take bus No 12, 13, 131 or 140 from stop No 9 of the bus terminal outside JR Nara and get off at 'Ikuei Gakuen mae'.

Where to eat

Deer is definitely not on the menu in Nara but there are plenty of fast-food choices along Sanjo-dori, including *McDonald's* and *Mos Burger*. A step up from these is *Capricciosa*, just off Sanjo-dori, serving huge helpings of pizza and pasta, and open daily 11am-10pm. Along Sanjo-dori, in front of Washington Plaza Hotel, is *Skylark,* a cheap Western-style family restaurant with an all-you-can-drink soft-drinks bar.

As well as fast food, Nara offers some excellent if expensive upmarket dining. If you're going to splurge on one good meal, Nara is a good place to do it. The tempura at *Asuka* (daily except Mon, 11:30am-2:30pm and 5-9:30pm, last order 9pm) is real melt-in-your-mouth stuff, with seating at the counter or tables. The cheapest lunch deal is the ¥1500 set meal that gives you a taste of everything, or opt for one of the tempura courses where you sit along the counter and the chef serves you directly. A menu in English is available for the counter courses, with set meal prices of ¥3500-5500. It's on an old, narrow street not far from Sarusawa-Ike.

Along a covered arcade off Sanjo-dori, *Hiten* (daily 11am-11pm, last order 10pm) serves a large range of Chinese dishes like dim sum, spicy pork, chicken, shrimps and beef. The best time to go is for lunch when there are set meals from ¥850. A large set lunch for two would set you back ¥1800. It's still good value in the evening when individual dishes start from about ¥500. They also serve take-out dim sum on the ground floor.

To really empty your pocket pay a visit to *Uma no Me,* close to Nara Hotel. This is about as traditional a Japanese place as you are likely to find. It's a very small restaurant decorated with Japanese *yakimono* (pottery), some of which dates from the early Meiji period. Seating is on tatami mats in the main part of the restaurant or in private rooms with a view over the garden. It's open for lunch (11:30am-3pm, from ¥3500), and for dinner (5:30-8:30pm, from ¥8000, reservation only); closed Thursdays. Finally, the Japanese restaurant in Nara Hotel, *Hanagiku,* serves skilfully prepared box-style lunches (*shokudo bento*) and is open 11:30am-2pm and 5:30-9:30pm.

⛩ Side-trip to Koya-san

Three thousand feet (900 metres) above sea level, a religious centre was founded on Mt Koya in 816 by the Buddhist monk Kukai. Pilgrims and tourists have been flocking here ever since. Where once the monks of Koya-san earned an income by begging to visitors, today they do so by providing accommodation for them. A night spent in one of the temples, with a superb dinner and breakfast of shojin ryori and the chance to take part in early morning prayers, should not be missed.

Think of a visit to Koya-san as an experience in two phases, namely the journey there and the place itself.

● **The journey** The private Nankai Railway operates services from Namba station in Osaka direct to Gokurakubashi station (90 mins; every 30-40mins; ¥850), from where a cable car runs up to Koya-san. Rail-pass holders can go part of the way by JR but have to transfer on to the Nankai line at Hashimoto station.

From Nara, take a train on the Kansai line to Oji (14 mins) and then transfer on to the Wakayama line for Hashimoto. **From Kyoto,** take a train to Nara and then follow the route above.

From Osaka, take a train from Tennoji station on the Yamatoji line to Oji (20 mins). From here, transfer to the Wakayama line and get off at Hashimoto (at least 60 mins). **From Wakayama** (see p178) there are two services an hour on the JR Wakayama line direct to Hashimoto (65 mins).

(cont'd opposite)

❑ Side trip to Koya-san (cont'd)

At **Hashimoto** cross via the overhead footbridge to the Nankai platforms and buy a ticket to Koya-san (45 mins, ¥810) from the booth on the platform. You might have to hang around a bit as connections between JR and Nankai are not always good. The final part of the route is quite possibly one of the finest rail journeys you can make in Japan. From Hashimoto, the train rattles and squeaks its way slowly upwards, until the track becomes surrounded by thick, pine-clad forests. As the train climbs (and your ears pop!), the temperature starts to drop. Here it's about 10° cooler (which makes it pleasant in the summer and freezing in the winter) than on the plains below. Inevitably, the train passes through a number of tunnels, though each time the train emerges into daylight, the scenery becomes more spectacular.

The train terminates at Gokurakubashi. The last part of the journey, one stop to Koya-san station, is a steep ascent by cable car. The five-minute, 870m ride uphill is included in the cost of the ticket from Hashimoto. From Koya-san station, buses take ten minutes to the centre (¥320); stop announcements are in English.

● **Koya-san** Koya-san is small enough to get around on foot. About the only reason for using a bus is to shuttle between the centre and Koya-san station. One-day bus passes (¥800) are available but not worth the money unless you plan to bus everywhere. In the centre of town, **Koya-san Tourist Association** (☎ 0736-56 2616, 🖹 56 2889, daily, 8:30am-4:30pm) has maps and also sells a guide book (¥1000). Cycles can be rented from here (1 hour ¥400; 5 hours ¥1200). Outside the office there are a few coin lockers suitable for day packs.

A combination ticket (¥1000) is available from the tourist office but is only worth buying if you intend to visit most of the sights charging admission. The main one to include on an itinerary is **Kongobu-ji**, the central monastery in Koya (daily, 8:30am-4:10pm, ¥350). This is the residence of the High Priest of Koya-san, responsible for around 3000 monasteries across the country that belong to the Shingon Buddhist sect. Next to the monastery is the 6 o'clock bell, rung by a monk every even hour between 6am and 10pm.

Sooner or later, you and everybody else will be heading for **Okunoin**, part of an enormous cemetery where the body of Kukai is enshrined. According to tradition, on 21st March 835, Kukai entered into 'eternal meditation'. From that day, he has been known as Kobo Daishi, and it is said he will not wake up until Miroku, the Buddha of the future, arrives. The cemetery is packed with tombs and gravestones of Kobo Daishi's followers. It's a good idea to visit early in the morning, when it's a long, peaceful walk from Ichinohashi Bridge on the edge of town through the cemetery towards the Hall of Lanterns, behind which is Kobo Daishi's mausoleum.

● **Where to stay and eat** It's a good idea to book accommodation on Koya-san in advance but tourist office staff will ring around the temples to see what's available if you arrive without a reservation. Either book directly with the temples or send a fax to the tourist office (see above) stating dates and preferred accommodation at least two weeks before arrival. They will send confirmation by fax. Payment is in cash only. At all the temples, overnight guests are invited to attend morning prayers, which usually start at 6 or 6:30am. The cheapest rates are offered by *Haryoin* (☎ 0736-56 2702), also called a 'National Lodging House'; ¥6500 with two meals, or ¥3500 without. Haryoin is a small temple on the edge of town and one of the first stops coming from the cable car station. All rooms share a common bath.

(cont'd overleaf)

❑ **Side trip to Koya-san**

(*Cont'd from p201*) Almost opposite Haryoin is the larger ***Rengejoin*** (☎ 0736-56 2233, 🖷 56 4743) which has rates starting from around ¥10,000 including two meals. Rooms are larger and better appointed, and some have views over a beautiful rock garden. Common bath only. Another bonus of staying here is that the head monk and his mother both speak English. My favourite was ***Sekishoin*** (☎ 0736-56 2734, 🖷 56 4429), founded in 923. The temple is next to Ichinohashi Bridge, which makes it very convenient for an early morning/evening visit to the Okunoin. Rooms in the new building are modern and more like a hotel than temple lodgings, rooms in the old temple building are more atmospheric; both kinds are available with/without bath. For two people sharing a room without bath the nightly rate (including two meals) is ¥16,000; add ¥8000 for a room with attached bath. To reach Sekishoin, take a bus heading for the Okunoin from Koya-san station and get off at Ichinohashi.

It may be worth knowing that most of the temples have beer vending machines so there's no problem having a drink in the evening. Also, if craving a bag of crisps or a bar of chocolate, there is one convenience store on Koya-san. *Coco!* is slightly hidden, on a back street behind the main road, on the opposite side to the tourist office. It's worth trying to find it as they even sell Ben and Jerry's ice cream!

Western Honshu – route guide

Many visitors to Japan take the shinkansen west along the Sanyo coast from Osaka to Hiroshima, perhaps en route to Kyushu (see p320). But western Honshu, also known as **Chugoku** (the 'middle lands'), has much more to offer than a hurried stop in Hiroshima. The Sanyo coast may have the fastest rail connections and the best-known sights but the less developed San-in coast provides a complete change of pace.

The journey from the Sanyo to the San-in coast offers yet another perspective, with spectacular mountain and river scenery and the chance to see a part of

Western Honshu
LOCATOR MAP

0   250   500KM
APPROXIMATE SCALE

SEA OF JAPAN

W. HONSHU

HOKKAIDO

PACIFIC OCEAN

HONSHU

SHIKOKU

TOKYO

KYUSHU

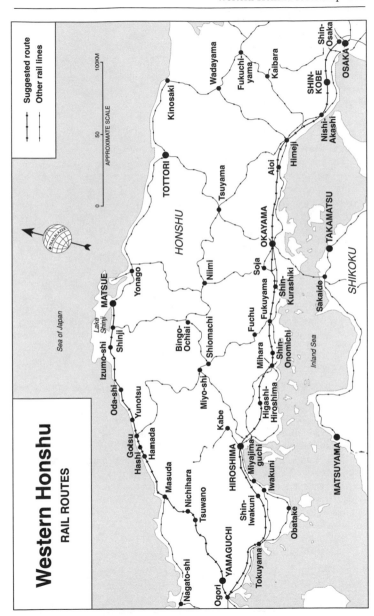

Japan that has not been bulldozed into the industrial revolution. The route along the San-in coast leads to Matsue (p237), justly famous for its splendid lake, Shinji-ko, and for being the former home of Irish writer, Lafcadio Hearn.

Two stations on this route are connection points for other rail journeys: Okayama (see p225) is the starting point for the Shikoku route guide (see p362) and from Ogori (see p211) it's only 20 minutes by shinkansen to Kokura, the starting point for the Kyushu route guide (see p321).

OSAKA (SHIN-OSAKA) TO OGORI BY SHINKANSEN

Distances from Shin-Osaka. Fastest journey time: 2½ hours.

The route below follows the shinkansen line; regular JR trains go on the Sanyo line which roughly parallels the route described but stops at more stations.

Taking the shinkansen, try to use the Hikari Rail Star which runs between Shin-Osaka and Hakata (the entire length of this part of the route). This train is modern, hi-tech and offers about the smoothest ride you'll get in Japan. A bonus is that car No 4 has been designated the 'Silence Car', a rarity in Japan and a welcome haven from the usual non-stop on-board announcements. Even the staff who wheel the refreshments trolley through the carriage don't say a word. All seats in the silence car are reserved so you do have to plan ahead to guarantee a noise-free ride. Don't be put off if some staff at JR ticket offices try to dissuade you from reserving a seat in this car by saying that you might miss your stop because there are no announcements. The Hikari Rail Star has no Green Car but does have private compartments which can be used by four people travelling together with ordinary rail passes – a chance to travel in luxury at no extra cost. Compartments should be booked in advance.

Osaka   [see pp101-8]

Shin-Osaka to Okayama   [Map 11, p205; Table 3, p400]

Shin-Kobe (37km)   [see pp219-25]
To find coin lockers (all sizes) go straight ahead after the ticket barrier until you reach the end of the station building. The entrance to the subway (one stop to Sannomiya station for Kobe) is downstairs. On the main station concourse are a few cafés and stalls selling the city's best-known souvenir, Kobe beef.

Shinkansen fans should note that Shin-Kobe is a good place to view the bullet trains speeding past. The station is unusual in that it has only two tracks (no middle track for trains not stopping at the station), so the services that don't stop at Shin-Kobe shoot straight past along the platform edge. A barrier on the platform closes automatically whenever a through train is about to go past.

The next stop along the line is **Nishi-Akashi (60km)** but only Kodama call here. Most Hikari call next at the castle town of Himeji.

Himeji (92km) As the train pulls in, look out on the right and you'll see Himeji Castle on a hill in the distance. Enquire at the tourist information desk on the concourse of Himeji's shinkansen station about the availability of an

English-speaking guide to show you around the castle. Usually staff will phone ahead and arrange for a guide to be waiting for you when you reach the castle entrance; alternatively take a chance on finding a guide when you get to the castle. All the guides are volunteers and their enthusiasm makes a visit to Himeji even more rewarding than a wander around the castle on your own.

From Himeji station, walk north for about 20 minutes up the tree-lined boulevard (Otemae-dori). About two-thirds of the way along, look out on the left for an udon restaurant, **Menme**, where you can get a filling bowl of noodles and a beer for around ¥1000.

Himeji Castle (daily, Sep-May 9am-4pm, June-Aug 9am-5pm, ¥500) is truly one of the most picture-postcard buildings in Japan. What makes Himeji so special it that it has never been bombed or reduced to rubble. Originally a 14th-century fort, it was rebuilt in its present style at the beginning of the 17th century. It will take you a good two hours to explore the castle and the grounds.

Heading through the main gate, Sakura-Mon, you enter the garden where there are plenty of outer fortifications to explore. Inside the main tower, quickly pass through the lacklustre displays of weapons and wall-hangings, and at the end of a flight of very steep, ill-lit steps, you reach the top, from where there's a great view of Himeji city, the station and surrounding area.

Only Kodama stop at **Aioi (112km)**.

Okayama (180km)   [see pp225-30]
The next stop is Shin-Kurashiki (see below). However, Kurashiki is better accessed by taking a regular JR train from Okayama along the Sanyo line to Kurashiki station (14 mins).

Okayama to Hiroshima   [Map 12, p207;
                             Table 3, p400]
Shin-Kurashiki (206km)   Only Kodama stop here. Shin-Kurashiki is not as convenient

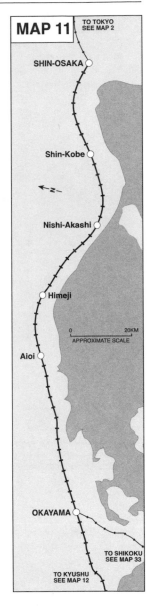

for Kurashiki as Kurashiki station, a nine-minute journey back along the JR Sanyo line (services are frequent).

It's worth stopping in Kurashiki to see the preserved **Bikan historical quarter** with its quaint old buildings, narrow lanes, small museums and canal. Theme park junkies will approve of **Tivoli Park**, a local version of the Copenhagen original. From Kurashiki station, not Shin-Kurashiki, take the north exit for Tivoli Park and the south exit for the Bikan historical quarter and Eki Rent A Car/Cycle (on street level, to the right as you exit the station). Cycles cost ¥350 for four hours or ¥650 for the day. There are coin lockers to the right after the ticket barrier (all sizes). If these are full, there are more by the Eki Rent A Car office at street level on the south side. Some staff at the tourist information centre (☎ 086-426 8681, daily Apr-Oct 9am-6pm, Nov-Mar 9am-5pm) on the station concourse speak English; they can help book accommodation and have a supply of maps. Pick up a copy of the monthly *What's Up in Kurashiki*, which has events listings and occasionally restaurant reviews.

To see Kurashiki in a day, the best plan is to hire a bike at Kurashiki station and cycle out to Bikan, less than 1km south along the main Chuo-dori. There are a number of museums and galleries in the Bikan district. Places with names such as the 'I Love Candy Museum' can be avoided; instead top priority should be given to **Ohara Museum of Art** (daily except Mon 9am-5pm, ¥1000). The museum was established in 1930 by Keisaburo Ohara, the then president of Kurashiki Spinning Corporation, to display the works of Western art that his friend Kojima Torajiro had collected on a number of visits to Europe – all this decades before bubble-economy rich Japanese businessmen were snapping up world-famous Western art work from Christies by telephone. Since then, the museum has expanded to house not only Western art but also a gallery of Asiatic art and a Craft Art gallery of ceramics and woodblock prints. But the biggest draw is its French Impressionist collection, as well as works by Picasso, Edvard Munch and Andy Warhol. An audio guide which introduces some of the works in the collection is available for hire (¥500).

Opened in 1997 outside the station's north exit, attractions at **Tivoli Park** (🖥 www.tivoli.co.jp/entivoli/) include a ferris wheel, roller coaster and log flume, as well as daily musical shows. The equivalent of Disneyland's Sleeping Beauty Castle is Tivoli Tower, a recreation of a medieval Danish castle. A day admission ticket is expensive (¥2000) and this doesn't even include entry to the paid attractions. If you're going to make a day of it, a one-day passport (¥4400), allowing unlimited use of all attractions, is the best deal. However, the best time to visit is after 5pm, when general admission tickets are reduced by 50% (¥1000). Opening times vary but are longest in the summer (check the website).

Check with tourist information about accommodation and rates at some of the small minshuku and ryokan in town. For proximity to the station, JR-run *Hotel Kurashiki* (☎ 086-426 6111, 🖷 426 6163; ¥8500/S, ¥12,000/D and ¥16,000/Tw) is the best choice. Rooms are above the station and some have views of Tivoli Park. Rail-pass holders receive 10% off advertised room rates.

Kurashiki Youth Hostel (1537-1 Mukoyama, ☎ 086-422 7355) has dormitory bunks at ¥2940 for YH/HI members and ¥3540 for others; reservations are required. Take a bus from stop No 6 of the bus terminal outside the south exit and get off at 'Shiminkaikan-mae', from where you have to walk 15 minutes up the hill to the hostel. For ¥400 per bag (paid directly to the youth hostel), you can leave your luggage in the morning at the Rent A Cycle office by the south exit of the station (8:10am-4pm), spend the day at leisure in Kurashiki, then collect your bags from the hostel after 5pm.

In summer, Hotel Kurashiki has a top-floor beer garden called *Alligator-son*, with all-you-can-drink-and-eat deals (two-hour time limit) for ¥3000, or ¥3300 for a view of Tivoli Park lit up at night. In the station is a *McDonald's* and a branch of the tonkatsu chain *Saboten*, with a take-out counter.

Fukuyama (239km)

As the train arrives look out on the right for a glimpse of Fukuyama Castle. This former castle town suffered extensive damage from WWII bombing raids. The view of concrete blocks as far as the eye can see is not an encouragement to linger but Fukuyama has a couple of quirky museums worth a half-day stop on the way to Hiroshima.

There are two sides to Fukuyama station. Take the north exit for the Castle Park, Prefectural Museum of History and Fukuyama Automobile and Clock Museum. Coin lockers are outside and to the right as you take the north exit (a few ¥600 lockers). Within the station is a shopping mall called 'Suntalk' with a few restaurants and a branch of *Andersen* which has a good selection of take-out sandwiches and cakes.

Staff at the tourist information counter (☎ 0849-22 2869, daily, 8:30am-5pm) on the main concourse give out leaflets and maps but don't deal with hotel reservations. The Seto Inland Sea Welcome Card (see p46) is available free from here.

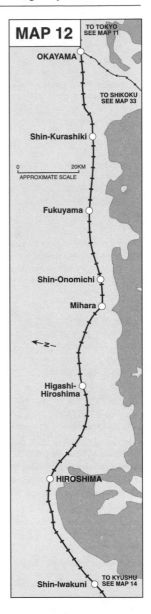

MAP 12 — TO TOKYO SEE MAP 11

OKAYAMA

TO SHIKOKU SEE MAP 33

Shin-Kurashiki

0   20KM
APPROXIMATE SCALE

Fukuyama

Shin-Onomichi

Mihara

← z →

Higashi-Hiroshima

HIROSHIMA

Shin-Iwakuni — TO KYUSHU SEE MAP 14

⛩ **Miracle cures by the Headless Jizo**
Twenty-four kilometres north-west of Fukuyama is the small town of **Fuchu**, known for its **Kubinashi Jizo** ('Statue of Headless Jizo'). The history of this statue, guardian deity of children, travellers and pregnant women, and how it came to be headless, remain something of a mystery. Nobody knows who the stone statue represents but the story goes that at dawn on 18 May 1977, the image of the Jizo appeared in the dream of a local resident. In his dream, the man heard a voice telling him: 'I am buried in the ploughed field on the hill. If you unearth and enshrine me, I will answer the prayers'. A taskforce began digging up the field and it wasn't long before the statue was found and duly enshrined. Ever since, the Jizo has kept his half of the bargain by answering the prayers of those who make a pilgrimage to the statue. There are numerous reports of the sick or infirm visiting the shrine and making a full recovery.

News of the headless statue's healing powers have since spread; there is now a steady stream of visitors to the shrine from all over Japan. The Jizo is also said to offer advice on everything from business and finance to personal relationships. A leaflet from the shrine office advises on how to pray at the shrine. The most popular method involves lighting a candle, chanting a sutra and then including your wishes in a prayer to the Jizo. Many visitors also touch the headless statue and towels can be bought from the shrine office for ¥500, with the purpose of rubbing them over the Jizo and taking them home for use in the bath to relieve aches and pains. It's worth noting before you begin to ask the Jizo for assistance that there is no guarantee of immediate pain relief. Some visitors 'temporarily fall in worse condition suddenly' before they get better.

Fuchu is reached by local train (40 mins; twice hourly morning and evening, hourly at other times) on the JR Fukuen line from platform No 8 at Fukuyama. A Jizo Festival is held at the shrine on the 18th of each month.

Fukuyama Castle, built in 1619 and situated in a park by the north exit of the station, has a reconstructed castle tower and museum of no great interest (daily except Mon, 9am-5pm, ¥200, 20% off with Welcome Card).

Much more fun is **Fukuyama Automobile and Clock Museum** (daily, 9am-6pm, ¥900 or ¥700 with Welcome Card), a 15-minute walk north of the station. You're allowed to get in all the cars on display, including a 1954 Mercedes Benz and some original 1960s Mazdas. But it's much more than clocks and cars; there are also gramophones, early TV sets, electric organs, a horse-drawn carriage, light aircraft and waxworks of famous Americans. This is a place where you are encouraged to touch and feel, live and breathe, 1960s America.

If you need to stay in Fukuyama, one of the cheapest places is *Fukuyama Terminal Hotel* (☎ 0849-32 3311, 🖹 32 3322), five minutes west of the station. Single rooms at ¥5500 with TV and aircon are not bad for the price.

Shin-Onomichi (259km) Only Kodama stop here.

Mihara (270km) Only Kodama stop here. Mihara is the nearest station to **Buttsu-ji**, a centre for training in Zen meditation, 40 minutes to the north by bus

🏮 The sole of Japan

Matsunaga, Japan's top production centre of traditional geta (wooden clogs), is between Fukuyama and the next shinkansen station at **Shin-Onomichi** (see opposite). To reach here, take a local train two stops (approx 10 mins) from Fukuyama along the Sanyo line; services operate about four times an hour between 9am and 7pm.

'As long as footwear continues to be made here,' says a travel brochure, 'Matsunaga will be the "soul" of Japanese feet'. To prove it, the town is home to the unique **Japan Footwear Museum** (daily, 9am-5pm, ¥1000, 20% off with Welcome Card). Laid out here in pairs is a sweeping history of footwear, from the earliest straw sandals to the latest in high-street fashion boots. Don't miss the glass cabinet that contains a few of the more quirky uses for shoes: a red, stiletto-heeled telephone, a geta-shaped ashtray and a large ceramic boot that doubles as a German beer mug. The museum coffee shop is a good place to put your feet up, but not for too long since museum staff might just snatch your footwear to add to the collection. Tickets are also valid for the adjacent **Japan Folk Toy and Doll Museum**. Most of the toys, dolls, kites and talismans on display are connected with religious festivals.

The Japan Footwear Museum is five minutes on foot (how else?) from the south exit (to the right as you pass through the ticket barrier) of Matsunaga station. Turn left on leaving the station, walk up to the junction, then turn right; the entrance is just up this road on the right.

From Matsunaga, rejoin the route by taking a train on the Sanyo line four stops to Mihara (approx 20 mins; see opposite), on the shinkansen line.

(four/day, ¥600). The temple is surrounded by cedar and maple trees, which attract visitors during the 'autumn leaves viewing' season, when admission costs ¥300.

Higashi-Hiroshima (310km)   Only Kodama stop here. For central Hiroshima, get off at the next stop.

Hiroshima (342km)   [see pp230-7]
For the island of **Miyajima** (see p235), transfer here to the Sanyo line.

Hiroshima to Ogori   [Map 13, p210; Table 3, p400]
Shin-Iwakuni (383km)   Only Kodama stop here.
The first major stop after Hiroshima is the town of Iwakuni, known for the five-arched **Kintaikyo Bridge** which spans Nishiki-gawa. The scenery is certainly picturesque and there is the added attraction of a ride by ropeway up to **Iwakuni Castle**.However, a stop here shouldn't be considered a top priority, more a pleasant diversion if you have the time.

Iwakuni has two main stations: Shin-Iwakuni, the shinkansen station, and Iwakuni, which is on the Sanyo line. The tourist area is roughly equidistant between the two, about a 15-minute bus ride away. JR Bus and Shiei Bus operate shuttle services between Shin-Iwakuni station, Kintaikyo Bridge and Iwakuni station (¥240 from Iwakuni and ¥280 from Shin-Iwakuni). JR buses are

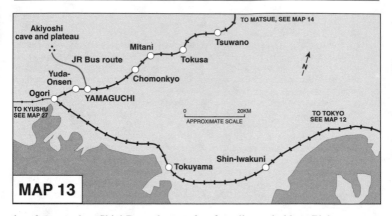

MAP 13

less frequent than Shiei Buses but are free for rail-pass holders. Pick up a map of Iwakuni at the tourist information booth (daily except Mon 9:30am-4:30pm) in Iwakuni station. A tourist information office with similar opening times is in Shin-Iwakuni station.

When the feudal lord of Iwakuni constructed the five-arched bridge in 1673 his aim was to ensure that it could never be washed away, but it duly has been twice. Crossing the bridge costs ¥220 when the toll booth is open. Over on the other side, you'll see a ropeway up to Iwakuni Castle (¥320 one-way, ¥540 return, ¥800 return plus castle entry). Destroyed in 1615 at the time of the Tokugawa shogunate, the castle was rebuilt in 1962 and moved to the top of a hill – not for reasons of military defence but to improve the view. There's little of interest inside (samurai armour you can see in any other castle in Japan and a

model of Kintaikyo Bridge, which you can see for real down below) but the top-floor lookout commands excellent views in good weather of Nishiki-gawa, the bridge and the Inland Sea in the distance. In the summer, it's a little cooler up here, and there are some walking trails.

If you show the Seto Inland Sea Welcome Card (see p46) at the toll booth just before you cross the bridge, there's a discount on the package ticket which includes bridge, ropeway and castle (¥840 becomes ¥670). This ticket is sold up to 3:30pm, to give you time to get up and down by 5pm.

❏ **The Holy Grail**

Monty Python star turned globetrotter Michael Palin visited Buttsu-ji (see p208) during his *Full Circle* travel documentary (episode 2, 14th Sept 1997) for BBC Television and attempted to interview the chief abbot:
'As I am only here for one night, what will I be able to learn in that time from being here, do you think?'
'You?'
'Yes.'
'But that is your problem. You must not ask me.'
'Oh well, interviewing never was a Zen activity.'

Buses to Shin-Iwakuni and Iwakuni stations depart from the bus terminal close to Kintaikyo Bridge.

Tokuyama (430km) A stop for Kodama and a few Hikari but the majority of the latter zoom past before stopping at Ogori.

Ogori (474km) Ogori is the starting point for the JR Yamaguchi line which runs inland across western Honshu all the way up to the San-in coast. It is not an attractive city and functions only as a useful transport hub. Ogori is a stop for both shinkansen and Sanyo line services. The JR ticket office is on the second floor of the shinkansen side, as is the tourist information office (daily, 8:30am-5pm). No English is spoken.

An overnight stay in Ogori may be necessary if planning to catch the morning steam train that runs along the Yamaguchi line to Tsuwano (see box below). Unfortunately, there's little in the way of accommodation apart from a few run-down business hotels. One exception is *Yamaguchi Grand Hotel* (☎ 0839-72 7777, 🖹 72 7393; ¥5500/S, ¥11,000/D, ¥11,000 and ¥13,000/Tw), opposite the station (shinkansen side). For a quick snack, on the ground floor of the station there is a branch of the *Vie de France* bakery that includes a café. Otherwise, Yamaguchi Grand Hotel has a Chinese restaurant and a bar that serves yakitori and beer in the evenings.

If heading for **Kyushu** (see p321), continue on the shinkansen from Ogori to Kokura (23 mins) and pick up the route guide starting on p322.

OGORI TO MASUDA   [Map 13, p210; Map 14, p215; Table 11, p405]

Distances by JR from Ogori. Fastest journey time: 1 hour 35 minutes.

Ogori (0km) Transfer to a Yamaguchi line train. It's mostly local trains on this line but three times a day the Oki LEX runs from Ogori to the San-in coast.

The Lady of Rank – a grand steam experience
At weekends from March to November every year, the SL Yamaguchi (C571, nickname: 'Lady of Rank') runs between Ogori and the picturesque rural town of Tsuwano (see p214). All seats on this steam locomotive are reserved but there are no additional charges for rail-pass holders. Without the pass, the fare from Ogori to Tsuwano is ¥1620. The train leaves Ogori in the morning and steams for just over two hours through the countryside, arriving in Tsuwano in time for lunch. It then waits for around three hours before making the return journey.

Apart from the steam locomotive itself, the highlight is a ride in one of the carefully preserved carriages, each designed to recall a different era of Japan's railway history. The best place to sit, however, is at the back of the train, where there's an observation car with (non-reserved) armchairs facing the window. Staff dress up in old railway uniforms and a huge crowd lines up to take photographs as the train pulls out of the station. The train departs from the old-fashioned platform 1 at Ogori station. There are daily services during Golden Week and most of August.

However, the Oki's noisy diesel engine, lack of trolley service and Japanese-style toilets make it a rather unglamorous experience. Car No 1 is reserved and non-smoking, cars 2 (smoking) and 3 (non-smoking) are unreserved. The name 'Oki' comes from the Oki islands, a group of 180 islands in the Japan Sea.

Yuda-Onsen (10km) Just before the train reaches Yamaguchi, there's a brief stop at this small hot spring resort favoured by Japanese looking for a cure for arthritis and other aches and pains.

Yamaguchi (13km) Off the shinkansen track, if not quite off the beaten track, Yamaguchi must be one of the smallest prefectural capitals in Japan. The main reason for pausing here is to take a trip to **Akiyoshi Cave** (see box opposite).

Yamaguchi Tourist Association (☎ 083-933 0088, daily, 9am-6pm) is on the second floor of Yamaguchi station. Staff will help book accommodation and can advise on travel throughout the area. A day or half day is good enough to see the main sights in Yamaguchi. Enquire at the bus ticket counter outside the station for Rent A Cycle (daily, 8am-5:30pm, 2 hours ¥320, each additional hour ¥100, or one day costs ¥840). If you rent a cycle, they'll store your luggage for free – considering it can cost up to ¥600 to use a large coin locker (some by the bus ticket counter), it can work out a lot cheaper to rent a cycle and leave your lug-gage there – even if you just leave the cycle round the corner.

The most unexpected sight in Yamaguchi is the modern **St Francis Xavier Memorial Church** at the top of Kameyama Park, 15 minutes on foot north-west from the station. The original church, built in 1952 to commemorate the 400th anniversary of Xavier's stay in Yamaguchi, burnt down in 1991. It was rebuilt in 1998 and now has a modern, pyramid design with two 53m-high square towers. Beyond the church, you'll really need a cycle to reach the Five-Storey Pagoda at Ruriko-ji. The temple grounds are part of Kozan Park, 1km north of Kameyama Park.

The cheapest lodgings are offered at *Yamaguchi Youth Hostel* (☎ 083-928 0057; ¥2600 YH/HI mem, ¥3300 non-mem), though it's an inconvenient 20-minute bus ride away in Miyano. The English-speaking manager is helpful but the place is a little down-at-heel. Accommodation is in shared tatami rooms, with supper an additional ¥1000 and breakfast ¥500. Staff at the tourist office have produced a useful guide to reaching the hostel. At the other end of the scale is *Hotel La Francesca* (☎ 083-934 1888, ▤ 934 1777), at the foot of the road leading up to Xavier Memorial Church. It's a Tuscan-style villa with bright,spa-cious twins from ¥30,000 and even larger suites from ¥40,000.

If you leave the station and turn left on to the main road, the first large building you'll see on the left is Pal-Lu Plaza. Run by the post office, the build-ing is part cinema, part restaurant and part conference hall. On the ground floor plaza is *Enchanté* (daily except Mon, 11am-9pm), which does a buffet dinner. For lunch, there are a variety of mainly Japanese set meals at reasonable prices. *Hotel La Francesca* (see above) has a classy Italian restaurant with the best deal at lunchtime when there are reasonably-priced pasta lunches. It's open daily for lunch from 11am to 3pm, as a café from 3 to 5pm and for dinner from 5 to 9pm.

⛩ Akiyoshi cave and plateau

Though not accessible by rail, it's worth considering a trip to Akiyoshi cave and plateau, since the route from Yamaguchi is operated by JR Bus so rail-pass holders can travel for free. The cave is 100m below Akiyoshi plateau and is the largest limestone cave either in Japan or in Asia – depending on who you talk to, or which leaflet you pick up.

After buying an entrance ticket (¥1240 or ¥1050 using the Seto Inland Sea Welcome Card, see p46), you enter an area that resembles a rain forest; it's an unexpected scene, especially after the man-made shopping arcade just outside. The entrance to the cave is no less impressive. A crashing waterfall (almost) drowns out the noise of microphone-clutching, flag-waving tour guides, who appear to have no fear of wearing high heels inside a slippery limestone cave. The path is obvious, so there's no danger of disappearing down a dark tunnel. For anyone wanting a bit more of an adventure, near the entrance there's a more off-the-beaten track that can be tried for an extra ¥300 (throw your money in the box and pick up a torch). The path winds its way past various rock formations, some of which have been given unusual names like 'big mushroom' and 'crepe rock'.

Though it's hard to gush quite as much as the publicity leaflet – 'the colours and shapes of stalactites, stalagmites, flowstones and limestone pools are so fantastic that you feel as if you are in an underground palace' – there's no denying that the interior is breathtaking. If visiting in the winter, it's advisable to put on several layers as the temperature drops considerably inside the cave. In the summer, the temperature is a good reason for heading on in, to beat the humidity.

At the end of the trail inside the cave, an elevator whisks you up 80m to within an easy 300m walk of Akiyoshi plateau. The change of temperature hits you as you leave the lift and begin the short ascent towards the plateau, which spans the horizon in front of you as if part of an extravagant Scottish Highlands film set (the plateau even boasts its own 'Akiyoshi Thistle'). The size of the plateau varies according to what you read but the largest estimate suggests it covers an area of 130 sq km. The plateau dates back 300,000,000 years (the impressive figure is displayed on a board close to the viewing area) to the time when a coral reef formed in the sea; the rocks that exist today were once lumps of coral reef. Only 500,000 years ago, rhinoceros, giant deer and elephant roamed around the tree-covered plateau.

At the top, there's a lookout observatory, souvenir shop and a place to buy drinks and ice cream. To return to Akiyoshido bus centre, you can retrace your steps (¥100 to take the lift back down) and walk back through the cave; alternatively, you can walk, or catch a bus down from the plateau.

From Yamaguchi station, JR buses (¥1300 one way for non-pass-holders) take around 50 minutes to reach Akiyoshi-do Bus Center close to the cave entrance. There are currently nine services a day in each direction. You can pick up a guide to the cave and plateau from the tourist information desk (☎ 08376-21620, daily, 8:30am-4:30pm) in the bus centre. From here, follow the signs to the cave entrance, which is a five-minute walk through a parade of shops.

Next to the hotel and under the same management is *Xavier Campana* (daily, 9am-8pm), a bakery which sells a range of cakes, sandwiches and salads. Look also for restaurants along the main street which leads up from the station towards a covered arcade, and along the arcade itself. Less than a minute from the station, on the right side of the main street, is the Indian restaurant *Shiva* (daily, 11am-3pm, 5-9pm). The weekday lunchtime set menu (¥800) is a bargain, though the ¥1500 course menu is also good value. A 10% discount is offered to holders of the Seto Inland Sea Welcome Card (see p46). Following the main road up from the station, turn right onto the covered shopping arcade. A few minutes' walk along on the right is Chimakiya, a department store with a basement food hall. Next door is a branch of Mister Donut.

♦ **Chomonkyo (32km)** The limited express does not stop at this small station, popular with photographers looking for a suitable vantage point to snap the Yamaguchi steam train (see box p211). Enthusiasts/photographers should make sure they are on a local train from Yamaguchi (about 30 mins) or Tsuwano (about 50 mins; see below) so that they can stop here. Services in either direction operate approximately hourly in the morning and evening and every 90 to 120 minutes during the day.

After Chomonkyo, the train passes through a succession of small stations before pulling in to Tsuwano. The final approach has some amazing views of the countryside. From the elevated track, you can look down on villages of black-roofed houses – a rural side to Japan rarely seen and mostly forgotten. The limited express calls at **Mitani (39km)** and **Tokusa (50km)**.

Tsuwano (63km) Tsuwano is not the only town in Japan to hanker after the name 'little Kyoto' – Takayama (see p155) also claims that title, as do others – but it is certainly one of the most picturesque stops on a journey through western Honshu. A former castle town of samurai lodgings and small canals filled with plump koi, Tsuwano can trace its foundation back over 700 years. During the Edo period (1600-1868), a number of persecuted Christians were banished

---

⛩ Hidden Japan

More than just rattling off the main sights, the real pleasure of Tsuwano is to wander around the old streets. With no obligation to tick off a list of must-see historical monuments, here is a luxury in waiting to watch time pass by slowly. No convenience stores, few cars, hardly any of that mind-numbing noise blaring out from shops, pachinko parlours and restaurants you find elsewhere in Japan. Not quite frozen in time, Tsuwano has at least decided not to follow slavishly the pace that other parts of Japan rush to keep. Armed with the excellent bilingual guide book, which contains a comprehensive list of all the town's sights, restaurants, lodgings and cafés, it is very tempting to spend several days here.

Being so picturesque, Tsuwano invites the crowds, but once they've departed after a frenetic day of sightseeing, in a puff of smoke as the steam locomotive heads back to ugly Ogori, it's very gratifying to wander around the quiet roads and savour the atmosphere. Many visitors to Japan justifiably complain that travelling here is never relaxing. Tsuwano is one of the few places to challenge the perception of a fast-paced, hi-tech, can't-wait, non-stop country that, in its desperate rush to meet the future head on, rarely has time to dwell in the past.

to Tsuwano, a place presumed to be suitably out of the way for the troublemakers to be forgotten about.

The steam locomotive from Ogori (see box p211) terminates in Tsuwano. Coin lockers are on the left side of the station as you exit (a couple of large ¥600 lockers). A tourist information office (☎ 08567-21771, daily, 9am-5pm) is in a small building to the right as you leave the station; the best source of information is the bilingual English/Japanese booklet (¥200). It's updated every two years and contains detailed information about the key sights in town. Rent A Cycle at the station charges ¥500 for two hours or ¥800 for one day.

The main sights are the ruins of **Tsuwano Castle**, the colourful **Taikodani Inari Shrine**, known for its tunnel of 1000 red gates, and **Washibari-Hachimangu Shrine**, venue for an annual display of yabusame (Japanese horseback archery) on the second Sunday in April.

Virtually all accommodation in Tsuwano is in ryokan or minshuku. Staff at the tourist office will make bookings and provide directions to the places mentioned below. *Wakasaginoyado* (☎/📄 08567-21146) is a small, friendly minshuku where English is spoken. Rates (including two meals) are from ¥7000 per night. *Tsuwano Youth Hostel* (☎ 08567-20373; ¥2900 YH/HI mem, ¥3900 nonmem) is about ten minutes by bus from the station. The bus service is not that regular (tourist information has an up-to-date schedule), so it doesn't make for a very convenient base.

If you really need a Western-style bed, try *Hotel Sunroute Tsuwano* (☎ 08567-23232, 📄 22805), just above the town and visible from the station. Old-fashioned singles cost from ¥7800 and twins from ¥12,600. If Tsuwano takes visitors back in time, the interior of this hotel will whisk you more specifically back into the 1970s. It has a restaurant and a hot spring bath, though be prepared for tasteless carpets in the guest rooms.

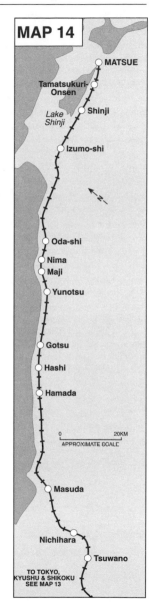

MAP 14

MATSUE

Tamatsukuri-Onsen

Lake Shinji

Shinji

Izumo-shi

Oda-shi

Nima

Maji

Yunotsu

Gotsu

Hashi

Hamada

0   20KM
APPROXIMATE SCALE

Masuda

Nichihara

Tsuwano

TO TOKYO, KYUSHU & SHIKOKU SEE MAP 13

There is no shortage of places for lunch, with restaurants catering to the day tourist. *Tsurube* (daily except Fri, 11am-7pm) serves excellent hand-made noodles in huge bowls for around ¥700-800. From the station, turn right on to the road in front of you, walk for about five minutes and look out for it on the right.

If you're looking for a snack, *Talk Saloon Tsuwano* (daily, 8:30am-5pm) shares a building with telephone company NTT and does excellent all-day coffee-and-waffles sets. From the station, turn right and go straight down the main road. It's a five- to ten-minute walk down this road on the left. Most restaurants shut by 7pm, though this isn't really a problem since virtually all the ryokan/minshuku in Tsuwano include an evening meal in the nightly rate.

The 'Tsuwano Express Highway Bus' departs nightly (9:40pm; ¥9000 one way) for Osaka from in front of Tsuwano station. For details, contact Iwami Kotsu (☎ 0856-24 0085, daily, 9am-6pm). Reservations are required.

Nichihara (73km) After Tsuwano, the Oki LEX stops briefly at this town of astronomy. Nichihara's link with the stars is evident from the constellation design by the platform. There's no tourist office at the station but there is a 'plaza' with a small branch post office and souvenir stand. The staff are friendly but don't speak English.

Nichihara Astronomical Observatory (*Tenmondai* in Japanese) (¥500, daily, 12-10pm; closed Jan-Mar) is a 50-minute walk uphill from the station. There is no bus service so the alternative to walking is an eight-minute taxi ride. During the day, you can see the telescope inside the observatory and visit the small museum, but star gazing itself starts after dusk. *Pension Hokutosei* (☎ 08567-41010, 🖹 41647; ¥6000/pp, ¥8500/pp with two meals), a Western-style pension next to the observatory (under the same management), is a good place to crash out after an evening gazing into deep space.

From Nichihara, the train continues north towards the San-in coast, roughly following Takatsu-gawa all the way out to the Japan Sea. If you've already travelled around Shikoku (see p362), you might notice the similarity of the landscape – lush and green, with rivers, forests and the occasional village and rice field.

Masuda (94km) A couple of minutes before arriving in Masuda, the scenery changes dramatically. After a slow journey through the rural spine of western Honshu, it's a rude awakening to emerge into a sea of smoke stacks and factory buildings. Masuda is an important railway junction, as it marks the end of the line from Ogori and is the connecting point for lines running along the San-in coast.

There's no need to change trains here for the next part of the route if travelling on the Oki LEX, which continues east along the San-in coast.

MASUDA TO MATSUE [Map 14, p215; Table 11, p405]

Distances by JR from Masuda. Fastest journey time: 2 hours 40 minutes.

Masuda (0km) From Masuda, the Oki LEX heads east along the San-in line. A few minutes out of Masuda, the train finally reaches the Japan Sea, dotted with rock formations. The sea here is rough and much less inviting than the calm water of the Inland Sea. For sea views, sit on the left side.

Hamada (41km) About 45 minutes east along the line from Masuda by limited express is the town of Hamada, an unremarkable stop recently put on the map thanks to a new aquarium. To reach the aquarium, change to a local train here and continue three stops to Hashi.

From Hamada, the train heads a little inland, so views of the Japan Sea are less frequent.

♦ Hashi (51km) Nearest stop to **AQUAS** (daily except Tue, 9:30am-5:30pm, ¥1500), an aquarium where you can see three white dolphins, seals, crabs, jelly fish and the like. Follow the signs to the aquarium from Hashi station.

Gotsu (60km) Change here to a local train if planning to visit Nima Sand Museum (see Nima below). Local/rapid trains from Gotsu and Oda-shi (see below) to Maji or Nima leave approximately hourly though less frequently in the middle of the day and not all rapid services stop at Maji.

Yunotsu (77km) Not all limited expresses stop at Yunotsu, a spa town popular with elderly holidaymakers. Forest surrounds both sides of the track along this section of the route but you might catch the odd glimpse of the sea.

♦ Maji (83km) Nearest station to the 'singing sand' beach of Kotogahama. The beach is named after Princess Koto, a member of the Heike clan who fled north to the San-in coast after the Heike were defeated by the rival Genji clan in the 12th century (see p33). To thank the people who lived by the beach for offering her protection, she played the koto (Japanese zither) every day. According to legend, after her death the sand itself began to make a noise similar to that of the koto. To this day it's said that whoever walks along the beach will hear the sound of the sand 'singing' to them.

To test this theory, leave Maji station and walk straight ahead to the beach. A volleyball tournament is held here annually at the end of July.

♦ Nima (86km) Just before the (local/rapid) train arrives at this small station, you might catch sight of an unusual glass pyramid building on the left which looks a bit like the entrance to the Louvre in Paris. This is **Nima Sand Museum** (daily except Wed, 9am-4:30pm, ¥700). Its main attraction is a giant egg timer which lasts for one year before needing to be turned over again. Passing by the self-playing piano by the entrance, there are various machines that revolve and pump sand round and round, displays of coloured sand, and jars of the stuff collected from beaches across Japan and around the world, including a sample from Waikiki Beach in Hawaii. The flow of sand in the egg timer, towering above the central atrium, is affected by outside temperature so the only way of ensuring that the year doesn't end too quickly is to use a computer which regulates the flow. Every year at midnight on 31st December, 108 people help to turn the hourglass round and welcome in the new year; visitors are welcome to join in.

⛩ **Side trip to Tottori**
From Matsue (0km), the San-in line continues east towards the city of Tottori (122km). First take a Yakumo or Super Yakumo LEX as far as the industrial city of Yonago (29km), see Table 11, p405. Yonago functions as a regional transport hub since it is a stop on the San-in line as well as a junction of the Hakubi line which runs south to Okayama (see p225) two hours away by Yakumo or Super Yakumo LEXs. To continue east, the Super Kunibiki LEX runs five times a day from Yonago to Tottori in 70 minutes. The Tottori Liner is slower, taking just over 90 minutes, but runs more frequently.

Tottori is known for its sand dunes which extend east to west along the coast for some 16km. The dunes are 20 minutes by bus (¥360) from platform 3 of the terminal outside Tottori station. It's hard to believe unless you actually make the effort to travel out here that Japan really does have its own mini desert. Just in case you forget where you are once you've arrived, non-native camels wait on the edge of the dunes for a classic Japanese photo opportunity (for a fee) or to take you for a ride. Horse-drawn carts are also on standby.

If you need somewhere to stay, ***Tottori Green Hotel Morris*** (☎ 0857-22 2331, 🖹 26 5574) is a few minutes walk north of Tottori station, just past Daimaru department store. Tiny 'business' singles go for ¥5000 while more spacious 'comfort' singles cost ¥5500. Twins are ¥9800 and doubles ¥8800. Included in the price is a newspaper (in English) outside your door in the morning. A coin laundry is available.

For food, there's a UCC coffee shop on the second floor of the station and a variety of ekiben are sold on the main concourse. *Kanizushi* (strips of crab meat on a bed of rice) is the best known. Opposite the station is a ***Mister Donut***, and Daimaru department store has a basement food hall. More upmarket dining possibilities are to be had next door at ***Hotel New Otani Tottori*** (☎ 0857-23 1111, 🖹 23 09225. The best deal is at ***Parier*** on the second floor, where there's an all-you-can-eat buffet lunch for ¥1500 (11am-2pm). Staying the night at the New Otani is not such a good deal, with singles from ¥8800 and doubles/twins at ¥18,000.

From Tottori, the Inaba LEX takes two hours to run south along the Inbi and Tsuyama lines to Okayama (see p179), while the Super Hakuto takes just over three hours to Kyoto (see p180). Note that part of the track on the route between Tottori and Okayama/Kyoto (between Chizu and Kamigori) is operated by the private Chizu Kyuko railway, which means rail-pass holders must pay a ¥1770 supplement (payable on board).

JR Nima station is very small and has no tourist information office. It's an eight-minute walk to the Sand Museum – leave the station, cross the train tracks and head towards the glass pyramid building.

Oda-shi (97km) A commuter stop on the limited express but of little interest to the tourist. There are great views of the Japan Sea on the approach to Izumo-shi as the train runs on an elevated track. You might see the odd fishing boat out in the distance.

Izumo-shi (130km) Izumo-shi is the nearest JR station to **Izumo Taisha**, site of a well-known shrine and a popular side trip from Matsue (see p242). The shrine can be reached by private Ichibata Railway.

From the north exit of the JR station, go straight and turn right on to the main road. Ichibata's station is just up this road on the right. It's a new station with attached department store which opened at the end of 2001. From Ichibata Izumo-shi, take a local train four stops to Kawato, where you change trains again for the final leg to Izumo-Taisha-mae.

For a speedy return to the Sanyo coast, the Yakumo LEX, a more modern train than the Oki, takes three hours to Okayama (see pp225-30).

Shinji (146km) This station is right on the edge of Lake Shinji but trees block all views until just before the train reaches Matsue.

Tamatsukuri-Onsen (156km) This popular hot spring resort, where it is claimed the gods once enjoyed bathing, is on the shore of Lake Shinji. The tourist information office in Matsue (see p240) can provide information on hotels and bath houses here.

During the last few minutes of the journey towards Matsue, there are views of Lake Shinji on the left.

Matsue (163km) [see pp237-42]

MATSUE BACK TO KYOTO/OSAKA

The fastest way back to the Sanyo coast is to take a Yakumo or Super Yakumo LEX along the Hakubi line to Okayama, a stop on the shinkansen (see p205). From Okayama, pick up a Hikari east (see p204) or Kyoto (p168). The fastest journey time from Matsue to Okayama is 140 minutes.

Western Honshu – city guides

KOBE

Short on sights but big on food, shopping and entertainment, Kobe is a good place to break a journey along the Sanyo coast. Like Nagasaki (see p343), Kobe developed as an international port city and is today popular as a tourist spot for Japanese interested in seeing the foreign settlements and Western-style houses that lent the city an 'exotic' feel in the decades following the Meiji Restoration.

The biggest event of the more recent past took place at 5:46am on January 17th 1995 when Kobe was struck by the Great Hanshin Earthquake. Over 6000 people were killed, more than 100,000 buildings destroyed, and much of the city and surrounding area reduced to rubble. But, such is the speed of recovery from natural disaster in Japan that few outward signs of this tragedy remain.

What to see
There's not a great deal to see in the area around **Shin-Kobe**, so if you've only got a little time it's best to catch a subway one stop to Sannomiya, the centre of

KOBE 神戸

Where to stay/eat

1	Kobe Kitano Youth Hostel	1 神戸北野ユースホステル
3	Shin-Kobe OPA	3 新神戸OPA
4	Holiday Inn Express Shin-Kobe	4 ホリディインエクスプレス新神戸
5	Super Hotel Kobe	5 スーパーホテル神戸
6	Hotel Monterey Amalie	6 ホテルモントレアマリー
7	Hotel Monterey Kobe	7 ホテルモントレ神戸

Other

1	Kitano Tenman Shrine	1 北野天満神社
2	Shin-Kobe Ropeway	2 新神戸ロープウェイ
8	Phoenix Plaza	8 フェニックスプラザ
9	Visa ATM (International)	9 Visa ATM （インターナショナル）
10	Kobe International House	10 神戸国際会館
11	Post office	11 郵便局
12	Kobe Harbor Circus	12 神戸ハーバーサーカス
13	Mosaic	13 モザイク
14	Kobe Maritime Museum	14 神戸海洋博物館
15	Meriken Park	15 メリケンパーク
16	Port Island	16 ポートアイランド
17	Rokko Island	17 六甲アイランド

downtown Kobe. That said, a short excursion can be made from Shin-Kobe by taking the **Ropeway**, a few minutes on foot from the station. Head towards Shin-Kobe Oriental Hotel just below the station and follow the signs to the rope-way entrance. The ropeway (return trip ¥1000) connects Shin-Kobe with 'Nunobiki Herb Park' on a hill behind the station. The herb park is a tourist trap and isn't worth bothering with on a cloudy day, but if the weather is co-operating it's possible to see as far as Kansai Airport.

Next to the tourist information booth in Sannomiya is **Phoenix Plaza** (daily, 10am-7pm; free), built to provide a permanent record of the destruction wrought by the 1995 earthquake. Most of the displays are in Japanese, though there's an excellent pamphlet (in English) that provides plenty of background information. Available at the entrance are headphones that provide an English translation to the series of films shown about the earthquake.

North of Sannomiya station lies the **Kitano district**, with Western-style buildings such as an 'original Holland house' and 'Wien Austrian house', which are probably of more interest to the domestic tourist. Many of the buildings had to be reconstructed after the 1995 earthquake and aren't really worth seeking out. It is, however, worth visiting **Kitano Tenman Shrine** which also houses a youth hostel (see p223). The shrine dates from the late Heian period (794-1185) and is popular for the views it offers over the city. On a clear day this is the best place to take in Kobe's geography. By the entrance to the shrine is a small kiosk

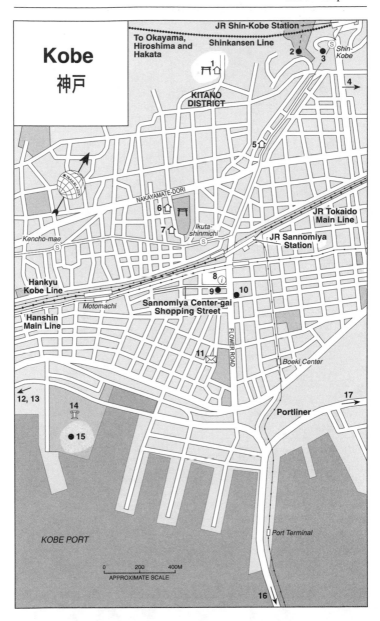

that sells cold drinks and ice cream. Just below here is a tourist information branch office, though not all the staff speak English.

Two stops west along the Sanyo line by local train from JR Sannomiya station is JR Kobe station, access point for **Harborland** and its shopping malls, department stores and small amusement park with ferris wheel. Head either underground as you exit the station or overground, walking under the elevated express way towards the main shopping and entertainment area. A good walk can be made by following the bay around from Harborland all the way to **Meriken Park**, a popular place for young couples searching for a romantic bay view. **Kobe Maritime Museum** (daily except Mon, 10am-5pm, ¥500), in Meriken Park, is more impressive from the outside than in.

Port Island and Rokko Island are man-made constructions off the coast and are accessible from the centre of Kobe via unmanned light transit railways. One of the biggest attractions on the larger **Port Island**, reached from JR Sannomiya via the Port Liner transit system, is Kobe Portopia Land (daily except Wed, 10am-5:30pm). A loop-the-loop roller coaster and giant ferris wheel are two of the attractions at this theme park by Minami-koen station. It's a classic example of what Kobe's all about – a city of entertainment without any kind of educational headache. Entry costs ¥1400 (no rides included); a one-day pass valid for all rides costs ¥3800. The smaller **Rokko Island** is home to **Kobe Fashion Museum** (daily except Wed 11am-6pm, Fri until 8pm, ¥500). The permanent exhibition of costumes, from sleek evening dresses to flowing Imperial gowns, is housed in the fashion wing. Temporary exhibitions are staged in the art wing. To reach Rokko Island, take a train from JR Sannomiya along the Tokaido line two stops east to Sumiyoshi station, and transfer on to the Rokko Liner. For the museum, get off at Island Center station.

PRACTICAL INFORMATION
Station guide
The main JR stations in Kobe City are **Shin-Kobe** (for shinkansen) at the foot of Mt Rokko, **Sannomiya** in the city centre, and **Kobe,** a gateway to the city's Harborland shopping and entertainment area. Sannomiya is a major rail junction, with the Hanshin and Hankyu railways, subway and JR stations all crossing through here. This means that Sannomiya, far more than Shin-Kobe, is the centre for commerce, shopping and entertainment.

Tourist information
The main tourist office is on Flower Rd in Sannomiya (☎ 078-322 0220, daily, 10am-7pm, July-Aug until 8pm), in a booth opposite Hanshin Sannomiya station. There's also an information counter at Shin-Kobe station (daily, 10am-6pm), though the staff here don't have as much information at their fingertips. On the 20th floor of Kobe International House in Sannomiya is the **Kobe International Community Center** (☎ 078-291 8441, Mon-Sat, 9am-5pm), which has foreign newspapers, magazines and organizes monthly cultural events. Another reason for coming here is the free view of the Shin-Kobe area.

Volunteer guides
Kobe Student Guides is a volunteer group of students from Kobe and Osaka. Volunteers are happy to guide foreign visitors around sights in Kobe, Osaka (see pp101-8) and around Himeji Castle (see p204). The only costs involved are the guide's transport, admission fees and lunch. Contact details for the group change from

time to time, so pick up a leaflet from the tourist office or check 🖳 www.geocities.co.jp/CollegeLife/3136/.

Access to/from Kansai International Airport

For rail-pass holders, the best way of getting to Kansai Airport (see p45) is to take a shinkansen to Shin-Osaka, one stop along the line from Shin-Kobe, and from there to take the Haruka LEX. The quickest way of reaching the airport, however, is to take the K-JET high-speed boat which shuttles between the K-CAT terminal on Port Island and Kansai in under 30 minutes. Tickets cost ¥2400 one-way or ¥4560 return, including the bus journey from K-CAT to Sannomiya station. If flying on JAL, ANA or JAS, you can also check in at K-CAT before taking the boat across to the airport.

Getting around

Kobe has a modern and efficient subway. Arriving in Shin-Kobe station, it's best to take the Yamate subway line one stop to Sannomiya. The new Kaigan line, opened in time for the 2002 World Cup, runs from Sannomiya to the football stadium outside Misaki-koen station.

On the 20th of every month a one-day city bus and subway ticket is sold for ¥500. The subway is very user-friendly, with signs in English and a button for an English translation on the ticket machines (look for the British flag).

The City Loop tourist bus service, which circles downtown Kobe in around one hour, is another option. Individual rides cost ¥250 or a one-day pass is ¥650. Passes are available from the tourist information offices at Sannomiya or Shin-Kobe, or on the bus. Pick up a copy of the timetable and route guide when you buy the pass.

Festivals

The biggest annual event is **Kobe Matsuri**, which lasts for about 10 days towards the end of July. On the last weekend there's a big fireworks display and a parade of floats through the city. Check with the tourist office for exact dates/times.

Where to stay

For peace and comfort, a good place to head is *Holiday Inn Express Shin Kobe* (☎ 078-222 1212, 🖹 222 1222, 🖳 hxkobe@nyc.odn.ne.jp; ¥8000/S, ¥13,000 /D, ¥16,000/Tw), in a quiet residential area five minutes on foot south-east of Shin-Kobe station. The rooms have neat touches like Japanese screens across the windows and the rate includes continental breakfast.

A cheaper option, midway between Sannomiya and Shin-Kobe, is *Super Hotel Kobe* (☎ 078-261 9000, 🖹 231 9090; ¥5800/S inc continental breakfast). Part of a growing national chain, this place has functional rooms that are fairly comfortable. All have aircon, TV, wide beds and attached bath but no telephone or fridge. Payment is in cash only, which you feed into a machine. Instead of keys, guests receive a receipt with a code number to unlock the door.

Just below the Kitano area, not far from Sannomiya, is *Hotel Monterey Kobe* (☎ 078-392 7111, 🖹 322 2899; ¥8800/S, ¥19,000/Tw/D). The theme is Italy, with whitewashed walls, patio courtyards and fountains. The guest rooms are less ambitious but pleasant enough with wide beds and wooden floors. Still more intriguing is the newer annex, *Hotel Monterey Amalie* (☎ 078-334 1711, 🖹 334 1788; ¥8000/S, ¥18,000/D, ¥19,000/Tw). The theme here is apparently nautical – most striking are the extraordinary lifts, worth a look even if you're not staying here. There's a good French restaurant with a ¥1500 lunch menu.

Kobe Kitano Youth Hostel (☎ 078-221 4712, 🖹 251 5682; ¥3200 YH/HI mem, ¥4200 non-mem, no meals), attached to Kitano Tenman Shrine (see p220), has modern four- and six-bed bunk dorms. Each bed can be curtained off for a bit more privacy and you even get an in-bed reading light! From the hostel meeting room, there's a fantastic view over Kobe. It's wise to book ahead in high season.

To get to the hostel, head for Tenman Shrine and go up the hill past the shrine entrance. The entrance is via a flight of stairs on the left side. Kitano is hilly, so be prepared for a bit of a slog if you've got a lot of luggage.

Where to eat

There are plenty of restaurants where Kobe beef is on the menu. One of the best known is *Wakkoku*, on the third floor of the Shin-Kobe OPA Center adjacent to Shin-Kobe station. An evening meal at Wakkoku doesn't come cheap, with course menus averaging ¥11,000 per head; it's better value at lunchtime, with the cheapest set course at ¥2500. There are many other restaurants and cafés at Shin-Kobe OPA, including places specializing in ramen, teppanyaki, tonkatsu and two beer restaurants, *Budweiser Carnival* and *Asahi Pier 21*. For fast food, there's a branch of the hamburger chain *Wendy's*.

The area in, around and underneath the railway stations in Sannomiya is packed with places to eat. Kobe International House, along Flower Rd, has a concert hall and cinema as well as two basement floors of cafés and restaurants. The cinema is on the 11th floor, next to a café with a roof-top garden called 'Tooth tooth the dining garden: gastronome and sensuality'. It's a good place to relax and forget the bustle of city life.

The Harborland district around JR Kobe station also has countless dining possibilities. Two big shopping and restaurant complexes close to Kobe station are Kobe Harbor Circus and Mosaic. The latter is probably the busiest and includes restaurants, shops and cinemas.

Whether or not it has anything to do with Kobe's Western influence, the coffee culture is big here and shows no sign of slowing down. *Starbucks* long ago smelt a major business opportunity in Japan and has opened several branches in the Kobe area. One is in the basement of Kobe International House in Sannomiya, and another is on the first floor of Kobe Harbor Circus in Harborland.

Side trip from Kobe

Probably the most popular side trip from the city is to the **Rokko mountains** behind Shin-Kobe, considered the perfect escape from frenetic city life. As with many natural escapes that lie so close to densely populated areas in Japan, the Rokko area has its charms – gentle hikes and views of the Inland Sea – but also shameless tourist traps, such as a museum of music boxes, Mt Rokko pasture and a 'Kobe Cheese Castle'.

Before setting off, pick up a copy of the excellent *Mountain Trails in Kobe* from the tourist information office; this has suggested routes and hiking courses. A trip on a cable car and ropeway into the mountains can be combined with a visit to **Arima-Onsen**, a hot spring resort on the other side of the mountain range. Arima-Onsen is one of the 'three ancient springs' in Japan, along with Kusatsu and Dogo-Onsen (see p386), but the future has caught up with the past in the modern hotels that cater to tourists.

There are a number of possible approaches to Arima-Onsen; the best way for rail-pass holders is to take a train from JR Sannomiya one stop east to JR Rokkomichi, then take a city bus (No 16) to Cable-Shita station, the starting

Opposite: The O-torii gate to Itsukushima Shrine (see p236), which at high tide appears to be floating on the water but which looks no less dramatic at low tide. (Photo © Bryn Thomas).

⛩ **Momotaro – the Peach Boy**

You can't wander around Okayama for long without noticing one of Japan's most celebrated folk heroes. The city has declared itself home to Momotaro, the legendary Peach Boy.

A well-known fairy tale begins with an old woman washing her clothes in a river, when she discovers an enormous peach floating by. She fishes it out and drags it home to her husband. Salivating at the prospect of tucking into a juicy peach, the old man takes a knife and is about to cut it when the fruit suddenly breaks in half and a baby boy jumps out. The 'peach boy' grows up with superhuman strength and soon leaves his parents to sail off to the Demon's Isle where, in the best traditions of good against evil, he defeats the Demon King – with the help of a spotted dog, a monkey and a pheasant he picks up along the way.

Okayama claims the heroic figure of Momotaro for its own, partly because the prefecture is known for peaches but also because the legendary Demon's Isle is thought to be the island of Megishima, in the Inland Sea between Okayama and Shikoku (see p363). On the plaza, outside the east exit of Okayama station, is a statue of Momotaro and his entourage on their way to fight the demon. Momotaro's face appears on some of the city's manholes, on the Momotaro credit card and in most souvenir shops. The Okayama Momotaro Festival takes place in spring (usually on the third Saturday and Sunday of April). International mail sent from the central post office receives a peach boy stamp and there's even a naked peach boy statue (holding a peach) in Korakuen (see p228).

---

point for a ten-minute cable car ride (¥1460 return) into the mountains. At the top of the cable car, it's possible to connect with the Rokko Arima Ropeway which takes 30 minutes (¥2640 return) to reach the terminus at Arima station.

OKAYAMA

One of the largest cities in western Japan, Okayama faces the Inland Sea, enjoys a mild climate and is known for its large stroll garden called Korakuen. The city expanded politically and economically during the Edo period (1603-1867) but suffered a devastating air raid on 29th June 1945. The bombing of Okayama has been largely forgotten, even though an area of almost 8 sq km was razed to the ground, because it happened just a few weeks before the atomic bomb was dropped on Hiroshima. Over 25,000 buildings – including Okayama Castle – were destroyed and more than 1700 people lost their lives.

What to see

Korakuen, part of Okayama's 'culture zone', is the city's star attraction. The zone is on both sides of Asahi-gawa across town from the station. Take a tram

---

Opposite: Hiroshima's A-Bomb Dome (see p231), originally the city's Industrial Promotion Hall, was one of the few buildings to remain standing after the world's first atomic bomb was dropped on the city in 1945. (Photo © Richard Brasher).

from the terminus outside the station all the way down Momotaro-dori to Shiroshita (¥100). At this junction, turn left and walk north for a minute to find on the left side **Okayama Orient Museum** (daily except Mon, 9am-5pm, ¥300), a recommended stop which houses a collection of ceramics and glassware mainly from Syria, Egypt and Iran. The displays are well lit and there is some English signage. A pamphlet is available at the entrance and there's a tearoom on the second floor.

Just past the Orient Museum on the same side of the road is **Okayama Prefectural Museum of Art** (daily except Mon, 9am-5pm, ¥300), displaying the work of local artists. It's also a venue for temporary exhibitions.

OKAYAMA　岡山

Where to stay

1 Okayama-ken Seinen Kaikan YH	1	岡山県青年会館YH
2 Okayama International Center	2	岡山国際センター
3 Matsunoki Ryokan	3	まつのき旅館
4 Hotel Granvia Okayama	4	ホテルグランヴィア岡山
5 Mielparque	5	メルパルク
6 Okayama City Hotel	6	岡山シティホテル

Where to eat

11 Heaven/Maruhachi	11	ヘヴン/丸八
13 La Melodie	13	ラ メロディ

Other

7 Hunter Bar	7	Hunter Bar
8 I Plaza	8	アイプラザ
9 Desperado	9	Desperado
10 Central Post Office	10	中央郵便局
12 Mitsui Sumitomo Bank	12	三井住友銀行
13 Okayama Symphony Hall	13	岡山シンフォニーホール
14 Okayama Orient Museum	14	岡山オリエント美術館
15 Okayama Prefectural Museum of Art	15	岡山県立美術館
16 Korakuen	16	後楽園
17 Okayama Castle	17	岡山城

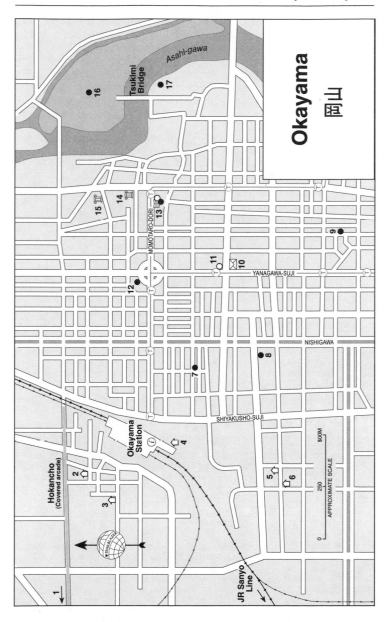

Okayama
岡山

Continue north until you see on your right a road leading across a bridge towards the entrance to Korakuen. The highlight of a stroll around the landscaped gardens of **Korakuen** (April-Sep 7:30am-6pm, Oct-Mar 8am-5pm, ¥350) is the 'borrowed' view – the black façade of Okayama Castle tower looming down from the hill above. The garden was constructed in 1700 by Tsunamasa Ikeda, feudal lord of Okayama, and it remained in the hands of the Ikeda family until 1871 when it was given to the prefecture. Built on an island on Asahi-gawa, Korakuen was the first garden in Japan to include grass lawns.

After strolling around, instead of backtracking to the main entrance, head for the smaller south exit (towards Okayama Castle). Straight in front of you as you go out is a small path that leads down to the river and a hut where rowing/paddle boats can be rented. Turning to the right after passing through the south exit, cross Tsukimi Bridge which leads to the castle entrance.

Okayama Castle (daily, 9am-5pm, ¥300) is known as *Ujo*, or 'crow castle', after its black exterior. The original 1597 donjon was destroyed during a heavy WWII air raid; the present reconstruction dates from 1966. Nevertheless, it's an impressive sight as you approach the donjon, with gold glittering from its roof. A volunteer guide service runs tours of the castle (from the booth to the left of the entrance), but only in Japanese.

Various combination tickets offer modest reductions on individual entrance fees; Korakuen plus the castle costs ¥520. If you don't want to visit the garden, you can buy a castle plus Oriental Art Museum ticket for ¥480.

Heading back to Shiroshita junction, opposite the tram stop is **Okayama Symphony Hall**. The concert hall has a seating capacity of 2001; it's worth checking the event programme to see what's on. There are several shops inside the complex, including a Maruzen bookstore and Okayama Tourism and Products Center (daily, 10am-8pm), on the first floor; the latter sells a variety of locally-made crafts.

PRACTICAL INFORMATION

Station guide

Okayama station has two sides connected by an underground passage.

The east side is the main exit for Momotaro-dori and Korakuen/Okayama Castle.

The west side is much smaller and is the exit for the International Center, Matsunoki Ryokan and Okayama-ken Seinen Kaikan Youth Hostel. Rent A Cycle offices (4 hours/¥350; 1 day/¥650) are on both sides of the station (east side daily 7:30am-7:30pm, west side daily 7am-7:30pm). Most coin lockers (all sizes) are on the east side.

Tourist information

The staff at the tourist information desk (☎ 086-222 2912, 🖷 224 2572, daily, 9am-6pm), by the station's east exit, speak some English and can provide maps and a list of accommodation. Just next to this desk is a separate hotel reservation desk where you can make same-day reservations (daily, 12-9pm; cash only, ¥525 commission per booking).

For more detailed information in English go to **Okayama International Center** (☎ 086-256 2914, daily except Mon, 9am-9pm, ground floor information counter 9am-5pm), a five-minute walk north-west from the station's west exit. The information counter has one internet terminal (¥300/half hour), CNN on TV, an information board and any number of brochures about places to visit in Okayama prefecture and the rest of Japan. Upstairs, there is a library (daily except Mon 10am-7pm) with books, magazines and newspapers. *Okayama Insider* is published monthly by the International Center and has cinema/event listings.

Alternatively go to **I Plaza** (☎ 086-234 5882, daily except Mon and 2nd Sun, 10am-6pm), a ten-minute walk south-east from the station, which has an international exchange corner on the fourth floor. Here, they organize free Japanese culture classes and also arrange home stays.

Getting around

Okayama's tram network has a terminus in front of Okayama station. There's a flat fare of ¥100 for journeys within the central area, any further afield is ¥140. The nearest tram stop to Korakuen (see opposite) is Shiroshita.

A limousine bus (¥680) takes 30 minutes from Okayama station to Okayama Airport, which handles mostly domestic flights.

Money

Mitsui-Sumitomo Bank, on a corner of the Yanagawa intersection, accepts foreign-issued Visa cards for over-the-counter cash advances. A passport and a considerable amount of patience are needed.

Where to stay

Top of the range is the JR-run *Hotel Granvia Okayama* (☎ 086-234 7000, ▤ 234 7099), right outside the east exit of the station. It's expensive even with a 10% discount to rail-pass holders. *Okayama City Hotel* (☎ 086-221 0001, ▤ 221 7100, ▭ cityhtl@mocha.ocn.ne.jp; ¥7000/S, ¥12,000/Tw) is one of the newest business hotels in the city and its rooms are surprisingly spacious. It's a seven-minute walk from the east exit of the station. Opposite is *Mielparque* (☎ 086-223 8100, ▤ 223

9152), one of a chain of hotels run by the Post Office (hence the post office flags out front). Basic singles are ¥4700, though for ¥1000 more you get a much larger room. Basic twins go for ¥9000 or ¥15,000 if you want more space. If you're looking for a Japanese inn, *Matsunoki Ryokan* (☎ 086-253 4111, ▤ 253 4110; ¥5000/S, ¥8000/Tw and ¥10,500/Tr) has tatami rooms with air con and attached toilet/bath. It's a friendly place that attracts a mix of Japanese and foreigners. Dinner (optional) costs ¥1300 and breakfast ¥700. The ryokan is a couple of minutes' walk west from the station's west exit. If in a fix, the *International Center* (☎ 086-256 2000, ▤ 256 2226) has a few rooms with attached bath and shared kitchen facilities. Singles are ¥5600, twins ¥4000 per person or a triple is ¥3500 per person. Book in advance, check-in is 4-10pm and you're asked to be in by 11pm.

The accommodation at *Okayama-ken Seinen Kaikan Youth Hostel* (☎ 086-252 0651, ▤ 252 7950, 1-7-6 Tsukura-cho; ¥2800/YH(HI), ¥3400/non-members) is in shared tatami rooms that have seen better days. Take city bus No 5 from Okayama station and get off at the 'Seinenkaikan-mae' stop, then turn right on to the next street after the bus stop. The hostel is the building with the pink exterior.

Where to eat

Beneath the station is Okayama Ichibangai, an underground shopping mall, with a selection of cafés, restaurants and take-out bakeries. For lunch, a number of places do good-value all-you-can-eat buffets.

Heaven, on the 20th floor of the Cred Building opposite the central post office, has a ¥1500 buffet lunch (daily, 11am-2:30pm). Window tables have great views of Okayama city. Also on the 20th floor, and offering similar views, is the Chinese restaurant *Maruhachi*, open all day from 11am. They offer a 'service lunch' for only ¥500. On the 6th floor of the same building there's a variety of Japanese restaurants serving ramen, udon, tonkatsu and the like. On the 3rd floor of Okayama Symphony Hall, next to the main auditorium, *La*

Melodie offers a ¥1500 buffet lunch including coffee (daily, 11:30am-2pm).

If visiting the International Center, *Café Fossette* is a small place that serves drinks and light snacks just to the right as you enter the building. Finally, a couple of places worth checking out if you want to meet some of Okayama's foreign residents:

Hunter Bar (known as 'Hunter's') has a couple of pool tables and shows music videos. It gets busy on Friday evenings. *Desperado* sometimes has live bands and guest DJs on Saturday nights but is really more of a bar than a club. The music varies, so check the listings in *Okayama Insider* for details of who and what's on.

HIROSHIMA

For most visitors, the story of Hiroshima begins and ends with the dropping of the world's first atomic bomb at 8:15am on August 6th 1945. But it was the city's historical importance that made Hiroshima an obvious target to the American military.

The largest castle town in the Chugoku region throughout the Edo period, Hiroshima continued to be a centre of political and economic affairs right up to and beyond the Meiji Restoration of 1867 (see p35), when the city became the seat of the prefectural government. In the decades following the Meiji Restoration the city grew as a centre for heavy industry, while the nearby port of Ujina expanded to become a base for the Imperial Army.

The atomic bomb wiped out the military garrison in an instant but what is remembered is the human devastation – it's estimated that 140,000 had died as a direct result of the bombing by the end of 1945. Some feared it would be decades before grass would grow again, while others believed the scorched land would remain desolate for ever. Clocks and watches froze at 8:15am but time did not stand still after the blast. It only took 17 days to rebuild the railway between Hiroshima and Ujina, and only three for the first tram line to restart. Many survivors took heart in seeing the trams back in service so soon after the blast.

In the decades since 1945, Hiroshima has reinvented itself as a centre for world peace and now, as you pull into the station by shinkansen, what you see is a thriving city of shops, restaurants and open spaces.

What to see and do
● **The Peace Memorial Park area** The park is on the west side of the city, sandwiched between the Honkawa and Motoyasu-gawa rivers. Before the A-bomb razed the city to the ground, this area was Hiroshima's main shopping and entertainment district. Now it is home to the **Peace Memorial Museum** (daily, 9am-5/6pm, ¥50, 20% off with Welcome Card), the one place everybody should visit when in Hiroshima. Divided into east and west exhibition halls, the first displays you see are two scale models of Hiroshima, before and after the explosion.

Just one second after detonation, the bomb created a fireball 280m in diameter – the aftermath and appalling effects of the A-Bomb are detailed in the west hall, where the most powerful exhibits are personal objects, such as a twisted pair of spectacles and a mangled bicycle frame. Don't leave the museum without stopping at the video booths, where some of the A-Bomb survivors – known as *hibakusha* – have recorded their own testimony of the day Hiroshima's sky turned black.

The Peace Park itself contains numerous memorial statues and peace monuments. Just across the river, and clearly visible from the tourist office, is the **A-Bomb Dome**, the burned-out shell of what was once the Hiroshima Prefectural Industrial Promotion Hall. A car park close by marks the actual hypocentre but the A-Bomb Dome is the only monument to be preserved as a reminder of the devastation.

The **Children's Peace Monument** is easily identifiable by the colourful paper cranes draped over it. The monument was erected in memory of Hanako Sasaki, a young girl who contracted leukaemia a decade after the bomb and who died in hospital before she could achieve her goal of making 1000 paper cranes.

The annual peace ceremony takes place in front of the **cenotaph**, underneath which is a chest containing the names of all those claimed by the city as atomic bomb victims. In 2000, the names of 5021 people were added to a list which now exceeds 217,000.

Some of the monuments in the park are more unexpected. Near the tourist information centre, look out for the large stone, cut from Ben Nevis in Scotland and presented to the city as a symbol of goodwill and of the wish for reconciliation and world peace. The newest addition to the park is the **Korean A-Bomb Victims Monument**, the base of which is a turtle because in Korean legend dead souls are carried to heaven on the back of a turtle. There are 2527 registered Korean victims but it's thought that as many as 20,000 were killed. For years, the monument was only allowed to stand outside the Peace Park, on the other side of the river. It was finally allowed into the park in 1999.

● **Away from the Peace Park** Try to fit in a visit to **Shukkeien** (daily, 9am-6pm, Oct-Mar 9am-5pm, ¥250, 20% off with Welcome Card), a beautiful Edo period garden originally designed in 1620 by a feudal lord and located on the banks of the Kyobashi-gawa. Another good place for an early evening stroll is **Central Park**, just west of the reconstructed Hiroshima Castle.

Finally, **Hiroshima City Transport Museum** (daily except Mon, 9am-5pm, ¥440 or ¥350 with Welcome Card) has interactive exhibits geared mostly towards children – the train simulator is the most popular. Serious trainspotters will find the place a bit gimmicky but there's just about enough here (old train posters, tickets, model engines and the like) to make the visit worthwhile. Pride of place in the museum goes to a huge model city, which is either a dream-like vision of how we will all be moving around in the future, or a futuristic urban nightmare, where the quaint idea of walking on foot has long ago been abandoned. Outside, there are 'fun cycles' and battery-powered cars (chargeable). Rail enthusiasts will enjoy the journey to the museum, by

Astramline, Hiroshima's 'new transit system', as much as the place itself; take the Astramline from Hondori station in the city centre north to Chorakuji (¥390). The museum is next to the large Astramline office outside Chorakuji station.

PRACTICAL INFORMATION
Station guide

There are two sides to Hiroshima station: the south (for the city centre), and the shinkansen, also known as the 'Hotel Granvia', side. An underground passageway connects both. On the south side, you'll find the unfortunately-named Asse department store, with restaurants on the sixth floor and a food hall in the basement. The tram terminus is outside the south exit. For coin lockers (all sizes) turn left and follow the station building until you reach the locker room. The shinkansen side is really only of use if staying at Hotel Granvia (see p234).

Tourist information

There are tourist information offices on both sides of Hiroshima station. The staff at the south side office (☎ 082-261 1877 daily, 9am-5:30pm) can't help with reservations but there is a hotel booking desk (daily, 11am-9pm) which charges a commission of ¥525 per booking. Less busy is the desk (☎ 082-263 6822, daily, 9am-5pm) in the JR ticket office on the shinkansen side. Staff here will help with reservations.

The main tourist office in the city centre is **Hiroshima City Tourist Association** (☎ 082-247 6738, daily, Apr-Sep 9:30am-6pm, Oct-Mar 8:30am-5pm), in the Rest

---

HIROSHIMA 広島

Where to stay

1 Ikawa Bekkan	1 いかわ別館
2 World Friendship Center	2 ワールドフレンドシップセンター
3 Hiroshima International Youth House/Aster Plaza	3 広島市国際青年会館/アステールプラザ
6 Rihga Royal Hotel Hiroshima	6 リーガロイヤルホテル広島
15 Dormy Inn Hiroshima	15 ドーミーイン広島
17 Hiroshima Youth Hostel	17 広島ユースホステル
20 Hiroshima Ekimae Green Hotel	20 広島駅前グリーンホテル
21 Hotel Granvia Hiroshima	21 ホテルグランヴィア広島

Where to eat

8 One Coin Bakery	8 ワンコインベーカリー
11 Andersen	11 アンデルセン
12 Pronto	12 プロント
13 Mario Espresso	13 マリオエスプレッソ
14 Okonomi-mura	14 お好み村

Other

4 Peace Memorial Museum	4 平和記念資料館
5 A-Bomb Dome	5 原爆ドーム
7 Sogo Book-kan	7 そごうBook館
9 Visa ATM (international)	9 Visa ATM(インターナショナル)
16 Central Post Office	16 中央郵便局
18 Hiroshima City Transport Museum	18 広島市交通科学館
19 Shukkeien/Prefectural Art Museum	19 縮景園/広島県立美術館

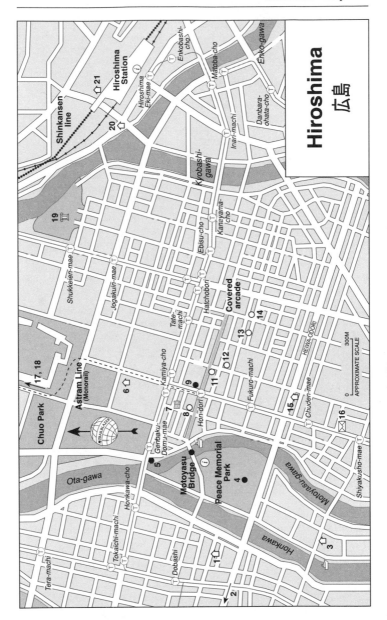

Hiroshima
広島

Shinkansen line

⇧21

Hiroshima Station

Hiroshima Eki-mae

⇧20

Enkobashi-cho

Matoba-cho

Enko-gawa

Danbara-ohata-cho

Inari-machi

Kyobashi-gawa

Ebisu-cho

Kaneyama-cho

19 🏯

Shukkeien-mae

Jogakuin-mae

Tate-machi

Hatchobori

Covered arcade

14 ○

13

Kamiya-cho

○12

11 ○ ●9

Fukuro-machi

HEIWA-ODORI

17, 18 ⇦

Astram Line (Monorail)

Chuo Park

6 ⇧

7

8 ○

Hon-dori

15 ⇧ Chuden-mae

0   300M
APPROXIMATE SCALE

⊠16

Shiyakusho-mae

Genbaku-Dom-mae

●5

Ota-gawa

Honkawa-cho

Motoyasu Bridge

ⓘ

Peace Memorial Park

●4

Motoyasu-gawa

Tera-machi

Tokaichi-machi

Dobashi

Honkawa

1 ⇧

⇧3

2 ⇩

House on the edge of the Peace Park, just after you cross over Motoyasu Bridge.

If you're interested in visiting a Japanese home for a couple of hours, apply in person (with your passport) at the **International Exchange Lounge** (☎ 082-247 9715, daily 10am-6pm Dec 1st-Apr 30th, 9am-7pm May 1st-Nov 30th), on the first floor of the International Conference Center in the Peace Memorial Park. Volunteer Peace Park guides can be arranged through the World Friendship Center (☎ 082-503 3191, see Where to stay).

The **Seto Inland Sea Welcome Card** (see p46) is available from these offices.

A useful on-line resource for information is Get Hiroshima (💻 www.gethiroshima.com); up-to-date listings of sights, hotels, restaurants, bars, cinemas and events in and around the city are provided.

Getting around

Hiroshima is one of Japan's best-known tram cities; provided the trams don't get stuck in traffic they are by far the best way of getting from the station to the downtown area. Single tickets cost ¥150 within the city limits or a one-day pass is ¥600. Alternatively, a ¥1000 pre-paid card gives ¥1100 worth of travel. Pick up a map of the tram network either from the tourist offices or from the tram ticket booth outside the station.

Rail-pass holders can get to the ferry port for the trip to Miyajima (see opposite) for free; if you don't have a rail pass consider taking the tram from Hiroshima station to Hiroden Miyajima (¥270).

A less conventional way of seeing Hiroshima is by **pleasure boat**. Though there are no great views, you do get an alternative perspective on the city and the boats at least don't get snarled up in heavy traffic. There are two departure points: one is close to Motoyasu Bridge which crosses into the Peace Park, the other (with fewer daily departures) is behind Aster Plaza (see map, key No 3). The 50-minute boat cruise costs ¥1100. For further details, contact Hiroshima River Cruise Company (☎ 082-240 5955).

Internet

Multimedia Station I Love You is an Internet café (with free drinks) in the basement of Sogo Book-kan, behind the Deo Deo electrical store in the centre of Hiroshima. Open 24 hours, you need to show some ID (a passport is OK) to 'join' the café. Membership costs ¥100; one hour of surfing costs ¥390, plus ¥90 for every 15 minutes thereafter.

Festivals

The annual **Peace Ceremony** is held on August 6th inside the Peace Park. In the evening, thousands of paper boats lit by candles are set afloat on the rivers and are left to drift towards the sea.

Where to stay

Book well in advance if planning to visit Hiroshima for the annual Peace Ceremony on August 6th.

Outside the shinkansen side of Hiroshima station is *Hotel Granvia Hiroshima* (☎ 082-262 1111, 📄 262 4050; ¥9300/S, ¥17,500/Tw, ¥15,500/D), an upmarket member of the JR Hotel group. Despite being right next to the station it's a peaceful place with an impressive lobby, spacious rooms and a choice of restaurants. Close to the south side of the station is *Hiroshima Ekimae Green Hotel* (☎ 082-262 2669, 📄 264-3939; ¥6400/S, ¥10,000 /D, ¥12,000/Tw), a standard business hotel.

Opened in late 2001, *Dormy Inn Hiroshima* (☎ 082-240 1177, 📄 240 1755, 💻 www.dormy-in.com; ¥6500/S, ¥11,000 /Tw) is close to the Peace Park and offers rooms which are a cut above the usual business hotel standard. A bonus is the hotel's own hot spring on the eighth floor. The in-house café/restaurant on the first floor is called 'Big Mamma'.

The *World Friendship Center* (☎ 082-503 3191, 📄 503 3179) is a small house run by a very welcoming American couple. The centre, founded in 1965 to promote world peace, is non profit-making and has a couple of tatami rooms at ¥3500 per person (inc Western breakfast). Take the tram to Dobashi, walk along the tram line to the main boulevard, turn right and cross Midori-ohashi bridge, turn immediately left, go to the fourth street and turn right. The centre is just a few yards up the road, behind the fifth house on the right.

Hiroshima's grandest hotel in the downtown area is *Rihga Royal Hotel Hiroshima* (☎ 082-502 1121, 🖹 228-5415; ¥12,000/S, ¥17,000/Tw). *Ikawa Bekkan* (☎ 082-231 5058, 🖹 231 5995), a five- to ten-minute walk west of the Peace Park, is a small, modern Japanese inn with friendly owners. All rooms have toilet, air con and TV and some have attached bath. A single room with bath costs ¥5500 (or ¥4500 without). Two sharing is ¥9000 with bath (or ¥8000 without).

There's little to recommend about *Hiroshima Youth Hostel* (☎ 082-221 5354, 🖹 221 5377) except the rate it offers to foreign visitors: ¥1770 (Apr-Jun and Oct-Nov) or ¥1940 (Jul-Sep and Dec-Mar). The 10pm curfew is inconvenient and accommodation is in very basic dorms. Another drawback is its location, 25 minutes by bus north of the station, which means you're reliant on public transport. From the station, take bus A, B or C from bus stop No 7 or 8 and get off at 'Ushita shinmachi-ichome', from where the hostel is a 10-minute walk uphill. Far better is *Hiroshima International Youth House* (☎ 082-247 8700, 🖹 246 5808), just south of the Peace Park and in Aster Plaza. Rooms are brightly decorated and an absolute steal for foreign guests who get special reduced rates of ¥3620 for a single and ¥3130 per person for two people sharing a twin. Facilities include a coin laundry and a reasonable restaurant – the only

downside is a midnight curfew. Take bus No 24 from stop No 3 outside the south side of Hiroshima station and get off at 'Kosei Nenkin Kaikan mae', from where it's one minute on foot to Aster Plaza.

Where to eat

Hiroshima is known for *okonomiyaki* (savoury pancakes); the best place to try one is at *Okonomimura*, a building packed with three floors of small okonomiyaki places. Try *Sonia* (daily, 11:30am-2am) on the fourth floor (turn right as you exit the elevator and it's on the right-hand side). They'll give you chopsticks and a plate but the real way to eat it is straight off the griddle.

There are plenty of places to eat along the covered Hondori shopping arcade, one of the most popular being the enormous branch of *Andersen* (daily except 3rd Wed, 10am-8pm), which has a bakery, delicatessen, salad bar, restaurants and an Honorary Danish consul all under one roof. The pizzeria *Mario Espresso* (daily, 11am-10:30pm) is on three floors opposite a small park, a couple of minutes from Okonomimura. The pizza is hand made and very popular but you can stop just for a drink on the first floor which opens out on to the street. Also in this area is a branch of *Pronto*, the coffee house by day that turns into a pub at night.

On the top floor of Rihga Royal Hotel, the ¥2500 all-you-can-eat lunchtime buffet is a feast and you get great views of the city. Finally, don't overlook the *One Coin Bakery*, on a street that runs off from the Hondori shopping arcade. All the cakes, buns and rolls inside are ¥100, making this a good place to put together a cheap packed lunch.

Side trip to Miyajima

Three of the most compelling reasons for going to Miyajima are: (1) Itsukushima Shrine, considered one of the top three scenic spots in Japan, (2) the chance to visit somewhere that has no convenience stores or traffic lights and (3) the ferry to the island is free for rail-pass holders.

From Hiroshima, take a local train eight stops westbound along the Sanyo line to Miyajima-guchi (25 mins). Local trains leave Hiroshima every ten minutes at peak times so there's no need to work out exactly which one to catch – just turn up and go! Head out of the station and walk straight down the road to

⛩ **Hiking Mt Misen**   (see map opposite)

At 530m, Mt Misen is the highest peak on Miyajima; there are excellent hiking trails (or a cable car) which lead up to the summit. A good place to start the hike is **Daishoin Temple**, from where the 'Daishoin Course' winds its way uphill, passing by a number of picnic huts along the way. About a third of the way up the path becomes steep, though it's nothing really challenging (but pack water in the summer, as there's no river for over half the walk and no vending machine until you reach the top).

The route is easy to follow but stick to the path to avoid treading on any snakes. As you reach the top, there's the welcome sight of a vending machine (beer and soft drinks) and there are great views out over the Inland Sea from Mt Misen Observatory. Next is a short walk down to the top cable car station. Note that the monkeys marked on the map are wild and there's no guarantee of spotting any. (Every year a few visitors complain to the tourist office that they went up Mt Misen to see the monkeys and then demand a refund for the cable car ride when they can't find any). At the bottom of the cable car, there's a stream that's good for paddling in. From here, follow the 'Nature Walk' back to the ferry terminal.

The cable car (daily, 9am-5pm, ¥1500 return) starts from Momijidani Park. Note that it is closed for safety checks twice a year, usually for about five days in June and December.

the ferry terminal. From here, JR Ferry services (daily, 6am-11pm, ¥340 return, free to rail-pass holders) take ten minutes to Miyajima and operate every 15 minutes at peak times and every 30-50 minutes at the beginning/end of the day. JR shares the terminal with Matsudai Ferry, which runs an identical service, but rail passes are not valid on Matsudai ferries.

A tourist information desk (☎ 0829-44 2011, daily, Mar-Nov 9am-7pm, Dec-Feb 9am-6pm) is inside Miyajima ferry terminal. The office has maps and information and staff the can help book accommodation. FM radios (¥300) can be rented for a commentary in English but you may find you're spending more time trying to locate the nearest antenna than seeing any of the island. Rent A Cycle (daily, 8am-5pm, 2hrs/¥320, then ¥110/per hour) is available from the JR ticket office on Miyajima.

Tour groups walk straight from the ferry terminal round to **Itsukushima Shrine** (6:30am-5/6pm, ¥500), which according to legend was founded in 593 when three goddesses were led to Miyajima by a crow. It was remodelled in its present structure, with long corridors connecting the main shrine halls, in 1168. Noh performances are occasionally staged at the shrine, which even became the venue for a recent fashion show – the long corridors doubling as the perfect cat-walk. The real attraction of the shrine is the vermilion **O-Torii** (Grand Gate), rising out of the sea (or, depending on the tide, sticking out of the silt) 200m from the main shrine. At high tide the gate appears to float in the water.

To stay overnight, opposite the station is the small but welcoming *Yamaichi Bekkan* (☎ 0829-44 0700, 🖹 44 0701; ¥7000/pp, no meals). There are only a few rooms, all but one of which are Japanese style with attached toilet and bath.

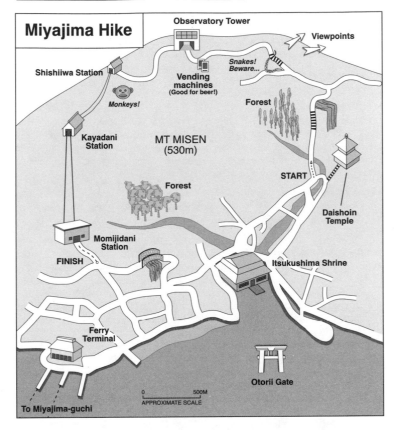

Miyajima Hike

Observatory Tower

Viewpoints

Shishiiwa Station

Snakes! Beware...

Vending machines (Good for beer!)

Forest

Monkeys!

Kayadani Station

MT MISEN (530m)

START

Forest

Daishoin Temple

Momijidani Station

FINISH

Itsukushima Shrine

Ferry Terminal

Otorii Gate

0   500M
APPROXIMATE SCALE

To Miyajima-guchi

The cheapest place is back on the mainland at *Miyajima-guchi Youth Hostel* (☎/▤ 0829-56 1444), a small, old place very close to JR Miyajima-guchi station. Turn right on to the main road in front of the station and it's less than a minute down the road on the left. Accommodation is in plain bunk-bed dormitories or tatami rooms each sleeping four to six people; ¥2730/pp (no reduction for YH/HI members).

MATSUE

'There seems to be a sense of divine magic in the very atmosphere, through all the luminous day, brooding over the vapoury land, over the ghostly blue of the flood – a sense of Shinto'.

Thus wrote Irishman Lafcadio Hearn of Matsue's Lake Shinji, which glistens out to your left as the train pulls into Matsue station. The seventh largest lake in

Japan is unusual in that it's a combination of fresh and seawater, depending on the tide.

Divided into north and south by Ohashi-gawa, Matsue well deserves its title 'city of water'. Matsue is an old castle town and the perfect place to break a journey along the San-in coast. Lafcadio Hearn (1850-1904) took up an English teaching appointment here in 1890; though he only lived in Matsue for a total of 15 months, his former residence is now one of the city's big draws. In his books Hearn often voiced his regret that Meiji-era Japan, in its rush to catch up on centuries of isolation from the outside world, was abandoning many of its ancient traditions. He would probably have been dismayed at the tourist industry that has grown up around his name. As well as the usual postcards, souvenir trinkets and T-shirts, more unusual Matsue souvenirs include Hearn chocolates and bottles of locally-brewed Lafcadio Hearn beer.

What to see and do

Consider spending a couple of days in Matsue as this will give you a chance to see the city and fit in a trip to nearby Matsue-Onsen (see p240) or Izumo-Taisha shrine (see p242).

● **Matsue Castle area** The main city sights are all around Matsue Castle. From the station, take the Lakeline Bus to the castle and then walk between the sights described below. A Universal Pass (¥920) includes entry to the Lafcadio Hearn Memorial Museum, Buke-Yashiki samurai residence and Matsue Castle, and offers small discounts at a number of other sights. The pass is available at the entrance to all three places and is valid for three days, though you can only enter each property once.

The **Lafcadio Hearn Memorial Museum** (daily, Apr-Sep 8:30am-6:30pm, Oct-Mar 8:30am-5pm, ¥300) exhibits objects from Hearn's house and other items relating to his stay in Matsue. Unusual items include a pair of iron dumb bells and a trumpet shell which Hearn 'blew half for fun when he wanted his maid to bring him a light for his tobacco'. Look out also for the high desk Hearn used to compensate for his poor eyesight. Enya plays softly as you walk around.

Next door, the **Lafcadio Hearn Former Residence** (daily, Mar-Nov 9am-5pm, Dec-Feb 9am-4:40pm, closed Dec 16th-Jan 1st, ¥250, 20% discount with Universal Pass) is now completely bare but there's a useful leaflet that describes how the rooms would have looked in Hearn's day. The small house looks out on to an even smaller Japanese garden that's similar to the one Hearn enjoyed when he lived in Kumamoto (see p351).

Further along the same street is **Buke Yashiki** (daily, Apr-Sept 8:30am-6:30pm Oct-Mar 8:30am-5pm, ¥250), a samurai house built in 1730. Although you can't actually go into the house, there is an outside path around the rooms which contain displays of samurai swords and artefacts used in daily life. If you go up the path behind the house, you'll come to a small building where you can watch a film about Matsue's Drum Festival which takes place every November.

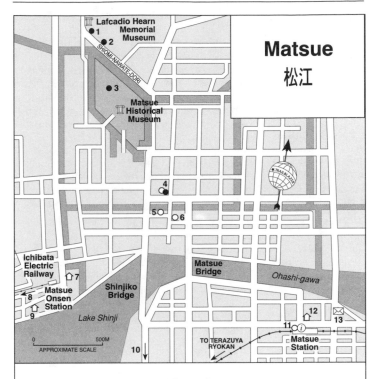

MATSUE 松江

Where to stay

7 Hotel Hakuba	7 ホテル白馬
8 Matsue Lakeside Youth Hostel	8 松江レークサイドユースホステル
9 Hotel Ichibata	9 ホテル一畑
12 Matsue Tokyu Inn	12 松江東急イン

Where to eat

5 Coffee-kan	5 珈琲館
6 Yamashina	6 ヤマシナ
11 Matsue Terrsa	11 松江テルサ

Other

1 Lafcadio Hearn Former Residence	1 小泉八雲旧居
2 Buke Yashiki	2 武家屋敷
3 Matsue Castle	3 松江城
4 Karakoro-kobo/Hermitage	4 カラコロ工房/エルミタージュ
10 Shimane Art Museum/ Vecchio Rosso	10 島根県立美術館/ ベッキオロッソ
13 Central Post Office	13 中央郵便局

Lastly, **Matsue Castle** (daily, April-Sep 8:30am-6:30pm, Oct-Mar 8:30am-5pm, ¥550) was built by the feudal lord Yoshiharu Horio in 1611, though what stands today is a 1950s reconstruction. Hearn often climbed the castle tower which he described as 'grotesquely complex in detail, looking somewhat like a huge pagoda'. On the ground floor of the donjon, the original dolphin and gargoyle-shaped roof tiles are displayed – these were too fragile to be used in the reconstruction. On other floors, there are scale models of the castle and city over which it once presided, and photos of other well-known castles in Japan. But the best part of the climb is the tremendous view from the top floor observation gallery over Matsue and Lake Shinji.

One hundred metres south of Matsue Castle, look out for the large, white, Western-style building that houses the **Matsue Historical Museum** (daily, 8:30am-5pm, free). Inside there's a random assortment of odds and ends from the late samurai period to the present day, including a portable shrine, a Japan Olympic team blazer and various medals from the Tokyo 1964 Olympics.

● **Other areas** The new **Shimane Art Museum** (daily except Mon 10am-6:30pm, ¥300) opened in 1999 in a modern glass building on the banks of Lake Shinji. This is the place to head just before dusk to watch the sun set over the tiny tree-studded island in the lake. The museum building threatens to overshadow the collection of art and sculptures it houses, which include a few minor works by Monet and Gaugin, and a bronze cast of Rodin's 1897 *Monument to Victor Hugo*, which takes pride of place in the second floor entrance hall.

A new addition to Matsue's cultural scene is **Karakoro kobo**, in the former Bank of Japan building on the north side of Ohashi-gawa. Here you'll find temporary art exhibitions, a café, restaurant, art and craft shops. The word 'karakoro' comes, of course, from Lafcadio Hearn. It's said that when Hearn woke up after his first night in Matsue, he heard the noise of wooden geta shoes in the street outside his ryokan. To Hearn's ears, the noise each footstep made was 'kara, koro, kara, koro…'.

Finally, **Matsue-Onsen** is the city's hot spring resort, on the banks of Lake Shinji close to Ichibata Railway's Matsue-Onsen station. The source of the spring is 1250m underground near the banks of the lake. At source, the water temperature is around 77ºC, though it's cooled down by the time it reaches the bath houses of the lakeside hotels and ryokan. The best way of enjoying the area is to stay at one of the resort hotels by the lake (see opposite), most of which have their own hot spring with a lakeside view. To reach the resort, take the Lakeline Bus from outside Matsue station.

PRACTICAL INFORMATION
Station guide
Matsue station has two exits, the north and south gates. Take the north gate for tourist information and bus platforms. The station has no large lockers, but large suitcases and packs can be stored at the 'temporary parcel storage' office (daily, 9am-5:45pm, price varies according to luggage size) along the south exit.

Tourist information
A tourist information office (☎ 0852-21 4034, daily 9am-6pm) is opposite the bus

platforms in front of the station. Turn left as you head out of the north gate and it's next to Mister Donut. The staff will assist with accommodation booking and can hand out city maps.

Various tours can be booked here and passes purchased: the Lakeline Bus plus Horikawa Moat Tour costs ¥1500. Lakeline Bus plus Horikawa Moat Tour and Lake Shinji Boat Tour is ¥2500. Lakeline Bus plus train journey on the private Ichibata Railway to Izumo Taisha (see p242) costs ¥1000. Finally, the 'Perfect Ticket' is a two-day pass which allows you to ride the Ichibata Railway, Lakeline Bus, Shiei city bus and Ichibata bus services for ¥2500.

Getting around

The best way of seeing Matsue's sights is to hop on the tourist Lakeline Bus (daily, 8:45am-sunset Mar-Nov, 9am-4:40pm Dec-Feb) which runs in a loop around the city and stops outside the station. Single rides cost ¥200, or a one-day pass is ¥500 and this also entitles you to a discount (usually the group rate) at Matsue Castle, Hearn Memorial Museum, Buke Yashiki and Shimane Art Museum.

As the 'city of water', Matsue naturally enough offers opportunities for boat rides. First is a one-hour **Lake Shinji Boat Tour** (☎ 0852-24 3218, daily Mar-Nov, 11am-5pm, ¥1200). There is also a daily sunset cruise (check with the tourist office for exact times).

The **Horikawa Moat Tour** (☎ 0852-27 0417, daily March-Nov, 9am-5pm, ¥1200) is a 45-minute cruise around the moat of Matsue Castle. The boats have to pass under some very low bridges on their way round but this is Japan so a flick of the switch lowers the boat canopy and allows a safe passage underneath.

Festivals

At the end of July/beginning of August is the Suigo-sai Festival, the highlight of which is a massive fireworks display over Lake Shinji.

The most raucous annual event is the Drum Festival on November 3rd.

Where to stay

Directly opposite the station is *Matsue Tokyu Inn* (☎ 0852-27 0109, 🖹 25 1327; ¥7200/S, ¥15,600D/Tw). The hotel has recently undergone a major refit; there are now two floors of non-smoking rooms.

Terazuya Ryokan (☎ 0852-21 3480, 🖹 21 3422) is a small family-run inn which has tatami rooms for ¥4000 per person, or ¥7000 with two meals. Dinner is a real feast and eaten with the family, so there's a very homely atmosphere. Turn left out of the station and follow the train tracks round for about 10 minutes until you hit the ryokan on the left side. Call for a lift from the station.

An alternative base is around Matsue-Onsen, where there is a mixture of Western hotels and traditional ryokan. One of the best value, outside Matsue-Onsen station, is *Hotel Hakuba* (☎ 0852-21 6195, 🖹 23 5299). It's an ugly building from the outside but Western singles with bath/toilet are good value at ¥5500 or there are twins at ¥5100 per person.

The top place to stay in Matsue-Onsen is *Hotel Ichibata* (☎ 0852-22 0188, 🖹 22 0230). Ask for a room in the new annex – many of the rooms in the original building are dated and not worth the money anyhow. Some rooms, for which you'll pay more, have views over Lake Shinji. The cheapest twins without a view are ¥15,000.

You need to take the Ichibata Railway one stop from Matsue-Onsen station to Furue to reach *Matsue Lakeside Youth Hostel* (☎/🖹 0852-36 8620; ¥2800 YH/HI mem, ¥3800 non-mem). Breakfast costs ¥600 and dinner ¥1000. The hostel is a 12-minute walk uphill from Furue station.

Where to eat

Matsue is known in Japan for the 'seven delicacies of Lake Shinji'. Since the lake is a combination of fresh and sea water, the seven fish are an unusual mix: carp, eel, shrimp, *shijimi* clams, whitebait, bass and smelt.

The fish don't all appear in the same season, so there are usually only two or three of the 'seven delicacies' on one plate but it's occasionally possible (for a lot of money) to eat all seven in one sitting. Ask at the tourist information office (see p240) for the best places to try the dish; wherever you go take a wallet full of cash.

Inside the station, look for a few cafés and restaurants along 'New Orleans Walk'. On your left as you leave the north side of the station is **Matsue Terrsa**, a glass building which houses a café and restaurant. The ground floor café serves excellent coffee and cake in a corner of the impressive atrium. On the second floor is *Capricciosa* (daily, 11am-10pm), the popular Italian pizza and pasta chain.

In Shimane Art Museum is an upmarket Italian restaurant, *Vecchio Rosso* (daily except Mon 10am-9pm, last order 7:30pm). This place takes advantage of its lakeside location with floor-to-ceiling windows. It's a great place for watching the sunset over the lake. Dinner is expensive, with ¥3000 or ¥5000 courses but lunch deals are more reasonable at ¥1500-2000, or there's a cheaper pasta lunch at ¥1250.

The French café/restaurant *Hermitage* (daily except Tue 11am-9pm, lunch 11:30am-2pm, dinner 5:30-9pm) is inside Karakoro kobo (see p240). The lunchtime menu (¥1000) usually includes soup and a choice of fish or meat as main course. Close by, on the other side of the river, is Karakoro-hiroba, a small courtyard square with a large red umbrella.

Just off this square is an excellent Japanese restaurant, *Yamashina* (daily except Mon 6pm-1am), where you sit either at the counter or at a large wooden table. Fish is often on the regularly-changing menu and there's Guinness on tap, as well as a range of alcoholic and non-alcoholic cocktails. Finally, a good place to stop for coffee is directly across the river from Karakoro kobo at *Coffee-kan*, where there are tables overlooking the river.

Side trip to Izumo Taisha

Some 30km west of Matsue, at the foot of Yakumo Hill, is **Izumo Taisha**, a shrine complex known as the home of the god of marriage. Expect to see lots of happy couples, or unhappy ones trying for a spiritual repair job. Lafcadio Hearn, who himself found love in Matsue when he married Setsu Koizumi, the daughter of a high-ranking samurai, visited Izumo Taisha twice and became the first foreigner to be allowed to enter the *honden* (inner shrine).

Izumo Taisha is accessible from Matsue-Onsen station via the private Ichibata Railway (55 mins, ¥750). Change trains at Kawato for the final leg to Izumo-Taisha-mae. To save money, rail-pass holders need to backtrack along the JR San-in line from Matsue to Izumo-shi (see p218), and from there transfer on to the Ichibata Railway for the last part of the journey.

Tohoku (Northern Honshu) – route guide

INTRODUCTION

When Japanese TV programmes poke fun at rural life and local dialects, more often than not their targets are the 'country folk' of Tohoku. Some Japanese will only reluctantly venture into the region, fearing that the dialects they encounter will be so strong that they might as well be speaking a different language. Such is the power of television, but a trip around northern Honshu

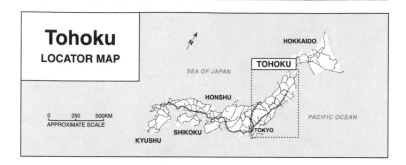

offers a rare chance in an overcrowded island to go off the beaten track.

In contrast to other parts of the country, Tohoku offers little in the way of famous temples or shrines. Volcanoes, lakes, mountains and rivers predominate, a geography which explains why northern Honshu lagged behind in the industrial race of the late 20th century. But, like many areas of Japan, traditional life – old farmhouses, small rural communities and local festivals – has not remained untouched by the modern age. The region is not without its large cities and industry. Yet more than enough remains of traditional Tohoku for the short-term visitor to experience something of what Japan's greatest haiku poet Matsuo Basho (1644-94) discovered, when he set off in the spring of 1689 on a five-month walking tour of the region: 'I had seen since my departure innumerable examples of natural beauty which land and water, mountains and rivers, had produced in one accord.' (*The Narrow Road To The Deep North*, translated by Nobuyuki Yuasa, Penguin, 1966).

Rail access to the north is fast and efficient, thanks to the Tohoku shinkansen which extends as far as Morioka (to Hachinohe from the end of 2002). Beyond this, running off to the east and west, is a network of local lines which are the best means of seeing Tohoku close up – the shinkansen is fast but due to the proliferation of tunnels the views are nearly always fleeting.

The following route travels in a loop around the region, starting with the journey north from Tokyo, on the eastern side of Tohoku to Aomori, on the northern tip of Honshu and the rail gateway to Hokkaido (see p271); then back towards Tokyo down the more off-the beaten track western side.

For details of JR East's regional rail passes, see p14.

TOKYO TO AOMORI

Tokyo to Sendai   [Map 15, p245; Map 16, p246; Table 12, p405]
Distances from Tokyo by shinkansen. Fastest journey time: 1 hour 40 minutes.

Tokyo (0km)   [see pp85-101]
Pick up the Yamabiko (or double-decker Max Yamabiko) which runs north to Morioka via Fukushima and Sendai.

Tohoku
RAIL ROUTES

Ueno (4km) Most trains call at Ueno, Tokyo's main terminal for the north. If joining the train here rather than at Tokyo station, it's worth reserving seats because at certain times the non-reserved cars are full by the time the train leaves Tokyo.

Omiya (30km) Omiya is so close to Tokyo it's impossible to see where one ends and the other begins. There's little incentive to stop so soon unless you're a Beatles fan and want to visit the **John Lennon Museum** (daily except Tue, 11am-6pm, Fri to 8pm, ¥1500). The museum opened on October 9th 2000, the day Lennon would have celebrated his 60th birthday. It's on the fourth and fifth floors of the Saitama Super Arena, centrepiece of a huge city redevelopment project. About 130 items are exhibited, including Lennon's first guitar, his trademark glasses, and clothes he and Yoko Ono wore on their frequent visits to the mountain resort of Karuizawa (see p117). From Omiya, change on to the Utsunomiya line and go one stop back (towards Tokyo) to Saitama Shin-Toshin, from where you should follow signs to the Super Arena (a three-minute walk).

Omiya is the last chance to change to the Asama for Nagano (see p116). After Omiya, some shinkansen call at **Oyama (81km)**.

Utsunomiya (110km) The first ekiben, two rice balls and pickles wrapped in bamboo leaves, is said to have been sold at this station at the end of the 19th century. Change here for **Nikko**, a beautiful shrine and temple town containing the mausoleums of Tokugawa Ieyasu and Iemitsu (see p34). Nikko (see p101) is 50 minutes by local train along the JR Nikko line; services operate hourly or twice hourly.

After Utsunomiya, some shinkansen call at **Nasu-Shiobara (158km)** and **Shin-Shirakawa (185km)**.

Koriyama (227km) It's only after Koriyama, over 200km from Tokyo, that the views start to improve as the landscape becomes more rural,

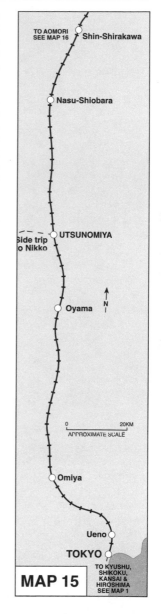

TO AOMORI
SEE MAP 16 Shin-Shirakawa

Nasu-Shiobara

Side trip
to Nikko UTSUNOMIYA

N

Oyama

0   20KM
APPROXIMATE SCALE

Omiya

Ueno

TOKYO

MAP 15

TO KYUSHU,
SHIKOKU,
KANSAI &
HIROSHIMA
SEE MAP 1

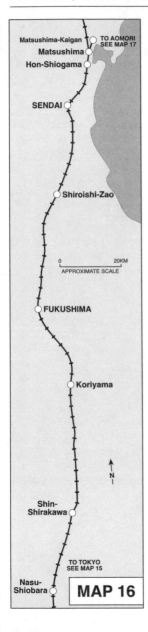

offering the first glimpses of what Tohoku has to offer. The view, however, is frequently blocked by tunnels.

Koriyama is a terminus for the Banetsu-sei line that runs some 190km across Honshu to Niigata (see p265).

Fukushima (273km) Since the shinkansen line splits here some trains divide. Therefore, you should make sure you're in the right part of the train (if you have a seat reservation you will be); the Yamabiko part continues on to Sendai and Morioka, and the Tsubasa branches off to Yamagata and beyond on the extension to Shinjo. After Fukushima some shinkansen stop at **Shiroishi-Zao (307km)**.

Sendai (352km) [see pp265-71]

Sendai to Ichinoseki via Matsushima
[see tables 13 and 14, p406]

The fastest way to Ichinoseki is by shinkansen (see Table 12, p405); if you choose to go by shinkansen the route starts again on p249.

The following route goes off the beaten track and includes a stop at Matsushima Bay. Distances are by JR from Sendai. Fastest journey time: 1³/₄ hours.

Sendai (0km) From Sendai, take the Umikaze rapid train on the JR Senseki Line (from platform 9). The train ride begins underground and then passes through an urban area.

Hon-Shiogama (16km) Shiogama is connected with Matsushima by a regular ferry service. The ferry is an alternative to taking the train to the next stop.

In the station, next to the View Plaza travel agency, is a small tourist information office (daily, 10am-4pm). The staff don't speak English but can advise on ferry times. It's a 10-minute walk from the station to the Marine Gate ferry terminal. Turn right on to the main road running parallel with the station. At the lights, turn right and go straight until you reach the terminal building. Tickets for the ferry ride to Matsushima (50 mins) cost ¥1420. The boat tour goes past some of the many tiny islands that are a familiar sight along this coastline but the journey is marred by two forms of pollution; one is the chimney stacks and factories that occasionally rise up behind the islands, the other is the non-stop commentary in Japanese that pours out of speakers strategically placed around the boat.

Matsushima-Kaigan (23km) Confusingly, Matsushima has two rail stations, separated by a five-minute taxi ride (no bus). Trains do not connect the two stations since they are on different lines. Matsushima-Kaigan station is on the Senseki line and is the most convenient for the sights, being just five minutes on foot from Matsushima Bay. But the next part of the rail route begins at Matsushima station (see p249), which is on the Tohoku line.

Over 260 islands are scattered around Matsushima Bay; collectively they count as one of the top three scenic spots in Japan, along with Miyajima (see p235) and Amanohashidate. For centuries, poets have journeyed here in search of inspiration – indeed, the islands themselves are sometimes compared to verses of a poem. In the station there is even a small haiku box where travelling poets can deposit their own work. Matsuo Basho visited on his epic journey through the region and wrote that Matsushima was the 'most beautiful spot in the whole country of Japan'.

Matsushima Information Center (☎ 022-354 2263, daily, 10am-4:30/5pm) is in a booth to the right as you exit Matsushima-Kaigan station. If you took the ferry from Shiogama to Matsushima you'll have arrived at the boat pier where there is a smaller tourist information desk (daily, 8:30am-5pm), but the staff here don't speak English.

A few of the islands just off the shore are linked by bridges to the mainland. The most popular is tiny **Godaidojima**, on which stands a hall containing five Buddhist statues which are put on view only once every 33 years (the next time is in 2006). Pleasant though it is, the tranquillity of the island is spoilt by the souvenir stalls set up along the approach to it. Much more relaxing is nearby **Fukurajima**, connected to the mainland via a long, red footbridge (¥200 to cross). This island has wooded paths free from souvenir stands and (almost) out of sight of any vending machines. From here, there are views to some of the other islands. Set just back from the port area is **Zuigan-ji** (daily, 8am-4pm, ¥700), a Zen Buddhist temple built in 828 and later reconstructed by Date Masamune (see p265). On the right as you walk through the pine trees towards the temple entrance are some caves inside which monks used to train before the temple was built. Look out for the rail monument near the caves, a tall column flanked by railway wheels on pieces of track. It was built to remember those who died during the construction of the railways or in rail accidents.

If you didn't take the ferry from Shiogama to Matsushima and want to take a boat cruise around the bay, a regular service operates from Matsushima Port (¥1400). Departures are hourly in the summer (9am-4pm).

For an overnight stay, *Folkloro Matsushima* (☎ 022-353 3535, 🖹 353 3588) is up behind Matsushima-Kaigan station. The rooms in this pension, operated

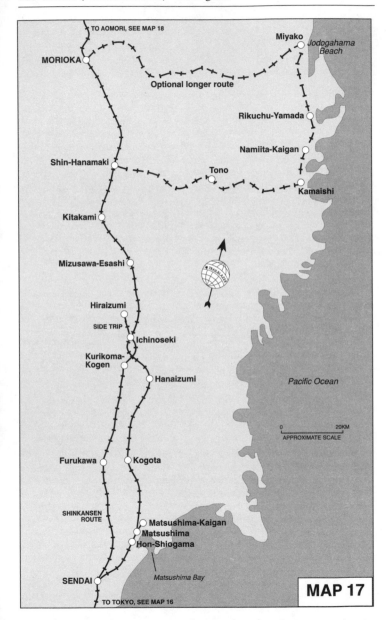

TO AOMORI, SEE MAP 18

Miyako

Jodogahama Beach

MORIOKA

Optional longer route

Rikuchu-Yamada

Shin-Hanamaki

Namiita-Kaigan

Tono

Kitakami

Kamaishi

Mizusawa-Esashi

Hiraizumi

SIDE TRIP

Ichinoseki

Kurikoma-Kogen

Hanaizumi

Pacific Ocean

0   20KM
APPROXIMATE SCALE

Furukawa

Kogota

SHINKANSEN ROUTE

Matsushima-Kaigan

Matsushima

Hon-Shiogama

Matsushima Bay

SENDAI

MAP 17

TO TOKYO, SEE MAP 16

by JR East, are Western style and feel very homely. Twin rooms cost ¥12,000, but better value if travelling in a group are the family rooms which can sleep up to four adults for ¥20,000. Room rates are reduced on the second and third nights. To reach the Folkloro, turn right on leaving Matsushima Kaigan station, then sharp right under a short rail bridge and follow the road up for about three minutes. It is on your left.

Alternatively, six stops along the Senseki line (two stops by rapid train) from Matsushima-Kaigan brings you to **Nobiru**, from where it's a 15-minute walk to *Paira-Matsushima Youth Hostel* (☎ 0225-88 2220, 🖃 88 3797; ¥3500/YH(HI), ¥4100 non-members). It's a clean, modern hostel with good facilities and a choice of Western and tatami rooms. Supper costs ¥1000 and breakfast ¥600. Just off a road lined with pine trees and not far from Nobiru Beach, the hostel is an excellent overnight base. Facilities include cycle rental (3 hours/¥500) and tennis courts (rackets can be hired). Before setting out for the hostel, pick up a map from the information centre (☎ 0225-88 2611, daily, 8:30am-5:30pm) in Nobiru station. From the station, cross the bridge and head straight towards the beach. Look out for the 'JYH' sign along the way.

▲ **Matsushima (23km)** Transfer to Matsushima station for the next part of the journey north along the Tohoku line (see Table 14, p406). This station is 30 minutes on foot from Matsushima-Kaigan (pick up a map from the tourist information desk outside the station) or a five-minute taxi ride.

Kogota (43km) About 20 minutes from Matsushima. Some trains on the Tohoku line terminate here (Table 14 includes direct services only), so you may have to change on to another local train for the rest of the journey to Ichinoseki.

Hanaizumi (79km) This rural town briefly hit the headlines when the bones of mountain buffalo thought to be 100 million years old were discovered here in 1956.

Ichinoseki (93km) The first major stop after Matsushima, Ichinoseki is a transport hub and stop on the Tohoku shinkansen line and is divided by Iwai-gawa. The main reason for stopping here is to take a side trip to the temple town of Hiraizumi (see box p250).

An overhead passageway connects the shinkansen side of the station with other JR lines. A small tourist information counter (☎ 0191-23 2350, daily, 9am-5:30pm) is next to the ticket barrier on the JR lines side. The staff do not speak English but you can pick up leaflets on Ichinoseki and Hiraizumi (see below). There's little reason to overnight in Ichinoseki, especially since the temple lodgings in nearby Hiraizumi are such an attractive option. Just in case, *Ichinoseki Green Hotel* (☎ 0191-23 8616, 🖃 23 8813; ¥6000/S, ¥10,000/D, ¥11,200/Tw) is modern and has clean, comfortable Western-style rooms. It's on the right-hand side of the main road that leads off from the station.

Ichinoseki to Morioka by shinkansen   [Map 17, p248; Table 12, p406]
Distances from Ichinoseki. Fastest journey time: 43 minutes.

⛩ **Side trip to Hiraizumi**

Eight kilometres north of Ichinoseki and reached in less than 10 minutes by local train along the Tohoku line (services operate hourly), is Hiraizumi. At first glance it's hard to believe that this rural town once boasted a population of over 100,000. In the 12th century it was a major centre of politics and culture, a period dominated by the wealthy Fujiwara family who ruled for four generations. Today, a couple of historic temples remain as a reminder of the place that once rivalled Kyoto in wealth and national influence.

Hiraizumi station is small with a few ¥300 coin lockers. A tourist information office (☎ 0191-46 2110, daily, 8:30am-5pm) is in the small house with wooden doors to the right as you leave the station. Maps and local bus times are available. Next door is a small Rent-a-Cycle booth (2 hours ¥500, ¥200 for each additional hour). You receive a map with a recommended three-hour cycling trip around the town, including stops at both the temples described below.

The construction of **Chuson-ji** (daily, 8am-5pm Apr-Oct, 8:30am-4:30pm Nov-Mar, ¥800) began in 1124 and the temple compound once boasted over 300 buildings. Not all have made it into the 21st century but the temple is still an impressive sight. Allow a couple of hours to explore as many of the buildings as possible. There's no fee to enter the compound and there are plenty of places, including the Honden (main hall), that don't charge admission. The most important surviving building is the **Konjikido** (Golden Hall). Entry tickets allow access to the Konjikido as well as to a few other temple buildings, including the modern **Sankozo**, a treasure house with an attached ATM. If you go as far as is possible along the tree-lined avenue through the temple compound and then take a path off to the right, you'll reach **Hakusan Shrine**. After the opulence of Konjikido, the austerity of this Shinto shrine is a pleasant surprise. From a corner of the shrine area there are great views down below of plains typical of the Tohoku region. Also here is the temple's thatched-roof Noh stage (Noh is performed here on the evening of August 14th). Take a bus to Chuson-ji from Hiraizumi station (¥140).

Motsu-ji (daily, 8:30am-4:30/5pm, ¥500) was founded in 850 and is known today for its well-kept garden. The main reason for visiting here is to overnight at *Motsu-ji Youth Hostel* (☎ 0191-46 2331). As well as dormitory accommodation, private *shukubo* (temple lodging) rooms are available. Guests are welcome to take part in early morning zazen meditation sessions (July to September) with one of the resident priests. Since this is a temple hostel you're also asked to keep strict hours; lights are switched out in the public rooms and the front door is locked promptly at 9pm. Rates are ¥4200/pp for a private room or ¥2800 for a hostel bed; breakfast costs ¥600 and dinner ¥800. Guests are exempt from the temple/garden admission fee. Motsu-ji is a 10-minute walk up the main road that runs away from the station. The temple is on the left side of the road. Note that the hostel is usually closed on Sundays, and for the New Year holiday (Jan 1st-3rd).

Ichinoseki (0km)

Mizusawa-Esashi (25km) Not all shinkansen stop at Mizusawa, known for the 'Mizusawa Gourmet Festival' held in the autumn. During the event, the largest cast-iron pan in Japan is used to cook a soup which is shared out among festivalgoers. After Mizusawa, some shinkansen also call at **Kitakami (42km)**.

Shin-Hanamaki (55km) Hanamaki, a small city, is known for its hot springs and as the birthplace of the poet Kenji Miyazawa, who achieved popularity as a writer of children's stories, such as *Night on the Milky Way Train*.

The city's major annual event is the Hanamaki Festival held on the second weekend of September, when large floats and portable shrines are carried through the streets in time to music. On February 11th, Hanamaki Public Auditorium plays host to the 'All Japan Noodle Eating Contest', where contestants gorge on bowls of soba until they can eat no more.

Shin-Hanamaki is a major junction, with shinkansen running north and south, and conventional rail lines east and west. To reach Hanamaki city from Shin-Hanamaki, take a local train two stops west along the Kamaishi line to Hanamaki station. If you're interested in exploring the city, there are tourist offices in Shin-Hanamaki (☎ 0198-31 2244) and in front of Hanamaki (☎ 0198-24 1931) stations.

From Shin-Hanamaki, it's just 13 minutes to the terminus of the shinkansen at Morioka. If you're in a hurry to head further north, continue on the bullet train for the blink-and-you'll-miss-it ride to Morioka and pick up the next part of the route from p253. Alternatively, take the extended rail journey described on p252, very slow-going in parts but one of the best ways of seeing traditional Tohoku close up. Although it's just about possible to complete this alternative route in one day, it's far better to break the journey by spending the night somewhere along the way.

Morioka (90km) Morioka is the terminus for the Tohoku shinkansen from Tokyo, although a branch line (the Akita shinkansen) runs west from Morioka to Akita (see p260). Shinkansen services depart from the second floor of the station. Coin lockers (up to ¥400) are available. On the second floor, English-speaking staff at the Northern Tohoku TIC (☎ 019-625 2090, daily, 9am-7pm) can help with accommodation bookings in Morioka, as well as provide more general information on sightseeing in the area.

⛩ Side trip from Morioka

North-west of Morioka lies the volcanic peak of Mt Iwate. For a closer look, take a local train on the Tazawako line (approx 8/day) to Koiwai, from where a 10-minute bus ride takes you to **Koiwai Farm**. The views are good but the farm itself is a tourist trap. However, rail enthusiasts may be impressed by the unusual *Steam Locomotive Hotel* (☎ 0196-92 4316, ▤ 92 0986) here; you can stay in the sleeping compartments of the D5168 train for ¥4000.

Further along the line is **Tazawako (Lake Tazawa)**. This is the deepest lake in Japan (423.4m) and is renowned for being a nearly perfect circle. Forty-minute boat tours on the lake cost ¥1170 (Apr-Nov). Tazawako station is also a stop on the shinkansen branch line from Morioka to Akita (take the Komachi shinkansen from Morioka). The lake is a short bus ride (¥350) from the bus terminal opposite Tazawako station. The tourist information office (☎ 0187-43 2111, daily, 8:30am-6:30pm) in the station has some leaflets.

♯ Shin-Hanamaki–Tono–Kamaishi–Miyako– Morioka
Optional route   (Map 17, p248; Table 15, p407)

From **Shin-Hanamaki (0km)**, pick up a local train or one of the Rikuchu LEXs heading east along the Kamaishi line that runs through the rice fields of the Tono Basin and over Sennin Pass, a total journey of 90km, towards Kamaishi on the coast. This is Tohoku as you might imagine it, a landscape of green rice fields and occasional thatched cottages which are a long way from the big cityscape of Sendai.

The first major stop is at **Tono (46km)**, which in the feudal era enjoyed prosperity as a market and castle town thanks to its strategic location between the plains and the coast. Today, most people know Tono as the location for a series of folk tales contained in *The Legends of Tono*. Many of these legends feature *kappa*, mischievous creatures that live in rivers and streams and are instantly recognizable from the 'shell on their back, a dish on their head, webbed hands and feet, and a sharp beak-like mouth'. Kappa stories were originally told to warn children of the dangers of playing near rivers.

Tono tourist information centre (☎ 0198-62 1333, daily, 8am-6pm) has maps and also rents out bicycles; turn right as you leave the station and it's a little further down on the right. There are a couple of museums within walking distance of the station but to reach most of the sights, including **Tono Furusato Village**, where a number of old farmhouses are preserved, you need to rent a car – the tourist office can provide details.

Tono is a good place to break the journey, with an excellent accommodation deal in the *Folkloro Tono* (☎ 0198-62 0700, 🖺 62 0800), a B&B pension immediately above the station. Rates vary according to season but in July/August a family room (up to four adults) costs ¥22,000 on the first night, reduced to ¥18,000 and ¥14,000 on the second and third nights. In high season, twins start at ¥10,000, falling to ¥9000 and ¥8000 on the second and third nights.

After Tono, the train begins to climb toward the Sennin Pass. It runs through many tunnels before making its final descent into **Kamaishi (90km)**, once a major centre for steel production in Tohoku and still home to the giant Nippon Steel Works, right outside the station. The Kamaishi line terminates here, so change trains and continue north along the Yamada line (local trains only) up the Rikuchu Coast to Miyako. Sit on the right for sea views.

It takes a while before you see the coast and the view is sometimes obscured, but this section is still enjoyable. About 25 minutes after leaving Kamaishi, look out for **Namiita Kaigan (108km)**. This is a very popular local beach – it's said that while tourists head for the much-hyped Jodogahama Beach in Miyako (see below), locals prefer Namiita. Even if you don't stop here, look out on the right-hand side for a great view from the train down on to Namiita Beach. The coastal views disappear after **Rikuchu Yamada (119km)** and trees tend to surround the track.

It's all change at **Miyako (146km)**, the nearest station to Jodogahama Beach. According to legend, a Buddhist priest visited the beach 300 years ago and declared that it was 'just like paradise'. Don't buy too much of the publicity about the contrast between pine trees, blue ocean and white rock. The beach is fine as a place to go for a swim or to lounge around for a few hours but it's not worth seeking out just for its natural beauty. Buses to the beach run from outside Miyako station (20 mins, ¥210). Miyako TIC (daily, 9am-5pm) is in a booth to the right as you go out of the station; maps are available.

❏ **Optional route (cont'd)**
Suehirokan Youth Hostel (☎ 0193-62 1555, 🖹 62 3052) is two minutes on foot
from Miyako station and has tatami rooms. To reach the hostel, head up the main
road from the station to the first set of traffic lights. Turn right; the hostel is a few
buildings along on the right. Look for the blue JYH sign at the entrance. YH/HI
members pay ¥2850 and there's a small supplement for non-members. Miyako is
known for its sushi; the best place to try some is at ***Janome Sushi*** (daily except
Wed, 10am-9pm). Janome is a couple of buildings up on the left-hand side along
the main road that leads away from the station (look for 'Janome' written in English
in small letters along the shop front). The set meals are good value and portions are
large – try the salmon onigiri as a side order.

The final part of the journey continues inland along the Yamada line to
Morioka (248km). Only very infrequent local trains run on this route. The inland
views are impressive for much of the time, though if you're taking the last, early
evening service back to Morioka it's hard to resist nodding off as the train winds its
slow way inland. By taking this optional route, you have now covered nearly 250km
between Hanamaki and Morioka. By shinkansen, the distance is only 35km. The
extra distance is worth it for the views.

Morioka calls itself the 'castle town of Northern Japan' but only the stone wall
ruins remain. Apart from a possible side trip to Lake Tazawa (see box, p251),
there's little reason to hang around in the city – unless you're passing through
between August 1st and 4th, when **Sansa-odori** is held. Groups dressed in traditional costumes dance down the main street to the accompaniment of taiko
drums and flutes. Festival stalls line the streets and there's a real street party
atmosphere. The best place to spend the night in Morioka is at the friendly
Ryokan Kumagai (☎ 0196-51 3020, 🖹 26 0096), an eight-minute walk from the
station across Kitakami-gawa. Tatami rooms are ¥4500 for one or ¥8000 for
two. Breakfast costs ¥800 and dinner ¥1500. For a selection of restaurants under
one roof, try the basement of the 'Fezan' department store, on the left of the
main station exit. Here you'll find places that serve ramen, tonkatsu and sushi
as well as fast food such as McDonald's.

Morioka to Aomori   [Map 18, p255; Table 16, p407]
Distances by JR from Morioka. Fastest journey time: 2 hours 10 minutes.

Morioka (0km) From Morioka, take a Hatsukari LEX or the newer Super
Hatsukari. On the Super Hatsukari, there are six cars with 2x2 seating; cars 1-3
are non-reserved and 4-6 are reserved. Part of car 6 is the Green Car.

For the first part of the journey, the view on both sides is blocked by a line
of trees. When the view does open out, the countryside consists of wide green
fields and hills, interrupted by small towns.

Ichinohe (65km), **Ninohe (71km)** and **Sannohe (88km)** After the fields
come the forests: dense pine forests begin to take over as you pass this series of
stations. 'Ichinohe' means the 'first door'. In medieval times, the northern part

---

Shinkansen – the next step
Look out to your left as you approach Hachinohe. The familiar raised tracks of the shinkansen are being constructed ready for the opening of the extension from Morioka in late 2002. The new line is a classic example of the way views are being sacrificed for speed; from Morioka to Hachinohe shinkansen passengers will pass through no fewer than 21 tunnels, including one, between Iwate and Ichinohe, which will be the world's longest tunnel on land.

JR East has announced that 15 shinkansen services will run daily between Tokyo and Hachinohe (and vice versa). The journey time from Tokyo to Aomori will be reduced by 30 minutes to four hours (change at Hachinohe on to the Super Hatsukari LEX for Aomori).

---

of Iwate and southern part of Aomori prefectures were divided into different political districts. Each district was known as a 'door', meaning the door or gateway to that district. After Ichinohe comes Ninohe (the second door) and Sannohe (the third door). The next 'door' to be found on the train line is Hachinohe (the eighth door).

Hachinohe (108km) Hachinohe is an industrial and port city but is not a major tourist centre. The reason for stopping here is to embark on an unusual side trip into the mountains to a small village where it's claimed that Jesus Christ is buried (see box p256).

Misawa (129km) About five or six minutes after leaving Misawa, look out on the right for the blue water of Lake Ogawara in the distance. It really is blink-and-you'll-miss-it, since for the most part trees block the view.

Noheji (159km) Noheji is a point of interchange for the JR Ominato line that runs part of the way up the Shimokita Peninsula.

Leaving Noheji, look out to the right for views over Mutsu Bay. It's frustrating at first, since thanks to the ever-present trees along the track you don't get a full view of the bay. It's not until just before the train approaches Aomori that the track gets close enough to the shore for a sweeping view of the bay. Look out for a beautiful pine-clad island that is impressive enough to make people look up from their newspapers.

Asamushi-Onsen (187km) The last limited express stop before Aomori, right outside the station is **Yusa Asamushi**, a modern building which contains a great hot spring (daily, 7am-9pm, ¥350) with views over Mutsu Bay. Small towels are sold but bring your own soap.

Aomori (204km) [see pp271-5]
It's a shame after the brief views of Mutsu Bay that the final approach into Aomori is less impressive, with the usual city glut of concrete buildings.

Most Hatsukari LEXs from Morioka terminate here but three a day continue on through the Seikan Tunnel to Hokkaido. For details of the journey, see p282.

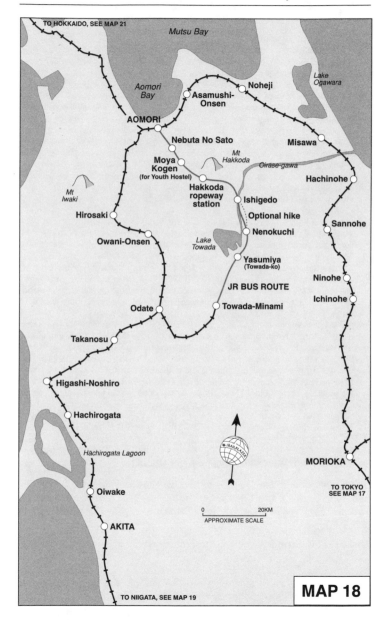

TO HOKKAIDO, SEE MAP 21

Mutsu Bay

Aomori
Bay

Noheji

Lake
Ogawara

Asamushi-
Onsen

AOMORI

Nebuta No Sato

Misawa

Moya
Kogen
(for Youth Hostel)

Mt
Hakkoda

Oirase-gawa

Hachinohe

Mt
Iwaki

Hakkoda
ropeway
station

Ishigedo

Optional hike

Hirosaki

Sannohe

Nenokuchi

Owani-Onsen

Lake
Towada

Yasumiya
(Towada-ko)

Ninohe

JR BUS ROUTE

Odate

Towada-Minami

Ichinohe

Takanosu

Higashi-Noshiro

Hachirogata

Hachirogata Lagoon

TRAILBLAZER

MORIOKA

TO TOKYO
SEE MAP 17

Oiwake

0   20KM
APPROXIMATE SCALE

AKITA

TO NIIGATA, SEE MAP 19

MAP 18

Jesus in Japan?

The journey to the remote village of Shingo, deep in the mountains west of Hachinohe, certainly feels like a pilgrimage. There is no rail line and the only way of reaching the village is to take two buses. Your destination is the **Christ Park**, so called because locals claim that it contains the grave of none other than Jesus Christ. The story goes that instead of dying on the cross, Jesus escaped at the last minute, fled to Siberia, made his way to Alaska and finally boarded a boat bound for Japan, where he landed at the port of Hachinohe. He quickly found his way to the village of Herai (now called Shingo) where he married a Japanese woman called Miyuko, had three daughters and lived to 106. In his latter years, Christ is said to have travelled around Japan, 'endeavouring to save the common people, while observing the language, customs and manners of the various regions'. He is described in village records as being 'grey haired and rather bald with a ruddy complexion and high nose and [he] wore a coat with many folds, causing people to hold him in awe as a long-nosed goblin.'

The extraordinary story only came to light in 1935 when two graves were found in a bamboo thicket at the top of a small hill in the village. It wasn't until May 1936, when Christ's 'last will and testament' mysteriously turned up in the village, that the significance of these graves was revealed: one of the graves was Christ's, the other belonged to his brother, called Isukiri. Or rather, just his brother's ear. Supposedly Jesus managed to avoid crucifixion thanks to his brother who 'casually took Christ's place and died on his cross', allowing him to escape to Japan clutching one of Isukiri's ears along with some 'hair of the Virgin Mary'. Further 'proof' can be found down in the village: Herai, the ancient name of the village, is said to be a corruption of 'Hebrew' and a villager who died some years ago 'looked not like a Japanese, his eyes were blue like those of a foreigner'. Curiously, there has been little attempt to cash in on the story by turning the park into a tacky tourist trap. Indeed, there's so little publicity that it's almost as if the village is embarrassed by the legend and doesn't quite know what to do with its two graves up on the hill.

The Christ Park, which contains the two graves as well as a small museum (daily except Wed, 9am-5pm) telling the story in Japanese and English, is open to the public. From Hachinohe station, take a bus bound for Gonohe (37 mins). From Gonohe, connect with a bus that takes you direct to the Christ Park just outside Shingo Village (34 mins). Tell the driver you want to get out at Kuristo-koen. For up-to-date timetables, contact Nambu Bus (☎ 0178-44 7111, Japanese only).

AOMORI TO TOKYO VIA AKITA AND NIIGATA

The fastest way back to Tokyo is to take the Hatsukari LEX south to Morioka, and from there pick up a Tohoku shinkansen. However, the route described goes back to Tokyo via the western side of Tohoku.

Aomori to Odate   [Map 18, p255; Table 17, p408]
Distances by JR from Aomori. Fastest journey time: 65 minutes.

Opposite: Waiting for a bite to eat: hungry koi carp fight for space in a tank on the approach to Akiyoshi Cave (see p213). (Photo © Ramsey Zarifeh).

There are two routes for this section of the journey. The first is a combination of JR bus and train, heading south from Aomori on a spectacular mountain route to Towada-ko, a caldera lake (see box pp258-9), but this is possible in a day only during the summer months. The second (see the route below) doesn't offer such stunning scenery but is all by rail and includes a stop in the ancient town of Hirosaki.

Aomori (0km)   [see pp271-5]

From Aomori, take a train on the JR Ou line towards Akita – there are a few limited expresses called either Inaho or Kamoshika. The first part of the journey is through a residential area but gradually the landscape opens up. The main sight from the train is Mt Iwaki, spiritual symbol of the surrounding area. Look out for it in the distance to the right from about 20 minutes after Aomori.

Hirosaki (37km)   Hirosaki flourished from the early 17th century as a castle town of the Tsugaru feudal lords. The big festival of the year, **Neputa Matsuri**, rivals Aomori's Nebuta Matsuri (see p274) and takes place at the same time, August 1st-7th. There is a nightly procession through the town of colourful floats.

Turn immediately left as you leave the station and walk to the end of the building to find coin lockers (up to ¥600 size). A tourist information office (☎ 0172-32 0524, daily 8:45am-5/6pm) is to the right as you go out of the station. Staff here can provide you with maps and will also book same-day accommodation (you pay ¥2000 of the accommodation charge in cash here, then take a voucher along to your hotel where you pay the remainder). Alternatively, the modern Hirosaki Sightseeing Information Center (☎ 0172-37 5501, daily 9am-5/6pm) is west of the station opposite Hirosaki Park. The Aomori Welcome Card (see p46) is available at both tourist offices.

Top priority on a visit to Hirosaki should be given to the **Fujita Memorial Japanese Garden (Fujita Kinen Teien)** (daily except Mon, 9am-5pm, ¥300 or ¥240 with Aomori Welcome Card, closed Nov 24th-mid-April), a typical Edo period stroll garden built on two levels. From the upper level, Mt Iwaki can be seen in the distance. Across the street from the entrance to the garden is **Hirosaki Park**, inside which is the site of Hirosaki Castle, completed in 1611. The original five-storeyed castle tower was struck by lightning and burnt to the ground, so what stands today is a replacement three-storeyed tower that has been turned into a museum of samurai artefacts (daily, 9am-5pm, ¥200 or ¥160 with Aomori Welcome Card, closed Nov 24th-April 1st). To reach Fujita Kinen Teien and Hirosaki Park from the station, take the ¥100 tourist loop bus and get off at 'Shiyakusho-mae/Koen Iriguchi' (15 mins).

For accommodation, right outside the station is *City Hirosaki Hotel* (☎ 0172-37 0109, 🖷 37 1229), an upmarket member of the Tokyu Inn chain with a

---

Opposite: Though a little out of the way, it's worth making the effort to fit in a detour to rural Hiraizumi, justly famous for its ancient temple, Chuson-ji (see box, p250). (Photos © Ramsey Zarifeh).

⛩ Alternative route (summer only): Aomori to Odate via Towada-ko

This route (see map 18) is well served by JR buses from May to October, but during the winter months service is severely restricted because of heavy snow, making it impossible to complete the journey in a single day. The bus timetable is subject to seasonal and annual change so, before planning your itinerary, call in at the tourist information office outside Aomori station. Staff here have up-to-date timetables and can advise on making connections.

Alternatively, if you wish to plan your journey before arriving in Aomori, call the JR Information Line (☎ 03-3423 0111) for the latest timetable information in English. Please note that reservations should be made on the JR bus from Aomori to Lake Towada (free to rail pass holders) at the JR bus counter outside Aomori station. Without a rail pass, the journey from Aomori to Towado-ko (Lake Towada, 3 hours) costs ¥3000 but foreign tourists receive a 50% discount by showing the Aomori Welcome Card (see p46).

Pick up a JR bus from stop No 9 outside Aomori station bound for Moya Hills and get off at the **Moya Kogen** stop (40 mins). Along the way, you'll pass **Nebuta no Sato** (see p275). Walk back down the road from the Moya Kogen stop and look out for a small yellow house on your right, which is *Moya Kogen Youth Hostel* (☎ 0177-64 2888, 🖷 64 2889, 🖳 FZJ05604@nifty.ne.jp; ¥3200/YH(HI), ¥4200 non-members). This is a superb place to stay due to the peaceful location, clean tatami rooms and delicious meals; dinner costs ¥1000 and breakfast ¥500. The hostel's owner loves Ireland, so Irish cocktails, Guinness and Enya are optional extras.

In the morning, the owner will drop you at the bus stop in time to pick up the JR Bus to Towada-ko (Lake Towada). It's a $2^{1}/_{2}$-hour ride south to the lake. On the way, the bus calls first outside **Hakkoda Ropeway station** (30 mins from Moya Kogen), from where gondolas (daily, 9am-4:20pm, occasional closures, ¥1650 return, 10% discount with Aomori Welcome Card) take 10 minutes to climb Mt Tamoyachidake (1326m). On a clear day, it's possible to see as far as Hokkaido. In winter this is a busy skiing area. The bus journey continues along the winding mountain road, stopping at a number of rural hot springs, the best known of which is **Sukayu-Onsen** (40 mins), famous for its giant cedar bath house (9am-5pm, ¥500) that can fit 1000 people – not that you'll see many of them through the steam. It's possible to stay on the bus all the way to the lake but it's more fun to get off earlier at **Ishigedo** (1 hour 40 mins) from where an 8.9km hiking trail begins, following the course of Oirase-gawa to its source, Lake Towada. At the Ishigedo bus stop is a rest centre with toilets, a scale model of the path to the lake and a small snack bar where you can get noodles, ice cream and stock up on water. The path leads off from behind the rest area (it's very obvious). Ishigedo means 'huge slab of rock' – you'll see the rock supported by a tree at the trail start. According to the sign, an evil but beautiful woman who once lived here 'would kill travellers and steal their possessions'.

Assuming you survive this first obstacle the remaining 8.9km are unproblematic – the route is mostly sheltered under a canopy of trees and passes by a number of waterfalls. It's a very popular trail (I saw a group of businessmen walking in shirt and tie), but unless you're here during high season (July-August and again in October for the autumn leaves) there should be room to breathe. The only downside is that the path sometimes connects up with the main road, which means you have to compete with lorries and cars. Allow 2-3 hours to complete the hike.

❏ **Alternative route (cont'd)**
The hike ends with a set of stone steps leading up to a bridge and your first view of Lake Towada, formed from a volcanic crater. You are now at the small lakeside resort of **Nenokuchi**, from where boat cruises (¥1320) cross the lake to the main resort centre of **Yasumiya**. Alternatively, pick up the JR bus from Nenokuchi for the 20-minute ride to Yasumiya (in the timetable Yasumiya may just be called Lake Towada; either way it's the last stop).

The bus starts from outside Nenokuchi bus terminal (known as the 'JR House'), which also sells drinks and ice cream. You'll see it as you come off the hike. The bus terminates at Yasumiya JR bus terminal (also called 'JR House'). The lake is right in front of you, and all around are hotels, restaurants and souvenir shops. Motor and paddle boats can be rented on the lake. The best-known lakeside sight is the **Statue of the Maidens** (known locally as 'two old women in the buff reaching out for each other'). The statue is a 10-minute walk around the lake from the JR House. The temperature here can fall as low as -20°c in winter but because of its depth (327m), the lake never freezes.

To complete this route, pick up another JR Bus from the Yasumiya JR Bus terminal which runs to **Towada-Minami station** (60 mins; 4 times a day Apr 1st-Nov 10th), from where you take a local train on the Hanawa line west to **Odate** (40 mins). Services to Odate leave at 09:21, 12:23, 14:58, 17:12, and 18:37. (Services from Odate to Towada-Minami leave at 08:43, 11:22, 13:53, 16:00, 17:19, and 18:38.) From Odate, pick up the route starting on p260.

choice of restaurants and attached fitness club and indoor pool. The cheapest singles are ¥7800, with twins from ¥15,000. Rates rise during Golden Week and during the Neputa Matsuri. The new *Hyper Hotel Hirosaki* (☎ 0172-31 5000, 🖹 39 4800; ¥4800/S, ¥5800/D inc breakfast) has compact but comfortable rooms. Turn right out of the station and head straight up the main road for about 10 minutes. Keep going until you see Hirosaki Post Office on your left; the Hyper Hotel is just after this on your right.

The best budget choice is *Hirosaki Youth Hostel* (☎/🖹 0172-33 7066; ¥2900/YH(HI), ¥3900 non-members, breakfast ¥600), in an old building out towards Hirosaki Park. From the station, take a bus (¥170) from stop No 6 and get off at 'Daigaku Byoin-mae', or take the ¥100 tourist bus to the same stop.

Owani-Onsen (49km) Only 10 minutes down the line by limited express, this is a popular stop for skiers in winter thanks to nearby Mt Ajara (709m), a mountain which even boasts its own ski shrine. It's pine-tree territory on both sides of the line between Owani-Onsen and Odate.

After Owani-Onsen a few trains stop at **Ikarigaseki (73km)**.

Odate (82km) This station is a terminus for the JR Hanawa line coming from Towada-Minami and Morioka.

Odate looks and feels a bit run down, and there's little reason to spend time here unless you're particularly interested in Akita dogs. Even then, the **Akita Inu Kaikan (Akita Dogs Center)** (daily, 9am-4pm, ¥100), a 20-minute bus ride from the station, is a very depressing place housing a small museum about the dogs. The only live specimen is the poor mutt stuck in a cage outside. It's thought that Akita dogs were bred from the Nara Period (710-794) when rivalry between feudal leaders and frequent battles meant that there was a great demand for personal guard dogs. In the early 20th century, dog fighting was a popular form of local entertainment.

Odate to Akita   [Map 18, p255; Table 17, p408]
Distances by JR from Odate. Fastest journey time: 1 hour 25 minutes.

Odate (0km) Join, or continue along, the JR Ou line towards Akita.

Takanosu (18km) Takanosu once won a place in the *Guinness Book of Records* by building the world's largest drum, measuring 3.71m in diameter, 4.32m in depth and weighing in at 3.5 tons.

Higashi-Noshiro (48km) The Ou line, which has been roughly following Yoneshiro-gawa towards the coast, turns south at this point on its way to Akita.

Hachirogata (75km) There is a major land reclamation area out to the right along this stretch of the journey. Although there's not a great deal to see, it's an amazing project on paper: Hachirogata Lagoon, once the second largest lake in Japan, was reclaimed and is now a vast expanse of rice paddies – an area equal in size to the space inside Tokyo's Yamanote line (see p86).

♦ Oiwake (91km) Limited expresses don't stop here but this is the nearest point of interchange for the local Oga line that heads west to the **Oga Peninsula** (27km, 40 mins).

Oga is known for its Namahage Sedo Festival on December 31st, when men wearing demon costumes and masks, and wielding large knives and wooden buckets come down from nearby Mt Shinzan and invade the town. They knock on doors shouting the equivalent of 'Are there any cry babies in this house?' or, according to JNTO, 'Any good-for-nothing fellows around here?' – in short, threatening lazy children and adults to get their act together in time for the New Year.

Akita (104km) Akita is a large industrial city with a modern rail station which was rebuilt when the Komachi shinkansen opened along the Tazawako line, linking Akita with Morioka (see p251). The main exit is on the west side of the station. A tourist information office is by the ticket barrier (☎ 0188-32 7941, daily, 9am-7pm). A map is available but the staff do not speak much English. Coin lockers are located next to the waiting room, which is opposite the ticket barrier.

About the only reason for stopping in Akita is if you're passing through during the **Kanto Matsuri** between August 4th and 7th; men parade through the streets balancing bamboo poles topped with lanterns on their foreheads, shoulders, chins, heads and other parts of the body. During the rest of the year, the **Kanto Festival Center** (daily, 9:30am-4:30pm, ¥100) is the place to head to see a film of the action and a display of some of the lanterns and poles. At weekends from April to the end of October, volunteers demonstrate the astonishing pole-balancing act (visitors are welcome to join in). The centre is 20 minutes on foot west from the station.

For accommodation, try **Kohama Ryokan** (☎ 0188-32 5739, 🖹 32 5845), run by a very friendly couple (and a parrot who will say goodbye when you leave). The building is old but the tatami rooms are clean. There's even the chance to dress up in kimono and the owner sometimes performs a traditional Japanese dance for guests. The rate is ¥5000/pp, with dinner an additional ¥1000; a Western breakfast costs ¥800. Go down the left-hand stairs/escalator at the station's west exit, then head up the main road that goes past the JR East and Eki Rent A Car offices (on your left). The ryokan is about five minutes down this road on the right.

If in a hurry to return to Tokyo take the Komachi shinkansen that runs east to Morioka and from there on to Tokyo. The train travels 'backwards' as far as **Omagari**, the first stop after Akita – don't bother to turn the seats around, though, because the direction of the train reverses after leaving Omagari. Two places worth stopping at en route to Morioka (or visiting as day trips from Akita) are **Kakunodate**, a beautiful old town with a preserved samurai district, and **Tazawa-ko** (see p251), where you'll find the deepest lake in Japan.

Akita to Niigata [Map 19, p262; Map 20, p264; Table 18, p408]

Distances by JR from Akita. Fastest journey time: 3½ hours.

Akita (0km) The next part of the route continues south towards Niigata along the Uetsu line. Fifteen minutes after leaving Akita there are glimpses of the Japan Sea out on the right. These views last for another 15 minutes, before the line heads back towards more rice fields.

Ugo-Honjo (43km) and **Nikaho (57km)** Limited expresses make brief stops at both these stations but the surrounding area is not particularly noteworthy.

♦ Konoura (63km) Unless you're on a local train you won't notice this stop but Konoura was the birthplace of Nobu Shirase, the first Japanese to set foot on Antarctica.

Kisakata (68km) The next limited express stop after Nikaho, the area around Kisakata station is not at all attractive, so it's surprising to discover that up until the beginning of the 19th century, the area was similar to Matsushima (see p247), with tiny islands scattered along the coast. The islands disappeared for ever after a huge earthquake in 1804 pushed up the sea floor.

> ❏ *Although little more than a mile in width, this lagoon is not in the least inferior to Matsushima in charm and grace. There is, however, a remarkable difference between the two. Matsushima is a cheerful laughing beauty, while the charm of Kisakata is in the beauty of its weeping countenance.*
>
> **Matsuo Basho**, *The Narrow Road To The Deep North,* trans Nobuyuki Yuasa, Penguin, 1966

MAP 19

For the next 40km or so there are great views to the left of the mountains in Chokai Quasi National Park. The rail line skirts around the park, at the centre of which is Mt Chokai (2236m), a semi-dormant volcano known as the Mt Fuji of Akita. As the train moves into Yamagata prefecture, gradually the focus shifts towards the coast, with views out to sea on the right side. Between Kisakata and Sakata the train stops at **Yuza (93km)**.

Sakata (105km) Sakata is a large port town at the mouth of Mogami-gawa. The area around the station is rather drab and depressing but Sakata does boast a good example of the classic Japanese stroll garden, worth a look if you haven't visited one before.

Only small ¥300 coin lockers are available at the station, though ask at the JR ticket counter and they may keep your bags for ¥410. The tourist information office (daily, 9am-5:30pm) is in the building to the right as you leave the station but the staff do not speak English and maps are in Japanese only.

Fortunately, the main sight is only a short walk from the station. Turn right on to the main road that runs along in front of the station. Go straight, past the A1 Hotel, until you see Daiei supermarket at a junction on your right. The entrance to the **Homma Museum of Art** (daily Mar-Oct but closed Mon Nov-Feb, 9am-4:30/5pm, ¥700) is opposite Daiei. The Homma family were one of the wealthiest in Japan thanks to rice production on their land, and they remained the most influential family in the area until WWII brought an end to their power. The museum is housed in an ugly 1960s concrete building and the exhibition changes periodically. Far more interesting is the small Japanese garden and wooden guest house. Tea is served inside at tables overlooking the garden. A highlight of the garden used to be the 'borrowed' view of Mt Chokai in the distance; this has now been blocked out by karaoke signs and the Daiei supermarket outside.

Amarume (117km) Amarume is a stop on the Uetsu line and also a terminus for the Riku Saisen line running east to Shinjo. A quick way of returning to Tokyo from here would be to take a local train to **Shinjo** (50 mins), from where you can pick up the shinkansen which runs via Yamagata and Fukushima south to the capital.

⛩ **Yaya Festival**
If you're passing through Amarume on January 15th it would probably be more sensible to watch than participate in the annual Yaya Festival. On one of the coldest days of the year, the local male population strips off, puts on straw skirts and sandals and then proceeds to trek through the snow. This is followed by the main ceremony, during which the half-naked participants have buckets of cold water thrown over them. They are then required to walk through the town holding lit candles. Finally, offerings are made to the gods of the local shrine and prayers are said for good health in the coming year.

Less terrifying (depending on your point of view) is the annual karaoke competition in mid-September, for which contestants remain fully clothed.

In 1960, a small oil and natural gas field was discovered beneath Amarume town and fossil fuels are still pumped out of the ground for local consumption.

♦ **Fujishima (126km)** Limited expresses don't stop here but it's worth noting that Fujishima is the venue for the annual National River Rope Crossing Tournament in August; contestants attempt to cross from one side of Fujishima-gawa to the other via a series of ropes. Anyone who falls in is, well, out.

Tsuruoka (132km) Tsuruoka station has small ¥300 coin lockers (in the waiting room). The staff at the tourist information office (☎ 0235-25 7678, daily, 9:30am-5:30pm), to the right as you go out of the station, don't speak English but will help book accommodation.

Most people who stop here are usually on their way to Haguro-san (Mt Haguro). The 414m mountain to the east of Tsuruoka is part of a chain known as **Dewa-Sanzan** (Three Mountains of Dewa), the other two being Gas-san and Yudono-san. The mountains are considered to be the home of the *kami* (spirits), and pilgrims visit year round to undertake spiritual cleansing: first to be climbed is Haguro-san (2446 steps), which represents birth, followed by Gas-san, which represents death, and finally Yudono-san, representing the future or re-birth. The easiest to access, and possible as a day trip from Tsuruoka, is Haguro-san. Buses (operated by Shonai-Kotsu) take 45 minutes from Tsuruoka station to Haguro-san. Ask at tourist information for bus schedules.

Tsuruoka city has only a few sights, the most interesting of which is the **Chido Museum** (daily 9am-5pm, ¥620). There's an odd architectural mix of buildings here, including the former Tsuruoka Police station, a Western-style building from the late 19th century and the retirement residence of the former ruling Sakai lords. There's also a small Japanese garden. All signs inside are in Japanese, though a leaflet in English is available at the entrance. Take a bus from the station and get off at the Shiyakusho-mae stop (¥100), then keep following the road, past the park and look for the entrance on the right.

For accommodation, immediately opposite the station is the *Washington Hotel* (☎ 0235-25 0111, 🖷 25 0110; ¥6000/S, ¥9500/D, ¥10,000/Tw). Alternatively try *Tsuruoka Youth Hostel* (see overleaf).

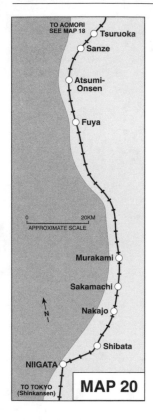

TO AOMORI
SEE MAP 18
Tsuruoka
Sanze
Atsumi-
Onsen
Fuya
0   20KM
APPROXIMATE SCALE
Murakami
Sakamachi
Nakajo
Shibata
NIIGATA
TO TOKYO
(Shinkansen)
MAP 20
N

♦ **Sanze (149km)** Three stops from Tsuruoka by local train, alight here for *Tsuruoka Youth Hostel* (☎/▤ 0235-73 3205, 💻 tyh@yamagata-npo.ne.jp; ¥2500/YH(HI), ¥3500/non-members). Local services operate approximately hourly in the morning and evening but less frequently during the day. Call in advance for a pick up. The hostel has recently reopened under new management. The building is old and the bunk-bed dorms (that sleep four or five) are only adequate, but the staff are friendly and the meals good (breakfast ¥500, dinner ¥1000). Activities such as paragliding can be arranged. The manager is involved with ecological projects and can advise hostellers on visiting the Dewa-Sanzan mountain range (see p263). To continue the route take a local train to Atsumi-Onsen.

Atsumi-Onsen (162km) More than 1000 years ago, Atsumi served as a border checkpoint for travellers entering Tohoku. Sandwiched between mountains and the coast, Atsumi is nowadays a busy hot spring resort. According to legend, the spring in question was discovered by none other than Kobo Daishi, the priest who founded the Shingon sect of Buddhism and established its headquarters on Mt Koya (see p200).

After Atsumi-Onsen, some limited expresses call briefly at **Fuya (176km)**.

Murakami (212km) As far as Murakami, the rail line runs along the coast, though views are limited due to the proliferation of tunnels (of various lengths) along this line. From here, the train heads inland and after 15 minutes passes a major industrial complex. The views gradually deteriorate as the surrounding area becomes more built up on the final approach into Niigata.

Before arriving in Niigata, there are three quick limited express stops at **Sakamachi (224km)**, **Nakajo (233km)** and **Shibata (246km)**.

Niigata (273km) [see pp275-80]

If not returning to Tokyo from here, Niigata also has direct rail connections with **Kanazawa**, just under four hours away by Hokuetsu LEX along the Hokuriku line. Pick up the route guide to Kanazawa from p124 as you pass Naoetsu (100 mins from Niigata). Direct access to **Nagano** (see p145) is also provided once a day by the Minori LEX, which takes 3 hours 20 minutes from Niigata.

🚂 Steam loco from Niitsu to Aizu-Wakamatsu
A good reason for opting to take the Banetsu-sei line from Niigata is that a steam locomotive operates between Niitsu and Aizu-Wakamatsu (Mar-Nov weekends only, daily during Aug).

All seats are reserved so you'll need to book a place in advance at any JR travel agency (reservations are free to rail-pass holders). Tickets go on sale one month in advance and are often sold out within the day. Demand has been so heavy since the service began in 1999 that extra carriages have been added.

Niigata to Tokyo

The fastest, though least scenic, way of returning to Tokyo from Niigata is by Joetsu shinkansen. The shinkansen line between Tokyo and Niigata is virtually all tunnels and the fastest journey time is 1 hour 40 minutes; there is at least one service an hour. Single and double-decker trains run on this line; the Max Asahi is a double-decker and it's worth reserving a seat on the upper deck for the snatches of mountain views in between the tunnels. However, these fill up quickly so book well ahead, or queue up early for a seat in the upper deck non-reserved cars.

If you have more time and are prepared to change trains you might consider the local Banetsu-sei line that runs inland from Niigata, via **Mikawa** (see p280) and the castle town of **Aizu-Wakamatsu**, to **Koriyama** on the Tohoku shinkansen line.

From Koriyama, you can complete the journey by jumping on a southbound shinkansen to Tokyo. Through services (Niigata to Mikawa to Aizu-Wakamatsu) depart at 08:23–09:15–10:40; 09:21–10:30–12:16; 11:07–12:18 –14:17; 17:18–18:15pm–19:50; 17:32–19:03–20:54; 19:46–21:01–22:51. Trains between Aizu-Wakamatsu and Koriyama leave roughly once an hour and take 70 minutes.

Tohoku (Northern Honshu) – city guides

SENDAI

Tohoku's largest city, Sendai, is located on the Pacific coast and shares the same latitude as Washington DC, USA, and the same longitude as Melbourne, Australia. The city was razed to the ground during WWII and consequently has few sights of historical interest. Sendai's history is dominated by the figure of Date Masamune (1567-1636), a feudal lord who earned the nickname 'one-eyed dragon' after he contracted smallpox during infancy and lost the sight in his right eye. Most visitors stop here briefly before heading on to Matsushima (see p247), billed as one the top three scenic spots in Japan.

What to see and do

The best way of seeing the main sights is to take the **Loople Sendai**, a bur-gundy-red tourist bus that departs from platform No 15 of the bus pool outside the station (9am-4pm; half-hourly). A one-day pass costs ¥600 or individual tickets are ¥250, available from the driver or from the ticket office at the bus ter-minal. The loop runs one way around the city, with 11 stops en route. Show your pass at the entrance to paid attractions for a small discount (usually the group rate). There are announcements in English before each stop. Ring the bell to stop at each place.

The following is a guide to the most interesting places along the way. A map at each bus stop shows the route to the place of interest.

At stop No 4, **Zuihoden** (daily, 9am-4/4:30pm, ¥550) is a temple-style mausoleum of the Date family reconstructed in 1985. There are statues of Masamune Date, and Tadamune and Tsunamune Date in the mausoleum, though they're off limits to visitors. There's a pleasant wooded area you can wander around and a museum with statues, artefacts and video – but the only English is in the guide you receive at the entrance to the mausoleum.

Sendai City Museum (daily except Mon, 9am-4:15pm, ¥400) at stop No 5 is more old fashioned than the hi-tech video show at Sendai Castle (see Stop No 6, below), but is very informative about the Date family with brief captions in English on most exhibits and an impressive scale model of the castle. A good pamphlet is available.

Stop No 6 is the site of the former **Sendai Castle**, built on top of the 132m-high Aoba Hill in 1602 by Masamune Date. Destroyed in 1945, it has now been resurrected as a massive tourist arcade and includes a restaurant and modern shrine. The only reason for heading out here is the view over Sendai – an impressive view of an ordinary city. There's an exhibition on the history of the castle with a computer-generated reconstruction video, but it's not particularly informative and could easily be skipped.

Finally, stop No 8 is **Miyagi Museum of Art** (daily except Mon, 9:30am-5pm, ¥300; extra charges for temporary exhibitions), 500m north of Sendai City Museum. The main gallery exhibits the work of 20th-century local artists and some minor works of foreign artists, including three early figurative paintings by Kandinsky. If you have time to spare, there's a pleasant modern sculpture garden and café.

PRACTICAL INFORMATION
Station guide

There are east and west sides to Sendai sta-tion but the main exit into the city is on the west side. On the third floor is the central shinkansen entrance and main JR ticket office (daily, 5:30am-10:30pm). There are lockers all around the station, though these are mostly only small size. On the second floor is the central entrance for all other JR

lines, including the Tohoku and Senseki Lines. Also on this floor is a large View Plaza travel agency where rail-pass vouch-ers can be exchanged.

Heading out of the station from the second floor brings you to the overhead walkways that run above the central streets in front of the station. On the first floor (street level) there's a 'parcel storage' office (daily, 6am-11pm) where you can leave luggage for ¥410 per item per day (¥820 overnight); the office is at the right-side end of the station building. There are plenty of places in the station for a snack – bakeries, cafés that do good value morning sets and a couple of beer restaurants that fill up in the evenings with businessmen.

Tourist information

The **tourist information centre** (☎ 022-222 4069, daily, 8:30am-8pm) is on the second floor of the station and has English-speaking staff. For more detailed information, contact **Sendai International Center** (English hotline ☎ 022-224 1919, daily, 9am-8pm, closed occasionally). This place is west of the city centre, across Hirose-gawa, and has a well-stocked library, foreign newspapers/magazines and travel brochures. The Loople Sendai tourist bus stops outside the centre.

Getting around

The best way of getting around is to take the tourist loop bus (see opposite). Sendai also has a network of buses and a subway line. City centre subway fares are ¥200.

Sendai airport has connections with Seoul, Hong Kong and Singapore. A limousine bus (¥910 one-way, 40 mins) operates between Sendai station and the airport.

Internet

Net U Internet is a swanky multimedia centre on the fifth floor of the AER building next to the station; you can surf the net for free (10am-8pm; 30 mins per visit).

Money

Cash advances from foreign-issued Visa cards can be obtained from the International Visa Card office on Aoba-dori.

Festivals

Sendai's biggest annual event is the **Tanabata Matsuri** on August 6th-8th. Along the main streets and in the station, colourful paper streamers and decorations are hung from bamboo poles. One of the largest summer events in Tohoku, the festival attracts around two million visitors.

Where to stay

Next to the station is the JR-run *Hotel Metropolitan Sendai* (☎ 022-268 2525, ▤ 268 2521), which has comfortable if not overly-luxurious rooms. Rack rates are ¥10,000 for a single and ¥18,000 for a twin but rail-pass holders receive a 10% discount.

Opened in 2001 and offering rooms of a high standard, *Holiday Inn Sendai* (1-4-1 Shintera, Wakabayashi-ku, ☎ 022-256 5111, ▤ 256 5211, 💻 www.holiday-inn-sendai.jp; ¥9500/S, ¥16,500/D, ¥17,500 /Tw, ¥20,500/Tr) is a six-minute walk from the station's east exit.

A 10-minute walk north of the station is *Roynet Hotel* (☎ 022-722 0055, ▤ 722 0056, 💻 sendai-info@roynet.co.jp), a cut above the standard business hotel, with reasonably-spacious singles going for ¥6953, doubles at ¥8191, twins at ¥12,667 and triples at ¥16,477. Facilities include a coin laundry and 24-hour restaurant. You pay into a machine in the lobby, though human staff are also on hand.

Fifteen minutes on foot from the station's east exit is *Mielparque Sendai* (☎ 022-792 8111, ▤ 792 8113; ¥6321/S, ¥11,862/Tw), a new addition to the chain of hotels run by the post office (hence the post office in the lobby). Rooms have wide beds but small bathrooms. The building is not easy to miss as it looks as if a boat has been built into one side.

Bansuitei Ikoi-so Ryokan (☎ 022-222 7885, ▤ 223 2222. 💻 bansui@ikoisou ryokan.co.jp) is less than 10 minutes on foot from Kita Yobancho subway station, three stops from Sendai station. It has a smart wooden interior with tatami rooms – a big selling point is the common bath that turns into a Jacuzzi. Japanese breakfast and evening meals are available; ¥5000/pp no meals (¥4500/pp for two people sharing a room), ¥7000/pp for two meals (¥6500/pp for two sharing a room). Take North Exit 2 at Kita Yobancho subway, turn right at the top of the steps that leads to street level, and walk for about eight minutes. The ryokan is on a quiet road off to the left, just before you reach Tohoku University Hospital.

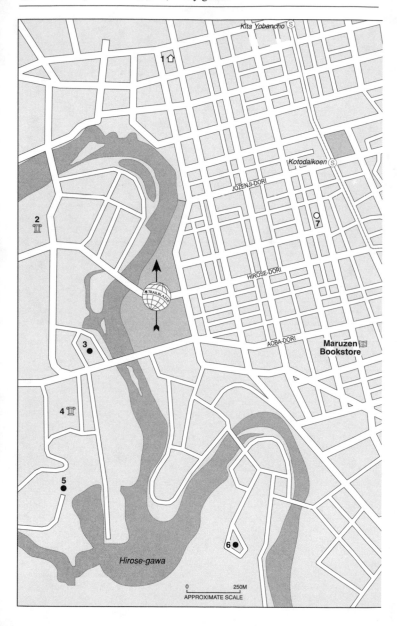

Kita Yobancho Ⓢ

1 ⌂

Kotodaikoen Ⓢ

JOZENJI-DORI

2 ⌁

7 ○

HIROSE-DORI

★ TRAILBLAZER

AOBA-DORI

Maruzen ▨
Bookstore

3 ●

4 ⌁

5 ●

6 ●

Hirose-gawa

0   250M
APPROXIMATE SCALE

SENDAI 仙台

Where to stay

1 Bansuitei Ikoi-so Ryokan	1 晩翠亭いこい荘旅館
8 Sendai Chitose Youth Hostel	8 仙台千登勢ユースホステル
9 Roynet Hotel	9 ロイネットホテル仙台
12 Hotel Metropolitan Sendai	12 ホテルメトロポリタン仙台
17 Hotel Mielparque Sendai	17 ホテルメルパルク 仙台
18 Holiday Inn Sendai	18 ホリデイ・イン仙台

[See p270 for continuation of key]

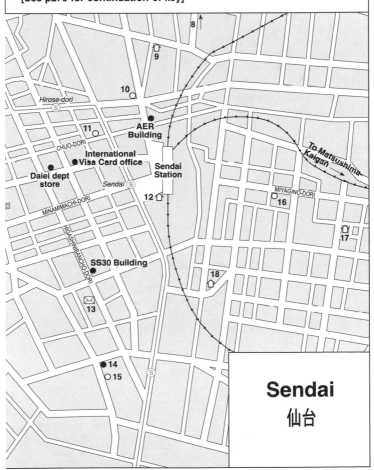

Sendai
仙台

SENDAI MAP KEY (continued from p269)

Where to eat

7	Chibou	7	千房
10	Samba Samba, Mojadar, Miconos	10	サンバサンバ／モジャダール／ミコノス
11	Capricciosa	11	カプリチョーザ
15	Silvia	15	シルヴィア
16	Michel	16	ミッシェル

Other

2	Miyagi Museum of Art	2	宮城県美術館
3	Sendai International Center	3	仙台国際センター
4	Sendai City Museum	4	仙台市博物館
5	Site of Sendai Castle	5	仙台城跡
6	Zuihoden Mausoleum	6	瑞鳳殿
13	Central Post Office	13	中央郵便局
14	Coin Laundry	14	コインランドリー

Sendai Chitose Youth Hostel (☎ 022-222 6329, 🖹 265 7551; ¥3000/YH(HI), ¥4000 non-members, breakfast ¥600, dinner ¥1000) is a good budget option with tatami rooms sleeping 2-4 people. In a residential area about 20 minutes on foot from the station (pick up a map from tourist information).

Where to eat

Over on the east side of the station, on the way to the Mielparque hotel, *Michel* (daily, 8am-10pm, early closing on Sun) is a boulangerie, patisserie and brasserie rolled into one. As well as simple food such as omelettes and sandwiches, they also do a more elaborate four-course evening set menu including coffee for ¥2800. In the summer, the doors are opened and you can sit at tables on the pavement-side terrace outside. The attached bakery sells sandwiches, pizza, cakes and the like. To find Michel, walk along the main tree-lined road that runs away from the station's east exit for about eight minutes. It's on the right side.

On the 20th floor of the Azur Sendai building, a five-minute walk north of the station, are three restaurants under the same management: *Samba Samba* does Latin American food and has live music most nights, *Mojadar* mostly Indian and *Miconos* is Mediterranean. All three serve buffet

lunches. Open for lunch from 11:30am to 2:30pm and in the evening from 5 to 11pm. *Chibou* is a D-I-Y okonomiyaki place (or they'll make it for you) with good-value lunch deals that include salad and a drink. A popular student haunt is the pasta-and-pizza chain *Capricciosa* (daily, 11:30am-10:30pm) that specializes in enormous portions. It's on the second floor along the covered Clis Rd arcade.

On the 28th and 29th floors of the SS30 Building there are several restaurants – from sushi to tonkatsu – with views over the city. Alternatively, head for the 30th floor observation gallery where you get a great view of Sendai by night for free. *Silvia* is above a branch of Lawson convenience store, a 15-minute walk south of the station. The bargain ¥480 Viking breakfast (not available during university holidays) is popular with cash-strapped students but anybody is welcome.

Finally, look out for branches of *Doutor Coffee* and *Pronto*, both of which are great for a quick breakfast. The steal Pronto has over Doutor is that in the evening the coffee shop turns into a pub, with beer on tap and well-priced spirits and cocktails. The transformation works surprisingly well and it's not as smoky as traditional Japanese bars.

Side trip to Yamadera

Some 50km west of Sendai lies Yamadera, a hillside temple founded in 860 by the priest Jikaku Daishi and considered to be of the holiest sights in northern Japan. The temple complex is within easy reach of Sendai, a 50-minute journey by 'rapid' train along the JR Senzan line to Yamadera station.

Once you pass the urban sprawl of Sendai city, the scenery begins to change. Unlike some rural rail routes that tend to be shut in by dense forest, along this line the views open up as the train weaves between the hills and passes from village to village. Yamadera station is small and has mostly ¥300 lockers. There's an overhead walkway from one side of the single-track line to the exit. There is no tourist information in the station but go to the ticket office and ask for a guide to Yamadera.

From the station, follow the signposted route up towards Yamadera, crossing Hoju Bridge. It's a two-minute walk to the entrance. Gates to the temple are open daily (6am-5pm) and admission costs ¥300. Give yourself an hour to climb 'about 1100' steps (it's easy to lose count). Getting to the top is like climbing a very long staircase: there's a handrail but some people buy wooden sticks to help with the climb. There are a few stalls on the way up selling soft drinks and the obligatory souvenirs. The best views into the valley are from about two-thirds of the way up, at **Godai-do**, a temple built like a stage, which doubles as a useful viewing platform. Your goal at the top is **Okuno-in Temple**, which contains a large golden Buddha.

If you need somewhere to overnight, *Yamadera Pension* (☎ 0236-95 2134, 🖹 95 2240, 💻 yamadera@mmy.ne.jp) is immediately to the left as you leave the station. Don't make the mistake of going past it thinking it must be much further away! All the rooms are Western style with low beds; the staff are friendly and speak some English. It's popular and as there's not much else in Yamadera is often booked up in the summer. Expect to pay around ¥8000 for a room with attached bath/toilet and two meals.

AOMORI

The last major city before Hokkaido, Aomori is best known for its red apples, considered to be the best in Japan, and for Nebuta Matsuri, one of the major summer festivals in Tohoku. Summer is mild but in winter temperatures drop well below freezing and snow becomes a fact of life for months on end. If visiting in the summer, look out for the phone boxes mounted well above street level with steps leading up to them. In winter, the steps – and sometimes much of the phone box – are buried in snow. Up until just over a decade ago, all rail travellers bound for Hokkaido had no choice but to stop here in order to transfer on to a passenger ferry for the journey across the Tsugaru Straits. Even though it's possible to travel straight through Aomori by train, it's still worth stopping for at least a day, particularly to visit the museum where some of the summer festival floats are displayed year-round (see Side trip, p275).

What to see and do

A good place to begin a tour of Aomori is at **ASPAM** (Aomori Prefectural Center for Industry and Tourism), the large triangular building by the port 10 minutes on foot from the station. On the 13th floor, there's an observation lounge and on the second floor a panorama theatre where Aomori prefecture is introduced on a 360° screen. The observation lounge costs ¥400 and panorama theatre ¥600; a combined ticket is ¥800. Show your Aomori Welcome Card (see p46) at the information desk next to the ticket vending machines on the first floor to receive 50% off these rates.

A five-minute walk from ASPAM, and visible across the water, is the **Memorial Ship Hakkoda Maru** (daily, 9am-6pm, ¥500), a former JR-operated ferry that used to plough the water between Aomori and Hakodate. You can go on board, look around and even put on a captain's jacket and cap and pose for photos. The ship has been preserved as it was, except that in the summer there's now a beer garden on the top deck.

Aomori Prefectural Museum (daily exec Mon and occasional days, 9:30am-5pm; ¥310) depicts the life of hunters and fishermen in Aomori prefecture from the Stone Age onward and has displays of wildlife found in the prefecture and a section devoted to Aomori apples. There's only a limited amount of English on the signs but a good pamphlet is available. Take a city bus from stop No 4 or 5 outside the station and get off at the Honcho 5-chome stop.

PRACTICAL INFORMATION

Station guide

Aomori station is small with two sides, east and west. The main exit is on the east side. Coin lockers (up to ¥500) are available. To the right as you exit the station is the Lovina department store and there are some lockers between the store and the station. As you leave the main east exit of the station look out for the bright new AUGA shopping, restaurant and library building.

Tourist information

To the left as you leave the station is the tourist information centre (☎ 0177-23 4670, daily, 8:30am-6pm), where staff can advise on accommodation and provide maps and travel information. Another desk is on the ground floor of ASPAM (☎ 0177-34 2500, daily, 9am-10pm), the triangular building by Aomori Port. Both places are staffed by English speakers.

Money

For Visa cash advances, visit the Saison counter in a corner of the fourth floor of Matsukiya department store along Shinmachi-dori.

Internet

Free Internet access is available on the eighth floor of ASPAM at the 'Aomori Prefectural Information and Communications Network System Center' (Mon-Fri, 9am-12pm and 1-5pm), a grand name for what is just a room full of people checking their email.

Getting around

The centre of Aomori is walkable but there is also a network of city buses. The Aomori Welcome Card gives a 50% discount on most local bus services. Collect a ticket when you board the bus and show the card to the driver as you get off.

Festivals

Nebuta Matsuri (August 1st-7th) is one of the most popular festivals in Japan. Every night, giant, colourful floats are paraded through the city and on the evening of the final day, a fireworks festival is held in the port area. The atmosphere of the city

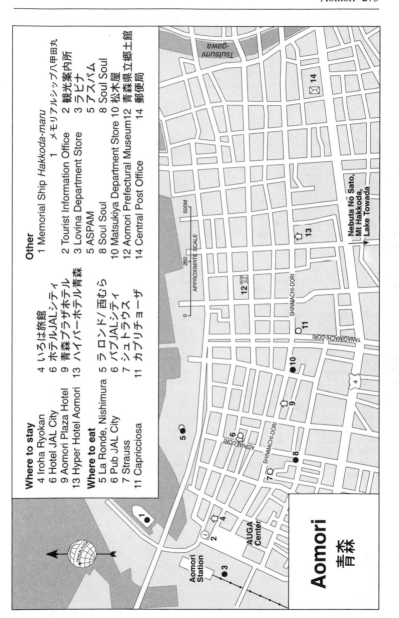

Aomori
青森

Where to stay
4 Iroha Ryokan　　いろは旅館
6 Hotel JAL City　　ホテルJALシティ
9 Aomori Plaza Hotel　　青森プラザホテル
13 Hyper Hotel Aomori　　ハイパーホテル青森

Where to eat
5 La Ronde, Nishimura　　ラロンド/西むら
6 Pub JAL City　　パブJALシティ
7 Strauss　　シュトラウス
11 Capricciosa　　カプリチョーザ

Other
1 Memorial Ship *Hakkoda-maru*　　メモリアルシップ八甲田丸
2 Tourist Information Office　　観光案内所
3 Lovina Department Store　　ラビナ
5 ASPAM　　アスパム
8 Soul Soul　　Soul Soul
10 Matsukiya Department Store　　松木屋
12 Aomori Prefectural Museum　　青森県立郷土館
14 Central Post Office　　郵便局

changes completely during the festival week. Thousands of visitors arrive from all over Japan, accommodation gets booked solid and even the plastic model of Colonel Sanders, outside the KFC along the main street, gets dressed up in a yukata and festival headgear for the occasion.

Where to stay

On a side street just outside the station is *Iroha Ryokan* (☎/🖹 0177-22 8689), offering tatami rooms but no attached bath/toilet or meals. It's a small place and gets booked up quickly. ¥4000/pp; cash only. It's on a small road just behind Aomori Grand Hotel.

A popular upmarket choice is *Hotel JAL City* (☎ 0177-32 2580, 🖹 35 2584; ¥8200/S, ¥14,000/Tw), with an elegant lobby and large rooms, close to the ASPAM building.

Aomori Plaza Hotel (☎ 0177-75 4311, 🖹 75 4317) has single rooms with wide beds for ¥5500 and twins at ¥10,000 including breakfast. It's a ten-minute walk up Shinmachi-dori from the station.

Hyper Hotel Aomori (☎ 0177-73 3000, 🖹 75 7373) is a similar place but has an automated check-in (cash only). Regular rooms (¥4800) sleep one adult, family rooms (¥5800) have two beds for adults and a small one for a child. Rates include breakfast and there's also a coin laundry. It's a 15- to 20-minute walk from the station up Shinmachi-dori. Look for the distinctive yellow/gold building with British, French and Australian flags flying outside the European façade.

Where to eat

A branch of the Italian chain *Capricciosa* has opened in Aomori, serving full and half-size portions of pizza and pasta. It's 12 minutes on foot from the station's east exit along Shinmachi-dori. It's on the corner of a major junction; look for the red, white and green veranda. If you're in the station area and need a quick coffee, there's a branch of *Doutor Coffee* within the station.

There are several restaurants in the **ASPAM** building down by the port which offer a modest discount with the Aomori Welcome Card. On the 14th floor, *La Ronde* (11:40am-10pm) is a French restaurant that revolves to ensure all diners get a share of the bay view. It's expensive in the evening but the lunch deals (from ¥1800) are more reasonable. Unfortunately, it feels very old-fashioned and the decor is dated. Much better is *Nishimura* on the 10th floor, a casual Japanese restaurant with low wooden tables. It specializes in local fish dishes.

Close to ASPAM is *Pub JAL City* (inside Hotel JAL City), a quiet place that does excellent value set lunches with soup, salad bar, main course of the day, dessert and coffee for ¥1000. Open for lunch 11am-2:30pm, dinner 5:30-9pm and 'pub time' (beer on tap) 9-11pm; get 10% off with the Welcome Card.

For a decadent treat, try *Strauss*, on a side road close to Vivre department store. Downstairs is a cake shop, but upstairs is a very smart café where waitresses in 1920s-style black and white uniforms serve rich slices of cake and various coffees. It's as near as you'll get to Vienna in Tohoku – the detail's there right down to the chandeliers and fireplace. There's no better place to escape a freezing Aomori winter than here with a hot chocolate and apple strudel.

Soul Soul (open evenings to late, daily except Mon) is a small but popular bar that plays a range of music. There's a ¥600 cover charge, and a good selection of beer and cocktails for ¥600-¥700. Some English is spoken and the chances are you'll meet some of Aomori city's foreign residents here.

Side trip from Aomori

Thirty minutes by bus (¥450) from Aomori station is **Nebuta no Sato** (daily, 9am-5:30pm, until 8pm in summer, ¥630). The route is operated by JR Bus and is free to rail-pass holders. It's a huge indoor space displaying several of the colourful floats used in Aomori's summer festival. Four times a day there's a show that introduces some of the flavour of the festival, with performers on stage playing the flute and drums, and visitors pulling one of the floats a few metres along inside the hall. The floats are incredibly heavy; just pulling them along for a few metres makes you wonder how participants manage to do it for two hours during the festival. The bus for Nebuta no Sato leaves from stop No 9 outside the station. Get off at 'Nebuta no Sato Iriguchi'. A visit here can be combined with the route from Aomori described in the box on pp258/9.

NIIGATA

Niigata is the largest city on the Japan Sea coast and was one of the first ports to open to foreign trade when Japan reopened to the outside world in 1869 after nearly 230 years of self-imposed seclusion. Visitors are put off spending time here – most press on without delay to nearby Sado Island – because it is a major industrial city. But it's difficult to write the place off as just another identikit Japanese city when it's home to a huge performing arts centre, a coastal area, quiet back streets and any number of shopping and dining opportunities. Winters here are cold (the average temperature in January is 2.1°C) but summers tend to be hot and humid.

What to see and do

A good place to start is across Bandai bridge, on the other side of the city to the station, at **Hakusan Park** inside which is **Hakusan Shrine**. A place of worship for more than 400 years, the shrine is frequently visited by couples seeking the support of a god of marriage enshrined here. From the shrine, walk through Hakusan Park, passing by the large lotus pond. Though the park is not big, it's a welcome escape from the noise of the city.

Also within the grounds of the park but entered from a street just outside, is **Enkikan** (daily except 1st and 3rd Mon, 9am-5pm, free), an old merchant home that has been moved here and transformed into a house for traditional Japanese arts like tea ceremony and flower arranging (see p40). Though modern, it's a beautiful example of a traditional Japanese house and there's no charge to look around and enjoy the view of the lotus pond. For ¥300 you'll be served a cup of Japanese tea in one of the tatami rooms. To reach Hakusan Park, take a bus from stop No 13 outside the station and get off at 'Hakusan Koen mae'.

Walking through the park and leaving the other side, you'll come to the **Prefectural Government Memorial Hall** (daily except Mon, 9am-4:30pm, free), which dates back to 1883. Used as the prefectural parliament for 50 years, it was apparently constructed in the same style as the Houses of Parliament in London, with Shinano-gawa in place of the Thames. Around the walls of the assembly hall, look out for some old photos of assembly delegates. It's interesting to note how the dress code has changed. In a group shot dated 1911, almost all the delegates are dressed in traditional Japanese clothes. By 1931, the vast majority were in Western-style suits.

Leaving the hall, look out for the huge, modern building that is the new Performing Arts Center, also known as **Ryutopia**. Opened in 1998 after three years of construction, the total cost is speculated to have been in the region of ¥26,600,000,000. What the citizens of Niigata got for their money was an enormous concert hall, theatre and separate Noh stage. It's a world-class facility and attracts international orchestras, theatre troupes and singers. Tickets can be purchased from the box office in the foyer, though you might want to check what's on with the English-speaking staff at the tourist office outside the station.

From here, it's an easy 10-minute walk to the central shopping area of **Furumachi**, where you'll find plenty of places for lunch. For a (free) bird's eye view of the city, the sea and on a clear day Sado Island, head for the 19th floor of the Next 21 Building, a landmark that's easy to spot because it's shaped like a pencil. Heading back towards the station, cross over Bandai Bridge and go straight. As you return towards the station, you'll see the **Rainbow Tower** on your right after crossing Bandai Bridge (daily except 2nd Wed/Thur, 10am-6pm, ¥450). However, it's not worth the expense when you can get a free view from the Next 21 Building.

Particularly in the summer, a good mini-escape from the city is down by the coast in the area around **Niigata City Aquarium**. The aquarium (daily 9am-

---

NIIGATA 新潟

Where to stay

12 Dormy Inn Niigata	12 ドーミーイン新潟
13 Tokyu Inn	13 新潟東急イン
14 Single Inn Niigata 1	14 シングルイン新潟第1
15 Single Inn Niigata 3	15 シングルイン新潟第3

Where to eat

2 Popolo Gelateria	2 ポポロジェラテリア
7 Essa	7 越佐
11 Immigrant's Café	11 mmigrant's Cafe

Other

1 Niigata City Aquarium	1 マリンピア日本海
3 Gokoku Shrine	3 護國神社
4 Hakusan Shrine/Park and Enkikan	4 白山神社/白山公園/燕喜館
5 Prefectural Government Memorial Hall	5 県庁記念館
6 Ryutopia/Rivage	6 りゅーとぴあ/リバージュ
8 Niigata Port	8 新潟港
9 Rainbow Tower	9 レインボータワー
10 Central Post Office	10 中央郵便局

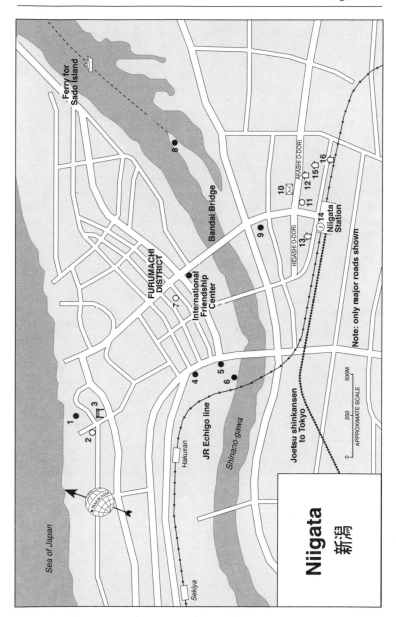

Sea of Japan

Ferry for Sado Island

Bandai Bridge

FURUMACHI DISTRICT

International Friendship Center

8

9

7

4

5

6

1

2

3

10

AKASHI O-DORI

12

15

16

11

13

14

HIGASHI O-DORI

Niigata Station

Note: only major roads shown

Hakusan

JR Echigo line

Shinano-gawa

Joetsu shinkansen to Tokyo

Sekiya

APPROXIMATE SCALE

0   250   500M

Niigata
新潟

5pm, ¥1500) is mainly of interest to children but the seafront area is a good place for a stroll. Near the aquarium are the Sea West restaurant/shopping blocks, numbered 1-3. *Popolo Gelateria* in Sea West 3 is open year-round and definitely worth seeking out as it serves probably the best hand-made ice cream anywhere in Japan. Down here, and with trees covering the concrete blocks behind, it's hard to believe you're in a major industrial city. Finally, don't miss **Gokoku Shrine**, surrounded by pine trees, just a couple of minutes from the aquarium. It was built in 1945 to console the souls of the war dead.

To reach this area, take a bus from stop No 11 outside the station and get off at the terminus, which is outside the aquarium. Instead of taking the bus back to the station, it's a very pleasant walk back into the city through quiet backstreets filled with old wooden houses and privately-owned craft shops. It's a complete contrast to the young and trendy Furumachi shopping district.

PRACTICAL INFORMATION
Station guide
Niigata is the terminus for the Joetsu shinkansen to/from Tokyo. The station is divided into the shinkansen side and regular JR lines side. For the city centre, follow signs for the Bandai exit. A passageway connects both sides, though access is only via stairs/escalator. The shinkansen side has the most shops and restaurants. Coin lockers are available on both sides.

The main rail lines are the shinkansen line to Tokyo, the local Echigo line to Yoshida, the Shinetsu line to Nagano via Naoetsu, the Joetsu line to Ueno and the Uetsu line that runs north to Murakami and Akita.

Tourist information
A tourist information centre (☎ 025-241 7914, daily, 8:30am-5:15pm) is to the left as you take the main Bandai exit. The staff here speak English, have information about ferries to Sado Island and can book same-day city accommodation. Pick up a copy of the monthly *Niigata English Journal*, which contains restaurant reviews and listings for concerts, exhibitions and movies. English speakers are also on hand at the Niigata International Exchange Foundation, also known as the International Friendship Centre (☎ 025-225 2777, daily except Wed, 10am to 6pm), on the left side just after Bandai Bridge coming from the

station. The centre is stocked with newspapers, has satellite TV and can supply excellent walking maps of the Bandai and Furumachi areas in Niigata.

Getting around
The central point for crossing over Shinano-gawa is Bandai Bridge. It's easy enough to walk around central Niigata but all city buses depart from the bus terminal outside the Bandai exit of the station. A flat fare of ¥180 operates within the city. Niigata is a major international gateway for flights to/from Russia. Scheduled services operate to Vladivostok (for connections to the Trans-Siberian Railway), Khaborovsk, Irkutsk, Hawaii, Seoul, Shanghai and Guam. A limousine bus to Niigata airport (¥350 one way) departs from bus stop No 11 at the bus terminal outside the station.

Money
The only ATM that accepts foreign Visa cards is along the Furumachi covered arcade, close to Daiwa department store. It's next to a sushi restaurant; look out for the sign 'UC Card Cash Station' on the door.

Festivals
Niigata matsuri runs from August 7th to 9th. This started as a festival to pray for the prosperity of the port and growth of the city; it still involves a procession and folk dancing over Bandai Bridge (on the 8th) and

ends with a huge fireworks display over Shinano-gawa on the evening of the 9th.

Where to stay
One of the newest places in town, five minutes on foot north of the station, is *Dormy Inn Niigata* (☎ 025-247 7755, 🖷 247 7789). The cheapest rooms are economy singles for ¥4800. If these are full, the deluxe economy single costs ¥5800. Both room types have sink and toilet but no bath. Singles with bath are ¥6600, and twins and doubles are ¥9600. All rooms have bilingual TV and mini-kitchen. The hotel has a good hot spring and sauna, and washing machines are free (you pay for use of the dryer).

Opposite the Bandai exit of the station is *Tokyu Inn* (☎ 025-243 0109, 🖷 243 0401), with singles from ¥7700, twins from ¥14,600 and doubles at ¥15,200. Rates fall by about ¥1000 between December and the end of March.

There are four branches of the Single Inn Niigata, all offering basic single and twin rooms for under ¥5000 per night. The nearest to the station is *Single Inn 1* (☎/🖷 025/241-3003), though *Single Inn 3* (☎ 025/243-3900, 🖷 243-2939) is marginally cheaper. Rooms at all Single Inns come with attached bath.

Where to eat
On the shinkansen side of the station is the PATIO restaurant/shopping area with coffee shops, a bakery, a cheap revolving sushi restaurant and a Chinese restaurant that does a range of lunches from ¥650-800.

An unusual dining experience is to be had at *Essa*, on a corner of the WITH building along Higashi-dori (look for the moving crab on the wall outside). This is the place to go for seafood; you eat at the counter around a big pool where the staff go and fish your food so you know your meal is going to be fresh. It's pricey in the evenings but at lunchtime (11am-2pm) the ¥1200 set meal is a feast. The crab on the outside of the building is actually a sign for the crab restaurant on the eighth floor. For Essa, take the stairs down to the basement.

Rivage (11:30am-2:30pm and 5-10pm) is a stylish restaurant on the third floor of the new Performing Arts Center; it is a quiet place to go for lunch with tables overlooking Shinano-gawa – and is especially good in spring when the cherry blossoms are out. A set lunch with soup, salad, main course, small dessert and coffee costs ¥1200.

A new addition to Niigata's dining scene is the *Immigrant's Café*, along Akashi-dori just across from the central post office, five minutes on foot from the station. It's popular with Niigata's foreign community as the staff (Japanese and foreign) all speak English and the place is run by a Japanese-Hawaiian. There are three different décors on split levels and a mixed menu of ethnic food like Vietnamese, plus Hawaiian and Mexican dishes. Most dishes are ¥780-980.

Side trips from Niigata
The most popular trip is to **Sado Island**, once a place of exile and now home to the world-famous Kodo drummers. Ferries and jet foils depart from Niigata Port. The ferry crossing takes 2 hours 20 minutes (¥2060 one-way). The jet foil takes only one hour but is more expensive (¥5960 one-way). To reach Sado Ferry Terminal, take a bus from stop No 6 outside the station and get off at Sado Kisen, the last stop.

An alternative side trip by rail could be made to **Mikawa**, some 46km from Niigata along the local Banetsu-sei line. Here, you can take a gentle boat cruise down Agano-gawa, the tenth longest river in Japan. Head out of Mikawa station and turn left on to the main road. Walk for about five minutes and the entrance for the boat cruise is on the right, just above the river. Cruises (¥2500, 50 mins) leave every hour on the hour from 9am-4pm. There's a chance of seeing wild deer and monkeys along this scenic route, which is especially beautiful in winter when snow covers the mountains; the river itself doesn't freeze over, so cruises run year-round as long as the weather is reasonable. Free shuttle buses are provided at the end of the cruise (in Iwama), 13km further down Aganogawa, to take you back to the start point, from where you can pick up the train. In winter call ahead (☎ 02549-92822) to check if cruises have been cancelled because of inclement weather. The manager speaks English.

Hokkaido – route guide

The northernmost of the major islands in the Japanese archipelago, Hokkaido represents one-fifth of the country's land mass but is inhabited by only one-twentieth of the total population. The island is the largest of Japan's 47 prefectures and is bordered by the Sea of Japan to the west, the Sea of Okhotsk to the north-east and the Pacific Ocean to the south.

Hokkaido is an island of stunning natural beauty, vast national parks with mountain ranges, volcanoes, forests, rivers, crashing waterfalls, wildlife ... and tourists. In the summer months, bikers, backpackers and cyclists descend on the island to feel what it is like to drive on the open road, unclogged by pollution, noise and urban development. Others come to escape the oppressive heat and humidity found elsewhere in Japan, to see cows, taste fresh Hokkaido milk, yoghurt and even Camembert-style cheese. In winter, when temperatures plummet and snow falls for months on end, skiers pour on to the slopes.

The bad news for the rail traveller is that as much as 45% of the Hokkaido network has closed in the last few decades. Spiralling costs, few passengers on remote lines and the difficulty of track maintenance in areas particularly exposed to the elements mean that some parts are no longer accessible by rail. But enough of the rail network remains to provide more than a glimpse of the spectacular natural environment. You'll be travelling on mostly rural lines, so don't expect lightning-fast services, but few other places in Japan offer such breathtaking scenery from the train window.

INTRODUCTION

Aomori (see p271), on the tip of northern Honshu, is the rail gateway to Hokkaido. The route in this chapter follows a loop around Hokkaido, starting and finishing in Aomori. Three weeks would be enough to enjoy the island without feeling rushed.

For a shorter 'taste' of what the island has to offer, the line between Abashiri and Kushiro (see p295) has some of the most impressive scenery. Since it's away from the major tourist areas, most visitors never make it this far but the views more than repay the distance and effort.

早稲の香や分け入る右は荒磯海

Through fragrant fields of early rice we went beside the wild Ariso Sea
(MATSUO BASHO)

卅 **Tunnel vision**
  The ferry service that had been in operation across the Tsugaru Straits
between Honshu and Hokkaido since 1908 was finally discontinued in 1988 with
the opening of the Seikan Tunnel. The idea for a tunnel had surfaced well before
WWII but the sinking of a JR ferry brought home the urgent need to turn the idea
into reality. On 26th September 1954, 1314 people were on board what was supposed to be just another routine crossing when the *Toya Maru* ferry foundered in
Hakodate port; 1155 people died, the world's second worst accident at sea after the
sinking of the *Titanic*, which claimed 1531 lives. It was to be another 34 years
before the rail line finally opened to passenger traffic. The tunnel (53.85km) is the
longest underwater tunnel in the world. It was built as straight as possible in antic-
ipation of the day (still decades away) that shinkansen trains would run through it.
  Though not recommended for claustrophobics, it's possible to go on a behind-
the-scenes tour. If nothing else, there's the chance to make a call from public phones
installed at the lowest point in Japan. Note that only selected local trains stop at the
two stations in the tunnel.
  Coming from Hakodate, the first stop is **Tappi-kaitei (64km)**. You are met by
a guide who walks you through the service tunnel to a cable car which provides a
scary journey up to the surface at Cape Tappi, the very tip of Honshu. There's a
small tunnel museum here but there's also time to walk over to the cape from where
there are great views of Hokkaido across the Tsugaru Straits. After a quick look
around the museum, it's time to take the cable car back down to the underground
station and pick up the train. Tickets for the cable car/tunnel museum option are
currently ¥2040 for adults, ¥1020 for children (rail passes not valid).
  The second stop in the tunnel is **Yoshioka-kaitei (87km)**. This is really only
for children since it's been turned into a 'Doraemon event', with displays relating
to the popular Japanese cartoon character and a live underground Doraemon stage
show. What this has to do with the tunnel is unclear but it's a popular family day
out. Tickets for this option cost ¥840 for adults and ¥420 for children (rail passes
are not valid).
  Reservations should be made in advance at Aomori or Hakodate stations. At
the time of writing, a local train departs Aomori at 11:08am, arriving at Tappi-kaitei
at 12:17pm. After the tour, another train picks you up from the station at 3:14pm
and arrives in Hakodate at 4:52pm. From Hakodate, a local train leaves at 8:04am,
arriving at Tappi-kaitei at 9:40am. After the tour, a train picks you up at 12:25pm
and arrives in Aomori at 1:27pm. Note that the trip by cable car to the museum and
the Doraemon event operate only in the summer. In winter, short underground tours
operate at both stations. Luggage can be stored in an underground locker for the
duration of the tour.

AOMORI TO HAKODATE   [Map 21, p284; Table 16, p407]

Distances by JR from Aomori. Fastest journey time: 2 hours.

Aomori (0km)   [see pp271-5]
From Aomori, take the Hatsukari LEX along the Tsugaru Kaikyo line bound for
Hakodate. In the days before the Seikan Tunnel (see box above) the journey
took 3 hours 40 minutes; it now takes less than two hours.

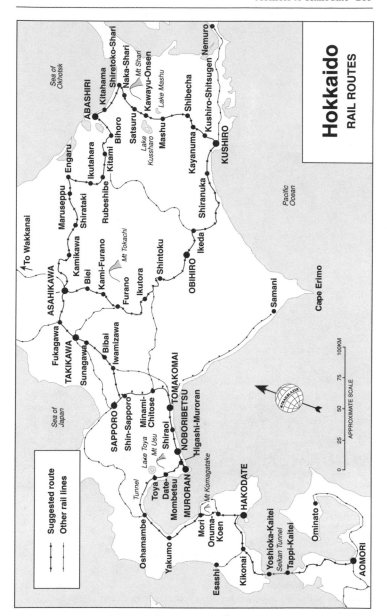

Hokkaido
RAIL ROUTES

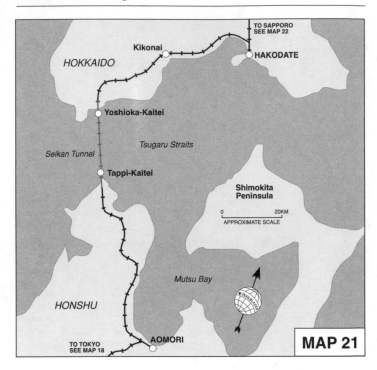

Leaving Aomori the line runs slightly inland from the coast on the journey to Tsugaru Peninsula, so the views are better from the left side of the train, where there are long stretches of rice fields. Towards the edge of the peninsula, the train passes through several tunnels, easing passengers gently into the long journey underground through the Seikan Tunnel.

Kikonai (119km) The first stop in Hokkaido after emerging from the tunnel, though some limited expresses do not call here.

Just as you begin to take in the Hokkaido scenery, the train abruptly plunges into a series of tunnels. Once past these, sit on the right side for views over the Tsugaru Straits and, in the distance, the tip of Shimokita Peninsula on Honshu. The train runs much closer to the coast than it does on the journey from Aomori and the views out to sea are superb. About 20 minutes before arriving in Hakodate you will see (or rather, should try to avoid) the large cement factory on the right that spoils the view.

Hakodate (160km)   [see pp304-9]
Hakodate is the terminus for limited expresses from Aomori.

Japan's forgotten people

Hokkaido was colonized by the Japanese only in the middle of the 18th century; prior to that it was known as Ezo and was almost exclusively inhabited by the Ainu, an indigenous population who all but disappeared as more and more Japanese moved north from Honshu. In recent years there have been efforts to revive the Ainu culture and its traditions but following decades when the Tokyo government barely acknowledged its existence it may now be too late to save one of the world's least-known aboriginal cultures. (For more information on the Ainu, see the box on p316).

HAKODATE TO SAPPORO [Map 22, p286; Table 19, p408]

Distances by JR from Hakodate. Fastest journey time: 3 hours.

Hakodate (0km) The quickest way to Sapporo is along the Hakodate line on the Hokuto or slightly faster Super Hokuto LEX. Some trains stop at **Goryokaku (3km)**.

Onuma-Koen (27km) A few minutes before arriving at the station (around 20 minutes after leaving Hakodate), look out to the left for views of Lake Konuma, with its tiny islands scattered across the water.

One of the most beautiful, if foreboding, natural backdrops you're likely to come across in Japan is **Mt Komagatake**; it last erupted in a big way in 1640 when it killed more than 700 people. Minor eruptions in 1998 and 2000 mean hiking trails around the peak are currently off limits. It's best to admire the volcano with its jagged peak from the safe distance of the lakes. Lake Onuma and two smaller lakes, Konuma and Junsainuma, were created when debris from an eruption of Komagatake settled as a natural dam.

To the right as you exit the small station (a few ¥400 coin lockers) is the International Exchange Plaza, a wooden building with a glass front, where there's a tourist information counter (☎ 0138-67 2170, 🖹 67 2176, summer daily 8:15am-6:45pm, winter daily 8:15am-5:45pm) staffed by an English speaker.

Between April and November, motor boats, paddle boats and canoes can be hired on the lakes. Alternatively, pleasure boats do 30-minute tours of Lake Onuma for ¥830. The best way of seeing the lakes and taking in the spectacular surrounding scenery is to hire a bike. There are rental places in the station area, the most obvious being Friendly Bear, opposite the station. Bikes cost ¥500 an hour or ¥1000 for the day. In winter the lakes freeze over and holes are cut in the ice for fishing.

By far the best place to stay is ***Onuma Koen Youth Hostel*** (☎/🖹 0138-67 4126). This small, friendly hostel set back from Lake Onuma offers pension-style 2- and 3-bed rooms at ¥2900 for YH/HI members and ¥3900 for others. Breakfast costs ¥600 and dinner ¥1000. The evening meal especially is a real feast. Cycles can be rented here for ¥500 per day. The only drawback is that the hostel is a good 30-minute walk from Onuma-Koen station, directly up the main

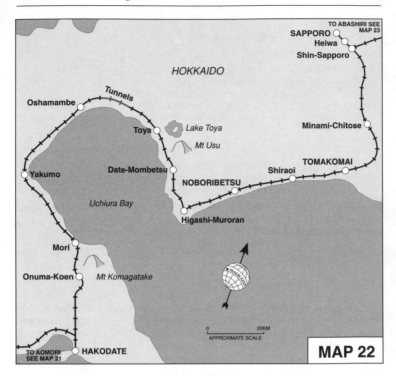

TO ABASHIRI SEE MAP 23

SAPPORO
Heiwa
Shin-Sapporo

HOKKAIDO

Tunnels

Oshamambe

Toya   Lake Toya
                    Mt Usu   Minami-Chitose

Yakumo   Date-Mombetsu   TOMAKOMAI
                    NOBORIBETSU   Shiraoi

Uchiura Bay

                                Higashi-Muroran

Mori

Onuma-Koen   Mt Komagatake

0   20KM
APPROXIMATE SCALE

MAP 22

TO AOMORI
SEE MAP 21   HAKODATE

road that runs alongside the lake. Alternatively, take a local train one stop back down the line towards Hakodate to Onuma station, from where you should change on to the Sawara line and go one stop to Ikeda-en station. At Ikeda-en, follow the grass path that leads off from the platform, rather than the overhead walkway. Turn left when you reach the surfaced path; at the end of that turn right and go straight until you see a wooden house on your left. Look for the JYH sign by the door.

A 20-minute walk further up the road from the hostel brings you to a viewing spot over the lake with Mt Komagatake reflected in the calm water. It's a great place to visit around dusk, when you can watch the sun set over the lake. If you're not eating at the hostel, try the ***Lumber House*** (daily except Mon 11am-7:30pm), in the log hut just a couple of minutes further up the road from the hostel. The speciality is steaks (hamburgers are ¥800, or get a real steak with fries for ¥2500); Budweiser is on tap.

Mori (50km) As the train leaves Onuma-Koen, look right then left as the line passes between Lake Onuma (on the right) and the smaller Lake Konuma (on the left). It's a fleeting but superb last view of the two lakes. Soon enough, the

---

⛩ The day the sky turned black

At 1:08pm on 31st March 2000 the resort area around Toya-ko was devastated when nearby Mt Usu erupted for the first time in 23 years, spewing out clouds of rock and steam for several days. The whole area was covered in a thick film of grey dust, turning broad daylight into dark night. Resort hotels, gearing up for a new season and for the coming Golden Week holiday, turned into grey shadows. Ten thousand people were evacuated and it was to be three months before anyone was allowed back into the area. The eruption has left a new crater on a slope just above the resort centre.

---

line becomes enclosed by a line of trees. Fittingly, it would seem, the next stop is called Mori (forest). Just before the station the train passes right by the sea. Mori, despite its name, is actually situated on the coast. The sudden change from lakes and mountains to dense forest and coast is proof of the amazing scenic variety Hokkaido has to offer.

After leaving Mori, the line begins to curve around Uchiura Bay. The track runs so close to the sea that you can see the different shades of blue in the water.

Yakumo (81km) The train runs further from the sea along this stretch of the line but look out to the left for views of the rolling green hills that are always featured on Japanese TV adverts for Hokkaido milk.

Oshamambe (112km) There is a long section of tunnels between Oshamambe and Toya, the next major stop along the line. About 15 minutes after the train leaves Oshamambe, just after emerging from another tunnel, look out to the right for a sweeping view around the bay (just before darting into yet another tunnel!).

Note that from Oshamambe the train now follows the Muroran line, not the Hakodate line (which branches off north from here) but you don't have to change trains.

Toya (154km) Toya-ko is a caldera lake formed by the collapse of a mountain following volcanic activity thousands of years ago. A hot spring resort has grown up along the banks of one side of the lake.

Turn right as you exit Toya station for buses to the lake (¥320 one-way; 35 mins). The eruption in March 2000 (see box above) damaged the old road into the resort; this currently means a long detour to reach the lake. Just before arriving in the resort you'll see the new crater bubbling away dangerously close to the shops and hotels just below it.

It's hard and perhaps unfair to knock a place when it's down but Toya-ko lacks the charm of Onuma-Koen (see p285). Huge resort hotels line the lake and spoil the scenery. In short, Toya-ko is just too much of a geared-up tourist resort to make it appealing. That said, the lake itself is worth a look and onsen fans might enjoy an afternoon wallowing in a hot spring or two in some of the larger resort hotels.

Date-Mombetsu (167km) This is the nearest the rail line gets to Sobetsu, the town which hosts an International Snowball Fight Tournament every February. Much more than just a bit of winter fun, this is a serious competition involving corporate sponsorship, prize money and a strict rule book.

After leaving Date-Mombetsu, the train runs along the coast again before entering more tunnels. Then, just to prove that it's not all unspoilt nature in Hokkaido, on the right there's a block of ugly factories, gas tanks, pipes and billowing chimney stacks.

Higashi-Muroran (190km) A branch line runs from here for 7km to the city of **Muroran**, known as a steel industry centre but of little interest to the tourist.

Noboribetsu (207km) Noboribetsu comes from the Ainu word 'Nupurupetsu', meaning 'a cloudy river tinged with white'. A bus ride from the station is a hot spring resort that draws water from **Jigokudani (Hell Valley)**, the centre of which is a volcanic crater where steam rises from the earth. It was only in 1858, when a businessman who was mining sulphur realized there was money to be made from tourism, that the first public bath house was opened using hot water from the crater. Since then tourism has taken off and the resort is now full of concrete hotel blocks and tourist attractions, such as a park full of caged brown bears, accessed by a cable car from the resort centre. Despite this, Jigokudani is worth seeing close up, as is bubbling **Oyunuma Lake**, and a visit here would not be complete without a trip to one of the hot springs in the resort.

From Noboribetsu station, buses run up to the terminal in the resort centre (¥330; 15 mins). Head up the road from the bus centre to find Noboribetsu Tourist Association (☎ 0143-84 3311, daily 9am-6pm), a couple of minutes up on the left-hand side. The staff do not speak English but maps should be available. Keep walking up the main road, past the hotels, until you reach Jigokudani.

In 1924, the whole area was designated 'Noboribetsu Primeval Forest', a fitting description for the haunting landscape. Though you aren't allowed to walk around Hell Valley (not that you'd want to with the bubbling and smoke rising from the ground), there is a short promenade walk that most people take for a close-up view. There's a better walk up into the hills above Hell Valley and down to Oyunuma Lake, a volcanic bubbling swamp, where temperatures reach 130°C. Look for the sign pointing towards the 'mountain-ash observatory'. Head up the path and Oyunuma is about 15-20 minutes on foot.

Having seen the source there are plenty of opportunities to test out the water by taking a bath in one of the onsen hotels. The most popular, but also the most expensive, are the baths at **Daiichi Takimotokan** (daily, 9am-5pm, ¥2000), the highlight of which is a rotemburo. This hotel is the last before Hell Valley; the

---

Opposite Top: Covered in snow in winter, Biei's sunflower fields turn bright yellow as summer approaches (see p303). **Middle:** Even in a predominantly industrial city such as Niigata, there are hidden surprises such as this lotus pond in Hakusan Park (see p275). **Bottom:** It may not be the Sahara but Tottori's sand dunes (see box, p218) are the closest thing to a desert in Japan. (Photos © Ramsey Zarifeh).

onsen entrance is at the back of the building. Less elaborate, but much better value, is **Sagiriyu** (daily, 7am-10pm, ¥390), the only municipal hot spring in the resort. Conveniently it's next door to the tourist office. The baths here are nothing fancy but it's a much more affordable option and you won't feel you have to spend all day in the water to get your money's worth. Look for the purple hanging curtain and wooden entrance, just before the tourist information office on the left side of the road heading up to Hell Valley.

The cheapest accommodation is at *Akashiya-so Youth Hostel* (☎/🖹 0143-84 2616), which has a mix of tatami and Western rooms for ¥3140 or ¥3640 if not a YH/HI member. Find the hostel by walking for about a minute back down the road from the bus terminal, past the post office, until you see a sign on the left side pointing to the hostel. The tourist office has a list of other accommodation and can assist with bookings.

As you leave, or arrive at, Noboribetsu station, you can't miss the enormous and kitsch, European-style castle. This is Noboribetsu Marine Park (¥2300), a large aquarium with dolphin, sealion and penguin shows.

◆ Shiraoi (226km) You'll need to catch a local train from Noboribetsu to reach Shiraoi, five stops along the line. Ten minutes on foot from the station is **Poroto Kotan**, a reconstructed Ainu village (daily, 8am-5pm Apr to Oct; 8:30am-4:30pm Nov to Mar, ¥650); see the box on p316.

To reach Poroto Kotan, turn left at the first set of lights in front of the station and go straight until the next lights. Turn left again, cross over the rail track and go straight until you see some shops on your right. Go past these, through a large souvenir shop, until you reach the entrance and ticket office. Apart from a few reconstructed huts and Ainu houses, where performances of Ainu dance and music are given, the most interesting part of the village is the Ainu Museum, which displays objects and garments used in daily Ainu life.

Tomakomai (248km) Tomakomai is a major railway junction and has ferry connections with Tokyo, Sendai, Nagoya and Hachinohe (all of which are on Honshu). It's not a very attractive place; the factories that can be seen from the train belong to the Oji Paper Company. Paper is Tomakomai's biggest industry.

Tomakomai is the starting point for the local **Hidaka line** which runs south along the coast towards Samani (3-3½ hours; 5 services a day), the nearest rail station to Cape Erimo. It takes just over three hours to Samani, from where irregular buses (one hour, ¥1300) can be caught to the cape.

Though not an appealing destination, Tomakomai does have an attractive accommodation option in the *Tomakomai New Station Hotel* (☎ 0144-33 0333, 🖹 33 0222). Spacious rooms cost ¥6200 for a single, ¥10,000 for a twin and

---

Opposite Top left: A 21st-century arcade game in Osaka: put your money in the slot, use the electronic hand to try to grab a live lobster from the tank and watch it drop out of the slot below. (Photo © Ramsey Zarifeh). **Top right:** Professional pachinko players (see p42) concentrate on the game in hand. (Photo © Richard Brasher). **Bottom:** Definitely not camera shy: these children in Nagasaki strike a familiar pose. (Photo © Richard Brasher).

¥11,000 for a double. The fitness club, indoor pool and sauna on the second floor can be used for ¥500 (no time limit). Head out of Tomakomai station's south exit and look on your left for the building with a couple of white birds painted on the side.

Minami-Chitose (275km) The penultimate limited express stop before Sapporo; change here for **Shin-Chitose Airport**, three minutes away by local train. This is the nearest airport to Sapporo, handling both domestic and (some) international flights.

Shin-Sapporo (308km) Some limited expresses make a brief stop here but stay on the train until the Sapporo terminus.

♦ Heiwa (311km) Only local trains call here. It's appropriate that the rail station here should be called Heiwa (Peace) because this place is home to an unusual museum, the **'No More Hibakusha Kaikan'**. *Kaikan* means hall, and *Hibakusha* is the term used to refer to the victims of the atomic bomb attacks on Nagasaki and Hiroshima who are still alive. Hibakusha are scattered across Japan; around 600 live in Hokkaido. It's a really small museum (daily except Sat, 10am-4pm; free), the size of an ordinary house, and is owned by people who experienced the atomic bombs. It's nothing like the scale of museums in Hiroshima (see p230) or Nagasaki (see p344) but it's certainly worth a look if you haven't visited either of these places. Photos of the horrific injuries and burns sustained by victims minutes, hours, days and years after the atomic blasts are accompanied by paintings.

Local trains leave Shin-Sapporo for Sapporo roughly three times an hour and take three minutes to Heiwa (the first stop after Shin-Sapporo). From Heiwa, trains leave with the same frequency and take 12 minutes to Sapporo. The frequency is the same in the other direction.

To get to the museum head up the flight of steps at Heiwa station, turn right and walk all the way along the bridge to the end. Right in front of you as you leave the bridge is a red-brick building which has a copy of Hiroshima's A-Bomb Dome on the roof. Ring the bell to be let in.

Sapporo (319km)   [see pp309-15]

SAPPORO TO ASAHIKAWA   [Map 23, p291; Table 20, p409]

Distances by JR from Sapporo. Fastest journey time: 80 minutes.

Sapporo (0km) From Sapporo, take the Lilac LEX or the slightly faster Super White Arrow on the Hakodate line to Asahikawa. Lilac trains do the journey in 90 minutes, the Super White Arrow in 80 minutes.

Iwamizawa (41km) Views are less than spectacular on the first part of the journey as far as Iwamizawa, as it takes some time for the train to leave Hokkaido's capital behind. But from here on, the familiar wide green spaces start to open up once more. Some trains stop at **Bibai (46km)** and **Sunagawa (64km)**.

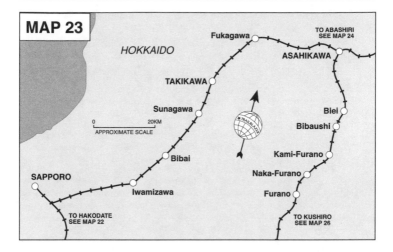

Takikawa (84km) The landscape is briefly interrupted by the small city of Takikawa, known throughout Hokkaido for its extremely heavy snowfall. The city plays host to an All Hokkaido Fancy Dress Tug-of-War Championship, held annually on the first Sunday in February. The Shibuki Festival, held the first weekend in August, is worth experiencing if you are in the area at that time.

In 1980, the fossil of a manatee (large plant-eating aquatic mammal) was discovered here. The fossil is on display at the **Museum of Fine Arts and Natural History** (2-5-13 Shinmachi, daily except Mon, 10am-5pm, ¥600). To reach the museum from the station, turn left on to the main shopping street ('Bell Road'), walk up it for about five minutes and turn right when you reach the intersection with a branch of Mister Donut. Walk straight down this road for about ten minutes and turn left when you see the 'Kaihatsu Kyokan' (Hokkaido Development Center). Go straight and you'll see the red-brick entrance to the museum on your left.

About 10 minutes after leaving Takikawa, the train crosses Ishikari-gawa.

Fukagawa (107km) At the weekend and on selected weekdays between May and September the **'Suzuran' steam train** (locomotive number C11 171) runs from Fukagawa along a branch line to the coastal town of Rumoi (see box p292). The train staff dress up in period costume. Seat reservations (¥800) should be made in advance from any JR ticket office.

About 10 minutes after leaving Fukagawa there is a series of long tunnels.

Asahikawa (137km)   **[see pp315-9]**

⛩ **Railway tear-jerker**
One of the most popular programmes broadcast by TV network NHK is a drama series that runs Monday to Saturday from 8.15 to 8.30am. Each series lasts for six months, and one of the biggest ratings winners of recent years was *Suzuran*, broadcast in 1999. 'It was a very moving story,' one viewer told me, 'and a lot of people cried once a day at the start of the morning'.

Set in the early 1900s, the story begins with a baby girl, abandoned on the bench of Ashimoi station. The girl is adopted by the station master and named Moe after the station Ashimoi. Thanks to her surrogate father she grows up to be very kind and everybody loves her – everybody, that is, but her evil stepsister and stepaunt. Thanks to the plotting of this pair, Moe is packed off to what must surely be the world's worst orphanage. All seems lost and inevitably the girl suffers while locked away inside this institution. At last she manages to escape and in the middle of an unrelenting snowstorm walks back along the railway line to Ashimoi, where her beloved stepfather is waiting for her. This was one of the most moving scenes in the drama and the child actress playing Moe won such acclaim that she was quickly snapped up to be the new face on JR Hokkaido posters. But the story does not end there. As she grows up, Moe faces the challenge of looking for her mother in Tokyo and her life becomes a series of setbacks, but she draws strength from the memory of Ashimoi station and her father. In the final scene she returns to Ashimoi, now an abandoned station on a discontinued local line, and dies on the same bench where she'd been left 80 years before.

The Suzuran steam train ride remains hugely popular and the set of the TV series can still be seen at Ebishima station between Fukagawa and Rumoi. The NHK drama was so successful that it was later remade as a film.

ASAHIKAWA TO ABASHIRI [Map 24, p293; Table 21, p409]

Distances by JR from Asahikawa. Fastest journey time: 3 hrs 50 mins.

Asahikawa (0km) From Asahikawa, take the Okhotsk LEX that runs along the JR Sekihoku Line to Abashiri on the Sea of Okhotsk. This train runs five times a day and originates in Sapporo. It's worth making a seat reservation as there are only a limited number of carriages. There's a Western-style toilet and trolley service on board.

All the clichés of Japan being a nation of no open space and houses packed together like rabbit hutches collapse on this stretch of the journey. The train travels slowly enough to see some of the tiny stations along the way.

Kamikawa (49km) Most tourists who alight here are heading to **Sounkyo-Onsen**, the highlight of which is a trip to Sounkyo Gorge for its waterfalls and rock formations. Neither is accessible by rail so it's necessary to transfer to a bus (¥770) for the 30-minute journey to the main resort area. Buses are timed to meet most trains; enquire at the bus ticket office to the right as you exit the station.

After Kamikawa the predominant scenery is forest, rather than open space. The track becomes hemmed in by trees on both sides and there are a number of semi-tunnels (with windows). There's one long tunnel about 15 minutes before arriving at Shirataki but then the countryside starts to open up again.

Shirataki (86km) Some limited expresses do not stop here but if you look out (even if you don't stop!), you'll see that Shirataki's station is supposed to recall the railway of yesteryear, with a clock tower topped by a weathercock. However, the re-creation of the golden age of the railways hasn't been entirely successful: as a concession to modern-day financial constraints, the station offices inside the building are closed and Shirataki remains unmanned.

Maruseppu (106km) Most limited expresses make a brief stop here.

Engaru (125km) Engaru used to be an important rail junction, with a line running from here up to Mombetsu on the east coast. The train waits for a few minutes here as everyone turns their seats around so as to continue facing the direction of travel.

Ikutahara (141km) Some limited expresses make a brief stop here.

Shortly after leaving Ikutahara (around 23 minutes after Engaru) the train heads into the Jomon Tunnel. The tunnel is very short but achieved notoriety some years ago when human bones (see box p294) were discovered nearby.

Rubeshibe (162km) Nothing to stop for here but it's worth noting that Rubeshibe is home to the world's biggest cuckoo clock.

From here to Kitami, the final major stop on the line to Abashiri, the wide plains seen during the early part of this journey return, with fields on either side of the track.

Kitami (185km) During the last few kilometres before Kitami, the surroundings get a little more built up (for Hokkaido) and there's a long tunnel just before arriving at Kitami station.

Kitami is a point of interchange with the private Furusato Ginga line which runs south to Ikeda. Frequently threatened with closure, peo-

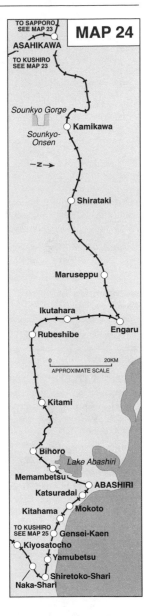

⛩ Human sacrifice?

It was once the practice in Japan, when a new bridge, tunnel or other major public works project was constructed, for an individual to be offered to the site as a human sacrifice.

One Hokkaido resident told me that when she was six or seven, human bones were found along the railway line at the Jomon Tunnel. The story goes that about 30 years before, a railwayman had been supervising the laying of additional track along the line. No doubt he had heard the stories concerning the ghosts that haunted the tunnel. Working alone late one evening he disappeared mysteriously and it was only years later that his skeleton was discovered near the track deep in the tunnel. Locals claim that he'd been pushed by a ghost into the path of an approaching freight train, a sacrifice required because none had been made after the construction of the tunnel.

---

ple living along this line have lobbied hard to ensure it remains open. The line should be safe for the next decade since two young train drivers were recently employed, one of whom is the son of a retired driver on the line.

Bihoro (210km) It's possible to rent a car from here and head over the beautiful Bihoro Pass towards Lake Kussharo and Kawayu-Onsen in Akan National Park (see p297).

Memambetsu (222km) This station lies just at the edge of Lake Abashiri. From here, though the track looks as if it will run right by the lake, trees block out any view and it is only about four minutes before arriving in Abashiri that there is finally a glimpse (on the left) of the northern tip of the lake. Just in case you miss it, the conductor makes an announcement urging passengers to look out of the window and savour the fleeting view.

Abashiri (238km) Abashiri is the terminus of the JR Sekihoku line from Asahikawa. In winter, people come here to see blocks of drift ice on the Sea of Okhotsk. Ornate, hand-crafted snow and ice sculptures are a highlight of the Drift Ice Festival in February.

Abashiri station is small but has some coin lockers (all sizes, but only a few ¥500 ones) in the space between the station building and the tourist information office. The staff at tourist information (☎ 0152-44 5849, daily, 9am-5pm), on your right as you exit the station, have maps and will help book accommodation.

The main sights are around Mt Tento; a bus runs on a loop around places of interest daily between 9:30am and 4pm. A one-day pass (¥900) is a good deal since it also gets you reductions on entry fees at the attractions mentioned below. The pass is available from the tourist office at the station. The bus departs from stop No 1, opposite the taxi rank in front of the station.

Taking the bus from Abashiri station, stop first at the old **Abashiri Prison** (Apr to Oct 8am-6pm; Nov to Mar, 9am-5pm, ¥1050), which during the freezing winters must have been a very bleak place to serve time. The prison relocated in 1984 and today visitors are allowed to wander around the rows of cells, bathhouse (with waxwork models of tattooed inmates), and outhouse buildings. Picking up the bus from outside the museum, the next stop is the **Okhotsk Ryu-Hyo (Drift Ice) Museum** (Apr to Oct 8am-6pm, Nov to Mar 9am-4:30pm, closed Dec 16th to Jan 14th, ¥500), which has a 'Drift Ice Experience Room', where lumps of ice are supposed to show what the Sea of Okhotsk is like in the dead of winter. Of more interest are the views of Lake Abashiri and the Sea of Okhotsk from the lookout points on the third, fourth and fifth floors. Next pick up the bus or walk 800m to the **Hokkaido Museum of Northern Peoples** (daily except Mon 9:30am-4:30pm, ¥300). This museum seems to attract fewer people than the other two, which is a pity since it's perhaps the best, with exhibits relating not just to the Ainu but to minorities across the northern hemisphere. The main exhibition hall displays everything from snow boots to a re-created winter home. TV screens show footage of events like reindeer herding and hunting for fish by cutting holes through the ice. A pamphlet is available.

From January 20th to the first Sunday in April the bus also stops at the Aurora Terminal, from where the **Icebreaker Aurora** runs one-hour trips (¥3000) on the Sea of Okhotsk. 'Feeling the ice cracking beneath the ship's hull defies description,' reads the publicity. This trip is by far the best reason for paying a visit to Abashiri in the dead of winter.

To reach *Abashiri Ryuhyo-no-oka Youth Hostel* (☎/🖷 0152-43 8558; ¥3250 YH/HI, ¥4250 non-mem), take the bus to Okhotsk Aquarium, from stop No 1 in front of Abashiri station, and get off at the Meiji Iriguchi stop. A youth hostel sign points you up a road off the main road. Follow this road up for about 15 minutes to reach the hostel. It's a small, clean, friendly place, with mostly bunk-bed dorms and a good view over the Okhotsk Sea from outside.

Exit the station, turn left on to the main road and look out on the right for *Victoria Station* (daily, 10am-1am), a family restaurant that specializes in steaks but also does pasta, an all-you-can-eat salad bar and all-you-can-drink soft drinks bar. This is one of the few places in town to stay open late.

ABASHIRI TO KUSHIRO   [Map 24, p293; Map 25, p296; Table 22, p410]

Distances by JR from Abashiri. Fastest journey time: 3½ hours.

Abashiri (0km) The next part of the journey has some of the most stunning scenery but is not for anyone in a hurry. Only local trains run along the single-track Senmo line that first heads east along the coast as far as Shari, before turning south through Akan National Park towards the port town of Kushiro.

Katsuradai (1.5km) First stop after leaving Abashiri, there's a short tunnel immediately after leaving here. Emerging from the tunnel, there are great views out to the left of the Sea of Okhotsk.

Mokoto (9km) Mokoto station has a coffee shop with views out to sea, but a personal favourite is the coffee shop at the next stop.

Kitahama (12km) Although only a few minutes out of Abashiri, it really is

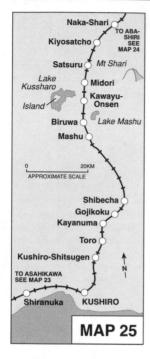

Naka-Shari

Kiyosatcho

TO ABA-
SHIRI
SEE
MAP 24

Satsuru   Mt Shari

Lake
Kussharo   Midori

Island   Kawayu-
              Onsen

Biruwa   Lake Mashu

Mashu

0   20KM
APPROXIMATE SCALE

Shibecha
Gojikoku
Kayanuma

Toro

Kushiro-Shitsugen

TO ASAHIKAWA
SEE MAP 23

N

Shiranuka   KUSHIRO

MAP 25

worth stopping here briefly; there can be no better location to have a coffee than here facing the sea, especially in winter when the water becomes a sheet of ice. The old railway seats and battered suitcase make this the ultimate café for passing travellers. The menu includes toast, pasta, and a daily set lunch. The station's waiting room is worth seeing as it is covered with old railway tickets and business cards left by travellers. The café is open daily (except 2nd and 4th Sat), 10am to around 8pm.

After leaving Kitahama, look out to the right for views of Lake Tofutsu which, between November and April, becomes home to around 1000 Siberian swans.

Gensei-Kaen (17km)   Gensei-Kaen station is a popular spot for viewing Lake Tofutsu.

Yamubetsu (26km)   If it's not too foggy, you should be able to see Shiretoko Peninsula on the left in the distance, though the view is blocked for much of the way by a pine trees.

After Yamubetsu, there's a long stretch without any stations.

Shiretoko-Shari (37km)   This is the nearest station to the **Shiretoko Peninsula** and the point to connect up with buses that run part of the way along it. The peninsula is considered an idyllic retreat from the man-made world, an unspoilt territory inhabited by wild eagles, brown bears and the world's largest owls.

Turn left as you exit the station for the Shari bus terminal (under the archway that reads 'Welcome to Shiretoko'). Most buses run from here along the peninsula to the bus terminal at Utoro (¥1490, 50 mins), from where it's about a ten-minute walk to the ferry terminal for tours of the peninsula. The longest ferry ride goes all the way around Cape Shiretoko (inaccessible by road) and back to Utoro for ¥6000 (3¾ hours; one a day). An alternative ferry ride that doesn't go as far is ¥2700 (90 mins; several daily). Note that in winter much of the peninsula is inaccessible.

Naka-Shari (42km)   First station after Shiretoko-Shari; just after leaving here a large and unsightly factory looms into view on the right-hand side. This eyesore aside, the journey from here is one of the best parts of a rail route round Hokkaido. This is the only line on the island that actually runs through a national park, between Lake Kussharo and the smaller, but more mysterious, Lake Mashu. Neither lake is visible from the train, though there are good access points to both along the way.

Kiyosatocho (49km)   After Kiyosatocho, look out for the 1545m Mt Shari which, unless the summit is covered in cloud, should be visible out to the left.

Satsuru (57km) and **Midori (65km)**   There's a long stretch of line between these two stations in an area where trees very definitely outnumber people. Midori ('Green') station has a green roof and blue trees painted on the side, and is the last stop before Kawayu-Onsen, in Akan National Park. The whole area, with the track surrounded by forest, is so lush and green that it is difficult to tell exactly where the national park officially begins. But about 10 minutes after leaving Midori the train passes through a tunnel. Emerging from this you are officially in Akan National Park.

Kawayu-Onsen (80km)   Built in 1936, the old station master's office has been turned into an excellent café. It's tempting to while away an afternoon right here but with such magnificent scenery so close to hand it would be a shame to miss out. Cycles can be rented for free (ask at the café) but they must be returned by 5pm. The station has no coin lockers but you should be able to leave stuff at the café.

From the station, head up to the main road and turn right. Go straight until the first set of lights and turn left onto Route 391. A few minutes down this road, on the left-hand side, is the stunning **Mt Iwo**, still very much an active volcano. If you don't see it first, you'll almost certainly smell it. Smoke pours out from different places around the mountain and the sulphur turns the rock a bright yellow. Most people take a brief closer look at the smoke then rush back covering their mouths and noses.

Continue along the main road for another 2km until you reach the centre of Kawayu-Onsen. As you arrive in the centre, look for an orange Seicomart convenience store on your right. Then look on the left for a sign pointing to the new **Kawayu Eco Museum Center** (EMC) (daily except Wed, May to Oct 8am-5pm; Nov to Apr 9am-4pm; free); this shows films of the area's wildlife, flora

---

⛩ Sumo in Hokkaido
Kawayu-Onsen was once the home of sumo wrestler **Taiho-san** who reached the rank of *yokozona*, sumo's highest honour. His record of 32 tournament victories, twice winning six consecutive titles, has yet to be beaten. Now in his 60s, Taiho-san is a sumo trainer in Tokyo, but a small museum (daily, 9am-5pm; June to Sep 6:30am-9pm, ¥310) is close to EMC (see above) in Kawayu-Onsen. On display are all 32 sumo tournament trophies won up to his retirement in 1971, along with photos and other memorabilia including one of the wrestler's oversize suits hanging next to more traditional sumo gear.

Taiho-san was born in Sakhalin (now part of Russia) but moved to Hokkaido and attended school in Kawayu-Onsen before leaving for Tokyo at the age of 16 to begin his sumo apprenticeship. Kawayu-Onsen's link with sumo explains why it is the venue for the annual Women's Sumo Championship.

and fauna, has scale models of Akan National Park and free tea and coffee! Ask at the information desk for the *Let's walk around EMC* leaflet, with details of walks in the woods around the centre.

If not in a hurry to return to Kawayu-Onsen station, energetic cyclists might consider continuing on for a further 3km to **Lake Kussharo**, where Kussie – the local equivalent of Scotland's Loch Ness Monster – is said to live. Around the lake are a number of outdoor hot springs (some free) and summer activities on the lake include canoeing and kayaking.

After a cycle tour of Kawayu-Onsen, head back to the station in time to pick up a train to Mashu, as Mashu-ko Youth Hostel is a good place to overnight.

Biruwa (87km) This is more of a portakabin than a station.

Mashu (96km) A small station with a few ¥300 coin lockers by the exit. The tourist information office (9am-5pm) is open in summer only.

Lake Mashu, 20km in circumference, is known as the lake 'of mystery and illusion'. No river flows in or out of the lake which is completely surrounded by trees. The only way of seeing the lake – if you are lucky and there isn't a blanket of fog over the water – is from elevated observation points. I arrived early in the morning but within 30 minutes the lake was completely swallowed up by mist. It's almost as if this mystical natural phenomenon becomes disgruntled by the unwanted attention, so cloaks itself in a mist to avoid the gaze of tourists. All the tour buses pull up at the Rest House, which has an observation platform but is also crammed full of souvenir stalls. If the weather is good, consider walking, hitching or taking the infrequent bus to the less crowded 'third observation platform' further along the road.

From Mashu-ko Youth Hostel (see below), it's a three-hour walk up the road that runs outside the hostel to the lake but it should be easy to hitch a lift with a fellow hosteller. Alternatively, the very infrequent bus stops right outside the hostel and goes to the first rest house (check times with hostel staff).

The ideal place to stay is *Mashu-ko Youth Hostel* (☎ 01548-2 3098, ▤ 2 4875, 🖥 www.masyuko.co.jp; YH/HI ¥3360, non-members ¥4410, 10-20% discount for online reservations; closed Dec 1st-20th), situated on the way to the lake. Call ahead for a pick-up from the station. Meals are served in *The Great Bear*, the restaurant next to the hostel (dinner ¥1050, breakfast ¥630). Hostel staff organize summer and winter activities including cross-country skiing and canoeing (extra charge). Accommodation is in tatami or modern four-bed dorms and there is a coin laundry and internet access (¥10 per minute).

Mashu station lies just outside Akan National Park but the views from the train remain tremendous, with long gaps between isolated stations. The next major sight is Kushiro-Shitsugen National Park; it's a good idea to plan to spend a whole day on the journey between Mashu and the terminus at Kushiro.

Shibecha (121km) At the far end of the platform is a monument to an old steam locomotive that used to run along this line; you can ring the bell in memory of C1171.

Gojikoku (130km) This station is on the edge of the last national park before Kushiro, Kushiro-Shitsugen National Park. The park is mostly marshland, inhabited by Japanese cranes. Though not as well known as Akan National Park it still has some beautiful scenery.

Kayanuma (135km) A sign above the station name says that this is a 'station where Japanese cranes come'. During the mating season, between January and March, cranes perform elaborate mating dances on the snow-covered ground.

From here, there's a long stretch of track through marshland, so look out for swamp marshes on both sides.

Toro (142km) Bikes can be rented (¥700 per hour) from the coffee bar in this station. Ask the owner for a map of the area, which includes Lake Toro, the major lake in the marshlands area.

From April to September a semi-open train called the 'Kushiro-Shitsugen Norokko' runs between Toro and Kushiro. The seats face the windows, which are open so that you feel you are closer to the rivers, hills and marshland. Seat reservations can be made in advance but there are also non-reserved cars. The train runs four times a day between Toro and Kushiro in August, dropping to twice a day thereafter.

Kushiro-Shitsugen (152km) All the stations along this stretch of the line are tiny wooden buildings. There are plenty of hiking opportunities around Kushiro-Shitsugen.

Views from the train remain impressive until about 10 minutes before Kushiro, where modern life begins to encroach on the unspoilt environment.

Kushiro (169km) Kushiro is the terminus for the Senmo line from Abashiri and also a stop on the Nemuro line that runs east to Nemuro and west to Obihiro. Facing the Pacific Ocean, Kushiro is the most easterly city in Japan.

Turn left after the ticket barrier to find coin lockers (all sizes). The staff at the tourist information booth (☎ 0154-22 8294, daily, 9am-5:30pm) in the station do not speak English. On the concourse level you'll find a *Mister Donut* as well as a couple of noodle places. The horrendously kitsch chapel that sits incongruously outside the station is a fake, rented by couples in search of a white wedding (see also p139). Inside is a tea lounge open to the public. Kushiro was the first station in Japan to open a **Station Museum** (daily except Mon, 10am-6pm, ¥100), which displays the work of local artist Eimatsu Sasaki.

Kushiro City Museum (daily except Mon, 9:30am-5pm, ¥360) is 15 minutes by bus from the station. Here you can get an overview of the city and the Kushiro-Shitsugen marshland you have just travelled through. There are also exhibitions on Ainu traditions and on the Japanese crane (the feathered variety). Several buses go to the museum from the bus terminal to the left as you exit the station. Get off at Kagaku-kan-dori.

Fifteen minutes down the main road that leads from the station is **Fisherman's Wharf**, a large waterside shopping and restaurant complex popularly known as MOO. (MOO, I was told, stands for Marine Aqua Oasis. MAO was presumably deemed not capitalist enough for a Japanese shopping complex). As well as a fish market on the ground floor and various shops, cafés and restaurants on the second and third, Kushiro Fitness Center (daily 10am-9:30pm, Sun until 6:30pm; closed in winter on Thur) is on the fifth floor and has an indoor pool (¥810). While at MOO, don't forget to take a brief look at EGG (Ever Green Garden), a greenhouse tacked on to one end of the building. On the ground floor of MOO, opposite a small branch post office, is the ticket desk for the **Sea Grace sightseeing boat** (Apr to Oct only, ¥1400) that does a 50-minute tour of the Kushiro waterfront. The boarding point is right in front of MOO. Six departures a day in August, dropping to three a day outside the peak season.

The best accommodation in town is at the *ANA Hotel* (☎ 0154-31 4111, ▤ 24 8640; ¥9000/S, ¥18,000/Tw, ¥15,000/D), directly across the street from MOO. *Tokyu Inn* (☎ 0154-22 0109, ▤ 24 5498; ¥6900/S, ¥12,800/Tw and ¥12,000/D) is just to the left across the street as you leave the station. *Kushiro Makiba Youth Hostel* (☎ 0154-23 0852; ¥2680 YH/HI, ¥3980 inc two meals) is an old hostel in a quiet residential area 20 minutes on foot from the station. To reach the hostel, turn left out of the station, follow the road (with the railway tracks on your left) until you reach a point where you can cross over the tracks at the railway crossing on your left at street level (don't cross the bridge that goes over the tracks). After crossing, head up the road until you see a taxi office with taxis outside on your left. Turn right here and go straight for about five minutes. The hostel is on your left (look for the HI sign on the fence outside).

From Kushiro, the Nemuro line extends east to its terminus in **Nemuro**, known for its locally-caught crab and also for the view of the Habomai Islands, currently disputed territory with Russia. The train to Nemuro takes just over two hours, from where it's a further 40 minutes by bus (¥1040 one-way) to the cape.

KUSHIRO TO SAPPORO & ASAHIKAWA [Map 26, p301 & Map 23, p291]

Distances by JR from Kushiro. Fastest journey time: 4 hours.

Kushiro to Shintoku
Kushiro (0km) From Kushiro, pick up the Ozora LEX, or the slightly faster Super-Ozora which has Western toilets and plenty of luggage space. The reserved-seat carriages are more comfortable than the older, non-reserved ones.

The first Super-Ozora leaves Kushiro at 7:39am, then further departures are at 8:40am, 10:56am, 1:21pm, 3:16pm, 6:35pm. The Super-Ozora takes just under two hours to Shintoku and the Ozora just over 2 hours. To Sapporo the fastest time is 4½ hours on the Ozora and 3½ hours on the Super-Ozora. Services from Sapporo leave at 7:05am, 8:56am, 1:27pm and 2:27pm and arrive in Kushiro at 10:52am, 1.43pm, 5.21pm and 7:05pm respectively. An overnight Ozora leaves each city at 11pm and arrives the next morning at 5:50am.

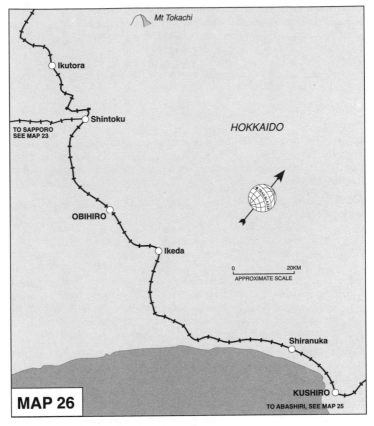

There are occasional glimpses of the Pacific Ocean during the first part of the journey. Some trains stop at **Shiranuka (27km)**.

Ikeda (104km) The first major stop after Kushiro. The only landmark of note is a large ferris wheel on the right a minute before arriving in Ikeda. Five or six minutes after leaving Ikeda, the train crosses Tokachi-gawa.

Obihiro (128km) The Hidaka mountains lie to the south and west of Obihiro. There is little of interest in Obihiro itself, but in case you need to stay here the JR-run *Hotel Northland Obihiro* (☎ 0155-24 1234, 🖷 28 3553, 🖳 www.netbeet.ne.jp/~jrhotel/eframe.html; ¥9000/S, ¥12,500/D, ¥17,000/Tw; 10% off for rail-pass holders) is right outside the station. There are special rates (¥6500/S, ¥10,000/D, ¥12,000/Tw) for those who book on-line.

Obihiro is a distant access point for **Cape Erimo** (Erimo-Misaki), the south-ernmost point on Hokkaido. Tokachi buses run from the bus terminal outside Obihiro station to Hiroo (120 mins, ¥1830), part of the way along the coast to the cape. From Hiroo, a JR bus runs down to Erimo-misaki (60 mins, ¥1510). The same bus continues around the cape up to Samani, where you can pick up a local train on the JR Samani line that takes three hours to run up to Tomakomai (see p289).

Shintoku (172km) From here, the Ozora and Super Ozora continue towards Sapporo along the Sekisho line.

▲ To follow the route described below, change here to a local train continuing along the Nemuro line to Furano. Stations along this line are spread out and there's a whole series of tunnels, one of the longest being about 25 minutes after leaving Shintoku.

Shintoku to Asahikawa [Map 26, p301; Map 23, p291; Tables 23/24, p410]
Ikutora (210km) Ikutora station, the second stop after Shintoku (on some trains, the first stop), was the setting for the movie *Poppoya*, another nostalgic story of a stationmaster who loses his young daughter (see box p292). Voted best film at the 1999 Japan Academy Awards, 'Poppoya' means railroad work-ers, while 'poppo' is the sound of a steam locomotive's whistle. The film grossed at least ¥3 billion at the box office, proving that the nostalgic combina-tion of rural railway and rugged Hokkaido landscape will always be a smash hit.

After leaving Ikutora, the train runs past Lake Kanayama on the right-hand side. The track then crosses the lake before entering a tunnel. After this, it's a pleasant ride through the hills and plains to Furano.

Furano (254km) Known in winter for its powder snow and in summer for its fields of lavender, Furano is one of the most popular tourist resorts in Hokkaido. In summer, the Furano Lavender Express runs direct from Sapporo; in winter the Furano Ski Train is packed with skiers from the big city – Furano Ski Ground is 10 minutes by taxi from the station.

Lavender was introduced to Furano by a local farmer and it's now big busi-ness; lavender ice cream is available nearly everywhere and even the JR station has its name painted in purple above the entrance. The main attractions are lavender fields, dairy farms and cheese-making factories. Furano feels a little like the south of France and is probably of more interest to the domestic tourist. The official lavender-viewing season is July; during this month it's probably best to avoid Furano completely.

On the second floor of the white building across the street from the station is Furano Information Center (☎ 0167-23 3388, daily, 9am-6pm) where there are a few leaflets in English. Furano does have a bargain 'railway hotel' – a disused coach next to the station where people can sleep on a thinly carpeted space for ¥700 a night (July to September). No bedding is provided, so bring your own sleeping bag. Ask about staying here at the JR travel centre inside the station.

Change trains here and take another local train along the Furano line towards Asahikawa. In the summer months, a 'Norokko' train with open-air carriages runs along this line between Furano and Biei (see below). It operates daily from June to August, but has more limited services in September.

Naka-Furano (262km) Leaving Furano, look out on both sides of the train. On your immediate left are low hills and fields but in the distance to the right are the more impressive peaks of the Daisetsuzan mountains.

The new *Furano Youth Hostel* (☎/🖹 0167-44 4441; YH/HI ¥3150, ¥4200 non members) is six minutes on foot behind this station. There are only five rooms and they are all pension-style. Dinner costs ¥1000 and breakfast ¥600. The tourist office outside Furano station has a list of other accommodation in the area and can assist with bookings.

Kami-Furano (269km) Three buses a day run from here to two hot springs in Daisetsuzan National Park. The bus goes as far as Tokachi-dake-Onsen (¥490), but it's better to get off along the way at Fukiage-Onsen (the stop is called Hakuginso). This is a completely natural (wild) hot spring where bathing is mixed and there are no admission fees. It's just there in the open for anybody to take a dip. If mixed bathing in the wild is not your thing, just down the road from the spring is *Fukiage Onsen No Hakuginso* (☎ 0167-45 3251; no English spoken), with a variety of segregated baths at different temperatures as well as a sauna and rotemburo affording views over the mountains. Buy a ticket (¥600) from the vending machine in the entrance lobby and hand it in at the desk. If you fancy a night in the mountains you can stay here, either in a tatami mat room or in bunk-bed dorms, for only ¥2600 per night.

Bibaushi (278km) There are opportunities here for cycling and walking. In addition, **Guide no Yamagoya**, in the wooden building across the street from the station, is an outdoor pursuits centre which arranges canoeing and rafting trips, and guided mountain bike rides out to Daisetsuzan National Park. From December to March, the main activity is cross-country skiing. Reductions on activities and equipment rental are offered to youth hostel guests (see below). This place also has a café, showers, coin lockers and laundry.

The bright white house right outside the tiny station is *Bibaushi Liberty Youth Hostel* (☎ 0166-95 2141, 🖹 95 2142, 🖥 bibaushi@hokkai.or.jp; ¥3200 YH/HI, ¥4200 non-members), where accommodation is mostly in four-bed dorms. The couple who run the hostel are really welcoming and it's small enough to feel very homely. The food is also excellent (breakfast ¥600, dinner ¥1000). The hostel is closed in November.

Biei (285km) The building on your left outside the station is Shikino Johokan, the tourist information centre (☎ 0166-92 4378, daily, 8:30am-7pm May to Oct, 8:30am-5pm Nov to Apr). Luggage can be stored here for ¥300 per item. The tourist information counter on the ground floor is well stocked with leaflets and maps.

> ⛩ **Ken and Mary's tree**
> Many Japanese come to Biei in search of 'Ken and Mary's tree'. Ken and Mary were two characters who starred in a Nissan commercial which ran for six years in the 1970s. The ad featured the couple out on a summer's drive in their new Nissan Skyline, before pulling up to relax under a large tree.
> The tree still stands and is even marked on local maps. Today, nobody may remember who Ken and Mary really were but the number of people who still make a pilgrimage to Biei to have their photo taken under the tree debunks the old media adage that adverts are here today and forgotten tomorrow.

If descriptions of 'the greens of the rolling pastures, the delicate pinks of the potato flowers, the rusty yellows of the ripened seeds' appeal, Biei will be the perfect place to stop for an extended cycle ride (outside the snow season). The area is very hilly, so be prepared for a bit of legwork – but your efforts will be rewarded with magnificent views. Mountain and ordinary bikes can be hired from *Matsuura Rent A Cycle* next to the tourist information centre (one hour ¥200, five hours ¥1000). Luggage can be left at the shop and staff will give you a cycling tour map.

There are plenty of small cafés and private art galleries to explore in and around the hills above the station. *Biei Potato-no-Oka Youth Hostel* (☎ 0166-92 3255, 🖹 92 3254) is just over 4km from the station and charges the same rates as the hostel in nearby Bibaushi (see p303). If you call ahead, the hostel staff will pick you up from the station.

From Biei, stay on the train for the rest of the journey along the Furano Line to Asahikawa.

Asahikawa (309km)   [see pp315-9]

ASAHIKAWA TO SAPPORO, SAPPORO TO HAKODATE, HAKODATE TO AOMORI

Follow the route starting on p282 in reverse.

Hokkaido – city guides

HAKODATE

The first major stop on a journey through Hokkaido, Hakodate is the third largest city on the island and was one of the first port cities in Japan to open to foreign trade in the 19th century. The first commercial treaty was signed with the USA in 1858, followed by similar agreements with Holland, Russia, Britain and France. Foreign consulates opened up near the port in order to oversee international trade, redbrick warehouses and churches were built, and many of the original buildings still stand as a reminder of the city's Western influence. Its proximity to Honshu means Hakodate gets packed out in the summer when tourists come to eat fresh crab and gaze down at the 'milky way floating in the ocean', a lyrical description of the night view of the city from the top of Mt Hakodate.

What to see and do

Outside the station's west exit is the busy **Morning Market**. Early in the morning the market-stall tanks are filled to bursting with fresh catches of crab and squid. Fruit (particularly musk melons) and vegetables are also big business. The market is up and running by 5am and most of the traders are packing up by midday, so get here as early as possible. Closed on Sundays in winter.

Behind the station is Seaport Plaza, moored next to which is the **Memorial Ship *Mashumaru*** (daily, 9am-6pm, ¥500). This old JR ferry plied the water between Aomori and Hakodate in the days before the Seikan Tunnel (see p282). Similar to the preserved ship in Aomori (see p272), this one has a small museum and visitors can tour the bridge and radio control room, and even put on the captain's jacket and gloves.

● **Motomachi** Motomachi is the the city's old quarter, where the former consulate buildings were located. The most interesting of the four main sights in this area is the **Museum of Northern Peoples**, housed in the former branch of the Bank of Japan. Displays include a collection of clothes and accessories worn by the Ainu as well as a number of ceremonial objects and everyday items such as a sled and fishing harpoons. Five minutes' walk uphill from the museum is the **Old British Consulate**, first opened in 1859. The building that stands today was constructed in 1913 and was used up to the closure of the consulate in 1934. Look out for the rusty 'Dieu et mon Droit' royal crest that used to hang on the consulate gate, and for the various kitsch models depicting life in Hakodate a century ago. One scene has the consul's wife 'teaching Western-style washing to the women of Hakodate'. The gift shop does a roaring trade in Beatrix Potter, Paddington Bear, shortbread biscuits and tea cups; hardly the image of 21st-century Britain the embassy in Tokyo is trying to promote.

A little further up from the consulate is the **Old Public Hall**, a large Western-style building completed in 1910, with a number of guest bedrooms and a large hall on the second floor that commands a great view of the harbour in the distance. Free concerts are held here occasionally between June and October. Finally, the least interesting is the **Museum of Literature**, which has displays on the life and works of novelists, poets and journalists who are connected with Hakodate. Individual tickets for any one of these cost ¥300, any two ¥500, any three ¥720 or all four ¥840. All are open daily 9am-7pm from April to October and 9am-5pm from November to March.

Other sights to look out for in Motomachi are the **Roman Catholic Church**, the **Hakodate Russian Orthodox Church** and **Hakodate Episcopal Church**. To reach Motomachi, take the tram from the station to Suehiro-cho.

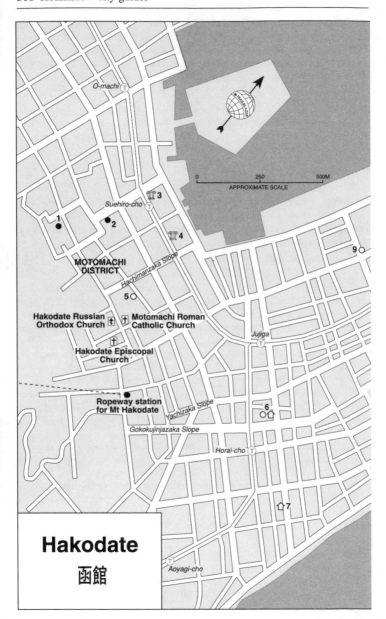

O-machi ⓣ

0   250   500M
APPROXIMATE SCALE

Suehiro-cho ⓣ 🏛 3

1 ●   ● 2

🏛 4

**MOTOMACHI
DISTRICT**

Hachimanzaka Slope

5 ○

Hakodate Russian ✝ ✝ **Motomachi Roman**
Orthodox Church   **Catholic Church**

Jujiga ⓣ

✝
Hakodate Episcopal
Church

● **Ropeway station**
for Mt Hakodate

Yachizaka Slope

6
○⌂

Gokokujinjazaka Slope

Horai-cho ⓣ

9 ○

⌂ 7

Hakodate

函館

ⓣ
Aoyagi-cho

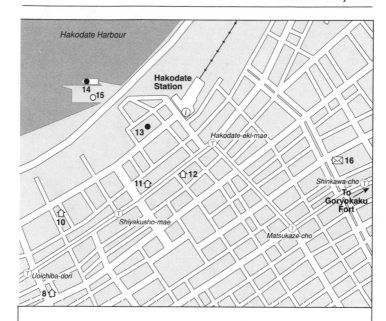

HAKODATE 函館

Where to stay
6 Hotel JAL City
7 Hakodate Youth Guest House
8 Hotel Chocolat Hakodate
10 Niceday Inn
11 Aqua Garden Hotel
12 Fitness Hotel 330

Where to eat
5 Tao Tao
6 Capricciosa
9 Hakodate Beer
15 Beelong's

Other
1 Old Public Hall of Hakodate Ward
2 Old British Consulate
3 Hakodate City Museum of
   Northern Peoples
4 Hakodate City Museum of Literature
13 Morning Market
14 Memorial Ship *Mashumaru*
16 Central Post Office

6 ホテルJALシティ
7 函館ユースゲストハウス
8 ホテルショコラ函館
10 ナイスディン
11 アクアガーデンホテル函館
12 フィットネスホテル330

5 タオタオ
6 カプリチョーザ
9 函館ビール
15 ビロングス

1 旧函館区公会堂
2 旧イギリス領事館
3 函館市北方民族資料館

4 函館市文学館
13 朝市
14 メモリアルシップ摩周丸
16 中央郵便局

Three kilometres south-west of the station and 334m above sea level, **Mt Hakodate** offers a panoramic view of the city. A ropeway runs up to the top (¥1160 return) from Motomachi, or a walking path is open from spring to autumn. The cheapest way of reaching the summit is by bus from stop F at the bus terminal opposite Hakodate station. Bus services (¥360 one-way, 20-25 mins) operate April 25th-November 14th and mostly in the evening, when the view is considered the most spectacular.

About 4km north-east of Hakodate station is **Goryokaku,** the first Western-style fort in Japan. Built between 1857 and 1864 as a strategic location from which Hokkaido could be ruled, the fort is a pentagonal star shape (called 'the most beautiful star carved on earth'). Warriors from the fallen Tokugawa shogunate escaped from Honshu to Hakodate and occupied the fort in October 1868. Seven months later they gave themselves up to the Imperial Army, bringing Japan's feudal era to a dramatic end. At the main entrance is the 60m-high Goryokaku Tower (daily, Apr to Oct 8am-7pm, Nov to Mar, 9am-6pm, ¥630). It's a modern-day eyesore but does have an observation platform affording views over the fort.

To reach Goryokaku, take the tram to Goryokaku-Koen-mae and then walk north along the main road for about 10 minutes. Look for signs pointing towards the fort. You'll see the concrete Goryokaku Tower in front of you.

PRACTICAL INFORMATION
Station guide
In a bid to revive the somewhat depressed area immediately around it, Hakodate station is to be completely rebuilt on the same site (to a Dutch design) by 2003. There are plenty of coin lockers (¥500) around the current station. Most of the shops in the station are souvenir places, though there are a couple of noodle counters, a café and a small bakery. There is, however, a wide choice of seafood ekiben; even a Seikan Tunnel lunch box for ¥1050.

Tourist information
When the new station opens, the tourist information centre (☎ 0138-23 5440, daily 8am-7pm in summer, daily except Sun, 8am-5pm in winter) will be inside it. For now, the office is on the right as you take the main exit. Some staff speak English and they will help book accommodation.

Getting around
Hakodate's tram system has been in operation since 1913 and it's still the best way of getting around the city. A one-day pass

(¥1000, two days ¥1700) allows unlimited travel on all trams as well as city buses (except Hakodate Bus). The pass also covers the summer bus service to the top of Mt Hakodate. Purchase the pass either from the tourist office or from tram drivers.

Money
Foreign-issued Visa cards are accepted for over-the-counter cashing at Hokkaido Bank (Mon to Fri, 9am-2:30pm) across the street from the station. Bring your passport.

Festivals
In late July/early August, an outdoor dramatic performance is staged at Goryokaku Fort. It's an astonishing theatrical event that tells the story of Hakodate using dry ice, fireworks, canons, motor boats, stampedes of horses, acrobatics, ballet, dance and an amateur cast of thousands.

A Frenchman had the idea for this when he visited Goryokaku and saw that the old fort was the perfect backdrop for a son-et-lumière-style spectacle. Tickets can be purchased in advance (¥1800) or on the door (¥2000). Enquire at the tourist office.

> **Ħ Karaoke tram**
> The tram used to be just a means of getting from A to B, but in Hakodate it's now become a night out in itself. Groups can hire a tram fully equipped with karaoke machine, flashing lights and microphones. Beer and snacks are allowed on board to get people in the mood for singing as the tram makes as many loops of the city as those on board can stand. Net curtains are installed to ensure passengers' anonymity.

Where to stay

The rates quoted below are for high season (June to Oct), except in the case of the Niceday Inn, where the rate remains constant throughout the year.

Hotel Chocolat Hakodate (☎ 0138-26 1330, 🖷 26 0393) is a good, mid-range choice that is quiet and elegant without being overly pricey or stuffy. All rooms have wide beds, minibar, TV and phone as standard. 'Moderate' rooms are singles with large beds that go for ¥8000, or ¥10,000 for two sharing. Twins from ¥13,000. Take a tram from the station to Uoichiba-dori. The hotel is part of the same chain as the larger *Fitness Hotel 330* (☎ 0138-23 0330, 🖷 23 5377; ¥9000/S, ¥16,000/Tw), close to the station, which has a fitness club (additional charge). Across the street is the cheaper *Aqua Garden Hotel* (☎ 0138-23 2200, 🖷 23 4757; ¥6500/S, ¥13,000/Tw/D, and ¥18,000/Tr).

In Horai-cho, *Hotel JAL City* (☎ 0138-24 2580, 🖷 27 2581; ¥9500/S, ¥18,000/Tw and ¥16,000/D) is a bit overpriced for its small but upmarket rooms. The nearest thing to a youth hostel is *Hakodate Youth Guest House* (☎ 0138-26 7892, 🖷 26 0989; closed late Nov/early Dec, mid-Jan and mid-April), near Hotel JAL City. It's more like a pension than a hostel, with mostly twin Western-style rooms (no attached bath). The price ranges from ¥3800 (Oct 1 to June 30), to ¥4500 in summer; rates include a simple breakfast. Even cheaper is the *Niceday Inn* (☎ 0138-22 5919; ¥3000/pp) which has small bunk-bed rooms. It's on the narrow street right across from Hakodate Kokusai Hotel. Look for the sign in English and Japanese on the door.

Where to eat

The morning market by the station is a good place to hunt around for an impromptu meal; you can be sure that the fish is fresh at the many restaurant stalls in the area.

Capricciosa (daily, 11·30am-10pm), on the second floor of Hotel JAL City, serves huge pizzas and pasta to a mostly young crowd. *Hakodate Beer* (daily, 11am-10pm) is a lively place near Kokusai Hotel where you can try various meat and seafood dishes and wash them down with locally-brewed beers. In the summer, there's space to sit on a verandah outside. Another popular drinking place is *Beelong's*, a large pub in the Hakodate Seaport plaza behind the station.

In Motomachi, *Tao Tao* is a South-East Asian restaurant serving a range of Asian beers, soft drinks such as guava juice and great spicy food. It's open in summer from 12 noon-11pm (in winter, Tue to Fri 5-11pm and Sat/Sun 12 noon-11pm. Closed on Mon).

SAPPORO

The biggest city in Hokkaido and venue for the 1972 Winter Olympics, Sapporo is frequently voted the city where most Japanese would like to live. It certainly feels relaxed and cosmopolitan, with green parks, turn of the century red-brick buildings and a thriving entertainment district. It's also one of the easiest cities to get around, thanks to the north-south grid layout. If you need further incentive to spend a couple of days here, time your visit to coincide with one of the many summer and winter festivals, the most famous of which is the annual Snow Festival in February (see p312). Like the rest of Hokkaido, Sapporo receives a thick blanket of snow in the winter but summer is mild and provides the perfect opportunity for relaxing in the city's central Odori Park.

What to see and do

Even the shortest visit should include a tour of **Sapporo Beer Museum** (daily, 9am-5pm, last entry 80 mins before closing), since it costs nothing and, at the end, everyone gets a free glass of draught beer. Inside is a working brewery, the smallest of Sapporo Beer's factories. Guided tours are in Japanese only (tape in English available), but you're rushed around at such high speed that there's barely time to take in any of the exhibits. If you like what you taste on the tour, walk over to Sapporo Bier Garden (see p314). To reach the museum and beer garden, take the special Factory Line bus from the stop outside Seibu department store opposite the station. Alternatively, take bus No Higashi 63 from the north side of the station and get off at the Kita 8 Higashi 7 stop.

Another well-known Hokkaido company is **Snow Brand Milk**, which offers tours of its Sapporo plant and museum (daily, 9-11am and 1-3:30pm), tracing the history of milk in Hokkaido and around the world. Visits are by reservation only (☎ 011-704 2329) and tours are in Japanese. The museum is at N6 E19; take bus No 63 from the station.

Directly south of the station is **Odori Park** which stretches for 1.5km through the centre of the city between West 1 and West 12. In summer, people come here to relax, play games and hang out. In the eastern corner of the park is the 147.2m-high **TV Tower** (daily, 9am-9pm, ¥700) with an observatory that's not really high enough for exceptional views. (Much better is the revolving bar on the top floor of Century Royal Hotel outside the south exit of Sapporo station where, for the price of a drink, you can get a bird's eye view of the city).

To the north of Odori Park is the former **Hokkaido Government Office Building** (Mon-Fri 9am-5pm, free), nicknamed 'Red Brick'. Built in 1888, it was gutted by fire and had to be completely rebuilt in 1911. Entrance is free, though not all the rooms inside are open to the public. One block south is Sapporo's famous **Clock Tower** (daily except Mon, 9am-5pm, ¥200). If you don't see the clock immediately, you'll no doubt see the tourists lining up at the official photograph point in front of it. The tower was constructed in 1878 but had to be redesigned when the clock that arrived from the USA was too big. Inside, the ground floor is used as an exhibition space and concerts are sometimes staged on the second floor.

West of the Hokkaido Government Building are the **Botanical Gardens** (Apr to Sep 9am-4pm; Oct to Nov 9am-3:30pm, ¥400), good for a summer stroll. The ticket includes entry to a small Ainu museum in the grounds but there's a better museum devoted to preserving Ainu heritage and culture in the

Kaderu 2.7 Building, across the street from the entrance to the gardens. On the seventh floor is a permanent **Ainu exhibition** (daily except Sun 9am-5pm, free) with a range of exhibits including items of Ainu clothing and equipment used in daily life. Pop into the office next door to pick up a leaflet.

In the evening, the place to head for an eyeful of Japan by night is the **Susukino** entertainment district. Susukino is (in)famous for its soaplands, but the streets are also packed with pachinko parlours, pubs and bars. Billed as the 'largest amusement area north of Tokyo', the area boasts between 4000 and 5000 bars and restaurants, all of which rely on evening trade when the district is flooded by businessmen. Take the subway to Susukino.

PRACTICAL INFORMATION
Station guide
Sapporo station has north and south exits; take the south exit for the main city area. Inside, the station building is split into east and west sides with ticket barriers and access to the platforms on both sides. You don't have to hunt around for food in this station; look out for branches of Doutor Coffee and Mister Donut, both good for a quick breakfast. Paseo department store is on both sides of the station concourse and there are more shops/cafés under the station.

The station has recently been redeveloped and construction continues outside the south exit. A department store (Daimaru), another shopping mall and cinema complex, and a tower which will have 38 floors and will contain a 350-room hotel (JR Tower Hotel Nikko Sapporo; 🖳 jr-tower.com) on the 23rd-34th floors, will open in spring 2003.

Tourist information
The **International Information Corner** (☎ 011-213 5062, daily 9am-5pm; closed 2nd and 4th Wed) is in Twinkle Plaza travel agency on the west side of the station. Staff speak English and are well supplied with leaflets and maps. **Sapporo**

International Communication Plaza 'i' (☎ 011-211 3678, daily 9am-5:30pm) is in the city centre, on the ground floor of the Sapporo MN Building across the street from the Clock Tower. At either place, pick up a copy of the monthly *What's on in Sapporo?* and bi-monthly *Xene*, a magazine with listings for restaurants, bars and clubs.

Getting around
Sapporo has a modern subway system with three lines that interconnect at Odori station, one stop south of Sapporo station. There is also a tram line. One-day subway passes (¥800) can be purchased from vending machines at subway stations. The 'common-use one-day card' (¥1000) is valid on the subway, tram and most buses.

Bikes can be rented from **Rent A Cycle** (daily, 10am-6pm, ¥500/2 hrs, ¥300 each additional hour) on the 1st floor of the TV Tower.

Between May and November cycles can be rented for free at the **Toyohira-gawa Jitensha Kashidashi jo** (S9; daily except Mon, 9am-4:30pm). Bikes are supposed to be used only for cycling on the bike course along Toyohira-gawa. To reach the centre, take the subway to Nakajima-Koen. Exit the station and walk towards the river. The

---

❏ Sapporo orientation
Thanks to Sapporo's grid system, it's easy to find your way almost anywhere in the city. Nearly all addresses include a grid reference, so a building at 'N3, W6', for example, is three blocks north and six blocks west of the grid apex on the eastern corner of Odori Koen in the city centre.

bike centre is in a red-brick building next to Hotel North City. The entrance is slightly hidden down a ramp.

Money
For credit cards issued overseas, try the ATM (hidden behind a lottery/cigarette stall) on the east side of Paseo department store on the ground floor of Sapporo station.

Internet
On the east side of Paseo shopping mall beneath Sapporo station is Bon de Bon Café (daily, 10am-9pm), where you can surf the net for ¥200/30 minutes.

Festivals
The biggest event of the year is the **Yuki Matsuri** (Snow Festival) in February, when tourists from around the country and the world flock to see the huge ice sculptures on display in Odori Koen. The **Yosakoi Soran Festival** in June brings together dance teams from all over Japan, who compete to win over the judges with their own

interpretation of a dance rhythm that originated in Kochi (see p384). The festival dates back to 1991, when a student attended the Yosakoi Festival in Kochi and decided to organize a similar event in Sapporo.

The first festival attracted 10 teams and a total of 1000 dancers. By 1999, the number of dancers had risen to 34,000 representing a total of 333 teams, watched by a crowd of nearly two million.

In summer the **Pacific Music Festival** (July to August), originally started by Leonard Bernstein, brings together young musicians from all over the world who stage a series of concerts around the city. Some performances are free.

Where to stay
The grid references for each of the hotels listed below are given in brackets.

Sapporo has far too many hotels; they only fill up completely during the Snow Festival in February. This hasn't put companies off building new ones and the latest addition is set to be JR Tower Hotel Nikko

---

SAPPORO 札幌

Where to stay
- 2 Hotel Sapporo Met's
- 6 Nakamuraya Ryokan
- 11 Sapporo International YH/ Nakajima-Koen/Toyohira-gawa Jitensha Kashidashi jo
- 12 Hotel New Budget Sapporo
- 14 The Hamilton Sapporo

Where to eat
- 7 Aji no Tokeidai
- 9 Aozora/Lilac

Other
- 1 Former Hokkaido Government Office Bldg
- 3 Sapporo Beer Garden/Museum
- 4 Central Post Office
- 5 Botanical Gardens
- 8 Clock Tower
- 10 TV Tower/Rent A Cycle
- 13 Odori Koen

2 ホテル サッポロ メッツ
6 中村屋旅館
11 札幌国際ユースホステル/
　中島公園/
　豊平川自転車貸出所
12 ホテルニューバジェット札幌
14 ザハミルトン 札幌

7 味の時計台
9 あおぞら/ライラック

1 旧本庁舎

3 札幌ビアガーデン/博物館
4 中央郵便局
5 植物園
8 時計台
10 テレビタワー/レンタサイクル
13 大通り公園

Sapporo
札幌

Hokkaido University

Former Hokkaido Government Office Building

Kaderu 2.7 Building

International Communication Plaza

Sapporo Station

To Asahikawa and Historical Village of Hokkaido

To Susukino

Kinokuniya Bookstore

Maruzen Bookstore

Tram line

Nishi-Juitchome

Nishi-Juhatchome

APPROXIMATE SCALE
0   250M

N 6 N 5 N 4 N 3 N 2 N 1
E 1 E 2
W 1 W 2 W 3 W 4 W 5 W 6 W 7 W 8 W 9 W 10 W 11 W 12 W 13 W 14 W 15 W 16 W 17

Odori

Sapporo (see Station guide). *Nakamuraya Ryokan* (N3, W7, ☎ 011-241 2111, 🖻 241 2118; ¥7000/S, ¥13,000/Tw, ¥18,000/Tr) is a typical Japanese inn with tatami rooms (all with small attached bath/toilet). The ryokan is in the city centre, on the road between the Botanical Gardens and Hokkaido government buildings.

A couple of stops on the Nanboku subway line north of Sapporo station to Kita-Juhachijo station is *Hotel Sapporo Met's* (N17, W5, ☎ 011-726 5511, 🖻 716 1082, 🖳 info@hotelmets.co.jp; ¥6800/S, ¥10,000/ Tw inc breakfast). For the price of a business hotel, you get a mini-apartment, including washing machine, tumble dryer and small kitchen area. *The Hamilton Sapporo* (S1, W15, ☎ 011-632 0080, 🖻 632 0081, 🖳 sapporo@the-hamilton.co.jp; ¥8500/S, ¥13,500/Tw, ¥18,500/Tr) is a new mid-range choice in a quiet part of town. Take the Tozai subway line to Nishi Juhachi-chome station or the tram to Nishi-jugo stop, a minute from the hotel. *Hotel New Budget Sapporo* (S3, W6, ☎ 011-261 4953, 🖻 261 4960; ¥4900/S, ¥8000/Tw inc breakfast) is a new business hotel with automated check in (cash only).

The best budget choice by far is the *Sapporo International Youth Hostel* (☎ 011-825 3120, 🖳 kokusai@youthhostel.or. jp; ¥3800, breakfast ¥850). The family-size tatami rooms as well as the Western-style dorms are very comfortable and kept spotless. All rooms are equipped with individual lockers; in the basement there's a hot spring bath and coin laundry. From the station, take the Toho subway line to Gakuen-mae station and follow the signs for Exit No 2.

Where to eat

Check the latest issue of *Xene* for the newest restaurants and bars. The shopping mall that runs underneath Sapporo station has a wide range of places to eat. Head down to subway level; on your way you'll pass even more restaurants and cafés.

A Sapporo speciality is *jingiskan* (Hokkaido ram and vegetables grilled in a special pan), named after Genghis Khan and served in a pan shaped like a Mongolian hat. The best place to try jingiskan is *Sapporo Bier Garden* (daily, 11:30am-9pm) where there are various all-you-can-eat-and-drink deals (from ¥3100/ pp for 100 minutes). In the summer, there's seating in the garden as well as in the large hall. The beer garden is close to Sapporo Beer Museum (see p310).

Another local speciality is Sapporo ramen, the broth of which is made from *miso* (fermented soybean paste) and is rich with garlic and butter. A popular place to try it in the city centre is *Aji no Tokeidai*, sandwiched between a convenience store called 'Community Store' and a branch of Sanwa Bank. The reasonable prices and large portions mean this place gets crowded at lunchtime.

For a budget lunch, head for City Hall, where there are two café restaurants on the 18th and 19th floors that have good views as well as cheap food. *Aozora* on the 19th has simple meals like chicken with rice or noodles for ¥500-600 and there's a similar menu at *Lilac* on the 18th. Even cheaper is the basement canteen, where you buy a ticket from a vending machine (choose what you want from the plastic foods on display in the entrance and match up the kanji with the descriptions on the machine); take the ticket to one of the serving counters to collect your food. Prices start at around ¥300. If you arrive shortly before 12 noon, you'll be able to get a seat and witness the arrival of white-collar workers en masse.

Side trip from Sapporo

Though not accessible by rail, it's worth considering a trip to the **Historical Village of Hokkaido** (daily except Mon 9:30am-4:30pm, April to Nov ¥610, Dec to March ¥500) in Nopporo Forest Park in the suburbs of Sapporo, since the route is operated by JR Bus and is free to rail-pass holders. A large number of buildings from the Meiji and Taisho periods (mid-19th to early 20th century) have been restored and moved here. It's a very atmospheric place to wander around and there are explanations in English. The main entrance to the village is through the old Sapporo railway station, in use from 1908 to 1952.

Although the village is the main attraction of Nopporo Forest Park, it's by no means the only reason for heading out here. Locals joke that tourists visit for the historical village, while residents head here for the 30km of trails through the forest. Pick up a map of the forest park from the tourist office in Sapporo; it has details of footpaths and distances along various routes.

Three buses a day run to the village from Sapporo station (leaving at 9:05am, 9:40am and 10:20am; 60 mins). Alternatively, take the train to Shin-Sapporo, from where more buses go to the village. Buses leave from stop No 10 on the north side of the bus terminal outside Shin-Sapporo station and the last bus leaves Shin-Sapporo for the village at 1:50pm. Some of the return buses from the village continue on to Sapporo station after stopping at Shin-Sapporo, but it's quicker to take the train from Shin-Sapporo back to Sapporo.

See p70 for details of **Otaru Transportation Museum**, a worthwhile side trip for rail enthusiasts.

ASAHIKAWA

Despite the backdrop of the Daisetsu mountain range, Asahikawa is not an attractive place by Hokkaido's standards. The second biggest city in Hokkaido after Sapporo serves mainly as a transport hub and a gateway to Daisetsuzan National Park (see p319).

What to see and do

There is little of interest in the city. However, to kill time, consider a visit to **Kawamura Ainu Memorial Hall** (daily, 9am-5pm, ¥500). It's a very small museum with a few exhibits on Ainu traditions. (Continued on p318)

⛩ **Racing with carthorses**

Apart from snow and ice, Asahikawa is known for a special type of horse race, unique to Hokkaido, known as *banba*. Horses, twice the weight of thoroughbreds (or so it is claimed), compete in a test of strength, racing to pull one-ton sleighs and a driver around a track.

This unusual sport, which has its roots in France and Belgium, first appeared in Japan a century ago during the Meiji era when the pioneers who came to Hokkaido used horses to plough the fields. Today's race track includes a number of steep hills which the horse and driver have to negotiate. Unlike in a normal horse race, the winner is not the horse whose nose crosses the finishing line first. Both horse and attached sleigh must cross the line before the winner can be declared.

Racing takes place only on certain days each year so check details at the tourist information booth inside the station or call ☎ 0166-75 3100. Races take place outside the city at the race track in Kamui-cho.

⛩ The Ainu: fight for survival

When Kenichi Kawamura visited the National Museum of Natural History in Washington, USA, in April 1999 for an exhibition of Ainu artefacts, he was joined by the late Japanese prime minister, Keizo Obuchi. Kawamura overheard the prime minister enquire of another visitor to the museum, 'Are there still Ainu in Hokkaido?'

The Ainu have long been almost invisible to the outside world. In a speech to the United Nations in 1992, a representative of the Ainu people told how the Japanese government had 'denied even our existence in its proud claim that Japan, alone in the world, is a "mono-ethnic nation"'. The Ainu originally populated parts of northern Honshu as well as Hokkaido, living in small communities of up to 10 families, fishing from the rivers and hunting bear – a sacred animal in Ainu tradition – in the forests. There was never any question of land rights until the *wajin* (Japanese) moved further north, calling the Ainu 'dogs' (the Japanese word for dog is *inu*) and forcing them off their land. The only work that some could find was manual labour with logging companies – thus the Ainu found themselves in the extraordinary position of having to earn a living by destroying the very land on which they had lived.

In 1899, the Hokkaido Former Aborigine Protection Law was passed, giving the island's governor power to 'manage the communal assets of the Ainu people for their benefit', on the pretext that the Ainu were unable to manage these assets themselves. Almost a century was to pass until the law was repealed in 1997, replaced with a new act to promote Ainu culture and return assets totalling around ¥1.5 million that had been 'managed' by the prefectural government. Endless legal wrangles in court over the exact amount and how it should be paid suggest a quick resolution is unlikely.

There has been some attempt to revive Ainu traditions and in particular the Ainu language, now spoken by fewer than a dozen elderly people. Weekly Ainu language radio courses have started and storytellers are being trained to continue the Ainu oral tradition. In 1994, Shigeru Kayano became the first Ainu to win a seat in the Upper House of the Japanese Parliament, and in a landmark 1998 ruling a Hokkaido judge recognized the indigenous status of the Ainu people for the first time. Nobody yet knows if all this is too little too late to save the Ainu from cultural extinction.

ASAHIKAWA 旭川

Where to stay
8 Asahikawa Terminal Hotel	8 旭川ターミナルホテル

Where to eat
2 Le Montrachet	2 レ モントラシェ
3 Mister Donut	3 ミスタードーナッツ
4 Doutor Coffee	4 ドトールコーヒー
5 Aji no Tokeidai	5 味の時計台
6 McDonald's	6 マクドナルド
7 Capricciosa	7 カプリチョーザ

Other
1 Central Post Office	1 中央郵便局

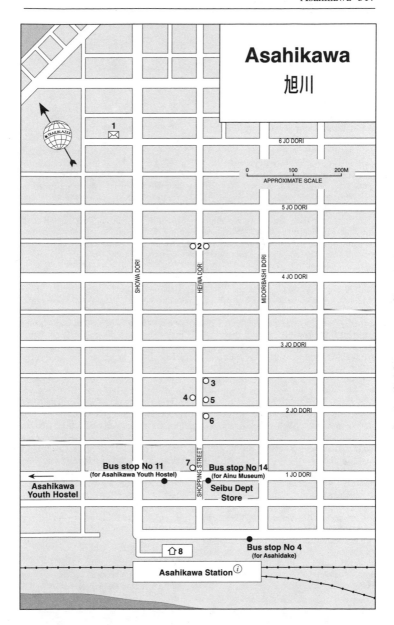

(*Continued from p315*). The museum was founded by Kenichi Kawamura, an eighth generation Ainu who has campaigned for many years for greater recognition of Hokkaido's indigenous population (see box p316).

It's a ten-minute bus ride (bus No 24) from bus stop No 14 outside Seibu department store. Get off at Ainu Kinenkan-mae.

PRACTICAL INFORMATION
Station guide
Asahikawa celebrated 100 years of connection to the rail network in 1998.

At the bottom of the stairs from the platforms up to the station concourse is an intercom that can be used to request assistance with getting up the stairs.

The main exit, in front of you as you pass the ticket barrier, leads out to a shopping street popularly known as 'Kaimono-dori' (shopping street). On the ground floor is a small bakery, Lotteria hamburger bar, branch post office and a row of coin lockers (all sizes).

Asahikawa is a major rail junction with lines going north to Wakkanai, east to Abashiri, south to Furano and west back to Sapporo.

Tourist information
The staff at the tourist information booth (☎ 0166-22 6704/5139, daily, 9am-7pm; earlier in winter) in the station speak little English, though a guide to Asahikawa and the surrounding area is available and staff will make reservations for you. Pick up a copy of *AIC Information*, a monthly newsletter published by Asahikawa International Committee (☎ 0166-25 7491), with information on local events, concerts and film listings.

Money
Asahikawa is really the last chance to change money before heading further off the beaten track. None of the ATMs accepts foreign-issued Visa cards but you can apply for an over-the-counter cash advance at the Saison desk on the sixth floor of Seibu department store (the 'A' building) just outside the station. A passport is required.

Festivals
In early February (usually around 11th/12th), the city celebrates the **Asahikawa Winter Festival**. It's not as vast or commercial as Sapporo Snow Festival (see p312) but is just as impressive. The World Ice Sculpture Competition brings together international teams who compete to build giant sculptures in Tokiwa Park, about 15 minutes' walk north of the station. A fireworks display takes place on the opening night. For precise dates, contact the tourist office or Asahikawa International Committee (see above).

Where to stay
Asahikawa Terminal Hotel (☎ 0166-24 0111, 🖹 21 2133, 🖳 www.asahikawa-th.com; ¥7700/S, ¥12,650/D, ¥14,850/Tw) is right outside the station and is an ideal overnight base. There's a good Japanese restaurant on the sixth floor, or there are other places to eat in the adjacent Esta department store.

Alternatively, take a 20-minute bus journey to *Asahikawa Youth Hostel* (☎ 0166-61 2800, 🖹 61 8886; YH/HI ¥3200, ¥4500/Tw). Most accommodation is in tatami dorms but there are a few twin rooms with attached bath/toilet. Excellent meals are served in the café; the huge breakfast is especially recommended. In the winter, you're perfectly placed to take advantage of the Inosawa ski slope next to the hostel. To reach the hostel, take bus No 444 or 550 (¥200) from stop No 11, just along from Malsa department store, a couple of minutes from the station.

Where to eat
Sapporo ramen may be better known but Asahikawa is proud of its version, where the pork is stewed in shochu.

Along the main street that runs north from the station is a branch of the Sapporo ramen restaurant *Aji no Tokeidai* with a handy picture menu. In the basement of the 'A.s.h.' building along the same street is a branch of the Italian chain *Capricciosa*. Further up is *Le Montrachet*, a bakery/café that sells a range of cakes, buns and sand-wiches and does light meals. Directly across the street is Le Montrachet's more upmarket French bistro, with prices to match. Along this street you'll also find a variety of fast food outlets, including *McDonald's*, *Doutor Coffee* and *Mister Donut*.

Side trip to Asahidake

An 80-minute free bus ride from Asahikawa brings you to **Mt Asahi** or **Asahidake**, in Daisetsuzan National Park. Alpine flowers bloom in spring on the slopes of this, the highest mountain in Hokkaido. In winter, powder snow attracts skiers keen to take advantage of Japan's longest skiing season, from December to early May.

The bus runs to the resort of Asahidake-Onsen, stopping outside the newly renovated **Asahidake Ropeway** (¥2800 round trip July to Sep, ¥1800 rest of the year; operating hours vary according to season; July to Sep daily 6am-7pm; closed for inspection May 16th to 31st and Nov 11th to 30th).

The ten-minute ropeway journey takes you up to 1600m, where it's a few degrees cooler than at the foot of the mountain. At the top station, there's a small photo gallery of Asahidake through the seasons and a video show – good if you're waiting for a ropeway back down. From the top station, it's a gentle 1km walk to the main lookout point. Asahidake is similar in appearance to Mt Iwo in Kawayu-Onsen (see p297), with smoke pouring out from rock turned yellow by the sulphur. From here, it's a further 2.6km to the summit, which at 2290m is sometimes covered in cloud. The hike to the summit takes around two hours (allow a further hour to get back down to the top ropeway station); it's advisable to wear strong trainers or hiking boots as the path is rocky.

Before going up the mountain, pop in to the Asahidake Visitor Center (daily, 7am-5/6pm, early closing in winter), on the main street just before the ropeway entrance. Inside are some displays of local nature and wildlife, and you can pick up a map from the reception desk.

The best place to overnight is at the newly-renovated *Daisetsuzan Shirakaba-so Youth Hostel* (☎ 0166-97 2246, ▤ 97 2247; YH/HI ¥2900, ¥3900 non-members, breakfast ¥600, dinner ¥1000), less than five minutes on foot down the main road that leads up to the ropeway station. Campjo-mae bus stop, the final stop before the ropeway terminus, is right outside the hostel. The visitor centre has a list of other accommodation in the area.

From June to October, three buses a day run between Asahikawa and Asahidake ropeway. Buses leave from stop No 4 outside Asahikawa station at 9:10am, 1:10pm and 3:10pm, and return at 12:05pm, 4:05pm and 6:05 pm. The service is less frequent in winter. The service is free from Asahikawa to Asahidake, and for the return journey if you pick up a coupon from the ropeway station when you buy your ticket or from the hostel (otherwise it costs ¥1000).

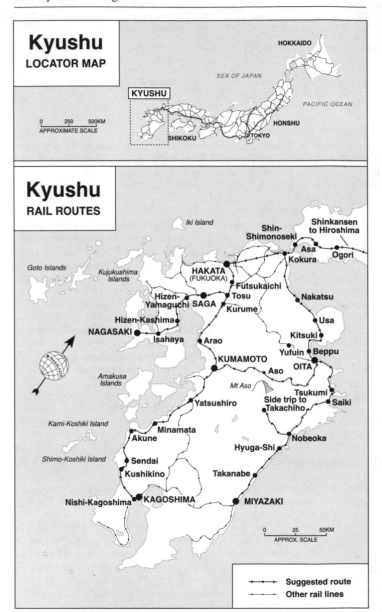

Kyushu – route guide

Despite its modern-day reputation as something of a backwater, Kyushu's history has been more linked with the West than any of the other main islands. The port of Nagasaki, in particular, was the only place in the country where trading with the outside world was permitted during Japan's nearly 300 years of self-imposed isolation under the Tokugawa shogunate.

Today, the majority of visitors to Kyushu pause briefly in Fukuoka (see p336), the island's capital, before making a beeline for Nagasaki (see p343), the second city in Japan to be hit with an atomic bomb in 1945. But if you're prepared to devote more time to seeing the island, it really is worth travelling further south.

Perhaps because of its relatively mild climate, Kyushu feels more relaxed and the people more laid back than on Honshu. This may also have something to do with the popularity of shochu, a strong spirit found in every bar that becomes even stronger and more popular the further south you go.

A trip down the west coast brings you to the shochu capital, Kagoshima (see p355), sometimes described as the 'Naples of the East', and neighbouring Sakurajima (see p361), one of the world's most active volcanoes.

Over on the east coast, fans of water parks, flumes and a year-round tropical climate shouldn't miss a trip to the giant Ocean Dome in Miyazaki (see p333). And right in the centre of the island, a perfect side trip by rail from either the east or west coasts, lies formidable Mt Aso (see p334), where visitors can peer over the top of an active volcanic crater.

Kyushu can be reached easily by rail from Honshu via the Tokaido and Sanyo shinkansen lines which run from Tokyo to the terminus in Hakata (Fukuoka). JR Kyushu runs an efficient network that will take you just about anywhere and uses limited expresses on most of its lines. For details of JR Kyushu's rail pass, see p14.

Nagasaki can be seen in a couple of days but allow at least a week if you're travelling down either coast and planning to fit in a visit to Mt Aso as well.

山の温泉や裸の上の天の川

Hot spring in the mountains:
high above the naked bathers
the River of Heaven
(SHIKI MASAOKA)

ㅠ   How to fillet a fugu

Two stops west from Shin-Shimonoseki along the Sanyo line, right on the tip of Honshu, is Shimonoseki. This city is known for *fugu* (blow fish), the notorious fish that can kill when eaten if it is not correctly prepared; 70% of Japan's fugu is traded at a fish market in Shimonoseki. A unique method of bidding for fugu at the market involves the fisherman and buyer haggling over a price by grasping one another's fingers in a cloth bag.

At the restaurant table, fugu is served raw, as a fish jelly or deep fried. In a bid to ensure there are no foreign casualties, the local government has produced step-by-step instructions in English on how to fillet a fugu. According to the manual, one should 'hit the fugu's head to knock it out', 'put the tip of the knife to the fugu's nostril and cut off the snout', 'scrape out the guts', 'take out the eyes' and 'chop the head'.

If you can do or read all this without wincing, it's likely you could apply for a licence to prepare the fish; all would-be fugu masterchefs are required to have a licence before opening a fugu restaurant. This requirement should mean there is no risk to diners, though very occasionally reports of death-by-fugu creep into the national press. All the same, it's best not to think too much about the fugu swimming around above you as the shinkansen speeds through the underwater tunnel on its way to Kyushu.

OGORI TO HAKATA BY SHINKANSEN   [Map 27, p323; Table 3, p400]

Distances from Tokyo by shinkansen. Fastest journey time: 45 minutes.

Ogori (1027km)   Ogori is a point of connection with the route guide around western Honshu (see p211).

From here, continue on the shinkansen to Kokura, the first stop in Kyushu. Most Hikari run non-stop to Kokura but the Kodama stops twice at **Asa (1062km)** and then **Shin-Shimonoseki (1089km)** before heading into the tunnel for the journey through the narrow Kammon Straits to Kyushu.

Kokura (1108km)   Heading out of the tunnel that connects Honshu with Kyushu, the train soon arrives at the sleek, modern Kokura station.

Kokura made the American military's shortlist as the next A-Bomb target following the attack on Hiroshima, but cloud cover over the city on the morning of August 9th 1945 meant the plane carrying the bomb was forced to change direction and headed instead towards Nagasaki.

From Kokura, the shinkansen line continues on to Hakata (see p336), and the Nippo line runs along the east coast of Kyushu towards Oita and Miyazaki (see p333). Regular trains to Hakata run on the Kagoshima line.

JR West runs the shinkansen tracks at Kokura, so if you're changing from the shinkansen follow the signs for 'JR Kyushu Lines'. The main station concourse, with a central plaza and large TV screen, is on the third floor. Since the station has been rebuilt there is good disabled access, with either lifts or ramps in addition to stairs/escalators to get from the concourse to street level.

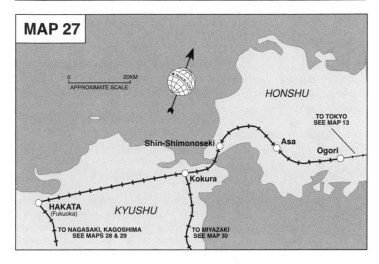

Maps of Kokura are available from the tourist information booth on the central concourse (☎ 093-531 9611, daily 9am-6pm).

The **Kitakyushu Welcome Card** (see p46) is available from the main tourist information office (daily 9am-6pm), hidden away in a corner on the floor below the central concourse. From the main concourse, head towards the shinkansen entrance, next to which is an escalator that leads down to the north exit. Turn right at the bottom of the escalator and the office is in the corner. Show your passport to receive the card.

Kokura is of limited appeal to the traveller. That said, with a couple of hours to spare, it's worth fitting in a trip to the **Kokura Castle** area, a 15-minute walk from the south exit of Kokura station. Head up the main street, Heiwa-dori, turn right on to Komonji-dori and cross the bridge.

The entrance to the castle area is just past City Hall on your right. The castle itself (daily 9am-5pm, ¥350) is a 1990 reconstruction of the original 1602 building and now contains a kitsch puppet show. The only reason to stop here would be for the views from the top floor but you get much better views (for free) from the top floor of City Hall.

It's better to skip the castle and head to the newly-constructed **Kokura Castle Japanese Garden** (daily, 9am-5pm, ¥300), the entrance to which is opposite the castle. An Edo period home has been reconstructed overlooking a small Japanese garden, an unexpected oasis of calm in the middle of an industrial city. The only downside is the view of City Hall that looms overhead. For ¥500 extra, you'll be served a bowl of green tea and a Japanese sweetmeat by shuffling, kimono-clad women and you can briefly imagine yourself transported to a private house in Kyoto.

Having seen **City Hall** from the castle gardens (one of the most unfortunate examples of a 'borrowed view'), it's worth going in and taking the lift to the top, where there's an observation gallery (Mon-Fri, 8:45am-5pm). You can walk all the way around and get a bird's eye view of Kyushu's industrial heartland and of the shinkansen gliding away from Kokura back towards Honshu. Take the lift up to the 15th floor and then the stairs to the top. There are vending machines and chairs here, and a restaurant on the 15th floor that serves cheap pasta, ice cream parfaits and coffee.

Families flock to northern Kyushu to visit the **Space World** theme park (see 🖳 www.spaceworld.co.jp for opening times/latest prices and an attraction guide in English); it even has its own station (JR Space World), five stops from Kokura along the JR Kagoshima line. A one-day passport costs ¥3800 (12-17 years ¥3900, 4-11 ¥2800); ¥200 less if bought in advance from any JR station in Kyushu.

The most convenient place to stay the night is *Station Hotel Kokura* (☎ 093-521 5031, 🖹 512 0345, 🖳 www.kosta.co.jp/hotel; ¥7800/S, ¥14,000/D, ¥15,000/Tw) built into the JR station building. A 10% discount off rack rates is offered to rail-pass holders. A package deal combining one night's accommodation, breakfast and a one-day passport to Space World is available for ¥10,000/pp; for further details check the Space World website (see above).

From Kokura, it's one more stop by shinkansen to Hakata/Fukuoka. If heading down the east coast (on the route starting on p329), change trains here rather than at Hakata, otherwise you'll have to backtrack.

Hakata/Fukuoka (1175km) [see pp336-43]

It's mostly tunnels on the short journey between Kokura and Hakata; in the brief snatches of daylight it's surprising to see how lush and green the countryside is between these two cities.

Hakata, also known as Fukuoka, is the shinkansen terminus and a major transport hub for onward trips west to Nagasaki and south to Kumamoto and Kagoshima.

HAKATA TO NAGASAKI [Map 28 opposite; Table 25, p411]

Distances by JR from Hakata. Fastest journey time: 2 hours.

Hakata (0km) A blueprint for an extension of the shinkansen line to Nagasaki was drawn up in 1973 – it still exists only on paper. For now, the fastest way is by Kamome LEX from Hakata along the JR Kagoshima line.

❏ **Using the rail route guides**

The fastest point-to-point journey times are provided for each section of the route. Even though each route has been divided into different sections it may not be necessary to change trains as you go from one section to the next. Occasionally, however, it is essential to change train in order to complete the route described. Such instances are denoted by the following symbol ▲. Places which are served by local trains only are marked ◆. **(For more information see p84)**

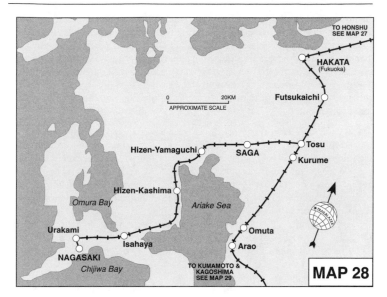

The Kamome was introduced with great fanfare in 2000 under the slogan 'it's white, it's fast, it's beautiful' – well, it does have wooden floors and comfortable leather seats.

Futsukaichi (14km)   Some trains make a brief stop at this hot springs resort. Of more interest is Tenmangu Shrine, home to Sugawara Michizane, god of scholars and literature, in neighbouring Dazaifu. From Futsukaichi, it's four minutes by bus to Nishitetsu Futsukaichi station, where a local train runs two stops to Dazaifu. If there are no buses, it's easy enough to walk the short distance between the two stations in about ten minutes. From Nishitetsu Futsukaichi, take a local train two stops to Dazaifu (rail passes are not accepted on the private Nishitetsu line). Train services run every 5-40 minutes (in both directions); services are most frequent during peak times.

The tourist information office at Dazaifu station can provide a list of accommodation and a map. Cycles can also be rented here (¥200 per hour). The former Dazaifu Youth Hostel has now been renamed ***B&B Guest House Dazaifu*** (1553-3 Dazaifu, ☎ 092-922 8740, 🖨 922 8762; ¥3300 for dormitory accommodation, ¥5000 for a twin-bed room). Breakfast costs ¥700. It's a 12-minute walk from Dazaifu station (pick up a map from tourist information).

Tosu (29km)   Nothing particular to see here but Tosu is a major rail junction. From here, the Nagasaki line heads west towards Nagasaki; this is the route followed here. For details of the Kagoshima line south to Kumamoto and Kagoshima, see p327.

There are few facilities at Tosu station, apart from a small branch of the *Train D'Or* bakery and a convenience store. Exit the station and you'll see the 'Joyful Town' shopping complex a couple of minutes' walk away. Here, there's a selection of cafés and restaurants and a large department store. On Sunday, you could join the crowd at the stadium next to the station. This is the home of 'Sagan Tosu', the local soccer team currently in J-League Division Two. If the size of the crowd is anything to go by, they could do with some extra support. The team's motto is 'the 3C's – Cooperation, Communication, Challenge'.

Saga (54km) Everyone passes through Saga on their way to Nagasaki but few stop at this prefectural capital, venue for an **International Balloon Festival** in November. Sandwiched between the greater tourist draws of Nagasaki and Fukuoka, Saga offers little to the passing tourist. Saga prefecture is best known for its hand-made pottery, a centre for which is the small town of **Karatsu**, 80 minutes away on the local Karatsu line. Located on the coast, Karatsu was once a prosperous port town and a gateway to China.

Saga station has north and south exits and a tourist information office (☎ 0952-23 3975, daily, 8:30am-5/6pm) on the concourse. Also here is a *Train D'Or* bakery and a branch of *Mister Donut*. In case you decide to stay the night, *Saga Tokyu Inn* (☎ 0952-29 0109, 🖷 29 0141; ¥6900/S, ¥12,800/Tw, ¥14,000/D) is right outside the station's south exit.

In Saga city, the main sight is Kono Park, inside which is the **Tea House Kakurintei** (daily except Mon 9am-5pm, free), a reconstruction of the original built in 1846 by Lord Naomasa Nabeshima, 10th lord of the Saga Clan. It's small but has been faithfully reconstructed with a veranda commanding great views of the surrounding lake (and less impressive views of a concrete water tower). Green tea (¥300) is served.

Hizen-Yamaguchi (68km) This station is the junction for the Sasebo branch line. Travelling to Nagasaki there's no need to change trains because the Kamome LEX continues along the Nagasaki line.

Hizen-Kashima (83km) After Hizen-Kashima the line follows the coast, affording great views of the Ariake Sea on the left side. The train briefly comes to a halt along the coast to allow the train returning to Hakata to pass. The view is occasionally blotted out by the odd tunnel and gradually the train moves more inland before arriving at Isahaya.

Isahaya (129km) Isahaya is a gateway to **Shimabara Peninsula** which juts out east of Nagasaki into the Ariake Sea, with Mt Unzen at its centre. On a plateau south-west of Mt Unzen is the hot spring resort of **Unzen Jigoku**. Today, people visit for the scenery and the chance to bathe in the public spas but 350 years ago, during the time of religious persecution in Japan, 30 Christians were sent there for refusing to renounce their faith, and were promptly thrown into the boiling hot springs.

The private Shimabara Railway (JR passes not valid) runs from Isahaya around the peninsula, stopping at the port town of Shimabara on the eastern side. Turn right out of the JR station; the entrance to the Shimabara Railway is between Mister Donut and the Joyroad travel agency. Purchase tickets from the ticket machine in the JR station (Isahaya to Shimabara costs ¥1330). Unzen Jigoku is not accessible by rail. Buses to Unzen (90 mins; ¥1300 one-way) leave from the bus terminal directly opposite Isahaya station.

For the last ten minutes of the journey to Nagasaki the train goes at full speed and there's one long tunnel about five minutes before arrival.

Urakami (152km) When it first opened in 1897, Urakami was Nagasaki station. But the growth of the downtown port area and land reclamation meant traffic shifted further away so a decision was made to construct a new Nagasaki station; in 1905 the station's name was changed to Urakami.

The atomic bomb exploded at 11:02am on August 9th 1945 over this district; Urakami is the nearest JR stop to the A-Bomb Museum and Peace Park (see p344).

Nagasaki (154km) [see pp343-50]

HAKATA TO KAGOSHIMA VIA KUMAMOTO
[Map 28, p325 & Map 29, p328; Table 26, p411]

Distances by JR from Hakata. Fastest journey time: 3 hours 45 minutes.

Hakata (0km) [see pp336-43]
From Hakata, the fastest way south to Kagoshima is on the Tsubame LEX, silver trains that speed down the west side of Kyushu. There's a buffet car in one of the carriages, on-board toilets are Western style, luggage racks are in each carriage and seats are airline style (a light above your seat and an individual footrest). The first carriage is the Green Car.

Tosu (29km) A major rail junction as tracks diverge: one line heading west to Nagasaki, the other, the Kagoshima line, continuing south to Kumamoto and Kagoshima. If heading to Nagasaki from Kumamoto or Kagoshima (or vice-versa), there's no need to backtrack all the way to Hakata since you can change trains here. Both Tsubame (for Kumamoto/Kagoshima) and Kamome (for Nagasaki) LEXs make brief stops here.

For information on Tosu and the route from Tosu to Nagasaki, see p325.

Kurume (36km) The area around Kurume is an unattractive mix of factories and industrial plants. Kurume station is the point of interchange for the Kyudai line that cuts across Kyushu (west to east), stopping briefly at the hot spring resort of **Yufuin** before terminating in **Oita**, a city on the east coast (see p330). The Yufu LEX runs three times a day in each direction: Kurume to Yufuin (99 mins); Yufuin to Oita (45 mins).

Omuta (69km) Omuta station is a run-down place but a few minutes out of here the train starts to speed through fields punctuated by villages and small towns as it heads towards the city of Kumamoto.

MAP 29

Kumamoto (118km) [see pp350-5]

Kumamoto is a point of interchange for the scenic Hohi line which runs straight across Kyushu to Oita on the east coast, via Mt Aso. For details of the side trip to Mt Aso, see p334.

Yatsushiro (154km)

The tourist information counter (daily except Wed 8:45am-5pm, closed 12-1pm, Sat 8:45am-12pm only) is at the window next to the JR ticket counter. The staff do not speak English and the only map available is in Japanese. A small number of ¥300 lockers are to the right as you exit the station.

Yatsushiro is home to a small but attractive Japanese garden and tea house called **Shohinken** (daily except Mon, 9am-5pm, ¥300), built in 1688 by the feudal lord of Yatsushiro as a gift to his mother. The garden's not as precious as the ones where you hardly dare walk for fear of untidying them; this one has the feel of having been trampled on for the last few centuries. It's best reached by bus (10 mins) from the station. Check schedules at the tourist information counter.

If you happen to be passing on November 23rd, stop here to take part in the **Myoken Festival**, and look out for the enormous imaginary creature called 'Kida', a cross between a turtle and a snake, which is paraded around the city.

From here, the train skirts Yatsushiro Bay, though it's more muddy rock than sand. On a clear day it would be easy to spot the Amakusa Islands out on the right. The line runs briefly inland before arriving in Minamata.

Minamata (204km)

In 1968, the Tokyo government announced that a chemical company with a factory in Minamata was responsible for illegally dumping mercury waste into Minamata Bay. Although first discovered as far back as 1956, untreated mercury continued to pour into the sea for another decade. Thousands of local residents contracted what became known as Minamata Disease as a result of eat-

> ⛩ **Alternative route back to Hakata**
> Instead of returning to Hakata the same way, it's possible to cut across
> Kyushu via the JR Nippo line (two hours by Kirishima LEX; services leave approx-
> imately every two hours) from Nishi-Kagoshima to Miyazaki (see p333). From
> Miyazaki, follow the route described on pp329-34 in reverse all the way up the east
> coast to Kokura (see p322). You can then take the shinkansen back to Honshu.

ing contaminated fish. As well as a number of fatalities, babies were born with
severe mental and physical handicaps. A compensation agreement was signed
in 1973 with Chisso Co Ltd, which finally admitted responsibility after years of
attempted cover-up. The sludge in Minamata Bay was dealt with by dredging
and through land reclamation (paid for by Kumamoto prefecture not Chisso),
and the water is now some of the cleanest in the prefecture.

Eco Park Minamata is home to the Minamata Disease Museum (daily
except Mon 9am-5pm, free) and Minamata Disease Memorial. In the museum,
headphones provide English translations of the video panels. Buses run from
Minamata station to the Eco Park's main entrance. A tourist information desk
(daily, 9am-5pm, except Sun/Tues am) is at the station. Cycles can be rented at
the station for ¥500 per day.

After Minamata, the Tsubame makes very brief stops (less than a minute
each) at **Izumi (220km)**, **Akune (240km)** and **Sendai (271km)**.

Kushikino (283km) Kushikino has ferry connections with two islands,
Kami-Koshiki and Shimo-Koshiki. There's one final, brief stop at **Ijuin
(300km)** before reaching the Kagoshima terminus.

Nishi-Kagoshima (317km) [see pp355-61]

Nishi-Kagoshima station is the main rail terminal for the city of Kagoshima and
the terminus for limited express trains from Hakata. Kagoshima station is one
stop further along but it's small and you'll probably only pass through it if heading towards Miyazaki on the JR Nippo line (see box above).

KOKURA TO MIYAZAKI [Map 30, p330 and Map 31, p331; Table 27, p411]

Distances by JR from Kokura. Fastest journey time: 5 hours.

Note: Although it's possible to start a journey down the east coast of Kyushu
from Hakata/Fukuoka (see pp336-43), you'll save a lot of time by taking the
shinkansen one stop from Hakata back to Kokura and picking up a limited
express from there.

Kokura (0km) Pick up a Nichirin LEX that runs straight down the east coast.
This train is also known as the 'Red Express' but in truth the journey is anything
but fast. From Kokura it takes just under five hours to Miyazaki. Another limited express, the Sonic, only goes as far as Oita but if you are on the 883 version

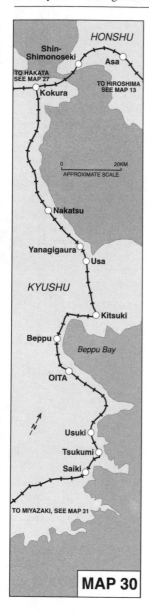

MAP 30

you may like the fact that it has headrests that make you look like Mickey Mouse. Sit on the left side for views of the coast.

Nakatsu (52km) Located on the coast, this is one of a few brief stops that the Nichirin makes on the journey down the eastern side of Kyushu. If you're on the Sonic, the next stop is Beppu. If on the Nichirin, you'll make brief additional stops at **Yanagigaura (69km)**, **Usa (76km)** and **Kitsuki (99km)**.

Beppu (121km) Infamous as one of Japan's most garish hot spring resorts, the classic image of the rustic hot spring is shattered by the view as the train arrives in Beppu. It's a sprawling city and somewhere amongst the mass of concrete buildings lie hot springs that have to be seen to be believed – or simply avoided. Tacky, overly commercial, a tourist trap – all of these apply. But Beppu sweeps away criticism levelled at it with a confident, 'so what?'.

Oita (133km) A 'humanistic city with rich greeneries', according to the town guide given out at the tourist information booth (daily, 9:00am-5:30pm) at the station. Oita can certainly lay claim to being an international city since it's twinned with Austin, Texas (USA), Wuhan in China and Abeiro in Portugal, and was also chosen as a host city for the 2002 Korea-Japan World Cup. The city's **Art Museum** (daily except Mon 10am-5:30pm, price depends on exhibition) is ten minutes by bus from the station and has temporary exhibitions that change throughout the year. Check bus times and the museum schedule at the information booth.

Turn right after the ticket barrier and walk straight to find coin lockers (mostly ¥300 size but a few large ¥600 ones) at the very end of the concourse. For a snack in the station, the *Train D'Or* bakery is infinitely preferable to the fast-food joint *Lotteria*. *Mister Donut* is just outside and to the left as you exit the station.

The main reason for stopping in Oita is to connect up with the JR Hohi line that cuts across Kyushu to Kumamoto via the Mt Aso tableland (see p334). Trains on this line depart from platform 6. Three times a day the Aso LEX runs along this line to **Mt Aso** (98km; 100 mins) before terminating in **Kumamoto** (148km; 2 hours 40 mins). All other services are local and several changes of train are necessary.

Continuing south from Oita, the Nichirin makes brief stops at **Usuki (169km)** and **Tsukumi (179km)**.

Saiki (198km) As you approach Saiki there are good views out to sea on the left side. The views become more spectacular as the train leaves the coast and begins to thread its way inland through the hills. One passenger I met on this train compared the landscape between Saiki and Nobeoka with that of Switzerland.

Nobeoka (256km) There is nothing to see in Nobeoka itself and you may well be disappointed that the verdant landscape enjoyed so far on the journey abruptly disappears as the train pulls in to the station. However, you can transfer here for the mountain railway to Takachiho (see box, p332).

Nobeoka was put on the literary map by Japanese author Soseki Natsume, who mentions the place in his most famous novel, *Botchan*. In the story, Koga, a quiet, well-mannered English teacher, is informed that he is to be transferred to a school in Nobeoka. His colleague, the novel's eponymous hero Botchan, later wonders why: 'It would have been different if he had been going to a fine place, like Tokyo, that had trams and trains. But Nobeoka, in Hyuga province? ... Nobeoka lies deep in the heart of the mountains, beyond range after range ... The very name sounded uncivilized. It made you imagine a place populated half by monkeys and half by men'. But the novel is not all bad press for Nobeoka. Later, at a party to

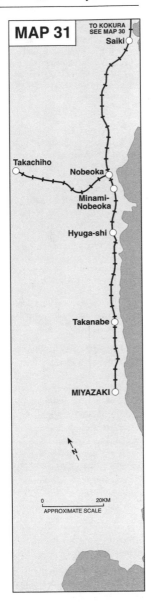

⛩ **Side trip by rail to Takachiho**

The main reason for stopping in Nobeoka is to take a trip on the private **Takachiho Railway** to the mountain town of Takachiho. Considered one of the most scenic mountain railways in Japan, the 80-minute, 50km journey is in a single carriage that winds its way slowly up into the mountains. Services operate 14 times a day in each direction but at irregular times. The first train from Nobeoka is at 6:16am and the last at 8:50pm; the first from Takachiho is at 5:33am and the last at 8:26pm.

Takachiho is known for *yokagura*, ancient dances which re-enact scenes from Japanese mythology. Traditionally, performances of yokagura take place in local people's homes and tend to last from early evening through to the following morning. Plenty of saké keeps everyone awake into the small hours.

Tourists are welcome at these performances, which are organized at the weekend between November and February (call Takachiho Tourist Association on ☎ 0982-73 1213 for times). Alternatively, a truncated one-hour version is performed nightly, at 8pm, year-round at Takachiho Shrine in the centre of town (tickets ¥500 at the shrine).

A high priority is also a visit to **Takachiho Gorge**, formed by the gradual erosion of lava that once flowed from Mt Aso (see p334). You can rent a boat and row around the gorge (daily, 8:30am-5pm; 30 minutes ¥1500). There is no bus from the train station to the gorge – you have to take a bus to the bus centre and then hop on another one. A taxi would be quicker and not too expensive. For information on this and on accommodation contact Takachiho Tourist Association.

To get to the Takachiho railway station in Nobeoka turn right out of the JR station. The one-way fare between Nobeoka and Takachiho is ¥1470.

bid Koga farewell just before he heads off into the unknown, the straightforward and outspoken maths teacher, Hotta, puts the record straight about the place: 'I know that Nobeoka is a remote, out of the way place, and that it may have some material disadvantages compared with here. But I have heard that it is a pastoral spot, where manners and customs are of the simplest and where both teachers and pupils are gentle and well-behaved, like the people of past ages.' (Excerpts from *Botchan*, translated by Alan Turney, Kodansha International, Tokyo, 1972, original text 1906).

To overnight in Nobeoka, *City Hotel Plaza Nobeoka* (☎ 0982-35 8888, 🖹 35-8977; ¥4800/S, ¥10,000/D/Tw) is to the left as you leave the station. Alternatively, a five-minute taxi ride away is the more upmarket *Hotel Merieges Nobeoka* (☎ 0982-32 6060, 🖹 32 6777; ¥7200/S, ¥11,500/D, ¥12,900/Tw). This place has a good Chinese restaurant and a rooftop beer garden (May-September only).

The short journey between Nobeoka and **Minami-Nobeoka (260km)** takes you through a mass of pipes that connect up the Asahi Kasei factories.

Hyuga-shi (277km) Hyuga has a number of beaches popular with local surfers but isn't really worth stopping at. There are, however, great views of the coast from the train.

🎐 Paradise within a paradise

Decades ago, when vacationing Japanese were not the world travellers they are today, Miyazaki was one of the most popular honeymoon spots in the country. As the demand for ever more exotic holidays increased, the number of visitors dwindled and it became the poor man's Hawaii. In a bid to recapture the tourist market, the huge Seagaia Resort (🖥 www.seagaia.co.p/index_e.htm) was built and opened in 1993 along the pine-tree clad Hitotsuba coast north-east of Miyazaki.

The big attraction of the resort is the enormous **Ocean Dome**, an indoor water paradise with an artificial beach at its centre. Body boards can be rented for surfing the artificial waves on the sea. Around this are flumes, roller coasters that dump you in water, ride-the-rapids simulators, whirlpools and water guns. Dubbed a 'paradise within a paradise', Ocean Dome is in the *Guinness Book of Records* as the 'world's largest indoor water park with a retractable roof' – the roof opens in fine weather to take advantage of Miyazaki's mild climate. Though it may seem bizarre to spend the day inside an artificial beach paradise just yards from the real Pacific Ocean, it's hard to find fault with Ocean Dome as a fun day out. One-day tickets cost ¥2500 (12-17 years ¥2000 and 4-11 ¥1400). Some attractions inside the dome are chargeable. The best deal is the 'attraction free' wrist band (¥1200) allowing unlimited use of all the attractions. Viewing tickets (¥600) are available for those who don't want to get their feet wet but this isn't really a place for anyone afraid of water. The dome is open daily from 10am to (at least) 7pm, the hours vary depending on the season. Aside from the dome, other facilities at Seagaia Resort include a zoo, bowling alley, professional golf courses and a tennis club.

The most luxurious place to stay in Miyazaki – indeed, one of the top hotels in Japan – is **Hotel Ocean 45** (☎ 0985-21 1133, 🖹 21 1144; ¥30,000/D/Tw). On the 43rd floor is an observation gallery which affords views of the ocean, coastline and Miyazaki city in the distance. All guest rooms have an ocean view and hotel facilities include any number of restaurants and bars, a cinema and a fully-equipped fitness centre, spa and pool. **Sun Hotel Phoenix** (0985-39 3131, 🖹 38 1147; ¥17,000/Tw) is set amidst the pine forests along the Hitotsuba coast.

Buses run to the Seagaia Resort from outside the west exit of Miyazaki station (25 minutes). A free shuttle bus runs between Ocean Dome, the hotels and all other resort facilities.

The Seagaia Resort sustained massive debt in 2001 but was saved from bankruptcy by a US-based company. Though it was unclear at the time of going to press if and how the facilities would change, it seems likely that Ocean Dome and the resort hotels will continue to operate as normal for the foreseeable future. For up-to-date information check the Seagaia web page.

Takanabe (314km) The line between Hyuga and Takanabe is one of the most rewarding parts of the journey. There are fantastic views of the coastline on the left as the train runs for one stretch just a few metres from the shore.

Miyazaki (340km) 'Welcome to Vitamin Resort Miyazaki' proclaims a sign outside the station. Miyazaki is known for its long hours of sunshine and mild climate, making the city feel very relaxed.

Miyazaki's modern station is small and easy to find your way around. For food, there's a convenience store, *Mister Donut*, *Train d'Or* bakery and *KFC*.

Inside the station, a tourist information counter is open daily, 9am-7pm (☎ 0985-22 6469). A map is available and some staff speak a bit of English.

There's only one local speciality you should not leave Miyazaki without trying and that's **chicken nanban**, pieces of fried chicken served with a sweet and sour sauce. Many restaurants in Miyazaki have chicken nanban on the menu but it's worth going to *Taku-chan*, about a 20-minute walk from Miyazaki station. Grab a seat at the small counter and ask the friendly owners for the 'chicken nanban teishoku' (set meal). To find Taku-chan, head up the main road in front of Miyazaki station (take the west exit) until you reach a major junction, with KFC on one corner. Turn left on to Tachibana-dori and head straight up this road until you see Hotel Big Man on your left. Taku-chan is just past the hotel on the opposite (right) side of the main road, before you reach the bridge which crosses Oyodo-gawa.

To move on from Miyazaki, instead of retracing your steps, it's possible to connect up with the west coast rail route by taking a train along the JR Nippo line to Kagoshima (see box p329) and then following the route (in reverse) from p329.

SIDE TRIP FROM KUMAMOTO OR OITA TO MT ASO   [Map 32]

A trip to the Aso Tableland with its spectacular mountain scenery and the chance to peer over the edge of a volcanic crater makes an excursion to the centre of Kyushu a highlight of any rail journey in Japan. An advantage of this journey is that it can be combined with a tour of both Kyushu's east and west coasts: from Kumamoto on the west side (see p328), follow this route to link up with Oita on the east coast. The following route runs **from Oita to Kumamoto**, so follow in reverse if starting from Kumamoto.

● **From Oita to Aso** Very soon after leaving Oita on the JR Hohi line (also known as the Aso Kogen line) the train starts a gradual climb into the mountains and forest scenery takes over. As the train chugs down the single-track line there are long stretches where the train passes small clusters of houses separated by fields and mountains. Heading towards Aso station, the craters that make up the Aso range should be visible in the distance.

● **Mt Aso (98km from Oita/50km from Kumamoto)** Mt Aso refers not to one particular mountain, but to the whole caldera area and all five of its peaks, called Nakadake, Takadake, Nekodake, Kijimadake and Eboshidake. All of these are contained within the enormous outer crater that is the Aso tableland. The most accessible and impressive is Nakadake, the only active volcano, reached by a combination of bus and ropeway. If weather conditions allow, you can peer over the edge of this volcanic crater and see the bubbling green liquid below. The last big eruption at Nakadake was in 1979, when a sudden explosion killed three and injured eleven. The ropeway to the crater is often closed because of sulphur gas, and sometimes when it is too foggy.

Aso station is the gateway to Aso National Park. The train only makes a very brief stop here, so be ready to jump off as soon as the doors open. After

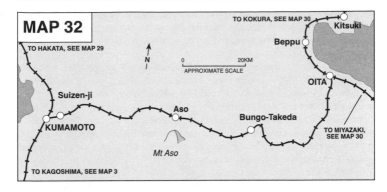

passing the ticket barrier, turn right for the tourist information desk (☎ 0967-34 0751, 🖳 aso-info@aso.ne.jp, daily except Wed 9am-5pm). The staff speak English and will help book accommodation. You can also store luggage here (9am-6pm, ¥300 per bag) if it won't fit into a coin locker. From the station, seven buses a day run up to Nakadake, taking 40 minutes to reach Asosan-nishi station (¥570). From Asosan-nishi, a ropeway (daily, 9am-5pm, every 8 mins, ¥410) completes the journey to the crater. Timetables are available from the information counter inside the station.

The ropeway deposits you just beneath the crater. It's an extraordinary experience to stand at the edge of the crater. Concrete bunkers have been built in the event of a sudden eruption and experts suggest that at the first sign of danger it's best to run backwards, looking at the crater, so as to dodge pieces of volcanic debris.

If the weather is not cooperative, **Aso Volcano Museum** (daily 9am-5pm, ¥840) displays footage of major eruptions and has real-time cameras for a close up of the crater without having to peer over the edge yourself. The museum is on the way to Asosan-nishi ropeway and the bus stops in front of it.

Aso Youth Hostel (☎ 0967-34 0804) offers the best budget accommodation in town – ¥3650 with meals or ¥2450 without. The manager has supplies of hiking route maps. Take the bus from the station bound for Asosan-nishi station; the hostel is the first stop along the route. Check-in is from 4 to 8pm and the front door is closed at 8pm. Right in front of Aso station is ***Kokumin Shukusha Nakamura*** (☎ 0967-34 0317), a small inn which charges ¥6800 with meals and ¥4500 without. The place boasts its own hot spring right next door, called Yumenoyu (daily, 10am-9:30pm), which is open to the public.

For a hearty meal, you can't beat ***Sanzoku Tabiji*** (daily except Wed, 11am-7:30pm). The set menus are huge and include mountain vegetables and wild potatoes. The staff do not speak English but are friendly. Head up the road from Aso station until you reach Route 57. Turn right on to this main road and the restaurant is a 10- to 15-minute walk along the road on the left.

● **From Aso to Kumamoto** It's just under one hour along the Hohi line towards Kumamoto; for the first half the train passes through the Aso valley and its rice fields. In the distance, the craters remain in view for a while after the train leaves Aso station.

The **Aso Boy Steam Locomotive** (SL) runs once a day between Kumamoto and Miyaji, via Mt Aso, most weekends between March and November (daily departures during Golden Week and August). Booking ahead is essential; all seats are reserved. The SL fare between Aso and Kumamoto is ¥1880. Rail-pass holders can travel for free but must reserve a seat on the train by going to the JR ticket office at either Oita or Kumamoto station. Rail passes are not accepted for seat reservations on the Aso Boy at Aso station; if you wait until arriving in Aso you'll have to pay the standard fare.

Kyushu – city guides

FUKUOKA (HAKATA)

Fukuoka, literally 'happy hills', was one of the first parts of Japan to come into contact with foreign culture, due to its proximity to the Asian mainland. The city's JR station is called Hakata not Fukuoka, a confusion of names that dates back to the time when the city was divided into the merchants' district (Hakata) and the old castle town (Fukuoka).

At the weekend, people flock here from all over Kyushu (and increasingly from further afield as well) to take advantage of Fukuoka's abundant shopping and entertainment facilities. There are a good few cultural sights as well, making a stopover in Fukuoka an excellent introduction to the rest of the island.

What to see and do

If you only have time for one sight, make it the **Fukuoka City Museum** (daily except Mon 9:30am-5:30pm, ¥200). The museum traces the history of Fukuoka, right back to the Yayoi period when the introduction of rice farming led to sporadic fights between villages and the beginning of the age of warfare. The star exhibit is the gold seal of a Chinese Emperor, discovered on nearby Shikanoshima Island in 1784. Exhibits examine how and why Fukuoka has always been at the forefront of international exchange in Asia. The number of rusty daggers, spears and swords on display is visual proof that 'international exchange' has not always been harmonious.

Fukuoka's rapid modernization after the Meiji Restoration is also covered. This was the time when streets were paved, ¥1 taxis hit the streets, waterworks were built to improve sanitation and French-style cafés became the place for intellectuals to meet and discuss issues of the day. A typical café has been reconstructed, inside which you can see footage of what the city looked like at the turn of the century, before much of it was reduced to rubble in a 1945 American air raid.

⛩ **Fukuoka – shopping paradise**
Fukuoka is Kyushu's shopping capital and **Tenjin** (accessible by subway
from Hakata) marks its centre. Wander just a little bit from here and you might find
yourself in trendy **Daimyo**, a chic enclave of local stores and designer-label shops
just west of Tenjin where you'd be lucky to find anyone over 30. Daimyo is an area
of narrow streets filled with an eclectic mix of shops selling everything from snow-
boards to fashion haircuts. You'll know you've stumbled into Daimyo when you
find stores with names like 'Garageland Seventies' and 'Modernize' – retro past
meets the future.

   Set away from all this is **Canal City**, a futuristic city within a city of shops,
restaurants, food courts, thrill rides and a 13-screen cinema. Finally, there's **Hawks
Town**, next to Fukuoka Dome where you'll find more shops as well as a United
Cinemas multiplex and the 'Wonder Park' which contains bowling alleys, karaoke
boxes and arcade games.

There are bilingual signs on exhibits and headphones can be rented (free; bring
passport) for an English commentary. To reach the museum, take bus No 306
from the bus terminal outside Hakata station to 'Hakubutsukan kitaguchi'
(¥220). This bus goes via Fukuoka Dome, Hawks Town and terminates outside
Fukuoka Tower (see below for details of all these attractions).

Fukuoka City Museum is in an area called Momochi, built on recently
reclaimed land. Also in this area is **Fukuoka Dome**, opened in 1993 as a home
for the Daiei Hawks, the city's professional baseball team. Backstage tours of
the dome (which boasts the world's first retractable roof) and its locker rooms
and practice areas operate daily except when the stadium is in use (¥1000,
hourly 9am-4pm). Though the dome is impressive, the tour is probably only of
interest to die-hard baseball fans. Take bus No 306 from Hakata station and get
off at the dome. Go up the stairs and walk around the building until you reach
the Information Center between gates 7 and 8. Next to the dome is **Hawks
Town**, a shopping and entertainment complex (see box above). The skyscraper
beyond the dome is the 234m-high **Fukuoka Tower** (daily, 9:30am-9/10pm,
¥800) which has a 123m-high observation deck open to the public.

Ohori Koen is popular with joggers and skateboarders. As well as a boat-
ing lake the park is home to **Fukuoka Art Museum** (daily except Mon 9:30am-
5:30pm, Jul/Aug until 7:30pm, ¥200). The museum contains two floors of
Western and Japanese art; on display are works by Salvador Dali and Andy
Warhol. Next to the museum is a small **Japanese garden** (daily except Mon
9am-5pm, ¥240), a pleasant place to stroll and avoid the joggers in the main
park. Go by subway to Ohorikoen and take exit No 6.

Fukuoka Asian Art Museum (daily except Wed 10am-8pm, ¥200) is a
modern gallery on the seventh floor of the Hakata Riverain complex. Artists in
residence from across Asia display their own works and there is also a small
permanent collection of contemporary Asian art. Take the subway to Nakasu-
Kawabata.

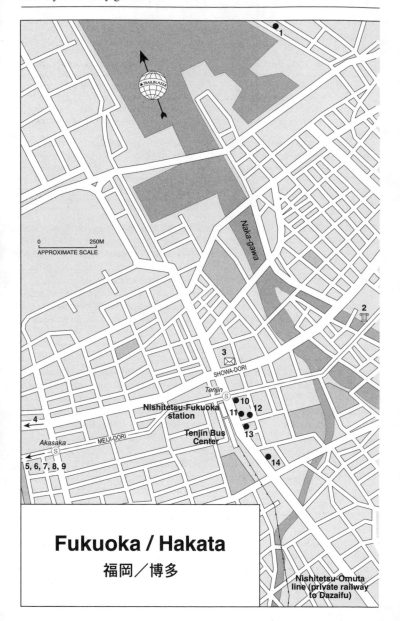

Fukuoka / Hakata

福岡／博多

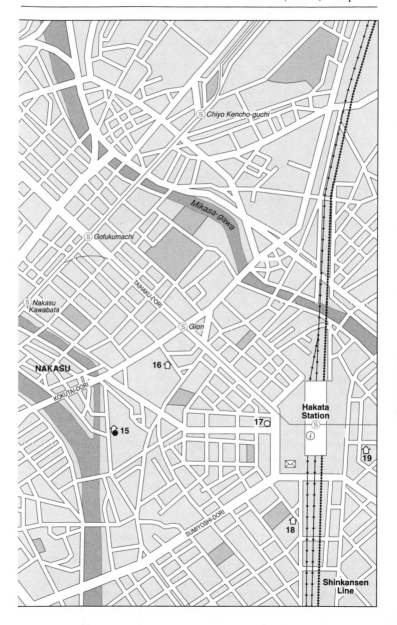

Ⓢ Chiyo Kencho-guchi

Mikasa-gawa

Ⓢ Gofukumachi

TAIHAKU-DORI

Ⓢ Nakasu Kawabata

Ⓢ Gion

NAKASU

16 ⌂

KOKUTAI-DORI

● 15

17 ○

Hakata Station

Ⓢ

ⓘ

⌂ 19

✉

SUMIYOSHI-DORI

⌂ 18

Shinkansen Line

FUKUOKA / HAKATA 福岡/博多

Where to stay
4 Hyper Hotel Akasaka   4 ハイパーホテル赤坂
15 Grand Hyatt Fukuoka   15 グランド ハイアット 福岡
16 Hotel Skycourt Hakata   16 ホテルスカイコート博多
18 Super Hotel Hakata Eki-mae   18 スーパーホテル博多駅前
19 Hotel Blossom   19 ホテル ブラッサム

Where to eat
17 Ichiran   17 一蘭

Other
1 International Ferry Terminal   1 博多港国際ターミナル
2 Fukuoka Asian Art Museum   2 福岡アジア美術館/
  (in Hakata Riverain)   博多リバーレイン
3 Central Post Office   3 中央郵便局
5 Ohori Park   5 大濠公園
6 Fukuoka Art Museum   6 福岡市美術館
7 Fukuoka Dome   7 福岡ドーム
8 Fukuoka Tower   8 福岡タワー
9 Fukuoka City Museum   9 福岡市博物館
10 Fukuoka Building   10 福岡ビル
11 Tenjin Core   11 天神コア
12 Vivre   12 天神ビブレ
13 IMS Building   13 イムズビル
14 Daimaru Department Store   14 大丸
15 Canal City   15 キャナルシティ

As an alternative to traipsing around the city sights, **a short excursion** that combines train and boat can be made from Hakata station. Take a local train on the JR Kagoshima line three stops to Kashii (11 mins). Change on to a local train on the JR Kashii line and go to the terminus at Saitozaki (20 mins). This is a pleasant ride out along a narrow peninsula but the best part is the boat journey from the ferry terminal at Saitozaki back to Hakata Port (¥430 one-way). On this short ride, there are great views of the Hakata skyline and bay area – Fukuoka Dome and Tower (see p337) are two major landmarks to look out for. The boat ride is also a superb way of getting another perspective on the city.

PRACTICAL INFORMATION
Station guide

Hakata station has two main exits: Hakata gate is the main exit for the city, while Chikushi gate (the shinkansen side) is the exit for Hotel Blossom (see p342). The main bus terminal is on the right as you exit the Hakata gate. There are plenty of coin lockers (all sizes) around the station. There are also separate entrances for the shinkansen (second floor) and the ordinary lines (ground floor concourse level).

A branch of *Mister Donut* and a *Train d'Or* bakery are on the main concourse level. One floor below, between the station and the subway, is the 'food market', full of cheap restaurants ranging from Western-style family restaurants, to fast food and okonmiyaki.

Don't confuse JR Hakata station with the private Nishitetsu Railway's Fukuoka station. Nishitetsu Fukuoka station is in Tenjin, the main shopping district (see p337).

Tourist information

The tourist information counter (☎ 092-431 3003, daily 9am-7pm) at the station is tucked away on the Hakata side (look for a small radio studio above it). It's not the greatest tourist facility in Japan as you're not guaranteed to find a member of staff who speaks English and they can't book accommodation, but along the same counter is a hotel reservation desk open until 8pm (same-day reservations only) and next to that a JR information desk.

Far more useful is **Rainbow Plaza** (☎ 092-733 2220, open daily except 3rd Tues 10am-8pm), on the eighth floor of the IMS Building in Tenjin. To reach the IMS building, ride the subway to Tenjin and take exit No 13. Here you'll find English-speaking staff, information on places throughout Kyushu and the rest of Japan, satellite TV, foreign newspapers, magazines and a notice board. Next to Rainbow Plaza is a small Magazine Club where you can sit and browse various foreign-language magazines free of charge.

The staff at Rainbow Plaza produce the monthly *Rainbow* newsletter with cinema listings, details of special events and festivals. *Fukuoka Now!* is a free monthly booklet with reviews of new pubs, clubs, restaurants and shops. If you're planning a night out in the city, or some serious shopping, it's definitely worth a look. *Fukuoka on Foot* is a very well-researched booklet of city walking tours. Pick this up either from the tourist information counter or at Rainbow Plaza.

Pick up the **Fukuoka Welcome Card** (see p46) from the tourist information counter at Hakata station or from Rainbow Plaza.

Getting around

Buses within Fukuoka city are operated by Nishitetsu Bus; the fare between Hakata station and Tenjin is ¥100. **Subway** fares are either ¥200 or ¥250. If unsure, buy a ¥200 ticket and use the 'fare adjustment' machine when you arrive at your destination station. A one-day subway pass is ¥850 and gives discounts on some attractions. Fukuoka's subway stations have good facilities for disabled, with lifts at nearly every station from the platforms to the concourse.

Fukuoka Airport has two domestic terminals and an international terminal serving a number of destinations in Asia (the international departure tax is ¥900 for adults and ¥450 children). The airport is connected to the city by subway – it's two stops to Hakata station (¥250). Free shuttle buses operate between the domestic and international terminals.

The **International Ferry Terminal** at Hakata Port has daily services to Pusan in South Korea. JR Kyushu (☎ 092-281 2315, 🖳 www.bcctlc.jrkyushu.co.jp) operates a high-speed jetfoil, the *Beetle II*, which zips between Hakata and Pusan in 2 hours 55 minutes (¥13,000 one-way or ¥24,000 return); online booking, up to three months in advance, is possible. Rail passes are not accepted (the point is to encourage travel around Japan, not let you flee to Korea at JR's expense).

Alternatively, Camelia Line (☎ 092-262 2323) operates an overnight passenger ferry to Pusan. The cheapest option is the common tatami area (¥9000 one-way or ¥17,100 return). From Hakata station, take bus No 11 or 19 for the port.

Internet

Surfing the net and checking email can be done at any branch of Kinko's (¥200 for 10 mins) in the city. Rainbow Plaza has a list of locations.

Money

Foreign-issued Visa cards can be used at several ATMs in the city – a list is available at Rainbow Plaza. The nearest to the station is on the first floor of Hotel Centraza

Hakata, on the left as you exit the Chikushi side of the station.

Festivals

The biggest annual event is **Hakata Gion Yamakasa** (July 1st-15th), the climax of which is a float race through the city; seven teams carry their respective floats a distance of 5km. The biggest sporting event is the **Kyushu Grand Sumo Basho**, the last tournament of the annual sumo calendar (see p39). It takes place in November at Fukuoka Kokusai Center.

Where to stay

Fukuoka has some world-class hotels at prices that would be impossible to find in Tokyo, as well as some cheap but clean business hotels.

Top of the range is *Grand Hyatt Fukuoka* (☎ 092-282 1234, 🖹 282 2817, 🖳 www.hyatt.com), in Canal City; it's *the* place to stay in Fukuoka if you can afford it. Large bathrooms feature a bath you can definitely sink into and separate shower – and a small TV screen you can watch while soaking in the tub. Hotel facilities include a gymnasium, swimming pool and saunas. Standard room rates start at ¥19,000 for a double, but ask about special offers or promotional packages.

Rail-pass holders receive a 10% discount on room rates at the JR-operated *Hotel Blossom* (☎ 092-413 8787, 🖹 413 9746, 🖳 fukuoka@jrk-hotels.com) where the cheapest singles are ¥7500 and twins are ¥12,800. Features include non-smoking rooms and a 'ladies floor' with pot pourri in the bathroom and pyjamas instead of the usual yukata. It's very convenient for Hakata station, since the hotel is only a three-minute walk from the Chikushi Gate exit. Go straight up the main road from the exit and it's just past Hotel New Miyako.

Super Hotel Hakata Eki-Mae (☎ 092-474 9000, 🖹 474 9050) is also close to the station but only has single rooms (¥4800 per night including a simple breakfast). Cash only, here, as it's an automated check-in. For proximity to Tenjin, a good budget option is *Hyper Hotel Akasaka* (☎ 092-732

0900, 🖹 732 0909; 🖳 akasaka@hyper-hotel.co.jp), an apartment-style hotel where rooms have mini kitchen units and small attached bath. Single rate is ¥4800 per night including simple breakfast. Add ¥1000 for another person sharing the same room and ¥2000 extra for three sharing. Take the subway to Akasaka. An alternative is *Hotel Skycourt Hakata* (☎ 092-262 4400, 🖹 262 8111) which offers reduced rates to YH/HI members – the standard ¥6500 for a single room is reduced to ¥4500. Take the subway one stop to Gion (exit 3).

Where to eat

Hakata is associated with ramen. There are plenty of places around the station that serve up cheap bowls of the stringy yellow noodles but one popular place is *Ichiran* (daily, 10am-10pm) on basement level 2 of the black building opposite Hakata station (take the Hakata gate), next to the large red-brick building that houses Fukuoka City Bank. It's hidden away in a corner, so look out for the hanging red curtain with 'Ichiran' in black kanji. Buy a ticket (¥650) from the vending machine and take a seat. You'll then be given a sheet to fill out (ask for the English version), specifying exactly how spicy, how much garlic and what kind of vegetables you want in your ramen. There are branches of Ichiran in other parts of Fukuoka – look out for one in the basement of **Canal City.**

The big shopping and entertainment complexes are also good places to look for food. Canal City has a good selection of other restaurants, including *Asian Kitchen* on the fourth floor, where people queue in long lines at the weekend. The main eating area is on the basement level, where you'll find the Grand Hyatt's *Food Live* court, packed with eateries. *Starbucks* has recently opened a branch in Canal City.

If you're shopping in Tenjin, the basement of Daimaru department store has a good selection of food to take out. On the ground floor of Tenjin Vivre department store is *Seattle's Best Coffee*, which serves Italian soda, organic juices and a range of sandwiches and cakes, in addition to great coffee. Floors 12-13 of the IMS building are designated the 'Party Court' with various restaurants including a *Sizzler* steak house on the 13th. The restaurant has rather bland décor and lacks atmosphere but you can't fault its large salad bar and lunch-time deal of ¥850 for one trip to each of the bars, salad, soup and dessert.

Side trip by rail from Fukuoka

Dazaifu (see p325), once the political heart of Kyushu and the town where the god of learning and literature is enshrined, is an easy day trip from Fukuoka but can equally well be visited en route to Nagasaki, Kumamoto or Kagoshima. From Fukuoka, the most direct way is to take the private Nishitetsu-Omuta line (¥390, rail passes not accepted) from Fukuoka station in Tenjin. The entrance to the station is in the large Mitsukoshi department store. Some trains run direct to Dazaifu, though you may have to change at Futsukaichi.

NAGASAKI

'I cannot think of a more beautiful place. There is a land locked harbour; at the entrance are islands…the ship winds up the harbour which is more like a very broad river, with hills on either side levelling down towards the extreme end where the town of Nagasaki stands.'

So wrote Elizabeth Alt, wife of William Alt, a 19th-century English merchant who lived and traded in Nagasaki. Nagasaki's history as a centre of international trade and its long period of contact with the West are still the reasons why tourists pour into the city, but it was the dropping of the second atomic bomb here on August 9th 1945 that ensured Nagasaki would become known throughout the world. More people were killed in this one blast than in all the bombing raids on Britain throughout WWII. Like Hiroshima (see p230), Nagasaki is now home to a Peace Park and A-Bomb Museum, both of which record huge numbers of visitors every year.

For sightseeing purposes, it's useful to consider Nagasaki as a city of two halves. North of the station, in the **Urakami district**, is the Atomic Bomb Museum and Peace Park. Down in the south, on the hills overlooking the harbour, is **Glover Garden**, full of 19th-century Western-style homes. One day would be just enough to visit both parts but it's preferable to allow a couple of days to do everything at a more relaxed pace and also include a tour of the central area including newly-restored **Dejima**, the island enclave which was the only point of contact with the outside world during Japan's period of national seclusion (1641-1859).

What to see and do

A good start to a tour of Nagasaki would be to take **Mt Inasa Ropeway** (daily 9am-10pm Mar-Nov, 9am-9pm Dec-Feb, ¥700 one-way, ¥1200 return) for a panoramic view of the city. The best time to go is at night when the city is lit up – take a wide-angle lens with you. Look back over the dark hills for a strange and slightly eerie contrast to the bright lights that dazzle below. Take Nagasaki Bus No 3 or 4 from the station and get off at 'Ropeway-mae', or take tram No 1 or 3 two stops north from the station to Takara-machi. From here, follow the main road underneath the railway line and over Urakami-gawa. Cross the river, turn right and follow the road round until you see a shrine entrance on your left. Walk through the entrance gate and turn left to find the entrance to the ropeway.

● **Urakami district** The atomic bomb dropped on Nagasaki at 11:02am on August 9th 1945 was meant for the city of Kokura (see p322). Poor visibility meant the plane carrying the bomb circled three times over Kokura before changing course for Nagasaki, where cloud also hampered visibility. A chance break in the clouds just after 11 o'clock sealed the city's destiny. It's estimated that over 70,000 (of a 240,000 population) were killed either instantly or in the period up to the end of 1945.

The bomb was intended for Nagasaki Shipyard, but exploded instead over Urakami, a centre of Christian missionary work in Nagasaki since the latter half of the 16th century. As the bomb was dropped, a service was underway at Urakami Cathedral – all that's left today is a melted rosary on display in the A-Bomb Museum and one piece of the cathedral wall in the nearby Hypocenter Park. Today, Urakami is home to the Peace Park and Atomic Bomb Museum.

Nagasaki Atomic Bomb Museum (daily, 8:30am-5pm, ¥200) is a high priority, though the constant stream of school groups through the museum can be waring. What you want most is the chance to walk around quietly on your own – and that's the one luxury you're nearly always denied here. Passing through into the first hall, the scene immediately transforms to the precise moment that the bomb was dropped – a clock ticks and black and white images of the devastation appear on screens. As with the Peace Memorial Museum in Hiroshima (see p230), the most memorable exhibits are individual objects, such as the glass bottles melted together from the heat of the blast and the burnt-out remains of a schoolgirl's lunchbox. Directly down the hill from the museum, and next to the main street, is the **Hypocenter Park**, marking the precise spot over which the A-bomb exploded.

The nearby **Peace Park** is filled with statues and memorials given to the city as a gesture of peace from all over the world – many are from former Eastern bloc countries. The centrepiece of the park is a giant Peace Statue, erected ten years after the bombing and now the backdrop for the annual peace ceremony held on August 9th. Throughout the year, visiting school parties hold their own peace ceremonies in front of the statue.

The nearest tram stop for the Peace Park and Atomic Bomb Museum is Matsuyama-machi, eight stops north of Nagasaki station on tram No 1 or 3.

● **Near Nagasaki station** Nagasaki's importance as a historical centre for Christianity in Japan is most obviously seen at Oura Catholic Church below Glover Garden (see opposite) and at the **Site of the 26 Christian Martyrs** in Nishizaka-machi, a memorial to six Spanish missionaries and 20 Japanese Christians who were crucified here in 1597. It's a very simple memorial, a few minutes' walk east from the station, heading up the road to Nishizaka.

Very much off the tourist trail is the **Oka Masaharu Memorial Peace Museum** (9-4 Nishizaka-machi, daily except Mon 9am-5pm, ¥200). This peace museum focuses on Japan's actions before and during WWII in Korea, China, and Southeast Asia. It's not an easy place to visit, some of the photos are shocking, but it provides a very different historical perspective to that offered at the 'official' A-Bomb Museum. The museum was founded in memory of the late Protestant Minister and peace activist, Oka Masaharu (1918-94), who devoted much of his life to relief efforts for Korean atomic bomb survivors in Japan. Signs are in Japanese and Korean but there's a pamphlet with some explanations in English; the photos that line the walls tell their own story. The museum receives few visitors and is not included in any of the tourist guides or brochures produced by the city. It's a little hard to find but follow the same road up to Nishizaka from the station as for the 'Site of the 26 Christian Martyrs'. The museum is just past this memorial.

● **Nagasaki Harbour area** **Glover Garden** (daily, 8am-6pm, ¥600), an area of Western-style houses built on a hill overlooking Nagasaki harbour, is usually swamped with visitors. The harbour views from the hillside repay the ticket cost, even if the houses are not overly exciting for Western visitors.

Best known of all the 19th-century residents was the man whom the garden is named after, Thomas Glover. Born in Scotland in 1838, Glover moved to Nagasaki in 1859, married a Japanese woman and involved himself in a number of key Japanese businesses, helping to set up the Japan Brewery Company in July 1885, predecessor to today's Kirin Brewery. Look out for the *kirin*, a mythical creature that sports a bushy moustache remarkably similar to Thomas Glover's, on cans and bottles of Kirin beer. Since the area was populated by merchants, it's appropriate that the management of Glover Garden has kept the financial spirit of Glover et al alive by bottling and selling off the gimmicky 'Thomas Blake Glover lager beer' at ¥500 a piece.

On the way up to the Glover Garden entrance, look out for **Oura Catholic Church** (March-Nov 8am-6pm, Dec-Feb 8:30am-5pm, ¥250), built by French missionaries in 1864 and the oldest church in Japan.

⛩ **Japan's first railway?**
   Though most history books conclude that the first railway line in Japan was built between Shimbashi and Yokohama, the estate of Thomas Glover begs to differ. In a corner of Glover's House a sign reveals that in 1865 the Scotsman purchased the 'Iron Duke', claimed to be Japan's first steam locomotive, and laid a 400m-long track in Nagasaki. He used Japanese coal to power the engine and opened the line up to an astonished public. It was not until 1872, seven years after the opening of this mini railway, that the Shimbashi–Yokohama line opened for business (see p66).

   An account of Thomas Glover's life can be found in Alexander McKay's *Scottish Samurai* (Edinburgh, Canongate Press, 1997).

To reach Glover Garden, take tram No 1 (bound for Shokakuji-shita) from Nagasaki station and change at Tsukimachi. From here, change on to tram No 5 and ride all the way to the terminus at Ishibashi.

Dejima From 1641 to 1859, the island of Dejima, just off Nagasaki, was Japan's sole point of contact with the outside world as the base for trade with the Dutch East India Company. A reconstruction of the Dutch enclave on Dejima (daily, 9am-5pm, ¥300) opened in 2000 to mark the 400th anniversary of relations between Japan and the Netherlands. Here you'll find replica 19th-century buildings and an excellent museum recounting the story of the Dutch traders who were forced to live in isolation on the island.

The reconstruction will not be complete until 2010; the plan is to recreate Dejima's traditional fan-shape, surrounded by water on all sides. Five of the scheduled twenty five buildings are already open to the public, some of which display objects found during ongoing excavation work. The obligatory gift shop is there too, selling Dutch chocolate and cookies. Take tram No 1 three stops south from Nagasaki station to Dejima, which drops you right outside the reconstructed complex.

NAGASAKI 長崎

Where to stay
1	Hotel Ship Victoria	ホテルシップ ヴィクトリア
9	Holiday Inn Nagasaki	ホリデーイン長崎
10	The Hamilton Nagasaki	ザ ハミルトン長崎
15	Nagasaki Youth Hostel	長崎 ユースホステル
16	JR Kyushu Hotel Nagasaki AMU Plaza	JR 九州 ホテル 長崎/ アミュプラザ
21	Minshuku Tanpopo	民宿たんぽぽ

Where to eat
6	Tia/Dejima Wharf	テイア/出島 ワーフ
11	Hamakatsu	浜勝
12	Coffee and Antique Nanbanjaya	南蛮茶屋
13	Bistro Pied de Porc	ビストロ ピエ ド ポー

Other
2	Glover Garden	グラバー園
3	Oura Catholic Church	大浦天主堂
4	Koshibyo	孔子廟
5	Dutch Slope	オランダ坂
7	You Me Saito Shopping Centre	夢彩都
8	Dejima	出島
14	Central Post Office	中央郵便局
17	26 Christian Martyrs Monument	日本２６聖人殉教地
18	Oka Masaharu Memorial Peace Museum	岡まさはる記念長崎平和資料館
19	Nagasaki Atomic Bomb Museum	長崎原爆資料館
20	Peace Park	平和公園

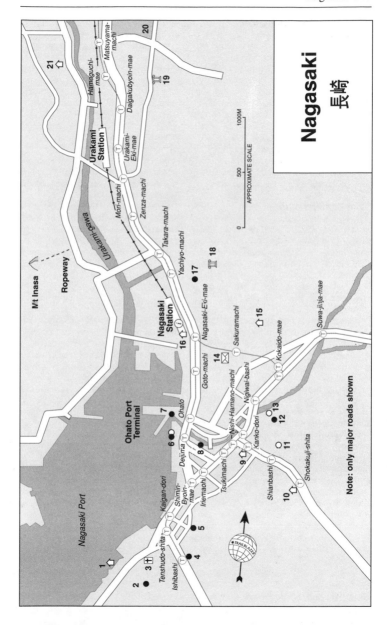

Nagasaki 長崎

APPROXIMATE SCALE

0   500   1000M

Note: only major roads shown

Mt Inasa

Ropeway

Urakami-gawa

Nagasaki Port

Ohato Port Terminal

Urakami Station

Nagasaki Station

Hamaguchi-mae

Matsuyama-machi

Daigakubyoin-mae

Urakami-Eki-mae

Mori-machi

Zenza-machi

Takara-machi

Yachiyo-machi

Nagasaki-Eki-mae

Sakuramachi

Kokaido-mae

Suwa-jinja-mae

Goto-machi

Nishi-Hamano-machi

Ngiwai-bashi

Kanko-dori

Shokakuji-shita

Shianbashi

Tsukimachi

Iriemachi

Dejima

Shimin-Byoin-mae

Kaigan-dori

Tenshudo-shita

Ishibashi

Ohato

20

21

19

18

17

16

15

14

13

12

11

10

9

8

7

6

5

4

3

2

1

PRACTICAL INFORMATION
Station guide
Nagasaki station was completely rebuilt in 2000 and now incorporates a hotel, department store and plaza under a giant canopy with a dragon suspended from the roof.

There is only one central exit, on the same level as the platforms. Turn left after the ticket barrier, skirt around the travel agency and follow the station building round to the main coin locker area.

In front of you as you leave the platforms is AMU Plaza department store. On the fourth floor is a United Cinemas multiplex and the fifth floor has restaurants.

Tourist information
As you exit the ticket barrier, **Nagasaki City TIC** (095-823 3631, daily 8am-7pm Mar-Nov, 8am-5:30pm Nov-Feb) is on your right and has maps and hotel information. Pick up a useful guide to the city tram network.

For more detailed information, **Nagasaki Prefectural Tourist Federation** (☎ 095-826 9407, daily except Sun 9am-5:30pm) is on the second floor of the Kenei Bus Center across the main road from the station. Use the overhead walkway to reach it. *The Nagasaki Beat*, a monthly newsletter with event listings, is available here.

Getting around
Nagasaki is known for its *chin chin densha*, old-fashioned trams that have been trundling around the city since 1915, and which are by far the best means of getting around.

One-day tram passes (¥500) are available from tourist offices and some hotels but not on board the trams themselves. Individual rides cost ¥100, regardless of the length of journey, so work out how many trips you're likely to make in one day before purchasing the pass.

Less useful but also available from the tourist offices are one-day bus passes (¥500).

The shuttle bus to Nagasaki Airport (domestic flights only) takes 60 minutes and costs ¥1200 from Nagasaki station.

Money
Foreign-issued Visa cards can be used for cash advances at the Saison Cash Dispenser, on the second floor of AMU Plaza department store at Nagasaki station. Don't go into the store but take the outside escalator that leads up to the Royal Host restaurant. The ATM corner is next to the restaurant.

Where to stay
JR Kyushu Hotel Nagasaki (☎ 095-832 8000, ≣ 832 8001, ⌨ nagasaki@jrk-hotels.com; ¥6000/S, ¥11,000/Tw) opened in 2000 as part of the new Nagasaki station. Rooms are good value.

Holiday Inn Nagasaki (☎ 095-828 1234, ≣ 828 0178, ⌨ holidayinn@holidayinn-nagasaki.co.jp; ¥8500/S, ¥15,000/D, ¥16,000/Tw) makes an excellent base for exploring the city. From the station, take tram No 1 and get off at Kanko-dori, right by the entrance to the Holiday Inn. *The Hamilton Nagasaki* (☎ 095-824 1000, ≣ 827 8111, ⌨ nagasaki@the-hamilton.co.jp; ¥9500/S, ¥18,000/Tw) is a smaller hotel further along the same road as the Holiday Inn. Its theme is yesteryear Britain. Beds are wide and the rooms are a generous size.

If you prefer to be based closer to the Peace Park, *Minshuku Tanpopo* (21-7 Hoeicho, ☎ 095-861 6230, ≣ 864 0032) is a good choice. Tatami rooms with communal bath cost ¥4000 for one, ¥7000 for two or ¥10,500 for three people. It's close to Matsuyama tram stop but if you call in advance and arrive at Urakami station (last stop before Nagasaki, see p327) you should be able to arrange a free pick-up.

The best budget option is *Nagasaki Youth Hostel* (1-1-16 Tateyama, ☎ 095-823 5032, ≣ 823 4321), which has bunk bed dorms for ¥3000/pp. The dorms are nothing special, but the bonus is a free breakfast. As this is a public youth hostel, there's no discount for YH/HI members.

Finally, how about a night on board *Hotel Ship Victoria* (☎ 095-822 8888, ≣ 820 4399)? Docked on the waterfront below Glover Gardens, this ferry once ploughed the water between Aomori and the port of Hakodate in Hokkaido before the opening of the Seikan Tunnel (see p282) but has now been turned into an upmarket hotel. A night on board costs ¥20,000 (breakfast included) for the cheapest twin room. You can even get married on board, though the auspices – being literally on a boat to nowhere – are not good.

Where to eat

In the station area, the obvious place to head is the fifth floor 'Gourmet World' of AMU Plaza department store. Here you'll find an Italian, a revolving sushi bar, a Chinese, and a flame-grilled steak restaurant. Popular with Nagasaki residents and visitors alike, **Hamakatsu** (Kajiyama-machi 6-50; daily 11am-10:30pm, last orders 10pm) is the place to eat tonkatsu. Seating is at tables or along the counter – or a take-out box of tonkatsu sandwiches costs ¥650. It's a five-minute walk north of Shianbashi tram station.

For a quiet drink surrounded by antiques, head for **Coffee and Antique Nanbanjaiya** (open daily from around 12 noon-10pm), beyond the Kanko-dori arcade. Mellow music plays in the background in this 160-year-old wooden building. Go to the end of the covered arcade along Kanko-dori, cross the next road, go straight until you reach the convenience store (Daily Store), turn left, and look on the left-hand side for a red lampshade. Next door is the tiny **Bistro Pied de Porc** (daily except Monday 11:45am-1:30pm and 5:30pm-9pm) with lunch courses from ¥1100 and dinner from ¥3800.

Another good area to look for food is the new **Dejima Wharf**, where there is a good selection of Western and Japanese restaurants. It's especially pleasant in the evening, where you can sit and enjoy views of the harbour. If you're hungry, head for the second floor of the wharf complex, where **Tia** has great organic food. Fill up with pasta, soups, tofu, brown rice, salads and wash it all down with herbal tea or lime juice. The all-you-can-eat-and-drink buffet lunch (11:30am-2:30pm) costs ¥1200 or dinner (5:30-8:30pm) is ¥1400.

Side trip to Huis Ten Bosch from Nagasaki

Huis Ten Bosch (🖳 www.huistenbosch.co.jp), the Dutch theme park overlooking Omura Bay north-east of Nagasaki, is one of Kyushu's most popular attractions for vacationing Japanese.

The idea for this bizarre re-creation of tulip fields and windmills in southern Japan came from Yoshikuni Kamichika, who visited Holland in 1979 and decided to build a city in Japan that would combine Dutch city planning with Japanese technology. The aim was to make the site a living, working, eco-friendly city 'to last 1000 years'. What you find is much more of a Disney resort, with hotels, rides and attractions, canals, shops that sell clogs and a cast of real Dutch who dress up in traditional costume and become walking photo opportunities. As one foreign resident in Nagasaki noted, Huis Ten Bosch can hardly be called authentic when the only grass to be had is in the green fields.

Plan to spend a full day at Huis Ten Bosch. A one-day passport allowing unlimited use of most attractions costs ¥4800 (12-17 years ¥3600 and 4-11 years ¥2600). Park operating hours vary according to the season, so check with the website or at the tourist information office in Nagasaki station.

From Nagasaki, take either the Sea Side Liner or (twice a day) the faster Super Express Siebold along the Omura line to JR Huis Ten Bosch (70 mins).

Called a 'European Classical Express with Panoramic Lounges', the Siebold has a monitor in every car showing the view from the front of the train. Alternatively, sit right up at the front in the lounge area where the driver should be (he or she is on top). Combined rail and one-day passport tickets are available from Nagasaki. Direct rail services also run from Hakata station in Fukuoka. The Huis Ten Bosch LEX takes 90 minutes from Hakata.

KUMAMOTO

Halfway down the west side of Kyushu, Kumamoto once flourished as a castle town; today the (reconstructed) castle still rates as the city's biggest tourist draw. Probably Kumamoto's best-known resident was Miyamoto Musashi (1584-1645), an exceptional swordsman who wrote a book during the last years of his life in which he is said to have 'tempered his samurai way of thinking with more serene views of life'. His serenity did not stop him from being buried in full armour, clutching his sword.

Miyamoto probably approved of the 'Kobori swimming technique', an unusual martial art originating in Kumamoto, which according to city publicity involved the 'art of swimming in the standing posture while attired in armour and helmet'.

What to see and do

Right in the centre of the city is **Kumamoto Castle** (daily, Apr-Oct 8:30am-5:30pm, Nov-Mar 8:30am-4:30pm, ¥500). Completed between 1601 and 1607, most of the structures that make up the fortifications were destroyed during the civil war of 1877, so what you see today is largely a 20th-century reconstruction. The castle is still an impressive sight, especially when lit up at night (until 11pm). Inside the donjon are displays on the civil war, the cultural history of the region and a scale model of the original castle. Enquire at the main gate ticket window about free guided tours of the castle in English. To reach the castle from the station, take the tram to 'Kumamotojo-mae' stop.

Flag-waving tour guides lead a constant stream of school parties around Kumamoto's other hot spot, **Suizen-ji Garden** (daily, 7am-6pm, ¥400), stopping briefly for a mass photo call in front of the main point of interest, a grass mound in the shape of Mt Fuji. Since it's much smaller than Kenrokuen in Kanazawa (see p160), it's very hard to enjoy the park in tranquillity.

Also in the grounds are **Izumi Shrine**, built in 1878 and a popular venue for New Year celebrations, and a **Noh theatre** (performances, lit by fire, are staged here during the summer festival, August 11th-13th). It's best to visit Suizen-ji as early as possible to avoid the crowds. Take the tram to 'Suizenji-Koen-mae' stop.

Down a narrow path behind Suizen-ji Garden is the **Former Residence of Mr Leroy Janes** from Philadelphia (USA), who worked as a teacher in Kumamoto from 1871 to 1876. The Western-style building (daily except Mon 9:30am-4:30pm, ¥200) seems ordinary enough today but it's claimed that the house once 'drew thousands of curious visitors who, bringing their lunches, made a day of their outing to the foreign house'. The son of devout Christian parents, Janes arrived in Japan accompanied by his wife Harriet to teach at the Kumamoto School for Western Studies.

The house is now virtually empty but does contain an upbeat account of Janes' achievements during his teaching tenure in Kumamoto. He is credited as being the first person to introduce co-education in Japan by allowing two girls to attend his class. 'When the class started, the male students tried to avoid them by sitting as far away as possible,' signs in the house record, but Janes 'taught them the spirit of chivalry, which was to be kind to ladies, and help weaker people'. From Suizen-ji, take the exit by the replica Mt Fuji, turn right, and follow the narrow path that runs along the back of the park to find the house.

Behind Tsuruya department store in the city centre is the former home of Irish writer **Lafcadio Hearn**. Hearn is better known as a former resident of Matsue (see p237), from where he moved to Kumamoto in 1891. He lived in a house owned by a local samurai family, now in the middle of the downtown shopping area.

The house is very small but it's still worth spending ¥200 (daily except Mon, 9:30am-4:30pm) to go inside, where panels in English tell the story of how Hearn was born on the Greek island of Levkas, lived in Dublin (Ireland), went to school in Durham (UK), travelled to the USA, worked as a reporter on the island of Martinique, and finally arrived in Yokohama in 1890 at the age of 40 on an assignment for *Harpers* magazine.

He spent the rest of his life in Japan, where he lived in Matsue before spending three years in Kumamoto teaching English. Later, Hearn moved to Kobe and in 1896 became a naturalized Japanese citizen. Koizumi Yakumo, as Hearn became known following his naturalization, died suddenly of a heart attack on 26th September 1904.

PRACTICAL INFORMATION
Station guide
Kumamoto station is south-west of the main city centre. On the second floor of the station is Fresta, a collection of shops and a few cheap restaurants, none of which is particularly recommended. On the ground floor is a Train D'Or bakery; just outside you'll find a Mister Donut, Mos Burger, KFC and an udon shop. For coin lockers (all sizes), exit the station and turn left. Also at the station is a branch post office and convenience store.

Tourist information
The tourist information counter (☎ 096-352 3743, daily, 9am-5:30pm) in the station is usually staffed by an English speaker who

can help book accommodation and provide a map.

Even better is the International Lounge, on the second floor of **Kumamoto City International Center** (4-8 Hanabatacho, ☎ 096-359 2121, 9am-8pm Mon-Fri, 9am-7pm Sat-Sun, closed 2nd/4th Sun), which has CNN, Internet terminals (¥50/5 mins), newspapers and magazines. The lounge is air-conditioned and a great place to beat the heat in the summer. While here, pick up a copy of *Yoka!*, a monthly newsletter that contains a calendar of events for Kumamoto prefecture.

Getting around
One-day passes (¥500) allow unlimited travel on the tram and Shiei Buses (mostly

KUMAMOTO 熊本

Where to stay
1 Ark Hotel Kumamoto
8 Suidocho Green Hotel
9 Suizen-ji Youth Hostel
12 Komatsu-so
13 Hotel New Otani Kumamoto

Where to eat
6 Mister Donut
10 Senri

Other
2 Kumamoto Castle
3 Kumamoto City International Center
4 Kumamoto Transportation Center
5 Iwataya Department Store
7 Former Residence of Lafcadio Hearn
10 Suizen-ji Garden
11 Central Post Office

1 アークホテル熊本
8 水道町グリーンホテル
9 水前寺ユースホステル
12 小松荘
13 ホテルニューオータニ熊本

6 ミスタードーナッツ
10 泉里

2 熊本城
3 熊本市国際センター
4 熊本交通センター
5 岩田屋
7 小泉八雲熊本旧居
10 水前寺公園
11 中央郵便局

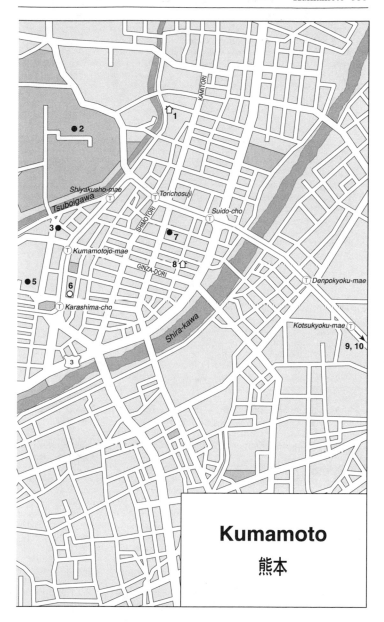

KAMITORI

Shiyakusho-mae

Tsuboigawa

Torichosuji

SHIMOTORI

Suido-cho

Kumamotojo-mae

GINZA-DORI

Denpokyoku-mae

Karashima-cho

Shira-kawa

Kotsukyoku-mae

9, 10

Kumamoto

熊本

⛩ Basashi – an acquired taste

That evening I learned that raw horsemeat was a speciality of the area...I went to a little restaurant near Kumamoto station with my mind made up to try some. It was disappointingly stringy, and having come straight out of the refrigerator, was hard with bits of ice. I sat for a long time sipping beer, waiting for the horsemeat to thaw, while the only customer in the restaurant had a conversation with the owner.   **Alan Booth**, *The Roads to Sata*, Kodansha International, 1985

Kumamoto's big culinary draw doesn't sound the most appetizing of regional specialities; the main problem with basashi (raw horsemeat), however, is not so much the taste but that most places offering it are prohibitively expensive. You could easily spend around ¥10,000 per person by dining at a restaurant specializing in the stuff.

If you decide to try basashi it's best to buy some from a butcher and take it back to your ryokan or minshuku. If you ask, the butcher will prepare it ready to eat and probably include some soy sauce. I got a 'basashi take-out' from a butcher and took it back to the minshuku I was staying in. The owner gave me chopsticks (and more soy sauce), so I ended up trying Kumamoto's speciality at a fraction of the prices charged in basashi restaurants. Also, I did not have to wait for it to thaw and found it tasty and not stringy.

---

green) within the city centre. Passes are available from the tourist information counter at the station, or on board the trams themselves.

One of the trams, called the San Antonio after Kumamoto's sister city in the USA, has an on-board commentary in English and Japanese on the relationship between Kumamoto and San Antonio.

A tourist bus does a loop around town (8:30am-5pm, two an hour, ¥130 flat fare), starting and finishing at the Transportation Center in the city centre, and includes a stop at the castle (see p350).

Internet

Internet access is available at Kumamoto City International Center (see p351).

Money

An ATM at Kumamoto station accepts credit cards issued outside Japan (follow the signs for 'cash dispenser').

Festivals

The biggest annual event is the **Hi-no-Kuni** ('country of fire') festival that takes place on August 11th-13th. Events include a fireworks display and late-night folk dancing.

Where to stay

Room rates in the station area are cheaper than in the centre near Kumamoto Castle and it's really not that much of a hassle to get into town – there are regular buses and trams from the station.

One expensive option outside the station is *Hotel New Otani Kumamoto* (☎ 096-326 1111, 🖷 326 0800; ¥11,000/S, ¥18,000/Tw/D), which has all the facilities you'd expect of this top-class hotel chain.

A five-minute walk from the station is *Komatsu-so* (096-355 2634), a small minshuku that is homely if a bit run down. It's cheap at ¥3500/pp without meals, so at that price you can't really complain about the dust. It's an extra ¥700 for breakfast or add ¥2000 for breakfast and dinner. The owner is very kind and will probably give you tea and rice crackers in the evening.

Get on to the main road in front of the station, turn left and walk past the Hotel New Otani; Komatsu-so is a little further down this road on the left. Look for the

'Welcome' sign. The entrance is up a narrow path.

It's advisable to book ahead at *Suizenji Youth Hostel* (☎ 096-371 9193; ¥2800/YH (HI), ¥3800 non-members) as they don't seem to like unannounced arrivals. There's a 10pm curfew. From the station, take the tram to Misotenjin-mae, turn the first right, go to the end of this road, turn right again, then first left, and you'll see the hostel sign on the left-hand side.

For a cheap hotel bed in the downtown area try *Suidocho Green Hotel* (☎ 096-211 2222, 🖹 211 2278; ¥6300/S). This newish business hotel has clean, compact singles.

Going up in price is the *Ark Hotel Kumamoto* (☎ 096-351 2222, 🖹 326 0909; ¥10,000/S, ¥16,000/Tw/D), with wide beds in fairly spacious rooms. Some twins have the option of a third child bed. It's situated just below the castle.

Where to eat
In the city centre arcades, there's a good selection of informal cafés and restaurants including the usual fast-food places.

If you're visiting Suizen-ji Garden, *Senri* (11am-2:30pm, 5-10pm) has set lunches in private dining rooms starting at ¥2000. Ask for a room with a view on to the park. You can try basashi here (see box opposite) as part of the set lunch.

Dinner courses are more expensive, starting at ¥4500, though you do get to view the park minus the tourists, since the restaurant stays open after the park closes for the day.

On the fourth floor of the International Center is *Miyuki*, a cheap place to grab a coffee or a bite to eat.

Adjacent to the downtown Kumamoto Transportation Center is *Iwataya* department store, which has a good-value restaurant floor.

KAGOSHIMA

Known as the 'Naples of the Orient', Kagoshima is on the eastern side of the Satsuma Peninsula facing Kinko Bay. The island of Sakurajima (see p361), with its brooding volcano, lies just 4km away. The volcano's proximity means umbrellas are sometimes needed to keep off the dust and ash blown across to the mainland.

If Sakurajima dominates the skyline, historically it is the Shimazu family who have dominated the political map of Kagoshima. Successive generations of the family remained in power from 1185 through to the Meiji Restoration in 1871.

The southern gateway to Japan, Kagoshima was also the place where missionary Francis Xavier landed on 15th August 1549. As his ship approached the city, Xavier is said to have been filled with excitement on seeing what he thought was the cross of Jesus Christ, but which turned out to be the sign of the ruling Shimazu family. Little of Xavier's legacy is left today, since the church he built was bombed during the Pacific War.

What to see and do
Apart from Sakurajima, Kagoshima's big draw is **Isoteien**, also known as Senganen (daily 8:30am-5:30pm, ¥1500). It was constructed in 1660 as a residence for Mitsuhisa Shimazu, 19th lord of the Shimazu family. The layout of the garden takes full advantage of its Sakurajima backdrop. The ¥1500 ticket allows entry into the gardens and tea house, where there are short guided tours in Japanese before you are served a cup of green tea. Alternatively, a ¥1000 tick-

et allows entry into the gardens only. To reach Isoteien, take the tourist City View bus from Nishi-Kagoshima station. The bus stops right outside the main entrance.

Either before or after visiting the garden, take a quick look at adjacent **Tsurugane Shrine**, dedicated to the heads and family members of the Shimazu family who reigned over Kagoshima. One of the deities enshrined here is Princess Kameju. Born in 1571 as third daughter of the 16th Shimazu Lord, Kameju became known as the guardian of female beauty. Legend has it that a woman who prays at the shrine will become even more beautiful.

Tickets for Isoteien are also valid for **Shoko Shuseikan Historical Museum**, on the site of the former factory used by the Shimazu family to manufacture iron and glassware. Inside, the history of the Shimazu family is told in great detail – there are plenty of signs in English. The museum is just across from the entrance to the garden.

The main attraction in the **Museum of the Meiji Restoration** (daily 9am-5/6pm, ¥300) is a 25-minute waxwork show, during which a model of Saigo Takamori (see box opposite) rises from the floor/grave and the story of his life is retold in dramatic fashion. The soundtrack is in Japanese only. Take the City View bus from Nishi-Kagoshima station; the museum is the first stop on the route.

The best place for a bird's eye view of Kagoshima and Sakurajima is from the Observatory on **Mt Shiroyama** which rises 107m above sea level. From the bus stop, walk up past the stalls selling Saigo Takamori T-shirts and trinkets to the observation area, from where there's a great view of the city and of Sakurajima. The colour of the volcano is supposed to change seven times a day, so if it burns bright red and orange for too long, it's at least reassuring to know you're on high ground. Shiroyama itself consists almost entirely of volcanic deposit and is famous as the death place of Saigo Takamori. Take the City View bus from Nishi-Kagoshima station all the way to the observatory (the stop after the 'Cave where Saigo hid').

Kagoshima City Aquarium (daily, 9:30am-6pm, last entry 5pm, ¥1500), next to Sakurajima Ferry Terminal, is in the building with a roof that looks like a rough copy of the Sydney Opera House. Star attractions are the dolphins, though the 3D movie in which you can get wet without having to bring a change of clothes will keep children amused.

PRACTICAL INFORMATION
Station guide
The main rail station, where all limited expresses from Hakata and Kumamoto terminate, is called Nishi-Kagoshima.

There are few facilities in the station apart from the Friesta shopping mall. Coin lockers (all sizes) are easy to find on the main concourse. It's unlikely you'll pass through the small Kagoshima station on the other side of the city; apart from a small tourist office (see below), there are no facilities there.

Tourist information
There are information offices outside Nishi-Kagoshima (daily 8:30am-6pm) and Kagoshima (daily, 8:30am-5pm, closed 12-1pm) stations; the latter is generally very quiet and has only one member of staff.

⛩ Saigo Takamori

It's impossible to walk very far around Kagoshima without seeing the name Saigo Takamori on the many statues and monuments around the city. Points of reference like the 'Birthplace of Saigo', 'Statue of Saigo', 'House where Saigo was resuscitated', 'Cave where Saigo Takamori hid' and 'Place where Saigo Takamori died' can all be seen at one glance on a city map – laid out around town is the chronicle of one man's life, his journey from humble birth to a glorious if tragic death.

Saigo Takamori (1827-77) was born into a lower-class samurai family in the province of Satsuma (now Kagoshima), the eldest of seven children. In 1868 he became one of the leading figures in the battle to defeat the shogunate and restore power to the Meiji Emperor. It wasn't long before Saigo's loyalties were stretched between support for the new power base and his unerring allegiance to the large numbers of samurai in Satsuma who were being deprived of their status by Imperial edict.

His change of heart reached a dramatic climax in 1877, when Saigo gathered a 15,000 strong army and announced his intention to march on Tokyo. He never even got as far as Honshu and died on Mt Shiroyama in his native Kagoshima at 7am on 24th September 1877 after a defiant last stand against the government he had helped to found.

The staff at Nishi-Kagoshima will assist with reservations. From Nishi-Kagoshima station, head out to the bus platforms and look for the tourist information booth.

Getting around

Like Kumamoto, Kagoshima has a tram network which is by far the best way of getting around town. There is a flat rate of ¥160. One-day passes (¥600) allow you to board any tram, Shiei Bus or the tourist City View bus, an old-fashioned bus that does a circuit of the main sights in just under one hour. Passes are available from tourist information offices.

Kagoshima Airport (mostly domestic flights) is accessible by limousine bus (¥1200 one-way) from Nishi-Kagoshima station.

Festivals

Two major festivals in Kagoshima are the **Natsu Matsuri** (summer festival) at the end of July and **Ohara Matsuri** in early November.

Where to stay

Right outside the station is the new *JR Kyushu Hotel Kagoshima* (☎ 099-213

8000, 🖷 213 8029, 🖳 kagoshima@jrk-hotels.com; ¥6500/S, ¥12,000/Tw), opened in 2001. Rooms are modern and brightly decorated and you're allowed to check in as early as 2pm (check-out at 11am).

Towards the centre of town, *Lexton Inn* (☎ 099-222 0505, 🖷 225 7989; ¥7000/S, ¥12,000/Tw, ¥16,000/D) has moderately spacious rooms with minibar and hairdryer. There's also a coin laundry, Japanese restaurant and a very small tea room/coffee shop squeezed into a corner of the lobby.

Close by is a new addition to the business hotel market, *Kagoshima Plaza Hotel Tenmonkan* (☎ 099-222 3344, 🖷 222 9911, 🖳 info@kag-plaza.co.jp). There's a big column outside with 'business hotel' written on it. 'Compact singles' cost ¥6000, though the 'studio single' at ¥7000 is good value since you get a small sofa and a bit more breathing space. The rate for two people sharing a studio single is ¥10,000. There are only a couple of twins at ¥12,000.

Nakazono Ryokan (☎ 099-226 5125, 🖷 226 5126, 🖳 shindon@satsuma.ne.jp) is close to City Hall and offers tatami rooms at ¥4000 for one, ¥8000 for two and

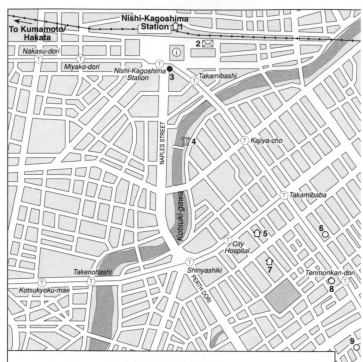

KAGOSHIMA 鹿児島

Where to stay

1	JR Kyushu Hotel Kagoshima	1	JR九州 ホテル 鹿児島
5	Lexton Inn	5	レクストンイン鹿児島
7	Kagoshima Plaza Hotel Tenmonkan	7	かごしま プラザホテル天文館
11	Nakazono Ryokan	11	中薗旅館
15	Shigetomiso Ryokan	15	重富荘

Where to eat

6	Capricciosa	6	カプリチョーザ
8	Häagen-Dazs	8	ハーゲンダッツ
9	Noboru	9	のぼる
12	Densuke	12	でんすけ

Other

2	Central Post Office	2	中央郵便局
3	Daiei Department Store	3	ダイエー
4	Museum of the Meiji Restoration	4	維新ふるさと館
10	Mt Shiroyama	10	白山
13	Kagoshima City Aquarium	13	鹿児島市水族館
14	Isoteien	14	磯庭園

Kagoshima

鹿児島

0   200M
APPROXIMATE SCALE

10

Asahi-dori

City Hall

Izuro-dori

11

12

Suizokukanguchi

Sakurajima
Sanbashi-dori

MIAMI DORI

Kagoshima
Station

Sakurajima Pier

13

Kagoshima
Station

14, 15

To Miyazaki

Kagoshima Bay

To Sakurajima

¥11,400 for three people sharing. Meals are not included but the owner is friendly and may well direct you to Densuke, a popular izakaya just around the corner (see below). All rooms have TV and telephone, though baths are communal (open 24 hours) and there's a coin laundry. Call ahead and, if he is free, Nakazono-san will collect you from the station.

Finally, top-of-the-range ryokan *Shigetomiso* (Shimizu-cho 31-7, ☎ 099-247 3155) deserves a mention for its location (close to Isoteien) and for its moment in history when part of the James Bond movie *You Only Live Twice* was shot there. Rates include two meals, though don't reckon on paying anything less than ¥20,000 per night to stay in one of the ryokan's eight rooms. Make a reservation through the tourist office if you don't speak Japanese. Originally built for Hisamitsu Shimazu, 29th feudal lord of the Kagoshima district, the ryokan commands great views of Sakurajima. If you do stay here it may be best not to mention Bond. When I enquired about Sean Connery's visit, the polite but firm response was: 'That was so long ago. Will it never be forgotten?'

Where to eat

There's not much inside Nishi-Kagoshima station (a branch of *McDonald's* in the Friesta shopping area within the station), but a good place to organize your own packed lunch is at *Daiei* department store opposite the station. On the ground floor is a bakery and there's also a good range of hot and cold food to take out. A branch of *Mister Donut* is attached to Daiei.

Within the covered mall that leads off from Tenmonkan-dori tram stop are a number of casual eating places. A branch of the Italian chain *Capricciosa* is just off from the covered mall, between a KFC and a convenience store, and within the mall is a branch of *Häagen-Dazs*.

Noboru, a short walk south from Izuro-dori tram stop, is a small place with only one item on the menu: ramen. You can either sit at the counter downstairs or head upstairs to one of the small rooms. For ¥1000 you'll be served a huge bowl of ramen, together with large slices of *daikon* (Japanese radish) and cups of tea.

Finally, *Densuke* is an izakaya close to Nakazono Ryokan. Though Nakazono-san, the ryokan owner, describes Densuke as 'traditional', don't go there expecting kimono-clad staff and wailing shamisen music. This is above all a drinking place (daily except Sun 5pm-late), where you can order up skewers of meat or fish to accompany your liquid refreshment.

Side trip to Sakurajima

Smoke, dust and ashes billowing out from Sakurajima are a common-enough sight in Kagoshima but the last major eruption was in 1946. The worst eruption of the last century was in 1914, when three million tons of lava buried eight villages and turned the island into a peninsula, completely filling a 400m-wide and 70m-deep sea.

Ferries to Sakurajima depart 24 hours a day from the terminal next to Kagoshima Aquarium (¥150, 13 mins). JR Kyushu operates one-day bus tours around the island (¥4000) but rail passes are not accepted. Tickets can be purchased from the JR ticket office on the second floor of Nishi-Kagoshima station. The bus starts and finishes at the station and includes stops around the city before heading to Sakurajima. Another bus (¥1700) starts from the port and runs twice a day on a three-hour tour of the island. Another option would be to hire a car for the day (or even half day).

⛩ **Swimming for their lives?**
   Every year in July there's a swimming contest from Sakurajima to Iso Beach in Kagoshima, a distance of around 4km. Though apparently all for fun, it's worth noting that the race always starts on the Sakurajima side. Could this be an emergency evacuation drill disguised as a sporting day out? If Sakurajima erupts, the practice will stand the competitors in good stead.

Your first port of call should be Sakurajima Information Center (☎ 099-293 2525) at the ferry terminal, where you can find out about cycle rental (one hour ¥400, two hours ¥600, each additional hour ¥300) and car rental (¥5000 for two hours, plus ¥1000 for each additional hour). Signposted from the ferry terminal a couple of minutes along the main road by car is the Sakurajima Visitor Center (☎ 099-293 2443, daily except Mon 9am-5pm, free) which has a model of Sakurajima, an explanation of the eco-system, displays of volcanic rock and footage of previous eruptions.

Just one main road circles the island; on the way round look out for observation points, lava fields and the *daikon* (giant radishes) that can grow up to 30kg on the fertile slopes. One of the most enjoyable stops is at Furusato-Onsen, a seaside hot spring in ***Furusato Kanko Hotel*** (☎ 099-221 3111, ▤ 221 2345; daily except Thurs, 8:30am-5pm). Entering the hotel, someone will direct you to the vending machine where you buy a ticket (¥1000), collect a yukata and head downstairs. It's easy to get lost in the corridors of the hotel, though staff are used to gaijin stumbling around, so eventually you'll open the door that leads outdoors and down some steps to the hot spring. The yukata is worn in the water because the spring is part of a shrine. Located right by the sea, this ranks as one of the most impressive places to bathe in Japan. Room rates at the hotel are ¥15,000-30,000.

Sakurajima Youth Hostel (188-1 Yokoyama, ☎/▤ 099-293 2150) charges ¥2600 (no discount for YH/HI members). Breakfast costs ¥500 and dinner ¥700. It's about 10 minutes on foot uphill from the ferry terminal.

❏ **Using the rail route guides**
The fastest point-to-point journey times are provided for each section of the route. Even though each route has been divided into different sections it may not be necessary to change trains as you go from one section to the next. Occasionally, however, it is essential to change train in order to complete the route described. Such instances are denoted by the following symbol ▲. Places which are served by local trains only are marked ◆.   **(For more information see p84)**

Shikoku – route guide

Shikoku ('Four Provinces') takes its name from the provinces into which the island was once divided. The old provinces of Sanuki, Tosa, Iyo and Awa are known today as the prefectures of Kagawa, Kochi, Ehime and Tokushima.

Predominantly rural, Shikoku has everything that the current image of Japan does not: wide open spaces, forests, rural villages and a dramatic natural landscape. However, the island is not just a provincial backwater. There's plenty to see and it's worth devoting at least a week to completing the loop route described below.

The route passes through all four prefectures and includes stops in the capital cities of three of them. Though a number of road bridges have opened in recent years, linking Shikoku with Honshu, the only entry/exit point by rail is across the Inland Sea via the Seto-Ohashi Bridge, opened in 1988.

This route starts in **Okayama** (see p225), taking the Marine Liner train across the bridge to **Takamatsu** (see p375). From here, the route heads south to **Kochi** (see p381) via **Kotohira** (see p366). The route continues in a clockwise direction to **Uwajima** (see p371), known for its bull fights and sex museum, then on to **Matsuyama** (see p385), the largest city on the island and a good access point for a visit to Dogo-Onsen, Japan's oldest spa town. The last part of the journey covers the route from Matsuyama back towards Okayama on Honshu.

It's worth noting that though plenty can be accomplished on a rail tour of Shikoku, the more isolated parts of the island, including the two southern capes at Muroto and Ashizuri, can be reached only by infrequent buses or by hiring a car and driving there.

Most weekends between April and September (except possibly in June due to the rainy season), open-air carriages are attached to two of the most scenic rail lines in Shikoku. These carriages are called 'Torocco' and carry an additional charge of ¥310. The first is on the Tokushima line that runs between Awa Ikeda and Tokushima; the open-air carriage is available between Tsuji and Sadamitsu stations, a 45-minute stretch as the line follows Yama-gawa.

The other is on the Yodo line between Kubokawa and Uwajima (see p369); an open-air carriage is attached between Tokawa and Ekawasaki. Seat reservations should be made in advance from any JR ticket office.

冬星の旅青鷺は番なり

Winter stars –
just two grey herons
as I journey by
(MINAKO KANEKO)

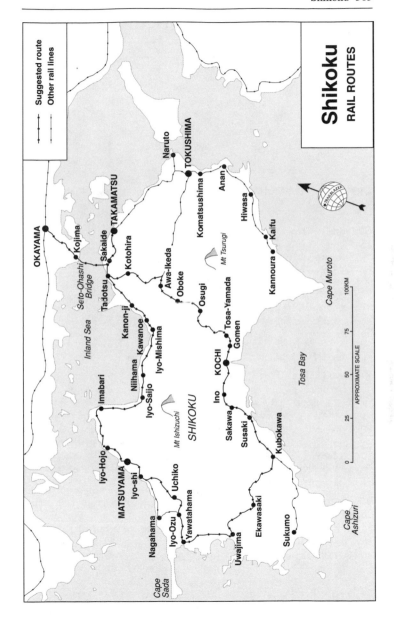

Shikoku
RAIL ROUTES

Suggested route
Other rail lines

OKAYAMA TO TAKAMATSU   [Map 33, p365; Table 28, p412]

Distances by JR from Okayama. Fastest journey time: 60 minutes.

Okayama (0km)   [see pp225-30]
Take the Marine Liner rapid train along the Seto-Ohashi line, which runs direct
to Takamatsu, across the Seto-Ohashi Bridge. On its way to the bridge the train
calls at **Senoo (8km)** and **Chaya-machi (15km).**

Kojima (28km) Last stop on Honshu before the train crosses Seto-Ohashi.
The bridge, or rather series of bridges, spans 9.4km and took nearly a decade to
build, opening in 1988 with a construction bill of ¥1120 billion. The view from
the train as it crosses the bridge is certainly impressive, though eclipsed by the
scale and design of the bridge itself. The downside towards the end of the crossing is the view to the left of the huge Kawasaki factory.

Sakaide (51km) First stop after crossing the Seto-Ohashi Bridge. Looking
back towards Honshu, you'll see the Seto-Ohashi commemorative park, where
there's a museum and observation tower; outdoor concerts are held here occasionally. Change here if planning to visit Kokubun-ji (see below).
    In the station are lockers up to ¥500, a convenience store with a few tables
where you can sit and have a drink, and, slightly hidden, a tourist information
office (daily, 8am-7pm) where only Japanese is spoken. There are elevators
between the concourse and platforms. Opposite one side of the station is the
SATY shopping complex with a variety of restaurants.

♦ Kokubu (60km) Only local trains stop here; services operate approximately every 30 minutes from Sakaide (11 mins) and from Takamatsu (15
mins). It's a five-minute walk from the station to **Kokubun-ji**, the 80th temple on the Shikoku pilgrimage. If coming from Takamatsu, cross the overhead
bridge, exit the station and walk straight ahead to the main road that runs parallel with the rail track. Turn right and about three minutes down this road on
the left is a sign pointing towards the temple. The entrance is just off the main
road on the left. Despite the numbers of pilgrims, the temple remains a calm

TO HIROSHIMA
SEE MAP 12

SHINKANSEN LINE

OKAYAMA

TO TOKYO
SEE MAP 11

Senoo

Chaya-machi

Kojima

Seto-Ohashi Bridge

Inland Sea

Utazu

Marugame

Tadotsu

Sakaide

TAKAMATSU

Takuma

Zentsu-
ji

Kokubu

Kotohira

Kanon-ji

Iyo-Saijo

Niihama

Kawanoe

TO MATSUYAMA
SEE MAP 34

Iyo-Mishima

Awa-Ikeda

SHIKOKU

Oboke Gorge

Oboke

Mt Tsurugi

0   20KM
APPROXIMATE SCALE

Osugi

TO UWAJIMA
SEE MAP 34

Tosa-
Yamada

KOCHI

Ino

Gomen

Ryugado Cave

MAP 33

and tranquil place. To the right of the main temple, Japanese music plays, guiding you into a store where you can buy assorted lucky charms and various pieces of the pilgrim's outfit, including the white shirt and walking stick.

Takamatsu (72km) [see pp375-81]

TAKAMATSU TO KOCHI [Map 33 above; Table 29, p412]

Distances by JR from Takamatsu. Fastest journey time: 130 minutes.

Takamatsu (0km) Pick up the Shimanto LEX heading south towards Kochi along the Dosan line.

Sakaide (22km) For details, see opposite.

Marugame (29km) For details, see p374.

⛩ **Shikoku 88 temple pilgrimage**

Pilgrims who start out on the journey around Shikoku's 88 temple circuit are following in the steps of Kobo Daishi, the Buddhist saint who first walked around the island and who now lies in eternal meditation at Koya-san, home to the Shingon sect of Buddhism founded by him in the 9th century.

Most *henro* (pilgrims) visit Koya-san (see box p200) either before or after completing the Shikoku pilgrimage. It's not necessary to follow precisely in Kobo Daishi's steps by walking between the temples. There are no rules to prevent modern-day pilgrims taking a bus, taxi or private car. Indeed, many of the pilgrims you see in the temples today, dressed in traditional white and carrying sticks to help them along the way, have a minibus waiting in the car park ready to whisk them off to their next destination.

The pilgrimage does not have to be completed in one visit, so many make return trips to Shikoku over a number of years. Some, however, such as the Buddhist monks who walk the circuit for spiritual cleansing, do it the hard way.

Tadotsu (33km) For information on Tadotsu, see p373.

The line splits here: the Yosan line heads west towards Matsuyama (see p385). The Shimanto LEX continues south along the Dosan line to Kochi.

Zentsu-ji (39km) Zentsu-ji is the birthplace of Kobo Daishi, the Buddhist priest who made a pilgrimage on foot around Shikoku (see box above). The temple here is the 75th on the 88 temple circuit and one of the busiest because of its link with Daishi.

Inside the temple precincts are a 45m-high five-storeyed pagoda, completed in 1884 for the 1050th anniversary of Kobo Daishi's death, and Mie-do Hall, said to be the very spot where Kobo Daishi was born in 774. The temple is a 20-minute walk west along the main road which runs away from the station.

Kotohira (44km) Just one stop along the line from Zentsu-ji, Kotohira is home to an interesting shrine and is the ideal place to break your journey for a few hours on the way to Kochi. JR Kotohira station has a ticket office, where you can make onward seat reservations, and a small udon restaurant but the only coin lockers are small ones. Walk straight up the main road from the station to find the steps leading up to the shrine.

⛩ **Squaring the circle**

An enterprising farmer from Zentsu-ji has taken Japan's cultural obsession with the melon a step further by creating what is surely a world first: the square water melon. The melons, which sell for ¥10,000 apiece, are grown in square glass boxes. The advantage square melons have over their round rivals is that they don't roll around the table and they fit neatly into the corner of a refrigerator. These melons have even been exported to the USA where they sell for over US$80 each.

⛩ **Naked Festival**
The highlight of February's Hadaka Matsuri (Naked Festival) at Zentsu-ji is *fukubai*, the 'scrambling for good luck sticks'. Hundreds of young people, wearing only a loincloth, battle to grab hold of the sticks and ensure they enjoy good fortune for the rest of the year. A local guidebook suggests that, even though participants are wearing next to nothing, 'the fierce fights make participants steaming hot. Nakedness signifies innocence like a newborn baby, while the white of the loincloth represents the purity of its wearer.'

Check with the tourist office in Takamatsu for the exact date of the festival as it changes every year.

The shrine of Kotohira-gu is better known as **Kompira-san**, the affectionate name for the guardian deity of seafarers. Kompira-san rises up the slope of Mt Zozu ('elephant's head'); the reward for making it up the first 785 steps to the main shrine is a view over the valley below and out over the Inland Sea. From here, there are a further 583 steps to Okusha Shrine, the Inner Sanctuary. Along the way are stalls that sell walking sticks to assist with the ascent, as well as drinks and noodles.

The **Stone Steps Marathon** is held on the first Sunday of October; hundreds of participants race from the station up to the inner sanctuary and back, running up and down a total of 2736 steps.

Before or after making the ascent, drop in at **Kanamaru-za** (daily except Tues 9am-4pm, ¥500), the oldest kabuki theatre in Japan. Take the road that leads left from the foot of the shrine steps and up a small hill. Built originally in 1835, the theatre later became a cinema, before falling into a state of disrepair. Restored in 1976, you can now go behind the scenes, check out the backstage dressing rooms and wander underneath the stage itself. Kabuki is only staged here once a year, during the spring, when a parade of kabuki players announces that the playhouse will once again be used for performance.

If you continue up the road past the theatre, you'll reach the statue of Jinnojo Okubo in Kotohira Park. At the end of the 19th century, Okubo mooted the idea of linking Honshu and Shikoku with a bridge over the Seto Inland Sea – an idea that took another hundred years to be realized.

From Kotohira, trains continue along the Dosan line towards Kochi. Pick up the Shimanto or Nanpu LEX. Reservations are recommended as some trains run with fewer carriages making it a scramble for the non-reserved seats.

Awa-Ikeda (77km) This is an interchange station for the Tokushima line. Although not included on this route, the Tokushima line makes for an enjoyable side trip by rail, the slowest trains taking around two hours to wend their way alongside Yama-gawa towards Tokushima.

From Awa-Ikeda, the Dosan line continues south towards the area's big sight, **Oboke Gorge**. Unfortunately, many of the passengers who use the limited express train to commute to Kochi shut the curtains and sleep through some

---

⛩ Borrowed from Belgium

One less well-known sight not far from Oboke Gorge is a copy of Brussels' best-known statue, Mannequin Pis (in Japanese, 'shoben kozo'). The naked boy is perched precariously on a clifftop looking down into the gorge, quietly relieving himself. The cliff-top vantage point is considered a place to prove your bravery. If you can stand next to the statue and look down at the gorge directly below, it's said that nobody will ever again question your courage. But you'd be more courageous – and possibly even make the local news – if you tried to imitate the boy and take a leak into the gorge below.

---

of the best views. If you don't want to miss out, reserve a window seat (both sides of the train have superb views).

Oboke (99km) Only a few limited expresses stop here. If you're planning to visit the gorge, confirm with JR staff whether the train you plan to catch stops here.

The gorge – or 'canyon', as the Japanese signposts call it – is one of Shikoku's hidden highlights. The starting point for boat tours of the gorge is about 1km from the station. Walk up to Oboke Bridge above the station, cross it, turn right and go straight. A short walk brings you to 'Lapis Oboke', in a modern building overlooking the gorge. Inside is a café, souvenir shop and Museum of Rocks and Minerals (daily, 9am-5pm, ¥500). This is not an essential stop, so continue past until you hit another building further ahead that contains a restaurant and souvenir shop. The ticket office for the 30-minute boat tours (daily 9am-5pm or earlier if not busy, ¥1000) is inside. No rowing is required – all you have to do is sit back and admire the view.

At Oboke, there's a minshuku (*Minshuku Oboke*, ☎ 08838-4 1226) which was firmly shut when I visited but which local residents assured me offered the cheapest night in the area at ¥2500 without meals. It's by Oboke Bridge, just above the station.

Osugi (120km) A few limited expresses stop here. Osugi means 'big cedar', named after a nearby tree which some people claim is 3000 years old. Most of the next 5km are spent in tunnels.

Tosa-Yamada (144km) By now, the gorge has receded and the landscape begins to prepare you for arrival in Kochi.

Tosa-Yamada is the nearest station to **Ryugado Cave** (daily, 8:30am-5pm, ¥1000), a 4km-long cave containing stalactites and stalagmites. Buses run out to the cave from here, or there's a bus service from Kochi station (check the times with tourist information in Kochi, see p382).

Gomen (149km) Last limited express stop before Kochi.

Kochi (160km)   [see pp381-5]

KOCHI TO UWAJIMA [Map 34, p370; Table 30, p412]

Distances by JR from Kochi. Fastest journey time: 3 hours.

Kochi to Kubokawa

If you're in a hurry and want to skip the next (slow!) part of the journey from **Kochi** to **Matsuyama** via Uwajima, consider taking a direct JR bus between the two cities. Buses depart on the hour 7am-7pm (same schedule for buses departing from Matsuyama) and the journey time is 3 hours 17 minutes. One-way costs ¥3700 but rail-pass holders travel free. You need to get a ticket from the bus centre ticket office, to the right as you exit Kochi station. The ticket office doesn't open until 8:45am, so if getting a bus before this time, or after the bus centre office closes, you can get one at the ticket office inside the station.

Kochi (0km) From Kochi, pick up the Nanpu LEX which continues along the Dosan line to Kubokawa, where you connect with the Yodo line that chugs slowly towards Uwajima.

Ino (11km) Few limited expresses stop at Ino, a paper-making town for over 1000 years. Water from Niyodo-gawa is used to manufacture the paper. Ino is the terminus for one of Kochi's tram lines, so streetcar enthusiasts might consider a trip by tram between here and Kochi station.

Sakawa (28km) Usually the first stop by limited express after Kochi. There are rice fields everywhere you look on this stretch of the journey. Kochi's mild weather and heavy rainfall means that it's the first place in Japan to harvest the year's crop of rice.

Susaki (42km) Approaching Susaki, and after the acres of rice fields spread out on either side of the rail line, it's something of a shock to come across factories, concrete buildings and industry; not the most attractive part of the journey. The next stop is at **Tosa-Kure (53km)**.

Kubokawa (72km) The JR Dosan line terminates here. From here, the private Tosa Kuroshio Railway runs further south to **Nakamura**, the nearest station to **Cape Ashizuri** (infrequent buses from Nakamura take 1 hour 40 mins to the cape and cost ¥1930). The JR Nanpu LEX continues along this private line, though rail-pass holders have to pay between Kubokawa and Nakamura.

▲ To follow the next part of this rail route, change trains here and connect up with the rural Yodo line, which runs along Shimanto-gawa before terminating in Uwajima. Pick up a Yodo line train from platform 4. If you don't have a rail pass, take a ticket when boarding the train and pay the fare when you get off. No limited expresses run along this line.

Kubokawa to Uwajima [Table 31, p412]

The Yodo line is one of the most scenic and rural in Shikoku; most of the stops are barely stations – just places where the train pulls up, often on the edge of a field. In theory, since the line between Kubokawa and Wakai (first stop after

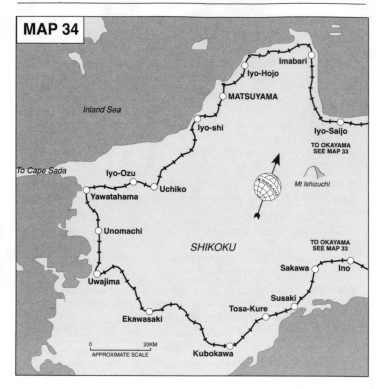

MAP 34

Imabari
Iyo-Hojo
MATSUYAMA
Inland Sea
Iyo-shi
Iyo-Saijo
TO OKAYAMA
SEE MAP 33
To Cape Sada
Iyo-Ozu
Uchiko
Yawatahama
Mt Ishizuchi
Unomachi
SHIKOKU
TO OKAYAMA
SEE MAP 33
Sakawa
Ino
Uwajima
Susaki
Tosa-Kure
Ekawasaki
0   20KM
APPROXIMATE SCALE
Kubokawa

Kubokawa) runs on private track, rail-pass holders should pay a ¥200 supplement. However, since nobody checks your ticket until you arrive in Uwajima, it seems that this additional fare is forgotten.

It takes around two hours for the train from Kubokawa to pull in to Uwajima, by which time the passengers will have probably changed several times. The train occasionally fills up with school children but then just as quickly empties again. For part of the way, the line follows the course of Shimanto-gawa, claimed to be the 'last great virgin river in Japan'. No man-made dams have been built near it; unimpeded by mechanical barriers, the water is probably the clearest you'll see anywhere. Trout and *ayu* (sweetfish) are popular catches.

Even though the chugging of the train can be sleep-inducing, the scenery is worth staying awake for, as you'll see farmers working in the fields and storks in water-logged rice paddies. More often than not, the rail line has been cut between fields, so you can stare right down at the cauliflowers, cabbages and individual rice plants. After **Ekawasaki (115km)** the line leaves the Shimanto-gawa, which winds its way towards the Pacific Ocean, and crosses into Ehime prefecture, on its way to Uwajima.

Uwajima (150km) Uwajima station was recently rebuilt with platforms on the same level as the exit. Station staff have ramps to assist with boarding trains. You'll find a *Willie Winkie* bakery and convenience store at the station. Only small coin lockers are available but the staff at the ticket barrier may allow you to store large luggage for ¥410. The tourist information office (look for the red letters on white background) is on the street opposite the station (☎ 0895-22 3934, daily, 8:30am-5pm). Pick up a map from here to locate the sights mentioned below.

As a staging post between Kochi and Matsuyama, Uwajima has a few attractions. Top of the bill is **Taga Shrine** and its **Sex Museum** (daily, 8am-5pm, ¥800). The museum is wall-to-wall penises, in various shapes and sizes, though the emphasis tends to be on the huge. The phallic models, pictures and works of art that leave nothing to the imagination are crammed into a three-floor building in one corner of the shrine. All the signs are in Japanese but it's not as if much explanation is needed.

Uwajima's other main attraction is **bull fighting**. The twist to this contest is that it's strictly bull against bull – no human risks getting hurt. Fights take place at the Municipal Bull Fighting Ring on the following days: January 2nd, the first Sunday in April, July 24th, August 14th and the second Sunday in November (tickets cost ¥3000).

At other times, a film of the fighting is shown (Mon-Fri, 8:30am-5pm, ¥500). The following extract from the promotional literature gives an idea of what to expect: 'Bouts between two bulls weighing nearly one tonne are quite dynamic. The bulls crash so hard against each other trying to push their opponent out that you may possibly hear the sound of their pant'.

If you need somewhere to stay, the new *Hotel Clement Uwajima* (☎ 0895-23 6111, 🖳 23 6666, 🖳 hotel@clement.shikoku.ne.jp; ¥6600/S, ¥11,000/D, ¥11,550/Tw) is immediately above the station – handy if you've got a lot of luggage. Rooms have modern furnishings, bilingual TV and fridge. There are also a couple of spacious tatami rooms that are worth paying for if you can afford the ¥16,500 for two; 10% off all rates with the rail pass.

Uwajima Youth Hostel (☎ 0895-22 7177; ¥3150/YH/HI, ¥4150 non-members) has an enviable location up on a hill overlooking the town, but this also means that it's inconvenient to reach. There are no buses up to the hostel, so avoid a painful walk up by taking a taxi from the station. Breakfast costs ¥600 and dinner ¥1000.

Sirene, at the station, is a very reasonable place to eat. The menu is French/Western and lunch courses (¥800-1000) are a good deal. It's just inside the entrance to the Hotel Clement. They sometimes serve Italian gelato from a stall outside.

UWAJIMA TO MATSUYAMA [Map 34, p370; Table 32, p413]

Distances by JR from Uwajima. Fastest journey time: 1¼ hours.

Uwajima (0km) From Uwajima, pick up the Uwakai LEX which runs along the Yosan line to Matsuyama. The first stop is **Unomachi (20km)**.

Yawatahama (35km) Yawatahama is home to one of the region's largest fishing communities and is the nearest station to Cape Sada peninsula. The best way to reach the cape is to drive there (enquire about car-hire prices at the JR ticket counter). The 50km cape juts out a little further up the coast from Yawatahama. It's the longest and narrowest in Japan and at the tip is Cape Sada Lighthouse, from where there are good views of the Seto Inland Sea.

Iyo-Ozu (48km) From here the rail line divides, with a choice of either the **inland route**, which this guide follows (served by limited express or local train), or the **coastal route** (served by local trains only). If you're on a limited express and want to follow the coastal route, this is the last place you can change before the lines diverge. Taking the coastal route, the line follows Hijigawa out to sea, then heads slowly up the coast before converging with the inland line at Iyo-shi station; services operate roughly hourly and take approximately 70 minutes.

Uchiko (59km) There are elevators from platforms 1 and 2 down to street level. The station has small coin lockers only. In the square outside the station is a steam locomotive that ran on the Uchiko Line from 1969 to 1970, transporting cargo between Uchiko and Iyo-Ozu. Built in 1939, its accumulated mileage would be enough to circumnavigate the globe 33 times.

Between the Edo and Meiji periods, Uchiko prospered as a manufacturing centre for Japanese paper and wax. Today, Uchiko is known for the **Yokaichi Historical Area**, a street of old, preserved houses, some of which are open to the public as museums or upmarket coffee shops. From the station, walk along the road into town until you reach a junction where there's a branch of Iyo Bank. Turn left at this junction and walk uphill to find the old street.

Uchiko must have been wealthy because it even boasts its own kabuki theatre, **Uchiko-za** (daily, 9am-4:30pm, ¥300). Built in 1919, it is similar in design to the theatre at Kotohira (see p367), with a revolving stage. Look for signs to the theatre on your way into town from the station.

Iyo-shi (85km) This is the point at which the coastal and inland rail lines re-converge for the final part of the journey to Matsuyama.

Matsuyama (97km) [see pp385-90]
As the train pulls in to Matsuyama, look out to the left for the silver Botchan Stadium. A new location for city baseball, the stadium is named after one of Matsuyama's most famous honorary citizens, the character from Soseki Natsume's novel of the same name (see p331). The character, Botchan, visited the Dogo-Onsen hot spring baths, still one of the city's biggest draws.

MATSUYAMA TO OKAYAMA   [Map 34, p370; Map 33, p365; Table 33, p413]

Distances by JR from Matsuyama. Fastest journey time: 2 hours 40 mins.

Matsuyama (0km) The final part of the journey around Shikoku runs from
Matsuyama back to Okayama. The Shiokaze LEX runs direct from here back to
Okayama. If returning to Honshu, make sure you're sitting in cars 4-8, as cars
1-3 split off at Tadotsu and head to Takamatsu.

Iyo-Hojo (18km) Some limited expresses stop here. Between Matsuyama and
Iyo-Hojo, the line roughly parallels the main 196 trunk road but there are occasional views of the Inland Sea out to the left. About 20 minutes after Iyo-Hojo
you should see, also out to the left, Shikoku's newest engineering feat, the Nishi
Seto Highway linking the island with Honshu.

Imabari (50km) Imabari is the starting point for the Nishi-Seto Highway which
connects Shikoku with Honshu via a road bridge. Completed in 1999, the bridge
uses six small islands as staging posts and runs across the Inland Sea to Onomichi.
This is the third road bridge connecting Shikoku with Honshu. Imabari's other
claim to fame is that it's the number one towel-producing city in Japan.

Iyo-Saijo (80km) If you happen to be passing this way around October 14th-
17th, drop in on the town's annual festival. The highlight is a parade of portable
shrines through the city on the morning of the 15th. Conveniently, Niihama (see
below) holds a festival at around the same time. On the way between the two
stations, there's some mountain scenery out to the right.

Niihama (91km) Expect **Niihama's Drum Festival** (October 16th-18th) to be
a noisy event. The drums that get paraded through the town weigh around two
tonnes each, and require 150 people to carry them.
    The limited express next calls at **Iyo-Mishima (116.8km)** and **Kawanoe
(122km)**, which is the last stop before the train crosses the border from Ehime
back to Kagawa prefecture.

Kanon-ji (138km) This is the best stop for Kotohiki Park, known for its massive and mysterious coin shape called Zenigata (see box, p374), carved about
2m deep in the sand. The park is a 20-minute walk north-west of the station,
across Saita-gawa.

Takuma (152km) Some limited expresses stop here. Between Takuma and
Tadotsu there are great views of the many tiny islands in the Inland Sea.

Tadotsu (162km) Tadotsu is a junction for the Yosan line between
Matsuyama and Takamatsu, and the Dosan line to Kochi (see p366). This is
where the railway network on Shikoku began in 1889, when the first steam
locomotive ran 15.5km from Marugame to Kotohira via Tadotsu.
    As soon as the Shiokaze LEX stops, a lightning-fast decoupling takes place,
allowing the front half (cars 4-8) to continue on to Okayama, while the remainder wait a couple of minutes before starting off for Takamatsu.

♯ **The Zenigata – coin-shape carved in the sand**
    There are a number of stories about how the Zenigata came to be here.
Some claim the coin is at least 350 years old, while others say it only dates back
130 years. The common consensus is that the coin was completed in just one
night by locals in 1633 as an unusual gift to the feudal lord of the area, Ikoma
Takatoshi, who was to arrive the next day on a tour of inspection. Everybody
knew that his lordship had to be pleased and a huge coin in the sand seemed the
perfect answer.
    Some claim that the coin was and remains to this day a UFO base (a Japanese
version of crop circles?), while others attribute it to the miracle-working of Kobo
Daishi. With a circumference of 345m, the biggest mystery is why the design does
not disappear in the rain or wind.
    Twice a year, the coin is reshaped by a group of volunteers who are shouted
orders by one person commanding a bird's eye view. A two-day **Zenigata Festival**
is held around July 20th (Maritime Day), highlights of which include a fireworks
display and dance contest in Kotohiki Park.

Marugame (166km) Marugame is a former castle town with a couple of
attractions. Take the south exit for tourist information (Mon-Fri 9:30am-6pm,
Sat-Sun 10am-5pm), just to the right as you exit the station. No English is spoken, but the place is well stocked with leaflets.
    Marugame Castle (daily 9am-4:30pm, closed Dec 25th-Feb 28th) was
originally built in 1597 on a hill overlooking the city. Its design may not be
unusual but the mason who built the ramparts was: legend records that he
always worked naked.
    The castle is about 15 minutes on foot down the main road which runs away
from the south exit. There's no fee to visit the castle tower if you show the
Kagawa Welcome Card (see p46) at the entrance.
    Right outside the station in a striking modern building is **Marugame
Genichiro Inokuma Museum of Contemporary Art (MIMOCA)** (daily
10am-6pm, occasional holidays). Permanent exhibitions on the second floor
display the works of Genichiro Inokuma, who attended school in Marugame
before heading off to Tokyo, Paris and New York (where he opened his own studio and stayed 20 years) before finally settling in Hawaii. Tickets to the permanent galleries cost ¥300. The museum café on the third floor is a great place to
relax and is much better than anywhere in the station for a drink and a quick
snack. Earl Grey tea and cinnamon toast are on the menu.

Utazu (169km) Heading out of the station, you can't miss the **Gold Tower**
(daily, 9:30am-6pm). It has a 127m-high observation gallery that, judging by
the soft music played and the two-seater booths, is a haven for star-struck lovers
who wish to gaze out over the Seto-Ohashi Bridge. There's even a noticeboard
where partners can leave romantic messages for each other.
    If you can stand the ghastly kitsch of the place and shut out the noise of
both the lift attendant and the romantic ballads pouring out of the speakers, the

---

☐ **World Toilet Museum**
The **World Toilet Museum** (daily, 9:30am-6pm) is housed in a small red building attached to the Gold Tower in Utazu. It's tiny, but does contain the world's only solid gold toilet and accompanying gold toilet slippers. This is followed by a brief history of toilets, along with replica lavatories from around the world. You'll find everything from primitive holes in the ground to ornate toilet suites from Versailles and Vienna (proving that citizens of culturally refined cities still have to submit to the demands of Mother Nature). Chopin plays in the background.

Curiously, all the toilets have signs on them in Japanese urging visitors not to use them. Since the toilets are all plumbed in, there is theoretically nothing to stop you giving them a go, except that they are on display in a museum. The museum is on the second floor. Public toilets are on the ground floor and worth a brief look in themselves.

---

view from the top is almost worth the expense. A combined entry ticket to the observation gallery and adjacent World Toilet Museum (see box above) costs ¥1000. There's a ¥100 reduction on presentation of the Kagawa Welcome Card (see p46).

Utazu is the final stop in Shikoku before the train turns to cross the Seto-Ohashi Bridge bound for Okayama. If you're not returning to Honshu and haven't yet changed trains, this is the last chance to do so.

Kojima (187km) First stop back on Honshu, and the point where JR Shikoku staff are replaced by their opposite numbers from JR West.

Okayama (214km)   [see pp225-30]
Back in Okayama, you can continue your journey either west towards Hiroshima (see p205), or east to the Kansai region (see p165), and beyond that back towards Tokyo.

Shikoku – city guides

TAKAMATSU

Capital of Kagawa Prefecture for over a century and a former castle town, Takamatsu is now attempting to become a major business and tourism centre for the 21st century with the construction of 'Sunport Takamatsu'. A brand new hotel, leisure and conference facilities, pier and an artificial beach are set to revitalize the port area behind JR Takamatsu station. The project is scheduled to be completed by 2004, though the first stage was opened in April 2001.

Kagawa may be the smallest prefecture in Japan but developments such as Sunport and the new Prefectural Office skyscraper suggest that it's probably not

TAKAMATSU 高松

Where to stay

2 ANA Hotel Clement Takamatsu	2 ANAホテルクレメント高松
4 Business Hotel Palace	4 ビジネスホテル パレス高松
6 Hotel Fukuya	6 ホテル 福屋
7 Rihga Hotel Zest Takamatsu	7 リガホテルゼスト高松
13 Wataya Ryokan	13 わたや旅館

Where to eat

1 Mikayla Restaurant and Bar	1 Mikayla Restaurant and Bar
9 Sea Dragon	9 Sea Dragon
14 Doutor Coffee	14 ドトールコーヒー
15 KFC/Capricciosa	15 KFC/カプリチョーザ
16 Sicily Island	16 Sicily Island

Other

3 Tamamo Koen	3 玉藻公園
5 Post Office	5 郵便局
8 Takamatsu City Museum of Art	8 高松市美術館
10 City Hall	10 市役所
11 I-PAL Kagawa	11 アイパル香川
12 Kagawa Prefectural Office	12 香川県庁
17 Ritsurin Koen	17 栗林公園

one of the poorest. The biggest attraction for tourists is Ritsurin Koen, a large park 2km south of the station area. Takamatsu feels very international – you might be surprised to see how many foreigners there are in town – and has sister-city relations with a number of places around the world including Tours in France.

What to see and do

The new **Prefectural Office**, in the centre of town and the tallest building in the area, has a free observatory on the top floor and is a good place to orientate yourself.

Tamamo Koen (daily, 8:30/9am-5/6pm, ¥150), by the harbour and next to Kotoden Takamatsu Chikko station, is a large park where Takamatsu Castle once stood. Some of the original castle turrets still remain but what makes the castle noteworthy is its unusual proximity to the sea. Originally built in 1590, waves crashed against the castle's northern ramparts up until 1900, when land was reclaimed to construct a new harbour. An air raid on Takamatsu on 4th July 1945 killed over 1300 people and destroyed over 18,000 buildings, including most of what remained of the castle.

Ritsurin Koen (daily, 8:30am-5pm; extended opening hours in summer, ¥350), Takamatsu's biggest draw, has a dramatic setting at the foot of Mt Shiun. One advantage Ritsurin has over other well-known Japanese parks is its size – the tour groups are there but there's much more space for them to spread out.

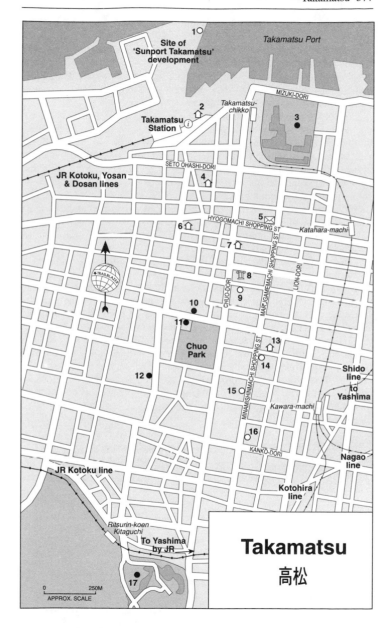

1 ○

Site of
'Sunport Takamatsu'
development

Takamatsu Port

MIZUKI-DORI

2

Takamatsu-chikko

Takamatsu
Station

3 ●

SETO OHASHI-DORI

JR Kotoku, Yosan
& Dosan lines

4

5 ✉

HYOGOMACHI SHOPPING ST

Katahara-machi

6

MARUGAMEMACHI SHOPPING ST

LION-DORI

7

CHUO-DORI

8

9 ○

10 ●

11 ●

Chuo
Park

13

MINAMISHINMACHI SHOPPING ST

14

Shido
line
to
Yashima

12 ●

15 ○

Kawara-machi

16

KANKO-DORI

Nagao
line

JR Kotoku line

Kotohira
line

*Ritsurin-koen
Kitaguchi*

To Yashima
by JR

Takamatsu

高松

0   250M
APPROX. SCALE

17 ●

There are plenty of narrow paths and observation points that give an impressive overview of the grounds which are divided into two, the Hokutei (northern garden) and Nantei (southern garden). The 'wild ducks' in the duck pond are disappointingly tame – perhaps they realize they will no longer be shot as sport, which they were about 370 years ago when the gardens were part of the local feudal lord's villa residence. Look out for turtles along the paths, apparently oblivious to the hordes of tourists storming by.

The Kikugetsu-tei ('moon-scooping cottage') is a restored tea house where it's thought that moon-viewing parties were once held. The tea house is sometimes open to the public for tea ceremony demonstrations (an extra ¥710 including tea and cake; check with tourist office for times). Also within the park grounds is the small Sanuki Folk Art Museum (free), containing a model portable shrine and various ceramics and masks. Animal lovers should avoid the zoo (an extra ¥600) in the park.

To ensure you have as much peace as possible, go early but check opening times with the tourist office. To get to the park take a local train from JR Takamatsu (on the Kotoku line towards Tokushima) two stops to Ritsurin-Koen Kitaguchi, just by the park's north gate.

Takamatsu City Museum of Art (daily except Mon 9am-5pm, Fri until 7pm), housed in a modern building downtown, has a permanent collection (¥200) of mostly contemporary Japanese art that is worth a look. The galleries are small but exhibits are changed every few months. Temporary exhibitions (separate admission charge) are held on the second floor. The museum occasionally stages classical and folk music concerts.

Takamatsu is also an access point for some of the islands on the Inland Sea. Check with the tourist office for ferry departure times and fares. The island of **Megijima**, also known as Onigashima, has a huge cave said to have been used as a pirate den. **Shodoshima** is much larger and is known as an island resort. Attractions here include a miniature version of the 88 temples on the Shikoku pilgrimage, useful for anyone in need of a fast-track spiritual cleansing.

PRACTICAL INFORMATION
Station guide

Takamatsu station was completely rebuilt in 2001. On the concourse level is a place that sells freshly-baked cookies, a fast-food restaurant and a convenience store.

Coin lockers are very easy to find as they are directly across from the ticket vending machines.

On the second floor are several Japanese restaurants, a souvenir shop and book store.

Tourist information

Takamatsu Information Plaza (☎ 087-851 2009, open daily 9am-6pm, 6-9pm for accommodation reservations only) is between the station and ANA Hotel Clement Takamatsu and staff can provide you with a map and help with accommodation. There's no guarantee that the staff will speak English and questions are answered efficiently if a little abruptly.

Far more helpful is **Takamatsu International Association**, based at I-PAL (☎ 087-837 5901, Tues-Sun 9am-6pm), a

> **Ⅲ Kotoden – trainspotters' paradise**
> The private Kotoden rail company operates three lines around Takamatsu and Kagawa, with its main Kawara-machi station beneath the former Sogo department store in the city centre.
>
> Particularly among trainspotters – called *tetsudo maniaku* ('railway maniacs') in Japanese – Kotoden is known as a good place to photograph some of Japan's oldest trains still in service. The company has bought old rolling stock from cities such as Tokyo and Osaka and put them back into service on local lines. The oldest train dates back to 1925.

modern building in a corner of Chuo Park. Facilities here include newspapers, CNN, and free Internet use. I-PAL also produces *Kawara-Ban* four times a year, a newsletter with events and cinema listings, as well as *Kagawa Journal*, with articles on life in Japan written by both local and foreign residents.

Pick up the Kagawa Welcome Card (see p46) from the tourist office at the station or from I-PAL.

Getting around

As well as JR train services, the private Kotoden Railway operates in Takamatsu and the surrounding area (see box above). Though you may want to take a train to Ritsurin Koen, over on the other side of the city, the best way of seeing the city centre is on foot.

Money

Unfortunately, the Sogo department store above Kawara-machi station closed after the company filed for bankruptcy, taking the ATM which accepted foreign-issued Visa cards with it. If another company takes over the store, the ATM may re-open, but for now the best bet is to try the ATMs in the central post office at the north end of Marugamemachi shopping street.

Festivals

The biggest annual event is **Takamatsu Festival** (Aug 12th-14th), when thousands of people dance through the main streets (anyone is welcome to join in) and there's a fireworks finale.

Where to stay

Right outside the station, *ANA Hotel Clement Takamatsu* (☎ 087-811 1111, 🖻 811 1100), centrepiece of the Sunport development project, is the most deluxe place to stay in town – with top-price room rates to match: singles from ¥10,500 to ¥14,000; doubles from ¥18,000 to ¥20,000 and twins from ¥21,000 to ¥35,000. A beer garden operates on the fifth floor of the hotel in the summer months.

If you're looking for a much cheaper bed near the station, a good place to try is *Business Hotel Palace Takamatsu* (☎ 087-851 3232, 🖻 851 3240). It's one of the cheapest places around. The rooms are small but there's a coin laundry. Using the Kagawa Welcome Card (see p46), a single works out at ¥4950 and a twin is ¥7560.

The price goes up a little at *Hotel Fukuya* (☎ 087-851 2365, 🖻 822 8724), 10-15 minutes from the station. The open-plan lobby is a welcome change from the tiny reception areas of most business hotels and rooms veer towards being spacious – the bathrooms remain tiny though. It seems they will only honour the Welcome Card for Western-style singles, which are reduced from ¥6600 to ¥6000. Otherwise, twins are ¥11,550 and there are tatami rooms at ¥7600 for one person, ¥12,705 for two people and ¥17,325 for three.

For a taste of luxury, head for *Rihga Hotel Zest Takamatsu* (☎ 087-822 3555, 🖻 822 7516). Rooms in the main building are nothing special (the smallest singles from ¥6800, twins from ¥15,000 and doubles from ¥13,000). More luxurious are the rooms in the newer annex, where a deluxe twin is ¥25,000. It's the same price for a combination Western/tatami room that can sleep four; 10% discount on all room rates with the Welcome Card.

Wataya Ryokan (☎ 087-861 3806, 🖫 861 4916) has tatami rooms for ¥9000 per person including two meals. Located within the downtown shopping area, Wataya is good value if a touch gloomy. The owner seems to be a bit discriminate about when to accept the Welcome Card even though it is included in the booklet, so ask the tourist office to help you make a booking.

Where to eat
Mikayla Restaurant and Bar (daily, 11am-12 midnight), part of Sunport Takamatsu, is located out on the pier and has a terrace café which affords great views over the Inland Sea. The evening menu is a little pricey (from around ¥1500) but the food (pasta, salads, fish and meat dishes) is excellent. There are cheaper set deals in the afternoon (pasta main course for ¥880) and the terrace is a great place to relax with a cocktail at sunset. The glass entrance is easy to spot as the name, Mikayla, is written in English above the entrance. It's a five-minute walk from JR Takamatsu station.

Sicily Island, on Tamachi shopping arcade, serves cheap pasta lunches from ¥500. Set menus are available 11:30am-4pm. Inside it's very plain but at the weekend there's usually a live band. The Italian theme continues at *Capricciosa* – they serve the usual huge portions but the half-portion lunchtime menu is good value and includes salad, pasta or pizza and coffee. The restaurant is on the second floor, on a street just off the covered shopping arcade.

Popular with Takamatsu's foreign community, particularly on Friday and Saturday nights, is *Sea Dragon*, which is mainly a drinking place but serves some food, such as tacos. It's a little hard to find as it's set below street level on a side street off the main covered arcade. Look for the dragon above the entrance. Finally, for cheap food with a great view, try the canteen inside **City Hall**. It's on the 13th floor; though it's supposed to be for City Hall staff, it's open to anybody. Plastic models of the meals (from ¥450) make selection easy and you can get a window table with great views of Takamatsu. It's only open Monday-Friday for lunch and gets very busy from 12 noon to 1pm, when everyone goes on their lunch break.

Side trip by rail from Takamatsu
To the north-east of Takamatsu lies **Yashima** ('roof-top island'), a plateau made of volcanic lava jutting out 5km into the Inland Sea. The plateau gained its place in national history as the site of a decisive battle between the Minamoto and Taira clans (see p33), both of which were vying to rule Japan in the 12th century. The plateau, accessed by cable car (daily, 8am-5:30pm, ¥1300 return), affords great views of the Inland Sea and is home to the 84th temple on the Shikoku pilgrimage, Yashima-ji. Below the plateau is **Shikoku Mura** (daily, 8:30am-4:30/5pm, ¥800), an open-air museum of traditional homes gathered from all over Shikoku.

After visiting Shikoku Mura the done thing is to stop for a bowl of *sanuki udon*, a traditional noodle dish, at *Waraya* (daily, last orders 6:30pm). The restaurant is in the building next to the water mill, by the entrance to Shikoku Mura. Alternatively, as you leave Shikoku Mura look out for a traditional British-style building with red phone box and pillar box outside. Inside is a café which serves tea and cakes. It's open daily, 9am-6pm.

Yashima can be reached from Takamatsu station by JR on the Kotoku line but it is more fun to travel on the private Kotoden line; this takes longer but drops you closer to the start of the cable car up to Yashima plateau. From Takamatsu-Chikko station (close to JR Takamatsu station) to Yashima, the fare is ¥310 (change at Kawara-machi station, beneath the former Sogo department store). As you exit Kotoden Yashima station you'll see the cable car going up the plateau. Shikoku Mura is a few minutes' walk east of the cable car entrance.

KOCHI

Bordered in the north by the Shikoku mountain range and to the south by the Pacific Ocean, Kochi is known for its mild climate, long days of sunshine and relaxed, friendly atmosphere. The city definitely feels very laid-back and is a great place for anyone wanting to sample an unhurried and less frantic Japan.

What to see and do

Harimaya-bashi junction in the centre of Kochi is unusual in that it's a bridge that no longer has any water flowing under it. It remains a recognizable landmark and is the only point at which Kochi's two tram lines converge.

Two of the main sights that can be reached by tram are Kochi Castle in the downtown area and Kochi Museum of Art, which is about 20 minutes by tram from Kochi station. You can easily fit both into one day, or even half a day.

East of the city centre, Kochi's **Museum of Art** (daily except Mon, 9am-5pm, ¥350) is housed in a modern building and is well organized, with large galleries for both regular and temporary exhibitions. The main collection is mostly expressionist works by both Japanese and Western artists. There's also a large hall used for films, concerts and theatre productions. Noh productions are staged here around twice a month; tickets are sometimes free. The museum prints a schedule of performance times (in Japanese only), which you should be able to pick up at Kochi station tourist information desk. Inside the museum, close to the entrance, is *Pizzicato*, a small but attractive café that serves sandwiches, cakes and drinks. From the station, take a tram or walk to Harimaya-bashi. From here, change for a tram heading for Gomen and get off at Kenritsu Bijutsukan-dori (Museum Road).

Completed in 1611 by a feudal lord, **Kochi Castle** (daily 9am-5pm, ¥400), at the end of Otesuji-dori, is the city's big sight. Look out inside the castle for the huge, pointed lance made entirely of feathers. It's worth heading out here for the view of Kochi and the surrounding area from the top floor of the donjon.

Chikurin-ji (daily 7am-5pm; small museum 8:30am-5pm, ¥400), a stop on the Shikoku pilgrimage (see box p366), is accessible by bus from Kochi station or from the bus terminal next to Seibu department store. Take a bus marked 'Godaisan Chikurinji'.

If here on a Sunday, visit the **Weekly Market** that runs along Otesuji-dori, the main street leading up to the castle. Stalls sell local produce, fruit and vegetables brought into Kochi from the surrounding countryside.

Worth a browse if you happen to be in town at the right time is the informal **Flea Market** that usually takes place on the second and fourth Sunday every month along Obisan Road, which runs parallel to but a couple of blocks down from Otesuji-dori.

PRACTICAL INFORMATION
Station guide
Renovation work on Kochi station is not scheduled for completion before 2004, so it's fair to assume that until then the station will not be the most user-friendly of places. During the building work, disabled access to the station and platforms is likely to be limited.

For a quick snack in the station, look for the Willie Winkie bakery (daily, 7am-7pm) and attached café to the right as you exit. JR buses to Matsuyama (see p369) depart from bus platforms to the right of the station exit. To the left as you exit are coin lockers of all sizes. On the second floor of the station is a small department store and Japanese restaurant serving run-of-the-mill set meals. The tram terminus is on the main road that runs parallel to the front of the station. Use the overhead walkway to reach the tram platform.

Tourist information
Kochi's well-informed tourist information counter (☎ 088-882 1634, daily 9am-9pm) is to the left as you exit the station. The staff speak English, will help with hotel bookings and can advise on travel around the prefecture as well as in the city.

Another point of information is **Kochi International Association** (☎ 088-875 0022, Mon-Sat 8:30am-5:15pm), in a small building opposite the castle park. It's on the second floor and has a selection of magazines and books. You might also enquire here about meeting up with volunteer guides – though, as ever, it's best to contact them ahead of your visit. The association also publishes the monthly Kochi International Magazine *Oi!*, with articles on events happening throughout Kochi prefecture, as well as film listings.

KOCHI　高知

Where to stay
4	Bright Park Hotel	4　ブライトパークホテル
9	Super Hotel Kochi	9　スーパーホテル高知
10	Tosa Bekkan	10　とさ別館
11	Kochi Pacific Hotel	11　高知パシフイックホテル

Where to eat
3	Doutor Coffee	3　ドトールコーヒー
5	Baffone	5　バッフォーネ
6	Irish Pub Amontillado	6　アイリッシュパブ
7	Tosa Ichiba	7　土佐市場

Other
1	Kochi Castle	1　高知城
2	Kochi International Association	2　高知県国際交流協会
8	Kochi Museum of Art	8　高知県立美術館
12	Central Post Office	12　中央郵便局

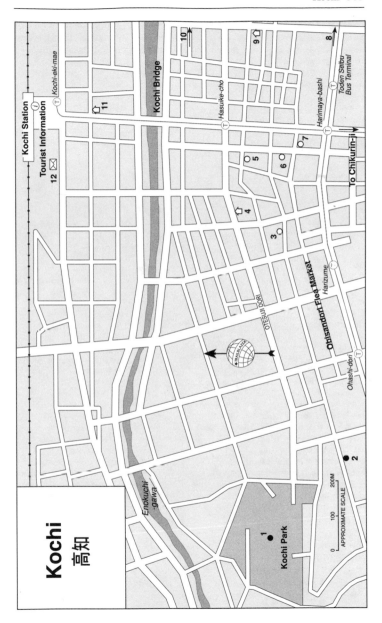

Kochi
高知

Kochi Station
Tourist Information
Kochi-eki-mae
Kochi Bridge
Kochi-eki-mae
Hasuike-cho
Harimaya-bashi
Toden Saitsu Bus Terminal
To Chikurin-ji
Obisandori Flea Market
Harizume
OTESUJI DORI
TRAILBLAZER
Ohashi-dori
Enokuchi-gawa
Kochi Park
APPROXIMATE SCALE
0   100   200M

Getting around

Kochi has an old but efficient tram system. There are two lines which intersect at Harimaya-bashi junction in the city centre. A flat fare of ¥100 is charged, or ¥180 if transferring between lines at Harimaya-bashi. A one-day pass costs ¥600, available from the bus centre ticket office at Kochi station. If changing tram lines at Harimaya-bashi, ask for a *norikae-kippu* which allows you to transfer without paying again.

Look out for the trams that have been brought from Germany, Portugal, Austria and Norway, each with a different design and interior layout.

Festivals

Yosakoi Festival (August 9th-12th) is a high-energy dance event involving over 14,000 people divided into teams. One visitor a few years ago was so impressed by the event that he went home and launched a copycat festival in Sapporo, Hokkaido (see p312). The one in Kochi, though, is the original and best.

Where to stay

A five-minute walk north-east of Harimaya-bashi junction is *Super Hotel Kochi* (☎ 088-884 9000, 🖹 884 9020), a new business hotel with singles at ¥4800 per night including breakfast; a good budget choice.

A short way up the main road that heads away from the station towards the Harimaya-bashi crossing is *Kochi Pacific Hotel* (☎ 088-884 0777, 🖹 884 8008; ¥6800/S, ¥15,000/Tw), opened in 1999. An upmarket business hotel (note the grandfather clock in the lobby), you pay for the space but the beds are wide. You can also check in here from 2pm, earlier than most business hotels allow.

Closer to the centre of town, handy if you want to investigate any of Kochi's many bars or visit the Sunday market, is *Bright Park Hotel* (☎ 088-823 4351, 🖹 823 7459; ¥6500/S, ¥10,000/D, ¥14,000/Tw). Renovated in 2000, this is a good-standard business hotel, with a small coffee shop on the first floor.

Tosa Bekkan (☎ 088-883 5685) is a small Japanese inn which gets booked up quickly; per person rates without meals start at around ¥4500 (rates vary according to the season/whether the place is busy). There's a handy coin laundry right outside.

The bad news for budget travellers is that Kochi Ekimae Youth Hostel, the local backpackers' haunt, has closed.

Where to eat

Freshly caught sea bream is popular and, according to one local gourmet guide, 'prepared so that it is still alive and in one piece before eating'. Less terrifying would be a bowl of *dorome*, tiny, clear fish that are the local speciality, available in many places including *Tosa Ichiba* (daily except Mon,11am-9:50pm), a popular local restaurant with a feast of plastic dishes to choose from in the window. They do reasonably-priced set meals. Look for the picture of the whale on the sign outside (a whale is also on the sign of the restaurant opposite).

Irish Pub Amontillado is close by, but open in the evenings only. Look for the green shop front and picture of the Guinness toucan outside. Guinness and Kilkenny are on tap.

For good coffee and sandwiches, try the branch of *Doutor Coffee* in the covered arcade, next to Toho cinema.

Baffone (daily except Wed, 12 noon-12am), a small bistro that opens out on to the street, is a laid-back place. They serve good pasta and wines, and coffee and cake in the afternoon. The menu changes regularly.

Side trips from Kochi

It's possible but expensive to arrange a day's **whale watching** from Kochi. The people who once hunted whales have now turned to tourism to save them from a ban on whaling. To reach any of the points along the coast from where boats can be hired requires your own transport. The tourist office at Kochi station keeps a list of companies that organize whale watching and can advise on who to contact. Reservations must be made in advance; expect to pay around ¥5000 per person.

MATSUYAMA

Matsuyama, the largest city on the island, became prominent as a castle town in the 17th century. The castle, along with Dogo-Onsen, the oldest hot spring in Japan, are the city's main tourist draws. In recent years the city has benefited greatly from the opening of new road links with Honshu, in particular the Nishi-Seto Highway, completed in 1999 and linking nearby Imabari (see p373) with the main island. Matsuyama is keen to project itself as an international city and has established sister-city relations with Sacramento, California, and Freiburg, Germany.

What to see and do

Two priorities are Matsuyama Castle, perched on a hill in the city centre and accessible by ropeway, and nearby Dogo-Onsen. Both could be done in one day, but an overnight stay in either Matsuyama or neighbouring Dogo would be more relaxed.

Matsuyama Castle (daily, 9am-5pm, ¥350) is at the top of Katsuyama Hill in the city centre. Construction of the castle was completed in 1627 but has since suffered fates similar to those of other castles in Japan. Struck by lightning on New Year's Day 1784, the donjon burnt to the ground. The castle was reconstructed in 1854, only to suffer bomb damage during WWII.

Today, the castle is reached by taking either the ropeway or a cutesy chair lift (daily, 8:30am-5:30pm, ¥210 one-way, ¥400 return). It's difficult to imagine what the castle lords who occupied this fortification would have made of the sight of people gliding up the hill in moving chairs but it's safe to assume that as intruders they'd have been easy targets. You can avoid the expense of the ropeway by walking up the hill – even if you take the chair/ropeway, there's still a fair way to walk before you reach the donjon. The views from the top (132m above sea level) make the effort worthwhile and even eclipse the main purpose of the journey, which is to climb up inside the donjon. The constant flow of tour parties and school groups means the donjon's entrance becomes a bottle-neck – you just have to go with the flow until you eventually emerge at the exit. Back outside there's a great view of the city and surrounding area, with mountains on one side and the Inland Sea coastline on the other.

The nearest tram stop for the ropeway up to the castle is Okaido. Discounts on the ropeway and castle entrance are available to Welcome Card holders (see p46) – a ropeway return plus castle entrance works out at ¥600. Otherwise, a round trip and castle combination ticket costs ¥750.

The French-style building lower down the hill is **Bansui-so** (daily except Mon, 9am-5pm) and was built in 1922 by a former feudal lord. Today it functions as an annex to the Prefectural Art Museum (see overleaf). Entry to the ground floor is free but the second floor houses temporary exhibitions for which the charge varies. The nearest tram stop is Okaido.

A couple of minutes north of Minami-Horibata tram stop is the **Prefectural Art Museum** (daily except Mon, 9:40am-6pm, ¥500) which houses a permanent collection of Japanese and Western art alongside special exhibitions.

● **Dogo-Onsen** Twenty minutes by tram from Matsuyama is the ancient spa town of Dogo. Today, Dogo is geared up to the tourist trade but a trip to the bath house is an excellent way to unwind after a day's sightseeing. Don't plan on doing any serious hiking after a trip to the baths though, since a visit here can leave you feeling extremely lethargic.

The hot spring dates back 3000 years and according to legend was discovered when a white heron put its injured leg into hot water flowing out of a crevice in some rocks. The main wooden bath house was built in 1894 and the cost of entry depends on the level of service you want. Tickets for the no-frills ground floor bath called Kami-no-yu (Water of the Gods) cost ¥300. For ¥620 you are given a yukata and served Japanese tea and a rice cracker afterwards on the second floor. The second floor also has its own bath, the more exclusive Tama-no-yu (Water of the Spirits), which costs ¥980 including yukata, tea and rice cracker. Finally, to use the second floor bath and have a private room for changing and relaxing afterwards the charge is ¥1240. This includes Japanese

---

MATSUYAMA　松山

Where to stay

1 Matsuyama Youth Hostel	1 松山ユースホステル
2 Hotel Patio Dogo	2 ホテルパティオドウゴ
3 Yamatoya Honten	3 大和屋本店
7 Matsuyama Tokyu Inn	7 松山東急イン
8 ANA Hotel Matsuyama	8 全日空ホテル松山
17 Terminal Hotel Matsuyama	17 ターミナルホテル松山

Where to eat

9 Minoru Café	9 Minoru Cafe
10 Sushitoku	10 すし徳
11 Lofty	11 Lofty
13 Tiny Restaurant Four Seasons	13 フォーシーズンズ
14 A Table	14 ア テーブル

Other

4 Dogo Onsen	4 道後温泉
5 Matsuyama Castle	5 松山城
6 Bansui-so	6 萬翠荘
12 Central Post Office	12 中央郵便局
15 Matsuyama International Center	15 松山県国際交流協会
16 Prefectural Art Museum	16 愛媛県立美術館

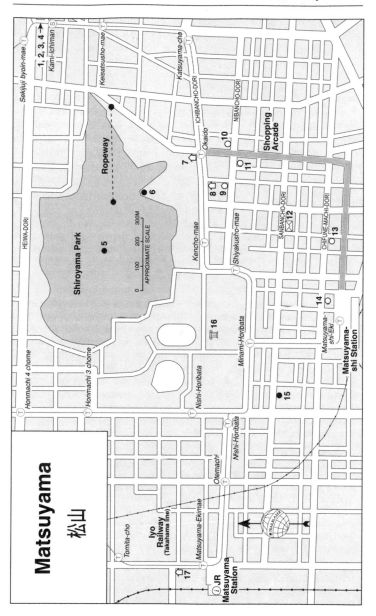

tea and Botchan Dango (dumpling-shaped sweetmeats) that Soseki Natsume, author of *Botchan*, used to eat when he was a teacher at Matsuyama Junior High School. The private rooms have a balcony from where you can look down on people in their yukata and geta wandering around town. There are some signs in English inside, so there's no problem about making an onsen faux-pas like stumbling into the wrong changing rooms.

The bath house is open 6:30am-10pm, except the ground floor which is open until 11pm. Take a tram from Matsuyama station bound for Dogo-Onsen. The last stop on this line is the old-fashioned Dogo-Onsen terminal, a 1986 reconstruction of the original (1911) European-style building. From the tram station, walk through the covered shopping arcade, turning right when you reach a large modern bath house on your left. The main wooden bath house will be straight in front of you.

PRACTICAL INFORMATION
Station guide
Access to the platforms is by stairs only. However, if you walk to the end of platform No 1 (turning left after passing through the ticket barrier), you can cross over the tracks to the other platforms without having to use the stairs.

The JR ticket office (daily, 5am-11pm) is combined with the travel agency. On the second floor of the station is a large souvenir shop. For a snack, try Aunt Stella's Cookies or Willie Winkie bakery. Coin lockers (all sizes) are to the right of the station exit. Next to the locker room is a Rent A Cycle office (daily, 8:50am-6:30pm), where the daily rate is ¥310.

Tourist information
The **tourist information booth** (☎ 089-931 3914, daily 8:30am-5pm), to the left as you exit the ticket barrier, has maps but the staff may not speak much English.

A quirk of this place is that from 8:30am to 5pm it functions only as a tourist information office and cannot help with accommodation reservations. However, from 5 to 8:30pm hotel reservation staff take over and can provide help with hotel bookings but won't have all the detailed knowledge of the sights. So if you time your arrival for around 4:30pm you'll get the best of both worlds.

Another tourist office is across the street from the tram terminus at Dogo-Onsen (see p386).

The staff at **Matsuyama Internation-al Center** (☎ 089-943 2025, daily except Mon, 9am-5:30pm) can offer some advice in English but information is mostly geared to foreign residents. However, this place does offer Internet access on the second floor (one hour, ¥100). The centre is a short walk south-west of Minami-Horibata tram stop.

At all these places, as well as in some hotels, you should be able to pick up a copy of *What's Going On?*, a monthly guide to events in Matsuyama.

Pick up the **Seto Inland Sea Welcome Card** (see p46) from the tourist information booth at Matsuyama station or Matsuyama International Center.

Getting around
The easiest way of travelling around Matsuyama is on one of its five tram lines – they're regular, cheap (¥170 flat fare) and go past all the major places in town. Enter at the back and pay as you leave at the front. A one-day pass costs ¥460 and can be bought from the tourist office at JR Matsuyama station or at Shi-eki station, the central tram terminal in the city centre.

Money
Try the ATMs in the central post office; the ATM that was in Sogo dept store (now called Rozunado Iyotetsu Hyakkaten) has closed.

Festivals
The highlight of **Matsuyama Festival** (August 11th-13th) is a night-time parade

of samba dancers. The event is kicked off by a fireworks display on August 10th.

Where to stay

All the below except the youth hostel offer discounts (the amount varies) to holders of the Seto Inland Sea Welcome Card.

As Shikoku's biggest city, Matsuyama is not short of top-class hotels. *ANA Hotel Matsuyama* (☎ 089-933 5511, 🖹 921 6053; ¥7500/S, ¥15,000/Tw/D) has the best location, right opposite the castle and in the centre of town. The spacious rooms have wide-screen TV, mini bar and room service. There's a good choice of restaurants including Castle Grill and a ground-floor coffee shop that sometimes has all-you-can-eat buffet lunches. Across the street is *Matsuyama Tokyu Inn* (☎ 089-941 0109, 🖹 934 3725), with a bright interior and smartly decorated rooms, some with views of Bansui-so (see p386). Rates are slightly lower than at the ANA Hotel.

The station area is not so convenient for sightseeing, though if you've got an early start and need to be close to the JR station, *Terminal Hotel Matsuyama* (☎ 089-947 5388, 🖹 947 6457) has functional single rooms for ¥5500 and a few twins at ¥10,000. Look for it to the left as you exit the station. Just by the entrance is a small coin laundry.

Matsuyama Youth Hostel (22-3 Dogo-Himezuka, ☎ 089-933 6366, 🖹 933 6378) is actually in the Dogo-Onsen area but the facilities and welcome make the trek out there worthwhile. Take tram No 5 to the Dogo-Onsen terminal and head for the steps that lead up to Isaniwa Shrine. Take the path to the right of these stairs and follow the 'Tsukasa View Hotel' signs along the way. The youth hostel is in an unmissable bright yellow building on the right before this hotel. The hostel has a restaurant but you can opt for the no meals rate which works out at ¥3200 for YH(HI) members and ¥4200 for others. Breakfast costs an additional ¥500 and dinner ¥1000.

A couple of other places in the Dogo-Onsen area are *Hotel Patio Dogo* (☎ 089-941 4128, 🖹 089-941 4129, 🖳 www.patio-dogo.co.jp; ¥8900/S, ¥13,000/D, ¥15,000/ Tw), offering Western-style accommodation right across from the bath house, and *Yamatoya Honten* (☎ 089-935 8880, 🖹 935 8881), which is definitely the place to stay if you can afford it. It's all kimonos and shamisen music in this upmarket ryokan which even boasts its own Noh theatre. Most of the rooms are tatami style though there are some Western singles and twins. The hotel has its own hot spring. Twin rooms with two meals go from ¥17,000. Room-only rates are available on request.

Where to eat

Tiny Restaurant Four Seasons (daily except Mon, 11:30am-2pm, 5-11pm) is tucked away on a side street and is billed as a 'rare ethnic restaurant in the Shikoku area'. It's highly recommended – the food is a mixture of Thai and Vietnamese with dishes such as spicy pork with ginger, fish in banana leaf, and coconut ice cream. There's also a good selection of cocktails and Welcome Card holders get a free drink. Expect to pay around ¥2000 a head for dinner.

Another place that does a take on Vietnamese food is *Minoru Café* (daily except Mon, 11am-11pm), near Mitsukoshi department store, where you can also get good coffee and cake sets in the afternoon.

Near here is *Lofty*, a place that serves pancakes, snacks and drinks from inside an imported London double-decker bus. Parked on a street corner by Mitsukoshi department store and with an enormous teddy bear locked in the driver's compartment, it's popular with young people dreaming they're extras on Cliff Richard's *Summer Holiday*. The pancakes, from around ¥250, are OK.

In *Sushitoku* (daily except 1st Wed, 10am-11pm) try to sit at the counter so that you can watch the staff rolling the fresh sushi; 10% off with the Welcome Card.

For authentic French cooking head for *A Table*, a small place with a counter and a few wooden tables which you share with other customers. The chef, who's lived in Matsuyama for nearly a decade, brings a taste of his native Lorraine to the menu; the ¥850 set lunches are the best value.

APPENDIX A: GLOSSARY

General

Basho sumo tournament
-bashi ..bridge
Bunraku puppetry
Conbini convenience store
Donjon the great tower or keep of a castle
-dori/odori ..street
-gawa ..river
Gaijin foreigner
Geisha person (usually a woman) trained to entertain at a party
Geta wooden clogs
Haiku poem of 17 syllables
Hiragana syllabary for writing Japanese words
Ikebana flower arranging
Izakaya Japanese-style pub/bar
-ji ..temple
-jo ..castle
Kaisoku rapid train
Kaiten-zushiya conveyor-belt sushi restaurant
Kami spirit/deity
Kanji Chinese characters used to write the Japanese language
Katakana syllabary for writing non-Japanese words
-ko ..lake
Koban police box
Koen park
Koto Japanese harp
Kyuko express train
Maiko trainee geisha
Manga comic
Meishi business card
Mikoshi portable shrine
Minshuku place to stay, similar to a B&B
Morning set a coffee shop's breakfast; usually coffee, boiled egg and toast
Onsen hot spring resort
Rotemburo open-air hot spring bath
Ryokan Japanese-style hotel
Shamisen wood instrument covered in cat skin with three strings made of silk
Shinkansen super express or bullet train
Shohizei consumption tax (5%)
Shojin ryori vegetarian food served and eaten by priests in temples
Shokudo canteen, dining hall
Shokudo bento lunch box

Tokkyu limited express train
Torii gate at entrance to Shinto shrine
Yakuza Japanese mafia
-yama mountain
Yokozuna grand champion in a sumo tournament
Yukata cotton garment worn as a dressing gown
Zazen Zen meditation

Food

Curry rice A uniquely Japanese take on the Indian curry. The sauce is more like gravy than curry but it's a cheap filling meal.
Dango Dumpling-shaped sweetmeat or confection.
Donburi A bowl of rice usually topped with chicken and egg (*oyakodon*) or strips of beef (*gyudon*). A very cheap meal. Restaurants are easy to spot as the counter is usually full of businessmen and meal tickets are bought from vending machines at the entrance.
Kakigori Crushed ice served with different fruit flavours, similar to Slush Puppy.
Kani Crab, which is usually expensive and served in dedicated crab restaurants, instantly recognizable from the giant crab with moving pincers above the entrance.
Meron pan Melon-flavoured buns.
Miso soup Served with practically every Japanese dish, miso (soybean paste) is a staple ingredient in Japanese cuisine. In Nagano there's even a shop where you can try miso-flavoured ice cream (see p148).
Mochi A rice cake; a special type of mochi is eaten to celebrate New Year.
Nabe A kind of Japanese hot pot; chicken, beef, pork or seafood mixed with vegetables and cooked in a large pot at your table.
Natto Fermented soy beans. Foreigners are often asked if they like *natto*. Answering yes will shock your listener since gaijin are not supposed to like it.
Okonomiyaki Japanese savoury pancake with vegetables and meat, cooked on a grill and served in front of the customer.
Onigiri A popular convenience-store snack, onigiri are triangles of rice wrapped in a sheet of nori (seaweed) and containing fillings such as salmon, tuna or pickled plums.

Pocky A snack food, thin biscuit sticks which are covered in icing (in a variety of flavours) and are available in every convenience store.

Ramen Stringy yellow noodles, served in a soup/broth with vegetables. Originally imported from China, ramen is a popular late-night snack. Some restaurants offer 'challenge ramen' which is incredibly hot, but which you don't have to pay for if you can finish it without exploding. Also sold as 'cup ramen' in convenience stores.

Sashimi Slices of raw fish, the most common are tuna, eel, prawn and salmon roe; not to be confused with sushi, which is arranged on a bed of rice.

Shabu-shabu Thinly sliced beef cooked at your table with vegetables and served with a special sauce.

Soba Thin buckwheat noodles eaten hot in a soup/broth, or cold when the noodles are dipped into a separate sauce made from soy, mirin (saké for cooking) and saké.

Somen Noodles served cold and eaten only in the summer.

Sukiyaki Thinly sliced beef with vegetables grilled in a special iron pan at your table.

Sushi Slices of fresh fish (particularly prawn and tuna) on a bed of rice. The most common kind, on small, oval-shaped rice balls, is called nigiri-zushi. Add soy sauce (and wasabi) to taste and eat with a few slices of pickled ginger.

Takoyaki Pieces of octopus in batter; popular at summer festivals.

Tempura Prawns/fish and vegetables deep fried in batter; served with a dipping sauce.

Tofu Soybean curd, delicious when dipped in soy sauce.

Tonkatsu A pork cutlet, dipped in breadcrumbs and deep fried. Always served with a mountain of shredded cabbage, miso soup and rice (all of which can be refilled on demand). Also made with chicken.

Umeboshi Sour, pickled plums. Some restaurants have bowls of umeboshi on the table for diners to pick at before/after a meal.

Udon Wheat-flour noodles, much thicker than soba, served hot in a broth.

Unagi Eel, basted in soy and saké sauce, cooked over a charcoal fire and served on a bed of rice. Traditionally eaten in the summer as stamina food for beating the heat.

Wasabi Hot mustard, similar to horseradish, served with sushi.

Yakisoba Pork mince and vegetables with fried noodles; popular at summer festivals.

Yakitori Chunks of chicken (wing, leg, heart, liver) and/or vegetables (usually leeks and pepper) on a skewer, dipped in a sauce made from saké, mirin (rice wine), stock and soy sauce and cooked over a charcoal fire. Usually served along with mugs of cold draught beer in small Japanese bars called *izakaya*.

Drink

Asahi Superdry One of the top two beers in Japan (see also Kirin).

Calpis A milk-based soft drink popular with children. Its name was changed to 'Calpico' when launched overseas.

CC Lemon A fizzy drink which claims to have 'a hundred lemons' worth of Vitamin C' in every can.

Kirin Rivals Asahi Superdry for the title of 'nation's favourite beer'.

Pocari Sweat A well-known energy drink in a blue can.

Saké Often refers generally to alcoholic drinks, while 'Nihonshu' is more specifically what is known in the West as the Japanese liquor saké. Made from white rice, saké is served hot or cold. Spiced saké is called o-toso.

Shochu A strong spirit popular in southern Japan (particularly Kyushu) and made from grain/potato. *Chulime* is shochu served with lime cordial.

Tea Cups of green tea are served free in nearly all Japanese restaurants. Earl Grey and English Breakfast are common in many hotels, while fruit and peppermint flavour tea infusions are also widely available.

Whisky No karaoke bar would be without bottles of Suntory whisky, the leading domestic brand. But really high-class establishments only serve imported whisky (Johnny Walker).

Yakult A 'lactic acid bacteria beverage' or, if you think it sounds more appealing, a fermented milk drink. Either way it is very popular in Japan.

APPENDIX B: USEFUL WORDS AND PHRASES

General words and phrases

Good morning	*ohaiyo gozaimasu*	Good evening	*konbanwa*
Good night	*oyasumi nasai*	Hello	*konnichiwa*
Please	*dozo*	Goodbye	*sayonara*
Thank you	*domo arigato*	Yes	*hai*
(very much)	*(gozaimashita)*	No	*ie*
No thanks	*kekko desu*	Excuse me	*sumimasen*
I'm sorry	*gomen nasai*	I don't understand	*wakarimasen*

What's your name?	*O-namae wa nan desu-ka*
My name is	*Watashi wa .... desu*
Where do you live?	*Doko ni sunde imasu ka*
I'm from Britain/America/Canada/ Australia/New Zealand	*Igirisujin/Amerikajin/Kanadajin/ Australiajin/New Zealandjin desu*
Do you speak English?	*Anata wa eigo ga hanasemasu ka*
Please write it down for me	*Sore o kaite kudasai*
Could you repeat that please?	*Mo ichido itte kudasai.*
How much does it cost?	*Ikura desu ka*

Japanese – Hiragana script

あ a		い i		う u		え e		お o	
か ka	が ga	き ki	ぎ gi	く ku	ぐ gu	け ke	げ ge	こ ko	ご go
さ sa	ざ za	し shi	じ ji	す su	ず zu	せ se	ぜ ze	そ so	ぞ zo
た ta	だ da	ち chi	ぢ ji	つ tsu	づ zu	て te	で de	と to	ど do
な na		に ni		ぬ nu		ね ne		の no	
は ば ぱ ha ba pa		ひ び ぴ hi bi pi		ふ ぶ ぷ fu bu pu		へ べ ぺ he be pe		ほ ぼ ぽ hobopo	
ま ma		み mi		む mu		め me		も mo	
や ya				ゆ yu				よ yo	
ら ra		り ri		る ru		れ re		ろ ro	
わ wa				を o				ん n	

Numerals

1	*ichi*	一	11	*ju-ichi*	十一	21	*ni-ju-ichi*	二十一
2	*ni*	二	12	*ju-ni*	十二	22	*ni-ju-ni*	二十二
3	*san*	三	13	*ju-san*	十三	100	*hyaku*	百
4	*shi/yon*	四	14	*ju-shi/yon*	十四	101	*hyaku-ichi*	百一
5	*go*	五	15	*ju-go*	十五	200	*ni-hyaku*	二百
6	*roku*	六	16	*ju-rokku*	十六	1000	*sen*	千
7	*shichi/nana*	七	17	*ju-shichi/nana*	十七	1001	*sen-ichi*	千一
8	*hachi*	八	18	*ju-hachi*	十八	2000	*ni-sen*	二千
9	*kyu/ku*	九	19	*ju-kyu*	十九	10,000	*ichi-man*	一万
10	*ju*	十	20	*ni-ju*	二十	20,000	*ni-man*	二万

Day/time

Monday	*getsuyobi*	Friday	*kinyobi*	yesterday	*kino*
Tuesday	*kayobi*	Saturday	*doyobi*	morning	*asa*
Wednesday	*suiyobi*	Sunday	*nichiyobi*	afternoon	*ogo*
Thursday	*mokuyobi*	today	*kyo*	evening	*yoru*
		tomorrow	*ashita*	hour *ji*	minute *fun/pun*

Japanese – Katakana script

ア a			イ i			ウ u			エ e			オ o		
カ ka	ガ ga		キ ki	ギ gi		ク ku	グ gu		ケ ke	ゲ ge		コ ko	ゴ go	
サ sa	ザ za		シ shi	ジ ji		ス su	ズ zu		セ se	ゼ ze		ソ so	ゾ zo	
タ ta	ダ da		チ chi	ヂ ji		ツ tsu	ヅ zu		テ te	デ de		ト to	ド do	
ナ na			ニ ni			ヌ nu			ネ ne			ノ no		
ハ ha	バ ba	パ pa	ヒ hi	ビ bi	ピ pi	フ fu	ブ bu	プ pu	ヘ he	ベ be	ペ pe	ホ ho	ボ bo	ポ po
マ ma			ミ mi			ム mu			メ me			モ mo		
ヤ ya						ユ yu						ヨ yo		
ラ ra			リ ri			ル ru			レ re			ロ ro		
ワ wa						ヲ o						ン n		

Directions

North	*kita*	(Go) left	*hidari (itte)*
South	*minami*	(Go) right	*migi (itte)*
West	*nishi*	(Go) straight on	*massugu (itte)*
East	*higashi*		

Where is...	*...wa doko desu ka*		
the train station	*Eki...*	the ticket office	*Midori-no-madoguchi..*
the bus stop	*Basu noriba ...*	a tourist information office	*Kanko annaijo...*
the tram stop	*Romendensha noriba..*	a toilet	*O-tearai* (polite)/
a taxi stand	*Takushi noriba ...*		*toire* (informal)

Railway vocabulary

Booking a ticket/making a reservation

adult	*otona*
child	*kodomo*
aisle (seat)	*tsuro (gawa no seki)*
berth	*shindai*
itinerary	*ryotei*
(railway) line	*sen*
no-smoking car	*kinen-sha*
refund	*haraimodoshi*
reserved seat	*shitei-seki*
reservation	*yoyaku*
seat	*seki*
sleeper train	*shindaisha*
ticket	*kippu*
ticket office	*midori-no-madoguchi*
(for seat reservations)	
timetable	*jikoku hyo*
transfer ticket	*norikae-kippu*
Travel Service Center	*ryoko senta*
unreserved seat	*jiyu-seki*

At the station

entrance	*iriguchi*
exit	*deguchi*
fare adjustment office	*ryokin seisanjo*
handicapped	*shintai no fujiyu*
platform	*platthomu*
station	*eki*
ticket gate/wicket	*kaisatsu-guchi*
underground/	*chikatetsu*
subway/metro	

On the train

departure	*shupatsu*
arrival	*tochaku*
buffet	*byuffe*
conductor	*shashosan*
Green car	*guriin-sha*
luggage	*nimotsu*
ordinary class	*futsu*
ordinary class coach	*futsu-sha*
railway lunchbox	*ekiben*

Railway phrases

How can I get to [Kyoto] from here?	*Koko kara [Kyoto] niwa made dousureba ikemasu ka*
I'd like to reserve a seat on the next train to [Kyoto]	*Tsugi no [Kyoto] iki ressha no zaseki o yoyaku shitai'n desu ga*
What time does the train to [Kyoto] leave?	*[Kyoto] iki ressha wa nan ji ni shupatsu shimasu ka*
Which platform does the train to [Kyoto] leave from?	*[Kyoto] iki no ressha wa dono homu kara shupatsu shimasu ka*
Excuse me, does this train go to [Kyoto]?	*Kono ressha wa [Kyoto] ni ikimasu ka*
Can you tell me where my seat is on this train?	*Kono ressha demo, watashi no seki o oshiete moraemasen ka*

Hotel

	Hoteru
I'd like to book a single/ double/twin room	*Singuru/daburu/tuin no heya o yoyaku shitai'n desu ga*

I'd like a room but no meals	*Sudomari onegaishimasu*
Can I check-in please?	*Check-in onegaishimasu*
I'd like to check out please	*Check-out onegaishimasu*
Do you accept Amex/Visa card?	*Amekkusu/Viza kaado wa tsukaemasu ka*

Restaurant

	Resutoran
I'd like to make a reservation	*Shokuji no yoyaku o shitai'n desu ga*
Do you have a menu in English?	*Eigo no menyuu wa arimasu ka*
What is this?	*Kore wa nan desu ka*
I'd like this please	*Kore o kudasai*
What time does the restaurant open/close?	*Resutoran wa nan ji kara/nan ji made desu ka*

Useful kanji

Male	男性	Day	日	Entrance	入口
Female	女性	Month	月	Exit	出口
Smoking	禁煙	Year	年	North	北
Non-smoking	禁煙	Hour	時	South	南
Reserved seat	指定席	Minute	分	East	東
Unreserved seat	自由席	Second	秒	West	西

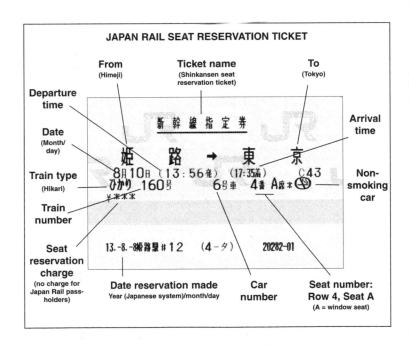

JAPAN RAIL SEAT RESERVATION TICKET

From (Himeji)
Ticket name (Shinkansen seat reservation ticket)
To (Tokyo)
Departure time
Arrival time
Date (Month/day)
Train type (Hikari)
Non-smoking car
Train number
Seat reservation charge (no charge for Japan Rail pass-holders)
Date reservation made — Year (Japanese system)/month/day
Car number
Seat number: Row 4, Seat A (A = window seat)

APPENDIX C: 2004 TIMETABLES

THE JAPANESE RAILWAY TIMETABLE

Even though the summaries contained in this appendix will give you an idea of the services available, the Japanese Timetable (see below) will always be the most up-to-date version so you may like to refer to one in order to check your plans.

How to use the Japanese Timetable

The route maps in the timetable use kanji to mark places so you need to know the kanji for where you are and where you want to go – a selection is provided below, or you can look at JNTO's *Tourist Map of Japan*. Find the route map which covers the area you are travelling in and then the places you want to travel between. Finally look for the number which appears immediately above or below it. This refers to the corresponding page in the timetable. For major services two numbers are given – one for each direction. Go to the relevant page. At the beginning of every timetable the names of all stops on a particular route appear in hiragana as well as kanji. Thus, even if you don't recognize the kanji, by using the hiragana syllabary on p392 you could work out the hiragana for eg Osaka. Working your

---

English/Japanese place names

Abashiri	網走	Nagano	長野
Aomori	青森	Nagoya	名古屋
Asahikawa	旭川	Narita Airport	成田空港
Atami	熱海	Naoetsu	直江津
Beppu	別府	Niigata	新潟
Furano	富良野	Nishi-Kagoshima	西鹿児島
Fukuoka	福岡	Nobeoka	延岡
Hakata	博多	Noboribetsu	登別
Hakodate	函館	Odawara	小田原
Himeji	姫路	Okayama	岡山
Hiroshima	広島	Ogori	小郡
Ichinoseki	一ノ関	Osaka	大阪
Kanazawa	金沢	Sapporo	札幌
Kansai Airport	関西空港	Sendai	仙台
Kochi	高知	Shin-Fuji	新富士
Kokura	小倉	Shin-Kobe	新神戸
Kubokawa	窪川	Shin-Osaka	新大阪
Kumamoto	熊本	Shin-Shimonoseki	新下関
Kyoto	京都	Shin-Yokohama	新横浜
Masuda	益田	Shizuoka	静岡
Matsue	松江	Takamatsu	高松
Matsumoto	松本	Takayama	高山
Matsushima	松島	Tokyo	東京
Matsuyama	松山	Toyama	富山
Mishima	三島	Tsuwano	津和野
Miyazaki	宮崎	Ueno	上野
Morioka	盛岡	Uwajima	宇和島
Nagasaki	長崎		

way around the Japanese timetable can take time but it is ultimately rewarding and since the information contained in it is up to date it is by far the most reliable way of working out which train you need to catch.

USING THE TIMETABLES IN THIS GUIDE

Timetables for shinkansen and limited express (LEX) services for most routes described in this book are provided below. Times for local/rapid trains are not included (except where they are the only option) even though these also operate on most routes.

The timetables below are included as an assistance to planning your trip but times should **always** be checked before heading to the station. Most services listed operate daily but weekend services can differ so checking is essential. It must also be noted that in most cases the timetables shown do not include all the services.

Table 1: Narita Airport to Tokyo via Narita Express (N'EX) [Only main stops shown]

1a: Narita to Tokyo

Narita Airport	07:43[1]	08:15[2]	08:47[1]	09:13[1,2]	09:43[1,2]	10:13[1,2,3]	14:43[2,4]
Airport Terminal 2	07:46	08:17	08:49	09:16	09:47	10:15	14:45
Tokyo	09:02	09:27	09:51	10:15	10:47	11:11	15:43

[1] Continues to Shinjuku and/or Ikebukuro. [2] Continues to Shinagawa and Yokohama.
[3] Hourly until 19:13 though subsequent times vary a bit.
[4] Hourly from 14:43 till 21:43 though subsequent times vary a bit.

1b: Tokyo to Narita

Tokyo	06:30[1]	07:00[1,2]	07:30[1]	08:00[2,3]	08:30[1]	10:03[1,2,4]	13:33[1,5]
Airport Terminal 2	07:26	07:54	08:32	08:57	09:25	10:56	14:24
Narita Airport	07:29	07:58	08:35	08:59	09:28	10:59	14:27

[1] Most services start in Ikebukuro (32 mins earlier) and stop in Shinjuku (23 mins earlier).
[2] Most services start in Yokohama (34 mins earlier), some stop at Shinagawa (13 mins earlier).
[3] Also at 09:00   [4] Hourly till 20:03 but subsequent times vary by up to 15 minutes.
[5] Hourly from 13:33 till 18:33 though subsequent times vary a bit.

Table 2: Kansai Airport to Shin-Osaka/Kyoto via Haruka LEX

	2a: Airport to Osaka/Kyoto				2b: Kyoto/Osaka to airport			
Kansai Airport	06:29[1]	07:59	08:48[2]	09:18[3]	▲ 07:09	07:40	08:52	10:02
Tennoji	07:17	08:41	09:22	09:50	06:39	07:09	08:09	09:32
Shin-Osaka	07:36	09:05	09:38	10:07	┃ 06:17	06:48	07:48	09:16
Kyoto	08:02	09:30	10:03	10:30	▼ 05:46[4]	06:22	07:16[5]	08:49[6]

[1] Also at 07:29   [2] Hourly till 20:48 though subsequent times vary by a few minutes.
[3] Hourly till 22:18 though subsequent times vary by a few minutes.
[4] Also at 06:46 and 07:46 though subsequent times vary by a few minutes.
[5] Hourly till 20:16 though services leave Kyoto at 18 mins past between 10:18 and 16:18, and arrive at Kansai Airport at 31, 32 or 34 minutes past the hour.
[6] Hourly till 19:46; services leave at 49 mins past the hour apart from 09:46, 16:46, 17:46, 18:46 and 19:46; some services after 16:46 arrive at the airport at 20 to 25 mins past the hour.

Table 3: Tokyo to Hakata (Fukuoka) by shinkansen

Note: The services listed below generally operate daily and hourly until approximately 18:00. The details given are accurate for the services shown but subsequent trains may not make all the same stops and some make additional stops. This therefore affects departure/arrival times. In addition this list is only a sample of the services available: the maximum number of departures every hour to/from Tokyo is now: 7 Nozomi, 2 Hikari, 3 Kodama. Thus the table should be used as a guide only.

The JR pass is not valid for Nozomi services and it is not possible to pay a supplement to use them. If travelling without a rail pass, it's worth noting that all Nozomi services now have three non-reserved carriages (there is no longer a compulsory additional seat reservation charge for Nozomi trains).

A new bullet train station has opened at Shinagawa (p87), on the Yamanote loop line which runs around Tokyo.

3a: Tokyo to Hakata (Fukuoka)

	To Oka-yama (Hikari)	To Shin-Osaka (Hikari)	Hakata (Nozomi)	To Shin-Osaka (Kodama)	
Tokyo	06:36	07:10	06:50	06:56	
Shinagawa		07:17	06:58	07:04	
Shin-Yokohama	06:53		07:09	07:15	
Odawara	07:10			07:35	
Atami				07:44	
Mishima				07:58	
Shin-Fuji				08:08	
Shizuoka		08:12		08:24	
Kakegawa				08:44	
Hamamatsu		08:34		08:59	
Toyohashi				09:18	
Mikawa-Anjo				09:35	
Nagoya	08:25	09:05	08:34	09:48	
Gifu-Hashima	08:37			10:00	
Maibara	08:57			10:17	
Kyoto	09:21	09:44	09:12	10:41	
Shin-Osaka (arr)	09:36	09:59	09:27	10:56	
				To Hakata (Kodama)	**Hikari**
Shin-Osaka (dep)	09:38		09:29	11:15	09:59
Shin-Kobe	09:52		09:42	11:29	10:12
Nishi-Akashi	10:02			11:40	
Himeji	10:14			12:01	10:30
Aioi	10:30			12:12	
Okayama	10:47		10:15	12:45	10:52
Shin-Kurashiki				13:06	
Fukuyama				13:19	11:09
Shin-Onomichi				13:32	
Mihara				13:42	
Higashi-Hiroshima				13:56	
Hiroshima			10:52	14:08	
Shin-Iwakuni				14:25	11:34
Tokuyama				14:44	
Shin-Yamaguchi				15:00	

Table 3 (cont'd)

3a: Tokyo to Hakata (Fukuoka)

	To Hakata (Nozomi)	To Hakata (Kodama)	To Hakata (Hikari)
Asa		15:15	
Shin-Shimonoseki		15:34	12:17
Kokura	11:35	15:45	12:26
Hakata (Fukuoka)	11:57	16:06	12:44

See Note opposite.

3b: Hakata (Fukuoka) to Tokyo

	To Shin-Osaka (Hikari)	To Tokyo (Nozomi)	Shin-Osaka to Tokyo (Hikari)	Okayama to Tokyo (Hikari)	To Shin-Osaka (Kodama)
Hakata (Fukuoka)	07:35	06:25			07:12
Kokura	07:53	06:41			07:33
Shin-Shimonoseki					07:47
Asa					08:06
Shin-Yamaguchi	08:13	07:00			08:17
Tokuyama					08:39
Shin-Iwakuni					08:54
Hiroshima	08:46	07:31			09:11
Higashi-Hiroshima					09:24
Mihara					09:39
Shin-Onomichi					09:49
Fukuyama	09:11				09:58
Shin-Kurashiki					10:21
Okayama	09:28	08:07		07:32	10:45
Aioi				07:53	11:07
Himeji	09:49			08:03	11:25
Nishi-Akashi				08:15	11:38
Shin-Kobe	10:07	08:38		08:27	11:49
Shin-Osaka (arr)	10:20	08:51		08:41	12:04

					To Tokyo (Kodama)
Shin-Osaka (dep)		08:53	08:20	08:43	08:23
Kyoto		09:09	08:37	09:00	08:40
Maibara				09:28	09:05
Gifu-Hashima				09:45	09:20
Nagoya		09:47	09:15	09:57	09:33
Mikawa-Anjo					09:46
Toyohashi					10:06
Hamamatsu			09:45		10:25
Kakegawa					10:40
Shizuoka			10:10		10:58
Shin-Fuji					11:11
Mishima					11:23
Atami			10:36		11:32
Odawara				11:09	11:46
Shin-Yokohama		11:10		11:26	12:03
Shinagawa		11:22	11:05		12:15
Tokyo		11:30	11:13	11:43	12:23

Table 4: Tokyo to Nagano by Asama shinkansen

Note: The services shown below are only a sample of the many on this route. During the day there are at least two an hour to/from Tokyo and one an hour to/from Ueno. The details given in the sample timetables below are accurate for the services shown but other trains may not make all the same stops and some make additional stops. This also affects departure/arrival times. Thus the table should be used as a guide only.

4a: Tokyo to Nagano

Tokyo	07:52	09:12	10:00	12:28	13:28	14:48	16:28	17:28	
Ueno	07:58	09:18	10:06	12:34	13:34	14:54	16:34	17:34	
Omiya	08:18	09:38	10:26	12:54	13:54	15:14	16:54	17:54	
Kumagaya	08:32	09:52		13:08		15:28	17:08		
Honjo-Waseda	08:43			13:19		15:39	17:19	18:20	
Takasaki	08:53	10:08	10:55	13:29	14:19	15:49	17:29	18:37	
Annaka-Haruna	09:02	10:17		13:38		15:58	17:38	18:46	
Karuizawa	09:15	10:30	11:12	13:51	14:36	16:11	17:51	18:56	
Sakudaira	09:24		11:21	14:00	14:45	16:20	18:00		
Ueda	09:34		11:31	14:10	14:55	16:30	18:10		
Nagano	09:47	10:54	11:44	14:24	15:08	16:43	18:23	19:09	

4b: Nagano to Tokyo

Nagano	08:58	10:12	12:24	13:10	14:20	15:21	16:35	17:55	
Ueda			12:37	13:23	14:33	15:34		18:08	
Sakudaira			12:48	13:34	14:44	15:45		18:19	
Karuizawa	09:23		12:58	13:44	14:54	15:55	17:00	18:29	
Annaka-Haruna	09:34		13:09		15:06	16:06	17:11		
Takasaki	09:43		13:19	14:01	15:16	16:16	17:21		
Honjo-Waseda					15:26	16:26			
Kumagaya	09:59		13:35		15:36	16:36	17:36		
Omiya	10:14	11:12	13:50	14:26	15:50	16:50	17:50	19:11	
Ueno	10:30		14:10	14:46	16:10	17:10	18:10		
Tokyo	10:41	11:35	14:16	14:52	16:16	17:16	18:16	19:36	

Table 5: Nagano to Nagoya via Matsumoto

5a: Nagano to Nagoya					5b: Nagoya to Nagano			
Nagano	09:00	10:50	12:50	14:50	11:54	12:49	15:43	17:48
Shinonoi	09:08	10:58	12:58	14:58	11:45	12:41	15:35	17:40
Hijiri-Kogen				15:18				
Matsumoto	09:51	11:42	13:41	15:42	11:03	12:00	14:57	17:00
Shiojiri	10:01	11:52	13:51			11:50	14:46	16:50
Kiso-Fukushima	10:28	12:19	14:19	16:19	10:23	11:23	14:19	16:23
Nagiso			14:43	16:44		10:58		15:58
Nakatsugawa	11:03	12:54	14:56	16:56	09:47	10:47	13:44	15:47
Tajimi	11:29	13:20	15:22	17:22	09:22	10:22		15:22
Chikusa	11:45	13:37	15:39	17:39	09:06	10:06		15:06
Nagoya	11:51	13:43	15:46	17:47	09:00	10:00	13:00	15:00

Note: There is generally one through service an hour from both Nagano and Nagoya.

Table 6: Nagano to Toyama (and Kanazawa) via Naoetsu

6a: Nagano to Naoetsu[1]		6b: Naoetsu to Toyama/Kanazawa[2/3]					
			H	H	H	H	H
Nagano	08:21	Naoetsu	09:37	11:18	12:31	14:46	17:19
Toyono	08:23	Itoigawa	10:01	12:12	12:53	15:09	17:43
Kurohime	08:43	Tomari					18:01
Myoko-Kogen	08:51	Nyuzen					18:05
Sekiyama	08:59	Kurobe	10:28	12:39		15:36	18:13
Arai	09:16	Uozu	10:33	12:44	13:23	15:42	18:19
Takada	09:26	Namerikawa	10:39	12:50			
Naoetsu	09:39	Toyama	10:51	13:02	13:38	15:57	18:34
		Takaoka	11:03	13:14	13:50	16:09	18:46
		Isurugi					18:57
		Tsubata					
		Kanazawa	11:29	13:39	14:18	16:25	19:14

6c: Kanazawa/Toyama to Naoetsu[2/3]						6d: Naoetsu to Nagano[1]	
	H	H	H	H	H		
Kanazawa	07:20	10:48	13:13	14:05	17:07	Naoetsu	08:12
Tsubata		10:57				Takada	08:21
Isurugi	07:35	11:06				Arai	08:41
Takaoka	07:45	11:27	13:38	14:30	17:32	Sekiyama	08:59
Toyama	07:57	12:04	13:49	14:42	17:44	Myoko-Kogen	09:08
Namerikawa	08:08				17:55	Kurohime	09:16
Uozu	08:14	12:20	14:07	14:58		Toyono	09:37
Kurobe			14:12	15:03		Nagano	09:50
Nyuzen	08:25				18:15		
Tomari				15:14	18:18		
Itoigawa	08:45		14:41	15:32	18:36		
Naoetsu	09:07	13:12	15:05	15:56	19:01		

H = Hokuetsu [1] There are no limited express services between Nagano and Naoetsu; the local service takes approx 90 mins and generally operates once an hour.
[2] The times shown are a sample of the almost hourly service (in each direction) between Naoetsu and Kanazawa.
[3] See Table 8 for details of other services between Toyama and Kanazawa.

Table 7: Toyama/Takayama to Nagoya[1]

	7a: Toyama to Nagoya				7b: Nagoya to Toyama			
Toyama	08:10	13:09	15:12	17:16	12:18	14:46	16:47	18:51
Hayahoshi	08:19	13:18				14:38		18:17
Hida-Furukawa	09:28	14:23	16:24	18:27	11:09	13:35	15:36	17:37
Takayama	09:47	14:42	16:42	18:48	10:56	13:22	15:23	17:24
Gero	10:28	15:26	17:26	19:35	10:12	12:37	14:35	16:34
Mino-Ota	11:23	16:15	18:29	20:26	09:22	11:43	13:43	15:43
Gifu	11:47	16:47	18:48	20:47	09:02	11:23	13:22	15:22
Nagoya	12:09	17:09	19:09	21:09	08:43	11:03	13:03	15:03

[1] Services for Nagoya that start in Takayama (and vice versa) are not given but generally operate once an hour during the day; some of these services stop also at Kuguno, Hida-Osaka, Hida-Hagiwara, Hida-Kanayama, Shirakawaguchi, Unuma and Owari-Ichinomiya.

Table 8: Toyama to Osaka

	8a: Toyama to Osaka				8b: Osaka to Toyama[2]			
Toyama	08:17	10:10[1]	14:16	16:08	11:50	12:53	14:59	17:00
Takaoka	08:28	10:22	14:28	16:20	11:38	12:42	14:47	16:48
Kanazawa	09:01	10:54		16:53	11:15	12:18	14:24	16:25
Komatsu		11:11	15:01	17:09			14:02	16:04
Kaga-Onsen		11:20	15:25	17:18		11:50	13:54	15:55
Awara-Onsen		11:30		17:28		11:40	13:43	15:45
Fukui	09:44	11:41	15:45	17:40	10:28	11:29	13:33	15:34
Sabae				17:48				15:25
Takefu		11:53		17:53			13:20	
Tsuruga		12:13		18:13			13:00	15:00
Kyoto	11:06	13:06	17:06	19:06	09:08	10:09	12:10	14:10
Shin-Osaka	11:28	13:28	17:28	19:28	08:46	09:46	11:46	13:46
Osaka	11:32	13:32	17:32	19:32	08:42	09:42	11:42	13:42

[1] Also at 11:10 and 13:10.　[2] Hourly, at 42 mins past the hour, until 18:42. However, the stops and therefore departure/arrival times vary so it is essential to check.

Table 9: Nagoya to Shingu[1]

	9a: Nagoya to Shingu[2]				9b: Shingu to Nagoya[3]			
Nagoya	08:14	10:06	13:06	19:45	09:34	12:17	16:17	20:40
Kuwana	08:32	10:24	13:24	20:03	09:14	11:57	15:58	20:20
Yokkaichi	08:42	10:35	13:35	20:14	09:02	11:46	15:48	20:09
Suzuka				20:22	08:54			
Tsu	09:02	10:57	13:57	20:35	08:41	11:37	15:27	19:48
Matsusaka	09:16	11:12	14:12	20:50	08:26	11:12	15:10	19:33
Taki	09:23	11:19	14:19	20:57	08:19	11:03	15:04	19:26
Misedani		11:41	14:41	21:19	07:57	10:41		19:04
Kii-Nagashima	10:12	12:10	15:09	21:45	07:30	10:13	14:14	18:27
Owase	10:33	12:31	15:30	22:08	07:08	09:50	13:51	18:15
Kumano-shi	11:00	13:02	15:57	22:34	06:41	09:23	13:23	17:48
Shingu	11:19	13:25	16:17	22:53	06:22	09:03	13:03	17:28

[1] Rail-pass holders have to pay an additional fare (¥490) between Yokkaichi and Tsu.
[2] All trains apart from the 19:45 from Nagoya continue to Kii-Katsuura.
[3] All trains apart from the 06:22 start in Kii-Katsuura.

Table 10: Shingu to Shin-Osaka and Kyoto (cont'd p403)

	10a: Shingu to Kyoto				10b: Kyoto to Shingu			
	SK	SK	OA	SK	K	SK	OA	SK
Shingu	08:43	10:41	13:11	15:47	14:10	15:03	16:38	19:03
Kii-Katsuura	09:01	10:56	13:25	16:02	13:54	14:48	16:25	18:49
Taiji	09:07							18:42
Koza	09:24	11:02		16:27	13:29	14:22		18:23
Kushimoto	09:32	11:31	13:52	16:36	13:21	14:11	15:58	18:14
Susami	10:02	12:08		17:07	12:44	13:35		17:43
Tsubaki	10:17					13:22		17:30
Shirahama	10:34	12:35	14:38	17:34	12:20	13:13	15:10	17:18
Kii-Tanabe	10:45	12:46	14:49	17:45	12:11	13:02	15:01	17:04
Minabe					12:03			

Table 10: Shingu to Kyoto (cont'd from p402)

| | 10a: Shingu to Kyoto | | | | 10b: Kyoto to Shingu | | | |
	SK	SK	OA	SK	K	SK	OA	SK
Gobo	11:11	13:12	15:15	18:12	11:42	12:35	14:35	16:37
Wakayama	11:49	13:49	15:51	18:49	11:02	12:00	14:00	16:01
Hineno	12:06				10:44			15:43
Otori				19:21				
Tennoji	12:31	14:31	16:31	19:34	10:20	11:20	13:20	15:20
Shin-Osaka	12:50	14:50	16:51	19:51	10:03	11:03	13:03	15:03
Kyoto			17:17	20:16	09:34	10:36	12:35	

SK = Super-Kuroshio   K = Kuroshio   OA = Ocean-Arrow

Table 11: Shin-Yamaguchi to Yonago via Masuda and Matsue

	11a: Shin-Yamaguchi to Yonago			11b: Yonago to Shin-Yamaguchi		
Shin-Yamaguchi	08:50	12:26	16:31	10:12	14:00	18:52
Yuda-Onsen	09:01	12:35	16:41	10:02	13:51	18:42
Yamaguchi	09:05	12:38	16:44	09:59	13:48	18:39
Mitani	09:33	13:02	17:09	09:33	13:23	18:13
Tokusa	09:44	13:13	17:19	09:23	13:13	18:03
Tsuwano	09:56	13:25	17:32	09:11	13:00	17:51
Nichihara	10:06	13:35	17:41	09:01	12:51	17:41
Masuda	10:29	13:57	18:03	08:41	12:30	17:14
Mihomisumi		14:15	18:21	08:21	12:07	16:50
Hamada	11:01	14:33	18:42	08:06	11:52	16:35
Hashi	11:10	14:42			11:43	16:17
Gotsu	11.18	14:49	18:56	07:44	11:36	16:05
Oda-Shi	11:48	15:01	19:23	07:11	11:10	15:50
Izumo-Shi	12:10	15:17	19:46	06:46	10:48	15:28
Shinji		15:46	19:58	06:34		
Tamatsukuri-Onsen	12:21	15:59	20:06	06:27	10:28	15:06
Matsue	12:35	16:13	20:12	06:20	10:22	15:00
Yasugi	12:50	16:27	20:27	06:05	10:07	14:44
Yonago	12:57	16:34	20:34	05:58	10:00	14:37

Table 12: Tokyo to Sendai, Morioka and Hachinohe by shinkansen

| | 12a: Tokyo to Sendai/Morioka/Hachinohe (cont'd overleaf) | | | | | | | |
	H	MY	H	MY	H	Y	Y	Y
Tokyo	08:52	09:24	09:56	10·16	11:56	12:16	16:16	18:08
Ueno	08:58	09:30	10:02	10:22	12:02	12:22	16:22	18:14
Omiya	09:18	09:50	10:22	10:42	12:22	12:42	16:42	18:34
Utsunomiya	10:15			11:07		13:07	17:07	18:58
Koriyama		10:48		11:40		13:36	17:38	19:30
Fukushima		11:04		11:56		13:51	17:53	19:46
Sendai	10:38	11:30	11:39	12:22	13:38	14:14	18:18	20:12
Furukawa		11:52		12:37		14:28	18:34	20:27
Kurikoma-Kogen		12:02		12:48		14:38	18:46	20:37
Ichinoseki		12:12		13:02		14:48	19:01	20:47
Mizusawa-Esashi		12:23		13:13		14:59	19:12	20:59
Kitakami		12:33		13:22		15:12	19:21	21:08
Shin-Hanamaki		12:42		13:31		15:21	19:30	21:17
Morioka	11:26	12:54	12:26	13:44	14:26	15:33	19:43	21:30

Table 12 (cont'd): 12a: Tokyo to Sendai/Morioka/Hachinohe

Iwate-Numakunai	11:40		
Ninohe	11:53	12:48	
Hachinohe	12:04	13:00	14:55

12b: Morioka/Sendai/Hachinohe to Tokyo

	H	Y	H	H	MY	MY	Y	Y
Hachinohe	07:58		08:55	10:04				
Ninohe	08:10		09:07					
Iwate-Numakunai			09:20					
Morioka	08:39	08:28	09:39	10:39	14:16	15:16	15:46	16:28
Shin-Hanamaki		08:41			14:29	15:29	15:58	16:41
Kitakami		08:54			14:38	15:38		16:54
Mizusawa-Esashi		09:03			14:48	15:48	16:11	17:04
Ichinoseki		09:15			15:04	16:04	16:22	17:15
Kurikoma-Kogen		09:25			15:14	16:14	16:32	17:26
Furukawa		09:35			15:24	16:24		17:37
Sendai	09:24	09:52	10:24	11:24	15:43	16:43	16:57	17:53
Fukushima		10:20			16:09	17:09		18:19
Koriyama		10:36			16:30	17:30		18:36
Utsunomiya		11:09			17:08	18:08		19:10
Omiya	10:42	11:34	11:41	12:42	17:34	18:34	18:18	19:37
Ueno	11:02	11:54	12:02	13:02	17:54	18:54	18:34	19:58
Tokyo	11:08	12:00	12:08	13:08	18:00	19:00	18:44	20:04

H = Hayate   Y = Yamabiko   MY = Max-Yamabiko (double decker)

Note: (i) The above is a selection of the many services on this route. Not all the stops are shown; however, none of the services shown stops at Oyama, Nasu-Shiobara or Shiroishi-Zao.

(ii) See p414 for basic details about the new service on the original route.

(iii) See Table 16 for details of other Hayate services between Morioka and Hachinohe.

Table 13: Sendai to Matsushima-Kaigan

	13a: Sendai to M'shima-Kaigan		13b: M'shima-Kaigan to Sendai	
	Rapid[1]	Local[2]	Rapid[3]	Local[4]
Sendai	10:10	09:23	▲ 10:07	11:39
Tagajo	10:21	09:43	│ 09:47	11:19
Hon-Shiogama	10:25	09:50	│ 09:42	11:12
Matsushima-Kaigan	10:37	10:02 ▼	09:35	11:02

[1] Also at 11:10 and 12:10, thereafter at 59 minutes past the hour till 17:59.
[2] Hourly till 17:22.   [3] Hourly till 17:34   [4] Hourly till 18:02.

Table 14: Matsushima to Ichinoseki

14a: Matsushima to Ichinoseki

Matsushima	08:27	09:25	11:04	13:04	15:07	17:05	18:07	19:20
Kogota	08:53	09:49	11:32	13:35	15:35	17:31	18:27	19:47
Hanaizumi	09:26	10:17	12:05	14:09	16:07	18:06	18:57	20:24
Ichinoseki	09:39	10:34	12:19	14:23	16:23	18:20	19:16	20:35

14b: Ichinoseki to Matsushima

Ichinoseki	08:00	10:48	12:51	14:53	16:43	17:55	19:01	19:54
Hanaizumi	08:15	11:02	13:04	15:06	16:58	18:10	19:15	20:08
Kogota	08:49	11:46	13:53	15:51	17:43	18:49	19:58	20:45
Matsushima	09:09	12:06	14:12	16:10	18:03	19:09	20:17	21:04

Table 15: (Morioka)–Hanamaki–Tono–Kamaishi–Miyako–Morioka

	15a: Hanamaki to Morioka				15b: Morioka to Hanamaki		
	R	**R**	**R**				
(Morioka)	08:41	11:22	17:01	▲	09:04	12:54	16:31
Hanamaki	09:11	11:53	17:31		08:36	12:26	16:25
Shin-Hanamaki	09:18	12:00	17:38		08:24	12:14	15:51
Tsuchizawa	09:25	12:07	17:45		08:17	12:07	15:44
Miyamori	09:38	12:20			08:03		15:30
Tono	10:02	12:45	18:23		07:42	11:27	15:03
Kosano	10:41	13:27	19:04		07:00	10:41	14:22
Kamaishi	10:47	13:34	19:10		06:55	10:35	14:17
	Lcl	**Lcl**			**R**	**R**	**Lcl**
Kamaishi	11:26	15:39	19:35		06:48	10:26	14:11
Namiita-Kaigan	11:47	16:04	20:00		06:23		13:44
Rikuchu-Yamada	12:11	16:26	20:17		06:07	09:52	13:29
Miyako	12:44	17:06	20:52		05:35	09:24	12:57
	Rpd	**Lcl**	**Lcl**		**R**	**Lcl**	**Lcl**
Miyako	09:26	15:49	18:11		12:48	15:47	18:53
Morioka	11:19	18:00	20:41	▼	10:48	13:46	16:30
					Rpd	**Rpd**	**Lcl**

R = Rikuchu LEX, Lcl = local, Rpd = rapid

Table 16: Morioka to Aomori (and Hakodate)
Note: See p414 for details about the route changes between Morioka and Hachinohe and Table 12 pp403-4 for details of additional Hayate shinkansen services.

16a: Morioka to Aomori (and Hakodate)

	HAY	**HAY**	**HAY**	**HAY**	**HAY**	**HAY**	**HAY**	
Morioka	07:59	09:26	10:26	11:02	13:26	15:26	16:26	18:26
Ninohe	08:26	09:53	10:48			15:53		
Hachinohe	08:37	10:04	11:00	11:31	14:04	16:04	16:55	18:55
(change to LEX)	**H**	**SH**	**H**	**SH**	**H**	**H**	**SH**	**SH**
Hachinohe	08:50	10:16	11:10	12:16	14:15	16:13	17:07	19:02
Misawa	09:04	10:29	11:24	12:29	14:29	16:28	17:21	19:16
Noheji	09:23	10:46	11:42	12:46	14:47	16:46	17:38	19:33
Asamushi-Onsen	09:40			13:01	15:03	17:02	17:53	
Aomori	10:00	11:20	12:17	13:21	15:22	17:22	18:12	20:06
Hakodate	12:04	13:12	14:19	15:16	17:31	19:23	20:09	21:54

16b: (Hakodate and) Aomori to Morioka

	SH	**SH**	**H**	**H**	**H**	**SH**	**SH**	**H**
Hakodate	07:00	08:48	10:40	11:30	12:51	13:40	15:40	16:51
Aomori	08:58	10:55	12:48	13:43	14:49	15:44	17:43	18:46
Asamushi-Onsen			13:01		15:02	15:57		18:58
Noheji			13:17	14:12	15:19	16:12	18:09	19:16
Misawa			13:36	14:30	15:37	16:29	18:26	19:34
Hachinohe	09:53	11:52	13:51	14:45	15:51	16:43	18:40	19:49
(change to shinkansen)	**HAY**	**HAY**	**HAY**	**HAY**	**HAY**	**HAY**	**HAY**	**HAY**
Hachinohe	10:54	12:04	14:04	14:55	16:04	16:55	18:55	19:58
Ninohe	11:07			15:07		17:07	19:07	20:11
Morioka	11:33	12:33	14:33	15:33	16:33	17:33	19:33	20:33

HAY = Hayate shinkansen   H = Hatsukari   SH = Super Hatsukari

Table 17: Aomori to Odate (and Akita)

	17a: Aomori to Odate & Akita				17b: Akita & Odate to Aomori			
Aomori	06:07[1]	09:57	13:46	15:45	11:54	12:25	15:17	20:03
Hirosaki	06:39	10:27	14:16	16:15	11:12	11:50	14:46	19:28
Owani-Onsen		10:36	14:26	16:25		11:40	14:36	19:17
Ikarigaseki		10:44	14:34	16:32		11:33	14:29	19:10
Odate	07:11	11:03	14:54	16:50	10:31	11:15	14:11	18:52
Takanosu	07:26	11:20	15:09	17:05	10:13	10:54	13:56	18:37
Higashi-Noshiro	07:51	11:45	15:35	17:28	09:48	10:31	13:23	18:15
Hachirogata		12:09	16:00	17:52	09:16	10:08	13:09	17:52
Akita	08:50	12:32	16:24	18:17	08:46	09:41	12:44	17:29

[1] Continues to Niigata (see Table 18a).

Table 18: Akita to Niigata

The services shown are the only direct services between Akita and Niigata.

	18a: Akita to Niigata			18b: Niigata to Akita		
Akita	08:50[1]	12:49	16:33	12:11	16:14	19:27[2]
Ugo-Honjo	09:24	13:25	17:06	11:38	15:42	18:54
Kisakata	09:46	13:47	17:26	11:18	15:22	18:33
Yuza	10:14	14:09	17:47	10:57	15:01	18:12
Sakata	10:31	14:22	18:00	10:47	14:51	18:02
Amarume	10:41	14:30	18:09	10:37	14:40	17:51
Tsuruoka	10:57	14:43	18:20	10:26	14:30	17:40
Atsumi-Onsen	11:18	15:03	18:39	10:05	14:09	17:19
Murakami	12:03	15:44	19:20	09:20	13:22	16:32
Sakamachi	12:12	15:53	19:29	09:11	13:13	16:23
Shibata	12:28	16:09	19:45	08:55	12:57	16:07
Niigata	12:55	16:31	20:07	08:33	12:35	15:42

[1] Comes from Aomori (see Table 17a). [2] Continues to Aomori (see Table 17b).

Table 19: Hakodate to Sapporo

	19a: Hakodate to Sapporo							
	SH	H	SH	SH	H	SH	H	SH
Hakodate	08:30	09:30	11:00	12:17	13:25	14:26	15:24	16:43
Goryokaku	08:34	09:35	11:04	12:21	13:29			
Onuma-Koen	08:49	09:53	11:21	12:36	13:48	14:44	15:44	
Mori	09:05		11:39			15:05	16:02	
Yakumo	09:25	10:30	11:57	13:08	14:16	15:23	16:23	
Oshamambe	09:43	10:49	12:15	13:26	14:46	15:41	16:44	
Toya	10:05	11:14	12:37	13:49	15:12	16:04	17:09	
Date-Mombetsu	10:15	11:25	12:47	13:59	15:23	16:13	17:19	
Higashi-Muroran	10:30	11:42	13:02	14:16	15:40	16:30	17:36	18:30
Noboribetsu	10:41	11:53	13:13	14:27	15:51	16:42	17:48	
Tomakomai	11:03	12:15	13:35	14:48	16:14	17:03	18:12	19:01
Minami-Chitose	11:19	12:31	13:50	15:03	16:29	17:19	18:28	19:16
Shin-Sapporo	11:39	12:50	14:09	15:22	16:50	17:40	18:50	19:35
Sapporo	11:47	12:59	14:17	15:31	16:58	17:49	18:59	19:43

Table 19 (cont'd)

19b: Sapporo to Hakodate

	H	SH	H	SH	SH	H	SH	SH
Sapporo	07:30	08:34	09:19	10:52	12:22	13:17	15:07	16:52
Shin-Sapporo	07:38	08:43	09:28	11:00	12:30	13:25	15:15	17:00
Minami-Chitose	07:51	09:04	09:47	11:19	12:48	13:45	15:34	17:19
Tomakomai	08:15	09:19	10:03	11:35	13:04	14:01	15:50	17:34
Noboribetsu	08:42	09:40	10:25	11:56	13:25	14:23	16:11	17:59
Higashi-Muroran	08:56	09:52	10:38	12:08	13:37	14:36	16:23	18:12
Date-Mombetsu	09:13	10:07	10:53		13:50	14:51	16:37	18:26
Toya	09:24	10:16	11:04	12:29	13:59	15:02	16:44	18:36
Oshamambe		10:40	11:29	12:53		15:27	17:10	18:59
Yakumo		10:57	11:48	13:10		15:46	17:28	19:17
Mori		11:16	12:09			16:07	17:48	19:35
Onuma-Koen	10:48	11:33	12:27	13:44	15:09	16:25	18:03	
Goryokaku						16:43	18:20	20:10
Hakodate	11:10	11:53	12:48	14:04	15:29	16:48	18:24	20:14

H = Hokuto   SH = Super Hokuto

Table 20: Sapporo to Asahikawa

	20a: Sapporo to Asahikawa		20b: Asahikawa to Sapporo	
	S	L	S	L
Sapporo	08:00[1]	09:30[2]	09:20	10:00
Iwamizawa	08:24	09:58	08:56	09:32
Bibai	08:34	10:08	08:46	09:21
Sunagawa	08:44	10:20	08:36	09:09
Takikawa	08:49	10:26	08:30	09:03
Fukagawa	09:02	10:40	08:18	08:49
Asahikawa	09:20	11:00	08:00[3]	08:30[4]

S = Super White Arrow   L = Lilac

[1] Hourly till 21:00   [2] Hourly till 19:30   [3] Hourly till 17:00   [4] Hourly till 17:30

Table 21: Asahikawa to Abashiri

	21a: Asahikawa to Abashiri				21b: Abashiri to Asahikawa			
Asahikawa	09:01	11:20	16:58	19:07	10:10	13:09	17:11	20:59
Kamikawa	09:42	12:01	17:48	19:48	09:25	12:30	16:32	20:20
Engaru	10:57	13:21	19:03	21:10	08:09	11:16	15:17	19:05
Kitami	11:55	14:20	19:58	22:04	07:13	10:19	14:20	18:08
Bihoro	12:19	14:43	20:21	22:28	06:49	09:56	13:56	17:45
Abashiri	12:45	15:09	20:47	22:55	06:23	09:30	13:30	17:19

These services originate (and terminate) in Sapporo and are the only direct limited express services between Asahikawa and Abashiri.

Table 22: Abashiri to Kushiro[1]

22a: Abashiri to Kushiro					22b: Kushiro to Abashiri			
Abashiri	06:41	10:01	16:18	18:50	09:18	12:06	18:49	21:25
Kitahama	06:57	10:15	16:36	19:08	09:02	11:52	18:23	21:00
Shiretoko-Shari	07:27	10:46	17:30	19:36	08:34	11:26	18:06	20:43
Kawayu-Onsen	08:17	11:40	18:25	20:36	07:46	10:36	17:22	19:59
Mashu	08:37	11:55	18:47	20:55	07:29	10:21	17:05	19:42
Toro	09:19	12:39	19:28	21:36	06:34	09:36	16:06	18:44
Kushiro	10:07	13:17	20:06	22:06	05:59	09:05	15:48	18:19

[1] The services shown above are the only direct services between Abashiri and Kushiro; times are given only for the stations where the route guide suggests stopping.

Table 23: Shintoku to Furano [All services shown are direct]

23a: Shintoku to Furano

Shintoku	05:54	07:57[1]	10:13[2]	11:32[2]	14:10[1]	19:21[2]	21:02[1]
Furano	07:20	09:41	11:32	13:03	15:45	20:32	22:06

[1] This service originates in Ikeda. [2] This service originates in Obihiro.

23b: Furano to Shintoku

Furano	07:22[1]	09:15[1]	11:06[2]	16:45	19:10[1]	21:58
Shintoku	09:04	10:44	12:36	18:09	20:37	23:24

[1] This service continues to Obihiro. [2] This service continues to Kushiro.

Table 24: Furano to Asahikawa

A steam train, SL Furano Biei, operates between Asahikawa and Furano in the summer months; check locally for details.

24a: Furano to Asahikawa

Furano	10:02	11:45	13:10	15:32	16:57	18:05	19:05	20:44[1]
Naka-Furano	10:12	11:52	13:21	15:46	17:07	18:13	19:15	20:51
Kami-Furano	10:22	11:59	13:31	15:55	17:21	18:21	19:24	20:58
Bibaushi	10:31	12:15	13:41	16:09	17:31	18:31	19:34	21:08
Biei	10:39	12:23	13:48	16:28	17:39	18:38	19:42	21:15
Asahikawa	11:10	12:55	14:23	17:02	18:17	19:13	20:17	21:41

[1] This service originates in Obihiro at 18:36 and departs Shintoku at 19:21 (see Shintoku to Furano above).

24b: Asahikawa to Furano

Asahikawa	09:29	11:30	13:36	15:25	16:30	17:46	18:27	20:38
Biei	10:02	12:08	14:15	16:00	17:03	18:20	19:02	21:15
Bibaushi	10:10	12:16	14:23	16:08	17:11	18:31	19:11	21:23
Kami-Furano	10:27	12:25	14:32	16:18	17:21	18:40	19:24	21:32
Naka-Furano	10:34	12:33	14:41	16:27	17:33	18:48	19:33	21:39
Furano	10:41	12:40	14:51	16:38	17:39	18:55	19:42	21:46

Table 25: Hakata/Fukuoka to Nagasaki

	25a: Hakata to Nagasaki		25b: Nagasaki to Hakata	
Hakata/Fukuoka	10:02[1]	10:22[2]	09:18	11:00
Tosu	10:23	10:48	08:58	10:38
Saga	10:38	11:03	08:44	10:23
Hizen-Yamaguchi	10:47	11:14	08:35	10:13
Hizen-Kashima	10:57	11:25	08:25	09:58
Isahaya	11:33	12:09	07:49	09:10
Urakami	11:51	12:27	07:33	08:53
Nagasaki	11:53	12:30	07:30[3]	08:50[4]

Note: Services operate before and after the given times but not regularly. Even though the service operates twice-hourly departure/arrival times can vary by up to five minutes.
[1] Hourly till 20:02   [3] Hourly till 20:30
[2] Hourly till 19:22   [4] Hourly till 18:50

Table 26: Hakata to Kagoshima-chuo (by LEX and shinkansen)

	26a: Hakata to Kagoshima-chuo	26b: Kagoshima-chuo to Hakata
Hakata (Fukuoka)	09:10[1]	10:53
Tosu	09:30	10:33
Kurume	09:37	10:27
Omuta	09:56	10:03
Kumamoto	10:27	09:30
Shin-Yatsushiro	10:47	09:06
(change to shinkansen)		*(change to LEX)*
Shin-Yatsushiro	10:50	09:03
Sendai	11.17	08:30
Kagoshima-chuo	11:29	08:17[2]

[1] Hourly till 20:10   [2] Hourly till 21:18
In both directions subsequent departure/arrival times sometimes vary by a few minutes.
Note: The route described in the text between Yatsushiro and Nishi-Kagoshima (now called Kagoshima-Chuo) is now served by local trains only; there are no direct services between these two places so it is necessary to change at either Izumi and/or Sendai. Rail-pass holders are advised to take the new shinkansen service from Shin-Yatsushiro.

Table 27: Kokura to Miyazaki

	27a: Kokura to Min-Miyazaki				27b: Min-Miyazaki to Kokura			
Kokura	10:48	12:46	14:46	16:46	12:31	15:31	16:31	19:05
Nakatsu	11:18	13:17	15:17	17:17	12:02	15:02	16:02	18:32
Beppu	11:56	13:55	15:55	17:56	11:23	14:23	15:23	17:43
Oita	12:10	14:10	16:10	18:11	11:11	14:10	15:10	17:34
Saiki	13:05	15:08	17:12	19:13	10:06	13:05	14:12	16:36
Nobeoka	14:08	16:04	18:15	20:14	09:10	12:06	13:11	15:35
Miyazaki	15:10	17:13	19:17	21:19	08:09	11:01	12:03	14:31
Minami-Miyazaki	15:13	17:16	19:20	21:22	08:06	10:58	12:00	14:27

There are four more services in each direction during the day, as well as a night service.

Table 28: Okayama to Takamatsu

	28a: Okayama to Takamatsu		28b: Takamatsu to Okayama	
Okayama	09:04[1]	09:34[2]	09:15	09:45
Senoo		09:40	09:09	09:39
Hayashima	09:14		09:05	09:35
Chaya-machi	09:18	09:46	09:01	09:32
Kojima	09:28	09:55	08:53	09:23
Sakaide	09:43	10:10	08:37	09:08
Takamatsu	09:58	10:26	08:23[3]	08:53[4]

[1] Hourly till 22:04   [2] Hourly till 21:34   [3] Hourly till 21:22   [4] Hourly till 20:52

Table 29: Takamatsu to Kochi

	29a: Takamatsu to Kochi				29b: Kochi to Takamatsu			
Takamatsu	08:08	09:10	12:09	20:14	11:06	17:06	20:37	21:34
Sakaide	08:23	09:26	12:24	20:27	10:53	16:53	20:23	21:16
Marugame	08:29	09:39	12:31	20:40			20:13	21:11
Tadotsu	08:34	09:44	12:45	20:45	10:49	16:49	20:09	21:07
Zentsu-ji	08:39	09:49	12:50	20:50	10:39	16:39	20:04	21:02
Kotohira	08:44	09:53	12:54	20:57	10:34	16:34	19:59	20:57
Awa-Ikeda	09:16	09:21	13:22	21:23	10:06	16:06	19:32	20:34
Oboke	09:34	10:39	13:41	21:41	09:48	15:48		
Osugi	09:56			22:00			18:55	20:01
Tosa-Yamada	10:16	11:00	14:16	22:19	09:13	15:13	18:35	19:42
Gomen	10:20	11:23	14:20	22:24	09:08	15:09	18:31	19:37
Kochi	10:28	11:31	14:28	22:31	09:01	15:01	18:23	19:29

Table 30: Kochi to Kubokawa

	30a: Kochi to Kubokawa				30b: Kubokawa to Kochi			
Kochi	09:53	11:39	13:28	15:22	09:52	12:54	14:56	16:56
Sakawa	10:15	12:01	13:50	15:44	09:30	12:33	14:34	16:29
Susaki	10:32	12:21	14:03	15:57	09:18	12:21	14:22	16:17
Kubokawa	10:58	12:47	14:28	16:22	08:51	11:50	13:55	15:50

Table 31: Kubokawa to Uwajima

	31a: Kubokawa to Uwajima				31b: Uwajima to Kubokawa			
Kubokawa	10:03	13:22	14:37	16:37	11:29	13:45	17:33	19:08
Ekawasaki	10:58	14:16	15:56	17:55	10:33	12:34	16:33	18:15
Uwajima	12:05	15:22	17:01	18:01	09:29	11:28	15:22	17:05

Table 32: Uwajima to Matsuyama

	32a: Uwajima to Matsuyama[1]				32b: Matsuyama to Uwajima			
Uwajima	08:32	09:51	12:47	14:48	09:26	10:22	11:26	12:32
Unomachi	08:52	10:10	13:05	15:08	09:08	10:01	11:09	12:15
Yawatahama	09:06	10:21	13:17	15:21	08:57	09:49	10:57	12:02
Iyo-Ozu	09:18	10:33	13:29	15:34	08:44	09:37	10:45	11:50
Uchiko	09:29	10:43	13:40	15:44	08:34	09:28	10:31	11:40
Iyo-shi	09:48				08:14	09:09		
Matsuyama	09:56	11:09	14:03	16:06	08:06	09:00	10:09	11:18[2]

[1] Services operate approximately hourly till 20:59 but at different times each hour.
[2] Hourly till 20:18 but not all trains stop at the stations shown and departure/arrival times vary by a few minutes.

Table 33: Matsuyama to Okayama

33a: Matsuyama to Okayama

Matsuyama	09:12	10:15	11:18	12:15	13:17	15:18	16:21	17:25
Iyo-Hojo	09:24							
Imabari	09:52	10:53	11:57	12:50	13:56	15:55	16:56	18:00
Iyo-Saijo	10:06	11:15	12:19	13:17	14:18	16:18	17:17	18:21
Niihama	10:22	11:23	12:27	13:25	14:25	16:25	17:25	18:29
Kanon-ji	10:59	11:58	13:00	14:00	14:57	16:59	17:59	19:01
Tadotsu	11:12	12:14	13:15	14:15	15:12	17:14	18:14	19:16
Marugame	11:16	12:18	13:19	14:19	15:17	17:18	18:18	19:20
Utazu	11:21	12:23	13:24	14:24	15:22	17:23	18:23	19:25
Kojima	11:37	12:37	13:38	14:38	15:26	17:36	18:36	19:38
Okayama	11:57	12:57	13:57	14:57	15:57	17:57	18:57	19:57

33b: Okayama to Matsuyama

Okayama	09:23	10:22	12:22	13:22	14:21	15:22	16:22	17:22
Kojima	09:46	10:47	12:47	13:46	14:46	15:47	16:47	17:46
Utazu	10:04	11:05	12:54	14:04	15:04	16:05	17:05	17:59
Marugame	10:08	11:09	13:09	14:08	15:08	16:08	17:08	18:09
Tadotsu	10:12	11:13	13:15	14:15	15:12	16:13	17:14	18:14
Kanon-ji	10:27	11:28	13:30	14:32	15:27	16:28	17:29	18:29
Niihama	10:59	11:59	14:02	15:09	15:59	17:00	18:00	19:03
Iyo-Saijo	11:12	12:07	14:09	15:15	16:06	17:08	18:20	19:19
Imabari	11:31	12:31	14:34	15:36	16:29	17:33	18:33	19:33
Iyo-Hojo					16:56	18:00	18:57	20:00
Matsuyama	12:07	13:09	15:10	16:12	17:08	18:12	19:10	20:12

UPDATE – 2004

Rail passes – p12
JR has a dedicated website in English which provides up-to-date information about the Japan Rail Pass and the regional passes. For more details, see 🖳 www.japanrailpass.net.

Regional Japan Rail Passes – p13
● JR Hokkaido (🖳 www.jrhokkaido.co.jp/global/index.html) has introduced a pass available in both ordinary (3 days, ¥14,000; 5 days ¥18,000) and green (first class; 3 days ¥20,000; 5 days ¥25,000) class. The passes can be bought before arriving in Japan or once there and are only valid for JR services on the island of Hokkaido. The pass does not include the cost of getting to Hokkaido by rail but a JR East rail pass (see p14) would be worth considering if coming from Tokyo. For alternative Hokkaido rail passes, see p77.
● Since the opening of the new Kyushu shinkansen (see p414), the price of the 5-day JR Kyushu Rail Pass (see p14) has increased by ¥1000 to ¥16,000. The 7-day pass has been discontinued. For more details, see 🖳 www.jrkyushu.co.jp.

Getting to Japan – p22
● All Nippon Airways (☎ 0870-837 8866, 🖳 www.ana-europe.com) now offers an online reservation service for its daily scheduled flights from London Heathrow to Tokyo's Narita Airport. Direct onward domestic connections are available from Narita to Sapporo (p309), Sendai (p265), Nagoya (p139), Osaka (p101), Hiroshima (p230) and Fukuoka (p336).
● Creative Tours (p24) is now called Jalpak International.

Arriving in Japan – p44
See p413 for details about Japan's newest international airport in Nagoya.

Arriving in Japan: Osaka – p45
The Passenger Services Facilities Charge is now included in the price of air tickets.

Japan Travel Phone – box, p45
The Japan Travel Phone service was discontinued in 2003.

Welcome Cards – p46
The Tokai region of Central Honshu (p109), which includes Aichi, Gifu, Mie, Shizuoka and Nagoya has introduced a Welcome Card. For more information visit 🖳 www.j-heartland.com.

JR Hotel Group – box, p49
JR now operates a website providing details of all the hotels which are part of the JR-Group: 🖳 www.jrhotelgroup.com/eng/.

Banks and money matters – p56
● ATMs in post offices nationwide now accept international VISA, MasterCard and Cirrus cards – useful if you run out of cash outside banking hours.
● Thanks to ongoing deregulation, all shops in Japan are now allowed to exchange foreign bank notes (previously, only authorized foreign exchange desks and banks could do so). Don't get too excited, though, since in practice most shops are not yet geared up to do this and the vast majority only accept payment in Japanese yen.

Japanese Railway Society – p69
The web address has changed to 🖳 www.japaneserailwaysociety.com.

Alternatives to a Japan Rail Pass – p77
The Kansai Thru Pass allows unlimited travel between Kyoto, Nara, Osaka, Himeji, Koyasan, Kobe and Kansai International Airport. The pass (2 days, ¥3800; 3 days, ¥5000) is valid on 32 private rail and bus companies. Note that travel on JR services is not permitted. For further information check 🖳 www.surutto.com/conts/ticket/3dayeng/.

Timetables – p79

The condensed JR timetable in English is no longer available. The updated timetables in the appendix give an idea of the services available but for up-to-date information in English look at 💻 www.hyperdia.com, 💻 www.world.eki-net.com (shinkansen services only) or contact your local JNTO office.

Making seat reservations – p79

Seat reservations can be made online (free for rail-pass holders) for all bullet trains as well as the Narita Express service (see p397). Seat reservation tickets must be picked up on arrival in Japan at one of a number of designated stations. Note that a charge is levied if you fail to pick up your ticket prior to travel. More details are available at 💻 www.world.eki-net.com.

> ❏ **Expo 2005**
> From 25 March to 25 September 2005, Japan plays host to the World Exposition (💻 www.expo2005.or.jp), the first global exhibition of the 21st century. More than 120 countries will have their own pavilions. The site covers 173 hectares and is 20km from Nagoya (p139). Tickets (¥4600) can be purchased in advance on the web.

Facilities for the disabled – p83

Accessible Japan (💻 www.wakakoma.org/aj/) is a useful website for information on hotels which offer specially adapted rooms, as well as trains with space for wheelchairs.

Tourist information – p96

The main tourist information centre has moved to the 10th floor, Tokyo Kotsu Kaikan Building, 2-10-1 Yurakucho, Chiyoda-ku. The building is just in front of Yurakucho station on the JR Yamanote line. The opening hours and phone number have not changed.

Where to stay – p97/8

● There is now an accommodation tax in the Tokyo metropolitan area: ¥100 for rooms costing from ¥10,000 to ¥14,999 per person per night; ¥200 for rooms costing ¥15,000 or more.
● One of Tokyo's newest and most stylish hotels is the *Four Seasons* (☎ 03-5222 7222, 🖷 5222 1255, 💻 www.fourseasons.com; ¥55,000/S, ¥60,000/D). Adjacent to Tokyo station, this 57-room boutique hotel is an ideal base for rail travellers looking for a quiet haven in the heart of the capital. Facilities include a spa and fitness studio. Style guru Tyler Brûlé calls the Four Seasons the 'new benchmark among boutique-size business hotels'. A sleek alternative is the new *Park Hyatt Tokyo* (☎ 03-5322 1234, 🖷 5322 1288, 💻 www.parkhyatttokyo.com; from ¥46,800/Tw), used as the location for Sofia Coppola's critically-acclaimed film, *Lost In Translation*.

Tokyo to Atami (by shinkansen) – p111

A new station has opened at Shinagawa on the Yamanote loop line.

Tokyo to Nagano by shinkansen – p116

A new station, Honjo-Waseda, has opened between Kumagaya and Takasaki.

Nagoya – p144

● Chubu Kokusai (Central Japan International) Airport, Japan's newest international airport, opens near Nagoya on February 17, 2005. It will replace Komaki airport. For more details about the new airport and the airlines which will operate from it, visit 💻 www.centrair.jp.
● The fastest journey time by rail from the airport to Nagoya city will be 28 minutes. Services are to be operated by the private Meitetsu Railway. Direct trains will also operate from the airport to Gifu (p128), Toyohashi (p115) and Inuyama (p145).

Matsumoto – p150

● *Ace Inn Matsumoto* (☎ 0263-35 1188, 🖷 35 1102, 💻 ace.alpico.co.jp/e/; ¥6700/S), immediately to the right as you exit JR Matsumoto station, is a good cheap option. Continental breakfast is included in the room rate and there's a coin-operated laundry.

Takayama – p155
● *Country Hotel Takayama* (☎ 0577-35 3900, 🖹 35 3910; ¥5900/S, ¥13,000/Tw) is a new business hotel across the street from the station offering basic but comfortable rooms.
● *Arisu* restaurant (p159) has become a wedding hall and is no longer open to the public for meals. Swiss restaurant *Belgins Bells* (p159) has closed.

Kansai – city guides – p180
For information on events throughout the Kansai region, check 💻 www.kansai.gr.jp.

Kyoto – p180
● The World Currency Shop on the eighth floor of the Kyoto station building exchanges cash and travellers' cheques in most major currencies.
● Kyoto City Air Terminal (KCAT) (p188) has closed and is now a staffed left-luggage office so it is no longer possible to check in here for flights from Kansai International Airport.
● The JNTO-run Kyoto Tourist Information Centre (p188) closed in January 2004. The three other tourist offices/information desks mentioned in the text are still open.
● The new *Budget Inn* (☎/🖹 344 1510 💻 www.budgetinnjp.com; ¥2500/night) is very close to and under the same management as the ever-reliable *Tour Club* (p190).

Hiroshima to Ogori – p211
Ogori station (see also p322) is now called Shin-Yamaguchi.

Kobe – p219
Japan's newest domestic airport opens in Kobe in spring 2005. Skymark Airlines (💻 www.skymark.co.jp) will operate four flights daily between Kobe and Tokyo's Haneda airport. A new transit system will connect downtown Sannomiya with the airport in 16 minutes.

Shinkansen: the next step – box, p254
● The bullet train line from Morioka to Hachinohe is now open. Fifteen shinkansen services, called 'Hayate' ('Swift Wind'), run daily between Tokyo and Hachinohe (2 hrs 50 mins on the fastest trains) in each direction: see p403-4 and p405 for timetable details. If travelling to Aomori/Hokkaido, the best bet is to pick up a Hakucho LEX from Hachinohe.
● The original line between Morioka and Hachinohe (as described in the text) has been divided, with the journey between Morioka and Metoki operated by Iwate Ginga Railway, and Metoki to Hachinohe in the hands of Aoi-Mori Railway. The fare from Morioka to Hachinohe is ¥2960; the service operates irregularly but approximately hourly taking about 90 minutes. Rail-pass holders and those in a hurry are advised to use the new shinkansen line.

Sapporo – p309
A good overnight base for rail travellers is the 350-room, JR-operated *Tower Hotel Nikko Sapporo* (☎ 011-251 2222, 💻 www.jr-tower.com; ¥16,170/S, ¥33,495/Tw). It's built onto the south side of the JR station and is part of a complex which also houses a department store and an 'observation spa' – a hot spring with commanding views of downtown Sapporo.

Kyushu: route guide – p321
● The new Kyushu shinkansen (opened in March 2004) operates between Shin-Yatsushiro (halfway down the island's west coast) and the new southern terminus of Kagoshima-Chuo (p355): see p409 for timetable details. Kyushu shinkansen services are all non-smoking.
● The 'Relay-Tsubame' limited express service links Hakata with Shin-Yatsushiro, from where you connect up with the 'Tsubame' ('Swallow') shinkansen to Kagoshima-Chuo.
● The section of pre-shinkansen railway line between Yatsushiro and Sendai (see pp328-9) is no longer operated by JR. It has been handed over to a private company, Hisatsu Orange Tetsudo, and the fare between Yatsushiro and Sendai is ¥2550. JR rail passes are not valid on this route so it is best to take the bullet train.
● Note that Ogori (p322) is now called Shin-Yamaguchi and Kagoshima-Chuo is the new name for a combined ordinary/shinkansen station formerly called Nishi-Kagoshima (p329).

INDEX